CRITICAL EXPLORATIONS IN SOCIAL SCIENCES

Essays presented to
Utsa Patnaik and Prabhat Patnaik

CRITICAL EXPLORATIONS IN SOCIAL SCIENCES

Essays presented to
Utsa Patnaik and Prabhat Patnaik

Edited by
Praveen Jha
Sudhanshu Bhushan

 Tulika Books

Published by
Tulika Books
86/1 (ground floor), Shahpur Jat, New Delhi 110 049, India
www.tfortulika.com

First edition (hardback) 2025

ISBN: 978-81-979383-4-4

Printed at Chaman Offset, Delhi 110 002

Contents

List of Tables and Figures

1

A Tribute to the Patnaiks

Praveen Jha and Sudhanshu Bhushan

This book, in honour of Professor Utsa Patnaik and Professor Prabhat Patnaik, is a tribute to two of our outstanding economists and public intellectuals in contemporary India. For well over half a century, the Patnaiks have been among the trailblazers in their generation of economists, and equally important, well acknowledged for their contributions to other related disciplines. In fact, it would be appropriate to say that, going well beyond their generation, they occupy a prominent place among formidable contributors to building India's critical and progressive intellectual tradition within the social sciences since the late nineteenth century. In particular, both of them are widely recognized, nationally and internationally, for extending and deepening the Marxist political economy approach.

Between them, the Patnaiks have contributed to an amazingly diverse range of themes, which have often set/altered the terms of discourse. Their seminal and critical engagements with alternative theoretical traditions in several areas are very well regarded. Deep and systematic investigations of the global political economy, both historically and for the current juncture, often from the perspective of the South, constitute a significant hallmark of their outstanding academic publications. To flag just one theme in this context: their sustained and hugely illuminating work on imperialism, for decades now, is widely appreciated as among the finest contributions on the subject. As it happens, much of the historical and analytical essence of their work on imperialism is contained in the 2021 book *Capital and Imperialism: Theory, History, and the Present*, which was published by the Monthly Review Press and awarded the Paul A. Baran – Paul M. Sweezy Memorial Award.

Specifically with respect to India's economic trajectory since Independence, there is hardly any major theme that has escaped the attention of the Patnaiks, if we catalogue all their scholarly outputs as well as more accessible writings aimed at a much wider audience of those not specializing in economics, and the general public at large; their reach has been truly exceptional. In short, both of them, apart from being academics of the finest calibre, have also been legendary teachers, not only for their direct students in 'formal' classrooms but also to a very large audience through their profound and much celebrated engagements as public intellectuals. Thus, across the length and the breadth of the country, and beyond, the Patnaiks have touched many lives, influencing and persuading them to reflect deeply on matters of economy and society, often with a sharp focus on justice and a better world, especially for the working people everywhere.

When we decided to embark on this project, we thought of it as a two-stage endeavour: first as a Special Issue of an established and reputed journal in India, then followed by a book. For the journal, we opted for the *Indian Economic Journal*, which is an organ of more than a century-old community of economists and social scientists, namely, the Indian Economic Association (IEA). The founder of the Indian Economic Association was Charles Joseph Hamilton, who was the Minto Professor of Economics at Calcutta University when he established the IEA in 1917; the journal has a footprint along the length and breadth of the country, and has had an illustrious history. The Special Issue of the journal was published a couple of years ago; this book includes all the articles published in the Special Issue and a couple of additionally commissioned contributions.

Of course, an exceptionally difficult issue that immediately confronted us when we conceived of our project was to settle on a list of invitees. Given a very large pool of worthy potential contributors – scholars, friends, colleagues, students, activists, public intellectuals and so on – all those close to the Patnaiks in a multitude of ways, how does one draw a small sample to be included in one special issue, with obvious limitations of space? We had to take this extremely difficult call which was unavoidable.

We hope that the select group of authors here is representative of the large pool hinted above and that their contributions reflect some of the important concerns that the Patnaiks have engaged with. And, indeed, we are immensely grateful to all the authors for accepting our request to be part of this project, to offer its token of appreciation for the Patnaiks, and celebrate their humongous and exceptional achievements as scholars, organic intellectuals and much more. Of course, our authors were free to choose the themes they wanted to engage with, and the result has been quite a broad range of diverse topics and very valuable contributions. If we may say so, this bouquet has served the intent of the endeavour.

The opening contribution, by Gopalkrishna Gandhi, titled 'Editor as Mediator: A Profile of Albert Cartwright in Early Twentieth-Century South Africa', chronicles aspects of the intellectual and political persona of Albert Cartwright (1868–1956), a distinguished journalist, who had worked in a number of newspapers in South Africa in the turbulent period around the Second Boer War and later, opposing the ruling order in some crucial respects, beyond the call of 'editorial' duty. The author informs us that as a friend of General J.C. Smuts, South Africa's most powerful politician, and interestingly that of M.K. Gandhi, who was pitted in an intense political struggle against the Smuts regime, Cartwright played the role of mediator during the latter's incarceration (1908). This resulted in a degree of conciliation between the two, creating space for the famous 'Agreement' of 1914. The essay is a very interesting profile of Cartwright and the power of his 'pen'.

The next essay, by Akeel Bilgrami, titled 'Economic Rights, the Very Idea', engages with the philosophical foundations underlying economic rights, comparable to the foundations that have long been available for the rights around the notion of liberty. Having done so, the author then situates his take on economic rights, within the realities of contemporary capitalist political economy; as it happens, the issue of 'economic rights' under capitalism has been a major preoccupation of Prabhat Patnaik in his several writings for decades now.

The next contribution, by Barbara Harriss-White, titled 'Awkward Classes and India's Rural Development', investigates a much-discussed and contentious theme in Marxian political economy. As the author suggests, Marx's stylized model of the evolution of capitalism, driven by ceaseless accumulation, ignores deviations from the polar classes of capital and labour, regarded as precapitalist outliers or as headed for extinction. However, as she argues, domains and instances of 'awkward classes', such as petty commodity production (and trade and services) and merchant's or commercial capital, persist widely. Harriss-White argues that petty production overlaps with both wage labour and small capitalist firms; it reproduces and expands by multiplication, not accumulation, and does not mobilize in a politically coherent way. Similarly, commercial capital is, in turn, suffused with productive activity, which encompasses petty trade and accumulating enterprises that preserve their independence.

The next essay, by C.P. Chandrasekhar and Jayati Ghosh, titled 'On Capitalism and Imperialism: A Note Based on Prabhat Patnaik's Contributions to Economic Theory', dwells on an extremely important theme in Prabhat Patnaik's work since his days as a doctoral student: that the expansion and relative 'stability' of capitalism can hardly be understood without incorporating the role of primitive accumulation and imperialism. The authors argue that without containing the spontaneity that is a central feature of capitalism, or without transcending capitalism, the quest for a just, egalitarian and sustainable social order remains elusive.

The essay by late Martin Khor Kok Peng and Jomo Kwame Sundaram, titled 'Surplus Transfers from British Colonial Malaya', connects very well with one of the themes central to Utsa Patnaik's work, namely, surplus transfers during the colonial era. Martin Khor's 1983 book is considered the first comprehensive attempt at estimating colonial surplus from British Malaya, extracted via different means. The contribution here by Martin Khor Kok Peng and Jomo K.S. builds on the earlier literature and throws considerable light on different channels through which financial surpluses materialized. They conclude that colonial Malaya was subjected to significant financial extraction.

The next essay, by Issa G. Shivji, titled 'The Peasant Question under Nyerere's Socialism', is a succinct overview of the changing course of addressing the peasant question by Julius Nyerere, the first president of Tanzania, from the immediate aftermath of independence to the 1980s. Shivji argues that, with the benefit of hindsight, it can be surmised that the consequences of the policy thrusts during the 1960s and the 1970s effectively discredited the regime and put tremendous pressure on Nyerere to change the course. Coupled with the fact that, during the late 1970s and the early 1980s, the country experienced its worst economic crisis, provided more than a foothold to imperialism and internal proto-bourgeoisie, which succeeded in imposing the notorious structural adjustment programmes, thus exposing the peasant to the vagaries of capitalism and its crisis. Shivji ends with outlining some elements of an alternative discourse to spearhead the peasants' struggle for autonomous, sovereign development.

The following essay, by K.P. Kannan, titled 'Revisiting the Kerala "Model" of Development: A Sixty-Year Assessment of Successes and Failures', seeks to revisit the much acclaimed Kerala 'model' of development since the formation of the state of Kerala and provides a panoramic view of Kerala's development experience for a period of six decades from 1960 to 2020. Kannan argues that the development experience of Kerala is largely shaped by its historical past, which privileged social development over purely economic development, based on the growth of the goods-producing sectors. High human and social development led to large-scale migration of persons, mostly men, to the Gulf countries that resulted in a kind of economic growth induced by outside money in the form of remittances. Furthermore, limited opportunities afforded by the national state or the increased flow of outside money could not be seized effectively by the regional state to transform goods-producing sectors such as agriculture and industry, resulting in major failures such as declining tax collection efficiency, increased net loss of state-owned public enterprises and massive waste of resources in implementing capital projects. Kannan concludes the essay with a call for a study of political economy of development by taking into account the specificities of the Kerala context within a larger national and international context.

The next essay, by Biswajit Dhar, titled 'WTO Agreement on Agriculture: Worsening India's Agrarian Crisis', maps and engages with several issues in the context of India's accession to the WTO in 1995. Dhar argues that, consequent to joining the WTO, most of the policies supporting agriculture, especially price support and input subsidies, labelled by the Agreement on Agriculture (AoA) as domestic support measures, came under the scanner, throwing up severe challenges. For instance, the price support measure that India uses, namely, the minimum support price (MSP) provided to most of the major crops, now faces a problem as the methodology of calculating the extent of subsidies on account of MSP is working against India. It is also worth noting that the AoA prevents India from using export subsidies since it was not using this instrument in the past. On the other hand, the agreement allows the advanced countries that were using export subsidies to continue using this instrument, albeit at a lower level.

The following contribution, by Paris Yeros, titled 'Generalized Semi-proletarianization in Africa', focuses on Africa's contemporary social formation. Yeros argues that the labour question in Africa has undergone a decisive transformation under neoliberalism. While under colonial rule, the formation of labour reserves was mainly the result of political engineering, especially in regions of white settlement, today, labour reserves are driven by the spontaneous operation of generalized monopoly capitalism and have become coextensive within the continent. The author suggests that the changing labour question is the most basic element of an apparent tendency of structural convergence among the continent's macro-regions; it amounts to a generalized condition of semiproletarianization, insofar as the bulk of the population is unable to meet its basic needs within the wage relation or outside it. Peasant and worker households straddle various labour regimes in rural and urban areas and seek to secure their social reproduction by a combination of wages, petty production and trade, simple use values and unpaid reproductive labour. Data sourced from the ILO are used to quantify some of these trends, including their gendered dimensions.

The subsequent contribution, by K.J. Joseph and Anitha Kumary L., titled 'India's GST Paradigm and the Trajectory of Fiscal Federalism: An Analysis with Special Reference to Kerala', explores the characteristics of India's GST paradigm from a fiscal federal perspective, its implementation and the tax performance of states under GST. The Indian GST paradigm built on the edifice of the GST Council and three key pillars of revenue neutrality, tax-sharing between the centre and the states, and the provision for GST compensation has been designed, ostensibly, towards fostering cooperative federalism. However, the essay demonstrates that the revenue neutrality has not been ensured and there were also issues with tax sharing and GST compensation. It is argued by the authors that both the edifice and the pillars of GST therefore were fraught with faultlines in both design and implementation. The tax effort of the states did not increase, indicating that GST has not been helpful in improving the revenue position of the states. The essay concludes that, although India's GST paradigm was supposed to foster cooperative federalism, the outcomes appear to lead us towards coercive federalism.

The following essay, by Arindam Banerjee, titled 'Capitalism, Imperialism and the Food Question', engages with some of the important debates pertaining to the trajectories of capitalist transition. In particular, it focuses on the claim that the emergence of industrial agriculture under successful capitalist transitions is supposed to have taken care of all food and raw material constraints that could have arrested the development of industrial economies and societies in the North. Connecting it with Utsa Patnaik's work, the essay debunks such a view. As is well known, Utsa Patnaik has been a severe critic of such a perspective and has explored multiple aspects of the contribution of colonies to the advance of capital accumulation in the North, delving deeply into the nineteenth-century 'international division of labour', the role of tropical food and raw materials exports by commercialized Southern agriculture, and deleterious implications for food security in the colonies. The author reiterates some of the major claims of the anti-imperialist scholarship of Utsa Patnaik with a specific focus on the evolution of the food question under capitalism in the world economy.

The next essay, by Rohit Azad and Shouvik Chakraborty, titled 'Imperialism of the Twenty-first Century: A Global Tripartite System', engages with a large and massively contested theme pertaining to the usefulness of 'imperialism' as an analytical category to understand the contemporary world. As is well known, while economists on the right either do not acknowledge or dismiss the notion of imperialism, many on the left, like Hardt and Negri, would agree that it is indeed dead and global hegemony has taken a different shape, which they call 'Empire'. The authors advance an interesting argument to understand the nature and mechanics of contemporary imperialism. They suggest that in varied frameworks of imperialism – world systems, dependency, unequal interdependence – the world has been theorized as constitutive of two parts: capitalist core (global North) and pre/semicapitalist periphery (global South). This neat classification has been smudged by the emergence of China from the global South as a major economic player in the global economy. The authors argue that its emergence, far from weakening imperialism, is a key factor in explaining today's imperialism. Imperialism of the twenty-first century constitutes three, not two, parts – capitalist core, periphery's core and periphery's periphery.

The following essay, by Vibha Iyer, titled 'A Tangible Concept of Imperialism: An Attempt to Explore Utsa Patnaik's Estimates of Colonial Transfers from India', engages with some of the conceptual and empirical issues in the context of colonial India. As the author notes, the earliest work on colonial transfers from India originated in the Drain of Wealth theory of the nineteenth-century nationalists, particularly Dadabhai Naoroji and R.C. Dutt. Iyer argues that while theories advanced by Naoroji and Dutt clearly show an implicit understanding of the linking of India's internal budget and its external accounts to facilitate tax-financed transfers to Britain – a feature unique to the colonial economy – they lack macroeconomic concepts to make its details explicit. The esaay argues that Utsa Patnaik's methodological framework over the last four decades has contributed significantly towards revealing the precise mechanisms of tax-financed transfers from India. The author has focused on two methodological contributions by Utsa Patnaik: first, the use of suitably modified modern macroeconomic concepts in a sovereign economy to lay bare the link between India's tax revenues and trade surplus; and second, the use of Council Bills as a proxy for India's merchandise surplus, which has helped in greater accuracy of estimates by overcoming conceptual lacunae in the existing trade data and literature.

The next essay, by Ritu Dewan, titled 'Patriarchy and Property: Goa's Uniform Civil Code', engages with the important theme of gender equality in all its myriad manifestations, particularly on the ownership and control over resources, especially land, in a developing economy. The author argues that nowhere in India are these direct and indirect interconnections between gender equality and resources so intricate, nuanced and simultaneously complex, as in the state of Goa, which is the only state in India where women are guaranteed equal property rights. Dewan attempts a demystification of the link between patriarchy and women's property rights in Goa, which is built on a combination of land, property and matrimonial rights. The foundation for these interconnections is provided by the Portuguese Civil Code and other relevant laws such as family laws, the code of comunidades the Goa Mundkar (Protection from Eviction) Act, 1975, and the recent Goa Succession, Special Notaries and Inventory Proceeding Act, 2012 which was passed in 2016.

The next contribution, by Sukhdev Thorat and Khalid Khan, titled 'Why Inter-Caste Inequality in Educational Attainment Still Persists: Wealth and Caste Discrimination Matters', uses recent data for 2017–18 to provide empirical evidence on the persistence of the inter-caste inequality in higher education, which generally reflects traditional caste hierarchies. Similarly, wealth and income inequality have a disproportionate adverse effect on low-income groups via low educational attainments. The essay shows that the shift in government policies towards privatization of higher education also has taken education beyond the reach of low-income households, leading to high dropout rates among the scheduled castes. Based on these results, the authors propose some policy recommendations to promote higher education among the low castes and low-income groups.

The next essay, by Sudhanshu Bhushan, titled 'Human Resource Development in Contemporary Indian Universities and Colleges', focusing on the debates on efficiency and ideological perspectives of technology, seeks to offer a critical engagement with technology in human resource development. It suggests that in the dominant discourses, the efficiency feature of technology tends to get prioritized; however, it makes a strong case to pay careful attention to the ideological dimensions of technology with respect to supporting the academic endeavours.

The final essay in the volume, titled 'Growth without Engines? The

Indian Transition to Lower Middle-Income Status', by Surajit Mazumdar, focuses on the growth trajectory of India during the period of neoliberal globalization since the early 1990s, with a focus on the period since the early years of the twenty-first century. As he notes, there was a significant growth acceleration from around 2003 which lasted for barely five years; in fact, as per the World Bank categorization, in 2007, India moved up from being a low-income to a lower middle-income country. However, as India entered the second decade of the twenty-first century, the factors which had been responsible for the spurt in growth rate during the first decade could not be sustained. Mazumdar argues that such a transition is not because of any deviation from the neoliberal path but precisely in the contradictions inherent in such a trajectory, given the specific historical context of India's economy, that one would have to locate the origins of this 'premature' exhaustion of the engines of growth.

As should be evident, the contributors to this volume have covered a spectrum of themes, with very substantive reflections on the past and the present, that include important theoretical concerns as well as in-depth examinations of a range of issues underlying development trajectories in India and elsewhere. We hope that readers of this book will be inspired by the excellent collection of essays here, and find them useful in their own quests for a better world. We invite everyone to join this celebration of the Patnaiks, to carry forward the conversations initiated by our esteemed authors, and, of course, on the wide-ranging canvas of economic, political and social questions that the Patnaiks have engaged with, and continue to do so.

2

Editor as Mediator

A Profile of Albert Cartwright in Early Twentieth-Century South Africa

Gopalkrishna Gandhi

Editor as mediator? Now what is *that* about? Editors helm newspapers and journals, they write editorials, sometimes fight their proprietors for their autonomy and more often capitulate to the owner's control. They come thereby to be admired and respected or neither admired nor respected. They resist political authority and pay a price for that, or they 'fall in line' and pay a higher price in terms of credibility. But mediation? How does that become part of an editor's role?

It can and does, because public life, as life itself, is not all black and white. There are areas which can be called a blend of both and, like black and white photographs and films are quite grey and misty, something that makes the films of Satyajit Ray, for instance, ring so true. And editors, who are not in politics but are situated on its rims, while not being players themselves are yet so close to the action that happens around them as to be indistinguishable from its voltage. They can find themselves sought for or seeking clarifications, being offered or offering suggestions. It is in them to exacerbate or alleviate tensions, encourage or discourage policy and programmes, and indeed, action including belligerence.

While doing so, they become mediators within themselves as well, mediating between their inner voice and prudence, the first impelling them to intervene and the second recoiling from overt action. That is the most difficult of the mediations they are called upon to attempt.

The 'loci' of this essay is South Africa and the role of the press in that country during the turn of the nineteenth century when war and brutality overwhelmed that part of the African continent. Two striking Africans appeared in the word of journalism there at the time. The first was John Tengo Jabavu (1859–1921) of the Eastern Cape who as a teacher began to write articles for some South African newspapers in English and after apprenticing himself to a printer, by 1884, founded his own newspaper, *Imvo Zabantsundu* ('Black Opinion'). This appeared in Xhosa, a brave and pioneering venture. Jabavu found himself at the intersection of liberal ideas in the Cape's South African Party and the repressive policies of Cecil Rhodes's 'Progressives'. The second was John Langalibalele Dube (1871–1946) of the Natal, an essayist, educator and articulate politician who with his wife Nokutela founded the first Zulu/ English newspaper *Ilanga lase Natal* ('The Sun of Natal') in 1903. Deeply influenced by Booker T. Washington, whose work he knew at first hand as a student in the USA, Dube wrote for and spoke to a mixed audience in South Africa, wanting to combine western education and mores with local customs and traditions.

Journalism, editorship and interventions by people of the eminence of Jabavu and Dube who belong to the place is important, and impressive and impactful. But when the person concerned is an 'outsider', such a role gets invested with an additional stamp – that of a somewhat lonesome individuality.

This is what happened with two of Jabavu and Dube's contemporaries, M.K. Gandhi (1869–1948) who founded and ran *Indian Opinion* from Durban and Phoenix in 1904, mainly on the issues facing the Indian South African community, and the British-born subject of Victorian Britain, and essentially a visiting Briton, Albert Cartwright (1868–1956).

Introducing Albert Cartwright

An excellent study (Derrick 2018) of a London-based weekly *West Africa* by Jonathan Derrick who worked on its staff for a number of years, gives us valuable details of the life of its founding editor – Albert Cartwright.

Born on Christmas day in 1868 in a Manchester town to Annie and Thomas Cartwright, a stationer, Albert studied in a semi-rural school. According to an unverifiable story, he 'ran away to sea' and by the time he was twenty, in 1889, found himself in Cape Town, South Africa, working for an empire-supporting and yet liberal-minded daily newspaper, *Cape Times*. Cartwright left that newspaper three years later to found *The South African* but abandoned the project to move from 'British' South Africa to Johannesburg in the South African Republic (The Transvaal) of the Boers and join *The Star* as a sub-editor.

'True-born' English as he was and married to the daughter of a Cape Town ship-owner, Cartwright belonged to the ruling race and naturally did not oppose the empire. Indeed, he supported its essential concept. But he was also a thinking and sensitive individual who was sharply aware of the immiserations caused by the imperial ambitions of the colonizers, the injustices perpetrated by them and the violations of what would now be termed 'human rights' that took place under their triumphalist and, by that time, increasingly fractious banners. While all nuances were lost on the blindness of the empire, nuances were precisely what populated Cartwright's vision. He could see there was little to choose between Briton and Boer in terms of what both were doing to and in South Africa, but as the stronger economic and military power, Britain had more to account for, more to remedy, more to prevent in terms of oppressive legislation, insensitive governance and plain governing–governed decencies.

Cartwright came to count as a journalist and editor between then and 1911, years when the people of that country, its African legatees, were witness to a major contestation for their lands and natural resources by two major European powers represented by the imperial British and the colonizing Dutch, known in South Africa as Boers. The former ruled over South Africa's coastal provinces, Cape Province to the west and the Natal to the east, while the Boers ruled the hinterland, the Transvaal and the Orange 'Free' State.

What was happening within the African mind then as these two powers fought for Africa's riches? Not much is known to be able to answer that. Mathew Arnold's words about the 'East' come to mind:

The East bow'd low before the blast
In patient, deep disdain;
She let the legions thunder past,
And plunged in thought again.

Anglo–Boer Rivalry

Oppression and exploitation were common to both powers, as were hubris and power-hunger. Rivalry, naturally, therefore, governed their relations and broke out in the grim and gory shape of the Anglo-Boer War (1899–1902), which had been growing ever since the discovery some three decades earlier of gold and diamond reserves in the Kimberley Boer tract, whetting British appetite for the whole of the loaf which saw the first Boer War (1880–1881) unfold and end in Boer victory with 401 British officers and soldiers killed and 480 wounded, against 25 killed and 41 injured on the Boer side.

With the Majuba Hill battle (27 February 1881), in particular, leaving a deep wound on British pride, it was inevitable that a Second Boer War should, sooner or later, shape itself. And it did, with the infamous, and disastrously again for the British, Jameson Raid (29 December 1895–2 January 1896) on the Boer Republic launched by the British from Cape Province under the instigation of the then Cape Prime Minister Cecil Rhodes.[1] *The Star* and its editor personally opposed the British venture which showed again British jingoists' craze for the gold and diamond reserves under Africa's Boer-ruled terrain and for power. Cartwright himself made no secret of his disapproval through his affinity with liberal Boer political figures in the Cape Province like William Schreiner[2] who had broken with Rhodes. Cartwright returned to the Cape Province in 1896 and accepting an invitation to be the editor of the Kimberley-based weekly *Diamond Fields Advertiser* – described by him in a letter to Schreiner as 'a thoroughly honest and independent paper' – became a figure of note. One might say, of dissenting note. Derrick tells us that under the paper's proprietor Roper and its new editor Cartwright, 'the *Advertiser*'s editorial pages (parts of which were in Dutch) quietly challenged Rhodes at the centre of his business empire[3] though not in a militant way'. The engagement with the *Advertiser* was not going to last. When in 1898 the paper was floated as a company, Rhodes got one of his trusted men to make heavy investments in it, virtually buying it up, and Cartwright was forced out of the editorship with his successor reversing the paper's policy on Rhodes.

Cartwright would, we may surmise, have liked to see the British and Boer parts of South Africa work non-competitively, and while advancing their imperial and colonial visions, treat the 'native' population with decency and human consideration, allowing for no violation of human rights and creating a progressive space for its participation through a widening non-discriminatory franchise in the affairs of the nation – an aim that falls far short of what today would seem politically appropriate and would be termed 'patronizing'. Mediation between the exploiters and the exploited would today be seen and rightly so as a weak method of redressing a fundamentally flawed binary. How can those two polarities 'agree'?

But in the South Africa of the 1890s, it required more than a measure of courage for a White editor to take a position that did not endorse the White establishment.

With the likes of Cecil Rhodes who was determined to use his wealth and power as a diamond heft and as Prime Minister of the Cape Province to further imperialism, there could, of course, be no mediation, no agreement. Nor could there be with Kitchener of Khartoum[4] whose intent and actions during the war to entrench colonialism Cartwright instinctively disapproved. But even when there was to be no meeting ground, a mediatory purpose was served in so far as Cartwright's written words appealed to the reason of people occupying the 'middle space' between those who supported the then order and those who suffered under it.

The Second Boer War

The Second Boer War (11 October 1899–31 May 1902) between the British empire and two independent Boer states, the South African Republic (Republic of Transvaal) and the Orange Free State, was set off by the discovery of diamonds and gold in the Boer states. It continued for two years with Boer guerrilla warfare harrying the British, until harsh British countermeasures including a scorched earth policy brought the Boers to terms. This period also saw the founding by John Dube of the Natal Native Congress, a precursor of the African National Congress, and his arrest on charges of sedition.

The war started with Boer irregulars and militia striking against British-ruled towns in colonies near Boer terrain such as Ladysmith, Kimberley and Mafeking in early 1900, and winning important battles at Colenso, Magersfontein and Stormberg. At first surprised, the British resistance met with little initial success.

Mohandas K. Gandhi, the 40-year-old Kathiawari barrister in Durban, was driven by the thought that as British subjects, Indian South Africans must offer their services, albeit non-combatant, to the British in this war. The resolve came after a mental tussle. He says, 'my personal sympathies were with the Boers' and he put together a 1,100 strong Indian Ambulance Corps for the purpose and waited to be called to service (*CWMG*, vol. 39, p. 173). 'The Boer', he writes, 'showing more pluck, bravery and determination than expected, our services came ultimately to be needed' (ibid.). The British Commander-in-Chief General Redvers Buller faced reverse after reverse, earning the searing nickname among his men of General Reverse. The Battle of Spion Kop was particularly disastrous for the British. Vere Stent, war correspondent for Reuters, has recorded this scene from the road to Spion Kop:

> I came across Gandhi in the early morning sitting by the roadside – eating an Army regulation biscuit. Every man in Buller's force was dull and depressed and damnation was heartily invoked on everything. But Gandhi was stoical in his bearing, cheerful and confident in his conversation, and had a kindly eye. He did one good. (Reddy 1999)

Buller was soon replaced and his successor Lord Roberts, with the famed Kitchener of Khartoum as his Chief of Staff, relieved the three besieged cities. The Indian Corps was disbanded around this time, its role mentioned in despatches. Towards the end of 1900, the British forces invaded the two Boer republics with heavy reinforcements from home aided by Cape Colony, the Colony of Natal, Rhodesia, some native African allies, and supported by volunteers from the British empire, including southern Africa, the Australian colonies, Canada, India and New Zealand. This advancing militia which boasted of well over 4,00,000 men was able to overwhelm the Boers who, despite their skills at guerrilla tactics of surprise attacks and quick escapes lasting almost two years under new generals Louis Botha, Jan Smuts, Christiaan de Wet and Koos de la Rey, and support from volunteers from 'neutral' countries as well as from parts of the British empire like Ireland, could not defend their territories. Boer fighters having got moral and material help from the farmlands which provided hiding places, supplies and horses, the victorious British turned to civilian farms where the properties, tillage and livestock were destroyed as part of a scorched earth policy with survivors on the farms, including large numbers of women and children were forced into concentration camps where as many as 26,000 of these civilians died of hunger and disease, especially and tragically, children.

His joining the British war effort, with more than a thousand of his compatriots notwithstanding, Gandhi was appalled by the atrocities perpetrated on the Boer population by the British under Roberts and Kitchener which he was to describe later in these words:

Lord Kitchener left no stone unturned to break their spirit. He confined them in separate concentration camps where they underwent indescribable sufferings. They starved, they suffered biting cold and scorching heat. . . . [W]hen the cry of agony raised by the women in the concentration camps reached England . . . through a few high-souled Englishmen and women who were then in South Africa, the English people began to relent. The late Sir Henry Campbell-Bannerman[5] read the mind of the English people and raised his voice against the war. The late Mr Stead[6] publicly prayed and invited others to pray that God might decree the English a defeat in the war . . . (Gandhi 1928)

At this point in the narrative enters an extraordinary Cape Town figure – Olive Schreiner (1855–1920), sister of William Schreiner, who along with her husband Samuel Cronwright-Schreiner opposed Cecil Rhodes's racism. Schreiner, who had received acclamation and respect as the author of the stirring novel *The Story of an African Farm* (1883) based on life lived by a mixed community of Whites and Africans, and had gone on to write another novel, this time on the plight of Africans in Rhodesia, *Trooper Peter Hallket of Mashonaland* (1879). Schreiner's dislike of Rhodes (after an initial period of admiration for him) stemmed from particular acts of his like the 'strop bill' in Rhodesia which made Africans liable to be whipped for even minor offences and Rhodes' orders (Farwell 2001) in Mashonaland at the time of an Ndebele uprising that no mercy be shown in putting down the rebellion, telling officers 'Your instructions are: do the most harm you can to the natives around you' and ordering a police officer to 'kill all you can', even those Ndebele who begged for mercy and threw down their arms'. Schreiner's opposition to Rhodes also came from the knowledge of his long-term acts like the wholesale marauding of the newspaper industry in South Africa, so much so that, as she wrote 'There is not one paper now not in Rhodes' hands' (quoted in Derrick 2018, chapter 3). Gandhi, who had come to know Schreiner and received support from her for the Indian cause was to describe her as 'a gifted lady popular in South Africa and well known wherever the English language is spoken' (Gandhi 1928, p. 34). Schreiner strove to have a newspaper started, presumably from out of Cape Town to counter Rhodes and his policies but, as Derrick tells us, going beyond that to a larger aim (in her words): 'If only Dutchmen, Englishmen and Natives would all see where the common danger lies and combine against the common enemy which is not a person but the system.' Derrick says that, by this Schreiner meant the capitalist system. Schreiner wanted the new paper to become the voice of non-racial progressivism, with Cartwright as its editor. But the idea did not materialize.

Cartwright did, however, go on to Cape Town to become editor of *South African News*. This change was to give the course of events and indeed his life an interesting turn. When Cartwright was editing *South African News* from out of Cape Town, in other words from within British South Africa during the height of the war, he was opposing the British in the Anglo-Boer War at its fieriest. He was doing with Lord Roberts and Lord Kitchener exactly what he had done with the Randlord Rhodes – pointing out the folly underlying it and the play of egos – that of the jingoists in Britain and of generals wedded to war irrespective of the right and wrong of things.

Cartwright was watching with dismay these acts and writing about them in *South African News*. Gandhi does not mention Cartwright in that passage but his description of 'a few high-souled Englishmen and women' most definitely would apply to the then editor of *South African News*.

The war ended with the Treaty of Vereeniging in May 1902 under which the former Boer republics were turned into the Transvaal and Orange River colonies, to be finally merged with the British-ruled Cape and Natal Colonies into the Union of South Africa in 1910, as part of the British empire – but not before the enactment of a not-so-small drama involving Cartwright, thanks to an overdrive act on the part of Kitchener's martial law administration.

The Cartwright Case

In early 1901, *The Times* of London carried an anonymous letter purporting to be from an officer in the army out in the Boer War. The letter alleged that Kitchener had sent instructions down to the fighting ranks that as and when the Boers were surrounded and raised the white flag of surrender, not one of them was to be taken prisoner. In other words, they were to be shot down to the last man. The scene sharply echoes Rhodes' instructions about the Ndebele. Cartwright re-published this letter in *South African News*. The country was under martial law and Kitchener was virtually the ruler of the Cape Province. Cartwright was charged, tried and sentenced for sedition to twelve months of imprisonment.

From all accounts, Cartwright was confined to a private accommodation in Cape Town and did not suffer any particular privation, but his health suffered and by the time his term as prisoner was to end, he sought permission to leave Cape Town, leave South Africa itself, and return to Great Britain to recoup his health and resume his journalism, a prospect he did not see available to him in Kitchener's South Africa. The permission denied, two discussions took place in the House of Commons – the first following a factual question put to the Secretary of State for War and the second being on an adjournment motion moved by the great Liberal and thinker John Morley (author of *On Compromise*) seeking to discuss Cartwright's plea to be allowed to return to England on the expiration of his prison term. This was lost after a lively and in many ways defining debate by the leading political players of the day. Among these, apart from a host of MPs that included C.P. Scott, the Left-inclined editor of *Manchester Guardian* were four future prime ministers of note – A.J. Balfour and Winston Churchill from the Conservative Party and H.H. Asquith and D. Lloyd George from the Liberal Party.

Interestingly, while the 'majority' in the House – Conservative as it then was – succeeded in preventing Cartwright's return at that point on the ground that he will be indulging in anti-British propaganda on his return, the editor unwittingly mediated from his seclusion in Cape Town between hardliners and more sensitive MPs, with Churchill himself, arch-Conservative as he was, saying Cartwright's plea has to be seen as an issue where a principle, a constitutional right – the right of the people of Britain to receive any opinion and the right of a Briton to express that opinion in Britain – was involved. In Cartwright's 'case', the majority defeated the motion, but the minority led by Morley and supported by three out of four future prime ministers across the party spectrum had won the moment. Cartwright's experience mediated between hardlining and liberal outlooks in Parliament and made the defeat seem technical, the small change of legislative numbers, before the dividend of principles that were reiterated.

The following discussion took place in the House of Commons on 25 March 1902.[7]

> Mr Channing:[8] I beg to ask the Secretary of State for War whether he is aware that Mr Albert Cartwright, formerly editor of the *South African News*, who is about to complete a year's imprisonment at Cape Town for reprinting from the press of this country a letter held to be a seditious libel, is in bad health, and has applied on that ground, and also on the ground that his means of making a living in South Africa no longer exist, for permission to come to this country; and that such permission has been refused by the military authorities; and whether he will, under these circumstances, request the military authorities to reconsider this application.
>
> Mr Brodrick:[9] I have no knowledge of the circumstances alluded to in the question.
>
> Mr Channing: Will the Right Hon. Gentleman inquire? I may say the question has been asked at the earnest request of the wife of this gentleman, who has been sent to England.
>
> Mr Brodrick was understood to reply that it was impossible for him to inquire into the cases of those who had got into trouble under martial law, and he would rather hesitate to interfere with their discretion. And the following discussion in the House of Commons is recorded in the Hansard for 24 April 1902.[10]
>
> Mr John Morley, Member for the Montrose District, rose in his place, and asked leave to move the adjournment of the house for the purpose of discussing a definite matter of urgent public importance, namely, 'the compulsory detention of Mr Cartwright in Cape Town without charge brought, and for indefinite length of time'.

Mr John Morley:[11] Mr Speaker, I make no apology to the House for this interruption of public business, because the matter to which I must draw their attention is one which involves, in the first place, extreme hardship to an individual, and in the second place, a gross and flagrant violation of the legal and constitutional principles of which this House is the guardian and the champion. The story is very short, very plain and very simple. Mr Cartwright was indicted in the ordinary way before an ordinary court in Cape Town for a defamatory and seditious libel, was tried before a judge and jury and was convicted and sentenced to undergo one year's imprisonment. That year of imprisonment terminated, as the Right Hon. Gentleman has just told the House, I think, on Tuesday. Upon all that part of the matter I have no comment whatever to make. It does not come within the scope of the subject to which I am drawing attention. About two months ago – I think in February – Mr Cartwright sent in a written application to the authorities in the Cape Colony for information whether upon the expiry of his sentence he would be allowed to travel. He gave two reasons for desiring this permission to leave Cape Colony and come to England. One reason was that he had been in the doctor's hands, so he alleges, for some time, and that his health required the change to England; and the second reason was that he had no chance whatever of earning his livelihood as a journalist, for there was no opening for him in Cape Colony, and therefore his only chance was to come here; and I may add further, that he stated that he was willing to show to the authorities a bona fide engagement for doing work of a purely non-political character in this country. Well, Mr Cartwright upon this received a refusal. No reason was given for this refusal. No charge was made or indicated. He was simply told that he would not be allowed to travel – that is to say, not allowed to leave South Africa. The House will observe that by this proceeding, by this refusal of the authorities, they took upon themselves to make an enormous and unmeasured extension of Mr Cartwright's legal penalty. A legal penalty had been imposed upon him, but he had undergone it. His offence was purged, and no additional offence could have been committed by him because, of course, he was in confinement. He was then by this refusal called upon to undergo a further penalty – namely, a compulsory detention in Cape Town, and the prevention of his performing his ordinary avocations. As the Secretary of State told us two or three nights ago, he is now a free man. But in what sense free? He is free to walk about in Cape Town, under supervision, as the Right Hon. Gentleman said. Therefore, I submit that, so far as that goes, the authorities in Cape Town, whose action is endorsed by the Secretary of State, have extended, without any law or intention to appeal to law, a legal penalty. Upon this state of facts, I put a question to the Secretary of State for War on 14 April, and I received, not from him, because he was unfortunately not present, but from the noble Lord, the Financial Secretary, in those unfaltering accents which make him a sort of impersonation of martial law – I received from him, I think, the most outrageous and indefensible answer ever given within these walls since Simon de Montfort invented Parliament. I will read the noble Lord's answer: 'The authorities in South Africa', he said, 'did not consider it desirable to grant Mr Cartwright permission to proceed to England. His views, as the Right Hon. Gentleman was probably aware.'

I do not know why I should be aware of his views: 'were strongly anti-British, and it was not deemed desirable by the authorities in South Africa to increase the number of persons in this country who disseminated anti-British propaganda' [quoting Mr Brodrick].

The House will observe there is no word said about the military necessities or about anything indeed in South Africa. It is the dissemination of anti-British views in Great Britain. Now I might put a question to the Secretary of State, and I might invite him to tell me first what he understands the authorities in South Africa to mean by anti-British views. I suppose they mean, and can mean, nothing else than views which are not palatable to His Majesty's Government. Therefore, Mr Cartwright is kept in exile – because it comes to that – by the arbitrary action of the military authorities, because he might disseminate views unfavourable to His Majesty's Government in this country. Now I will put another point to the Right Hon. Gentleman. Supposing Mr Cartwright holds obnoxious anti-British views – whatever anti-British may mean – will the Right Hon. Gentleman be kind enough to tell us where on earth the dissemination of anti-British views could be so entirely harmless as in Great Britain? If they prevented Mr Cartwright from going to Berlin, or Paris or The Hague, there might be something to be said for it; but he is not to be allowed to come to Great Britain, where, if anywhere, surely there are enough British views to outweigh the addition of one single individual to those who are alleged to disseminate anti-British propaganda. The one country, therefore, to which he cannot come is the country where we all know he would not do one atom or scintilla of harm of any kind, I say, not only is the action illegal, unconstitutional, tyrannical and arbitrary, but it is, on the face of it, impudently absurd and preposterous.

Brodrick, Secretary of State for War: On 6 February 1901, Mr Cartwright was guilty of what I think is the greatest crime from the journalistic point of view that a British subject can well be accused of. He published in the *South African News* a statement headed: 'How we are waging war. A dreadful disclosure. Lord Kitchener's secret instructions', and then follows: 'Lord Kitchener having, as he thought, caged his enemy, sent secret instructions to the troops to take no prisoners, that is, if the Boers surrounded on all sides found themselves unable to resist and hoisted the white flag as a token of surrender, they were to be shot down to the last man.'

Then there follows this, professing to come from an officer. Whether any person, having any title to be called an officer ever communicated to

the *South African News* we know not, but that it was an absolute and outrageous falsehood is well known. This 'officer' said: 'I received the order
personally from a General of the highest rank, holding one of the first positions in South Africa. The order was repeated twice, so that there might be
no mistake. I found that all the other senior officers were aware of the order.
What their private opinions and intentions were I do not know, but I heard
no word of condemnation.'

Well, Sir, that is an attempt, not merely to charge Lord Kitchener and
the highest authorities of the British Army, but all the senior officers engaged
in that particular operation, with a grave military crime, with the intention
of taking action, which from every standpoint would be abhorrent to the
feelings of the people of this country. That would be admirably calculated
to increase the violence of opinion between the two combatants and was
framed absolutely and solely for the purpose of damaging the British troops.

R. Winston Churchill:[12] I rise for the purpose of expressing to the
House how greatly I differ from the view my noble friend the Member for
Kensington has put forward, and my regret that one who so often delights
this House with his eloquence and well-reasoned arguments should have
committed himself to such a very bad position on this occasion. This is not
a question of Party at all, it is a very great question arising from a very small
incident in the course of the warfare in South Africa. It does not matter a row
of buttons who Mr Cartwright is. He may be a ruffian, perhaps he is. But
he has been tried by a court martial. He has been tried by a judge and jury;
he had been found guilty; and South Africa is not an atmosphere, I imagine,
in which a man would be likely to get less punishment than he deserved,
although I am bound to say, in view of what the Secretary of State has read,
Mr Cartwright appears to have been lucky in the sentence he received; but,
at any rate, he has served his sentence, and his offence is blotted out. There
is no right or power in this country which allows the Home Government,
in time of peace, to proceed against a man who has already served all that
the law has a right to require of him. If there is no right, there is no reason.
What reason has the Government to be afraid of Mr Cartwright? There are
many people in this country who spread what is called anti British propaganda, but does that alter the opinion of the British people? Has it in any
way impaired the security of the British Government? No Government has
benefited so much by the strong support and opinions of the masses of the
country as this Government. No Government has less right not to allow
those masses to receive any opinion within the law which may be properly
expressed to them. This is a great constitutional principle, and I should be
very sorry indeed if it were thought by those outside who read the debates in
this House that constitutional principles are valued and supported only by
Hon. Members opposite. There are some of us on this side of the House who
are not prepared to see a great constitutional principle violated, not, I think,

with any deliberate intent, but simply because those who administer the law have got used to an over exercise of power, and who, having overstepped themselves on this occasion, should be made by the due authority of this House to withdraw within the limits of the law.

Mr Bartley:[13] Lord Milner and Lord Kitchener, in the exercise of their high powers, have thought it desirable that this man should be kept where he is, and we are bound to support them in that action. . . .

Mr A.J. Balfour:[14] It appears to me that the man who published that seditious libel avowedly with a view of bringing discredit on our troops, officers and generals, with a view of embittering and prolonging the war, with a view of opening every sore and pouring poison into every wound – that man was guilty of as base and as horrible a crime as the imagination of any of us is able to picture. If the matter is to be argued upon its merits or demerits, I do not think there is anybody, or hardly anybody, in any quarter of the House who would dare to get up and defend this Gentleman's cause.

Mr Bryce:[15] Who is Lord Kitchener? He is our commander-in-chief in South Africa, and a brave and distinguished soldier, who deserves our confidence for the way in which he has conducted the war. But he is not a constitutional lawyer. It is not Lord Kitchener's duty to say what is the law of England, what are the rights of British subjects, or whether a British subject should or should not be allowed to leave South Africa. Suppose Lord Kitchener were to say, 'I think these persons ought not to leave South Africa' that does not give him the right to prevent them leaving. The guardians of the constitution are the Ministers of the Crown, and it is not possible for them to shuffle off that responsibility. But it appears to me that they are trying to get a responsibility which is theirs on to the military commander in South Africa. The real issue we have in this case is a simple one. We have nothing to do with the merits of Mr Cartwright. We have nothing to do with the justice of his sentence. We have nothing to do with martial law, as I have humbly submitted, because the only test of martial law is military necessity, and it cannot be alleged that there is that necessity applicable to England, although I do admit there may be in South Africa. The real issue is shortly and simply this: Whether there exists in the law of England any power or right by which the executive Government or the military Government can interfere with the rights of a British subject in England to write or speak what he pleases subject to his responsibility to the law, or to prevent him from coming to the shores of England. If that authority can be given let it be given. If it is not given, we are bound to protest against such a doctrine. The First Lord of the Treasury has asked what would be said in South Africa and other parts of the world if this action with respect to Mr Cartwright had not been taken. I should like to ask what will be said in all the countries of the world, which look to England as the home of constitutional freedom, if the House of Commons is found throwing away our constitutional rights in this fashion? There is an old maxim, 'That eternal vigilance is the price of freedom', and the House of Commons will be false to its responsibilities and traditions, if it neglects to mark, to check, and to denounce this monstrous infraction of constitutional rights.

Mr Lloyd-George:[16] The fact is that Mr Cartwright has not been guilty of wickedly inventing a slander, but of grave error of judgment in believing he was safe in publishing something which had appeared in *The Times*. For that error of judgment, he very properly got 12-months imprisonment. Here we have kept in Cape Town, the centre of activity, a man who is believed to be so dangerous that he cannot be allowed in England. What papers would Mr Cartwright write for? He would not be allowed to write for *The Times*. Every paper which is supposed to be anti-British is prohibited in South Africa. How would any of his writings reach that country? Would they ever have any access there? No. . . . His offence, which was really that of implicitly believing in *The Times*, has been expiated, and every man in this country, however foul may be his offence, once he has purged that offence, is free to go where he pleases. The worst that can be done is to subject him to police supervision. Why is not Mr Cartwright to be allowed to come to this country under ordinary conditions?

Mr Asquith:[17] . . . I can understand a man being locked up without reason assigned if he was thought to be dangerous to the peace of a colony, or if he was likely to give assistance to the enemy in the field. I can understand under the *régime* of martial law a man being deported from the colony on the ground that under existing circumstances his room would be preferred to his company. But never until tonight, never until this case, never until the noble Lord a few days ago told us what the grounds of detention of this gentleman were, never in the history of the law has it been suggested that a commander was entitled, under the *régime* of martial law, not to keep a man in gaol, but, to allow him to wander freely in the country where martial law prevails, and yet to keep him in that country which is the scene of disturbance against his will, unless he will give a pledge as to what he will do or not do when he gets away from the scene of disturbance to a free country where martial law does not prevail. That is the proposition, and the only proposition, which the House has to consider. Whatever your views may be about the war, its origin, and its conduct, whatever may be your admiration and confidence – and I yield to no one in that respect – in the generals and officers in the field. I say that the House is not bound by any consideration of patriotic reserve to abstain from discussing – aye, and condemning – a proposition of this kind put forward on the authority of Ministers of the day, a proposition in which I for one will never acquiesce, and against which I invite the House to protest.

Mr C.P. Scott:[18] Perhaps Hon. Gentlemen opposite would like to know that Mr Cartwright's case did not stand alone, but that there had been a

number of similar cases. It ought to be understood that the House was dealing with an attempt, not on the part of Lord Kitchener, but on the part of
certain other persons in the Colony, to prevent journalists who happened
to know a great deal about the facts in South Africa from coming to this
country and informing the mind of the British public. I know of at least two
or three other journalists who had been or who were now detained in South
Africa on the same kind of plea as that put forward in Mr Cartwright's case.

Mr Speaker: Order, order; I must remind the Hon. Member that he will
not be in order in discussing other cases.

Mr C.P. Scott said he merely wished to point out that there was a principle involved, and this was not simply the conduct of a single individual. It
was said that by carrying this motion they would be passing a vote of cen-
sure on Lord Kitchener, but he did not think Lord Kitchener knew anything
whatever about the cases of these journalists. He believed the course taken
had been decided upon by some official at Cape Town whom he did not
know. It would be a most salutary thing if they were to do something by way
of protest against the excesses of these irresponsible persons – something
which would clip their claws and teach them that Members of that House
had a little more respect for the rights of British subjects than they appeared
to have.

Mr Markham:19 Mr Cartwright is a man than whom no one is more
patriotic. I say that Mr Cartwright has made great sacrifices. He made a
grave error. It has been said that 'a man who makes no mistakes never makes
anything'. Mr Cartwright having made this mistake has paid the penalty. I
say that Mr Cartwright does not hold anti-British views but is animated by
the desire of seeing this country doing what is right in South Africa, and
nothing else.

The House divided: Yesses, 182; Noes, 259. Cartwright was denied permission to come to England.

Unbeknownst to it, the House of Commons did South Africa a good
turn by keeping Cartwright in that country. He moved from *The South African*
in Cape Town to Johannesburg – far more congenial to him politically – to
become editor of *The Transvaal Leader* and an influential member of the
Progressive Party which was strong enough in the new Transvaal Parliament.
This also meant that he came to know the Boer leadership which, in the
post-War altered circumstances was heading the Province of Transvaal with
accountability to London.

Cartwright and the Indian South African

Outside of the theatre of that war, Cartwright had observed the ugly
face of racism as it worked against the 'native' population as also against the
small but professionally vital community of South Africa's expatriate Indians.

And he did what he felt impelled to do with this nuanced assessment of the situation to blunt the imperial claw-nail.

Quite inevitably, Cartwright emerged as a mediator between authorities in the South Africa that he knew and worked in during the same time M.K. Gandhi did. The two got to know each other well and became thought-partnering friends. A shared thought or binding idea uniting the two was a belief in the innate goodness of the state as it is meant to be and dismay at the manifest un-goodness of the state as it showed itself to be, and a consequential belief amounting to a deep faith in the almost endless possibility of mediating settlements and conciliating differences through dialogue and persuasion, to make the state responsive and responsible – a process in which both saw journalism playing a crucial role. If Cartwright started his time in South Africa through journalism, moving from newspaper to newspaper, Gandhi added to his public initiatives the one impactful journal *Indian Opinion* which ran under his watch from 1903 to 1915.

In 1908, when Gandhi was arrested for resisting The Transvaal Immigration Restriction Act that required among other iniquitous provisions, Indians residing in the Transvaal to register themselves with fingerprints being taken from them. 'It is not a question,' Gandhi said to a gathering just before his trial and conviction 'of . . . giving a thumb impression or a ten digits' impression . . . but the sting lay in the spirit itself – the condemnation of the whole of the Indian community' (*CWMG*, vol. 8, pp. 36–37). The sentence, his first ever, was for two months without hard labour.

Cartwright got into action mode to find a method to defuse the tension and have Gandhi and many others imprisoned along with him released, and came to The Fort Prison in Johannesburg where Gandhi was lodged. Gandhi writes:

> On 21 January (1909) I had an unexpected visitor. Mr Albert Cartwright, editor of *The Transvaal Leader*, had himself suffered imprisonment for reasons of conscience and was as broad-minded as he was able. He had remained indefatigable in his support of the Indian cause. He and I had become good friends. When he came after securing special permission to do so, he and I discussed the whole issue, and we agreed that the law should be repealed during the following session of Parliament and the Indian community should immediately take out registers voluntarily. We put this agreement down in writing. He then met leaders of his party, the Progressive Party, who while accepting the suggestions asked that the Indians should write a letter from gaol volunteering to register. (Ibid. pp. 65–66)

Quite clearly Cartwright then met General Smuts, then Minister for the Interior, and as such in charge of law and order, to discuss his proposal, prisoner Gandhi's response and the Progressives' modification of it. Gandhi continues: 'Mr Cartwright then brought the draft letter to me on 28 January.

It had either been drafted or approved by General Smuts whom he met and found to be welcoming of his mediation.'

With some more modifications made at Gandhi's instance, a formula was arrived at that involved no loss of principles only of procedure, and Cartwright went back to Smuts with it. 'At five in the afternoon,' Gandhi writes, 'he rang to say General Smuts had accepted the draft with one suggestion for alteration which we accepted.' All the prisoners, including Gandhi, were released after a meeting that followed quickly thereafter between Gandhi and Smuts. The agreement did not hold, satyagraha was resumed with plantation workers and miners in the lead during the Great March of 1913 that saw some 10,000 Indians arrested, and the world knows the story of its eventual success in the Gandhi-Smuts Agreement of 30 June 1914 and the Indian Relief Act which met the aspirations of most of the Indians.

Behind that agreement lay the quiet mediation of Albert Cartwright and, one must not fail to acknowledge, the last-minute crucial mediation of the Rev C.F. Andrews sent from India by the statesman G.K. Gokhale.

In London, on his way back to India at the end of his struggle in South Africa, Gandhi and his wife Kasturba were accorded a reception (8 August 1914) at Hotel Cecil and feted for his leadership. Describing the agreement as 'the Magna Carta of the British Indians of South Africa not only because of its substance, which was great enough, but for its spirit, which indicated a change of attitude on the part of South Africa and the South African Government', Gandhi recalled the momentous times that had just ended. 'If we merited any approbation,' he said, 'how much more did those who were behind us and who went into the struggle with simple faith and no thought of appreciation?' He spoke of Harbut Singh[20] who was 75 years of age when he joined the struggle and entered prison and died there. He spoke of the young lad Narayanaswami[21] who was deported to Madras and on his return, starved and died. He also spoke of another Tamil youth Nagappen,[22] who was imprisoned and worked on the African veldt in the bitter cold of winter and died, and of Valliamma,[23] the girl of eighteen who went to prison and was discharged only when she took very ill and died shortly thereafter.

He said to the gathering that 20,000 workers left their tools and work and went out in faith. Violence was entirely eschewed. These men and women, he said, are the salt of the earth and on them will be built the Indian nation that is to be. We are poor mortals before these heroes and heroines.

First World War had just broken out and Gandhi was mediating in his mind his role exactly as he had done when the Boer War had begun. As a British subject, loyal to the empire and with expectations of the empire for India, he felt he should participate in a non-combatant capacity in the war. But his newly acquitted and deeply cherished adherence to non-violence and to Tolstoy's audience pointed to another direction. The life of the thinker and activist is ever fraught, never at ease. And so is that of a writer, journalist and editor if she or he is to hear the voice of the conscience above the din of the day. And a mediation takes place quite unceasingly in their minds between principles and prudence, courage and caution, proximate loyalties and permanent affinities.

In Gandhi's London audience that day were prominent Indians, current and future leaders of the Indian sub-continent who were visiting London – Lala Lajpat Rai, Mohammed Ali Jinnah, Sarojini Naidu, Bhupendranath Basu.

And also seated there, quietly listening to a story they knew from the inside, were two visitors from South Africa – Olive Schreiner and, now no longer barred from being in his home country, Albert Cartwright.

An Assessment

Cartwright deserves being recalled today because, quite simply, his is a tale worth retelling for its own sake but also because today when contemporary media struggles to 'breathe' through the strangulations of the majority-ruling market and the grasp of majority-manipulating supremacisms, his story contains a message to journalists and editors across the world: With sales, competition and profits becoming Gospel and editorial opinion looking over the shoulder in fear of authority's 'raised eyebrow', the Fourth Estate, with great exceptions, of course, is having to play its role below par. The imperialism of high-end market finance and the colonizing control of low-time majoritarian power politics have blurred the distinction between the real and the spurious, fact and fiction. Cartwright's example shows how, when occasion arises, a journalist and an editor can, mediating between courage and play-safeness, stand up to bullying and speak up for what is right.

The Cartwright story also serves to show that the current scene in many countries, so dispiriting, in the matter of free and frank and fearless expression is not new and, more importantly, has been overcome. Therein lies hope.

Albert Cartwright eventually did move to Britain to found in London in 1917 a weekly of which he was the editor for full thirty years – *West Africa*. That was his longest spell with any newspaper, journal or establishment. Derrick says the weekly's policy 'accepted British colonial rule and the established trade-based West African economic system as part of the landscape . . . and saw them as on the whole beneficial'. But Africans 'were visible in its columns' both as writers of articles and letters to the editor, who covered some of the early political movements of Africans 'well enough to help the modern historian'.

It is unlikely that in his London setting, Cartwright would have heard of his friend M.K. Gandhi's meeting the Rev. S.S. Tema of the African National Congress (ANC) in India on 1 January 1939, and of Gandhi saying to his visitor, 'The Indians (in South Africa) are a microscopic minority. . . . You, on the other hand, are the sons of the soil who are being robbed of your inheritance. You are bound to resist that. Yours is a far bigger issue. . . .' But there is no doubt that the reflexive opponent of Rhodes and of Kitchener would have endorsed that. As also the observation made by Chief Albert Luthuli, the ANC president from 1952 to 1967 in a hand-written statement preserved at Howard University, Washington: '[I have] no doubt that [Gandhi's] efforts for his people inspired people like John Dube[24] and others to concern themselves with seeking human rights for their people.' They were all mediating natural gulfs, Luthuli, Gandhi, Dube, Cartwright. And reducing them to the extent they or anyone in their situations could.

Retiring in 1947, Cartwright passed away in 1956. His niche in the history of South Africa's evolution from out of its imperialist and colonial past is as a counter-imperialist (as distinct from an anti-imperialist), opinion-maker, mediator and opponent by his own light.

In the interplay of the culture of print with politics in Rhodes' and Kitchener's South Africa, Cartwright's place is best seen in tandem with that of Jabavu, Dube and Gandhi, a role in which mediation and compromise – John Morley's passion – played a central role. Khwezi Mkhize (2018)[25] describes this tellingly, while writing about the nuanced roles of Jabavu and his newspaper, *Imvo*:

> I trace the making of *Imvo Zabantsundu* to the project of imperial liberal-ism. I argue that Jabavu and his peers were black Victorians who took their status as imperial subjects as a condition of possibility for their engagements with the colonial order. An encounter with *Imvo Zabantsundu* therefore means thinking through empire as both a political geography and a structure of feeling. In so doing, I suggest that we seriously consider imperial citizen-ship as a category through which to mark the making of the black intelli-gentsia and tune our senses to the long histories of liberalism that informed colonial belonging and its attendant contradictions.

Cartwright was an imperial liberal, a work-in-progress to become a White African to the more 'finished' works from the time of Imperial Liberalism – the 'Black Victorian' in Jabavu, Dube and Gandhi.

An Indian Postscript

Gandhi's association with editors was a strong feature of his political work in South Africa and India. Examples of journalists and editors being active and making huge sacrifices towards their people's and their nation's causes are inspiring, but they are legion. It is when these journalists and editors are 'foreigners' and despite their being so, they yet understand and identify themselves with these causes, at great risk to themselves, that they command special notice. Gandhi responded to such editors with instant appreciation. Two such equations with British-born editors in particular mirror the Gandhi-Cartwright one. The first of these is that between Gandhi and Benjamin Guy Horniman (1873–1948) who after a career in the *Portsmouth Evening Mail*,

Daily Chronicle and *Manchester Guardian* came out to India and edited *Bombay Chronicle*, making it a vigorously anti-imperialist and anti-colonial organ, fiercely opposing British policy after the Jallianwala Bagh massacre (1919) for which impudence he was famously deported, leading Gandhi and nationalists in India to hail his courage and denounce the Raj's hubris. The second is that between Gandhi and William Arthur Moore (1880–1962), who was appointed managing editor of *The Statesman* in Calcutta in 1933 and by the late 1930s had become a strong critic of the Viceroy, Lord Linlithgow, by writing in his paper for a greater role being given to Indians in the running of India and wanting a rapid move towards dominion status. This was less than what the Congress wanted but more than what the Raj was then prepared for, making Moore's role one of piquancy. But he earned the trust of Gandhi and also that of Lord Linlithgow's successor, Lord Wavell, during the Bengal famine by his transparent earnestness. During Gandhi's last fast in Delhi (January 1948) for communal harmony, Moore fasted parallelly in solidarity, breaking it only when, on getting assurances from community leaders and the newly installed government led by Nehru, Gandhi broke his. But this is Cartwright's space; Horniman and Moore must await another occasion for their stories to be told in greater detail. Suffice it to say that editors as mediators and gadflies are to be thanked for what they have done and can do in the cause of justice and equity – essential for us, in our times where a new illiberalism that is neither imperial nor feudal but crassly manipulative of social vulnerabilities and prejudices to further its agenda of commercial gain and political control, is at work.

I close this essay invoking the memory of Natal-based Manilal Gandhi (1892–1956), second son of Kasturba and Mohandas Gandhi, who edited *Indian Opinion* from 1920 to his death with courage and sagacity, mediating with no compromise on principles, between his firm opposition to apartheid and his equally firm adherence to non-violent methods, making him valued and yet distinct from both ends of the political spectrum. And that of his wife Sushila Gandhi *nee* Mashruwala (1907–1988) who, after her husband's death managed with fortitude and skill the Phoenix Settlement and edited *Indian Opinion* renamed *Opinion* (1957–61); a vociferous opponent of apartheid, participating in the defiance of petty apartheid laws in 1951 and also fasting at Phoenix in protest at the killings of African pass law protestors in 1960.

It is my great good fortune to be able to offer this essay to two deeply cherished friends, the scholar-teachers Prabhat Patnaik and Utsa Mukherjee, whose intellectual veracity and academic energy are an inspiration to observe and a joy to celebrate.

I gratefully acknowledge the usefulness of Jonathan Derrick's splendid work *Africa, Empire and Fleet Street* published by Hurst Publishers, the time and attention allocated by him to my queries, the help received from the lawyer-scholar and historian Anil Nauriya, Professor Venu Madhav Govindu, Eric Itzkin, Deputy Director, Immovable Heritage at City of Johannesburg, Professor Isabel Hofmeyr, Witwatersrand University, Johannes Kgoadi, Manager of the Johannesburg City Library, and Lungisani Silolo of the same, during the course of my preparing this essay.

This essay was originally published under the same title in *The Indian Economic Journal*, vol. 71, no. 1, 2023, pp. 12–29.

Notes

[1] Cecil John Rhodes (1853–1902): British mining magnate and politician in southern Africa, served as Prime Minister of the Cape Province from 1890 to 1896.

[2] William Philip Schreiner (1857–1919): barrister, politician, statesman and Prime Minister of Cape Colony during the Second Boer War.

[3] Cecil Rhodes entered the diamond trade at Kimberley in 1871 at the age of eighteen and, with financial backing from Rothschild & Co., started on a strategy of buying out and consolidating diamond mines gaining, over the next two decades, a formidable monopoly not just over South Africa's but over the world diamond market. His diamond company De Beers, formed in 1888, has, over the decades, been synonymous with this formidable grip.

[4] Kitchener of Khartoum (1850–1916): Irish-born senior British Army officer, colonialist and imperialist, came to prominence for his military campaigns, winning famously, in 1898, the Battle of Omdurman and securing control of Sudan; made Baron Kitchener of Khartoum; played a key role as Chief of Staff (1900–1902) in the Second Boer War during Lord Roberts' conquest of the Boer Republics, succeeding Roberts as commander-in-chief by which time Boer forces had taken to guerrilla fighting and British forces imprisoned Boer civilians in concentration camps; Commander-in-Chief (1902–1909) of the Army in India, embroiled in quarrel with Viceroy Lord Curzon who eventually resigned; aspired in 1911 to be Viceroy of India, but foiled by Secretary of State for India, John Morley, perhaps in part because Morley, after the recent grant of limited self-government under the 1909 Indian Councils Act, for a serving soldier to be Viceroy; appointed in 1914, at the start of the First World War, a Cabinet Minister as Secretary of State for War but blamed in 1915 for the shortage of shells – one of the events leading to the formation of a coalition government – and stripped of his control over munitions and strategy. On 5 June 1916, he was aboard HMS Hampshire headed for Russia to attend negotiations with Tsar Nicholas II when, in bad weather, the ship struck a German mine 1.5 miles west of Orkney, Scotland and sank. Kitchener was among 737 who died.

[5] Sir Henry Campbell-Bannerman (1836–1908): British statesman and Liberal politician, served as the Prime Minister of the United Kingdom from 1905 to 1908 and Leader of the Liberal Party from 1899 to 1908. A.J.A. Morris, in the Oxford Dictionary of National Biography, has called him 'Britain's first and only radical Prime Minister'.

[6] William Thomas Stead (1849–1912): British newspaper editor, pioneer of investigative journalism, editor of *The Pall Mall Gazette*, best known for his 1885 series of articles, written in support of a bill, later dubbed the 'Stead Act', that raised the age of consent from 13 to 16, died in the sinking of the RMS Titanic on 15 April 1912.

[7] H.C. Deb, Debates in the House of Commons, UK, which form part of what is popularly known as the *Hansard*, 25 March 1902, vol. 105.

[8] Francis Allston Channing (1841–1926): an American-born British barrister, academic and Liberal Party politician, elected as Liberal Member of Parliament (MP) for East Northamptonshire at the 1885 general election, held the seat until the December 1910 general election, made a Baronet in 1906 and in 1912 elevated to the peerage as Baron Channing of Wellingborough, in the County of Northampton.

[9] William St John Fremantle Brodrick, 1st Earl of Midleton, KP, PC, DL (1856–1942): a British Conservative and Irish Unionist Alliance politician. He served as a Member of Parliament from 1880 to 1906, as a government minister from 1886 to 1892 and from 1895 to 1900, and as a Cabinet minister from 1900 to 1905, as Secretary of State for War.

[10] H.C. Deb, 24 April 1902, vol. 106.

[11] John Morley (1838–1923): known as 'the last of the great nineteenth-century Liberals'; barrister, journalist, Liberal MP and statesman; as an anti-imperialist opponent of the Boer War; biographer in a three-volume work of his hero W.E. Gladstone; Chief Secretary for Ireland (1892–1895) in Gladstone's government; Secretary of State for India under the governments of Henry Campbell-Bannerman and H.H. Asquith, crafting, with the Viceroy of India Lord Minto, the major rubric for political reform in India known as the Morley-Minto Reforms in the Indian Councils Act, 1909; opposed imperialism and supported Home Rule for Ireland; opposed the First World War and as a consequence left Asquith's Government in which he was Lord President of the Council; author of celebrated work *On Compromise* (1874) and biographical monographs on Edmund Burke, Voltaire, Rousseau, Cromwell and Richard Cobden, and on literary themes such as Aphorisms. Liberal MP at the time of this discussion.

[12] Winston Churchill (1874–1965): Britain's most celebrated politician; Sandhurst-trained soldier seeing action in British India, the Anglo–Sudan War, the Boer War; MP from five constituencies and the Conservative Party between 1900 and 1964, opposing his party and government on some key issues like financial policy and free trade, labour union rights and in the Cartwright case under discussion; later switched to the Liberal Party under the governments of which he held key positions, returning to the Conservative fold, unabashed imperialist, twice Prime Minister (from 1940 to 1945 and from 1951 to 1955); Nobel Prize winning writer and prolific painter. Conservative MP at the time of this discussion.

[13] George Christopher Trout Bartley (1842–1910): Conservative politician, MP from 1885 to 1906, was in South Africa when the Second Boer War broke out.

[14] Arthur James Balfour (1848–1930): British Conservative statesman. Prime Minister from 1902 to 1905; gained some unpopularity by Britain's experience in the later part of the Boer War and over the question of importing Chinese labour into South Africa; as Foreign Secretary in D. Lloyd George's coalition in 1917, issued the Balfour Declaration proclaiming Britain's support for a Jewish homeland in Palestine; Conservative MP at the time of this discussion.

[15] James Bryce (1838–1922): Ulster-born academic, jurist, historian and Liberal politician. Regius Professor of Civil Law in Oxford, elected to the House of Commons from 1880 to 1907; in 1897, visited South Africa and published a volume of impressions of that country that had considerable influence in Liberal circles when the Second Boer War was being discussed, Ambassador of Great Britain in the United States of America from 1907 to 1913, after the First World War, authored the Bryce Report following a study conducted at Prime Minister Asquith's behest of German atrocities in Belgium; in 1915, with the help of Arnold Toynbee wrote on the Armenian Genocide in the Ottoman empire.

[16] D. Lloyd George (1863–1945): Welsh statesman and Liberal Party politician; while not an opponent of the British empire per se, in a speech at Birkenhead (21 November 1901) stressed that it needed to be based on freedom, including for India, not 'racial arrogance'; gained national fame by displaying vehement opposition to the Second Boer War; served as Prime Minister of the United Kingdom from 1916 to 1922; the last Liberal to hold the post of prime minister, holding the office through the last two years of the First World War, leading the British delegation at the Paris Peace Conference in 1919; Liberal MP at the time of this discussion.

[17] H.H. Asquith (1852–1928): British statesman and Liberal politician; served as Prime Minister of the United Kingdom from 1908 to 1916, the last Liberal prime minister to command a majority government, took Great Britain and the British empire into the First World War; was vigorously attacked in 1915 for a shortage of munitions and the failure of the Gallipoli Campaign; formed a coalition government with other parties but failed to satisfy critics; forced to resign in December 1916, never regaining power; Liberal MP at the time of this discussion.

[18] C.P. Scott (1846–1932): British journalist, publisher and politician, editor of the *Manchester Guardian* (now *The Guardian*) from 1872 until 1929 and its owner from

1907, maintaining a progressive, liberal policy, until his death; a Liberal Member of Parliament as elected at the 1895 election from Leigh; re-elected at the 1900 'khaki' election despite the unpopular stand against the Boer War that the *Guardian* had taken.

[19] Arthur Basil Markham (1866–1916): Industrialist, owner of coalfields and Liberal politician, served from 1900 to 1916 as Liberal MP for the Mansfield Division of Nottinghamshire.

[20] A fellow prisoner of Gandhi's, with other satyagrahis and mine workers in Volksrust jail, 1913. Gandhi (1928) writes in *Satyagraha in South Africa*: '. . . new prisoners came every day. . . . Among these was Harbut Singh, of about 75 years in age. He was not a miner and therefore was not one of the strikers. "Why are you in jail?" I asked him, alluding to his age. "How could I help it?," he replied, "when you, your wife and even your boys have gone to jail for our sakes? . . . And how happy I should be to die in jail!" My head bent in reverence before this illiterate sage. Harbut Singh who was shifted to Durban Jail, had his wish, and he died in Durban Jail on 5 January 1914. His body was cremated according to Hindu rites in the presence of hundreds of Indians.'

[21] Narayanaswamy was deported to India as a passive resister. He returned with other deportees under an arrangement to have such deportees return, but the ship was not allowed to land in South African ports. Debilitated and ill, Narayanaswamy died at Delagoa Bay on 16 October 1914.

[22] 'Sammy' Nagappen, eighteen years old, died on 6 June 1909 soon after release from prison, where he had suffered ill-treatment, though he had observed all jail rules and done the tasks entrusted to him which included road-construction where he contracted double pneumonia. Gandhi (1928) writes of him in *Satyagraha in South Africa*: '. . . if we consider his fortitude, his patience, his patriotism, his firmness unto death, there is nothing left which we might desire him to possess.'

[23] Valliamma Moonsamy Moodaliar died on 22 February 1914, a few days after release from prison. Visiting her when she was grievously ill, Gandhi asked her, 'Valliamma, you do not regret your having gone to jail?' 'Regret? I am even now ready to go to jail again if I am arrested.' 'But what if that results in your death?' 'I do not mind it. Who would not love to die for one's motherland?' (Gandhi 1928).

[24] John Dube (1871–1946) South African essayist, philosopher, educator, politician, publisher, editor, novelist and poet, founding president of the South African Native National Congress (SANNC), which became the African National Congress in 1923.

[25] An authority on Africana Literature, with PhD from the University of Pennsylvania, Dr Mkhize teaches at the University of Cape Town.

References

Deb, H.C. (1902a), 'Debates in the House of Commons, U.K. which form part of what is popularly known as the *Hansard*', vol. 105, 25 March.

——— (1902b), 'Debates in the House of Commons, U.K. which form part of what is popularly known as the *Hansard*', vol. 106, 24 April.

Derrick, J. (2018), *Africa, Empire and Fleet Street*, London: Hurst Publishers.

Farwell, B. (2001), *The Encyclopaedia of Nineteenth Century Land Warfare: An Illustrated World View*, New York: W.W. Norton & Co.

Gandhi, M.K. (1928), *Satyagraha in South Africa*, Ahmedabad: Navajivan.

——— (1962), *Collected Works of Mahatma Gandhi*, vol. 8, New Delhi: Publications Divisions, Government of India.

——— (1970), *Collected Works of Mahatma Gandhi*, vol. 39, New Delhi: Publications Divisions, Government of India.

Mkhize, K. (2018), '"To See Us as We See Ourselves": John Tengo Jabavu and The Politics of the Black Periodical', *Journal of Southern African Studies*, vol. 44, no. 3, pp. 413–30.

Reddy, E.S. (1999), 'India and the Anglo-Boer War', 29 July, available at https://www.mkgandhi.org/articles/boer_war.php

3

Economic Rights, the Very Idea

Akeel Bilgrami

Prabhat Patnaik (2010) has recently proposed that *fundamental economic rights* ('rights', properly so-called, rather than merely gestural 'directive principles')[1] should be inserted into India's constitution, thereby redeeming a commitment made during the freedom movement in the Karachi Resolution of 1931 and subsequently ignored by the constitutional developments in independent India. In this essay, I will first situate this proposal in a larger exploration of the philosophical foundations both of *the very idea* of rights, quite generally, as well as of economic rights, in particular. I will then situate his proposal on the larger canvas of his own life's work[2] (his persistent and deeply probing analysis of capitalism in the modern period of world history) with a view to making the earlier philosophical and foundational explorations of this article relevant to the actually existing realities of the political economy of our time. Patnaik's proposal is quite *specific*, both in being about economic rights in particular and because it is intended for a particular nation (India) at a particular time (the present, even though it traces the proposal's genealogy to a resolution adopted in 1931). But, when it comes to a subject like rights, however specific the proposal under discussion is, the force and rationale of the proposal, even in its specificity, cannot be fully explored without first getting clear in a quite *general* way about certain foundational questions regarding what rights *are* and *why* we speak of them at all. The specificity of the proposal may cancel *some* detailed points that surface in such a discussion of the foundational questions about rights in general (and, in what follows, I will mention where such a cancellation seems apt), but it cannot cancel all of them without changing the topic from rights to something else. Patnaik, after all, is not talking about economic and social welfare *policies* that are the outcome of a government's *cabinet* deliberations or the routine deliverances of a *legislature*. He is, rather, proposing (economic) *rights* that a *constitution* should adopt. So, there is no avoiding a more foundational discussion of two questions:

(1) What is *meant* by this quite distinctive suggestion that they are rights and not mere policies?

(2) *On what grounds* do we posit such a distinctive thing as rights in the first place? Let me, then, take up both these questions in turn.

What Are Rights? Two Features

Since whole books have been written on the question of what is meant by 'rights', it would be foolish to undertake any extended answer to it in a short article, but let me at least try to state some of the more elementary and defining features of rights so as to set the general context within which the idea of more specifically economic rights can be raised.

Even a glance at a good dictionary will tell one that rights are *entitlements* that all or some members of the public have and, as such, these entitlements entail *duties* (sometimes in the form of prohibitions) for others. If someone is entitled, by right, to something, it is standardly implied that others (individuals, institutions, including the state) are required to or made to do or not do something. My right to privacy entails that others have a duty to not do some things – set up apparatus for surveillance in my drawing room, for instance.

But bare definitions of this kind tell us very little about what rights are. We need to conceptually explore what features such – barely defined – rights have before we come to a full understanding of what rights mean.

This conceptual exploration can proceed from various angles.

One angle is to see what rights should be distinguished from. They are distinct from 'the good'. A way to put this distinction is to say that a right is the sort of thing that cannot be violated in order to maximize the good, under any understanding of what is 'good'. In the intellectual history of the subject, maximization of the good, understood in utilitarian terms, is the usual source of contrast with rights. But the contrast is not restricted to that, it holds for all conceptions of the good. This is because rights are, to use a phrase from John Rawls, *'prior* to the good'.[3] What this means is that the value we put on non-violation of rights cannot be weighed on the same scale as the good. Why not? Rights stand outside of considerations of the good and serve – from the outside – as a form of *constraint* on the pursuit of the good. That is to say, one cannot pursue the good when doing so violates a right. So, for instance, if one is seeking to maximize social aggregate utility, rights cannot ever be the object of a negotiation appealing to considerations of utility – or, indeed, any other good being maximized. This point about rights being a constraint is even more radical than I have put it so far because it is not restricted to constraints on the pursuit of the good or goods. It is a constraint on *any* maximization project. Hence, it is not just that rights cannot be weighed on the same scale as the good, they cannot be weighed *at all*. Even if the violation of a *particular* right were to serve the maximization of the non-violation of *rights in general*, the violation will not be justifiable. To think that it could be justified would be to confusedly treat the notion of a constraint as being on par with what it is a constraint on. A category confusion.

The second feature of rights is that in a society that adopts them, there is some sort of *obligation* to implement them. Since 'implement' is a success term, perhaps the more cautious way to put the point is that in that society, there must be some institutions (formal or, at the very least, informal) that strenuously *seek* to implement them, even if there is no guarantee that the attempt will be successful. So, it is not as if their implementation must be guaranteed, but what is guaranteed is some determined institutional attempt at correction or redress or protection, if it looks as if rights are being violated or threatened. Sometimes the term 'justiciable' is used to capture this feature of rights. Institutions in a polity, such as independent judicial courts, for instance, are *obliged* to take up the matter if rights are violated or threatened.

This feature of rights implies that they presuppose some authority, formal or informal, which undertakes these obligations that rights generate. There are two possible objections to this claim. First, it may seem that the longstanding talk of *natural* rights comes with no such presupposition, it is only conventional rights that do, because in a state of nature there is no authority of the state or courts, which only emerge after, and as a result of, a social contract. As Locke (1689b) puts it, in a state of nature, 'every man is a judge in his own case', simply making a claim to a right on the basis of an appeal to its justification *in (our) nature*. But given the fact that conflicts may arise between natural rights and given also that there will be unequal relations of power in the state of nature (some individuals are just stronger than others), some sort of (at least, informal) authority that assesses and adjudicates these conflicting rights claims and navigates these differentials of power is presupposed, if natural rights are to be effectively implemented. A second objection might be that individuals may justifiably be said to have some rights *against* the actions and judgements of a state and its institutions such as the judiciary, so talk of rights presupposing an authority such as the state to implement them, cannot be conceptually quite right. But I do not believe this sort of case should be viewed as a *counterexample* to the claim that a right presupposes some state-like authority or state-related institutions like the courts which undertake the obligation we call 'justiciability'. Rather, this sort of case provides a *limiting or degenerate* case of such a presupposition. The presupposition *is* in place, even if in a degenerate form, in these cases. Constitutions, which have escape clauses for conscientious objection, implicitly acknowledge this.

I will proceed, then, assuming that these two features of rights (their priority over the good and their justiciability) are necessary and defining features. A third feature, which I will divulge at the end of the essay, is much less discussed in the literature on rights but it is of vital importance in the context of Patnaik's more general analysis of capitalism.

The Foundations of Rights: The Rights of *Liberty* and *Economic* Rights

Turning from what rights mean to the other foundational issue, we must ask *why* do we introduce the notion of a right (understood as having these features that I have mentioned) into the discourse of politics in the first place? This is a much more difficult and complex question than the question of meaning and will need far more detailed attention and elaboration. It is also a question of the utmost significance because without a satisfactory answer to it, rights are not likely to be taken seriously.[4] There is an increasing number of both political and legal theorists, who are hostile to rights – in a way that I am not. They would happily allow the concept of the good to exhaust the realm of political morality, without any constraints coming from rights, and they would reduce the centrality of a constitution in a polity by saying *all* matters are up for political debate and negotiation. I, myself, do not subscribe to such latitude. It leaves too much to the consensual judgements that emerge in politics and morals and, in a sense, I think that is to be too idealistic about human beings. One does not have to be a cynic to think that it is *not up for negotiation* that on certain matters of fundamental moral and political and economic importance, human beings and the institutions they adopt need to be constrained – that is, need to be made to or required to do certain things or prevented from doing other things, by some fundamental constitutional commitments that stand apart from all the other commitments. Rights are where those principles are enshrined and, given the emphasis on their non-negotiability, one has to give them, at the very outset, firm foundations in considerations that speak to what is fundamental about human beings. It is these foundations that a satisfactory answer to Question 2 stated earlier must provide.

So, something special is being done when we introduce talk of a right into the discourse of morals and politics. In doing so, we are elevating a *value* to a *special* status among all the other values we have and pursue. We pursue all sorts of values that we have each day of our lives. But some of these values (such as *freedom* of speech, say, or *privacy*, or the value implicit in Patnaik's proposal – the *security* we gain from food and shelter and health), we are told, are to be elevated into something special and to be called 'rights'. And, what Question 2 is asking is: *On what grounds* is this elevation of some values being made? What makes these particular values special and deserving of this status and this name?

When it comes to a value such as free speech, we find that the question we have just posed about the grounds on which it is elevated to a right, has been getting answers (of varying degrees of soundness and sophistication) going as far back as Periclean Athens, with its notion of 'parrhesia', and again and again through the centuries since then – with Milton's (1644) *Areopagatica*, Locke's (1689a) *A Letter Concerning Toleration*, Kant's (1997) profoundly deep discussion of autonomy, Mill's (2011) widely influential *On Liberty* – providing only some of the most prominent answers. This entire rich tradition of thought grounds not just the right to free speech but a wide range of other rights tied to the notion of liberty in general, that is, such personal freedoms as the freedom of association, the freedom of religion and even the right to privacy. (The right to private property is frequently bundled with these, but that is restricted to liberal doctrines since socialist political ideals have long put it into question.)[5]

My own view is that the deepest source of such a grounding for these rights of personal freedom lies in the notion of *autonomy or self-governance* and this idea of autonomy is itself ultimately *grounded in the fact that human beings, by their very nature, are unique in possessing 'reason'*. That shows just how basic the ground is on which these rights stand. By tracing it all the way to the idea of human reason, what I mean is this. Individual human subjects are born into social contexts of one or another kind and are, from very early in their development, acculturated and habituated into their mores and customs and ways of thinking. But, unlike other creatures, say wolves, they are possessed of the capacity to ask of any social acculturation or social conditioning that they have been brought up on – *should I be doing (thinking) what the pack is doing (thinking)*? This just comes with the capacity for 'reason'. It defines human subjects *uniquely* (as far as we know). To possess reason is to be able to ask questions of this kind. And it is from this capacity to raise such a question that *self*-governance or autonomy (initially, autonomy from the established conventions of one's upbringing, one's social background and influences, etc.) emerges as a fundamental human trait that defines human subjects and is exercised in our choices of what we speak and express, of what we worship and of whom we form associations with. By protecting these rights, we, thus, preserve what is unique in human nature or what defines human subjects. Although, the point has not been put in just this way, all the many details that have been traversed in the liberal tradition of thought on this subject (as I said, from Socrates, through Milton, to Kant and Mill and after) stem, I believe, from these very fundamental considerations tied to human reason as it yields notions of autonomy or self-governance.

I should add that nothing in what I have said here about these rights being grounded in this notion of autonomy is intended to be individualistic in any dogmatic or invidious sense. Let me, in particular, distance what I have said from two such senses of individualism with which it might be confused.

First, autonomy, so conceived as intrinsically linked with the human capacity for reason, does not in the slightest amount to a conception of the individual as seeking his self-interest rather than the interest of the group to which he or she as an individual belongs. Just because reason from its earliest onset disposes us to ask 'should I be thinking or doing as the social group is doing?', it does not follow at all that it is asking whether it is in my *self-interest* to do what the group is thinking or doing. It *could* take that form but it does not *have* to do so. In its most general form, exercising autonomy consists in asking 'Do I think what the group is thinking or doing, is *right*?' (This use of the word 'right' is synonymous with 'correct' or 'morally correct' and – obviously – should not be confused or conflated with talk of 'a right'). That the notion of 'right' here is to be thought of as being elaborated as 'in my self-interest' is a very specific and substantive reading of what is right or correct. Some might well think of right that way, but many might not. So, there is no *logical tie* between the autonomy-reflecting question and a self-interested form of individualism. As it happens, it is quite possible that our reason itself might tell us that pursuing one's self-interest is *not* right. In short, nothing about autonomy, so conceived, generates free riders. I have, elsewhere, put the point by saying that the notion of reason or rationality in question, the one that underlies autonomy or self-governance, is a 'thin' notion of reason.[6] It can be developed into 'thicker' ideas of rationality in various directions (in the direction of individual self-interest, in the direction of the group's interest, or indeed in several other directions yet that are orthogonal to these), but such thick ideals should not be confused with what is the source of autonomy or self-governance and, therefore, what underlies the rights of personal liberty. What underlies these is 'reason' in the thin and most minimal sense that I expounded above (and in note 9).

Second, despite the example I gave of the autonomy-reflecting question ('should I do or think what the group does or thinks?'), there is nothing in what I have said about reason and its conceptual tie with autonomy that suggests that the notion of autonomy can only be exercised by individual human beings. That question can also be asked (and, therefore, autonomy can also be exercised by) a social *group*. A group can ask the same sort of autonomy-reflecting question. Of course, it is not (it logically cannot be) the same question that is asked by an individual human being; but it has the same general form as that question. Thus, a collective might ask, 'Should the group be following the customs or traditions that it has formed over the long past?' Now, of course, if the group does ask such a question and exercises its autonomy in this way, it is thinking (cognitively functioning and deliberating) as an individual, a *group*-individual, as it were, rather than an individual human organism. There is no reason why only the latter should count as individuals, capable of individual deliberation. There certainly can be rational deliberation carried out by more abstract kinds of individuals, such as a group-individual. Rousseau was precisely suggesting this possibility when he spoke of the 'general will'. That will was intended by him to be both 'general' (all the citizens in the polity) *and* 'individual' (i.e., singular). And since Rousseau, the idea has been metaphysically developed and considerably refined.[7] Thus, though, in political contexts, the reference of the terms 'individual' and 'human organism' mostly coincide, they can come apart in the case of group-individuals. I say all this to make clear that what I have said about autonomy is not any kind of dogmatic stand against collective forms of deliberation and autonomy.

It is not insisting on a *liberal* individualism that restricts itself to individual *human beings*. So, perhaps the best way to put the general lesson here is this: autonomy (and ultimately 'reason') is the fundamental grounding notion for the rights of liberty and both individual human beings and group-individuals can exercise autonomy (and reason) in the sense I have briefly outlined. I think, to see autonomy in this way, as being reflected in the notion of reason that itself is exercised in its most elementary and fundamental form in the raising (whether by an individual human being or a social collective) of questions of this kind, is a particularly attractive formulation, because it combines Kant's notion of autonomy with Hegel's (and Marx's) ideas about how autonomy and reason are to be seen in two respects that find no central place in Kant's thinking. By tying autonomy to questions of this kind – questions that are always asked by one about what is *given to one in one's socially and historically situated condition* – makes for the Hegelian and Marxian correction of Kant by always situating our subjectivity *in a historical context*. And by allowing the question that reflects autonomy to also be asked by a *collective* or group-individual, it corrects Kant's liberal individualism in just the way that Hegel and Marx were well-known to have sought to do. Yet this notion of autonomy, so formulated in the possibility of asking questions such as this, at the same time preserves what is deep in Kant's notion of it, the possibility of *self*-governance, despite one's historical and social situatedness. Although, at first sight, it may seem to do so, this deep Kantian element does not cancel the Hegelian element that I am trying to integrate with Kant in this formulation. Why not? Because any *answer* that these autonomy-reflecting questions (Should I be doing or thinking what the group is doing or thinking? Should the group be following the traditions it has been for so long shaped and defined by?) get will unavoidably be given from *within* the situated perspective of the society (or tradition) within which the individual (or group) finds itself when asking that question. There is no transcendent perspective or source from which these answers can be provided. In that sense, reason, even when it questions society or tradition, does so without losing its place in society or tradition. Autonomy, therefore, can be genuinely *autonomy* even as it is exercised only within history and within a social context. One cannot step outside of these contexts. Precisely what Hegel and Marx sought as a correction of Kant is thus preserved. In Hegel and Marx, this preserved element is famously presented in a notion of social and economic transformation that follows an *internal dialectic* of contradictions emerging in a society or economy and passing over into transformative resolutions of those contradictions. This is just their (more diachronically indexed) version of my more synchronically formulated point that answers to the questions that reflect one's autonomy from one's social context or one's tradition are nevertheless given from within the perspective of one's social context and one's tradition.

Since I am not a liberal, I am particularly concerned to stress both these caveats I have made because they both reveal that one can be committed, as I am, to these particular rights around the value of liberty and freedom, without a commitment to liberalism, as it is standardly understood.[8] Liberalism does not have exclusive claims to the notion of liberty nor to its enshrinement in these various rights. To drive home this point, I should add that, though the discussion of this notion of autonomy or self-governance, which grounds the notion of certain rights of liberty and freedom, has indeed been dominated in the modern period by a liberal tradition of thought, there have been very interesting dissenting offshoots: one claiming that the deepest notion of freedom at stake is best exemplified in a long *republican* tradition going back to Ancient Rome, recently inventively revived and with meticulous scholarly detail, by Quentin Skinner (2008), and another, owing to Rousseau and culminating in Marx, putting somewhat different points of pressure on the liberal tradition as being too exclusively focused on the negative notion of liberty (liberty as 'non-interference') and offering, by contrast, various more 'positive' elaborations of the notion of liberty.[9] All of these diverse ideas and doctrines, not just liberalism, can be mobilized into answering foundational questions about the rights surrounding liberty.

Nothing like this longstanding (and outstanding) intellectual history is to be found in the efforts to lay foundations for the rights that Patnaik's proposal is concerned to promote. Explicit foundational discussions of it are really only detectable as recently as the late 1940s and mostly owing to the fact that the 'United States Declaration of Human Rights' in 1948 contained some clauses (see in particular, articles 22–26) about the right to food, work and shelter.[10]

Why is this kind of inquiry such a latecomer in political philosophy and social theory? Why should the value of liberty and autonomy get a foundational discussion for some twenty hundred years while the value of security in the basic necessities of life is more or less entirely neglected until measurably less than a century ago? Given this striking differential, it is hardly surprising that such rights have to get the kind of special advocacy that Patnaik is urging for them now, while rights around the concept of freedom and liberty such as, for instance, free speech, need no such advocacy since they are already widely and deeply entrenched in the constitutions of liberal democratic polities.

Part of the reason, for this curious neglect of economic rights may be due to the fact that they are the kind of rights that the Left, rather than standard forms of liberalism, are likely to take up, and yet much of the Left, especially the Marxisant left, has shown an abiding hostility to the notion of rights in general. In fact, I cannot resist saying that when Patnaik's essay which made the proposal for economic rights for India was published in the *Economic and Political Weekly* (Patnaik 2010), a friend of mine wrote to me to ask, 'Why is a Marxist like Patnaik going soft and liberal?' This question, though it was put to me in a somewhat offhand manner, is not without point since Marx, as everyone knows, had famously written with dismissiveness about the very idea of rights precisely because it was embedded in a liberal ideology that, according to his analysis, had evaded aspirations to a more profound emancipation.[11] However, Marx, it must be remembered, was writing in, what Hobsbawm had dubbed, 'The Age of Revolution' (Hobsbawm 1962; 1848 was palpably in the horizon of his thinking, 1789 was not a very distant inspirational antecedent, and it is these very dates that serve as the bookends of Hobsbawm's 'Age'). So, quite understandably, he had hopes for Europe leapfrogging over an extended period of incubation in rights which were, in any case, predominantly theorized only in liberal doctrine, to a more radical transformation of society. But, as the question that was put to me reveals, Marx's sceptical attitude towards rights has influenced generations of Left thinking on the subject, even when the 'Age of Revolution' has receded into a distant past and there does not seem much scope for (what I called) the 'leapfrogging' that Marx held out hopes for. Yet his scepticism about rights seems to persist in much of the radical Left. It is partly this sceptical challenge that has prompted me to write the reflections of this essay.[12]

Although, as I said, this is, in part, no doubt responsible, the main reason why considerations of autonomy (and the various values of liberty and freedom that it underwrites) have occupied philosophers and thinkers for longer and more deeply is because they are considered *more fundamental* than the value of security that comes from the provision of food and shelter and health and so forth. This is so for various reasons and it is not at all obvious that the reasons are good ones. But before I get to those reasons, I will need to make some preliminary analytical points regarding the foundations of rights, including particularly, economic rights.

As a terminological point, let me just quickly say that I think we need a term other than 'security' to describe the value or values that are attained through these provisions that economic rights demand. The entire rhetoric around 'security' has been ruined by its recent association with the 'war on terror' which was said to be carried out in the name of attaining 'security' for one's people. It is not obvious what alternative vocabulary should replace it. In earlier rhetoric, these provisions were described as the fulfilment of our 'basic needs' and the term 'well-being' was often used to describe the value that was served by fulfilling basic needs. This term is not entirely satisfactory either since it may seem as if much more than the fulfilment of basic needs goes into bringing about our 'well-being'. But whatever word we use, the question remains: How can it be that what such a word represents can be *less* fundamental than autonomy? What it represents, that is, what is brought into effect by the fulfilment of basic needs, is just about the most fundamental value that human beings could seek since, without such basic needs being fulfilled, we could not function as the human beings we are. This point is surely very well understood and hardly needs to be said. (As a matter of fact, it has been said in such foundational discussions of economic rights as exists in the philo-sophical literature.)[13] Nevertheless, it has to be admitted, that there seems to remain a very strong strain in philosophy that views the basic needs and their fulfilment as less fundamental in underpinning rights foundationally than considerations of autonomy. That is one reason why economic rights remain without philosophical foundations unlike, say, the right to free speech and other rights of liberty. And that, in turn, it would seem is why economic rights seem to be excluded from constitutions and need the special kind of advocacy that economists like Patnaik are seeking.

A more important preliminary point of analysis requires me to lay down in a very elementary *schematic* form the nature of the answers that might be given to Question 2, the question that asks about how rights are to be grounded. In any schematic answer to Question 2, we have to say which value is being elevated by the rights in question, as well as what in human nature grounds the rights and the value being elevated.

With one set of rights regarding speech, association, worship and privacy, which have received long and careful answers over the centuries, we have already presented the following schema: The value that these rights *elevate* is liberty or freedom (for the purposes of this article, I use these two terms synonymously); and these rights and this value are *grounded* in the notion of autonomy, which itself is grounded ultimately in the very idea of human 'reason'.

What matching schema can we present for the other set of rights, economic rights, which have received far less long and careful attention? We have resisted saying that they elevate the value of 'security'. We have also resisted saying that they elevate the value of 'well-being'. Perhaps, then, it is best to simply say this as a matching schema: These rights *elevate* the value of 'basic needs fulfilment' (since the rhetoric of basic needs was widely used in the discussions of economic rights a few decades ago, we can simply describe the fulfilment of basic needs as itself the value that such rights speak to); and they are *grounded* in the notion of human vitality, that is, the living of a human life at its most fundamental existential level. (Sometimes this is described in terms of human 'survival' but, for reasons that I would not elaborate on here, I prefer to put it in terms of life and vitality.)

The idea of economic rights speaking to the value of the fulfilment of basic needs, and finding its constitutive ground in the very existence and sus-tenance of human life and vitality, is perhaps rather obvious. In the literature (see note 13), needs and rights have often been said to have a close conceptual tie and the schema offered above merely makes the tie explicit. But, obvious though it may be, this schema and this tie are not intended – at least not by me – as taking a misleadingly direct form. I am not suggesting that the very concept of a 'need' is such that one cannot hear that something is a need (or someone has a need) without feeling the tug of obligation to fulfil it. There is a temptation to say this because the concept of a need stands in contrast with the concept of a 'want' or 'preference'. And so, it may seem that it directly entails an obligation (on the part of the state, say, as propounded in the feature of rights that is called 'justiciability') to ensure that they are fulfilled. Wants, we all know, just by the fact of being wants, are not the sort of thing that impose any obligations on anyone to gratify them, not even on the possessor of the wants, leave alone on others or on the state. On the contrary, we say of many wants that they *ought not* to be gratified. As I said, even those who have the wants might sometimes say that. So, it might be thought, that one contrast with wants that needs stand-in, is that needs *do* impose such obligations to fulfil them. But that is not how the schematic argument for the foundation of economic rights presented above proceeds. This is because that is not the correct way to make the contrast between needs and wants. The contrast between needs and wants, no doubt, does turn on the fact that the former is more objective than the latter: If one *wants* something because it has a certain property, one necessarily believes that it has a certain property – but it could turn out that the belief is false. But if one *needs* something because it has a cer-tain property, it *does* have that property and if one also believes that it has the property (which, unlike in the case of wants, one might not), the belief *is* true. But needs being more objective than wants in this way does not directly give us any obligatory claim to having the needs fulfilled by way of right or rights. Why not? Because needs, despite being objective in the way just expounded, nevertheless are needs *for a purpose*. That is, when we say someone needs something, we can always be asked the question: Need it for what? And not all answers to this last question yield an obligation (in the form of a right) to have the need fulfilled. For instance, I might say, 'I need a cricket bat'. And, I will be asked: 'Need it for what?', to which I answer: 'To go out on to the pitch and face the bowling'. None of this, obviously, raises any issues about rights. It is only some answers to the question 'Need it for what?' that yield obligations of that sort. The schema we gave for economic rights suggested that the answer to this 'what for?' question, when applied to the needs that underlie economic rights, is human life and vitality. It is only when the answer goes as deep as that into the nature of human beings do we get into the terrain of rights with the obligatory feature we call 'justiciability'. All this suggests that the foundational relation between needs and rights is much more indirect than it might initially seem. They only ground rights via a justificatory grounding argument of the sort that the matching schema above tries to provide. There is no more direct certification that needs can provide for rights.

The point of these schemas is to bring out that the foundations of *both* sets of rights (one in notions of autonomy/reason, the other in notions of life/ vitality) go as deep as fundamental aspects of *human nature* itself and so it is not surprising that they have, for so long and recurringly, been described as 'natural' rights. If the foundational discussion takes us to a level as deep and fundamental as that, then whether or not we actually call them natural rights (a matter that turns on rather arcane issues), we can at least understand why many have thought it apt to call them that.

A final point of preliminary analysis requires me to explain why, since I am making the familiar appeal to basic needs and their fulfilment in the foundational discussion of economic rights, I have tended to focus on only three of the five economic rights that Patnaik (2010) mentions (and most others mention) when they speak of economic rights. I have restricted myself to talk about food, shelter and health and omitted the right to work or employment and the right to education. These are not omissions due to neglect. Let me take up the deliberate reason for each omission in turn. The reason I have not mentioned the right to employment at the outset is that, unlike food and shelter and health, it does not speak *immediately* to the value of basic needs fulfilment, it only *secondarily* speaks to it via the undeniable fact that food, shelter and health are only available in a productive economy, and such an economy requires that citizens be variously employed in production and distribution; moreover, even in a society which has adopted economic rights, there will be some minimum costs that citizens may incur in the purchase of food, and the maintenance of shelter and health costs which to be paid by citizens will require that they have income that presumably has its source in employment. So, a full understanding of what makes possible the implementation of the rights to food, housing and health requires one to see the secondary place of the right to employment within the schema that grounds these rights. Over and above this secondary place in the schema for economic rights, some may wish to argue (plausibly enough, though because this is a matter that could be debated, I have not stressed it) for a more immediate grounding of the right to work in considerations of human vitality, claiming that idleness goes against the vitality of a human existence and work is essential to vitality. As for the right to education, it has a slightly more complex and rather more interesting foundational base. It is important to make clear that the right to education should not get a very specific elaboration since what gets counted as a necessary education is highly contested – thinkers ranging from Gandhi to Paulo Freire to Bertrand Russell have argued that orthodox education of one or another kind prevalent in modern societies, far from being a right, is detrimental to human development. But even if one describes the education to which one must have a right in general enough terms to avoid these controversies, I would argue that, unlike the other economic rights, the grounding for such a right is not primarily and immediately tied to considerations of human vitality that underlie basic need fulfilment. Rather, the right to education is the one right which has a foot in each of the two schematic foundational grounds I outlined above. Like the rights to liberty, it has essential ties to the idea of human reason since education is essential for the nourishing and flowering of the capacity for human reason. But, equally, education is needed for some aspects of the functioning of productive economies that make possible the provision of food and housing and health – so, just as I said about employment above, it too is secondarily related to the values of basic need fulfilment that are grounded in considerations of vitality necessary for a functioning human life.

A Philosophical Bias and Its Sources

With these preliminary analytical points in place, let us return to the two schemas we had elaborated for the two sets of rights (the rights of liberty and economic rights) and ask again: Why, if these two sets of rights reach down to foundational values and notions that reflect something as fundamental as human nature itself, has one set of these grounding values and notions (liberty and autonomy/reason) been thought to be *more fundamental* than the other (the fulfilment of basic needs and human life and vitality)? I will present four factors (there may well be others) that are responsible for this bias.

One factor that may account for it being considered less fundamental is that, though these needs tied to the life and vitality of functioning human beings are defining of human beings, they are *not unique* to human beings and hold of the entire animal kingdom, indeed of the entire living environment. By contrast, 'reason' of the sort that goes into self-governance, and underlies the rights of freedom, *is* uniquely possessed by human beings. But this cannot be the basis for thinking that basic need fulfilment is less fundamental than freedom. If anything, it is a reason for making these rights based on the fulfilment of basic needs *wider* in scope so as to include the rights of animals and of nature. (It is not as if this point has not been registered quite widely by those who have been arguing for animal rights and the rights of the natural environment.) Something does not become more fundamental just because it is grounded in something that human beings alone possess. To say that it does would reflect a kind of parochialism about the human species that has no justification, no more than any other parochialism (of race or gender or caste or religion or nation) has a justification.

A *second* factor behind the tendency may be the fact that the threshold for what are *basic* needs shifts around, depending on how economically advanced the society is. This may make it seem as if rights tied to basic human needs are tied to something too indeterminate to be the grounds for something as fundamental as rights. To this sort of objection, either of the following two responses seems to me to suffice. We could, on the one hand, simply relativize the notion of what is 'basic' to different societies and tie rights to basic needs, so relativized. Or, on the other hand, one could say that if the idea of a basic need is grounded in the very idea of *human* life and vitality which, in turn, is uniform wherever human beings are found, then rights are tied to basic needs in some absolute and non-relativized sense, and some societies may wish to make *non*-rights form of policy commitments to higher thresholds once the rights to the basic needs, defined in these absolute terms, have been justiciably established. I am allowing either of these responses to this challenge with this kind of airy indifference only because *neither* answer nor the challenge itself, is relevant to Patnaik's proposal. The entire controversy about the indeterminacy of the notion of 'well-being' or of basic needs is beside the point in the context of his proposal, because he is, as I said at the outset, making a claim for a *very specific society and polity*, the national site of India in the present. Even though he may need to take up (as we have in this essay) foundational questions turning on universal considerations about human beings that ground the economic rights he is proposing, he is not making the proposal for all the human beings in the entire globe living in enormously diverse societies with very different levels of social and economic development. Therefore, if the foundational questions are answered by an appeal to the idea of basic needs, he can with confidence *assume* a relative *determinacy* of basic needs for the site he specifically has in mind.[14] The crucial point to keep in mind is that though the notion of rights (including economic rights) needs a foundational discussion of the kind we are exploring, and though any foundational discussion is going to be raising issues of *universal* human concern and relevance because (being foundational) they trace back fundamentally to features of human nature (such as autonomy and basic needs), *the 'universal' here should not be conflated with the 'global'*. This point is utterly obvious and the mistake of such a conflation, if made, would be elementary, but it may still be easy to slip into it because, as we know, rights (and economic rights particularly) came to have a new prominence a few decades ago at a global site as a result of being included in an *international* charter adopted by the United Nations. Moreover, on that global site and in that international charter, they were (and are) spoken of as 'human' rights to be contrasted with rights of citizens of particular nations. But the very use of the word 'human' there might give the impression of doing a quite different duty than just making this contrast. It may give the impression that the term 'human' there was intended to suggest a universality of the kind that has been in evidence in the foundational discussion of the foregoing pages in which we have spoken of autonomy and basic needs as fundamental facets of human nature that ground these rights. That is the confusion to be avoided. I repeat: the United Nations charter – with its international status, standing over and above particular nations – spoke of these rights as 'human' rights primarily with a view to contrasting them with the particular rights enshrined in the constitutions of particular nation-states. Thus, the ambiguous role of the term 'human' here makes it quite easy to fall into the confusion between 'global' and 'universal' when interpreting the charter's talk of 'human' rights. Patnaik's proposal, unlike the charter's articles on economic rights, is intended for a specific nation in the present time. Despite its specificity, we have been trying to explore the *universal* foundations for such rights. But, if we refuse the confusion of the universal with the global, that universality does not mean that the proposal, therefore, loses its specific earmark for a nation, and becomes a proposal in the global arena. And if earmarked specifically for a particular nation, it is not vulnerable to the objection that societies and countries with different levels of development will have different thresholds for what is *basic* in the understanding of 'basic needs'.

This last series of remarks (about the internationalist context within which the notion of economic rights has been discussed in recent years, ever since they were listed in three or four articles in the United Nations charter) leads into a *third* factor that has led to the neglect of serious discussion of the foundations of these rights. At the international level, rights talk is *necessarily merely aspirational.* This is for the simple and widely recognized reason that there is no state/judicial authority at the global level of the kind necessary to carry through the implementability or justiciability feature of rights that we mentioned earlier. A rhetoric of rights that is merely aspirational is not 'rights', properly so-called. It may be worthy rhetoric and it may be used (with a marginal degree of success sometimes, as by the Chiapas in Mexico and the Basques in Spain) to mobilize particular nation-states to implement rights, but this does not amount to 'justiciability'. That kind of success entirely depends on the extent to which national governments are willing to listen to and be shamed by chastising reports on human rights by international bodies such as the United Nations, and the plain fact is that most national governments committing human rights violations – such as our own today in India or Israel ever since 1967, to name just two – are shameless. What all this obviously reflects is the complete lack of authoritative sites of governance at the global level. In fact, when it comes to economic rights, it is a curious thing that, ever since its financialization in the neo-liberal period, the only global phenomenon of real significance in the last few decades is capital. Far from being a site of governmental authority, it is a phenomenon that desperately needs to be *constrained* by governmental authority, if any economic (or for that matter, environmental) rights are ever going to be implemented. But, as we know, there is no such authority at the global level to constrain capital. At the global level, there is only a high patchwork form of governance consisting of a toothless United Nations (and its Security Council), the international credit agencies and trade organizations, various multilateral and bilateral treaties and arrangements, and various elite associations (G20, G7), whose tendency has been to brazenly promote the hegemony of finance capital rather than to constrain it.

When rights talk is necessarily only aspirational in this way, lacking the feature of justiciability, the foundational considerations we appeal to will be unlikely to ground anything that is potentially effective. It will only ground rights as, at best, recommendations. This point applies to all rights, of course, not just economic rights. But since articles 22–26 of the United Nations charter brought attention to economic rights in a serious way for the first time, this merely aspirational element of rights at the global level made them ineffectual, a sort of window-dressing of loftiness while a capitalist political economy generated deprivations on the ground, especially from the 1980s onwards. As Samuel Moyn's (2018) recent work has ably demonstrated, it is not exactly accidental that *global*-level economic rights talk under the rubric 'human' rights has coincided almost perfectly with the phenomenon of global finance capital that we call neo-liberalism. But what Moyn does not recognize (because he provides no analysis of capitalism) is that what this should lead us to explore is the possibility that we begin to think of political economy for particular nations in ways that decathect from global finance capital and explore further how economic rights on distinct *national* sites, as clauses in the constitutions of national governments rather than in an international charter, may play a central role in such a transformation of their political economies. That is indeed Patnaik's proposal, restricted as it is to India, but as a proposal, it only really makes sense if one situates it in Patnaik's own analysis of the political economy of capitalism, to which I will turn shortly.

Before I do, I want to mention a *fourth* and final factor that prompts the tendency to view freedom and autonomy (which underlie the rights related to speech and association and privacy, etc.) as more fundamental than basic needs fulfilment and considerations of the vitality of human life (which underlie economic rights). This fourth factor is a much more sophisticated one than the previous three and derives from work that quite deliberately and explicitly seeks to deny a place of centrality to the idea of basic needs fulfilment, making it secondary by *folding it into notions of freedom and agency*. The most prominent and influential figure to take these issues in this direction is Amartya Sen, whose notion of 'capabilities' was first formulated via a critique of 'needs'. See Sen (1984) for these criticisms. I want to be clear that Sen's replacing 'needs' on centre stage with 'capabilities' is not a denial on his part that the fulfilment of basic needs is an important goal. He has spent much of a lifetime of thought and writing addressing the concerns of poverty and deprivation in a society. The sense in which he makes needs secondary is not by denying the importance of fulfilling needs – rather, as I said above, he makes them secondary, in a more sophisticated sense, by *subsuming* the notion of needs under another notion, the notion of capability. He does this because he thinks that capabilities have a property that makes them more fundamental than needs. That property is precisely the property of human autonomy and freedom. And since I am looking to diagnose why the considerations that ground one set of rights – considerations of freedom and autonomy – are generally considered more fundamental than the considerations that ground another set of rights – considerations of basic need fulfilment and human life and vitality – this sophisticated turn in the discussion of these issues is of immediate and direct relevance. Sen's refinement (words like 'refinement' and 'sophistication' are well chosen here since Sen is explicit in saying that the notion of needs is too crude for the purposes at hand) of the notion of needs via their subsumption under notions of freedom and autonomy is at once a reflection of the longstanding tendency to view freedom as more fundamental than basic needs fulfilment I am trying to diagnose and (because of Sen's great influence) a perpetuation of that tendency in our own time.

The basic idea in Sen is to knit together two notions that he labels 'functionings' and 'capabilities'. The former consists of human behavioural states as well as states of being. Someone voting is an example of a behavioural state. Someone being a cricketer is an example of a state of being. Both are examples of what he calls 'functionings'. Now, a society can arrange it so that I have the *option* to vote and the option to be a cricketer and in doing so it gives me some capabilities. By stressing options, capabilities stress freedom and autonomy. The subsumptive effect this has on the notion of needs is that something like the need for food or shelter, necessary for one's vitality in living a human life, is now filtered through options: Fulfilling these needs is an option that one has and one can choose to exercise this option and fulfil them. Freedom is thus primary, basic need-fulfilment is folded within it.[15]

An obvious criticism of Sen might take the form of saying that attributing a need to someone summons a certain sense of urgency and makes one sit up to the moral importance of addressing it, whereas capabilities lack that urgency and normative force.

But, we have to proceed slowly here. As we saw earlier, the urgency and normative force of someone needing x only really arises when the question 'needs x for what?' gets some answers rather than other answers, gets answers that speak to such fundamental considerations as human vitality requisite for the living of a human life. That is why economic rights speak to *basic* need fulfilment. But Sen can, then, respond by seeking to finesse this objection by speaking of *basic capabilities* (which, in fact, he has, though by this category he also has in mind to track innate human capacities such as the capacity for language), and he can declare that these are marked as having a certain urgency and normative force that other capabilities do not have. So where does that leave us on the matter of the difference between capabilities and needs?

This objection to Sen will, thus, have to be reformulated with greater care. Perhaps as follows. It might begin by saying that there is a qualitative difference between saying, (1) If a citizen opts to have their basic needs fulfilled, then a good society and polity, will seek to arrange it so that they are fulfilled and (2) A good society and polity will seek to arrange it so that the basic needs of its citizens are fulfilled, though, of course, it is up to particular citizens whether they opt to fulfil their basic needs. It should be clear that (1) expresses the basic capability view and (2) the basic needs view. And now, the objection must go on to claim that the difference between (1) and (2) is that (2) seems to have greater moral force and thus not only puts greater pressure on a state and society to make the requisite arrangements, but it motivates more than (1) does its own insertion into constitutions. Moreover, as a formulation, it is better suited to such an insertion than (1), which is formulated with a clause that gives a covering primacy to optionality and choice rather than to the basic needs. And proponents of the superiority of the formulation in (2) can, moreover, clinch their case by pointing out that, *in any case*, there are other aspects of constitutions (the other set of rights, the rights of liberty) that can recuperate the optionality that fails to find a place in (b).

It is, I suppose, still possible for Sen to say that though he can hear these subtle differences between (1) and (2), these differences do not show his initial response to be false. He can point out that what he was saying in his initial response was that basic needs and basic capabilities are co-*extensive*. These differences between (1) and (2) do not overturn that response because they only show that basic needs and capabilities are not co-*intensive*. To put it less cryptically, (1) and (2) are such that though they do not *convey the same idea* (i.e., are not co-intensive) because the idea of basic capabilities sophisticates the idea of basic needs in the direction of freedom and autonomy by filtering it through optionality, they nevertheless *pick out the same things* (i.e., are co-extensive) with their different respective concepts 'basic capabilities' and 'basic needs'. Be that as it may, the objection can still claim that not being co-intensive is significant because it has implications for politics if a greater moral pressure is exerted by the basic needs approach of (2) to make the requisite arrangements that fulfil those needs.

I think, so formulated, this objection does show that one should not be treating the foundational ground in autonomy for one set of rights as more fundamental than the foundational ground in basic need fulfilment for the other set of rights. So, the only question that remains, then, is whether Sen's urge to impose this filter of optionality on needs is not a kind of obsession with freedom and autonomy. And it particularly seems to be a kind of fetishization of freedom when it comes to viewing even *basic* needs through the filter of optionality; a sort of *bias* towards freedom over basic needs fulfilment. The only grounds I can think of, on Sen's behalf, for insisting on this filter of optionality is the somewhat strained possibility that someone might actually choose to exercise the option of *not* having his basic needs fulfilled, for example, an artist who feels that he cannot really do justice to his art unless he is existentially deprived – starving, say, or homeless, or suffering ill-health. I say 'strained' for more than one reason. First of all, such examples seem to be highly exceptional. Moreover, it might also plausibly be said that the artist needs the vitality of a basically functioning human life in order to make his art and this may require that the artist is *not* starving or homeless or suffering ill health. And finally, as I said above, constitutions (in any case) have the rights of liberty, so the optionality is (in any case) recovered there for this kind of exceptional artist. In response, Sen would have to say that this sort of 'in any case' recuperation somewhere else is not good enough. The optionality should be present *in* the formulation of basic needs and (2) does not do that. Without that, (2) is philosophically deficient. But I would think this demand is working with a very rarified and quite unreasonable conception of what is philosophically adequate and what is philosophically deficient. For all these reasons, I do find the example of the artist and the work it is being put to here, quite strained.

Even so, Sen can claim that his filter, which places freedom and autonomy in a more fundamental role than basic need-fulfilment, has the advantage of allowing in examples of this kind, however, strained they might seem. But, even if this is the response of last resort in favour of Sen's view, it is not decisive in establishing freedom and autonomy as being more fundamental than the vitality considerations underlying basic need fulfilment. This is because one can summon other examples (no doubt, also strained) which point in the opposite direction. Someone living in the hellish deprivation of chronic and severe malnutrition in India may think that life in Havana, even if he would be deprived there of the freedom and autonomy to speak freely, is a kind of paradise compared to the deprivations he is suffering. Anyone who has read Hegel will be alerted by this sort of example to one strand of thought behind . the philosophical myth of the master–slave dialectic, in which the existential struggle between Self and Other results in one person placing the value of life above the value of freedom and becoming the slave while the other, with these values inversed, becomes the master. Geist's dialectical development emerges from the pervading instability of this relationship because the master cannot get the recognition and acknowledgement from the slave. And one way to read Marx's upending (or upturning) of Hegel's idealism is precisely as seeing through to the point that nothing short of placing what I have called the value of 'life and vitality' *on a par* with the value of freedom and autonomy will yield the mutual recognition that sets history on the path to dissolving classes in an ideal state – not, in that case, the Prussian state, but the socialist ideal of an unalienated life formed by the appropriate distributive movement from abilities to needs.[16]

But, putting aside this suggestive philosophical messianism, one could just simply say, in a more sober register, that since (strained) examples can be given, in this way, in two opposing directions, what this implies is that the most plausible view would be an ecumenical one in which considerations of reason, freedom, autonomy *and* considerations of basic need fulfilment and vitality, *both* speak *equally* to fundamental aspects of human nature; and the hankering to place the one as having more fundamental status and the other as having a merely subsumed status within it is a misguided attempt at moral and political sophistication of the more elemental needs to which economic rights speak, revealing a philosophical bias in favour of autonomy and freedom.

Although all of this may sound like a criticism of Sen, in a sense it is not. By this I mean that there is an understandable reason why Sen does not see his way to the kind of ecumenism I have just suggested. This ecumenism comes into view only when one is focused, as I am in this essay, on the subject of rights. Sen's discussion of these issues is most often within a quite different focus, which is his longstanding and recurring interest in questions of equality (and inequality).[17] Given that focus, Sen is aspiring for something more ambitious than the fulfilment of basic needs. In one place, he even hints at something stronger than what I have just expressed in my last sentence, pointing out that often the advocacy of the fulfilment of basic needs might be a ploy to deflect from the more ambitious goal of equality. (This is quite of a piece with Samuel Moyn's conclusion that I mentioned a little earlier – that the entire movement of human rights grounded in the idea of basic needs of some decades ago nested quite comfortably with neoliberalism's widespread inegalitarian effects.) Sen's turn to capabilities, within the focus on that more ambitious goal of equality, can then be seen as a way of trying to ensure that equality is not at odds with freedom and autonomy and also that it is not conceived in the routinely rigid terms of equality of, say, income, but rather of ensuring that people are provided with what they, with the exercise of their autonomy, chose to value. The relation of capabilities to equality is perhaps that equality, when approached via capabilities, amounts to a dispersed version of 'equality of opportunity', where by 'dispersed version' I mean that, unlike the usual appeal to equality of opportunity which targets particular domains (as when we say: Everybody should have the opportunity of the same *education* or everybody should have the same opportunity for getting *bank loans*), Sen's version leaves the targets to the values that individual citizens opt for.

The overall point, however, is this. Whatever we think of the efficacies that capabilities yield in the aspiration to equality (there may be many who think that equality of opportunity is not the primary form of equality one should be seeking), the focus in this article – the question of economic rights – is on *a quite different set of concerns*. Although it can hardly be doubted that the implementation of economic rights will go some way in reducing inequalities, it is just as clear that their implementation will yield and will aspire to yield something that falls distinctly short of equality. Why then have I been concerned that this distinctly less ambitious goal of economic rights is being deflected by placing the values of freedom and autonomy above the values of basic needs fulfilment that these less ambitious goals aspire to? Why, in general, am I concerned with and focused on the much less ambitious goal (than equality) that Patnaik's proposal for economic rights speaks to? This is a good and sharp question. And we can only answer it, if we turn finally, as promised, to Patnaik's analysis of capitalism.

The Tendencies of Capital

To begin with, it is worth trying to get to grips with how his analysis of capitalism is relevant to understanding why his proposal that there should be economic rights is intended for a very specific national site, India in the present.

In two successive books,[18] co-authored with Utsa Patnaik, he argues that economic imperialism – the economic domination of one region of the world by another – is not a late-coming development in the history of capitalism, but an essential feature, built into the tendencies of capital from its earliest beginnings as an economic formation in Europe. On this analysis, capitalism in the metropole (Europe initially and then, by diffusion, other parts of the temperate belt such as North America and the Antipodes) is a dynamic system characterized by an incessant competitive drive, as a result of which an *external* stimulus is indispensable for the reproduction of capital. As a matter of empirical fact, due to the availability of essential primary commodities in the tropical and sub-tropical regions of the world (commodities which are not grown or not grown year-round in the North due to its climactic conditions), as well as because of the extensive external markets the populations of these Southern nations provide,[19] the chief external source of this stimulus needed to sustain capital accumulation (and capitalism as the economic formation it is), is provided by these distant lands. Imperialism, in the familiar traditional form of colonialism, was motivated by this need to secure this external source for capitalism and – until decolonization in roughly the middle of the last century – for its entire long duration it did so with methods and economic policies that imposed a range of economic hardships on the population of the colonized lands. In the period immediately after decolonization, there was a hiatus in this entire systemic relation between the metropole and its erstwhile colonies. This was due to independent sovereign states that had emerged in the latter seeking to gain greater control over their national economies than colonialism had allowed to these regions of the South, so as to pursue policies that would improve the conditions of their working people. This hiatus lasted no more than three and a half decades after which, as a result of measures adopted that made for the increasing financialization of capital and the globalization of finance, the ability of these newly emerging nation-states to exercise sovereignty over their own economies was drastically weakened in what has come to be called the 'neoliberal' period of capitalism; and thus the external element that is required to sustain capital in the form it requires was restored. This restoration amounts once again to imperialism because, though it employs methods and economic policies that are somewhat different from traditional colonialism due to the transformed nature of capital in the neo-liberal period of financial globalization, nevertheless, at a more abstract level of description (some of Patnaik's own descriptions at this abstract level are 'income deflation', 'demand compression'), they have the same essential features that imposed hardships on the populations during the colonial period.

For reasons of space, in an essay that is primarily about rights, I have put the analysis very abstractly and without any detail but, despite that, it is still easy to infer from this skeletal description that if one were to seek to oppose imperialism in this new formation of capitalism that we call neoliberalism, a first step will have to be that these nation-states of the southern regions of the globe will have to find ways to re-acquire greater control over their own economies. Since, because of the financialization and globalization of capital in recent decades, this cannot be attempted along the lines pursued immediately after decolonization, Patnaik argues that they can now only really do so by 'delinking' very substantially from the global economy of finance capitalism. It is in the context of this argument (an essentially anti-globalization argument, as the very notion of 'delinking' makes clear) that Patnaik's proposal about economic rights is made for *particular* nations, nations of the South suffering from this renewed imperialism, and his focus has been primarily on India. The idea presumably is that if India were to adopt a constitutional regime of economic rights, which had the two features mentioned earlier (justiciability and non-negotiable priority over the good), then in order to implement those rights, the state would willy-nilly have to adopt policies that, in the end, would amount to an assertion of control over their own economies by imposing constraints on global finance capital. Human rights articulated in a global arena, such as the United Nations charter, are simply not justiciable for lack of any serious structures of international governance. The only structure of governance that exists, with articulated constitutions and the requisite judicial and executive authority to implement rights, is on the site of the nation. It is hardly surprising, then, that, as Moyn has shown, the *global* human rights movement was entirely compatible with the form of imperialism that neo-liberalism exemplifies. In the neoliberal period, the global mobility of capital that its financialization has wrought weakens the states of countries like India and prevents them from pursuing policies that uplift the conditions of life of their working populations. Under neoliberalism, these policies, which would necessarily have to put constraints on capital, are hostage to the constant anxiety that capital will find these constraints intolerable and, given its new-found global mobility, it will move to other parts of the world which have not imposed the same constraints. For considerations such as these (and also familiar counterpart considerations having to do with trade in the neoliberal period), countries like India are helpless, while linked to the global economy. Delinking from the global economy is the only form of resistance to the hegemony of finance capital and setting up a constitutional regime of economic rights with the two features I mentioned earlier in the article, is the first substantial step in such resistance. In a word, in the current period of neo-liberalism, economic rights on the site of the nation and de-linking from the global economy to gain greater national sovereignty are *of a piece*.

The *full* extent to which they are of a piece, however, only comes into view if we understand another ineliminable aspect of capitalism that Patnaik has emphasized in his analysis and, once we do, we will be in a position to conclude this essay by specifying a third feature of rights which we left unspecified in the earlier discussion. This third feature, though it is a feature of all rights, not just economic rights, has a particularly vivid point and significance for economic rights, once we grasp this ineliminable aspect of capitalism.

Borrowing an expression of Oskar Lange, Patnaik characterizes capital as possessed of certain 'spontaneous tendencies', a prominent one of which is that *capital, by its very nature, is disposed to undermine all constraints that are put on it, rendering all such constraints unstable and impermanent*. Thus, under capitalism, human subjects do not have a certain kind of freedom, the freedom to impose permanent and stable constraints on capital. The undermining of the constraints that were imposed during what I called the period of 'hiatus' after the Second World War, is just one prominent example of this tendency. But the tendency is, in general, everywhere detectable on the surface of politics, as we well know, when governments that pursue social democratic policies (that require imposing constraints on capital) are never able to do so with much stability, even in the Scandinavian countries, and are constantly susceptible to being undermined and overthrown because such constraints are simply not tolerable, from the point of view of capital, given its built-in spontaneous tendencies. From this, Patnaik draws an interesting theoretical conclusion.

Given such tendencies, any effort to oppose capitalism is left with a disjunction. *Either* you transcend capitalism *or* capitalism will undermine the constraints you try to impose on it. To put it in terms of freedom and determinism, we, as human subjects in the modern period with its unique economic formation, are determined in the sense that we cannot (we are not free to) constrain that formation, but we are also *free*, free to *transcend* the formation. It is just *within* capitalism that we are determined and are not free to constrain it.

This leaves one with the question of how this transcendence is to be achieved. As the discussion earlier between Marx and Hobsbawm makes clear, we are not in an 'age of revolution', so, realistically speaking, a revolutionary transformation to another economic formation – such as socialism, say – is not in the cards. What options remain, then?

Patnaik himself does not answer this question in very detailed or elaborate terms. What he does say, though, is certainly in the right direction. He submits that one should *continue* to put constraints on capital and then, rather than leave things there (since, given his analysis of capital, we know that they will be sooner or later undermined), we should *build on them recursively* (those are his own words; emphasis added) till eventually capital is transcended. He does not specify what the further recursive steps would be because, as he says, they will depend on and be dictated by the contingent forms the crises and dysfunctionalities the constraints on capital will bring about, the exact nature of which cannot be predicted.

Although this is, as I said, a good schematic statement of the general direction of the answer to our overall question (the question, what options remain if the prospects of a revolution are nil?), an unanswered, indeed unasked, more specific question is: Even if the further recursive steps cannot be predicted, what should the *initial constraint* or constraints on capital be, on which the recursive steps must build? One should be able to specify these with some minimal theoretical description since we already have his analysis of capitalism in hand. What, then, is that significant minimal description? Clearly, the initial constraint will have to be carefully chosen so that it *addresses the central claim of his analysis of capitalism*. That means that one must seek to put a constraint on capital, which, *by its very nature*, confronts *explicitly and directly* the spontaneous tendency of capital to undermine constraints placed upon it. Previous constraints on capital were not constructed with full awareness of the disjunction mentioned above, they were not constructed with full awareness of the spontaneous tendency of capital to not tolerate constraints placed upon it. But if a constraint *is* constructed with such a full awareness (and I will say more about this constraint in a moment), it *would* address that tendency directly and explicitly and may therefore possess *relative* stability, not hitherto present in other constraints that have been placed on capital in the past. This, in turn, will allow scope (even as we know that the constraints are not going to be allowed to be permanent) to do what Patnaik thinks should next be done – recursively build on this initial constraint in the future till capitalism is transcended. And even if, as he says, these *further* recursive constraining steps that build on this initial constraint cannot be specified at the outset because the dysfunctionality and crisis that will be generated within capitalism by the imposing of this initial constraint cannot be predicted, one can nevertheless, if one chooses the *first* constraint along the theoretical lines I have just mentioned, be sure that *it will* generate a crisis and dysfunctionality. This is because, on the one hand, as Patnaik has pointed out, capital will not cease in its tendency to try to undermine the constraint and, on the other hand, the constraint in question (by its very nature, as I said) explicitly and directly addresses this tendency since it is self-consciously constructed with full awareness of the susceptibility of constraints on capital to being undermined. This would, then, be an unprecedented confrontation in the history of capital, creating conditions for a chronic crisis and dysfunctionality, which, though we cannot predict their exact nature, will be fertile ground for recursively strengthening this initial constraint with whatever future constraining steps those conditions of crisis and dysfunctionality will demand, till such point as transcendence from capital emerges as a serious possibility.

We have arrived at a crux point in the dialectic of this article and must ask: What kind of initial constraint is dictated when it is theoretically conceived as self-consciously addressing an innate spontaneous tendency of capital to undermine constraints upon it?

It will come as no surprise that its underlying nature is to be found in the insertion of economic rights in the constitution since I have already said that it is this insertion that will force nation-states to recover sovereignty over their own economies by imposing necessary constraints on capital. (I say 'force' because these economic rights will not be implementable – justiciable – if capital is not constrained.) But what exactly is it about economic rights that speak to the very specific nature that this initial constraint is supposed to have that distinguishes it from all previous constraints put on capital, namely that it is a constraint constructed out of a self-conscious awareness of the spontaneous tendencies of capital to undermine constraints put upon it and that, as a constraint, it contains properties that explicitly and directly address that tendency and oppose it. What about economic rights that speak to *this theoretical desideratum*?

It is to answer this crucial question that we need to introduce a third – relatively neglected – defining feature of rights, which I have so far suppressed.

What Are Rights? A Third Feature

Apart from the two features of rights that we had outlined earlier (priority over the good, and justiciability), rights, properly so-called, possess a third defining feature that I will call the 'Ulysses and the Sirens' feature.[20]

Ulysses, at a crucial moment in his travels, had tied himself to the mast because he was deeply and fundamentally committed to the value of marital fidelity (in his case, fidelity to Penelope), and he was concerned, knowing himself, that he might weaken and be seduced when the sirens sang their song. The idea is that even when he is weakened and seduced and no longer values fidelity, he is living by the value of fidelity. Commitments of this sort are, thus, relativized to times. At time t_1, a commitment to a value has the 'Ulysses and the Sirens' feature if, those who have the commitment, knowing that they might weaken at some future time *tn* and might cease to be committed to the value, arrange at t_1 to entrench the commitment to that value in such a way that they are living by it at *tn*, even when they have weakened and ceased to be committed to it at *tn*.

When we elevate some values to rights, properly so-called, we entrench the value and our commitment to it in constitutions, in just this way. Take the fundamental right to free speech in many constitutions. Apart from putting a constraint on various pursuits of the good in the way described earlier, and apart from its justiciability, making the value of free speech a fundamental right also amounts to saying that if at some point in the future, we find ourselves very upset by some offensive form of speech and allow those hurt feelings to weaken our commitment to free speech and demand that the speaker or writer to be censored, our demand should not and would not be indulged. By making the value of free speech a right, we have tied ourselves to the mast with it, and this future weakening and demand for censorship by us is thus going to be denied.

Similarly, if economic rights are rights, properly so-called, we will tie ourselves to the mast with them and will resist all tendencies to undermine them, because of a fundamental constitutional commitment to them in this 'Ulysses and the Sirens' form. *This feature of rights, then, explicitly and directly speaks to and resists what Patnaik calls 'the spontaneous tendencies' of capital.* If the effect of implementing economic rights in a particular nation-state like India will inevitably require the state to impose certain constraints on capital (for instance, to name just two, raising taxes on corporations and wealth and inheritance, and imposing capital controls to prevent capital flight that would otherwise ensue), and if, moreover, the economic rights are understood as having the 'Ulysses and the Sirens' like structure, then this *latter* feature of rights will necessarily amount to a more stable and sustained resistance against the spontaneous tendencies of capital to undermine the constraints placed upon it. Thus, economic rights (so understood as possessing this third feature) bestow on these constraints on capital that are required for their implementation, just the property that ought to be the first step in a recursive process of strengthening the constraints on capital till such time as capital might be transcended. If the tendencies of capital are to constantly destabilize constraints upon it, and if tying oneself to the mast with something, whose implementation requires, *as a result of being so tied*, those very constraints on capital *to be more stable than they have hitherto been*, we are set on a path which holds real possibilities for the recursive process that Patnaik's account envisages.

Various questions of detail remain. Some will be general questions about the consequences of de-linking from the global economy. One such is whether the envisaged delinking will not impose its own great hardships on the Indian economy. Patnaik's writings consider this issue in detail, warning against caving in to the punitive responses that global finance is bound to make, and making detailed proposals about how to address the hardships. What should be added is that the populations of nations of the south, which have undertaken such a delinking, must be persuaded to stay the course, despite the initial hardships that will follow upon delinking. This would mean a constant campaign of public education that would apprise them of the temporary nature of such hardships and of the mid- and long-term efficacy of the proposals to address them.

Another question will be whether the economies of some nation-states of the South will not be too small to survive such a delinking, and Patnaik addresses this too, though only briefly, by suggesting that there be South–South links, whereby a system of cooperation between larger and smaller economies of the South will emerge.

A third question, an anxiety really, about delinking is that it is a form of nationalism and nationalism is associated with a reversion to aggressive, narrow-minded ideologies, often driven by ethnic pride or religious bigotry, and often characterized by autarchic concentrations of power. Even Yannis Varoufakis, the radical economist and cabinet minister who walked out of the Greek government because it would not resist the domination of the banking elites set up in Brussels, refused delinking from Europe and a common currency as an option, saying he did not believe in autarchy. This anxiety is based on a fundamental confusion. There is no rational ground to conflate a delinking of the form that Patnaik is suggesting with nationalisms characterized along these lines, nor even any reason to think that they will generate such nationalisms. Indeed, there is good reason to think that delinking will, after an initial period of hardship, result in the upliftment of the conditions of the poorest sections of the working population of nations, a result that is likely to diminish their tendency to embrace the aggressive forms of nationalisms that prompt these anxieties. There is much more reason, in fact, to expect (as recent developments all over the world have manifestly shown) that if there is no delinking, and neo-liberalism and hegemonic finance continues to hold sway, that working people suffering under its policies will have nothing else to turn to than nationalism of this anxiety-inducing form.

Other questions will be more immediately connected with the idea of economic rights. For instance, how can a country like India afford to adopt and implement these economic rights? This is an obvious question and without an answer to it, the feature of justiciability of these rights is going to ring hollow. Patnaik considers the question of affordability in careful detail, makes highly specific assessments of the public expenditures entailed and how they will be provided for; in particular, what percentage of the GDP will be tapped by the extra expenditure entailed by introducing economic rights, and which segments of the population and which institutions will be targeted for taxation and for how much. Such details apart, at a more philosophical level, it seems at first sight that these questions arise only for economic rights and not for the other rights of personal liberty and freedom we discussed in our foundational discussion earlier in the article. The rights of liberty are to a large extent rights of *non-interference* and thus negatively formulated rights. By contrast, economic rights are more positively formulated as entailing *provisions* for the nation's citizens. For citizens to be left alone from interference, no questions seem to be raised about whether a state can afford their implementability. But when it comes to feeding and sheltering and sustaining the health of citizens, all sorts of issues arise because doing these things requires food to be grown, houses to be constructed, hospitals to be set up, doctors to be trained. So, it must be granted that the rights of liberty, unlike economic rights, seem to be rights that do not bring out immediately the extent to which individual citizens are embedded in contexts of social production and distribution. But this seeming difference is only a matter of degree. In fact, a very substantial regulatory force of policing and protection is involved in seeking to guarantee the rights of liberty. Just consider the enormous numbers of a police force that may have to protect publicly made speech that is controversial and generates conflict within a population, or consider the vast amount of public expenditure by the government of the United Kingdom which, in order to implement its free speech rights, gave Salman Rushdie twenty-four-hour police protection for years following the threats he received in the aftermath of the publication of *The Satanic Verses*. The implementation of *all* rights (the rights of liberty and economic rights) reflects some (if varying) degree of the fact that citizens are embedded in infrastructures of regulation, production and distribution. Rights may owe their foundations to our fundamental nature as human beings, but rights are not implemented for human beings in a state of nature, they are implemented for human beings in these highly embedded social, political and economic contexts.

A final question is about the third feature of rights which I have named the 'Ulysses and the Sirens' feature. What exactly does it mean to tie oneself to the mast with a right? It cannot, of course, be that masts – at least as under-stood in the constitutional context of rights – can simply *never* be untied. But even if that is so, the idea, in general, is that to the extent that one thinks these rights are fundamental rights and are to be deeply entrenched, then to that extent at least, one must make it as difficult as possible to undermine them. All sorts of detailed suggestions can be made regarding this entrenchment, which I cannot possibly elaborate here in an article that is already too long. But I will say this. No routine form of what often passes for 'judicial review' will suffice for such entrenchment. What may be required, if economic rights are going to be central to the initial set of constraints that will amount to a sustained resistance against the tendencies of capital, is a clear understanding that they will not be amended in their *basic structure* as commitments (even if they are periodically updated in the *detail* to adjust to changing contexts of needs) by anything more expedient than deliberations carried out after a re-formation of a constituent assembly of the sort that initially debated and then formulated the Indian constitution. That is how seriously we have to take fundamental rights.[21] That is what distinguishes them both from policies and from the variable forms of pursuit of the good.

Concluding Remarks

This essay, resisting current developments in political and legal theory (primarily critical race theory and critical legal theory), has proceeded on the assumption that rights are a necessary element of any rational understanding of a political framework for our time. Such an assumption equally stands in contrast with the overly idealistic political outlook that puts faith in the moral judgement of citizens to construct not just a theory of the common good but to put that theory into practice, without any framework of rights (possess-ing the three features I have outlined in the foregoing pages) that would, in some fundamental spheres of human life, *make* citizens and the institutions of governance they adopt do certain things and *prevent* them from doing other things. Policies and routine laws devised by the executive and legislative institu-tions of governance do not possess these three features and cannot, therefore, be counted on to be the deep commitments that will do the sort of 'making' and 'preventing' that rights are intended for. At the same time, as the expression 'fundamental spheres' that I have just used makes clear, this article has been careful to restrict the scope of rights to only those things that can get a foundational grounding in considerations of the most basic aspects of human nature. Rights cannot be proliferated (except as merely aspirational rhetoric and gestural, heuristic, principles) at the will of citizens. Rights are firm commitments, but they are *few* because they are chosen with the utmost rigour and care in such foundational discussion, some of which I have briefly presented.

It has been a central concern of the essay to include among these few and carefully chosen and defended rights, a range of economic rights. The extended discussion which sought to justify this inclusion had to situate economic rights in a foundational discussion, which inevitably led to detailed comparisons of the foundations of such rights with the foundations of the rights to liberty. But, even if economic rights were foundationally grounded along the lines this discussion brought out, the relevance of such rights for the political economy of our times does not come into view until we situate these rights further in an analysis of capitalism, one systematic example of which is provided by Prabhat Patnaik himself. The article briefly expounded that analysis and found, as a result, first that economic rights only get to have any bite in our time if they are inserted into the constitutions of *particular nations*, and second, that they can address the economic obstacles that capital constantly and effectively places in the path of the pursuit of the common good, if we stress a *third* defining feature of rights that has been relatively neglected in the discussion of the meaning of rights.

One recurring concern of the essay has been to try to diagnose why the rights surrounding liberty have received so much more foundational attention and discussion than economic rights. I have discussed at considerable length the factors that might lie behind this neglect of such a significant set of rights that speak to such fundamental aspects of human life and existence. That discussion raised a very wide range of issues. But one issue – perhaps the most obvious one – was not discussed earlier in the article because its significance is only manifest once we have an analysis of capitalism, which we did not have at that stage of the essay. So, let me conclude, then, with just one or two very brief remarks about it. I can do no better than to approach the issue by relating a conversation that I had with Ronald Dworkin (whom I have mentioned and cited in note 21). Quite some years ago, Dworkin had given the 'Dewey Lectures' at Columbia University on the subject of equality, in which he had made an elaborate case for a view of equality that stressed what he called 'equality of resources'. I had chaired the last of the three lectures and, as Chair, was expected to raise the first question to break the ice and get a public conversation going. I asked him why he had not mentioned the possibility that economic rights might be a first step in the direction of achieving greater equality. His answer came immediately, almost unreflectively, but it is obvious that he had long reflected on the subject. He said rights are only rights if they can be guaranteed to be implemented, and economic rights, he added, cannot be guaranteed to be implemented, so we should pursue them not as rights but as social welfare policies, to which he, as a liberal with social democratic commitments, was certainly committed.

Dworkin, however, did not pause to consider what was being presupposed by his avowed reason for excluding economic rights from rights proper. I believe that if we consider the relation between Dworkin's remark and the analysis given by Patnaik of the political economy of our time, it becomes quite clear that Dworkin's reason for saying that they should be the target of policies and not rights, implicitly presupposes that liberal democratic polities are always to be situated in a capitalist political economy and it is precisely in a capitalist economy that they are not implementable.

This, then, presents us with a choice. *Either* restrict the goal of fulfilment of basic needs to social welfare policies that, in effect, require putting constraints on capital *or* attempt – via the recursive strategy that includes adopting economic rights, outlined in the last few pages of this article – to transcend capitalism. Dworkin opts for the first, Patnaik for the second. Some wag, perhaps it was none other and none less than G.E. Moore, once said, 'One man's modus ponens is another man's modus tollens.' The relation between Dworkin's view and Patnaik's view does not quite fit this snowclone – because it is not a premise, but a background presupposition or assumption of Dworkin's that Patnaik is rejecting – but it is a close enough cousin of it.

Patnaik does not discuss the foundations of economic rights in much detail and to the extent that he does in the paper I have cited, he grounds them in the idea of democracy. I find this does not help as much as he thinks it does because notions of democracy are very variable and very contested, while the foundations we need for rights need to be much less variable and contested, if they are going to justify adopting commitments with the three features I have said are defining of rights. That is why, in probing their foundations, I have appealed to considerations that go to the most fundamental aspects of human nature, which are uniform among human beings and cannot be contested. But the strength of his discussion really lies in the fact that, unlike the philosophers who have discussed it foundationally, he motivates his proposal for economic rights, both in principle and in detail, within a deep and persuasive analysis of capitalism. A crucial element in that analysis is a disjunction – which I had presented earlier in the article – that it throws up. This disjunction has obvious bearing on the options – just mentioned – that are thrown up by a consideration of Dworkin's remarks. To repeat, the disjunction that Patnaik's analysis leads to is: *Either* you transcend capitalism *or* capitalism will undermine the constraints you try to impose on it. To repeat, the options that Dworkin's remarks lead to are: *Either* restrict the goal of fulfilment of basic needs to social welfare policies that, in effect, require putting constraints on capital *or* attempt – via the recursive strategy elaborated some pages ago (p. 54) – to transcend capitalism. The second of Patnaik's two disjuncts reveals exactly why one should not take the first of the two options that a consideration of Dworkin's account throws up.

All of this reveals a point of the utmost significance: Unless one situates the discussion of economic rights in a sound analysis of contemporary capitalism, as Patnaik does (but much recent discussion, whether it is by Dworkin or Sen or Moyn, does not), one will not find the really persuasive reasons for adopting economic rights, and one will have no answer to those (the very same gentlemen mentioned in the last parenthesis) who have expressed one or other sort of scepticism about economic rights and the foundational basis for them. At the same time, ironically, though not altogether surprisingly, it is precisely such an analysis of capitalism that satisfactorily addresses the other familiar quarter where scepticism about economic rights is most prevalent, those on the radical left who view Marx's historically contextual dismissive remarks about rights to be everlasting truths. I say this is not surprising only because it is how it *should* be – Marx is not shown to be wrong on terms that come from liberal doctrine, which implicitly presupposes a future without any conceivable terminus for capitalism as we know it, but rather on terms that are drawn from an appropriate Marxist analysis of capitalism, as we know it.

This essay was originally published under the same title in *The Indian Economic Journal*, vol. 71, no. 1, 2023, pp. 30–55.

Notes

[1] By 'properly so-called', what I am stressing is that the proposal is about fundamental rights, nothing less. The point is not merely that these are not vaguely declared directive principles, they are not rights in any low-profile sense of the term. They are fundamental rights, the deepest commitments of a constitution.

[2] I will be drawing mostly from Patnaik and Patnaik (2016, 2021) as well as from some of his essays in Patnaik (2012).

[3] This phrase gets a prominent discussion in Rawls (1971). It is also the main theme of Rawls (1988). In Bilgrami (2017), I argue that though rights are prior to the good in the sense of providing constraints on the good as expounded above, one nevertheless inevitably has to appeal to the good and often to variable conceptions of the good when one is trying to persuade people with diverse value commitments to embrace one or the other right. Even if, as I argue in the present essay, a right must have its foundations in deep and fundamental grounds that appeal to the most basic and universal aspects of human nature, the reasons by which one persuades people to adopt a right may have to appeal to *their* specific conceptions of the good, conceptions that may vary among them. There is no inconsistency in this. Foundational grounding and persuasion of people are distinct enterprises.

[4] See note 21 below for more on the words 'taken seriously'.

[5] This issue is utterly familiar and has been the topic of a great deal of discussion ever since the earliest formulations of socialist ideals. I will not be taking it up in this article. If it is not already obvious, the point here is not that socialism does not allow for the existence of any private property, only that it does not allow it as a right and

it does not allow it in the form that is defining of relations in a capitalist economic formation.

6 See chapter 10 in Bilgrami (2014) for the relevance of the distinction between thick and thin notions of rationality in the political sphere. Quite apart from the political sphere, speaking quite generally, for human subjects, thin rationality is *not optional*. To be capable of thought and action at all is to exemplify (not perfectly, but considerably) rationality in the thin sense. A massive or considerable failure of thin rationality in our thinking puts into doubt that it is thinking at all. Thin rationality can be codified, but we do not have to be self- consciously applying the codes or to be able to articulate the codes. We simply exemplify them in our thought from whatever early age the capacity for reason grows in us. (In this sense, it is just like our counting, say, marbles – after a certain early age – exemplifying the Peano axioms, without us either articulating them or in any way self-consciously applying them.) What sorts of notions of reason and rationality get counted as thin is an interesting question. Although perhaps no list can (or should) determinately be made, one can safely assume that something like deductive rationality, inductive rationality (that is, rationality roughly codified by inductive logic or 'confirmation theory'), and some spare understanding of the codifications of decision-theory, fall within thin rationality. But not all 'thin' ideas of reason are codified. What I am appealing to in this article, in stating what underlies autonomy, is something that there is no question of codifying. The autonomy-reflecting question is raised not from the point of view of any codified account of reason, it is rather simply the idea of rationality that is expressed by the most common or garden notion of 'reasons'. The autonomy-reflecting question is basically asking: 'Do I have *reason or reasons* to do or think what the group is thinking and doing?' It is the most general and common exercise of one's reason. Thus, 'thin'. The sense in which it contrasts with a thick conception of reason is immediately apparent when one puts the question (more thickly) as follows: Do I have a *self-interested reason* to do or think that the group does or thinks?

7 See Rovane (1998) for a detailed account of collective deliberation and rationality, and the idea of group agency and personhood.

8 I say 'standardly understood' with good reason. There is a tendency, in those who subscribe to liberalism as a doctrine, to seek to accommodate all sorts of dissenting ideas (such as those I mention later in the paragraph) within the doctrine. These efforts at non-standard liberalism are bootless and succeed in doing little other than bloating the doctrine to a point that it becomes all things to all and, thus, far less interesting than it is in its standard form, even if the standard doctrine is not, in the end, plausible.

9 The classic paper characterizing liberalism in terms of 'negative liberty' and expressing deep anxieties about positive ideals of liberty is 'Two Concepts of Liberty' by Berlin (2008). Both Rousseau and Marx and those whom they influenced are the explicit targets of Berlin's criticisms of positive liberty.

10 See https://www.un.org/en/udhrbook/pdf/udhr_booklet_en_web.pdf.

11 Marx (1844) is the most cited location for this vehement dismissal of rights, though it also surfaces in Marx (1848).

12 In my own case, I have also been grappling with the challenges to the idea of rights that come from Gandhi's criticisms of liberalism, as well. Since I am not a liberal, this challenge is partly congenial to me, though its relevance to rights is a subtle and delicate matter. Gandhi, as is well known, accepted the proposals for economic rights in the Karachi Resolution, that are invoked by Patnaik. In a curious way, Gandhi reverses the tendency of most liberals, who tend to emphasize the rights of liberty over the rights that would lift people from destitution. But I cannot elaborate on this here.

13 There is a small body of philosophical writing on basic needs and rights. See Doyal and Gough (1991), Mcloskey (1976), Wiggins and Derman (1987) and Braybrooke (1987).

14 Of course, some relativization may well be necessary despite this assumption of deter-

minacy – those who labour in fields or factories may need to ingest more calories than those sitting at a desk all day long.

[15] Of the many writings by Sen elaborating his notion of capabilities, see especially, Sen (1985) and Sen (1999).

[16] The familiar, relevant classic texts are, of course, Hegel (2018) and Marx (1977).

[17] Most explicitly in Sen (1979, 1992).

[18] See note 3 above for the references.

[19] These are two quite separate external sources. Should the external markets in the South even cease to matter, the first source – of supply of primary commodities – remains indispensable.

[20] The expression and the idea of 'Ulysses and the Sirens' is the theme of a book by Elster (1984) though it was anticipated by Derek Parfit (1984) in his example of the Russian Prince in his book and some papers by him that preceded that book. But Parfit and Elster are both focused on the moral psychology of individuals, not on politics and rights. I have exploited the idea of Ulysses and the Sirens to characterize a notion of subjective identity that is relevant to politics in various papers of mine, some of which are collected in the section on 'Identity' in Bilgrami (2014). Elster (2000) in a subsequent book is critical of my use of the idea in exploring the notion of identity. But I think the criticism is based on a misunderstanding, as Bykvist (2002) points out in her review of Elster's book. Sometimes, rights are described as pre-commitments and that is intended to capture something like the Ulysses and the Sirens idea, but the word 'pre-commitment' is incoherent since the idea of post-commitments makes no sense.

[21] When I say 'that is how seriously we have to take rights', I am harking back to the title of Dworkin's (2017). Dworkin, however, does not take up the Ulysses and the Sirens feature of rights and is focused much more on their priority over the good, which he is well known to have developed as the idea that rights can *trump* the good.

References

Berlin, I. (2008), *Two Concepts of Liberty,* available at https://mpra.ub.uni-muenchen. de/10039/1/MPRA_paper_10039.pdf

Bilgrami, A. (2014), *Secularism, Identity and Enchantment*, Cambridge, Massachusetts: Harvard University Press and New Delhi: Permanent Black.

—— (2017), 'Liberalism and Identity', in C. Laborde and A. Bardon, eds, *Religion in Liberal Political Philosophy*, Oxford, UK: Oxford University Press.

Braybrooke, D. (1987), *Meeting Needs*, Princeton, New Jersey: Princeton University Press.

Bykvist, K. (2002), 'Book Review: Jon Elster, *Ulysses Unbound: Studies in Rationality Precommitment, and Constraints*, Cambridge, UK: Cambridge University Press, 2000', *Ethics*, vol. 112, no. 2, p. 308, doi: https://www.jour- nals.uchicago.edu/doi/abs/10.1086/324252

Doyal, L., and I. Gough (1991), *A Theory of Human Need*, New York: Springer.

Dworkin, R. (2017), *Taking Rights Seriously*, Cambridge, Massachusetts: Harvard University Press.

Elster, J. (1984), *Ulysses and the Sirens*, Cambridge, UK: Cambridge University Press.

—— (2000), *Ulysses Unbound*, Cambridge, UK: Cambridge University Press.

Hegel, G.W. (2018), *Phenomenology of Spirit*, Cambridge, UK: Cambridge University Press.

Hobsbawm, E. (1962), *The Age of Revolution 1789–1848*, London: Weidenfeld and Nicholson.

Kant, I. (1997), *Groundwork of the Metaphysics of Morals*, Cambridge, UK: Cambridge University Press.

Locke, J. (1689a), *An Essay Concerning Toleration*, https://socialsciences.mcmaster.ca/~econ/ugcm/3ll3/locke/tol- eration.pdf

—— (1689b), *Second Treatise on Government*, available at https://www.gutenberg.org/files/7370/7370-h/7370-h.htm

Marx, K. (1844), *On the Jewish Question*, https://www.marxists.org/archive/marx/works/1844/jewish-question/

——— (1848), *The Communist Manifesto*, https://www.marxists.org/archive/marx/works/1848/communist-manifesto/

——— (1977), *Critique of Hegel's Philosophy of Right*, Cambridge, UK: Cambridge University Press.

Mcloskey, H.J. (1976), 'Human Needs, Rights and Political Values', *American Philosophical Quarterly*, vol. 13, no. 1.

Mill, J.S. (2011), *On Liberty*, https://www.gutenberg.org/files/34901/34901-h/34901-h.htm

Milton, J. (1644), *Areopagitica*, https://milton.host.dartmouth.edu/reading_room/areopagitica/text.html

Moyn, S. (2018), *Not Enough*, Cambridge, Massachusetts: Harvard University Press.

Parfit, D. (1984), *Reasons and Persons*, Oxford, UK: Oxford University Press.

Patnaik, P. (2010), A Left Approach to Development, *Economic and Political Weekly*, vol. 45, no. 30.

——— (2012), *Re-envisioning Socialism*, New Delhi: Tulika Books.

——— (2020), 'Globalisation and the Abridgement of Freedom', *Agrarian South: Journal of Political Economy*, vol. 9, no. 2, pp. 103–16.

Patnaik, P. and U. Patnaik (2016), *A Theory of Imperialism*, New York: Columbia University Press and New Delhi: Tulika Books.

——— (2021), *Capitalism and Imperialism*, New York: Monthly Review Press and New Delhi: Tulika Books.

Rawls, J. (1971), *A Theory of Justice*, Cambridge, Massachusetts: Harvard University Press.

——— (1988), 'The Priority of Right and Ideas of the Good', *Philosophy and Public Affairs*, vol. 17, no. 4, pp. 251–76.

Rovane, C. (1998), *The Bounds of Agency*, Princeton, UK: Princeton University Press.

Sen, A. (1979), 'Equality of What?', in S.M. McMurrin, ed., *Tanner Lectures on Human Values*, Cambridge, UK: Cambridge University Press.

——— (1984), 'Goods and People', in A. Sen, *In Resources, Values and Development*, Oxford, UK: Basil Blackwell.

——— (1985), 'Well-being, Agency and Freedom: The Dewey Lectures 1984', *Journal of Philosophy*, vol. 82, no. 4, pp. 169–221.

——— (1992), *Inequality Reexamined*, Oxford, UK: Clarendon Press.

——— (1999), *Development as Freedom*, New York: Alfred Knopf.

Skinner, Q. (2008), *Hobbes and Republican Liberty*, Cambridge, UK: Cambridge University Press.

Wiggins, D. and Derman, S. (1987), 'Needs, Need, Needing,' *Journal of Medical Ethics*, vol. 13, no. 2, pp. 62–68.

4

Awkward Classes and India's Rural Development

Barbara Harriss-White

Introduction

To this day, Marx's model of capitalism, based on his analysis of nineteenth-century British capitalist production relations, dominates critical materialist political economy. Focused on industrial production, including the industrialization of agriculture and the transition from pre-capitalist, peasant, feudal, artisanal or primitive communist production relations, Marx's model is driven by the class-differentiating contradictions between the forces and relations of production to which Utsa Patnaik has contributed germinal analyses (U. Patnaik 1976, 1987). On one side is the disciplining of capitalist wage labour (and the convulsive mass displacement of people necessary for this). On the other are the compulsive driving forces of accumulation through private property, the control of technology and the quest for profit (Marx 1887, chapter 24).[1] In the ongoing disputes over the transition to, and subsequent transformations of, capitalist relations, social classes which deviate from Marx's model have tended to be ignored, regarded as outliers or treated teleologically as headed for extinction (Aslany 2021; Bernstein 2001).[2]

Here we examine two such 'awkward' classes that are peripheral to the orthodox understanding of Marx's model but which persist and are expanding globally, play a vital role in social relations and politics, and are moreover now fully integrated with industrial and financial capital.[3]

The first is the class of petty commodity producers – also known as 'peasants', 'simple commodity producers' and 'the self-employed' – although these labels distinguish different aspects of the class, have different theoretical lineages and assign petty commodity production (PCP) different roles in development.[4] For India, Prabhat Patnaik has theorized PCP as the outcome of a 'perverse transformation' in which a truncated process of primitive accumulation of capital dispossesses labour outright through land seizure or intensifies its distress through progressively reducing rural incomes, yet is unable to absorb the free or semi-free labour it creates. So, PCP remains as a residue, effectively part of the reserve army of labour (P. Patnaik 2012). The second awkward class is the class presiding over circulation – 'merchant's capital', also known as 'commercial capital' (CC) and/or the 'produce traders' (Banaji 2016a; 2020; 2021;[5] Jan 2017).

As classes, they are certainly awkward. The concept of awkwardness in a class is owed to Teodor Shanin, who argued controversially that in Russia, a century ago, the differentiation of these classes into proletarians or capitalists faced a series of social and political, centrifugal and centripetal processes which countered the force of differentiation and led Shanin to suggest that peasants could not have a distinct political interest or become part of the long-term political vanguard (Shanin 1972).[6] Shanin's concept of awkwardness was therefore both analytical and political. Other scholars have developed the concept of awkwardness. For Bush (1992), the disjuncture between analytical categories and political activity, between a class which can be identified 'in itself', defined by conditions different from those of other classes yet which cannot organize politically 'for itself', is awkward.[7] He criticizes Marx for never having established links between class in and for itself (Bush 1992). The concept of awkwardness has also been expanded to include the discursive mismatches, first between state classifications and theoretical concepts, and second between the latter and those enshrined in regulative law (Sankaran 2008). And if we take seriously the dynamism, multifariousness and the social and spatial unevenness of actually occurring capitalist transformations (Adnan 2015; Braudel 1982; Dörre 2010), the polar classes of capitalists and workers themselves are not 'un-awkward' too.

In this volume, celebrating the signal contributions of Utsa and Prabhat Patnaik to Marxist scholarship and politics, we argue in this essay that the true awkwardness of petty commodity activity lies in its dynamics, structure and politics; in its persistence and capacity to reproduce without accumulation; in the internal contradictions of an apparently simple *form* which combines capital and labour and yet which also manages labour organized inside the family; and in its inability to act in a politically coherent way. We argue that the awkwardness of merchant's capital is different, lying in the tension between its structural and dynamic complexity and its political coherence. Although the theoretical concept is clear – capital for buying and selling in the sphere of circulation – in its concrete form it is permeated by productive activity. Further, actually existing commercial capital includes both large and sometimes oligopolistic firms, which accumulate through the concentration and centralization of capital, and very small or petty ('petit') firms which are prevented from accumulating but which persist and expand by multiplication into yet further small-scale operations. Oligopolistic commercial capital has a coherent politics in which, moreover, subordination, either to the state or to industrial capital, is successfully resisted. To overlook these two awkward classes is not just a matter of incompleteness, it is rather to misunderstand the dynamics of contemporary capitalist development.

The argument is developed for each awkward class as follows. First, concepts are introduced and critically discussed, since they have been developed at a relatively high level of abstraction and for general application. They are then applied to the case of contemporary India. India is not only a highly socially heterogeneous, unequal, regionally and politically complex, ecologically differentiated society, comprising nearly a tenth of the world's economy, a fifth of its people and a third of its poor (World Bank 2016); it has also long been a major focus of debates and of empirical research on the two awkward classes discussed here. In view of the enormity of the literature we focus mostly on rural and small-town society and politics.

Petty Commodity Production and Circulation in the Development of Capitalism

Petty commodity production (PCP) is economic activity in which the household is the unit of production and consumption, a contradictory class position combining capital and labour in gendered roles. Unable to reproduce itself without engagement in the commodity economy, the PCP household may be found in production and in circulation, with flexible and diverse portfolios of activity complicated by wage work: in agriculture, industry, trade, finance and services, in productive activity, in activity that is unproductive but necessary; and in activity which for some commentators is neither productive nor necessary but represents the reserve army of surplus labour, a sector of refuge, the non-capitalist economy or alternatively the socially excluded (Altvater 1993; Bhattacharya 2007; Sanyal 2007).

PCP in Agrarian Transformation

Combining the ownership of small holdings of land with family participation in the labour process, rural productive activity raises crops and animals primarily for subsistence, with sporadic or small surpluses being sold on markets. When markets are incompletely developed and producers are subordinated to other classes and the state, this definition also fits the standard conception of the peasant (Ellis 1993). While for many Marxist scholars the two terms are interchangeable, here, in order to clarify what is awkward about PCP, they need to be distinguished.

In his 'notorious epigrams' (Duggett 1975) Marx compared the French peasantry to potatoes in a sack (undifferentiated), representing 'rural idiocy' (social isolation) and 'barbarism within civilization' (political powerlessness).[8] In the European transition to capitalism, peasants were expected to disappear. Capitalism would grow on the peasantry's tomb, wrote Marx (1887, chapter 33). Engels wrote equally famously that 'their position is absolutely

hopeless as long as capitalism holds sway . . . capitalist large-scale production is absolutely sure to run over their impotent antiquated system of small
production as a train runs over a pushcart' (Engels 1892/2000, pp. 15, 23).
Later, both Lenin and Kautsky argued that peasants would be differentiated
into the polar classes of capital and labour, though while Lenin argued from
the Zemstvo statistics that the peasantry would be destroyed through struggles
between contradictory interests that forced most of them into the proletariat
(Lenin 1899/1964, chapter 2, p. 179 et seq), Kautsky thought that through
their 'superhuman industriousness' (Kautsky 1988, p. 116) peasants would
make possible the social reproduction of a distinctive reserve army of pau-
perized agricultural workers by producing at prices below those of capitalist
production. In addition, the seizure of peasants' assets in 'primary', 'original'
or 'primitive' accumulation,[9] later understood as not only an era of history
but as an ongoing process in logical and historical terms (Adnan 2015; Dörre
2010; Perelman 2001) was another violent force in addition to differentiation
that would threaten the peasantry.

While Hobsbawm famously nailed the late twentieth century as witnessing the 'death of the peasantry' worldwide, among scholars, the terminal
illness of this economic class is interminable, contentious (Bernstein 2001)
and unresolved. In Utsa Patnaik's foundational analysis of peasant class differentiation, the peasantry is alive, forms the nutrient base for capital while
subject to the concentration of the means of production, land, which compels
owners to exploit wage labour (U. Patnaik 1976).[10] For some, while the term
has fundamental historical significance, it has been liquidated as a concept
relevant to contemporary agrarian conditions (Friedmann 2013); yet for others, it has contemporary relevance as a cultural and political term (Edelman
2005; McMichael 2006).

While for Prabhat Patnaik, PCP is a non-capitalist form, a form outside
the capitalist sector whose persistence attests to the perverse transformation
unable to absorb labour virtually dispossessed by capital (P. Patnaik 2008,
2012), in other readings, the contradictory class position of the family farm
has been transformed and incorporated by the penetration of markets into all
aspects of production – except for the way in which family labour is deployed
and the family budget is allocated internally among its labour.[11] Indeed,
Bernstein and Byres, in their compendious retrospective review of research
in agrarian studies, conclude that '*peasant* production' (emphasis added) is

> constituted within generalized commodity production, conceived as the
> imperative of integration in commodity relations to social reproduction. . . .
> Among the implications of this approach are (i) its provision of an adequate
> theoretical specification of the *tendency* to class differentiation, postulated
> as the contradictory combination of the class places of capital and labour in
> peasant production in conditions of generalized commodity production; (ii)

the uneven allocation of those class places within PCP enterprises ('house-holds'), for example, by gendered divisions of property, labour and income; (iii) what determines whether, how, and how much, the tendency to class differentiation is realized in actual trends *of class formation (including the effects of counter-tendencies) and (iv) that one possible outcome of differ-entiation, according to specific circumstances, may be the consolidation of* middle peasant strata and/or 'capitalized family farms'. *(Bernstein and Byres 2001, pp. 26–27)*

So, PCP may be consolidated as one of the 'infinitely diverse combinations of this or that type of capitalist evolution' that are possible (Lenin 1899/1964, preface, pp. 25–28). And regardless of further debates over self-sufficiency, PCP is not a system of peasant or pre- or non-capitalist enterprise for three reasons. First, it is dependent on commodity relations in the circuits of produc-tion and reproduction. It cannot reproduce outside capitalist relations: they are its existence conditions. Second, while the units of PCP are households, petty commodity producers can develop 'micro-conglomerate' portfolios of gendered activity, varying seasonally, straddling economic sectors, displaced across territory, bridging rural and urban, fusing (migrant) wage work and its remit-tances with PCP, able to be destroyed yet easily resurrected (Chattopadhyay 1965; Harriss-White 2008; Jan 2017). While it may include a stream capable of differentiating into capital and wage labour, most PCP households repro-duce themselves as PCP while spaces are created into which PCP can expand. Third, Bernstein and Byres introduced Friedmann's distinction between the peasant form and the (American) 'capitalized family farm', and, with this, the idea that there are 'other ways of theorizing PCP/SCP'.[12] Here, peasant farms have become firms producing commodities, no longer meeting subsistence needs but agriculturalized, food crops in particular becoming cash crops, and spinning, weaving or brewing becoming specialist occupations rather than part of a complex way of life. And not only in agriculture, a clearer distinction between peasant production and PCP lies in the development of PCP as a form of independent activity for the market in the spheres of manufacturing, trade and services. As early as 1978, Moser, to take an influential instance, having critically reviewed all the ILO case material for informal economic activity in Latin America, Africa and South Asia, argued for the superiority of PCP as an analytical category, stressing the diversity and dynamism of its substantive urban forms and relations. Providing the bulk of urban livelihoods, it is to be considered a permanent feature of capitalism in developing countries, she concluded (Moser 1978, pp. 1056–60).

Actually Existing Petty Commodity Production in India

India's capitalist transition and ongoing transformations have created a complex, uneven and heterogeneous social formation (Mohanty 2016).

Rampant differentiation has occurred and advanced forms of corporate capital have been created with family dynasties, often grafted onto former colonial managing agencies, and now wielding global power (Mukherjee-Reed 2004) – and a substantial wage-working class (Hensman 2010). Yet the most common form of production is still PCP. In the 2013–14 Economic Census, 71.7 per cent of firms were own-account enterprises (GoI 2015). In terms of livelihoods, PCP is the robust backbone of the agrarian, manufacturing, service and commercial sectors, even though, due to the low purchasing power associated with PCP (P. Patnaik 2008), it is a constraint on the development of India's national market. It is not a transient or transitional form; if it is really only a stage in the differentiation of the peasantry into capital and labour, it looks likely to be an indefinitely long one (D'Costa 2014; P. Patnaik 2006, 2012).

Under liberalization, an explosion of activity officially classified as self-employment is now driving an expansion of the workforce and is a significant component of India's economic growth (Sinha 2007): own-account firms doubled in number between 1990 and 2011. Moreover, the average wage labour force per firm in India dropped from three workers to just two, while 95 per cent firms in India employ fewer than five people.[13] In India PCP is unevenly distributed, rarely dominating or even populating a whole state territory (refer Mishra 2015 for the exception of Arunachal; Harriss-White 2017, map 1).

It coexists with other forms of production, for some of which it may be functionally necessary for accumulation, while elsewhere it occupies niches in ways that are not directly exploited. Three types of coexistence can be distinguished. The first is 'process-sequential', in which PCP and wage work are deployed at different stages in a system of commodity production (as in the smelting and crafting of metal [Ruthven 2008]); the second is 'process-segregated' in which certain *sectors* of the informal economy are populated by PCP and others by firms with wage workers (e.g. local informal retail versus wholesale trade [Aga 2018]); and the third is 'process-integrated' in which PCP and factory production using wage labour are mixed at all stages of a commodity supply chain (e.g. garments) (Kaur *et al.* 2007) Under PCP, it is not that differentiation is impossible. Some households are able to invest in assets and expand by employing wage labour, while others slither into ever-greater dependence on wages. But its remarkable and theoretically awkward characteristic is how comparatively rare this is, and how much more common is its tendency to expand through multiplication rather than the concentration and centralization of capital. PCP exists and expands alongside other forms of capitalist production relations.

Why does it persist, and how?

The Economics and Internal and External Logics of PCP
The research literature has generated no consensus about the forces driving the persistence of PCP or its expansion through multiplication. Since

Figure 4.1 *Distribution of rural small and marginal holdings, India, 2011*

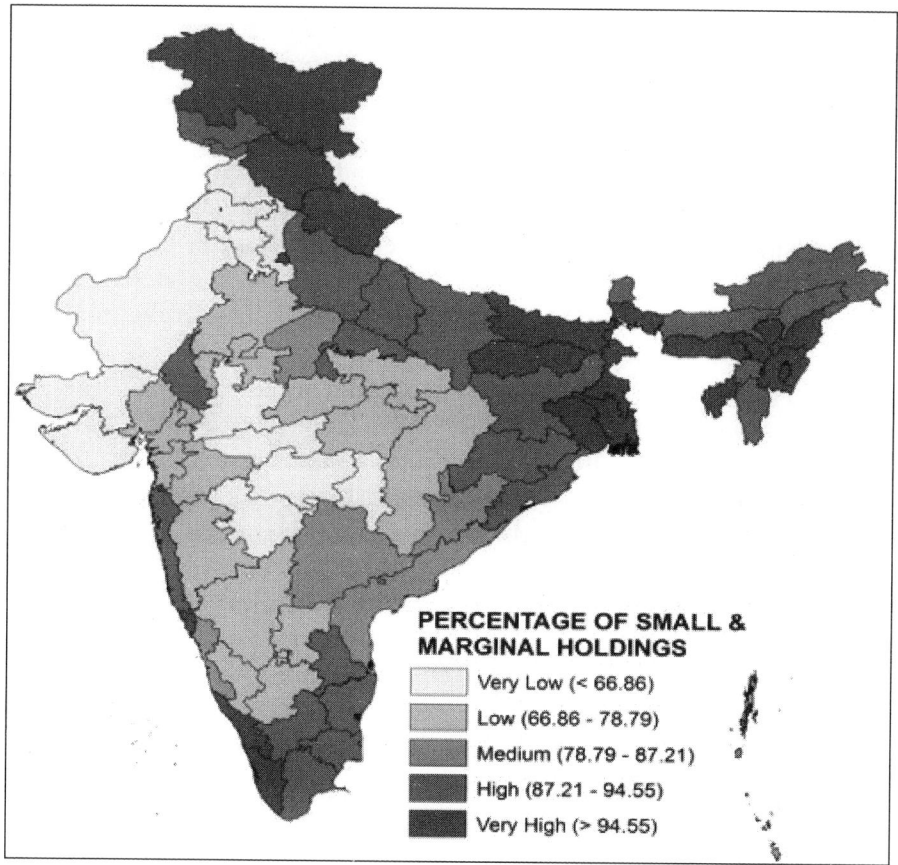

Source: Harriss-White (2017).

capital and labour are fused in PCP, it is not dynamized by contradiction – or at most through 'tensions' (Banaji 2016a).[14] These are specific to particular historical contexts. Although the term PCP is not found in Marx's own writings, three problematics related to PCP are found scattered there. Jan and Harriss-White (2019) have identified these themes as dissolution, conservation and the exploitation–autonomy dialectic. Distinguishing them may enrich theoretical–historical explanations for the persistence of PCP. In the first, PCP is transient; the English transition is used to show how the peasantry is transformed into a landless proletariat. In the second, labour is incompletely separated from the means of production and PCP persists formally subsumed to capital as disguised wage labour (DWL). The third is less well-established in Marxist scholarship. Here, Marx used nineteenth-century America to lay out ideas about 'independent producers'. He distinguished what he earlier called the 'twaddle' of conceiving individuals as capable of action in isolation from their societies (Marx 1857) from the concept of 'the producer' who is 'owner of his own conditions of labour' but without command over wage workers. This producer is 'awkward' because of being capable of resisting capitalist regimes, even when backed by their states. Marx held that to the extent that this kind of producer possesses the means of production and can accumulate for themselves, capitalist accumulation and its mode of production are not possible. Marx called these 'dramatically opposed economic systems' and thought that under 'independent production' wealth tends to be dispersed rather than accumulated (Marx 1887, chapter 33). So, capital and labour unified in PCP persists with some independence and may even reproduce at the expense of capital (Marx 1887).

In India's complex and historically uneven process of the subsumption of labour to capital, small-scale agriculture, subcontracting, out-sourcing, in-sourcing, home-working and such like are said not to be independent, and to be structurally no different from wage work, merely one of the 'classes of labour' differentiated by precarity, dependence and the scale of assets (Lerche 2010), or 'disguised unemployment' (Basu 2018, p. 5) or the 'reserve army' (P. Patnaik 2012). Here, petty production is being generalized as representing the formal subsumption of labour to capital – it is DWL – historically prior to wage work itself, which is the real subsumption, in turn delayed in India (Gupta 1980). In the transition to the polar classes of capital, the process of differentiation thus takes place after all, albeit extremely slowly. Distinguishing PCP as a class is said to mistake form for essence, to delegitimize labour politics and distract both scholarly and political attention from the struggle between capital and labour (Bhattacharya 2014).

However, while the phenomenon of DWL cannot be denied, several decades earlier, Adnan (1985) had already counter-argued that, where an owner of assets takes decisions about production[15] and is accountable for the outcome, the activity cannot be reduced to wage labour nor even to DWL but must be recognized as PCP.[16] Its persistence and expansion makes Adnan's position hard to resist and enhances the contemporary significance of Marx's third theme of an exploitation–autonomy dialectic.

Since PCP exists in all three forms, what halts differentiation? The persistence of independent production is due to their owning or controlling a restricted and specific means of production, on which the value of work–time, measured by the realized product, can be less than that of wage work. The capacity to self-exploit (and not to pay family labour) and the greater labour time invested in production at less than the prevailing wage does not just undercut capitalist production relations and labour-displacing technical change, it is also a mechanism for transferring resources/value from PCP to those consuming the product. Some rural economists interpret this capacity as efficiency (e.g. Lipton 1968) – and it can indeed result in the more physically efficient use of capital and scale-neutral production technologies than capitalist production (Hazell *et al.* 2010). Others see the partition and miniaturization of assets that underlies expansion by multiplication as 'involution' (Geertz 1963). But they are both forms of self-exploitation.

Another explanation proposed for the persistence of PCP involves the concept of simple reproduction in which surplus is invested only to the extent that production and consumption are constant. PCP depends on market exchange for day-to-day culturally defined subsistence, both food and non-food. Non-market forms of exchange, co-operation and sharing may be practised. 'Enrichment as such was not its direct purpose', observes Marx (1863, vol. 21, section 1305) of handicraft production. Inflation of the prices of consumption goods and inputs may provoke a 'simple reproduction squeeze' (Bernstein 1977), responses to which may include lowering food consumption and intensifying labour effort including, if necessary, withdrawing children from school to work in production (Pal *et al.*, 2016; U. Patnaik 2003).

Further, the need for consumption expenditure (including for housing and education), and spending on protection against risk (including health) constrain investment to expand activity and accumulate. So does the state's fiscal activity, which is in aggregate socially retrogressive, even if income tax itself is not (OECD 2017). Yet despite this tendency to produce adverse domestic balances, small social surpluses are accumulated and play a key part in the multiplication of small firms through the transfer of assets between and within families at marriages and through inheritance.[17]

The form of PCP cannot be analytically extricated in any pure and simple way from the social and cultural practices in which it is embedded, which generate further complexity. Marx (1863) called these 'patriarchal, political or even religious admixtures'. Accumulation is persistently constrained by micro-political relations of gender (in which women are normatively – and even forcibly – prevented from saving [Guerin, *et al.* 2013; Kapadia and Anandhi 2017]); and by caste and ethnicity – occupational choices are still mostly restricted for Dalits and Adivasis, the hours of toil are set customarily and the returns to effort can and do differ on ethnic- or caste-discriminating lines (Harriss-White and Rodrigo 2016). Further constraints on class differentiation are also found in the exchange relations in non-labour markets in which PCP is embedded. The persistence of tied contracts in several of the markets in which exchange takes place in both agriculture and non-agriculture (above all in the 'labour-intensive' textiles and garments sectors) has generated a large literature (reviewed in Mohan 2015). The social terms and conditions of tied labour reduce returns below the levels they might otherwise be expected to reach (Gill 2007). Less well acknowledged is the common addition to operating costs that happens when payments for what petty producers sell are delayed, while payments for what they need to buy are not (Harriss-White 2013). These asymmetrical payment periodicities combine to reduce the investible surplus.

Given the range of different logics and social relations at play in PCP and given the absence of contradiction between capital and labour in this form, it is not that PCP has no politics. Its politics are dynamic, incoherent and effectively neutralized in such a way as to avoid labour–capital confrontations of the classical kind.

The Awkward Politics of PCP in India

Insofar as PC producers are owners of capital, farmers' movements and business associations admit them to join mobilizations (such as for price support) (Lutringer 2010). But while these forms of collective action are often termed 'populist', they rarely allow for the political aspirations and interests of petty commodity producers to be represented if they differ from those of local capitalist elites.[18]

Considered as labour, the politics of PCP is just as disadvantaged as it is when seen as capital. Labour politics focuses on struggles to improve the terms of exploitation in labour markets. But if PCP is labour then it requires an expansion of the concept of exploitation to markets other than labour: rental markets for premises, land and machines, money markets, the supply of raw materials and of manufactured goods. To date, the politics of such markets is not recognized as labour politics by unions or labour policymakers or by scholars of labour.

As for the mobilization of PCP for itself, the Self-employed Women's Association which spread from Gujarat to cover 2 per cent of India's work-force is regarded as a political model for fighting for work security, income security, food security and social security.[19] But it is not generally replicable. Its unique attributes include the vast, complex range of activities it comprises (over 80 trades, and other activities ranging from housing and childcare to banks, education and eco-tourism), its capacity to cross-subsidize them until enterprises make profits, its engagement with the state rather than directly with employers, and a scale attracting international funding and engagement.

PCP has never generated a political party. The awkward political question for PCP is whether to try to remove the constraints to accumulation and to try to destroy PCP and DWL and accelerate the creation of a formal proletariat, or to try to transcend such forms by collectivized, cooperative and/or socialized forms of production. For lack of a clear analysis, state policy towards PCP has been incoherent and often self-defeating.

When the state engages in city beautification, when it invokes the law of eminent domain to seize land for public infrastructure or for corporate capital, it actively destroys PCP without compensation (Lieven 2018). PCP is also disenfranchised under Indian labour law, because for cases to be brought to court an individual employer must be identified. The labour laws not only disenfranchise, they also de-class petty capital, PCP and labour alike, because employers of up to five wage workers (recall, this is 95 per cent of all Indian firms) are themselves legally classified as 'labour' on grounds of their relatively small size and lack of access to social security (Sankaran 2008). Yet, when the state seeks to develop small-farmer agricultural technology and extension services, implement land reforms, build micro-industrial estates and expand micro finance, it deliberately promotes PCP. From 2005 to 2009, for example, the National Commission for Enterprises in the Unorganised Sector (NCEUS), despite its lack of consensus over self-employment, which it saw in 'good proportion' as being DWL, it treated PCP as a form of entrepreneurial capital, advocating credit, skills-training and secure sites as elements of 'pro-poor development' (NCEUS 2007). And when the state establishes safety nets of social protection it protects PCP along with wage labour. When it establishes municipal marketplaces and parking stands for carts and tempos, the state tolerates PCP. PCP is also both sustained and disadvantaged through unintended outcomes – as when the rural employment guarantee scheme incentivizes PCP by raising the formal wage floor under which PCP competes, or disadvantages it by expanding and formalizing credit for which PCP has no acceptable collateral (Harriss-White 2012). But it is for reasons other than the incoherence of state intervention that Prabhat Patnaik (2006) argued that PCP needs protection and promotion through collective and co-operative organization of the means of production. For Patnaik, the social costs of the alternative – mass unemployment – exceed the combination of the costs of state support for PCP (let alone the costs of its incoherence) and the threats to wages to labour and returns to self-exploitation of a ballooning reserve army of workers if PCP were to be eviscerated.

Threats to, and the Resilience of, PCP

Since threats to PCP would have wide ramifications, scholars of agrarian development have seen PCP's conditions of existence as being unprecedentedly threatened by the expansion of export agriculture, by contract production for supermarkets and corporate capital, by stricter phytosanitary regulation, by rising hedonic standards and by the speculation in food markets by finance capital. The commodification of applied life sciences also displaces agriculture from land to factories through the reconstitution of nutrients in bio-fortification, aquaculture, genetically modified seeds and the bonding of food processing with pharmaceuticals (Friedmann 2013; U. Patnaik 2003, 2008). These are indeed all serious threats.

In the Indian economy, however, such is its armoury of resistance that there is little evidence for anything but a continuing proliferation of PCP as a constitutive form of Indian capitalism. While PCP may undergo further transformations through capitalization, it seems all but proof against differentiation. It is not only the practical outcomes of state intervention which constrain differentiation. Over a span of several decades, characterizations such as 'blocked transition' (Harriss 1982) and 'blocked differentiation' (Jan 2017) have drawn attention to the roles of agro-commercial capital in preventing accumulation by PCP and in maintaining small-scale (often fragmented) production. This brings us to the role of the second awkward class: merchant's capital.

Marx's Merchant's Capital

Merchant's capital (MC) was peripheral to Marx's model of industrial capitalism and belonged to a historical epoch predating capitalism proper. For Marx, MC or 'circulation capital' was the oldest form of capital. It was money used in the sphere of circulation in which commodities are bought and sold. It was distinct from capital deployed in production. In *Capital*, Marx argued that there are no activities on the part of MC in the sphere of circulation which could increase the use value of the commodities which it buys and sells, because the act of buying and selling on markets does not change the physical nature of the commodity. MC is therefore unproductive – even though it is clearly necessary to the process of social reproduction. Its social value resides in the fact that 'a smaller part of society's labour power and labour time is tied up in this unproductive function' than would be the case were there to be no such mechanism for facilitating the turnover of capital (Marx 1887, chapter 4). Without MC, the mass of surplus value produced by agricultural and industrial capital would be less efficiently produced. Marx has been criticized for having an inadequate theory of the transition to capitalism.[20] However he can be read as seeing MC both as a transitional form of capital, and as an integral element of capitalism, subordinate to industrial capital in its mature stage. Marx introduces the idea that MC itself embodies contradictory relationships with respect to production.

For Marx, the role of MC is essentially ambivalent and has both progressive aspects – being conducive to the establishment of (industrial) capital – and regressive aspects – blocking this process. On the one hand,

> [t]he development of commerce and merchant capital gives rise everywhere to a tendency towards the production of exchange values, increases its volume, multiplies it, makes it cosmopolitan and develops money into world money. Commerce therefore has a more or less dissolving influence on the producing organization which it finds at hand, and whose different forms are mainly carried on with a view to use value. (Marx 1894, chapter 20)

Marx also recognized that MC, like primary accumulation, enables the concentration of capital which can then be invested in production. This is a process which is logically prior to the development of capitalist production because production takes place over time and investment capital is necessary for plant, raw material and wages before production can start.

On the other hand, MC could not avoid also having a regressive role because it was unable to avoid being dependent on (then) pre-capitalist labour processes to generate the products it buys and sells and thus prevented these processes from being superseded by capitalist production relations. Here Prabhat Patnaik makes two further points: first that merchants capital, while itself integrating regions, can isolate PCP production regionally, introduce impersonality, quash relations of clientage and cause reproduction crises; second (in an engagement with Irfan Habib), imperialist MC, aligned against national MC can rip, plunder and accelerate primitive/primary accumulation (P. Patnaik 2015). Furthermore, MC re-invests resources obtained by buying cheap and selling dear into markets and speculation, not in the expansion of production. 'The independent development of MC is inversely proportional to the degree of development of capitalist production' (Marx 1894, chapter 20). It is even 'synonymous with the non-subjection of production to capital' (Marx 1894 cited in Banaji 2016b). Thus, merchants' capital 'is an obstacle to the real capitalist mode of production' (Marx 1894, chapter 20).

The way Marx argues about the balance of contradictory effects is to privilege production relations:

> To what extent it [commerce] brings about the dissolution of the old mode of production depends upon its solidity and internal structure, and whither this process of dissolution will lead, in other words what new mode of production will replace the old, does not depend on commerce, but on the character of the old mode itself. (Ibid.)

Productive industrial capital is also privileged in Marx's prediction that the development of capitalism would force MC to be progressively subordinated to the role of a passive 'wing of industrial capital' (Marx 1894).

Despite the historical specificity of the MC to which Marx refers, this conception of MC has been influential in India. In part this is because, as the quotations show, he tended to elide the abstract concept of merchants' capital with the concrete one of commerce.

Commercial Capital

Over the decades since Independence, a few scholars of India have examined the concrete form of MC – Marx's 'commerce' – initially understood as money used for buying and selling in combination with money advances for production to secure post-production supplies of commodities. They have particularly asked whether the indirect control of petty production by merchant-moneylenders does or does not proletarianize producers who are dependent on loans for their reproduction (Banaji 1977; Harriss 1982). In a debate that brings together the two awkward classes of this essay, both sides also engage with the prevailing expectation in the Marxist tradition that commerce will eventually eradicate petty production before being itself subordinated to industrial capital. Yet in India, neither of these things has happened.

Marx's formulation of MC as having an unavoidably ambivalent developmental role, and of circulation as an analytically distinct and independent sphere, mixes the impurities of history with the pure concept of MC in a way that obscures the explanation of how the awkward class of MC persists. The actually existing counterpart to MC – commercial capital (CC) – needs reformulating, not as an autonomous independent entity floating above production relations and about to be subordinated to industrial capital, but as deeply rooted in productive activity.

As Marx acknowledged in *Capital*, volume 2, trade cannot take place without the processing of the traded goods ('an interruption of the process of circulation for productive purposes') (Marx 1885, chapter 6), and transport ('the use value of things is materialized in their consumption and their consumption may require a change of location') (ibid.) and storage (productively preventing deterioration in the way allowed by Marx for the repair of factory machinery) (Marx 1885, chapter 17). When CC does not undertake such activities directly, it advances money or loans-in-kind for purposes of production (or consumption), through a stratum of intermediaries which manage such loans. CC oligopolists seek the state's protection, including support for their roles as net contributors to the cascades of credit, and net recipients of the stream of commodities in repayment from debtors (Krishnamurthy 2015). As both Bernstein (1977) and Banaji (1977) argued forty years ago, such investment by MC/CC is an accumulation strategy capable of averting the subordination of MC to industrial capital expected by Marx. Commercial capital can also constrain the independence of PCP by subsuming it (Banaji 2016a, p. 417). The formal subsumption of labour through DWL is essential to this argument though, in deference to both the staggering variety and the blurring of forms in ground reality, both Banaji and Bernstein hedge their bets with vocabulary – sometimes substituting for DWL the concepts of 'artisanal production' or 'household commodity production' rather than outright PCP (ibid., p. 424).

How does CC invest productively and remain independent of industrial capital? The mechanisms invoked by theorists of capital are remarkably imprecise. Commercial capital presses household production 'into the service of capitalist production' (Marx 1887, chapter 25). Citing many historians who use the concept of commercial capital, Banaji invokes 'domination' and 'price domination' (forthcoming, pp. 13, 22). Chayanov is cited as calling the process 'economic dictatorship' (in Banaji, 2016a, p. 412). What are the criteria that count here?

Critical attributes are the difference in scale and reach of assets between MC/CC and those of household producers/PCP, the flexibility and fluidity of forms (Banaji 2016b), and the size and diversity of commercial portfolios (Jan 2017). It is the capacity of traders to buy at prices lower than average, store between seasons and sell above average; and their masterful skill in avoiding both tax and regulation (Basile and Harriss-White 2003). Banaji invokes their ability to extract 'the major share of the profit', of surplus value or of organization or of the management of production (2016a, p. 426). And in a convincing, virtuosic sweep through the history of MC/CC throughout the Islamic and colonial worlds, Banaji goes much further and argues for the existence not only of a mercantile-dominated form of industrial capitalism but also for the existence of a *merchant capitalism* (Banaji 2016b, 2017).

In order to compensate for the 'missing Marxist history' of this form of capitalism, Banaji proposes a new typology of 'the ways in which commercial and industrial capitals penetrate, control and/or reshape the countryside and its relations', which in his view explains this distinctive form.[21] 'This was [and is] a capitalism that invested widely in a range of economic sectors beyond commerce in its narrower definition'. . . . 'It was commerce that gave birth to industry' (Banaji 2016b, quoting Verlinden), becoming bound to it but not subordinated to it (Banaji 2016a). And as Banaji's wide-ranging examples show, MC/CC is as necessary to the non-agricultural capitalist economy as it is to agriculture.

However, one can accept Banaji's historical evidence while also suggesting another approach to the questions at stake – using a mass of primary fieldwork on 'real markets' in Indian rural-urban regions over the last five decades. This approach, less concerned with historical stages, breaks with both orthodox and unorthodox typologies of merchant's or commercial capital.

Actually Existing Commercial Capital in Non-metropolitan India
While historians have addressed CC in the export sectors, very large amounts of capital remain locked up in small-scale commerce for domestic circulation in forms of market exchange that are specifically not addressed by Banaji's histories of large-scale, vertically coordinated CC. In India, it is possible that the total capital controlled by family firms still outweighs that of corporate capital (RBI 2017). As with PCP, CC is unevenly distributed. Figure 4.2 shows the regional heterogeneity of commercial inputs to agriculture – similar to the spatiality of the marketed surplus but different from that of PCP displayed in Figure 4.1 (Harriss-White 2017).

Field evidence from districts in southeast India over forty-five years and North East India over twenty-five years, confirmed by recent studies in northwest India (Aga 2018; Jan 2017; Sinha 2017) and central India (Krishnamurthy 2011, 2015), shows that the structure of commercial assets is independent of land-based agrarian power. These commercial structures vary regionally and can even be specific to given towns and to crops/commodities; yet almost everywhere local oligopolies coexist with petty trade. Commodities are exchanged in combinations of wholesale, retail, processing, transport and storage that tend towards such diversity and complexity that they cannot be easily compared and the compulsion to compete is compromised (Harriss-White 1995, 2008). Commercial portfolios, built out of components controlled by individual family members, link apparently specialized trade with a range of productive activities. They are built up from rent, interest and profit from self-

Figure 4.2 *Commercialization of agricultural inputs, India, 2011*

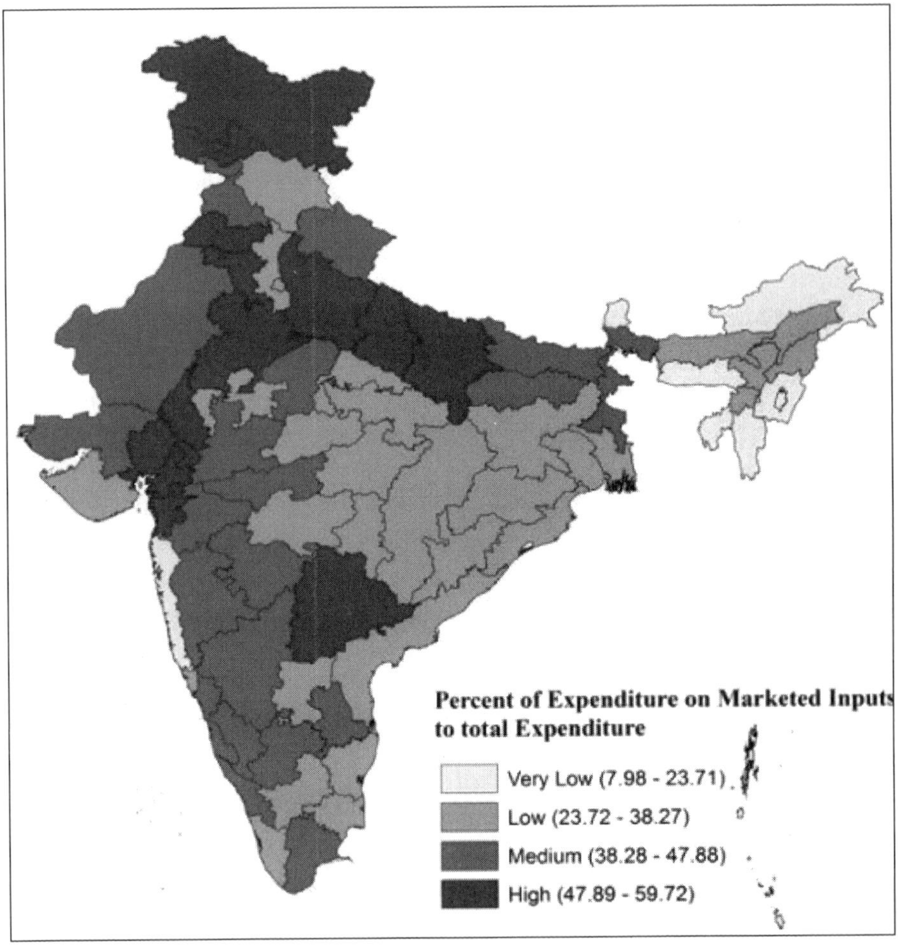

Source: Mishra and Harriss-White (2015).

exploitation, together with surplus extracted from relatively small and rarely permanent wage labour forces. Returns from these permutations, including trade, exceed those from productive sectors alone.

   Within a given structure of fluctuating prices, while some family firms accumulate, others persist without accumulating, yet without necessarily depending on larger-scale capitals (Aga 2018; Cohen 2013). Some petty trade may even lack sufficient collateral to be creditworthy and financially dependent on moneylenders. Yet corporate capital subordinates smaller scales of trade when it can – in Aga's case-study of agricultural inputs, by off-loading risk and reducing dealers' rates of return in the non-corporate sector and in Jan's cases, by manipulating quality assessments, prices and modes of payment. Elsewhere, mechanisms which limit domination and dependence include credit being rolled over at low or no interest, symmetries in payment periodicities, remote or mobile sites of operation, control over cheap second-hand technologies and spares and autonomy in the deployment of working capital (Guerin, *et al.*, 2013; Harriss-White 2008). From his extensive comparative fieldwork, Jan (2017) argues that while this kind of capital in trade, finance, processing and production is socially, technologically and functionally fragmented, it is sufficiently distinct from rural labour to be unified under the term 'rural commercial capitalism'.

The coexistence of varied forces of production, technologies and forms of organization of commercial activity and multiple modes of exploitation endows the system with resilience against risk and shocks. And this is in turn possible only due to the similarly awkward persistence of different kinds of social segmentation through forms of economic authority grounded in religion, *biradari*, caste, ethnicity, clan and gender. These too were expected to disappear altogether with the development of capitalism, or to become confined to the private sphere.[22]

The Politics of India's Commercial Capital

This structure of diversity is also reflected in the idiosyncratic politics of CC. Organized through local business associations (where possible federated in order to gain national influence) and Chambers of Commerce,[23] through factions and clientage, through lobbying, participation in and manipulation of state regulative agencies, through power over civic property (sometimes through management of the land of temples and mosques), and through a risk-minimizing participation in a range of political parties, throughout India, MC/CC confronts other classes and the state as 'masters of the countryside' (Lenin (1899/1964, chapter 2).

The many ways in which production and circulation are intertwined are not confined to rural commerce and class formation and the persistence of PCP in agriculture. Their variety is fundamental to India's capitalist economy. Their general implications for production have already been considered in the discussion of PCP. Their implications for commerce are of two broad kinds. First, CC which is large enough to be capable of accumulating secures average rates of profit which exceed those of purely productive activity. In complex portfolios, it is trade and commerce which yield the highest rates of return, and speculative activity which dominates the stream of profit. Second, in the numerically preponderant petty commercial capitalism, the margins between the prices of purchases and sales set by the mercantile activity of local oligopolies, together with their webs of credit, enable petty capital to enter, to generate small livelihoods, to multiply and be perpetuated in varying degrees of dependence – though less frequently to accumulate through the concentration and centralization of capital (Harriss-White 2008, 2016). The significant outcome is that far larger numbers of livelihoods are created than would be the case under generalized accumulation involving competition, labour displacement and scale economies, along classical Marxist trajectories.

While merchants' capital is a necessary theoretical concept, Marx did not theorize the composite forms of capital that have proved to be so persistent in India's economy, as elsewhere. Of CC, Banaji observes:

> It is logically absurd to imagine a history of capital using a notion of commerce that was developed by Marx for the kind of capitalist economy that evolved only in the 19th century. In practice that is largely what has happened. . . . There is a methodological impasse at work here, a staggering confusion of history and of logic. (Banaji 2007, p. 52)

Conclusions: Taking 'Awkward Classes' More Seriously

When euphemized as markets, the economy, growth or business, capitalism is de-institutionalized and de-politicized. Marx's analytical tools, privileging forces and relations of production and circulation, remain essential to the analysis of the myriad forms of social and political relations and institutions that exist alongside the development of the polar classes of (corporate) capital and labour. They occupy large spaces in-between these and have the capacity to persist in the contemporary era of neoliberal globalization.

Neither of the two explored here, PCP nor CC, is archaic, a backward form belonging only to history. While both stretch from the Middle Ages to contemporary times, they are as modern as is the corporation (Chandrasekhar (2017).[24] Although others differ, we conclude that PCP, in which capital and labour are fused and profit comes from self-exploitation, is neither a reserve army nor a pre-capitalist outlier. Though it may be being differentiated or surviving as DWL, a significant proportion of its vast numbers persists in a dialectic of exploitation and autonomy. Meanwhile actually existing CC is not confined to buying-and-selling, nor is it subordinated passively to industrial capital. Both involve complex bridging activities; both are rooted in the family and embedded in non-class social authority relations; both embody great internal variety and a wide range of exchange relations. This variety needs to be considered as normal.

To conclude, we summarize our findings about the concepts of class and of awkwardness, ending with some questions that they pose for politics.

Class

Are PCP and CC classes, what Marx called distinct social groups and Shanin defined through shared economic interests and united political action? Yes and no.

While PCP is identified in relation to the means of production through the fusion of micro-capital and labour, CC is less distinctly identified since it is so heterogeneous in function and scale that accumulation is possible through productive activity niched within the sphere of circulation.

While not in open contradiction with polar classes, both PCP and

CC create tensions with them. While it serves a functional role for corporate capital, PCP undercuts wage labour. While the management of corporate capital is skilled wage-work, that of CC results directly in a residual claim (profit). While corporate capital seeks to minimize wages, both CC and PCP self-exploit and exploit 'unpaid'[25] family labour.

PCP does not act as a class for itself. By contrast, the oligopolistic apex firms of CC have a distinctive politics involving the promiscuous and opportunistic alignment of business associations with political parties. Through the manipulation of the way regulative policy is implemented, CC acts to resist subordination to industrial capital and to maintain its independence. CC is thus a class that plays an active role in class formation. It can also prevent PCP from differentiating either to become disguised wage labour and then real wage labour or to accumulate. In both cases, the politics of identity is meshed with that of class – often reinforcing but sometimes acting at cross purposes with it.

Awkwardness for Political Economy

Both PCP and CC are awkward in the sense of having defied predictions about their transience. They are also awkward due to requiring detailed empirical evidence to interpret their overlaps with other categories. Found throughout the economy, reproducing despite or because of other forces, PCP overlaps with (disguised) wage labour and with accumulating capital.[26] Meanwhile MC/CC is not confined to circulation, meshes productive with unproductive but necessary activity, combines accumulating and non-accumulating firms, coexists with and may exploit PCP and trade. CC may also exploit and be exploited through markets other than labour markets. Relations between PCP and CC cannot be assumed: CC constantly reworks the relations that enable both to persist. Straddling the rural and the urban, the agricultural and the non-agricultural, understanding CC requires an expanded concept of the agrarian so that its ambivalent progressive-expansionary and retrogressive-exploitative roles can be integrated into political economy.

The balance between these roles is also awkward for state interventions, because the 'parametric' regulation of efficient private markets and the displacement of inefficient, exploitive markets (or the replacement of missing ones) by state-administered distribution of goods, which these classes call for, embody contradictions of principle (White 2016).

PCP is also awkward for labour politics because it undercuts wages, and because it is not possible to incorporate PCP into labour movements or mobilize it through access to labour law. The political question of whether PCP is an ally of the working class and hostile to capital is one only asked by Maoists (and answered positively [CPI Maoist 2004]). Meanwhile, the India state's NCEUS while recognizing PCP as DWL, regarded PCP for policy purposes as 'enterprise' requiring skills, sites and microfinance (NCEUS 2007).

Both PCP and CC are also discursively awkward for state policy because classifications and vocabulary differ.[27] CC is bundled up in official files called 'wholesale, retail trade and repair work, hotel and restaurant' and 'transport, storage and communications'.[28] And the question whether self-employment or small and marginal enterprise is to be encouraged or destroyed, and if so how, in a neoliberal era, given that 'markets' enable and force its persistence, has only ever been framed in this way by Prabhat Patnaik (2006) whose case for promotion requires collective/co-operative organization for PCP to reap economics of scale and enable technological upgrading.

Even if officially overlooked, the numerical importance to livelihoods of PCP and CC cannot be denied. India's corporate capitalist economy has failed to create jobs at the rate at which people reach the officially defined working age. Over three-quarters of India's agricultural sector consists of very small family farms, and nearly three-quarters of non-agricultural firms are operated by individuals. Excluding agricultural commodities and local distribution, interstate non-agricultural trade accounts for over half of GDP. In the structure of the macro-economy, the share of trade and services swells, while 'productive' manufacturing and agriculture are relatively stunted (Dasgupta and Kar 2018). Until the twenty-first century, the mutual embedding of production and exchange and the state's accommodation of CC have imposed strong constraints on challenges to this mass of livelihoods from any other class or class fraction. In the era of India's BJP government, the threat to CC is from above, from corporate capital with strong state support, rather than from below (P. Patnaik 2017; U. Patnaik 2020). As demonstrated by the year-long cross-class agrarian resistance to the attempt through thunderbolt politics to impose farm-market reforms favouring corporate capital, the impact upon livelihoods of a successful challenge from corporate capital would be nothing short of catastrophic to India's contemporary political economy.

This essay was originally published under the same title in *The Indian Economic Journal*, vol. 71, no. 1, 2023, pp. 56–77.

I am grateful to Shapan Adnan, Henry Bernstein, Ali Jan and colleagues and students at JNU's Centre for the Informal Sector and Labour Studies for discussions about contemporary petty production, and to Jairus Banaji for his historical work on merchant's and commercial capital. Errors are mine.

Notes

[1] Other driving contradictions have been theorized: between the predatory logic of capitalism and the complex logics of reciprocation (O'Connor, ed. 1994) including not just the necessity of collective activity but also the ecological conditions of production, and the absence of restitution under capitalism (O'Connor 1988).

[2] The latter is a view shared with bourgeois modernization theorists and their globally influential practitioners (refer the review in Hodgson 2001).

[3] There are others. Ancillary classes, the bureaucracy and the professions, were identified by Marx as necessary to the capitalist production–circulation process, though not per se productive and therefore dependent upon the polar classes of capitalism (Marx 1857, chapter 9). For Marx, the middle class is another category that he rec-

ognized both in an awkward manner and as being awkward for his model (Aslany 2021). For Kalecki (1972) and scholars such as Raj (1973) and Jha (1980) who found Kalecki's ideas relevant to a developing country like India, the concepts of intermediate capital, the intermediate classes and intermediate regimes are awkward for the Marxist mainstream.

[4] This set is far from exhaustive; it also includes artisanal production, cottage industry, craft, enterprise, family firm/farms, handicraft, home-work, household production/sector, micro-enterprise, out-sourcing, own account enterprise, small firms/farms, small-scale production, the tiny sector, village industry (Harriss-White 2012).

[5] The produce trades are one of Banaji's fourfold taxonomy of merchant capitalism, discussed later.

[6] Shanin's argument has been extensively criticized. Cox (1979) has re-interpreted Shanin's evidence to unearth signs of incipient capitalist relations. Politics as a *contingent* force has been solidly condemned (Pethybridge 1976) while Millar (1973) understands the countervailing forces privileged by Shanin as best regarded as a taxonomic model.

[7] Harvey (in Mahon 2012) goes so far as to generalize the modern working class as awkward on the grounds that it is more easily organizable politically through the neighbourhood than the factory.

[8] See the references to Marx on peasants in Duggett (1975).

[9] All translations of the German *ursprungliche*. Dobb's and Sweezy's debates about whether primitive accumulation can be achieved through market exchange or are the product of forcible seizure are discussed in Adnan (2015).

[10] Even in Marxist scholarship, the peasant is an unstable category used alongside terms, such as small farmers, peasant classes, small producers, self-employed workforce, subsistence farmers (Patnaik 2008; Ramana Murthy 2014).

[11] Though much is assumed and less known about the economic dynamics of family labour worldwide.

[12] SCP means simple commodity production, for the logic of which see later in this essay; also see Bernstein and Byres (2001, p. 26). Debates about the middle peasantry – whether its numbers and its self-sufficiency (which can be empirically disputed) give it power to dominate peasant politics – are found in Harriss (1982).

[13] See the discussion of sources in Harriss-White (2012).

[14] See Friedmann (2013) for an account that grounds some of these explanations in the changing conditions of modern world history.

[15] And for production, also read trade and services.

[16] Even Banaji in his recent paper on merchant's capital admits that households may have 'some degree of control over their own means of production' such that the distinction between DWL and PCP depends on judgements about what 'some degree' means (Banaji 2021, pp. 13, 22).

[17] These do not exhaust explanations. See Friedmann (2013), summarizing and commenting on Shanin, for others less relevant to South Asia.

[18] As in the case of small producers' need to protect common property resources being privatized by rural elites.

[19] See www.sewa.org

[20] See Bottomore *et al.* (1985) for a sympathetic treatment, and Hodgson (2001) for an unsympathetic one.

[21] These are (1) the *Verlagssystem* where the merchant capitalist is essentially a putting-out merchant; (2) international money markets (3) plantation businesses ('colonial trades') and (4) the produce trades. For their development, see Banaji (2021, pp. 9, 22).

[22] For the latter, see Myrdal (1968) and for their persistence and reworking as the social structure of accumulation see Harriss-White (2003).

[23] Forms of collective organization which act as an essential precondition to competition – in order for competitive behaviour to be socially defined and regulated.

[24] Even in 2011–12, as much as 86 per cent of workers in the private sector and 50 per

cent in the public sector were in units that could be designated as unorganized based on employment size. In fact, little is known about the allocation of returns to varied activity portfolios between the genders and generations of a family labour force.

[25] In fact, little is known about the allocation of returns to varied activity portfolios between the genders and generations of a family labour force.

[26] As a result, some scholars term PCP 'flexible' and 'unstable' (Aga 2018; O'Laughlin 2016, p. 400).

[27] See Cohen (2013) for a critical treatment of policy vocabulary.

[28] http://censusindia.gov.in/Census_And_You/economic_activity.aspx

References

Adnan, S. (1985), 'Classical and Contemporary Approaches to Agrarian Capitalism', *Economic and Political Weekly*, vol. 20, pp. 53–64.

———— (2015), 'Indian Capitalism in Development', in B. Harriss-White and J. Heyer, eds, *Primitive Accumulation and the Transition to Capitalism in Neoliberal India: Mechanisms, Resistance and the Persistence of Self-employed Labour*, Routledge, pp. 23–36.

Aga, A. (2018), 'Merchants of Knowledge: Petty Retail and Differentiation Without Consolidation among Farmers in Maharashtra, India', *Journal of Agrarian Change*, vol. 18, no. 3, pp. 658–76, doi: https://doi.org/10.1111/joac.12249

Altvater, E. (1993), *The Future of the Market*, London and Brooklyn: Verso.

Aslany, M. (2021), *Contested Capital: Rural Middle Classes in India*, New Delhi and Cambridge: Cambridge University Press.

Banaji, J. (1977), 'Capitalist Domination and the Small Peasantry: Deccan Districts in the Late Nineteenth Century', *Economic and Political Weekly*, vol. 12, nos 33–34, pp. 1375–404.

———— (2007), 'Islam, the Mediterranean and the Rise of Capitalism', *Historical Materialism*, vol. 15, no. 1, pp. 47–74, doi: https://doi.org/10.1163/156920607X171591

———— (2016a), 'Merchant Capitalism, Peasant Households and Industrial Accumulation: Integration of a Model', *Journal of Agrarian Change*, vol. 16, no. 3, pp. 410–31, doi: https://doi.org/10.1111/joac.12175

———— (2016b), Globalizing the History of Capital: Ways Forward', *Historical Materialism*, vol. 26, no. 3, pp. 143–66, doi: https://doi.org/10.1163/1569206X-00001530

———— (2017), 'Islam and Capitalism', paper presented at the workshop on 'Religion and Capitalism in South Asia and the Arab World', Oxford Brookes University, available at https://www.academia.edu/33746033/Islam_and_Capitalism

———— (2020), *A Brief History of Commercial Capitalism*, London: Haymarket.

———— (2021), 'Marxism and Merchant Capitalism', in S. Farris and A. Toscano, eds, *The SAGE handbook of Marxism*, available at https://cominsitu.files.wordpress.com/2020/09/marxism_and_merchant_capitalism.pdf

Basile, E. and B. Harriss-White. (2003), 'Corporatist Capitalism: The Politics of Accumulation in South India, in R. Benewick, M. Blecher and S. Cook, eds, *Asian Politics in Development*, Abingdon: Routledge.

Basu, D. (2018), 'An Approach to the Problem of Employment in India', Working paper, Department of Economics, University of Massachusetts pp. 2018–12.

Bernstein, H. (1977), 'Notes on Capital and Peasantry', *Review of African Political Economy*, vol. 4, no. 10, pp. 60–73, doi: https://doi.org/10.1080/03056247708703339

———— (2001), '"The Peasantry" in Global Capitalism: Who? Where? and Why?', *Socialist Register*, vol. 37, pp. 25–51.

Bernstein, H. and T.J. Byres. (2001), 'From Peasant Studies to Agrarian Change', *Journal of Agrarian Change*, vol. 1, pp. 1–56, doi: https://doi.org/10.1111/1471-0366.00002

Bhattacharya, S. (2007), 'Informal Sector Dynamics and its Role in the Capital Accumulation Process: The Contrasting Cases of India and South Africa', *Annual Conference on Development and Change, Cape Town, South Africa*, available at http://www. policyinnovations. org/ideas/policy_library/data/informal_sector_dynamics

———— (2014), 'Is Labour Still a Relevant Category for Praxis? Critical Reflections on Some Contemporary Dis- Courses on Work and Labour in Capitalism', *Development and Change*, vol. 45, no. 5, pp. 941–62, doi: https://doi.org/10.1111/ dech.12123

Bottomore, T., L. Harris, V. Kiernan and R. Milib (1985), *A Dictionary of Marxist Thought*, Blackwell Publishing.

Braudel, F. (1982), *Civilization and Capitalism 15th–18th Century, Volume II: The Wheels of Commerce*, Harper & Row.

Bush, M. (1992), *Social Orders and Social Classes in Europe since 1500: Studies in Social Stratification*, Routledge.

Chandrasekhar, C.P. (2017), 'India's Informal Economy', *The Hindu*, 23 September.

Chattopadhyay, B. (1965), 'Marx and India's Crisis', in P.C. Joshi, ed., *Homage to Karl Marx*, Peoples' Publishing House.

Cohen, A. (2013), 'Supermarkets in India: Struggles Over the Organization of Agricultural Markets and Food Supply Chains', *University of Miami Law Review*, vol. 68, no. 1, pp. 19–86.

Cox, T. (1979), 'Awkward Class or Awkward Classes? Class Relations in the Russian Peasantry before Collectivisation', *Journal of Peasant Studies*, vol. 7, no. 1, pp. 70–85, https://doi.org/10.1080/03066157908438092

CPI Maoist (2004), *Strategy and Tactics*, chapter 2, pp. 19–28, available at http://www.banned-thought.net/India/CPI-Maoist- Docs/index.htm

Dasgupta, I. and S. Kar (2018), 'The Labour Market in India since the 1990s', *IZA World of Labor*, https://wol.iza.org, https://doi.org/10.15185/izawol.425

D'Costa, A. (2014), 'Compressed Capitalism, Globalisation and the Fate of Indian Development', in D. Dutta, ed., *Inclusive Growth and Development in the 21st century*, chapter 2, Singapore: World Scientific Publishing.

Dörre, K. (2010), 'Social Classes in the Process of Capitalist Landnahme: On the Relevance of Secondary Exploitation', *Socialist Studies/Études Socialistes*, vol. 6, no. 2, pp. 43–74, doi: https://doi.org/10.18740/S4G880

Duggett, M. (1975), 'Marx on Peasants', *Journal of Peasant Studies*, vol. 2, no. 2, pp. 159–82, doi:https://doi. org/10.1080/03066157508437924

Edelman, M. (2005), 'Bringing the Moral Economy Back in to the Study of 21st-century Transnational Peasant Movements', *American Anthropologist*, vol. 107, no. 3, pp. 331–45, doi: https://doi.org/10.1525/aa.2005.107.3.331

Ellis, F. (1993), *Peasant Economics: Farm Households in Agrarian Development*, Cambridge University Press.

Engels, F. (1892, 2000), *The Peasant Question in France and Germany*, available https://www.marxists.org/archive/marx/works/download/Engles_The_Peasant_Question_in_France_and_Germany.pdf

Friedmann, H. (2013), 'Farming Households in 1973 and Today: One Path for Agriculture or Many Paths for Farming?', University of Toronto.

Geertz, C. (1963), *Agricultural Involution: The Process of Ecological Change in Indonesia*, Oakland: University of California Press.

Gill, K. (2007), 'Interlinked Contracts and Social Power: Patronage and Exploitation in India's Waste Recovery Market', *Journal of Development Studies*, vol. 43, no. 8, pp. 1448–74, doi: https://doi.org/10.1080/00220380701611519

Government of India (GoI) (2015), *Sixth Economic Census*, Ministry of Statistics and Plan Implementation, available at http://mospi-old.nic.in/Mospi_New/upload/census_2012/5_Highlights_6ecRep.pdf

Guerin, I., S. Morvant-Roux and M. Villarreal (2013), *Microfinance, Debt and Over Indebtedness: Juggling with Money*, Abingdon: Routledge.

Gupta, D. (1980), 'Formal and Real Subsumption of Labour Under Capital: The Instance of Sharecropping', *Economic and Political Weekly*, vol. 15, no. 39, pp. A98–A106.

Harriss, J. (1982), *Capitalism and Peasant Farming*, Bombay: Oxford University Press.

Harriss-White, B. (1995), 'Efficiency and Complexity: Distributive Margins and the Profits of Market Enterprises', in G. Scott, ed., *Prices, Products and People: Analysing Agricultural Markets in Developing Countries*, Lynne Reinner, pp. 301–24.

—— (2003), *India Working; Essays in Economy and Society*, Cambridge: Cambridge University Press.

—— (2008), *Rural Commercial Capital: Agricultural Markets in West Bengal*, Oxford University Press.

—— (2012), 'Capitalism and the Common Man: Peasants and Petty Production in Africa and South Asia', *Agrarian South: Journal of Political Economy*, vol. 1, no. 2, pp. 109–60, doi: https://doi.org/10.1177/227797601200100201

—— (2013), 'Credit, Finance and Contractual Synchrony in a South Indian Market Town', in I. Guerin, S. Morvant and M. Villareal, eds, *Microfinance, Debt and Over-indebtedness: Juggling with Money*, Abingdon: Routledge.

—— (2016), 'From Analysing "Filieres Vivrieres" to Understanding Capital and Petty Production in Rural South India', *Journal of Agrarian Change*, vol. 16, no. 3, pp. 478–500, doi: https://doi.org/10.1111/joac.12178

—— (2017), 'Constructing Regions Inside the Nation: The Economic and Social Structure of Space in Agrarian and Cultural Regions', *Economic and Political Weekly*, vol. 52, no. 46, pp. 44–55.

Harriss-White, B. and G. Rodrigo (2016), 'Discrimination in the Waste Economy: Narratives from the Waste-workers of a Small Town, *Journal of Social Inclusion Studies*, vol. 2, no. 2, pp. 3–27, doi: https://doi.org/10.1177/2394481120160201

Hazell, P., C. Poulton, S. Wiggins and A. Dorward (2010), 'The Future for Small Farms: Trajectories and Policy Priorities, *World Development*, vol. 38, no. 10, pp. 1349–61, doi: https://doi.org/10.1016/j.worlddev.2009.06.012

Hensman, R. (2010), 'Labour and Globalization: Union Responses in India', *Global Labour Journal*, vol. 1, no. 1, pp. 112–31, doi: https://doi.org/10.15173/glj.v1i1.1067

Hodgson, G. (2001), *Why Economics Forgot History*, Abingdon: Routledge.

Jan, M.A. (2017), *Rural Commercial Capital: Accumulation, Class and Power in Pakistani Punjab*, DPhil Thesis, Oxford University.

Jan, M.A. and B. Harriss-White (2019), 'Petty Production and India's Development', in S. Gupta, M. Musto and B. Amini, eds, *Karl Marx's Life, Ideas, and Influences: Marx, Engels, and Marxisms*, Palgrave Macmillan, pp. 345–67, doi: https://doi.org/10.1007/978-3-030-24815-4_16

Jha, P.S. (1980), *The Political Economy of Stagnation*, New Delhi: Oxford University Press.

Kalecki, M. (1972), *Essays on the Economic Growth of the Socialist and the Mixed Economy*, Unwin.

Kapadia, K. and S. Anandhi, eds (2017), *Dalit Women: Vanguard of an Alternative Politics in India*, Routledge. Kaur, R., P. Ghosh and R. Sudarshan (2007), 'Trade Liberalisation and Informality in the Rice Processing Industry', in B. Harriss-White and A. Sinha, eds, *Trade Liberalisation and India's Informal Economy*, chapter 4, Oxford University Press, pp. 128–233.

Kautsky, N. (1988), *The Agrarian Question*, volume 1, London and Winchester, Massachusetts: Zwan Publications.

Krishnamurthy, M. (2011), 'Harda Mandi: Experiencing Change in an Agricultural Market in Central India (1980–2010)', PhD Thesis, University College London.

—— (2015), 'The political economy of agricultural markets: Insights from within and across regions', in *India Rural Development Report 2013/14*, Indian Institute of Management Calcutta, Springer, chapter 4.

Lenin, V.I. (1899, 1964), *The Development of Capitalism in Russia*, Progress Publishers, https://www.marxists.org/archive/lenin/works/1899/devel/

Lerche, J. (2010). 'From 'Rural Labour' to "Classes of Labour": Class Fragmentation, Caste and Class Struggle at the Bottom of the Indian Labour Hierarchy', in B. Harriss-White and J. Heyer, eds, *The Comparative Political Economy of Development: Africa and South Asia Compared*, Abingdon: Routledge, pp. 64–85.

Lieven, M. (2018), *Dispossession without Development: Land Grabs in Neoliberal India*, New Delhi: Oxford University Press.

Lipton, M. (1968), The Theory of the Optimising Peasant, *Journal of Development Studies*, vol. 4, no. 3, pp. 327–51, doi: https://doi.org/10.1080/00220386808421262

Lutringer, C. (2010), 'A Movement of Subsidised Capitalists? The Multilevel Influence of the Bharatiya Kisan Union in India, *International Review of Sociology*, vol. 20, no. 3, pp. 513–31, doi: https://doi.org/10.1080/03906701.2010.511913

Mahon, M. (2012), 'Interview with David Harvey', *White Review*, http://www.thewhitereview. org/feature/interview-with-david-harvey/

Marx, K. (1857), Grundrisse: Foundations of the Critique of Political Economy, *Notebook IV-5*, available at https://www.marxists.org/archive/marx/works/download/pdf/ grundrisse.pdf

—— (1863), 'Formal Subsumption of Labour Under Capital', *Economic Manuscripts of 1861–63*, vols 20–21, no. 3, sections 1303–16, available at http://www.marxists.org/ archive/marx/works/1861/economic/ch37.htm

—— (1885), *Capital, A Critique of Political Economy, Volume II: The Process of Circulation of Capital*, https://www.marxists.org/archive/marx/works/1885-c2/

—— (1887), *Capital, A Critique of Political Economy. Volume I: The Process of Production of Capital*, available at https://www.marxists.org/archive/marx/works/1867-c1/

—— (1894), *Capital, A Critique of Political Economy, Volume III: The Process of Capitalist Production as a Whole*, available at https://www.marxists.org/archive/marx/ works/1894-c3/

McMichael, P. (2006), 'Peasant Prospects in the Neoliberal Age', *New Political Economy*, vol. 11, no. 3, pp. 407–18, doi: https://doi. org/10.1080/13563460600841041

Millar, J. (1973), 'Review: *The Awkward Class: Political Sociology of Peasantry in a Developing Society: Russia 1910–1925* by Teodor Shanin', *Soviet Studies*, vol. 24, no. 4, pp. 607–09.

Mishra, D. (2015), 'Agrarian Relations and Institutional Diversity in Arunachal Pradesh', in B. Harriss-White and J. Heyer, eds, *Indian Capitalism in Development*, Abingdon: Routledge, pp. 66–83.

Mishra, D., and B. Harriss-White (2015), 'Mapping Regions of Agrarian Capitalism in India', in E. Basile, B. Harriss- White and C. Lutringer, eds, *Mapping India's Capitalism: Old and New Regions*, Palgrave Macmillan, pp. 9–42.

Mohan, T. (2015), *Labour Tying Arrangements, An Enduring Feature of Agrarian Capitalism in India*, PhD Thesis, London School of Economics.

Mohanty, B., ed. (2016), *Critical Perspectives on Agrarian Transition: India in the Global Debate*, Routledge. Moser, C.O.N. (1978), 'Informal Sector or Petty Commodity Production: Dualism or Dependence in Urban Development', *World Development*, vol. 6, nos 9–10, pp. 1041–64, doi: https://doi.org/10.1016/0305-750X(78)90062-1

Mukherjee-Reed, A., ed. (2004), *Corporate Capitalism in Contemporary South Asia*, London: Palgrave.

National Commission on Enterprises in the Unorganised Sector (NCEUS) (2007), *Reports on the Financing of Enterprises in the Unorganised Sector and Creation of a National Fund for the Unorganised Sector*, NCEUS, Government of India.

O'Connor, J. (1988), 'Capitalism, Nature, Socialism: A Theoretical Introduction', *Capitalism Nature Socialism*, vol. 1, no. 1, pp. 11–38, doi: https://doi.org/10.1080/10455758809358356

O'Connor, M., ed. (1994), *Is Capitalism Sustainable?*, New York: Guildford Press.

Organisation for Economic Co-operation and Development (OECD) (2017), *Economic Survey of India, 2017*, OECD.

O'Laughlin, B. (2016), 'Bernstein's Puzzle: Peasants, Accumulation and Class Alliances in Africa', *Journal of Agrarian Change*, vol. 16, no. 3, pp. 390–409, doi: https://doi. org/10.1111/joac.12177

Pal, D., S. Kanungo, B. Bal, K. Bhowmik, T. Mahapatra and K. Sarkar (2016), 'Malnutrition Scenario Among Schoolchildren in Eastern India: An Epidemiological Study', *Epidemiology*, vol. 6, no. 1, pp. 1–9.

Patnaik, P. (2006), 'The Need to Protect Petty Production', *Macroscan*, https://www.macroscan. org/anl/jul06/pdf/ Petty_Production.pdf.

—— (2008), 'The Accumulation Process in the Period of Globalisation', *Economic and Political Weekly*, vol. 43, nos 26–27, pp. 108–13.

—— (2012), 'The Perverse Transformation', 22nd Rajan Lecture, Institute of Rural Management Anand, (IRMA), January, available at https://www.youtube.com/watch?v=Vy39RVvV_c4

—— (2015), 'Defining the Concept of Commodity Production', *Studies in People's History*, vol. 2, no. 1, pp. 117–25.

—— (2017), 'Contemporary Capitalism and the Shape it Takes in India', Interview, *The Wire*, 26 July, available at https://thewire.in/159148/prabhat-patnaik-interview-capitalism/

Patnaik, U. (1976), 'Class Differentiation Within the Peasantry: An Approach to Analysis of Indian Agriculture', *Economic and Political Weekly*, vol. 11, no. 39, pp. A82–A101.

—— (1987), *Peasant Class Differentiation: A Study in Method with Reference in Haryana*, New Delhi: Oxford University Press.

—— (2003), 'Global Capitalism, Deflation and Agrarian Crisis in Developing Countries', *Journal of Agrarian Change*, vol. 3, nos 1–2, pp. 33–66, doi: https://doi.org/10.1111/1471-0366.00050

—— (2020), 'The Global Angle to the Farmer Protests', *Network Ideas*, 31 December, available at https://www.networkideas.org/news-analysis/2020/12/global-angle-farmer-protests/

Perelman, M. (2001), *The Invention of Capitalism: Classical Political Economy and the Secret History of Primitive Accumulation*, Durham, NC: Duke University Press.

Pethybridge, R. (1976), 'Review: Teodor Shanin, The Awkward Class', *European History Quarterly*, vol. no. 2, pp. 269–72.

Raj, K.N. (1973), 'The Politics and Economics of Intermediate Regimes', *Economic and Political Weekly*, vol. 8, no. 27, pp. 1189–98.

Ramana Murthy, R.V. (2014), 'Conditions of Petty Commodity Reproduction and Agrarian Transition in Rural Andhra Pradesh: A Study in Three Villages', paper presented at the conference: 'The Return of the Land Question: Dispossession, Livelihoods and Contestation in India's Capitalist Transition', Institute of Development Studies, Kolkata, March 2014, available at https://www.academia.edu/9104419/Conditions_of_Petty_Commodity_Reproduction_and_Agrarian_Transition_in_Rural_Andhra_Pradesh_A_Study_in_Three_Villages

Ruthven, O. (2008), 'Metals and Morals in Moradabad: Perspectives on Ethics in the Workplace Across a Global Supply Chain', DPhil Thesis, Oxford University.

Reserve Bank of India (RBI) (2017), *Statistics*, available at https://www.rbi.org.in/scripts/PublicationsView.aspx?id=17789

Sankaran, K. (2008), 'Informal Economy, Own Account Workers and the Law: An Overview', *WIEGO Law Pilot Project on the Informal Economy*, Harvard University, 29 May, 2012, available at http://wiego.org/sites/wiego.org/files/resources/files/fow_background_note.pdf

Sanyal, K. (2007), *Rethinking Capitalist Development: Primitive Accumulation, Governmentality and Postcolonial Capitalism*, Abingdon: Routledge.

Shanin, T. (1972), *The Awkward Class: Political Sociology of Peasantry in a Developing Society Russia 1910–1925*, Oxford: Clarendon Press.

Sinha, A. (2007), 'A SAM Framework of the Indian Informal Economy', in A. Sinha and B. Harriss-White, eds, *Trade Liberalisation and India's Informal Economy*, New Delhi: Oxford University Press, pp. 233–306.

Sinha, S. (2017), 'Agrarian Accumulation in Liberalised India: A Study of Capitalist Farmers in Punjab', PhD Thesis, School of Oriental and African Studies.

White, G. (2016), 'Towards a Political Analysis of Markets', *Bulletin Institute of Development Studies*, vol. 47, no. 2A, pp. 45–58.

World Bank (2016), *India, World Bank Open Data*, available at https://data.worldbank.org/country/india

5

On Capitalism and Imperialism

A Note Based on Prabhat Patnaik's Contributions to Economic Theory

C.P. Chandrasekhar and Jayati Ghosh

The Nature of Imperialism

Imperialism is a concept that has been used by different writers to signify very different socioeconomic formations or versions of capitalism, as well as very different mechanisms supporting capitalist accumulation. These differences are also seen among those sharing a broad progressive position or claiming adherence to Marxism in some form. Is imperialism capitalism itself at a particular stage? Or an expansionism that is driven by the need for markets and critical raw materials to sustain accumulation in the advanced nodes of capitalism, that reorders agrarian modes of production and destroys traditional industry in the less developed regions? Or a search for territory, geographic and economic, that allows for the extraction of surplus to finance capitalist development in the metropolitan centres of a capitalism that in its very nature develops unevenly? Individual authors can explicitly or implicitly use one or more of these aspects of a system to designate it or its actions as imperialist. What is common is that the identified features are used to characterize a developed core and its relationship and even dependence on an underdeveloped periphery.

Marx's own writings point to very different aspects of the core–periphery relationship and its relevance to capitalist accumulation, as illustrated even by his analysis of capitalist development in the 'classic case' – Britain. The discussion in *Capital*, especially the first volume, speaks of the ways in which the process of capital accumulation is fuelled by plunder (primitive accumulation) and is catalysed by the benefits derived from access to the markets, underpriced raw materials and enforced cheap labour in the underdeveloped regions of the world economy, especially the colonies. A corollary is that capitalism is in some sense 'global' from the outset, and the underdeveloped regions were essential appendages for the capital accumulation process. It is another matter that Marx's detailed analyses of the consequences of colonial rule were featured in his (and Friedrich Engels') writings in the *New York*

Herald Tribune, rather than in *Capital*, his epic exploration of capitalism and capitalist accumulation.

In work undertaken over decades, Prabhat Patnaik has individually and jointly with Utsa Patnaik drawn attention to two crucial aspects of imperialism. The first aspect is that capitalism is inherently imperialist by nature, requiring an underdeveloped, precapitalist periphery to sustain expanded reproduction. This imperialist character is both central to accumulation, thereby ensuring that the system does not get stuck in a stationary state; and crucial to imparting a degree of stability to the system. As stated in the preface to *Capital and Imperialism*: 'not only has capitalism always been historically ensconced within a pre-capitalist setting from which it emerged, with which it interacted and which it modified for its own purposes, but additionally . . . its very existence and expansion are conditional upon such interaction' (U. Patnaik and P. Patnaik 2021, p. ix). A corollary is that the interaction between the metropolitan core and the periphery of this interdependent system must, as part of the process of accumulation, reproduce some version of the backward periphery. The second aspect is that there are multiple forms of the relationship of domination of the periphery by the metropolis and the mechanisms of exploitation of and surplus extraction from the periphery. As the geographical, social and historical context changes, so do these forms and mechanisms. But the dependence of the metropolis on the periphery is a constant feature of the system.

However, three features of Marx's analysis of capitalism, which did recognize the presence and a role for 'imperialism' in some form, resulted in an underestimation of the crucial role of the periphery in this system of accumulation.

The first feature was the restriction of his analysis of capital accumulation to a closed capitalist system, even though the logic of such accumulation points to the need for 'exogenous' stimuli to prevent the system from either being stuck in a stationary state and or being in steep decline. While it is possible to imagine the system as experiencing business cycles with periods of decline and periods of recovery, those cycles would tend to occur around a trend that reflects a stationary state.

The second feature was a tendency to suggest that primitive accumulation involving not just the accumulation of investible capital at one pole and doubly free labour on the other, but of the extraction of unrequited surpluses through unequal exchange or state-mediated transfers often ensured through the use of force, is typical of the early phases of capitalism and less true of its later phases. It was suggested that later capitalist phases are dominated by the extraction of relative surplus value, by denying workers of their share of the fruits of technological progress, rather than absolute surplus value.

The third feature was the idea that as capitalism subordinates pre-capitalist regions of the world system, it transforms the mode of production, putting the latter on a trajectory that takes them through the same stages of development seen by the former. In the words of Marx (1867): 'The country that is more developed industrially only shows, to the less developed, the image of its own future.' This has been interpreted as suggesting that imperialism does not disarticulate and retard development in the regions and countries it subordinates, thereby reproducing backwardness in the periphery, but instead progressively transforms production relations to allow for the development of productive forces.

As compared with this, central to Patnaik's understanding of the unevenness of capitalist development and the presence and persistence of backwardness in the periphery, is the idea that exogenous stimuli are needed for expanded reproduction of a capitalist economy. Endogenous stimuli cannot generate trend growth because atomistic decision makers in capitalist economies must make 'guesstimates' of potential demand when deciding on investment, based on implicit or explicit assumptions of what other capitalists would do, thereby shaping the future trajectory of demand and supply. Such expectations of demand must be partly based on current and or recent experience. That is, capitalists do not decide on investments based on the likely future outcomes of their own actions, or the fact that their investments, through purchases from other capitalists and payments of wages to workers employed by them, would spur demand, including demand for their own output. In such circumstances if endogenous factors were the only stimuli for investment, individual capitalists would find their capacities fully utilized only by accident or in special circumstances. If unutilized capacities rise, investment could fall and growth could slow. That slowdown of growth would be cumulative, and so, even periods of positive growth, if any do occur, would prove to be ephemeral (P. Patnaik 1972).

Prabhat Patnaik elaborates on what constitutes an exogenous stimulus as follows:

> Once we reject Say's Law and recognize that capitalism is prone to deficiency in aggregate demand, we have to accept that sustained growth in this system requires exogenous stimuli. By exogenous stimuli I mean a set of factors which raise aggregate demand but are not themselves dependent upon the fact that growth has been occurring in the system; that is, they operate irrespective of whether or not growth has been occurring in the system. Moreover, they raise aggregate demand by a magnitude that increases with the size of the economy, for instance with the size of the capital stock. They are in other words different from 'erratic shocks' on the one hand, and 'endogenous stimuli', such as the multiplier-accelerator mechanism, on the other: the latter can perpetuate or accelerate growth only if it has been occurring anyway. (P. Patnaik 2013, pp. 12–22)

The differences between exogenous stimuli and the endogenous stimuli referred to earlier is that while the latter can explain the persistence of growth once it has been triggered, 'they cannot explain why the system does not remain stuck at a stationary state; and they cannot also explain why, if growth perchance falters for some reason, it should revive again' (ibid., p. 12). These differences also imply a complex interaction between exogenous and endogenous stimuli.

Identifying Exogenous Stimuli

Defining the required exogenous stimulus as a factor that raises aggregate demand without itself being dependent on growth in the system helps to identify the elements that drive capitalist growth in different periods. Those normally referred to in the literature are external markets, state expenditure and innovation. Exports are an obvious and important 'external' inducement to invest, but their role in explaining capitalist growth is controversial. One way in which exports can drive investment and growth within a given tariff area is when exports to other countries or markets exceed imports from them. But such surpluses are difficult to sustain and not all countries can have surpluses vis-à-vis the rest of the world. Success itself – by raising wages, generating supply bottlenecks in areas like infrastructure, strengthening the domestic currency and leading to losses of trade preferences typically provided only to more backward economies – results in a loss of competitiveness. Historically, individual countries have benefited from net exports for periods of time, and then lost that advantage to new competitors. Growth can occur, but this cannot be a *permanent* inducement to invest in an individual nation. Nor does it resolve the problem for capitalism as a system.

Luxemburg (1964) had argued that a pre-capitalist periphery, the destruction of which provides markets and, thereby, an external source of demand for the capitalist sector, was a prerequisite for accumulation under capitalism. This view was questioned (Kalecki 1971) on the grounds that it confused between total exports and net exports. What matters for a bounded capitalist sector, it was argued, is *net exports*, since a part of the additional demand generated by exports would be neutralized by the inflow of imports that satisfied some fraction of domestic demand, dampening the aggregate demand stimulus because of 'leakages' to the international system.

There is, however, a point to what Luxemburg emphasized. The aggregate demand effects of positive net exports are obvious. But even when exports do not exceed imports, the presence of a pre-capitalist sector is an 'inducement' to invest. Increases in exports, by triggering investment in individual sectors benefiting from growth in external demand, can spur growth through multiplier effects on consumption and investment. For a number of reasons, such multiplier effects of the investment induced by exports could make exports a stimulus to growth even when trade is balanced. The opening up of external markets can cause a net increase in investment or consumption. This could result partly because the very process of opening up would itself require investment such as in transport facilities; partly because the expansion of export industries and contraction of import-competing industries need not be identically equal; and partly because the opening up may provide access to new commodities that stimulate additional capitalist consumption and do not displace domestic production (P. Patnaik 1972).

It should be obvious that, conceptually, this stimulus to investment and growth under capitalism cannot be equally effective and powerful across time. In fact, Rosa Luxemburg argued that the complete destruction of the available pre-capitalist periphery would in time undermine accumulation in capitalism, leading to its own stagnation. This presumes that the pre-capitalist periphery mainly serves as a market for capitalism, and that it is the only exogenous stimulus driving investment and growth under capitalism. While that is obviously not true, it does point to the fact that any single exogenous stimulus cannot be a continuous and persistent driver of growth. External, export markets can induce investment and drive growth in different regions and periods to different degrees but cannot be the consistent and sole driver of capitalist accumulation.

A second important source of stimulus to capitalist accumulation is state expenditure. Through the direct demand it gives rise to as a result of purchases made and the indirect demand resulting from the employment and incomes it generates, state expenditure is an obvious inducement for private investment. Such expenditure is essentially autonomous, since it is not itself induced by current and/or past incomes or profits; and can be financed by debt that can be serviced through taxes imposed on the consequent output increases. Therefore, state expenditure, by acting like an internal external market, serves as an exogenous stimulus for capitalist growth. In practice, for much of the recent history of capitalism in both developed and underdeveloped countries, this has been the leading driver of growth. However, state investment can be constrained for extended periods of time depending on particular conjunctures and political economy circumstances, making it a stimulus that is difficult to consistently sustain in many contexts. For example, if inflation results when demand induced by state expenditure runs up against supply bottlenecks (say in agriculture) that are not easily relaxed, this could lead to a reduction in such expenditure and a dampening of the stimulus involved.

A third potential exogenous stimulus is innovation. Kalecki emphasized the role of a continuous stream of innovations, which 'need not be identified with changes in technology. We can broaden the concept to include such a phenomenon as the opening up of new sources of raw materials, which induces additional investment in the productive and transportation facilities required' (Kalecki 1962, p. 147). In fact, the emergence of new industries too can have a positive impact on growth and even enable recovery from a crisis. According to Kalecki, 'the overcoming of the crisis in the USA in 1921 was unquestionably accelerated by developing the production of inexpensive cars, radio sets, electrical household equipment, rayon, etc.' (Kalecki 1932, p. 54). This is because,

> as in business fluctuations in general, a major role is played here by the time taken to construct industrial plants. While factories that are to produce new articles are under construction, such articles have not yet appeared in the market, whereas investments have already caused an overall increase in employment and an expansion of the domestic market. Hence, for the moment, 'old' branches of industry gain from the construction of factories for new articles. (Ibid.)

It is necessary to underline here the reference to a 'continuous' stream of inventions or innovations as a requirement for sustained growth. Only then would their impact be the same as a 'continuous increase in profits' or a 'continuous increase in output'. 'Each new invention, like each increment of profits (or output), makes certain projects ceteris paribus more attractive. Thus, a stream of inventions causes investment over and above the level which would otherwise obtain' (Kalecki 1962, p. 147).

This, however, makes innovation a different kind of exogenous stimulus as compared with public expenditure, since the government can for long periods maintain a certain fiscal deficit relative to GDP, or a continuous stimulus, if it chooses to. But there is no guarantee that capitalist evolution will be characterized by a continuous stream of innovations of equal or even substantial significance. In fact, Schumpeter, who gave an important role for innovations or 'new combinations' in taking capitalism out of its circular flow, saw them as not being 'evenly distributed through time' but as appearing, 'if at all, discontinuously in groups or swarms', leading to cycles of different durations (Schumpeter1961, p. 223).

Moreover, invention and innovation are not completely exogenous. With the growing integration of science and production, invention depends on research and development (R&D) spending, which in turn depends on firm growth and profitability. Moreover, inventions can remain in existence for long without being commercialized and exploited. The degree to which that happens, leading to innovation, also depends on economic circumstances. Finally, gross investment is the carrier of innovation or the application of invention in production. So, the greater the inducement to invest, the higher the level of investment and, therefore, faster the pace of innovation. Other prior stimuli that are more persistent can be more important than innovation as long-term drivers of growth.

This requirement for a persistent or continuous stimulus also makes the pre-capitalist periphery more significant than innovations. So long as the periphery exists and can be broken into and its production systems dismantled to yield new markets and sources of raw materials, it is a source of inducement for capitalist investment. And whatever investment occurs on that account unleashes many rounds of the multiplier process, generating further expansion. Actual exports to the periphery may not be as important as the very existence of such potential markets.

But the pre-capitalist periphery has in practice not just served as the market that provides the inducement to invest. In addition, and possibly even more importantly, it has been the location from which surpluses have been expropriated to finance capital accumulation in the metropolitan centres, often induced by those markets. This occurs not just in the form of the expropriation of surpluses through the use of force in the primitive accumulation epitomized by colonial rule and transfers. Rather, the transfer of surplus continues through unequal exchange in various forms.

Primitive Accumulation in Marx

While this was recognized by Marx, it was not central to his analysis of capitalism in *Capital*, which rather paid considerable attention to the ability of capitalism to sustain expanded reproduction purely on the basis of equal exchange. In Marx, what makes a commodity-producing system quintessentially capitalist is the generalization of commodity production in the sense that labour power too is a commodity. Unlike under slavery or feudalism, where the slave owner or feudal lord controls the labourer and has access to his or her labour time because of bondage and coercive power, the capitalist confronts the worker as the owner of labour power with the freedom to work for whomsoever she or he chooses. Since labour power is the capacity to labour, the labourer must also be in a position and willing to alienate this capacity and offer it for sale to the capitalist. For these choices to be made, she or he must be free in a double sense: free to dispose of her/his labour power as a commodity and free of or separated from all commodities that would allow her/him to use and realize the value of her/his own capacity to labour.

Marx did at times present the realization of this dual freedom as the *first step* in the development of capitalism through a process of 'so-called' *primitive accumulation*, in which peasants and petty producers are separated through expropriation from possession, control or ownership of the means of production. Such expropriation was defended by bourgeois political economy as being the result of the accumulation of wealth by an elite that was 'diligent, intelligent and above all frugal'. However, as Marx documented, it was in actual history the result of 'conquest, enslavement, robbery, murder, in short, force', which divorced producers from the means of production (Marx n.d., p. 873). While 'emancipating' these producers from serfdom and the fetters of guilds, it also left them with nothing to sell but their labour power.

There were also other forms in which non-market processes were used to accumulate capital as part of the processes of primitive accumulation.

The rising bourgeoisie needs the power of the state, and uses it to 'regulate' wages, i.e. to force them into the limits suitable for making a profit, to lengthen the working day, and to keep the worker himself at his normal level of dependence. This is an essential part of so-called primitive accumulation. (Ibid., pp. 899–900)

In fact, at the end of the seventeenth century in England, it took the form of a combination of moments that 'embraces the colonies, the national debt, the modern tax system, and the system of protection' (ibid., p. 915). Once this 'first step' was complete, capital accumulated at one pole confronts the doubly free worker and that is how capital accumulation based on surplus value extraction in production proceeds.

Accompanying and following this process is another transition that Marx presented as reflective of the development of capitalism proper. Since the magnitude of surplus value depends on the total length of the working day and the value of labour power, it can be increased either by lengthening the working day (*absolute surplus value*) or by reducing the value of labour power (*relative surplus value*), through productivity increases in the sectors producing the goods entering the worker's subsistence consumption basket.[1] In either case, since the ratio of surplus value to variable capital (or capital outlaid to cover the value of labour power) rises, so does the 'rate of exploitation', s/v, or the ratio of surplus labour to necessary labour or the value of labour power expended. But, in Marx's view, it is the extraction of relative surplus value through productivity-enhancing investments that was characteristic of capitalism in its fully developed form.

Since capital must confront 'doubly free' labour in the market for capital accumulation based on relative surplus value extraction to occur, the fact that labour power in that form must emerge through a process of primitive accumulation affects the dynamism of the system in its early stages. When money capital first seeks to realize the circuit M-C-M', it does not have ready at hand enough 'doubly free' workers. It extracts surplus by bringing the existing world of peasants and petty producers operating with pre-existing techniques of production under its sway, or through what Marx identifies as the 'formal subsumption of labour to capital' (ibid., p. 645). In those conditions, only absolute surplus value can be extracted, since the technical conditions of production are given.

It is only when workers who have nothing to sell but their labour power confront capital accumulated in the hands of a few, that the conditions where the owners of capital can transform the process of production and enhance surplus value extraction in the form of relative surplus value are created. This is the phase of 'the real subsumption of labour by capital'.[2] Here again, at many points in his analysis, Marx appears to suggest that the extraction of relative surplus value based on the real subsumption of labour by capital inevitably displaces the extraction of absolute surplus value through the formal subsumption of labour by capital. In Marx's view, the production of surplus value 'requires a specifically capitalist mode of production, a mode of production which, along with its methods, means and conditions, arises and develops spontaneously on the basis of the formal subsumption of labour under capital. This formal subsumption is then *replaced* by a real subsumption' (Marx n.d., pp. 645–46; emphasis added).

Once the process of primitive accumulation had created the conditions for extraction of surplus value in a system with equivalent exchange, accumulation in its quintessentially capitalist form begins and crudely coercive primitive accumulation moves into the shadows. And once the force of capitalist accumulation unleashes the productive forces, productivity increases ensure the expansion of surplus product and value, with surplus being extracted in the form of relative surplus value, rather than as absolute surplus value, or largely through an extension of the working day and an increase in the intensity of labour. This at times tends to be interpreted as an almost linear shift from primitive to normal modes of capital accumulation and from absolute to relative surplus value extraction. A corollary is that, from the point of view of the logic of expanded reproduction under capitalism, the use of predatory force and imperialist expansion was an early-stage phenomenon. Vestiges of that may remain and instances of recurrence may abound in later stages, but they are not seen as an essential requirement of capital accumulation.

As Marx noted in his preface to the first German edition, his intention was to examine the capitalist mode of production and the conditions of production and exchange corresponding to that mode, by analysing the capitalism of England of that time, which was its classic ground. The fact that other countries, including Germany, were not characterized by the dynamism that England displayed did not undermine the generality of that analysis because: 'The country that is more developed industrially only shows, to the less developed, the image of its own future' (ibid., pp. 90–91). This approach to the analysis of capital accumulation missed out on the tendency of capital accumulation to reproduce backwardness in peripheral regions and underplayed the role of that periphery in sustaining capitalist accumulation.

This kind of reading of the nature of actually existing capitalism was also encouraged by the fact that in *Capital* as it came to be published, Marx did not undertake an extensive analysis of the role of the state in supporting capitalist accumulation and providing a site for the *persisting* primitive accumulation of capital. Nor did he analyse the impact that capitalist expansion had on the peripheral countries and the colonies, where its 'modernizing' influence did not exclude coercive extraction of surplus, subordination of producers operating with primitive techniques and reproduction of backward relations of production so as to maximize the extraction of absolute surplus value.

The resulting optimism about the transformative potential of capitalism and the increasing assertion of the collective will of the working class possibly explains why Marx: (1) considered primitive accumulation as being confined to the early stages of capitalism, before the capital–wage labour relation is to a substantial extent 'universalized'; (2) saw a sequential movement away from the formal to the real subsumption of labour by capital and from the extraction of absolute surplus value to the extraction of relative surplus value; and (3) argued that this transition would be hastened by the ability of the working class to both limit the length of the working day and raise the level of wages.

Any reading of world history over the last 150 years would indicate that the first two of these features have not been confined to specific phases of capitalism but have persisted to differing degrees in different contexts across capitalist history. Even to the limited extent that Marx's analysis was true of the 'classic ground' of capitalism he analysed – England – it was by no means overwhelmingly the rule. And even though the expectation that capitalism would not survive through the nineteenth or the first part of the twentieth century has been belied, capitalism's persistence has not been accompanied by the expected transformations like the end of primitive accumulation, the shift away from absolute surplus value extraction to relative surplus value extraction, and the strengthening of the power of collective labour to win concessions from capital.

It is true that Marx did recognize that capital focused on maximizing surplus value and accelerating capital accumulation would continue to seek ways of extracting absolute surplus value and the workers' effort to limit that might be only partially successful. This is clear from his detailed discussion on the failure of the Factory Acts, the constant struggle to limit the working day, the tendency to increase the intensity of work within a given working day, and the resort to payment of time and piece wages. He therefore recognized that capital is constantly aiming to maximize surplus value through 'primitive' means. So, while a 'merely formal subsumption of labour under capital[3] suffices for the production of absolute surplus value', the 'unrestricted prolongation of the working day turned out to be a very characteristic product of large-scale industry' (Marx n.d., p. 646), even long after relative surplus value extraction had begun. In sum, it is completely possible that the generation of absolute and relative surplus value go hand in hand throughout the capitalist epoch and independent of the level of capitalist development.

This remains true even 150 years after the publication of *Capital*. The growing presence of casual, temporary and self-employed workers, and the unleashing of competition between the reserve army of cheap labour constantly reproduced in the peripheral countries and workers in the metropolitan centres only aggravate this. They create conditions where workers are forced to self-exploit themselves, thereby creating opportunities for the extraction of absolute surplus value, even when technological advance helps enhance relative surplus value. Moreover, inasmuch as these conditions and the proliferation of finance result in indebtedness that leads to the loss of ownership or control over assets on the part of workers, the middle classes and the peasantry, the expropriation of assets that can be sold or used later in surplus-value generating productive activity becomes the means to extract surplus without the mediation of productive activity in the first instance.

Capitalism as a World System

A corollary of this experiential evidence is that any study of actually existing capitalism must treat it as a world system and not just an English phenomenon. Marx's discussion of imperialism outside of *Capital* (in his *New York Tribune* articles for example) did recognize (1) the role of surplus transfer and market access in the colonies in sustaining capital accumulation in capitalism's classic ground well past its early history; and (2) the role of the subordination of the petty peasantry and capture of the state by capital in extracting the surplus that was transferred. Such transfers and market invasion continued to play a role through the twentieth century and do so even today, now under the aegis of finance as well. So, the transformation that Marx took for granted, though visible and significant, has not been taken to completion even in the developed capitalist world, and definitely not in the large, underdeveloped or less developed periphery of capitalism.

It is no doubt true that in the period after the Second World War, unemployment in the developed world was low and welfare state measures were in place. But the benefits of that accrued largely to workers in the advanced nations, and that period was an exception rather than the rule in the history of capitalism. A feature of contemporary capitalism is the large size of the so-called 'informal sector' and high proportion of 'informal employment', with workers employed in precarious conditions earning low and stagnant wages. This is obvious in the less developed countries where the informal economy accounts for between half and three-quarters of all non-agricultural employment with poor employment conditions, involving lack of protection when wages are not paid, compulsory overtime, lay-offs without notice or compensation and the absence of benefits such as pensions and insurance. But with unemployment in the developed countries soaring and remaining high after the 2008 crisis, descriptions of the labour market point to precarious conditions there as well. This has affected youth in particular, as they increasingly experience long or repeated spells of joblessness, suffer from large exposure to temporary and precarious jobs, and are forced to accept reductions in working time.

The dominant conclusion from the 150 years that have passed is the persistence of the extremely intensive exploitation of workers and petty producers, especially in the periphery, through 'primitive' forms of subsumption, albeit in changed forms. Related to this is the persistent reliance on various forms of absolute surplus value extraction, especially as the bargaining power of labour is weakened with help from the state. The intensity of these means of exploitation increases when the correlation of power favours capital and both 'society' and state do not restrain it. Such exploitation is still intense in the peripheral regions that are being increasingly integrated into global capitalism, even though the specific types of exploitation characteristic of the long period of colonial domination are no longer available to metropolitan capital.

The recognition of the persistence of forms of imperialism has also been coloured by Lenin's analysis of the monopoly phase of capitalism. Lenin's discussion of imperialism and inter-imperialist rivalries that gave rise to war focuses on a capitalism that has transcended the phase of free competition, in which the operation of competitive markets and the drive to substitute dead for living labour result in the concentration and centralization of capital. That takes the system to its monopoly phase, in which monopoly power helps to raise the level of surplus value and constricts markets. This in turn necessitates expansion abroad to sustain accumulation, facilitated by the greater 'seeing power' of big capital. From this argument it was just a short step to Lenin's characterization of imperialism as the 'highest' stage of capitalism, in which the battle for colonial territories intensifies inter-imperialist rivalry. This was a specific use of the term imperialism, which did not in any sense imply a denial of metropolitan influence over the peripheral regions in the century before Lenin wrote. Meanwhile, in this monopoly phase, other forms of primitive accumulation gained in intensity. Thus, ever since the onset of the monopoly phase of capitalism in the quarter century after *Capital*, Volume I, was published, the role of the state as the means and site for primitive accumulation has hugely increased.

Decolonization and After

A major change that occurred in the years following the Second World War was the wave of decolonization, driven not least by Britain's loss of its hegemonic position. The loss of political control over the dominions controlled by the earlier colonial powers had multiple implications. To start with, it meant that the ease with which the imperial powers with subordinate territories could use the colonial periphery to ensure stability and accumulation in the metropolis was eroded. It was now far more difficult, if not impossible to find ways to cover deficits of the metropolitan centres with countries and regions from which they imported more than they exported, such as China, through triangular trade. It was also more difficult and costly to access the capital that was, for example, exported along with labour from the metropolis to the regions of recent settlement in North America, Australia and elsewhere. Besides expanding the dynamic poles of capitalism, this capital export had also helped sustain the export of labour from the core metropolitan centre, enabling the system to reduce substantially the unemployment that would otherwise have been the inevitable outcome of capitalist accumulation, as Marx had argued in *Capital*. The loss of this 'privilege' obviously significantly reduced the dynamism of metropolitan capitalism.

Moreover, national governments of newly independent states in the underdeveloped regions intervened to set up protectionist barriers to reduce foreign access to domestic markets, set regulatory ceilings on where, how much and under what conditions foreign capital could enter the country, and intervened to encourage domestic capital and strengthen indigenous capabilities in the pursuit of import-substituting industrialization strategies, reducing the ability of metropolitan capital to use these countries as markets and as locations from which to extract surpluses as part of a system of accumulation on a world scale.

The debilitating effect these developments could have had was mitigated by two factors. The first was the step up in public expenditure and the launch of the welfare state, first necessitated by the Great Depression and then by the need to appease the metropolitan working class especially in the context of the 'threat' from socialism and of the Cold War. This triggered a strong version of one of the three exogenous stimuli discussed earlier. The second was the construction of a neocolonial international order, where international inequality was exploited to rebuild access to markets, intensify debt and foreign investment dependence, and ensure that the prices of commodities imported from the periphery, especially of energy products, remained low. This allowed inflation in the metropolis to be reined in despite large public expenditures and the near full employment that entailed. But as the oil shocks of the 1970s and after made clear, ensuring this subordination was no easy task, requiring periodically direct or proxy military intervention to secure the inequality within global capitalism that was needed to support accumulation and stability at the metropolitan core.

Neocolonialism achieved many objectives. It helped to keep markets partially open. It used the absence of technological capability and a capital goods industry in underdeveloped countries to help transnational firms jump tariff barriers and establish a significant presence in these countries and dominate some markets. It exploited the balance of payments vulnerability of inadequately diversified underdeveloped economies to make them dependent on foreign debt, in effect giving developed countries leverage over policy in the underdeveloped regions.

But at least for a couple of decades after the Second World War, countries with strong independent governments managed to limit such influence, even if not fully escape it. This was perhaps the weakest phase of imperialist influence, encouraging analyses which suggested that imperialism was dead and that the constraints imposed by the unequal international economic order on the development of capitalism in peripheral countries had weakened or were no more operative.

However, the persistence of domination and subordination was even more starkly illustrated by subsequent developments, even though some processes initially seemed to redress the international balance of economic power. Both the oil shocks of the 1970s, following the nationalization of oil resources and the formation of OPEC, and the shift of global manufacturing production to a few developing countries that became successful exporters, which reshaped the international division of labour, seemed to give less developed countries a larger share of the world's surpluses. But in time these advantages were either dissipated, or given the overall deflation in the world economy, the surpluses earned by the developing countries were diverted from productive accumulation to the global financial system controlled in the metropolitan countries.

Optimistic assessments of the immediate post-Second World War years were soon proved wrong. Paradoxically, this process started as metropolitan capital experienced a crisis in the late 1960s and 1970s, when the golden age characterized by creditable growth, near full employment and low inflation in the core capitalist countries came to an end. The crisis paved the way for a backlash led by Finance Capital against a fiscally proactive and regulation-inclined state, forced a shift to fiscal conservatism in the name of 'prudence' and triggered waves of deregulation and liberalization in both metropolitan and peripheral countries. Utsa Patnaik and Prabhat Patnaik (2021) argue that this shift initiated an era of income deflation in the peripheral countries. This enlarged the pool of cheap available labour in the peripheral countries and released for export a range of cheap commodities as well as offshored manufactured goods, which underlay the low inflation characteristic of the years of the 'Great Moderation' in the west. In addition, easy and cheap money policies, justified on the grounds that inflation was under control, became the principal macroeconomic instrument used to both drive growth and address economic downturns. The speculative lending and investment that this supported allowed growth to ride on financial bubbles, but led to periodic crises in the system, the costs of which were socialized through the intervention by government treasuries and central banks. A whole new framework of unequal exchange was established, in which the state consciously assisted capital behind the smokescreen of liberalization, inflated financial and corporate profits in the metropolis while keeping inflation low and growth at moderate levels. That framework underpinned the neocolonialism of this phase.

The ability to find new avenues to extract surpluses using new means from the periphery, is among the reasons for the accumulation that occurred in this phase of neoliberal capitalism. Neoliberalism as a policy regime has been the highly effective instrument of imperialism in this age of finance. The creative significance of Patnaik's work lies in recognizing the changing nature of imperialist subordination of the periphery by the centre, with neocolonialism partially substituting for colonialism and providing in multiple forms the exogenous stimuli and the resources needed to sustain capitalist accumulation.

Thus, since the inception of capitalism and the rise of the late nineteenth-century imperialism, the tendency to crises inherent in capitalism was partly counteracted by capitalism's subordination and exploitation of the underdeveloped and less developed regions of the world. As has been underlined elsewhere, Marx recognized and discussed this, but because of his focus on capitalism as a closed system, he paid less attention to it in *Capital*. In the period since the Second World War, despite decolonization, neocolonial relationships ensured that this relationship of subordination with the periphery continued, explaining to a substantial extent the resilience of the capitalist mode. Not surprisingly, increased economic integration of far-flying regions of global capitalism was a part of the restructuring that followed the 1960s crisis.

Significantly, in another illustration of the contradictory character of the capitalist system, the process of integration has also increased the instability of capitalism. The international expansion triggered by the process of resolution of the 1960s crisis saw the increased sourcing of goods and services from and relocation of production to less developed countries with a large and cheap reserve army of unemployed labour. Metropolitan capital became increasingly globalized, as policies that prised open the markets for goods, services, labour and finance were promoted across the world in the name of liberalization and economic 'reform'. One consequence of the resulting reordering of global production was an increase in global trade imbalances. With some countries turning out to be the dominant hosts to and exporters of manufacturing and primary commodities, and others their consumers and importers, the global trade balance reflected differential levels of surpluses and deficits. Cross-border flows of finance help to restore some balance. But since flows may not match requirements in all periods, balance of payments problems result in more frequent disruptions of the system of reproduction in individual countries.

On the other hand, global sourcing through purchase and production, by expanding the reserve army of labour available to the now globalized metropolitan capital, directly addressed the issue of any squeeze of profits as a result of wage increases. It also indirectly served the objective of maximizing surplus extraction by keeping wages in the metropolitan countries low, because of competition from labour abroad and the fragmentation of labour markets with precarious employment conditions at home. In addition, since it was the more labour-intensive segments of manufacturing that were relocated abroad, employment growth was limited and unemployment high. Finally, policy measures aimed at rendering labour markets 'flexible' were used to prevent existing institutional structures (especially unionization and labour market regulation) from becoming obstacles to their transformation. A consequence of all these tendencies, Patnaik argues, is an increase in the share of surplus incomes in global product, a corollary of which is a squeeze in mass consumption demand and a tendency towards overproduction, slow growth and recurrent recessions.

As discussed, the crisis in the late 1960s and 1970s necessitated a restructuring of capitalism, and besides the forms it took as discussed above, it included elements to address inflation, the banking crisis it gave rise to and the deceleration in real economic growth which followed the immediate contractionary response to inflation in the form of expenditure cuts and stringent monetary policy. In the course of that restructuring, two kinds of tendencies were unleashed. One was a radical shift in favour of restricted public expenditure or contractionary fiscal policies in the metropolitan core and the peripheral underdeveloped countries, which depressed mass demand and held down prices of primary commodities (including energy) and kept real wages stagnant. The other was the sourcing from or relocation to low-wage locations of manufacturing production that helped keep price increases low in metropolitan markets. These tendencies only increased the vulnerability of the global capitalist system.

Meanwhile, in the less developed countries, the invasion by global finance facilitated by the surfeit of cheap liquidity massively increased instability. The destabilizing nature of financial flows became clear with the debt crisis in Latin America in the 1980s and was driven home by the Southeast Asian financial crisis in 1997. From then on, hardly any less developed country has escaped becoming a victim of an external crisis precipitated by footloose finance in search of profit. In the case of Southeast Asia, even countries performing strongly, including so-called 'miracle' growth countries like South Korea, experienced major disruptions of economic activity, the effects of which are still visible. The recovery from the crisis did not mean a return to 'miracle' status. Instead, it was accompanied by significant acquisition, at deflated prices, of productive assets in these economies by foreign firms. It involved a substantial restructuring of the financial sector. It changed domestic macroeconomic tendencies with lowered investment rates and capital export becoming prominent features. It altered the nature of engagement with the world system of these economies, and their subordination by imperialism and global finance shows through in multiple ways. As the global system has been continuously flooded by cheap liquidity in the wake of successive crises, such instability and subordination in the less developed regions have been aggravated.

Throughout this latest period as well, the deep underlying reliance of capitalism on the pre-capitalist or non-capitalist institution of the family persisted. This has served as a central means for the extraction of the unpaid labour of women not only for social reproduction but for some forms of marketed production. Its interplay with the geospatial inequalities that mark contemporary neocolonialism, deserves to be noted, though it is still inadequately studied and understood. In addition, global capitalism has proved adept at creating new forms of 'economic territory' that effectively generated new markets. Some that are increasingly significant as arenas for imperialist penetration and competition today are the basic amenities and social services that were earlier seen to be the sole preserve of public provision; and those that concern the generation and distribution of knowledge, now privatized and commercialized in the form of intellectual property rights.

There are a number of implications that flow from this changing relationship between the metropolitan core of capitalism and its less developed periphery in which pre-capitalist segments are still predominant. The first is that if imperialism is seen as the mechanism by which the metropolitan centres of capitalism subordinate and exploit the periphery to ensure accumulation and stability at the core, the phenomenon has been an abiding feature of capitalism since its inception. Second, the periphery is not necessarily confined to less developed nation states with their own governments and geographical boundaries but is often present within 'core' capitalist nations. Third, mechanisms of exploitation varying from the use of force to plunder or extract absolute surplus value, by getting the working classes and the peasantry to sell their labour power at wages below the cost of reproduction of that labour power, were not confined to the early phases of capitalism alone but proliferated in the peripheral regions within and outside the metropolitan core even in later stages.

Fourth, with the transition of metropolitan capitalism to its monopoly phase, the concentration and centralization of capital that gave rise to monopoly capital has only intensified. Consequently, the enhanced 'seeing power' of big capital and the aggressive non-price competition between monopoly firms and nexus involving big capital, big finance and the state, have resulted in an intensification of exploitation of the periphery even as inter-imperialist rivalry is on the increase. The rise of truly international firms producing globally in integrated global production chains for global markets shows that imperialist exploitation can be internalized within these transnational firms. Finally, as rising global surpluses and constricted mass markets have adverse effects on the potential for physical accumulation, a feature of imperialism noted by Lenin has become dominant. Capital has made 'clipping coupons' to rake in financial profits, made up of shares in both relative and absolute surplus value, the principal means of its expanded reproduction.

This essay was originally published under the same title in *The Indian Economic Journal*, vol. 71, no. 1, 2023, pp. 78–91.

Notes

[1] The aim of the productivity increase is not to shorten the working day of the labourer but to shorten the necessary labour time in a given or even expanded working day. An increase in surplus value due to a change of this kind in the lengths of the two components of the working day amounts to an increase in relative surplus value.

[2] The production of absolute surplus value turns exclusively on the length of the working day, whereas the production of relative surplus value completely revolutionizes the technical processes of labour and the groupings into which society is divided.

[3] Or 'that handicraftsmen who previously worked on their own account, or as apprentices of a master, should become wage workers under the direct control of the capitalist' (Marx n.d., p. 645).

References

Kalecki, M. (1971), 'The Problem of Effective Demand with Tugan-Baranovsky and Rosa Luxemburg', in *Selected Essays on the Dynamics of the Capitalist Economy*, Cambridge, UK: Cambridge University Press.

——— (1932), New Industries and the Overcoming of a Crisis', in J. Osiatynski, ed., *Collected Works of Michal Kalecki (Volume 1): Capitalism: Business Cycles and Full Employment*, 1990, Oxford, UK: Oxford University Press.

——— (1962), 'Observations on the Theory of Growth', *The Economic Journal*, vol. 72, no. 285, pp. 134–53.

Luxemburg, R. (1964), *Accumulation of Capital*, New York: Monthly Review Press.

Marx, K. (n.d.), *Capital: A Critique of Political Economy* (Das Kapital series Book 1), Penguin Books Ltd.

——— (1867), *Capital, Volume 1*, Preface to the first German edition, available at https://www.marxists.org/archive/marx/works/1867-c1/p1.htm

Patnaik, P. (2013), 'Finance and Growth under Capitalism', in B. Dasgupta, ed., *Non-mainstream Dimensions of Global Political Economy*, New Delhi: Routledge, pp. 12–22.

——— (1972), 'A Note on External Markets and Capitalist Development', *The Economic Journal*, vol. 82, no. 328, pp. 1316–23.

Patnaik, U. and P. Patnaik (2021), *Capital and Imperialism: Theory, History and the Present*, New Delhi: Tulika Books.

Schumpeter, J.A. (1961), *The Theory of Economic Development: An Inquiry into Profits, Capital, Credit, Interest, and the Business Cycle*, Oxford, UK: Oxford University Press.

6

Surplus Transfers from British Colonial Malaya

Martin Khor Kok Peng and Jomo Kwame Sundaram

It is often presumed that the study of economic exploitation of colonial empires began with the recognition of western imperialism, perhaps beginning with the pioneering work of John Hobson from the end of the nineteemth century. Contemporary interest in understanding modern capitalist imperialism had been greatly stimulated by the European scramble for Africa at the end of the nineteenth century. Although Hobson was associated with the UK Liberal Party, this presumption ignores the pioneering contribution of his contemporary, early Indian nationalist Dadabhai Naoroji, who was a Liberal Party Member of the UK Parliament.

From the last quarter of the nineteenth century, Naoroji identified various dimensions of the external wealth drain from India to Britain. India was subject to external imperial power, which influenced the deployment of labour and capital for economic growth. India not only paid for Britain's colonial bureaucracy but also appointed foreigners to highly remunerated jobs over equally qualified Indians. The colony not only paid the costs of its own military occupation but also bore the expenses of imperial expansion and defence beyond its own borders. The imperial power also determined the nature of the colony's international economic relations. The recipients of the main incomes from the colony spent most of their earnings on imports or outside India. Utsa Patnaik and Prabhat Patnaik have long acknowledged and highlighted Naoroji's early work, especially as Utsa advanced her earlier work to estimate the colonial surplus from India.

Early efforts to estimate elements of the colonial surplus from British Malaya go back a century, but Martin Khor Kok Peng's (1983) book on Malaysian economic dependence was undoubtedly the first comprehensive estimate of the same. Based on his master's thesis, which would put many doctoral dissertations to shame, his effort involved a creative elaboration of dependency theory, first developed by Latin American economic nationalists in the 1960s. Using his own creative adaptation of dependency theory, inter alia, Khor addressed two interrelated issues. He described how Great Britain secured a surplus from the economy of Malaya (now Peninsular Malaysia) and tried to estimate various types of surplus from different sources.

Colonialism and Economic Surpluses

English East India Company rule in Malaya was limited to the Straits Settlement ports of Penang, Singapore and Melaka from 1786. A new stage of imperial expansion began from 1874 as the British extended 'indirect rule' to secure control of tin supplies, which had become more important following the Industrial Revolution, especially the US Civil War. Soon, the British established large plantations or estates with cash crops, most notably rubber. Thus, the peninsular was transformed into a commodity-exporting economy, dominated by large British firms. The colonial Malayan economy was thus transformed to better serve the interests of Britain and its empire. As a result, Malaya's economy, trade and finance came under more British and other western ownership and control.

Second, these various modes and forms of economic and political control sought greater surplus generation and transfer abroad. These included profits from foreign rubber, tin and trading companies. Khor estimated foreign profits at a third or more of total income in British Malaya before the Japanese Occupation during the Second World War (WW2) (also see Nazrin Shah 2017).

Colonial monetary arrangements, to issue Strait dollars (S$) for use in the Straits Settlements (SS), typically involved more than full or 100 per cent backing in the form of sterling reserves in London. Colonialism also required most public sector savings to be held in sterling in Britain for little or no interest. But British Malaya had to pay much higher 'market' interest rates for loans, for example, to finance infrastructure development. Significant additional transfers involved contributions from Malaya to the Imperial War Chest to fund the British imperial military. From 1915 to 1938, British Malaya contributed £50 million or S$431 million for the defence and expansion of the British empire. (This was equivalent to three-quarters of the estimated foreign tin profits of S$570 million over the same period).

With Malayan terms of trade declining, lower export prices meant less imports for the same amount of exports. Like Naoroji, Khor also considered generous remuneration payments to expatriate British civil servants and company managers as involving surplus transfer.

Despite increasing productivity, output, incomes and prosperity for some, most Malayans continued to live in poverty and deprivation. Benefits to most of the Malayan population were modest as wages were kept low. Labour remained largely unfree before WW2, initially due to indenture arrangements but also other forms of debt bondage. Living conditions did not significantly improve among workers in such production, even when prices were high (Jomo 1986). Colonial administrations spent the minimum on social development, mainly for public health (Chee 1982) and schooling (Jomo 1983). With much of the colonial economic surplus transferred to Britain, little was invested in developing the economy beyond what was necessary to enhance the productivity and profitability of the colonial economy, for example, for transport infrastructure (Kaur 1985).

Colonial Surplus Transfers

As colonial territories were subject to foreign economic control, large shares of their economic surpluses were not domestically invested but instead transferred abroad to benefit imperial countries. Perhaps the most research on colonial surplus transfers has been done for India inspired by Naoroji's pioneering work. Before Utsa Patnaik's significantly revised estimates, Clairmonte (1960, p. 79) estimated tribute to Britain, 'between Plassey and Waterloo', at £1,000 million. Mukerjee (1972, p. 200) estimated that between 1840 and 1900, £335 million went to pay 'home charges', i.e., the cost of debt charges, military expenditure 'abroad', administrative charges to London, etc. Through the loss of so much surplus, colonies lost much of the potential benefits of increased output.

Malaya was the most profitable colony in the British empire, at least in the first half of the twentieth century, except during the Japanese Occupation. Imperial Britain greatly benefitted economically from Malaya, the territory contributing most economically to it. After the first quarter of the twentieth century, an official government-commissioned report by Ormsby-Gore (1928) noted:

> Malaya has the greatest natural resources among colonised countries. In 1926 exports from British Malaya was worth more than all the other British dependencies combined – more than India, Ceylon, Nigeria, the Gold Coast, Uganda, Kenya, Egypt, and Fiji put together. The export value per head of population of British Malaya in 1925/26 was the highest in the world. (Labour Research Department 1926, p. 21)

The importance of Malaya to Britain was especially evident in the immediate post-war years when its own industrial production capacity had been significantly destroyed by Nazi bombing during the War. Malaya was thus crucial to Britain's economic survival and recovery after the Japanese surrender: 'In the period after WW2, Malayan rubber exports saved the United Kingdom from bankruptcy after the war by earning more dollars in the critical five years 1946/47 to 1951 than all the industries and trades of the metropolitan country put together' (Fisher 1964, p. 610).

Colonial surplus extraction meant much of the potentially investible funds generated in Malaya were transferred to Britain. This transfer of surplus from colonial Malaya involved various channels involving capital ownership, international trade, the Currency Board monetary system, commercial banks, public finance and managerial privileges. These were some of the most significant ways by which surplus was extracted from the peninsula for Britain's benefit.

Foreign Capital Ownership

During the first four decades of the twentieth century, a large and growing share of major productive assets in Malaya was under foreign ownership and control. Among foreigners, the British were dominant, accounting for 70 per cent of a total US$455 million of western capital in Malaya in 1937 (Emerson 1937). Expansion of merchant, finance and industrial capital in the colonial economy was principally led by large-scale foreign-owned businesses.

In the export-oriented colonial economy, the key areas of primary commodity production, trade and finance were foreign owned and controlled. The dominance of foreign capital in colonial Malaya was well established by the time of the 1929 Great Crash, well before WW2 (Li 1955; Nazrin Shah 2017). James Puthucheary (1960) detailed the extent of foreign ownership and control in British Malaya before the colonial period formally ended in 1957.

In the early twentieth century, ownership and control of the economy was heavily concentrated in international trade, finance and rubber plantations. Although present, British companies failed to wrest control of the tin mining industry before the advent of dredging required government-sanctioned access to larger mining concessions (Yip 1969). However, by 1940, foreign companies accounted for 72 per cent of tin output, and owned 74 per cent of total rubber estate land (over 100 acres in size) in Malaya. Such foreign ownership was highly centralized in a few holding companies, both mining and plantation agencies. Such agencies were not necessarily specialized, with some, known as agency houses, also engaged more broadly in international trade.

These large European-owned agencies dominated the upstream end of commodity supply or value chains. These involved primary commodities exported abroad such as smelted tin and smoked rubber sheets after some degree of processing to minimize transport costs. Agency houses also imported consumer items from Britain, the west and elsewhere, distributing them wholesale through 'local' retailers, many, but not all ethnic Chinese (Tan 1982). In 1953, 60 per cent of Malayan imports and 65–75 per cent of exports were in European hands (Puthucheary 1960, p. 73). Such commercial supply chains were typically intertwined with and complemented by credit lines.

In international shipping, British companies dominated, with their privileged positions and profitability assured by cartel agreements. Such shipping arrangements typically involved lucrative insurance deals. While most were for transportation between Malaya and the west, such control extended to other shipping routes as well.

Throughout the colonial period, three British banks dominated the Malayan banking scene (Lee 1974). In 1955, overseas banks controlled 75 per

Table 6.1 *Malaya: Estimated foreign profits' shares from rubber and tin, 1937*

	Output (S$m)	Estimated value-added (S$m)	Foreign profits (S$m)	Share of foreign profits in value-added (%)
Tin (FMS)	151	133	58	44
Rubber (Malaya)	341	304	70	23
Tin and rubber	492	437	128	29

Note: FMS is Federated Malay States.
Source: Khor (1983, Table 5.2).

cent of total deposits, while mainly ethnic Chinese-owned banks held the balance.

Puthucheary (1960) showed how much the British consolidated their grip over much of the Malayan economy after WW2. In 1953, European companies owned 1.6 million acres of rubber estate land, or 83 per cent of the total 1.91 million acres, i.e., not including rubber smallholdings under 100 acres in size. European estates were generally much larger than the mainly smaller Chinese-owned estates and large smallholdings. Most rubber, oil palm and coconut estates were controlled by about twenty agencies, with the largest five controlling more than three-fifths of total European acreage.

The European grip on tin mining was even stronger. In 1954, about 108 European mines owned by 76 companies produced 62 per cent of the Malayan tin output, while around 600 Chinese-owned mines produced the remaining 38 per cent. Concentration of control in mining was also very strong, with three big agencies managing forty-seven companies, producing 73 per cent of all European-owned output, or 45 per cent of Malaya's output (Puthucheary 1960, pp. 84–86). In 1953, 60 per cent of the Malayan imports and 65–75 per cent of the exports were in European hands (Puthucheary 1960, p. 73).

Thus, British colonialism changed the nature of the Malayan economy and society. Meanwhile, British capital unevenly took control, if not ownership, of much of the rubber, tin, banking and international trade of Malaya. Despite a decade-long communist-led insurgency during the Emergency from June 1948, foreign control abated little, at least during the Korean War boom years. By the time of independence in 1957, foreign ownership ranged from half to three-quarters of Malaya's major economic assets.

Profits for Capital Owners

Investment income outflows from colonial Malaya included profits repatriated by foreign-owned companies in various sectors – commerce, banking, tin and other mining, rubber and other cash crops such as coconut and oil palm. Poor and uneven statistical data are a major obstacle to more comprehensive analysis.

Martin Khor estimated that during 1913–39, foreign tin profits came to S$631 million, or half of all profits, and 32 per cent of value-added in the industry (Khor 1983). The foreign profits share of value added had risen dramatically from under a fifth before 1920 to between 40 per cent and 50 per cent in the 1930s due to fast-growing foreign control with the rapid rise of tin dredging. These high foreign-profit figures nonetheless still significantly understated the actual position. Using data from other sources, he estimated the actual foreign profit share for 1913–39 was probably over 40 per cent.

Despite patchy data, Khor (1983) used various sources to estimate foreign rubber profits from during the colonial period. Cumulative net profits of sterling rubber companies in Malaya up to 1921 were estimated at £47.2 million, or S$405 million or a fifth of gross rubber output. He also estimated total foreign profit share at a quarter of value-added by Malayan rubber production, including smallholdings. Although lack of data does not allow comparable estimates for 1922–39, estimates for 1937 suggest that foreign companies' profits came to S$70 million, or 21 per cent of the total rubber output of S$341.2 million, a ratio similar to that for the preceding period (Li 1955). Thus, foreign profits were 23 per cent of the total rubber value-added.

Table 6.1 estimates foreign profits from rubber and tin at about three-tenths of the total value-added. Reasonably assuming the two industries accounted for about 70 per cent of the total commodity production in Malaya at the time, foreign profits constituted a fifth of the total income from the Malayan production. The share would be even higher if foreign profits from coconut (including copra), oil palm and other agricultural produce, gold, coal and other minerals, as well as manufactures, are included. If services' income is also included, the foreign share of income in Malaya would be even higher, as international trade was also foreign dominated. *Hence, foreign profits accounted for a third or more of the total income from British colonial Malaya before WW2.*

Colonial International Trade

As colonial rule transformed the Malayan economy, changing the nature and purposes of production, it became much more engaged in international trade. Production for export became central to colonial Malaya, as higher proportions of goods for domestic consumption and investment were imported. Of the total income of the FMS in 1931, output income was S$154 million. Rubber and tin output were valued at S$105 million, or 68 per cent, with S$54 million from rubber and S$51 million from tin. Meanwhile, rice output accounted for only S$3 million, or less than 2 per cent.

The high ratio of exports to total output made Malaya the most valuable colony in the empire. Export primacy in production also meant heavy reliance on imports of foodstuffs, manufactured consumption as well as capital goods. In 1932, for instance, 66 per cent of total rice consumed in Malaya had to be imported.

The colonial, mainly open economy implied great economic instability due to volatile fluctuations in demand for and prices of Malayan exports. Trade instability had several repercussions for the economy. Prices of both commodities fluctuated widely, affecting the value of exports, government finances, employment and incomes, especially of estates and mines. The early 1920s and early 1930s were notable for extreme economic instability. During the nadir of the Great Depression between 1929 and 1932, the rubber price fell by more than three quarters, while tin prices fell, to a lesser extent, by a third. Export values dropped to only a quarter of its 1929 level, while the total estate and mining workforce fell 54 per cent by 196,000. Government revenue and expenditure in 1932 were less than half levels four years earlier.

The Great Depression affected not only the capitalist sector of estates and mines but also the hundreds of thousands of peasants engaged in cash crop, especially rubber cultivation. Citing a contemporary estimate, Khoo (1977, pp. 78–94) noted 450,000 unemployed Chinese in the Malayan peninsula in 1931. Many unskilled labourers, besides skilled workers and craftsmen were retrenched from mines, related industries and docks. For political reasons, ethnic Chinese were not repatriated during the Depression. Instead, the towns were choked with beggars, and Chinese farmers 'squatting' on vacant state land greatly increased. Despite much outcry, during 1930–33, there was net repatriation of 243,000 Indians from Malaya to India, another British colony.

Besides the export–import trade, foreign businesses dominated trade services – such as shipping, freight and insurance – in pre-WW2 Malaya. Western steamships led the flows of goods and labour between India and Malaya, and then between China and Malaya from the mid-nineteenth century. As trade rapidly expanded in the first half of the twentieth century, western shipping companies formed 'freight conferences'. These cartels shipped the region's trade with Europe and America, and much of the commerce within Asia. Linking Malayan commerce to western shipping companies were mainly British-owned trading agencies and merchant houses. Typically based in Singapore, they held lucrative agencies for the predominantly European shipping and insurance companies.

Colonial Trade Surplus

Declining terms of trade for Malayan primary commodities meant the same amount of exports fetched lower incomes. As rubber and tin prices fell relative to the prices of imports, for example, of capital and consumer products, the same amount of exports only bought a fraction of earlier imports, implying more 'unequal exchange' involving greater transfer of value due to colonial international trade.

Terms of trade declines experienced by colonies thus enhanced imperial advantage. Estimating such 'unequal exchange' due to colonial Malaya's poor and often worsening terms of trade is fraught with methodological

Table 6.2 *Malaya: Average rubber and tin prices, 1905–39*

Half-decade periods	Average tin price (S$/pikul)	Average rubber price (cents/lb)
1905–09	78	197
1910–14	90	177
1915–19	109	86
1920–24	109	47
1925–29	128	64
1930–34	83	15
1935–39	108	27

Source: Khor (1983, Table 5.3; Appendix 5.1).

controversies and hence not included in this study. Nevertheless, rubber and tin price trends suggest considerable terms of trade losses for Malayan commodity exports.

Table 6.2 shows the average tin price rising from 1905–09 to 1925–29, and then falling sharply during the Great Depression. But the five-year average price of rubber, which had become the most important export commodity by the mid-1910s, fell steadily, but even more dramatically, by 86 per cent, until after the Depression. Export price trends indicate very volatile terms of trade for Malaya which fell sharply after the Great Crash led to the Depression.

Colonial Financial Surpluses

Khor (1983) argued that colonial Malaya's 'financial dependence' involved three main means of surplus extraction, namely the Currency Board monetary system in which Malayan finances operated, private banks and colonial public finances. The Currency Board system, commercial banking and colonial fiscal policy all sought to ensure the British empire's monetary and financial interests.

The Board's substantial assets, the British banks' reserves and colonial public financial surpluses were primarily held in London as sterling cash or securities. Rather than serve the interests of the colony, the imperial financial system largely channelled Malayan funds – from its balance-of-payments surplus, public finance surplus and private bank deposits – for the empire's priorities. Instead of using the financial sector to regulate the economy and reduce its fluctuations, its systemic priorities served to magnify problems.

Currency Board System

The Currency Board monetary system was first introduced in the Straits settlements (SS) in 1899. However, the Straits dollar (S$) was the main currency used in British Malaya from the early twentieth century, even beyond the SS.

From 1938, it was officially adopted in the FMS and the Unfederated Malaya States (UMS) as well. Under the system, the Straits dollar (S$) was 'pegged' to sterling, with the currency at least 100 per cent backed by Currency Board's foreign exchange assets, mainly sterling. In practice, assets were maintained at 110 per cent to 200 per cent of the currency in circulation during 1920–38.

Under the system, money supply in Malaya supposedly depended on the Currency Board's foreign assets. Since its assets depended on Malaya's balance-of-payments, money supply was ostensibly determined by this 'external balance'. Increased sterling holdings – associated with a favourable balance of payments – would be exchanged for the Straits and later Malayan dollars issued by the Currency Board via commercial banks. These banks would then deposit the corresponding additional foreign assets in London, either as sterling currency or securities. The increase in currency was thus automatically matched by a corresponding increase in the Board's sterling assets. Thus, this automatic mechanism ensured full sterling backing for every Malayan or Straits dollar.

In effect, this system meant the Board did not have the power to increase or decrease the Malayan currency in circulation. Nor could it use monetary policy to regulate the economy. Its function was merely to exchange Malayan dollars for sterling assets. It is often claimed that this Currency Board system benefited colonies by providing foreign confidence in its currency, besides ensuring the colony's external financial position was in balance.

However, with no monetary policy independence, the Currency Board system did nothing for economic development in the colony. Although currency stability is desirable, it has to be weighed against its economic costs, often considerable. There was certainly no economic need to provide over 100 per cent backing for the Straits or Malayan dollar. Much less currency reserves would have sufficed as it was most unlikely that all holders of the currency would simultaneously demand converting them into foreign currencies. Lee (1974, p. 32) observed, 'The 100/110 per cent reserve in sterling was tantamount to an investment or an outflow of capital from Malaya and Singapore to the United Kingdom', and its empire. During 1920–38, the Currency Board's total reserves ranged from S$100 million to S$200 million. Their value ranged between 110 per cent and almost 200 per cent of total currency liabilities.

This implies that the Straits and Malayan dollars were typically more than 100 per cent backed, and almost 200 per cent backed in some years. Moreover, the returns to these invested foreign assets were minimal as they were mainly held in interest-free sterling currency or low interest-bearing securities. The Currency Board's considerable sterling assets comprised foreign exchange resources, much of which could have gone to finance development projects requiring imported materials and capital equipment.

Ensuring 'external balance' in these circumstances thus came at the expense of the colony's economic stability and development. The increase in Malayan currency was supposed to be automatically matched by a corresponding increase in the Board's sterling assets. This automatic mechanism was thus supposed to ensure full sterling backing for every Malayan dollar. But this rigid 'self-correcting mechanism' also proved to be pro-cyclical, deepening economic downturns, for example, during the Great Depression.

Thus, lower export prices had to be compensated by increasing output, not easily achieved with agriculture. Increasing supply would typically lower prices, deepening the problem. As the Board could only be a currency or 'money-changer', there was no scope for countercyclical monetary policy. Hence, maintaining balance-of-payments stability came at the expense of output, employment and income instability, as became evident after commodity prices fell during the Great Depression.

Incredibly, colonial Malaya's payments balance was in deficit for most of the first three decades of the twentieth century before the Great Depression of the early 1930s. The huge positive Malayan trade balance due to commodity exports more than offset the considerable net capital outflows. Profit outflows to mainly expatriate shareholders greatly exceeded net inflows of foreign rubber, tin, trade and other investments. Thus, the ratio of foreign reserves to the Straits dollar money supply greatly exceeded the Board's 100 per cent requirement.

Although helpful to the British empire as the gold peg and sterling monetary hegemony came under growing stress, the outcome was detrimental to the economic interests of Malaya. On the one hand, foreign exchange earnings from its exports went to London to increase low interest-bearing sterling currency reserves. On the other, it had to borrow from London at much higher cost for colonial infrastructure and other development purposes. As S.Y. Lee noted:

> Although the sterling securities in the Currency Fund yielded some interest, that yield was not sufficient to counterbalance the cost of borrowing, after taking account of the cost of issuing securities, interest rate, commissions, etc. From the colonies' standpoint, it would be better to use part of their currency reserves to purchase their own local securities in the manner of 'self-finance' for saving interest costs and avoiding other inconvenience, rather than to lend all available funds out to the London market and to borrow all requirements therefrom. Thirdly, in the long run, it would be better for the colonies to develop their own local money and capital market along with the growth of their monetary and banking system, instead of depending always on the London market. (Lee 1974, p. 34)

Commercial Banks

Despite growing ethnic Chinese-owned banks, mainly serving generally much smaller, less capital-intensive Chinese-owned tin mines and rubber plantations, British-owned commercial banks dominated banking in colonial

Malaya. Although banking statistics before WW2 are scarce, the post-war years saw continued British domination of banking in colonial Malaya. In 1947, liquid assets of Malayan and Singaporean commercial banks amounted to S$361 million. This represented 50 per cent of total assets and 57 per cent of total deposits, implying a very high liquidity ratio.

Of the total liquid assets of S$361 million, net foreign assets comprised up to S$215 million, or 60 per cent, mostly due to the transfer of funds by foreign bank branches to headquarters in the UK that is seen there as net balances due from banks abroad. *Thus, 34 per cent of the funds deposited by Malayan customers was mainly invested in London.* Further, the S$116 million, or 18 per cent of deposits, held in cash was fully invested in sterling through the Currency Board. Hence, lending in Malaya was limited, amounting to S$321 million, i.e., including loans and advances of S$223 million and local investments worth S$98 million, or only 50.6 per cent of total deposits.

The banks primarily financed trade, with few significant efforts to finance other investments. The mainly British commercial banks in colonial Malaya primarily served British capital, rather than the mainly ethnic Chinese Malayan business interests. The banks' portfolio choices were largely 'reduced to a simple formula, that is, to provide loans and advances in accordance with trade conditions and then remit the balance funds to London, as shown in statistics in the accumulation of foreign assets' (Lee 1974, p. 119).

In the absence of any scope for countercyclical monetary policies, commercial banks' trade-oriented lending were pro-cyclical in effect, worsening trade fluctuations and their effects. For P.J. Drake:

> A favourable balance-of-payments increased bank deposits of itself and created all the necessary conditions for secondary increases in deposits through increased bank lending. The reverse held for a balance-of-payments deficit. Instead of offsetting the effects of fluctuations in the balance-of-payments on economic activity in Malaya, bank credit tended to aggravate them because of this so-called 'classical link' between the balance-of-payments and the local money supply. (Drake 1969, p. 43)

Colonial Public Finances

Public finance policy in colonial Malaya was also subordinated to imperial considerations. For Khor (2019), colonial public finance sought to (1) 'as far as possible, maintain a surplus of revenue over expenditure'; (2) 'transfer funds from the colony to the metropolis'; and (3) 'play a major supportive role in encouraging western capitalist enterprise. In all three functions, the colonial Malayan government excelled'.

Malaya generated more tax revenue per capita, by far, than all other British colonies. In 1936, such revenue per capita in the FMS was S$33.17, compared to S$8.99 in Kenya and S$4.30 in India (Li 1955,

p. 25). As the Malayan economy grew, FMS revenue rose from S$8.4 million in 1896 to S$68.1 million in 1936. In the Straits Settlements (SS), it rose from S$5.4 million in 1900 to S$35 million in 1935.

In most years, revenue exceeded expenditure. Thus, a considerable colonial public finance surplus was amassed. Under colonial rule, the SS, FMS and UMS saw considerable revenue savings. Despite the Depression, British Malaya still had an accumulated overall public surplus of about S$260 million in the mid-1930s, half from the SS, with the balance from the FMS and UMS.

As with Currency Board assets, the government's accumulated revenue implied foregone public expenditure, for example, for social spending and development opportunities. Although accumulating a public finance surplus when the economy was buoyant was supposed to serve as a buffer in bad times when output or prices fell, yet, such surpluses continued to grow during the Depression, reflecting the absence of countercyclical fiscal policy.

Most colonial government assets were held in sterling. For example, of total FMS assets of S$125.3 million in 1928, sterling securities comprised S$16.3 million while short-term loans to Crown Agents came to S$12.1 million. Meanwhile, much of Opium Fund investments (S$17.8 million), fixed deposits (S$10 million) and Singapore Naval Base Contributions investments (S$7.8 million) were also held in sterling (Khor 1983). Hence, about half of FMS assets then were low interest-bearing loans to the United Kingdom. Besides investments in sterling, the FMS also loaned S$40 million to Siam in the early 1920s, with repayment scheduled over twenty-six annual instalments from 1924. The loan was for railway construction, unsurprisingly with contracts given to British engineering firms (Lim 1980).

While investing its public finance surpluses in low-yielding UK securities, colonial Malaya had to take loans from London at a much higher cost. Loans obtained by the SS included: £6.9 million issued in 1917 and 1910 at 3.5 per cent per annum, £2.4 million at 7 per cent in 1921, £5.2 million at 6 per cent in 1921 and £4.2 million at 4.5 per cent in 1922. These loans to the SS totalled £18.7 million, or S$160 million. In taking these loans, substantial payments were made to 'expenses of issue': for instance, of the two loans in 1921 and 1922, about £700,000, or 8 per cent of the total of £9.4 million, was deducted for such financial costs of issue (Mukerjee 1972).

Almost all these loans were to finance the construction of transport infrastructure – railways, roads and harbours – needed by British-dominated private businesses. The main direct beneficiaries of these large public works programme were the

> British iron and steel companies which make their profit out of contracts for materials; British financial groups which take commissions on loans raised for railway development and on the various financial transactions involved in every large contract; and mining and rubber companies which get a sub-

stantial return in the form of cheap transport on whatever they contribute in taxation. (Labour Research Department 1926)

Thus, both the low-yielding investments of the colonial public finance surplus and the high costs of borrowing to finance public investments in Malaya enriched British business interests at the expense of its colony. Besides these surplus and investment implications, the contribution of colonial public finance to surplus transfers can also be seen from the revenue sources and expenditure headings.

Colonial Fiscal Policy

The public sector in colonial Malaya was a major means by which significant surplus was siphoned off to the UK. Government revenues were largely from the private sector, but mainly from the incomes of labour, rather than capital. Expenditure patterns reflect the way such revenue was utilized and whom they benefited. Examination of the sources and use of public finances enables considering how the colonial government burdened and benefited various groups in society, including those with business interests in the colony, but not resident there. Hence, the colonial state advanced regressive economic redistribution by fiscal means through regressive taxation and expenditure.

Colonial Malaya did not collect direct taxes, for example, of company profits or personal incomes, let alone impose progressive taxes. Hence, the main fiscal mechanisms for progressive direct corporate or personal income or wealth taxation were absent. Instead, the main revenue source was from indirect taxation, borne not by business or the better off, but largely by those least able to afford them. Hence, the bulk of revenue was not derived from the ones with most means, such as the tin and rubber industries, but rather, from 'indirect' consumption taxes on four 'vices'– opium, tobacco, liquor and prostitution – seen by some as 'sin taxes'. Such excise duties, plus the revenue of government monopolies such as from the sale of opium, constituted the main sources of colonial government revenue, especially in the SS and Johore.

Opium importation, preparation and distribution became an explicit government monopoly from 1910. Its price was regularly raised by the SS authorities – from S$3 per tahil in 1910 to S$12 in 1919, i.e., by 300 per cent in less than a decade. In 1929, the price of SS government opium was S$12.50 per tahil, though its cost was only S$2.23 per tahil (Li 1955, p. 30), that is, less than a fifth. The main smokers and thus biggest contributors to government revenue were ethnic Chinese labourers whose addiction cost them much in terms of necessities such as food foregone.

In the SS, the opium monopoly was, by far, the largest revenue-earner, providing almost half of total revenue in 1900–20. Its share of colonial tax revenue had dropped to a quarter by 1934, but the combined tax contribution of opium, tobacco, liquor and petroleum was 55 per cent (Emerson 1937,

p. 303). The same revenue pattern also prevailed in the UMS, with opium, tobacco and liquor as the main sources of the government income. Such dependence on vice taxes for revenue was reduced by modest FMS export duties on tin and rubber. However,

> even in the exceptionally prosperous year 1938, when rubber and tin furnished the largest fractions of the total revenue, we find that the income derived from opium, liquors and tobacco was still larger than that coming from tin and rubber with S\$21,670,000 for the former group of commodities and S\$19,740,000 for the latter group. (Li, 1955, p. 31)

While the bulk of revenue was derived by taxing consumers, most of whom were low-income earners, significant shares of public finance were transferred abroad or spent to benefit business interests in the colony. These transfers included:

(1) *Contributions to the imperial war chest*: One of the largest public expenditure items was for the military, mainly contributions to imperial Britain's war efforts. Li (1955, p. 33) wryly noted that: 'A large amount of revenue was consumed by the military budget, a strange but interesting situation in the light of the fact that for the entire period (1895–1938), there was never any war in which British Malaya was directly involved.' The heaviest burden fell on the SS, which had to pay £100,000 annually for military expenses during 1890–1894: 17.5 per cent of its total budget in 1895–1898, 20 per cent of its total annual budget in 1899–1932, and S\$4,000,000 annually from 1933 until the outbreak of WW2 in the west. Such military contributions were thus the main expenditure item in the SS budget. Besides these 'regular contributions', the SS, FMS and UMS were required to make 'special contributions' to specific imperial military causes. The SS contributed £15 million and the FMS £13 million to British imperial war efforts in the First World War, i.e., £28 million or S\$240 million. Other special FMS contributions included S\$65,000 for the Boer War in 1899, £2,250,000 (S\$19 million) to build a battleship and £2 million (S\$17 million) to build the Singapore Naval Base. Li (1955, p. 35) estimated that 'from the end of World War I to 1938, a period of twenty years, British Malaya contributed to the cost of imperial defence no less than £22,250,000 – or as much as S\$191 million'. Hence, from 1915 to 1938, British Malaya contributed at least S\$431 million to defend the British empire, that is, equivalent to three-quarters of foreign tin profits of S\$570 million over the same period (Khor 1983). Thus, imperial military spending drained considerable public finances out of Malaya.

(2) *Debt charges*: Interest paid on colonial public debt and the high costs of contracting loans also claimed much of the public budget. As most

colonial government borrowing involved foreign loans, these debt charges were mainly paid abroad. In the FMS, for example, public debt charges amounted to S$6.9 million, or 12.8 per cent of total recurrent expenditure of S$53.7 million in 1932 (Emerson 1937, p. 191). Such charges on sterling loans amounted to S$80 million compared to local loans of S$16 million (Khor 1983).

(3) *Pensions, retired allowances, gratuities, etc.*: This expenditure item – including 'political pensions' and 'compassionate allowances' – was a major drain on colonial government revenue. In the FMS, it came to S$1.6 million or 4.4 per cent of recurrent expenditure in 1922 and S$4 million or 4.7 per cent in 1929. By 1932, it had risen to S$6.1 million or 11.3 per cent of recurrent expenditure. As the colonial bureaucratic elite receiving most of the pensions was European, much of these were paid abroad as the pensioners typically retired overseas.

(4) *Personal emoluments*: With its relatively large revenues, the colonial bureaucracy in British Malaya was especially well treated compared to others in the empire. British officers received high salaries and emoluments, including generous pensions, long vacations and other privileges. Periods of greater expansion quickly followed high rubber or tin prices. But when commodity prices fell, these generous conditions were invariably maintained. Reports of Retrenchment Commissions established to advise on staff and public expenditure cutbacks in the FMS and SS provide information on the colonial bureaucracy's extravagances. According to the FMS Retrenchment Commission Report (1932):

> the finances are now burdened with a public debt, increasing pensions, and the cost of swollen departments, at a time of revenue ebb. In the face of a crisis the establishments stand out as costly encumbrances which for want of means can no longer be maintained in their existing form. The administration in the past has relied too much on the mere momentum of prosperity to carry it through times of depression.

Discussing the causes of administrative expenditure over-expansion, the Commission concluded that ' [i]n general, we have reached the conclusion that the present standard of administration is unnecessarily high, that too many highly paid Europeans are employed and that their responsibilities are often insufficient to justify their pay' (FMS 1932: 21).

As examples of such unnecessary spending, the Commissions cited the S$8,325 salary for a European Council reporter, noting 'the country cannot afford to pay so large a sum for services so seldom required' (FMS 1932, p. 33), the 'entertainment allowance' for the Governor's Deputy, the Colonial Secretary and Resident Councillors, and allowances for 'entertainment of distinguished visitors' (SS Retrenchment Committee Report 1932, p. 425).

Such generous salaries and emoluments to European civil servants can also be considered a means of colonial surplus transfer via public finances. Resources used to pay them could instead have employed Malayan staff at lower cost, with the balance used for the population's welfare or development spending. British officers repatriated much of their high 'expatriate salaries'. Their expenditure while in Malaya typically involved imports, i.e., not generating much in terms of other Malayan incomes via 'linkages' and 'multiplier effects'.

The public expenditure pattern reflected colonial government priorities, including bias favouring British business. Apart from recurrent expenditure, much was expended on public works, mainly for the development of port, rail and road infrastructure, especially on the West Coast. These provided essential transport infrastructure for export commodities. The first East Coast railway line from Gemas in northern Johor in the south to Tumpat in northeast Kelantan was due to the British expectations of significant gold discoveries in highland Kelantan and the difficulties of transporting heavy gold ore from there. By 1934, the FMS government had spent over S$235 million to develop the peninsula's railway system (Emerson 1937, p. 187) largely financed with government revenue, typically involving costly loans from British banks.

The government budget for social services, such as education and health, was comparatively meagre. In 1932, for instance, education and health in the FMS received allocations of S$3.2 million and S$4.4 million. respectively (Mukerjee 1972) for a total of only 14 per cent of the recurrent budget, much less than the 24 per cent spent to service debt and to pay pensions. Even for the SS, which had the best health services in Malaya, 'from 1909 to 1938 expenditures for medical services were always considerably less than for military purposes' (Li 1955, p. 36).

Summing up colonial economic and financial policy, the inescapable conclusion of the American professor Rupert Emerson was unsurprising:

> If the economic base of the Federation (i.e., FMS) can be broadened by an effective encouragement of food crops and of other export crops and industries, if the Malay and the Chinese and Indian coolie can be given a real and significant place, it will begin to take on some of the characteristics of an economically sound and socially healthy community; but even this minimum program is more than can be expected within the framework of imperialism. (Emerson 1937, p. 193)

Thus, colonial finance and monetary or currency arrangements (Khor 1983, chapter 4) served as channels by which surpluses of different types were transferred from Malaya and other colonies and territories in the empire. Colonial monetary arrangements and public finance arrangements provided cheap credit to Britain. Conversely, colonial borrowers had to pay high interest rates and other charges to borrow for long-term investments, for example, for infrastructure.

Malayan sterling currency reserve holdings yielded no interest, UK government bond holders got very low interest. Thus, colonial public finance arrangements involved two types of losses. Khor (1983) estimated these as due to:

(1) the difference between the low interest from sterling bonds and higher interest from making alternative investments; and

(2) the difference between zero interest from sterling reserves and usurious interest payable for borrowing from British banks as well as exorbitant charges for floating such loans to finance development in the colony.

Thus, colonial financial arrangements bled the Malayan economy by three main means – via the Currency Board monetary system, commercial banks and colonial public finance arrangements, sometimes working in concert. The financial system in colonial Malaya served the British empire and foreign capital, rather than Malayan interests. The Currency Board, private banks and colonial public finances thus benefited from, but also served to enhance imperial financial stability. The Currency Board's substantial assets, commercial banks and colonial public finance arrangements also strengthened London's role as an international financial centre beyond serving as the political centre of the empire.

Hence, rather than prioritize the interests of the colony, the financial system channelled significant Malayan resources to London via its Currency Board reserves requirement, public finance surplus and private bank deposits. Returns to investments in trade and production in the colony also enriched the imperial centre. Besides the Currency Board reserves requirement, Malaya's colonial status compelled it to maintain a balance-of-payments surplus besides favouring big British capital, especially over Malayan economic interests. Rather than use financial and fiscal resources to grow and stabilize the Malayan economy, colonial currency, banking and public finance arrangements served to amplify rather than moderate business cycles due to commodity price volatility and financial vicissitudes.

Colonial Managerial Privileges

In the colonial context, there is considerable evidence of large payments secured by typically non-Malayan managers ostensibly for their expertise. Such remuneration included:

(1) Payment of directors' fees for companies in various sectors, especially tin, rubber, banking and international trade. In the rubber industry, for instance, 'the directorate . . . imposed a heavy recurrent sum of expenditure on companies, and this made up a significant percentage

of overhead costs. . . . The 2,121 directorships in British and Dutch territories cost the European plantation industry £424,200 a year, and the 479 chairmen a further £23,950' (Voon 1976, p. 161).

(2) Payment of very high managerial salaries, especially to foreigners in large European-owned companies. Thoburn estimated that before WW2, the relatively few in rubber plantation management receiving such salaries received the equivalent of 30 per cent of the entire wage bill for such estates (Ormsby-Gore 1928). Meanwhile, wages of skilled personnel and management salaries in tin dredging were equivalent to half the total unskilled tin dredging wage bill (Puthucheary 1960).

(3) Payment of high salaries, allowances, gratuities and pensions to European officers in the Malayan Civil Service and other related state organs such as statutory bodies and state-owned enterprises.

Khor (1983, 2019) saw these as 'forms of surplus related to technical dependence'. However, such remuneration can alternatively be seen as 'managerial rents' secured by taking advantage of their discretionary 'decision-making' privileges in private enterprises and the colonial state apparatus. These are comparable to contemporary executive remuneration, for example, in large modern enterprises, especially transnational corporations and international bureaucracies.

Such surplus transfers were enabled by colonial monetary and public finance arrangements. Thus, the relatively wealthy Malayan colony had to transfer funds to London at zero or very low interest rates and then had to borrow from British banks at exorbitant interest rates, also paying very high transactions charges. Through such colonial surplus transfers, Malaya lost significant financial resources. These could have been alternatively deployed to improve the condition of colonial subjects or to develop their economies.

This essay was originally published under the same title in *The Indian Economic Journal*, vol. 71, no. 1, 2023, pp. 92–107.

Martin Khor Kok Peng summarized two chapters of his seminal 1983 book, *The Malaysian Economy: Structures and Dependence*, when it was republished in July 2019. Entitled *Dependence and Surplus Transfers in Colonial Malaya*, it was presented at a conference on 'the colonial surplus'. Khor, Utsa Patnaik and Alec Gordon were expected to make major contributions on Malaya, India and Indonesia, respectively, at the conference. As Khor was too ill to present the paper himself, it was presented in absentia. Unfortunately, Gordon was not well and passed away over a month later. I have edited and published his remarks. Not long after, Khor succumbed in April 2020.

With the permission of his widow, Meenakshi Raman, this essay was revised to honour Khor as well as the Patnaiks. Khor was an economics undergraduate at Cambridge from 1971, where Prabhat taught while Utsa became a major figure in the debate then on Indian peasant agriculture. Jomo owes a great intellectual debt to both Utsa and Prabhat Patnaik having been inspired by their work and example from the time he was an undergraduate. While this chapter draws heavily on Khor's pioneering empirical work, Jomo alone should be held responsible for controversial interpretations and analyses.

References

Chee Heng Leng (1982), 'Health Status and the Development of Health Services in a Colonial State: The Case of British Malaya', *International Journal of Health Services*, vol. 12, no. 3, pp. 397–416.

Clairmonte, F. (1960), *Economic Liberalism and Underdevelopment*, London: Asia Publishing.

Drake, P.J. (1969), *Financial Development in Malaysia and Singapore*, Canberra: Australian National University Press.

Emerson, R. (1937), *Malaysia, A Study in Direct and Indirect Rule*, New York: Macmillan.

Federated Malay States (FMS) (1932), *Federated Malay States: Report of the FMS Retrenchment Commission*, FMS Government Printing Office, Kuala Lumpur.

Fisher, C. (1964), *Southeast Asia*, London: Methuen.

Jomo, K.S. (1983), 'Schooling for Disunity: Education in Colonial Malaya', *Jurnal Pendidikan*, vol. 8 (1978–83), pp. 63–84.

——— (1986), *A Question of Class: Capital, the State and Uneven Development in Malaya*, Oxford University Press.

Kaur, A. (1985), *Bridge and Barrier: Transport and Communications in Colonial Malaya (1870–1957)*, Oxford University Press.

Khoo K.K. (1977), 'The Great Depression: The Malaysian Context', in Khoo K.K., ed., *The History of South East and South Asia*, Singapore: Oxford University Press, pp. 78–94.

Khor Kok Peng, M. (1983), *The Malaysian Economy: Structures and Dependence*, Institut Masyarakat/Third World Network, Penang.

——— (2019), *Dependence and Surplus Transfers in Colonial Malaya*, paper presented to the seminar on the 'The Colonial Surplus', History Department, University of Malaya, Kuala Lumpur.

Labour Research Department, (1926), *British Imperialism in Malaya*, Labour Research Department, London.

Lee, S.Y. (1974), *Monetary and Banking Development in Malaysia and Singapore*, Singapore University Press.

Li Dun Jen (1982 [1955]), *British Malaya: An Economic Analysis*, second edition, Kuala Lumpur: INSAN.

Lim M.H. (1980), *Ownership and Control of the One Hundred Largest Companies in Malaysia*, Oxford University Press.

Mukerjee, T. (1972), 'Theory of Economic Drain: Impact of British Rule on the Indian Economy (1840–1900)', in K.E. Boulding and T. Mukerjee, eds, *Economic Imperialism: A Book of Readings*, University of Michigan.

Nazrin Shah, S.R. (2017), *Charting the Economy: Early 20th Century Malaya and Contemporary Malaysian Contrasts*, Singapore: Oxford University Press.

Ormsby-Gore, W.G.A. (1928), *Report by WGA Ormsby-Gore on His Visit to Malaya, Ceylon and Java*, Command Paper 3235, London.

Puthucheary, J. (1960), *Ownership and Control in the Malayan Economy*, Singapore: Eastern Universities Press.

Straits Settlements (1932), *Report of the Straits Settlements Retrenchment Committee, (1931)*, Singapore.

Tan T.W. (1982), *Income Distribution and Determination in West Malaysia*, Kuala Lumpur: Oxford University Press.

Voon Phin Keong (1976), *Western Rubber Enterprise in Southeast Asia, 1876–1921*, University of Malaya Press.

Yip, Y.H. (1969), *The Development of the Tin Mining Industry*, Kuala Lumpur: University of Malaya Press.

7

The Peasant Question under Nyerere's Socialism

Issa G. Shivji

Celebrating a Committed Marxist Couple

Writing an essay in honour of Utsa and Prabhat Patnaik is overwhelming if not intimidating. This remarkable Marxist couple has been on the radical intellectual landscape for the last half a century. I had the honour of inviting both of them to Dar es Salaam. In April 2010 when we were celebrating the Second Julius Nyerere Intellectual Festival, Utsa was invited to give a special lecture. She took the famous Nkrumah Assembly Hall at the University of Dar es Salaam by storm. The faculty, students and invited guests were transfixed, as she spoke effortlessly with passion and conviction which is unusual for modern celebrity intellectuals. With Sam Moyo's commentary, the lecture has been published in a book *The Agrarian Question in the Neoliberal Era* (U. Patnaik and S. Moyo 2011).

After five years of my incumbency as the Mwalimu Nyerere University Professorial Chair in Pan-African Studies (popularly called *Kigoda cha Mwalimu* in Kiswahili), the organizer of the Nyerere Intellectual Festival, I left, or rather, had to leave the Chair. I often tell my colleagues half jocularly that the life expectancy of any good initiative in the country is a maximum five years! Together with like-minded friends and colleagues, we founded the Nyerere Resource Centre (NRC, popular as *Kavazi la Mwalimu Nyerere*) which was hosted by the Tanzania Commission for Science and Technology. Two years before NRC was also closed down in 2020 (again lasting for just over five years!), I had invited Prabhat to give the Nyerere Dialogue Lecture. Prabhat's lecture titled 'Capitalism, Socialism and Petty Production' was published by Kavazi la Mwalimu Nyerere (2018).

At personal level, there are two things I have learnt from the Patnaiks: one, disarming humility, and two, unwavering and consistent commitment to the cause of the working people of the world. In this day and age of intellectual fashions, that is saying a lot (P. Patnaik 2019). A significant number of our former comrades have gone with the wind. They have not only changed geographical locations as they have moved from the periphery to the centre but also their former radical outlook. But Patnaiks have stood their intellectual ground with renewed vigour and passion. Notwithstanding the constraints of life they have faced (as we all do) over the years, between them and individually, they have produced a formidable corpus of both popular and academic writing which has been an educative and inspiring source of analysis for many of our upcoming Marxists and progressives. When their latest *A Theory of Imperialism* (U. Patnaik and P. Patnaik 2017) came out a few years ago, I devoured it within days. Admittedly, I did not quite understand all their fine economic arguments but got the gist of it. I must admit that I was taken aback by David Harvey's patronizing commentary on it which was included in the book. Since reading his impressive *A Brief History of Neo-liberalism* (2005), I have held Harvey in great esteem. Both the tone and some content of Harvey's commentary, particularly his near denial of the existence of imperialism made me, to put it mildly, uncomfortable.

As a tribute to my two remarkable comrades, I pen this essay on the topic, which is close to their hearts, the agrarian question. At the core of the agrarian question in many countries of Africa lies the peasant question. The peasant question has been at the heart of many Marxist debates since at least Kautsky (1976) and Lenin (1899). For African Marxists, the peasant question has been a veritable elusive issue. Samir Amin and Sam Moyo, amongst others, have been the leading African Marxists to address the peasant question in its various dimensions (see Shivji 2019).

The African Debate in a Nutshell

The debate on the peasant question among African intellectuals in the East African region has gone almost a full circle (for a partial review of the Kenyan debate, see Orvis 1993). In much of the 1970s, many left intellectuals took the traditional Marxist view of peasants as a 'sack of potatoes' (Marx's phrase) destined to die with the march of capitalism. Industrial large-scale agriculture was lauded; the peasant sector was derided. It was expected that through the 'normal' process of peasant differentiation, capitalist agriculture with intensive cultivation, economies of scale and higher productivity would flourish. The rural population would decline, and the surplus evicted from farms would find employment elsewhere, presumably in the industrial sector. Supposedly, this is the trajectory of agriculture and industrial revolution that had happened historically in the European countries, particularly in Britain in its transition from feudalism to capitalism. But as Utsa has shown in her numerous writings, there was no agriculture revolution in Britain as such (Patnaik and Moyo 2011; U. Patnaik 2012, pp. 203–54). The development of industrial revolution in Britain was very much tied with the importing of cheap food from tropical countries to feed the proletariat on the one hand, and the export of its 'surplus' population to settler colonies, on the other. The argument therefore that the surplus population flushed out of the countryside through enclosure movement was absorbed in the industrial sector is only partially true and is selective history at best. Since the countries of the global South do not have that option open, the European path of development is closed to them.

A variant of the above debate found expression among the Marxist left. Their argument was premised on the fact that African countries found themselves under imperialist-capitalist hegemony in which the surplus generated by the peasant sector was siphoned off from the agriculture sector. Thus, no surplus was left in the agriculture sector for accumulation or for what was then called accumulation from below (Neocosmos 1993). Thus, even the so-called normal differentiation of the peasantry from below was truncated and more or less arrested at the stage of rich peasant unable to make the transition to large-scale capitalist agriculture. This is what accounted for the fact that the peasantry persisted not so much as the lingering past of the pre-capitalist mode but rather as an integral part of the actually existing capitalism under the hegemony of imperialist capital. In essence, capital shifted the burden of social reproduction on the peasant household itself within which patriarchal relations ensured that the peasant woman bore the brunt of both production and reproduction (Shivji 1987). With little investment in agriculture, constant capital was minimal thus countering the tendency for the rate of profit to fall. It was the peasant labour mainly, though not exclusively, of women and children which yielded the surplus sucked by capital. The peasant producer in fact cuts into her necessary consumption to produce the surplus for capital thus augmenting a fairly high rate of surplus value. (This is what I have called the new form of primitive accumulation under neoliberalism). The result is that the peasant sector is sucked dry leaving the peasant to live a subhuman life while exerting superhuman labour.

Over the last few decades, the argument has been fine-tuned with more empirical research and also sharpening of analytical tools. The debates among African Marxists have been increasingly rooted in actually existing conditions in the villages and peasant communities of Africa. Happily, the most important factor in the equation of exploitation – the organized resistance and struggles of working people – which was to some extent ignored in earlier debates has been brought back as may be witnessed in the pages of the *Agrarian South* (AS) and the books published by the Agrarian South Network (ASN), both the product of Sam Moyo's imagination (Moyo, Jha and Yeros 2019; Monjane 2021). The journal AS and the books published by ASN have provided an independent, alternative space for debates on the agrarian question to the intellectuals of the global South. Both Patnaiks have been consistent contributors to these debates.

Increasingly, African Marxist intellectuals are focusing their research and debate on the financialization of the agriculture sector and its impact on the African peasantry. This work is still very much in its infancy. Young researchers are producing some interesting empirical work in this area. What is needed is the sharpening of the tools of analysis and the theoretical framework to understand the concrete conditions of the African peasantry in the context of increasing financialization of African agriculture (see, for instance, Castel-Branco and Greco [2022] for a very useful case study of financialization).

In this essay, I have chosen to paint a picture in broad strokes of the way Nyerere's socialism in Tanzania presented and addressed the peasant question during the country's nationalist phase.

The World Bank Experiment Goes Awry (1961–1966)

The peasant is venerated as well as vilified in equal measure. Venerated as a vote-bank for politicians while vilified as a backward, unproductive, traditional producer who resists change and modernization. Yet, ironically, it is the peasant generally and the woman peasant particularly, who is the greatest source of surplus in many an African economy. It is the woman peasant who bears the burden of production and reproduction in her multi-tasked labour-intensive life, producing food, caring for and feeding the family, which goes unaccounted for, thus subsiding capital and enabling local comprador and international multi-national capital to suck profits from the peasantry (Tsikata 2003; Mbilinyi 2016; Ossome 2021).

Nyerere's peasant was no different. For the first six years of independence, Tanzania followed the recommendations of the World Bank (World Bank 1961). Guided by modernization ideology prevailing then, the Bank recommended dual pathways to agricultural development called the improvement and transformation approach.

The Improvement Approach

The improvement approach advocated pumping government funds into agriculture in the form of credits, extension services, chemical pesticides and insecticides, irrigation projects, etc. to enhance the productivity of peasant production. This path was not novel. It was a continuation of what had already started in late colonialism (Coulson 1977). It did bring about some improvement in agriculture along two lines. First, reinforcing peasant differentiation through which infant capitalist elements got a boost as they managed to garner public resources for themselves through various means, fair and foul. Pockets of a class of African capitalist farmers which had begun to develop in the late fifties got a further fillip in the post-Independence period. But they remained local pockets. Agrarian capitalism was not generalized at the national level. The large majority of the peasantry was constituted by the middle and poor peasants who etched out a living by exerting superhuman labour while living subhuman lives. Exploiting itself, the peasantry continued to be the source of surplus to sustain the local merchant class and the mushrooming state, parastatal and cooperative bureaucracy.

Second, given the overall nature of the extraverted neocolonial economy wherein the main form of accumulation was commercial and related activities such as real estate and service sector, even the rich peasantry and capitalist farmers quickly turned to these latter activities rather than invest in agriculture. The net effect was that there was minimal accumulation of agrarian capital. Whatever surplus that was produced in agriculture was siphoned off by external capital, local and international.

The Transformation Approach

The transformation approach involved identifying so-called progressive farmers, as they were called, and settling them in specially created villages under a hierarchical management system. This venerated village settlement scheme was recommended by the World Bank in its report on the eve of independence (World Bank 1961). The rationale was rooted in the modernization ideology which saw the peasantry in its traditional environment as backward, unproductive and conservative. The solution was to uproot them from their backward environment and settle them in specially created modern villages. Nyerere, driven by his developmentalist vision to lift his people out of poverty, bought into the World Bank recommendations.

Volunteers coming to these new areas will become modern farmers in every sense; they will use machinery and perhaps irrigation because land tenure will be such as to ensure areas permanently large enough to justify the investment; they will have to follow laid-down crop rotations; and they will live in villages, going daily to their shambas. 'The effect of this settlement will be far-reaching, for planned Settlement does not only mean farms. It also means roads, commerce, and some local industries, as well as schools for the children, and health centres to help people enjoy the life they are creating' (Nyerere 1964, pp. 13–14).

A similar project was envisioned for pastoralists. Under the Range Development and Management Act of 1964, pastoralists, especially Maasai, would be removed from their traditional areas and settled in large-scale ranches to live sedentary lives like their brethren peasants. The project was funded by USAID (United States Agency for International Development). The rationale was to overcome their customary nomadic lives. The real intention, as one researcher showed, was to provide beef for foreign markets and conserve wildlife for tourists (Tenga 1986, p. 102). What was village settlement to agriculture, conservation and tourism was to pastoralism. Both projects were extraverted looking outwards to foreign market and foreign investment by external multinational capital (Århem 1985). The tendency in both was to decimate small producers on land in favour of large-scale agribusiness, hunting companies and tour operators, which respectively require exclusive game-controlled areas and national parks. Århem sums up the tendency succinctly.

Indeed, the national park can be seen as the direct counterpart of the beef ranch: a huge monocultural estate, producing services for consumption by foreign tourists. People, the indigenous producers, are no longer seen as a resource and a basis for development, but as an obstacle to development. Like the ranch, the national park is easier to handle and control than traditional human-use systems, easier to gear towards the overriding national development goal of increased, export-oriented production under firm state control. (Århem 1985, p. 206)

In effect, peasants settled in village settlements and supervised by a bureaucratized expatriate management, who had no understanding of rural Tanzania, were reduced to semi-proletarians. Both the village settlement schemes and the range development project proved to be an unmitigated disaster at a great cost to the treasury. The Nyerere government admitted its mistake. The second vice-president Kawawa announced the end of the settlement scheme and admitted that the schemes were 'heavily over-capitalized' and that it would be a lifetime burden on the settler farmer to repay the debt (Kawawa 1966, p. 8). The failure led to a fundamental shift in the paradigm away from the modern–traditional binary. Rather than impose modernization from the top uprooting tradition, it was now considered prudent to modernize tradition. As the second vice-president put it: 'In future, it has been decided that, instead of establishing highly capitalized schemes and moving people to them emphasis shall be on modernising existing traditional villages, by injecting capital in order to raise the standard of living of the villages' (Kawawa 1966, p. 8).

The scrapping of the village settlement schemes and the range development project dovetailed into the national policy change with the adoption of the Arusha Declaration in February 1967, Tanzania's blueprint for socialism and self-reliance. Under the Arusha Declaration, the commanding heights of the economy including large plantations were nationalized. On the heels of the Declaration, Nyerere wrote a paper on 'socialism and rural development' which was adopted by the party and the government as its policy on agriculture development. How did the peasantry fare under the policy of socialism or Ujamaa, its popular Swahili rendering?

The Peasant under Ujamaa

The Arusha Declaration identified workers and peasants as the builders and beneficiaries of socialism. Rural development would be spearheaded by peasants working together on communal farms and sharing the fruits of their labour under, no doubt, the supervision of agriculture extension officers. Very little was said about the development of productive forces in the rural sector nor on the transformation of the export-oriented nature of the rural economy producing exotic foods and raw materials for metropolitan markets.

Tanzania was still very much a colonial economy dependent on the export of its agriculture products to get necessary foreign exchange.

In spite of political exaltation, the number of registered Ujamaa villages was small. Nyerere had all along emphasized that living in Ujamaa villages would be voluntary and that peasants could not be forced to be socialists. Six years later the number of Ujamaa villages was still insignificant. Party zealots and bureaucrats, including Nyerere, were getting impatient. In a regional tour in 1973, Nyerere could not hide his anger and frustration at the recalcitrance of the peasants to live in Ujamaa villages. In the course of his speech, he reprimanded the peasants saying that the government had abolished poll tax, brought water and health to peasants but the peasants had not reciprocated. While he could not force them to be socialists, Nyerere said, he could force them to live in villages. By 1976, the whole of the rural population should have moved into villages, he ordered (Shivji, Yahya-Othman and Kamata 2020, p. 182).

Thus started the process of forced villagization under what was a semi-militarized operation. Crops and homesteads were set to fire, peasants were bundled onto trucks and moved into newly demarcated villages. A typical scenario is painted by a researcher in Iringa region.

> 'We were treated like animals,' some said. Government representatives (militia, Tanu Youth League member, government and party employees) simply told people they must move to a particular place by a given date. . . . To assure that people remained in the new villages, former houses were usually made uninhabitable by ripping out doors and windows and knocking hole in the mud walls or by setting fire to the thatch roof. In some cases grain stored in or near the house also caught fire and the family's food supply was destroyed. . . . (Shivji 2020, p. 182)

Pastoralists were not spared either. Traditionally pastoral communities have borne the brunt of modernization ideology. Their kraals were burnt; some Maasai fled across the border to Kenya, fleeing away from Ujamaa, as one research report put it (Shivji 2020, p. 183). By 1977, Nyerere boasted, almost 13 million were living in villages. The number may have been exaggerated. Estimates of people moved vary from five to seven million. Whatever the correct number, the movement was undoubtedly massive, yet it was neither voluntary nor participatory. Peasants moved because of coercion or because of fear of coercion or because they were lured to move with promises of better facilities (Shivji 2020, p. 183).

Forced villagization left an indelible adverse mark on Nyerere's socialist policy. It could have alienated Nyerere's peasant base though given his popularity, often boosted by party propaganda, it was not obvious at the time. True, school enrolment and dispensaries in the villages improved but production did not rise in the same measure. What is more, when the economy entered crisis in the late seventies and early eighties, the achievements in social services were wiped out as peasants withdrew their children from schools and dispensaries lacked vital medical supplies. Meanwhile, the peasant, as always, continued to be sucked dry as surplus was siphoned off by the sprawling bureaucracy managing state crop authorities. One way of computing the surplus drawn from the peasantry is to compute the difference between producer and market prices. In a time series, computing producer price as a share of sales price for export crops, Frank Ellis found that over the ten-year period from 1970 to 1980, it fell from 70.3 per cent in 1970 to 41.7 per cent in 1980. His estimate for the eleven-year period from 1970 to 1981 was that 4.6 billion Tanzania shillings was pumped out of the peasantry of which 2.2 billion went to the central state as taxation and 2.4 billion to crop parastatals as 'marketing costs'. This is an underestimate because he took the 1970 producer share of 66.5 per cent as his base which was much lower than the producer share in earlier years (cited Shivji 2020, pp. 197–98).

All in all, the peasant under Nyerere's Ujamaa did not fare well. The peasant question remained unresolved. However, on one issue Nyerere remained consistent. He refused throughout to commodify land and make it a freely marketable commodity. Although land sales did take place in both rural and urban areas this was done under the counter. Bare land could not be transacted on the market because the ultimate title to land was vested in the state. While there were cases of land being alienated to parastatals and other institutions of the state such as the military and prisons, the incidence of land alienation to private interests remained relatively low. With the advent of neoliberalism, the likes of the World Bank put increasing pressure on Tanzania to privatize land and make it freely available on the market. We now turn to the peasant under neoliberal Tanzania.

The Peasant under Neoliberalism

After putting up a valiant fight, albeit unsuccessful, against the International Monetary Fund (IMF) which typically wanted change of country's policies in return for a standby loan, Nyerere stepped down from the presidency in 1985 leaving it to his successor Ali Hassan Mwinyi to negotiate the terms of 'surrender' to the IMF. Mwinyi's ten years were a kind of transition from Nyerere's nationalism to neoliberalism. Trade and finance were liberalized. The process of parastatal reform, a euphemism for privatization of the public sector, was set in motion. The shilling was periodically devalued to meet IMF's shifting goal post. The market was flooded with used clothing, which was a respite in the short run but extremely harmful to the textile industry which in any case did not survive the privatization onslaught which was to follow under the next ten years of Mkapa presidency (for a full story see Shivji 2020, chapter 11).

As social services – health, education, water, sanitation – were com-

modified one after another under the World Bank advice of cost-sharing, the
social wage saw a big cut throwing the working people to the ravages of the
open market. The result was a perceptible fall in school enrolment, literacy
rates and infant mortality. Corruption shot through the roof as government
bureaucrats and private merchants colluded to take advantage of shortages
and siphon off state resources into private pockets (see Gibbon 1995, p. 15).
Inequality, which had been reasonably suppressed through deliberate income
policy during Nyerere, began to rise. Land alienation began to gather storm.
The most scandalous of them which still haunts the country was what came
to be called 'Loliondogate'. In 1993, the then minister of tourism leased the
entire Loliondo Game Controlled Area at Ngorongoro to an army brigadier
from the United Arab Emirates as a private hunting ground (ibid., p. 16).

The Land Commission

In 1990, President Mwinyi formed a Presidential Commission of
Enquiry into Land Matters the first of its kind since independence in 1961.
For reasons unbeknown, this author was appointed the chairman of the commission. Other members of the commission were veteran politicians or civil
servants or members of parliament. The terms of reference of the commission
were broad enough to allow the commission to visit villages and listen to the
grievances of the rural and urban working people. Given the policy changes
that were taking place at the time, it was expected that the commission would
come up with recommendations that would facilitate privatization of land
through the registration and formalization of the land tenure system – in the
event that was not to be.

I summed up for the commission the widespread opinion heard from
peasants and pastoralists during the commission's visits as a demand for security of tenure of small producers and the democratization of the land tenure
system in which peasant communities would participate in the control and management of their resources, the most important being land. Recommendations
of the commission were based on what the commission called the peasant path
of development predicated on what it called accumulation from below or a
kind of autochthonous process of accumulation. In the words of the commission, which need to be quoted in extenso:

> We begin from the premise that Tanzania is a country of the smallholder
> (the peasant and the herdsman). We accept that it is likely to remain so for a
> foreseeable future. While not wanting to make a virtue out of necessity, we
> also recognize that a substantial body of thought has fundamentally changed
> its perception of the peasantry in Africa, its role in the nation and its destiny.
>
> During the 60s and the 70s the future of Africa was seen in terms
> of large-scale industrial and agrarian development. The smallholder was
> considered inefficient and unproductive destined to disappear with develop-

ment. Models of large-scale, capital-intensive agrarian and pastoral ventures were tried to induce development. Most of these failed miserably. [. . .]

Recent studies and experiences in Africa have shown that the legendary inefficiency and low productivity of the African peasant were predicated on artificial measures adopted by the colonial and post-colonial state in favour of the settler farmer or the foreign multinational or the parastatal monopolist. The unfair advantage given to this type of large-scale land holder through various mechanisms [. . .] was in effect based on a hidden subsidy from the smallholder. It simultaneously impoverished the peasant thus perpetuating the myth of his inefficiency and low productivity while raising the profits of the large-scale holder thus upholding the latter's claim to superior economic performance. [. . .]

Ultimately though the scales of operations and economic performance are not really the main argument. The main argument should rest on the character of accumulation. The main issue is whether the surplus generated by the rural producer is accumulated within the rural sector, thus enhancing its capacity for self-sustained development, or is siphoned off to other centres of accumulation both within, but more often, outside the country. If the latter, neither the rural sector nor the country can take-off on the path to self-sustained national development. The economy is reproduced as an extraverted, dependent economy perpetually in crisis and constantly living off aid. (Ministry of Lands, Housing and Urban Development & the Scandinavian Institute of African Studies 1994, p. 137; paragraph numbers omitted)

The Commission's report generated intense debate. Broadly, the report was supported by public opinion. Many of the detailed recommendations of the commission were accepted by the government but two fundamental recommendations were not. The commission had recommended that the radical title vested in the state should be diversified; that the state should not have the monopoly of radical title; that the radical title in village land should be vested in the respective village assemblies and that that the residents of the village will hold land under customary tenure from the village assembly. The radical title in national lands would be vested in an extra-ministerial body called National Land Commission.

Second, it recommended that the village assembly (a body constituted by all adult residents of the village) should be entrenched in the Constitution of the country as the lowest rung of local government, and that customary land holding should be secure and occupy the same legal status as statutory titles. This, in the Commission's view, would provide peasant and pastoral communities security of tenure while at the same time give them control over village land through their village assemblies. There could not be a better democratic system which combined in it both political and economic governance.

The government flatly refused to accept that the state be divested of the radical title. Vesting of radical title in the state gave the bureaucracy control over the major resource of the country, land, from which they reaped political rents which they were not ready to forego. Vested interests trumped democracy as indeed we observe throughout the history of capital. New land laws were passed in 1999 recognizing among other things customary titles and giving them same security as statutory titles. But the radical title remained vested in the president to hold land as a trustee for the benefit of Tanzanians. A couple of years later, following the pressure exerted by banks, the law was amended stipulating that bare land had value and could be transacted on the market thus paving the way for the commodification of land and making it a marketable commodity (for the antecedents and the aftermath of the Commission report, see Shivji 1998).

Since then, the pressure from the private sector and sections of the bureaucracy has continued to facilitate alienation of land to investors. Modernization theory in its various incarnations has continued to haunt the agrarian landscape in the country at the expense of small peasants.

If Mwinyi's period was a transition to neoliberalism, the next ten years were a consolidation under his successor Mkapa. Mkapa (1995–2005) single-mindedly embarked on a privatization spree, one of his most controversial privatizations being the selling of the National Bank of Commerce, a state bank established during the Nyerere era, to a South African conglomerate at a fire-sale price. The other two neoliberal policies for which Mkapa is notoriously remembered at least in more critical circles is the rushing through parliament the Mining Act in 1998 whose effect was no less than diluting the sovereignty of the state over its most precious natural resource. And the second was uncritically buying into Hernando de Sotto's formalization of property thesis. De Sotto was sold to the Third World by the World Bank and neoliberal pundits through having set up a successful programme of formalizing informal settlements in Lima, Peru. A study made of the project showed that titling of informal housing in no way increased credit, which was the original promise of the project, but increased the number of hours of work that the occupants spent labouring outside their homes now that they had a feeling that their housing was secure. The latter finding as Mitchell (2005) has shown was dubious. Its premises and assumptions have been questioned

In Tanzania, funded by the Norwegian government, De Sotto's Institute for Liberty and Democracy (ILD) was invited by the government to lead the formalization programme. De Sotto's programme was squarely within the neoliberal framework promoted by all the big names in the neoliberal world. In Tanzania, the programme operated under the Kiswahili acronym of MKURABITA (*Mpango wa Kurasimisha Rasilimali na Biashara za Wanyonge – Tanzania*) – programme to formalise the property and businesses of the poor. De Sotto's IDL continuously stressed that there should be a single statutory land tenure system. It looked upon the customary land titles stipulated in the Land Laws of 1999 askance. Notwithstanding President Mkapa's admiration for De Sotto, it would have been politically imprudent for his government to abolish the customary land tenure. So, it continues to exist presumably awaiting an opportune moment when it can be abolished.

Ten years of President Kikwete (2005–2015) walked the same neoliberal path as Mkapa's, except this time around under an extremely laissez-faire regime. *Kilimo Kwanza* or 'Agriculture First' and 'Big Results Now' was the initiative taken in the agriculture sector under President Kikwete. Ostensibly, its aim was to remove all constraints on the development of small, medium and large-scale farming. Typically, in practice, the beneficiary was large-scale agriculture. One example dramatically epitomizes how *Kilimo Kwanza* was translated into practice. In 2010, a massive project called Southern Agricultural Growth Corridor of Tanzania (SAGCOT), presented as a public–private partnership, was launched. It emanated from the World Economic Forum Africa Summit held in Dar es Salaam in 2010. SAGCOT covers almost one-third area of mainland Tanzania. It envisaged that, over twenty years, it would invest 1.3 billion US dollars coming from the government and donors. It was expected that this would attract another 2.1 billion US dollars from local and international private investors (Sulle 2020, p. 336). The main issue which has doggedly faced the project is to acquire land which is under the jurisdiction of villages. This has faced stiff resistance from villagers and occasionally villagers have successfully frustrated the project's plan of acquiring land through court cases. Some actors within SAGCOT therefore adopt out grower and contract farming schemes thus inaugurating an indirect way of integrating small producers in commercial agribusiness.

SAGCOT stalled during President Magufuli's six years which saw a dramatic backlash to neoliberal policies. Deploying resource nationalism, albeit without being guided by a bigger picture or vision, the Magufuli government overturned several projects of the Mkapa and Kikwete periods. In the case of SAGCOT, the government withdrew from the financial agreement to provide matching funds. Furthermore, it adopted a more positive pro-small holder stance, both of which were a slap on the face of SAGCOT promoters (Sulle 2020). The project, however, survived Magufuli who died in office in March 2021. The successor regime under President Samia Suluhu Hassan seems to have made a 180-degree turnabout back to Kikwete's rampant neoliberal policies. Under this atmosphere, it would not be surprising if SAGCOT makes a comeback.

Peasant's Fate and Fight Under Neoliberalism

An in-depth empirical investigation of thirteen large-scale agro-investments and projects in Tanzania since the 2000s concludes that formalization of land, under whatever name, has gone hand in hand with land acquisition by or in the interest of outside investors (Engström, Bélair and Blache 2022). In collusion with district authorities and at the behest of directives from the central government, district officers have resorted to all kinds of subterfuges to alienate village lands. The researchers found a blaring discrepancy between 'the purported development benefits and the actual outcomes of the development orientations of land formalization and land acquisition for investment in Tanzania' (ibid., p. 11). The researchers continue: '[O]ur aggregate analysis confirms findings from previous smaller scale case studies and shows with clarity that rural smallholders are not only randomly but *systematically* dispossessed from their land' (ibid.).

The researchers furthermore assert that

> the increased pace and frequency of land formalization is not coincidental, but rather linked to the promotion of large-scale agro-investment since the early 2000s. . . . It is therefore not surprising that commercial initiatives such as SAGCOT constitutes a major source of such dispossession – six out of thirteen cases are located within the SAGCOT corridor. (Ibid.)

In many ways, SAGCOT is the quintessential of neoliberal agrarian policies dramatically revealing a political alliance between the state bureaucracy, local capital, multinational agri-business, donors and international financial institutions. The neoliberal attack on the village commons has not gone without resistance. It is persistently resisted by peasant and pastoral communities. It is in this context that I have argued elsewhere that the political task of the Left is to raise the slogan of reclaiming the commons (including peasant sovereignty over seeds) which should be put in the hands of village communities to be governed by their democratic organs such as village assemblies and new type of multifunctional cooperatives.

In concluding this tribute to the Patnaiks, I believe I can say without hesitation that the Patnaiks would readily align with the political task of the working people summed up above to address the contemporary agrarian question. Resolution of the peasant question does not lie in the elimination and marginalization of the peasantry but rather in the recognition of the peasant as a central actor in the emancipatory project of the working people.

This essay was originally published under the same title in *The Indian Economic Journal*, vol. 71, no. 1, 2023, pp. 108–19.

References

Århem, K. (1985), Two Sides of Development: Maasai Pastoralism and Wildlife Conservation in Ngorongoro, *Journal of Anthropology*, vol. 49, nos 3–4, pp. 4186–210.

Castel-Branco, C. and E. Greco (2022), Capital Accumulation, Financialisation and Social Reproduction in Mozambique, *Review of African Political Economy*, vol. 49, p. 171.

Coulson, A. (1977), 'Agricultural Policies in Mainland Tanzania', *Review of African Political Economy*, vol. 4, no. 10, pp. 74–100, https://doi.org/10.1080/03056247708703340.

Engström, L., J. Bélair and A. Blache (2022), 'Formalising Village Land Dispossession? An

Aggregate Analysis of the Combined Effects of the Land Formalisation and Land Acquisition Agendas in Tanzania', *Land Use Policy*, vol. 120, 106255, doi: https://doi.org/10.1016/j.landusepol.2022.106255

Gibbon, P. (1995), 'Merchantisation of Production and Privatisation of Development in the Post-Ujamaa Tanzania: An Introduction', in P. Gibbon, ed., *Liberalised Development*, Nor diska Afrika Institute.

Harvey, D. (2005), *A Brief History of Neo-Liberalism*, Oxford: Oxford University Press.

Kautsky, K. (1976), 'Summary of Selected Parts of Karl Kautsky's: The Agrarian Question', translated and summarized by J. Banaji, *Economy and Society*, vol. 5, no. 1, pp. 1–49.

Kawawa, R.M. (1966), 'New Approaches to Rural Development', *Nbioni*, vol. 2, no. 11, pp. 4–15.

Lenin, V. (1899), *The Development of Capitalism in Russia*, Moscow: Progress Publishers.

Maghimbi, P.S., ed. (1992), *The Roots of Agrarian Crisis in Tanzania—A Theoretical Perspective*, Aldershot: Avebury.

Mbilinyi, M. (2016), 'Debating Land and Agrarian Issues from a Gender Perspective', *Agrarian South: Journal of Political Economy*, vol. 5, nos 2–3, pp. 164–86.

Ministry of Lands, Housing and Urban Development, and the Scandinavian Institute of African Studies (1994), *Report of the Presidential Commission of Inquiry into Land Matters, Volume 1: Land Policy and Land Tenure Structure*, [Shivji Commission report].

Mitchell, T. (2005), 'The Work of Economics: How a Discipline Makes Its World', *European Journal of Sociology*, vol. 4, no. 2, pp. 297–320.

Monjane, B. (2021), *We Rise for Our Land: Land Struggles and Repression in Southern Africa*, Daraja Press & Sam Moyo African Institute of Agrarian Studies.

Moyo, S., P. Jha and P. Yeros (2019), *Reclaiming Africa: Scramble and Resistance in the 21st Century*, Singapore: Springer.

Neocosmos, M. (1993), *The Agrarian Question in Southern Africa and 'Accumulation from Below'*, [Research Reports 93, Scandinavian Institute of African Studies.

Nyerere, J. (1964), *Address by the President Mwalimu Julius K. Nyerere on the Tanganyika, Five Year Plan and Review of the Plan*, Tanganyika Information Services.

Orvis, S. (1993), 'The Kenyan Agrarian Debate: A Reappraisal', *African Studies Review*, vol. 36, no. 3, pp. 23–48, https://doi. org/10.2307/525172.

Ossome, L. (2021), 'Pedagogips of Feminist Resistance: Agrarian Movements in Africa', *Agrarian South: Journal of Political Economy*, vol. 10, no. 1, pp. 47–58.

Patnaik, P. (2019), Capitalism, Socialism and Petty Production, Marxist, vol. 35, no. 1, pp. 28–43, available at https://cpim.org/wp-content/uploads/old/marxist/201901-marxist-prabhat-patnaik-capitalism-socialism.pdf

Patnaik, U. (2012), 'Some Aspects of the Contemporary Agrarian Question', *Agrarian South: Journal of Political Economy*, vol. 1, no. 3, pp. 233–54, https://doi.org/10.1177/227797601200100301.

Patnaik, U. and S. Moyo (2011), *The Agrarian Question in the Neoliberal Era: Primitive Accumulation and the Peasantry*, Tanzania: Pambazuka Press.

Patnaik, U. and P. Patnaik (2017), *A Theory of Imperialism*, New York: Columbia University Press.

Shivji, I.G. (1987), 'The Roots of Agrarian Crisis in Tanzania: A Theoretical Perspective', research review, *Eastern African Social Science*, vol. 3, no. 1, pp. 111–34.

——— (1998), Not Yet Democracy: Reforming Land Tenure in Tanzania, International Institute for Environment and Development (IIED), HAKIARDHI and University of Dar es Salaam, Tanzania, available at https://www.iied.org/sites/default/files/pdfs/migrate/7383IIED.pdf

——— (2019), 'Sam Moyo and Samir Amin on the Peasant Question', *Agrarian South: Journal of Political Economy*, vol. 8, nos 1–2, pp. 287–302.

Shivji, I.G., S. Yahya-Othman and N. Kamata. (2020), *Development as Rebellion: A Biography of Julius Nyerere*, Dar es Salaam: Mkukina Nyota.

Sulle, E. (2020), 'Bureaucrats, Investors and Smallholders: Contesting Land Rights and Agro-Commercialisation in the Southern Agricultural Growth Corridor of Tanzania', *Journal of Eastern African Studies*, vol. 14, no. 2, pp. 332–53, https:// doi.org/10.1080/175 31055.2020.1743093

Tenga, R.W. (1986), 'The Historical and Socio-Economic Approaches in Learning the Law: Dar es Salaam and Third World Perspectives in Jurisprudence', Faculty of Law, University of Dar Es Salaam, Tanzania, pp. 95–116.

Tsikata, D. (2003), 'Securing Women's Interests Within Land Tenure Reforms: Recent Debates in Tanzania', in S. Razavi, ed., Agrarian Change, Gender and Land Rights, Oxford: Blackwell Publishing Ltd.

World Bank (1961), *The Economic Development of Tanganyika*, Baltimore: Johns Hopkins University Press, available at https://documents1.worldbank.org/curated/en/231391468760788974/pdf/11144.pdf

8

Revisiting the Kerala 'Model' of Development

A Sixty-Year Assessment of Successes and Failures

K.P. Kannan

Introduction

This article is a revisit of the development experience of Kerala, often referred to as the Kerala Model of Development, by examining its growth performance along with human development, employment and associated structural transformation for a period of 60 years. While our starting point is the remarkable achievements in Kerala's human development record, we also find that Kerala has come to occupy a high position even in comparative terms in the south and South-East Asian context. While the overall growth performance has also kept pace with the national record, we find several areas of failure that are in sharp contrast to the successes in human development. The findings may be summarized as follows.

First, Kerala enjoyed a historical advantage in the form of favourable initial conditions in pursuing higher levels of human development that continue to be way ahead of the all-India scenario. As such we find a favourable historical path when the notion of public action emerged as a critical factor in its human development trajectory. This public action made possible by social reform, radical politics and the emergence of an active public sphere and a social economy helped create an effective political demand for human development.

Second, this process of human development did contribute to the growth process through a demographic transition that helped to reap a premium in per capita growth in income to the extent of 1 per cent per annum compared to the national performance in per capita growth.

Third, during the first phase of this 60-year trajectory, growth performance was unimpressive and lower than the national average. However, growth started picking up a few years after the acceleration in growth in the national economy in the mid-1980s. This was largely contributed by the increasing flow of remittances to the Kerala economy made possible by large-scale migration of its people to work in the countries in West Asia called the Gulf countries. In that sense, the process of human development leading to the migration of educated people could be seen as contributing to the higher growth performance of the Kerala economy in the second phase beginning from 1987.

Fourth, the heightened growth performance was largely led by the construction sector but more importantly by the service sector. This led to a further lopsidedness of the sectoral growth performance of the Kerala economy. This period witnessed large-scale movement of workers away from the primary sector of the economy to the construction sector and the service sector.

Fifth, from an employment point of view this pattern of growth could not address the problem of unemployment especially that of the educated unemployed. While unemployment in the restricted sense of 'seeking work' was found to be declining for men, this was not the case for women. Unemployment among the younger generation was high and increasing. However, when unemployment is measured as those seeking and not seeking work (called labour underutilization [LU]), the situation is a challenging one with increasing proportion of women in the category of out of work and education. The problem was acute among the younger generation. Such a high rate of underutilization of labour despite high human development and high economic growth along with an advanced stage in demographic transition is nothing short of a spectacular failure. The overall situation in the national economy was hardly conducive to the alleviation of this problem since the rate of labour underutilization at the national level is no different from that of Kerala.

Sixth, while seeking answers to this question, we embarked on the performance of the state in creating economic opportunities through resource mobilization, management of public sector enterprises and avoiding waste of time and resources in implementation of public projects. In all these, the performance of the state of Kerala has been a dismal one. These therefore constitute another set of spectacular failures.

Finally, we hypothesize that while public action played an active role in enhancing human development, such an experience was not evident in the case of governance especially in the management of public finance and public enterprises and projects. It is possible that the scope for public action was limited in these areas since the benefits are collective unlike in human development where there is a convergence of public and private (individual) benefits as, for example, in education and health.

The Kerala Model and Its Critiques

A word about the Kerala Model of Development (henceforth KMD). When the Centre for Development Studies was established in Thiruvananthapuram (also referred to as Trivandrum) in 1971, its first major study called 'Poverty, Unemployment and Development Policy: A Case Study of Selected Issues with Reference to Kerala' was commissioned by the United Nations Committee on Development Planning (henceforth CDS Study 1975). This study brought to the fore that Kerala, a provincial state in India, has been able to achieve within a little less than two decades of its formation in 1956 a critical minimum of human development and welfare to its people despite a very low per capita income by international standards. It then came to be known as the Kerala Model of Development although the CDS Study 1975 did not use such a term. Many scholars, especially those associated with the CDS, do not consider Kerala's development experience as a 'model' although the term gets repeatedly used in both popular and academic discussions.[1] I also do not subscribe to the view that there is a 'Kerala Model of Development' simply because there was no preconceived formal strategy specific to Kerala's developmental challenges as in the case of say, Indian Planning Models. At the most, one could say that Kerala's specific developmental trajectory evolved out of its social and political processes over a long period of time starting from even before the formation of the state of Kerala in 1956. I am therefore using the term KMD in the sense of Kerala's development experience keeping in mind that this acronym has become part of the vocabulary in popular dialogue as well as scholarly discussions.

The fact that the growth performance of the Kerala economy, despite a high human development record, was poorer than the all-India level during the first three decades of the formation of the state led to the characterization of the KMD as a lop-sided one with 'high human development but low economic growth'. Several studies followed to understand this phenomenon. It also led to a situation where several scholars praised the model notwithstanding its poor economic growth record and many critics severely criticized and brought out the various failures of the state in managing public finance and delivering economic services. Kerala's highly organized labour – both in the organized and unorganized sectors – were also blamed for the poor economic performance.[2]

However, another CDS study (2006) brought into sharp focus the changing growth scenario by which a new phase of growth, beginning with the late 1980s, was noted characterizing the KMD as one of 'a virtuous cycle of growth' that fitted well with the theory that early human development ultimately leads of high economic growth. However, the growth engine was located in the international labour migration to Kerala that started in the early 1970s but assumed significant proportions from the late 1980s. That led to a measurement of annual remittances and its significance and impact on the Kerala economy. Both the remittances and the high growth of the Kerala economy has continued until 2019–20 when the worldwide pandemic induced by Covid-19 resulted in a break in the high-growth regime.

Why Revisit the KMD at This Juncture?

If the KMD has moved away from its human development lopsided-ness to a virtuous one characterized by high human development (HD) and high economic growth (EG), one may legitimately ask: why is there a need to revisit? There are two compelling reasons for me to undertake this revisit.

First, it is now almost two decades since the last exercise was undertaken (CDS 2006). And it is important to find out as to how Kerala has managed to sustain the 'virtuous' phase and, if so, how has it addressed its historically persistent problem of educated unemployment. This opportunity is also being utilized to examine some crucial aspects of the emergent issues of gender unfreedom despite the impressive achievements of women in the realm of human development. The second reason is the need to bring the story of the KMD up to 2020 since the year is likely to emerge as a watermark in Kerala's developmental journey along with the rest of the country due to the as yet unassessed impact of the worldwide Covid-19 pandemic.

Our revisit takes into account the entire period of the developmental trajectory since the formation of the state of Kerala in 1956. Based on availability of data, we have taken a long period of 60 years, from 1960 to 2020. For purposes of comparison, we have taken the all-India scenario for the same period.

Periodization of the Developmental Trajectory

While progress in human development has been a secular one, the trajectory of economic growth has several ups and downs. Based on the long-term trajectory of aggregate economic growth as per the official net state domestic product (NSDP) statistics presented in Figure 8.1, we have divided the six decades into two phases; the first phase being 1960–61 to 1986–87, and the second phase being 1987–88 to 2019–20. The first phase representing a lop-sidedness with high HD and low EG and the second phase representing a virtuous one with high HD and high EG. However, we have divided each of these phases into two periods, based on the pace of growth, with a total

Figure 8.1. *Growth performance of Kerala economy, 1960–61 to 2019–20,* NSDP in constant 1999–2000 prices in Rs crores

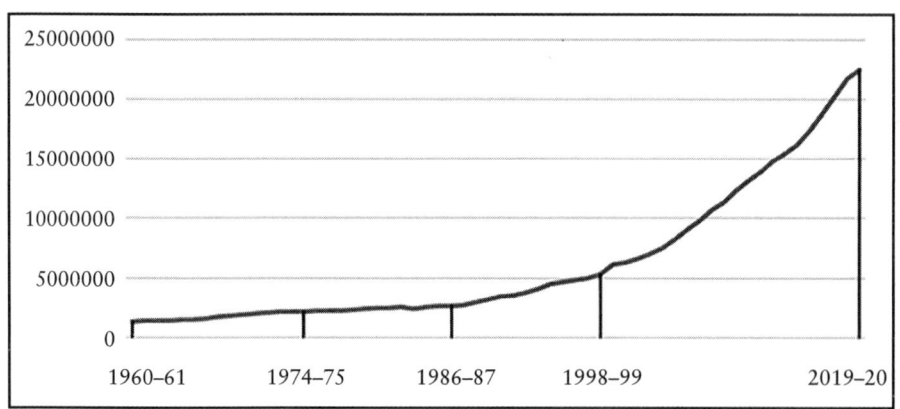

Source: Government of India, *National Accounts Statistics,* Central Statistical Organisation, New Delhi, various issues.

Table 8.1 Economic growth and human development in Kerala compared to all-India

Period 1	Period 2	First Phase	Period 3	Period 4	Second Phase	Whole Period
1960–61/ 1974–75	1975–76/ 1986–87	1960–61/ 1986–87	1987–88/ 1998–99	1999–2000/ 2019–20	1987–88/ 2019–20	1960–1961/ 2019–2020
14 years	11 years	26 years	11 years	20 years	31 years	59 years
High HD	High HD	High HD	High HD	High HD	High HD	High HD
High EG	Low EG	Low EG	High EG	EG > Period 3 but < India	High EG but < India	High EG but < India
High PCY growth	Negative growth in PCY	Low PCY growth	High PCY growth	High PCY growth	High PCY growth	PCY growth > India

Note: 'High' and 'Low' are used in relation to the all-India trend; EG stands for economic growth, HD for human development and PCY for per capita income.
Source: Author's own classification.

of four periods. The moderate growth of the Kerala economy during period 1 gives way to a deceleration bordering on stagnation during period 2. The revival of growth since 1987–88 takes Kerala to a higher-level growth path on par with the national economy. In the subsequent period, period 4, there is a marginal acceleration in growth. This periodization is based on the growth in NSDP that reflects the internal growth dynamics of the Kerala economy. Later, we have modified this series by adding the annual remittances and called it the modified state income (henceforth MSI) (see Kannan and Hari 2020). This MSI represents an important link of the Kerala economy with the global economy dictated largely by events in the six oil-rich Gulf countries in West Asia that employs Kerala's labour force equivalent to nearly a fifth of its domestic labour force.[3]

What we find is that the impact of initial investments in HD helped Kerala in triggering a steady process of economic growth but with a fairly long time-lag of close to three decades. In the subsequent three decades, Kerala registered a growth rate close to the national average. Correspondingly, the second period also witnessed an impressive progress in several of the crucial human development indicators for children, women and men. In fact, the achievements are clearly much above the national average as well as that of South Asia and eminently comparable to the average in the East and South Asian developing countries. Comparison in per income (in PPP dollars) is also commendable although some of the countries that have similar human development record as Kerala have already reached much higher levels of per capita income (see Table 8.1).

Our analysis of the six decades of Kerala's development trajectory brings out the secular increase in several human development indicators. In some respects, the progress made has been faster than earlier periods belying the hypothesis of a 'limit to Kerala Model of Development'. Economic growth picked up from 1987 onwards has also showed an acceleration in recent times (period 4). In several respects of human development, the gap between Kerala and all-India has increased.

The Importance of Initial Conditions

The CDS (1975) study had indeed highlighted some of the historically favourable factors in Kerala's ability to pursue a pattern of development that privileged distributional issues for reducing poverty and enhancing human development over growth per se issues. Two notable realms of initial favourable conditions that contributed to the characterization of the Kerala Model of Development were public policies on health and education. But studies have shown that these public policies were not autonomous decisions of ruling regimes but rather the pressures generated from the society, especially those deprived classes and segments, for a life of dignity (see Kabir and Krishnan 1996; Nair 1981). In that sense, one may characterize it as public action broadly understood. However, the dynamic element that resulted in favourable public action of a decisive kind after the formation of the state of Kerala was the creation of what we have earlier called 'effective political demand', that is, demands backed up by collective and organized power (see Kannan and Pillai 2004). In that sense, the historical path that emerged during the late nineteenth century and expanded continuously through various public demands seems to have exerted a powerful influence in Kerala's developmental journey since 1956 by privileging human and social development over expanding the directly productive activities.

This notion of historical path is often characterized as historical path dependency in economic development literature to emphasize the influence of the past over the present (see Liebowitz and Margolis 2000, for a survey). In most cases, it is used in a negative sense – as a barrier to change as in the case of technology, location-specific industrialization and so on. We would however like to use this notion of historical path dependency in a neutral sense that could result in either a positive outcome or a less positive or even negative one. In the case of Kerala's long-term development, the historical path created since the late nineteenth century took a powerful turn from the hitherto feudal social and economic systems and induced the development of a social consciousness for greater dignity and rights made possible by the freedom movement that also gave birth to a radical political movement for human emancipation. Therefore, the initial conditions that the new State of Kerala found itself as a single political-cum-unit within the larger constitutional democracy of India within a federal-type governance set-up was favourable to the expansion and strengthening of the human development administrative agenda of the Kerala society and for public measures to reduce absolute poverty.

However, the initial conditions arising out of a new historical path was not a favourable one for the development of the directly productive sectors of the Kerala economy that could perhaps explain its later stagnation or slow development and consequent lack of employment creation. We shall deal with this later.

The favourable initial conditions were mostly in the realm of education and health that were visible as early as the turn of the twentieth century that ultimately led to a demographic transition at least three decades earlier than all India. During the freedom movement, the space for public action expanded that got a further boost through the emergence of a radical political movement. It led to public action in demanding land reforms, minimum wages and better conditions of work, public distribution system and so on. The notion of public action was wide enough also to include social action in spreading literacy, formation of sociocultural organizations and flourishing of art and literature. All these also led to an expansion, through public action, to the realm of what may be called 'social economy' as well as the cultural realm that is an extension of the realm of human development. The social economy in Kerala is a dense one consisting of charitable societies and trusts running a large number of educational, health care, cultural and women's collectives providing employment and income. Cooperatives are another set of social economy institutions functioning in the areas of consumer marketing, dairying and primary agricultural credit and other activities. A number of trade union organizations also run cooperative institutions as well as workers welfare funds providing employment and income. As part of the national statistical system's initiative (see GoI 2012), a survey conducted in 2008, revealed that the total number of non-profit institutions (those registered under Charitable Societies and Trusts Acts) in Kerala was estimated at 3.26 lakhs as against 31.74 lakhs in India that gives a share of 10.3 per cent for Kerala as against its population share of 2.6. The total paid employment was estimated at 16.3 lakhs that works out close to 13 per cent of the total workforce in Kerala in 2011. The total number of volunteers was estimated at 91.28 lakhs that works out to 35 per cent of the adult population in Kerala as against 8 per cent for all-India. The last two indicators may be taken to represent the density of voluntarism in a society. The activities of all these organizations are overwhelmingly focused on the service sector of the economy with a heavy emphasis on educational activities broadly defined.

The unfavourable as well as the not-so-favourable initial conditions are partly structural and institutional. The agroclimatic conditions were more suitable for cash crops which had a steady demand and this resulted in limited land availability for food crops. However, the absence of any major drought or famine also resulted in a population growth that saw Kerala as the state with the highest density of population[4] resulting in a low land–man ratio, high incidence of landless labour in a context of highly unequal distribution of assets

Table 8.2 *Percentage of working age population (WAP) with educational levels secondary and above, and graduate and above, Kerala and India*

	WAP (15–59 years)				Younger Age (20–39 years)			
	Secondary and above		Graduate and above		Secondary and above		Graduate and above	
	India	Kerala	India	Kerala	India	Kerala	India	Kerala
1983 Men	16.3	18.5	3.8	2.9	20.0	19.7	5.5	4.0
2018 Men	45.8	56.6	13.2	12.6*	52.0	67.8	35.9	19.2*
1983 Women	6.6	15.4	1.4	2.3	8.0	16.4	2.3	3.7
2018 Women	34.0	58.4	10.1	17.5	39.6	73.4	15.5	29.0

Note: * The much lower percentage of younger men in this graduate and above group is largely due to the disproportionate emigration of young higher-educated men to the countries in the Gulf for employment.
Source: Calculated from unit level data from the 38th NSS Round for 1983 and from PLFS for 2017–18.

Table 8.3 *Kerala's human development record compared with selected Asian countries*

HDI rank	Country	Annual growth in HDI	HDI value	Life expectancy at birth	Mean years of schooling*	GNI per Capita (PPP$)	GNI/ Capita rank minus HDI rank
		1990–2017	2017	2017	2017	2011	2017
57	Malaysia	0.72	0.802	75.5	10.2	26,107	- 11
58	Kerala	0.64	0.779	75.3	9.3	11,153	- 19
76	Sri Lanka	0.69	0.770	75.5	10.9	11,326	19
83	Thailand	0.66	0.755	75.5	7.6	15,516	- 7
86	China	0.62	0.752	76.4	7.8	15,270	- 9
113	Philippines	0.64	0.699	69.2	9.3	9,154	- 7
116	Indonesia	0.61	0.694	69.4	8.0	10,846	- 19
116	Vietnam	0.58	0.694	76.5	8.0	5,859	14
130	India	0.52	0.640	68.8	6.4	6,353	- 5
136	Bangladesh	0.49	0.608	72.8	5.8	3,677	9
148	Myanmar	0.46	0.578	66.7	4.9	5,567	- 15
149	Nepal	0.47	0.574	70.6	4.9	2,471	12
150	Pakistan	0.47	0.562	66.6	5.2	5,311	- 14
	East A&P	0.62	0.733	74.7	7.9	13,688	
	South Asia	0.53	0.638	69.3	6.4	6,473	

Notes: East A&P stand for East Asia and Pacific; *for those 25 years and above; for India, the value for life expectancy at birth is 69.4 as per Registrar General of Census Operations for 2014–18; for Kerala, the HDI value is taken from: Sub-national HDI – Area Data Base – Global Data Lab) Downloaded; mean years of schooling computed from PLFS unit level data for 2017–18; GNI for Kerala represents net state domestic product.
Source: All data except for Kerala from UNDP (2018), *Human Development Indices and Indicators: 2018 Statistical Update*, New York.

and a hierarchical caste system resulting in widespread poverty, low level of industrialization and so on. As if to offset such crucial barriers, we also find a somewhat expanded service sector as in the case of financial intermediaries – banking density – and the existence of cooperative organizations mostly in service provisioning. A powerful outcome of these unfavourable initial conditions is the high incidence of unemployment.

In sum, what we would like to emphasize is that, first, the unified state of Kerala enjoyed an initial advantage in human development that was the result of a historical path created since the last quarter of the nineteenth century. There has not been any interruption in this process of human development both during low as well as high growth phases of the economy. A particularly striking feature of this is the remarkable progress attained by women in the sphere of education as borne by the figures given in Table 8.2.

Such a process of uninterrupted human development and later high economic growth has catapulted Kerala into one of the front-ranking places among a set of select developing countries in South, South-East and East Asia. In fact, Kerala's performance is well above the regional averages for South and South-East Asia (see Table 8.3).

High Growth in HD and the Delayed High EG

From the point of the emergence of a virtuous cycle of growth led by high HD, the results presented in Table 8.4 is of crucial importance. First and foremost, the poor aggregate growth performance of Kerala during the first phase gave way to a high performance during the second phase.

The second phase trend growth has been two-and-a-half times that of the first phase. In comparison, the national growth performance was much better than Kerala – higher by 26 per cent in the first phase but only 9 per cent in the second phase. It is during this second phase that Kerala reduced its gap

Table 8.4 *Annual growth rate* in NSDP at 1999–2000 prices for Kerala and all-India*

Particulars	First phase (FP)			Second phase (SP)			Whole period
	P1	P2	FP	P3	P4	SP	
1. Kerala economy (NSDP)	3.9	1.5	2.7	6.0	6.8	6.7	4.8
2. Kerala economy (MSI)	3.9	1.9	2.8	6.2	6.9	6.8	4.8
3. Indian economy	3.0	3.9	3.4	5.5	7.6	7.3	5.9
4. Population growth (K)	2.3	1.5	1.9	0.9	0.5	0.7	1.2
5. Population growth (I)	2.3	2.2	2.2	2.0	1.5	1.7	1.9
6. Per capita growth (K) (NSDP)	1.6	0.0	0.8	5.1	6.3	6.0	3.6
7. Per capita growth (K) (MSI)	1.2	0.7	1.1	6.2	5.8	6.2	3.8
8. Per capita growth (I)	0.7	1.7	1.2	3.5	6.1	5.6	4.0
9. PC growth (K) assuming IPG	1.6	- 0.7	0.5	4.0	5.3	5.0	2.9
10. Demographic dividend-1 of Kerala (6–9)	0.0	- 0.7	0.3	1.1	1.0	1.0	0.7
11. Demographic dividend-2 of Kerala (7–9)	- 0.4	0.0	0.6	2.2	0.5	1.2	0.9

Notes: P1=1960–61 to 1974–75; P2=1975–76 to 1986–87; P3=1987–88 to 1998–99; P4=1999–2000 to 2019–20. *Kinked exponential growth rates were calculated to reflect the trend in growth performance; per cap growth = total economy growth minus population growth; P1, P2, P3, and P4 represent the four periods; FP and SP stand for first and second phase, respectively; IPG stands for India's population growth.

Source: Author's computation based on data from Government of India, *National Accounts Statistics*, Central Statistical Organisation, New Delhi, various issues.

in growth performance with that of the national economy. For the 60-year-period as a whole, the national aggregate growth performance was still higher than that of Kerala by a margin of 22 per cent.

However, the story changes when the per capita growth in income is examined which is more appropriate because it neutralizes the population growth rate. Kerala's per capita income growth was only two-fifths of that of all-India during the first phase but gets reversed during the second phase due, obviously, to the demographic transition that was in the making during the first phase.[5] However, for the whole period of six decades, the per capita trend growth in income in Kerala was almost close to all-India but still short by a small margin. There is no doubt that despite a lower aggregate growth even in the second phase, Kerala managed to maintain a marginally higher per capita growth due to its early demographic transition. In that sense, the demographic transition's contribution to Kerala's economic growth works out to one percentage point during the second phase. This is derived by the difference between the actual per capita growth and a per capita growth assuming a population growth as that of all-India. We call this demographic dividend-1 (DD-1) and the figures based on MSI are called DD-2. The results based on the MSI data show that the DD-2 is double that of DD-1 during the first phase and in excess of 0.2 percentage point for the second phase at 1.2 per cent per annum. For the 60-year period DD-2 is also higher by 0.2 percentage points higher than that of DD-1 at 0.9 per cent per annum.

The conclusion that we draw from this exercise is that the demographic transition in Kerala helped it to achieve an additional growth rate of 0.7 per cent per annum for a period of six decades. But a more accurate representation would be the difference between the first and second phases. If the contribution of the demographic transition in the first phase was 0.3 to 0.6 per cent per annum, it jumped to 1.0 per cent to 1.2 per cent for the second phase (see Table 8.4, rows 10 and 11). Given the fact that the demographic transition was an outcome of early policies and investment in human development this quantification could be reckoned as the direct contribution of human development to economic growth in a relative sense, that is, in comparison with the all-India situation.

High HD and High EG but a Lopsided Growth Performance

A sector-wise examination of the growth performance reveals (see Table 8.5) a very poor performance of the primary sector that employed a majority of workers till the end of period 3 (1999–2000).[6] The long-term growth of this sector of agriculture and related activities has been less than 1 per cent per annum that was only one-third of the growth rate for all-India. The performance of the secondary sector was not a disappointing one even in the first phase in comparison to all-India and its performance in the second phase almost matched that of all-India with an impressive trend growth rate.

Of course, the secondary sector consists of manufacturing as well as construction and it was the latter that was responsible for the dynamism especially in the second phase. For the whole period of the 60 years, Kerala's construction sector growth rate was one-and-a-half times higher than the all-India average whereas manufacturing sector growth rate was lower by almost one-third (see Table A1). The overall secondary and service sector growth for the whole period in Kerala is however only marginally lower than that of all-India. However, it increased by a 0.3 per cent point when remittances are included. As in the case of all-India, it was the service sector that led the overall impressive growth performance. Even the low growth performance in the first phase was supported by relatively higher growth in the service sector. We have added the annual remittances to the service sector (shown with * in Table 8.5) for Kerala and it shows a higher long-term trend growth compared to all India for the second phase. To the extent that remittances are driven by emigration that in turn is an outcome of initial high human development, the contribution of remittances to growth has largely taken place through the service sector in Kerala that has now considerably expanded its share in both state income and employment.

When the sectoral growth rates show such a wide disparity, it also indicates that the high growth sectors are increasing their share in the total income. This in turn would indicate which sector is leading the overall growth in the economy. This sectoral contribution to growth (see Table 8.6) shows the steady emergence of the service sector as the leading sector in both the Kerala as well as the Indian economies. What is significant to note is the faster growth in the share of the service sector in Kerala; from contributing 42 per cent of the overall growth in period 1 to 78 per cent in period 4. To begin with, the contribution of the service sector to growth in the Indian economy in period 1 was higher (51 per cent) than Kerala (42 per cent); that changed in period 4 to 65 per cent and 78 per cent, respectively. That the contribution of the service sector in both the national economy of India and the regional economy of Kerala was higher than the two material-producing sectors is an interesting contemporary historical datum that needs to be kept in mind.

The growth performance of Kerala and all-India in terms of a detailed (15-sector) format presented in Table A1 (see Appendix) show the sub-sectors in the service economy leading the overall high growth performance. Construction and Mining & Quarrying are the only two sub-sectors in the non-service sector with high growth especially in Kerala. By arranging the growth performance in a descending order for Kerala, one gets an idea of the relative importance of the sub-sectors in the Kerala as well as the all-India economies.

Though the human development trajectory of Kerala's development seems to have a historical path dependency via education and health care and the importance of trade, commerce and banking arising out of the export-orientation of commercial crops, the service sector was not a dominant sector in Kerala's economy until the mid-1980s. But its steady rise powered by

Table 8.5 *Sectoral growth rates for Kerala based on MSI, 1999–2000 prices*

Sector	Region	P1	P2	FP	P3	P4	SP	WP
Primary	Kerala	2.91	- 0.98	0.84	4.14	- 0.77	0.21	0.98
	India	1.94	2.43	2.28	3.53	3.03	2.95	2.81
Secondary	Kerala	4.72	4.95	4.94	4.01	6.83	6.16	5.33
	India	4.02	4.01	3.95	5.76	7.15	6.55	5.44
Tertiary	Kerala*	5.07	2.32	4.56	8.47	8.09	7.85	6.6
	India	4.16	5.55	4.54	6.82	8.24	7.84	6.53
All sectors	Kerala	3.90	1.85	2.75	6.18	6.92	6.80	4.80
	India	3.03	3.87	3.41	5.53	7.62	7.25	5.49

Notes: P1=1960–61 to 1974–75; P2=1975–76 to 1986–87; P3=1987–88 to 1998–99; P4=1999–2000 to 2019–20. P1 to P4 refer to periods; period years as shown in Table 8.3; FP and SP stand for first and second phases; WP stands for the whole period; * denotes that the entire international remittance amount is treated as part of tertiary sector income.
Source: Author's computation based on data from Government of India, *National Accounts Statistics*, Central Statistical Organisation, New Delhi, various issues; also see Kannan and Hari 2020.

Table 8.6 *Sectoral growth contribution to overall growth in Kerala based on MSI, 1999–2000 prices*

Sector	Region	P1	P2	FP	P3	P4	SP	WP
Primary	Kerala	39.0	- 21.1	14.2	21.3	- 1.6	0.7	6.7
	India	28.3	23.4	27.4	20.2	8.8	10.3	15.1
Secondary	Kerala	19.2	59.0	32.9	15.2	23.2	21.4	23.8
	India	21.0	16.2	21.2	24.5	22.1	25.1	24.0
Tertiary	Kerala*	41.8	62.2	52.9	63.5	78.4	77.9	69.5
	India	50.7	60.4	51.4	55.3	69.1	64.6	60.9
All sectors	Kerala	100.0	100.0	100.0	100.0	100.0	100.0	100.0
	India	100.0	100.0	100.0	100.0	100.0	100.0	100.0

Notes: P1=1960–61 to 1974–75; P2=1975–76 to 1986–87; P3=1987–88 to 1998–99; P4=1999–2000 to 2019–20. P1 to P4 refer to periods; period years as shown in Table 8.3; FP and SP stand for the first and second phases; WP stands for the whole period; Kerala* indicates that all remittances are accounted for in the service sector; two points on sectoral growth calculation: (1) share of each sector is based on geometric mean of the annual shares of sectoral NDP to total NDP at current prices for a given period; (2) overall growth rate is based on kinked-exponential growth in MSI/NDP at constant prices.
Source: Author's computation based on data from Government of India, *National Accounts Statistics*, Central Statistical Organisation, New Delhi, various issues; also see Kannan and Hari 2020.

remittances and the resultant expansion of the non-traded sector (construction, banking and finance, trade, transport, education and health) was such that it became the major sector by the end of the twentieth century coinciding with the beginning of our period 4 in the second phase (51 and 57 per cent in 1998–99 and 1999–2000, respectively). Within the next twenty years, that is, by the end of period 4 (2019–20) the service sector became the dominant sector accounting for 77 per cent of the state income and a little more than half of total employment. Such a lopsidedness in sectoral growth performance is also visible for all-India but it is lower than Kerala mainly because of the relatively higher share of agriculture in national income (see Table 8.7).

This is the result of a significant share of job loss in the agriculture sector that was not fully compensated by the non-agriculture sector especially for women, as we shall see later. In terms of chronology, Kerala's structural transformation, that is, a major share of both income and employment in the non-agricultural sector, started around the late 1980s and continued uninterruptedly such that the share of agriculture in state income and employment reduced from 30 and 51 per cent, respectively in 1987 to 4 and 18 per cent, respectively in 2020. This covers exactly our second phase characterized by high growth of the Kerala economy. Such an early structural transformation may also be attributed to an early process of human development that continued steadily over the whole period of six decades. For men, the structural transformation in employment started as early as 1983 whereas for women it started from the beginning of the twenty-first century.[7]

The results of sectoral contribution to overall growth – where three-fourths of the overall growth is contributed by the tertiary (service) sector throws important questions of the nature of economic development both nationally and regionally. The increasing contribution of the service sector is not on the shoulders of an already developed primary and secondary sectors as in the case of economically developed countries. The low level of productivity in the primary and secondary sectors are matters of concern since it also contributes to intersectoral inequality that spills over to group inequality as between those dependent on the low productivity sectors and high productivity sectors. In the case of Kerala, the fact that close to 77 per cent of the overall economic growth is driven by the dynamism in the service sector has led to a lopsided growth and consequently development. Of course, as noted in the Kerala Human Development Report (KHDR) 2006, service sector is not an unproductive sector as a whole and there are important segments including the newly emergent ones such as information and communication technology that are as valuable as the goods producing sectors. However, state policy has to balance the sectoral growth rates by focusing on productivity-enhancing interventions in the primary and secondary sectors.

Table 8.7 *Structural transformation of the Kerala and all-India economy: sectoral percentage shares of the total income and employment*

Sector	Indicator	1983–84		1987–88		1999–2000		2019–20	
		Kerala	India	Kerala	India	Kerala	India	Kerala	India
Primary	Income	35.3	34.2	30.4	28.7	17.4	22.2	4.4	9.9
	Employment	57.3	67.9	50.6	64.2	37.3	60.2	18.4	43.9
Secondary	Income	21.1	17.4	21.5	17.3	16.4	16.0	18.2	14.9
	Employment	19.1	13.5	20.4	15.6	25.6	15.7	30.7	23.8
Tertiary	Income	53.6	48.4	48.0	54.0	66.2	61.8	77.4	75.2
	Employment	23.6	18.6	29.0	20.2	37.1	24.1	50.9	32.2

Note: Income data in 1999–2000 prices; NSDP data from CSO's National Accounts Statistics, various issues; Kerala's state income data including remittances attributed to the service sector. *Source*: Employment data calculated from unit level data from NSS 38th (1983), 43rd (1987) and 55th Rounds (1999–2000); data for 2019–20 calculated from PLFS data.

Failures Amidst Success

Spectacular Failure 1: Educated Unemployed and Gender Unfreedom

One of the unresolved challenges of Kerala's development experience is the persistence of the problem of unemployment, especially educated unemployment. Earlier in the 1970s, it was a case of both educated and non-educated unemployment that later emerged as one of predominantly educated unemployment. For adult educated men, part of this problem was overcome by large-scale international migration in search of jobs focused on the Gulf countries in the Middle East. Given the continuing and increasing aspiration for higher education, this problem has now become one of high unemployment and underutilization of labour among educated women. This we flag as a spectacular failure of the Kerala 'model' of development.

The conventional wisdom in development economics is that as an economy goes through a growth phase, it helps in the growth of employment, since growth is usually driven by the relatively higher productivity in the non-agricultural sector, especially manufacturing. This in turn also results in the growth of employment outside agriculture. Since manufacturing is associated with a higher labour ratio with respect to output as well as higher backward and forward linkages than other sectors, it is the expansion of this sector that economists advocate both for growth and employment.

We have seen that the growth performance of the Kerala economy in the second phase spanning over more than three decades was as impressive as the all-India economy, if not better. However, this did not result in the creation of additional jobs to absorb the surplus labour, that was getting increasingly educated, in the economy. The all-India scenario is also not dissimilar points to the overall national context in which growth was not adequately accompanied by net employment creation. In the case of Kerala, a good part of the problem of unemployment and underemployment of men was taken care of by the window of opportunity provided by international labour migration. When the growth is not accompanied by employment creation to the expected extent, what it suggests is that the employment content of growth is declining which is measured by employment elasticity. This could be due to technological or organizational changes taking place in the low-productivity sector or new investments in the less employment-generating high-productivity sector. We have presented in Table 8.8 the employment elasticity in the Kerala economy including the sector-wise figures. The period is limited by the availability of detailed data but covers a time-span of thirty-six years including periods 3 and 4 that comes under our second phase.

The results show that the declining employment elasticity in the Kerala economy has reached a stage (period 4) when it is a case of jobless growth. But the devil is in the detail. It is entirely contributed by the exodus of labour from the agricultural sector right through the whole time-span. While the secondary and tertiary sectors also show a decline, they continue to have positive employment growth. It is quite plausible that the phase of labour exodus from agriculture is over – only 19 per cent of the workforce in 2019 – and the future trajectory of employment elasticity could be a brighter one if new investments are attracted to the non-agricultural sector.

Since net employment creation is the result of a process of employment creation and destruction, we are in a position to measure the magnitude of employment lost and gained. Table 8.12 presents the relevant figures. The labour exodus from agriculture is to the tune of 32 lakh while the new employment created is to the tune of 56 lakh thus giving a net employment creation of 24 lakh during a period of thirty-six years. However, what is critical is the rise in net unemployment (except for a brief period, period 3) but a much more increase in the net unutilized labour that is equivalent to three-and-a-half times the net increase during 1983 to 1987. This translates itself to a low rate of actual growth in employment compared to the warranted growth dictated by growth in labour force (i.e., employed + unemployed in the sense of those seeking work), let alone the growth in labour underutilization (i.e., those who are out of workforce and in education, LU for short).

But what is significant from the point of what we call 'spectacular failure' of the KMD is the gender dimension in the net employment creation out of the dynamic process of employment creation and destruction. Our exercise reported in Table 8.12 show that despite a significant decline in employment in the primary sector to the tune of 13 lakh between 1983 and 2019, men stood to gain due to new employment creation to the tune of 39 lakh thus securing a net employment of close to 26 lakh. This, along with their migration to outside the state to the rest of India and abroad (mainly to the Gulf countries), men have brought down their additional unemployment to an insignificant level.

But the experience of women is exactly an opposite one. Their loss

Table 8.8 *Employment elasticity in the Kerala economy*

Sector	1983 to 1987	1987 to 1999–2000	1999–2000 to 2018–19
Primary	- 2.86	- 0.55	- 7.43
Secondary	0.74	0.50	0.23
Tertiary	1.11	0.27	0.24
Economy	0.31	0.11	0.06

Note: * including remittances.
Sources: Computer from unit level data from NSS 38th, 43rd, 55th Rounds and PLFS 2018–19.

in agricultural employment exceeds their gain in employment in the non-agricultural sector. This means a decline in the total number of workers during the last thirty-six years despite an increase in average level of education, reduction in fertility rate and a consequent increase in the working age population. This has increased the additional entrants to the pool of unemployed. But more significantly, those who are out of work and education (called LU) increased four times from 12 to 48 lakhs. It is this category that includes not only the unemployed (in the sense of seeking work) but also those who could be characterized as discouraged workers indicated by an increase in the share of LU in the working age population. These 48 lakhs are an addition to the stock in 1983. This has increased for men too but at 9 lakhs this is only less than one-fifth of the women in this category.

From an earlier analysis of the employment trends in the Indian economy, we had found (Kannan and Raveendran 2019) that those who lost jobs in recent times is the category of the less educated in both men and women, that is, those with less than secondary level of education. It is therefore pertinent to check this dimension with reference to Kerala. Our findings reported in Table 8.9 show that the entire net loss in employment between 1983 and 2019 fell on those with less than secondary level of education. Of course, women's loss is double that of men. What is significant is that those educated (secondary and above) has not experienced a net loss of employment in any of the broad three sectors or the detailed single-digit industrial classification (see Table 8.9). This should be a matter of concern as those with low education are usually found in poorer households. It is also possible that with a generalized upward shift in education even those who are currently engaged in manual work have a higher level of education, and that they stand to gain whenever new employment opportunities come up even in the casual labour market.

It is in this complex process of large-scale loss of employment in agriculture and new employment creation in non-agricultural activities where those with low education have been left out that Kerala has experienced a structural transformation. For the economy as a whole, 1993–94 seems to be

Table 8.9 *Net gain/loss in employment differentiated by gender and major activity sector between 1983 and 2019*, in lakhs

Sector	Secondary and above		Below secondary	
	Male	Female	Male	Female
Agriculture	4.011	0.233	- 16.675	- 19.027
Mining & quarrying	0.062	0.023	- 0.457	- 0.237
Primary sector	4.073	0.256	- 17.132	- 19.264
Manufacturing	3.945	2.141	- 3.092	- 3.416
Electricity, GWS	0.428	0.033	- 0.062	0.000
Construction	6.776	1.032	8.747	4.277
Secondary sector	11.148	3.205	5.593	0.862
Trade	7.615	2.248	0.962	0.504
Hotels & rest	0.774	0.159	0.777	0.368
Transport, St &C	3.626	0.229	2.439	- 0.163
Financial intermediation	1.237	1.328	0.019	0.590
Real estate, renting & BS	2.436	1.072	0.567	0.113
Public admin & defence	0.541	0.790	- 0.493	0.030
Education	0.239	2.896	- 0.190	0.320
Health & social work	0.737	1.760	- 0.069	0.340
Other CS & PS	1.020	0.354	- 0.148	0.059
Private HHs with EPs	0.020	0.102	- 0.213	0.000
Tertiary sector	18.246	10.935	3.651	2.162
Total gain/loss	33.467	14.397	- 7.887	- 16.240

Note: GWS means Gas and Water Supply; St & C means Storage and Communications; BS means Business Services; CS & PS means Community Services and Personal Services; Eps means Employed Persons; 2019 represents 2018–19.
Source: Computed from unit level data from NSS 38th Round and PLFS 2018–19.

the turning point when the employment in the primary sector fell below 50 per cent of the total employment. In income terms, the share of the primary sector had already fallen below the 50 per cent mark as early as the 1970s. Such a structural transformation took place in the national economy after a gap of close to two decades, that is, around 2011–12.

The sum and substance of a jobless growth process in Kerala, as it has later been in India, is a kind of structural transformation whereby both income and employment in the primary sector has become insignificant. In income terms, it is just 4 per cent in 2019–20, whereas employment is just 20 per cent. From a future growth and development point of view, it will be the non-agricultural sector that will drive the process. However, the challenging issue here is the low share of manufacturing in both income and employment. Such a scenario becomes all the more challenging when we view the sectoral product per worker ratio in the three sectors. The exodus of workers from agriculture is not due to an increase in labour productivity but a loss of labour-intensive rice cultivation that got substituted by annual and perennial cash crops. But later, the gross cropped area has also started declining as a result of the high pressure or demand for land for non-agricultural activities especially building construction.

It is in such a context of the lacklustre performance of the material-producing sectors accompanied by a jobless growth of the overall economy that international migration emerged as a safety valve for the increasingly educated adult male members of the society. That option was not available to the adult women members in general. In fact, the required mobility to secure employment even within the state is limited by social norms, institutions and concerns about security. These kinds of 'unfreedom' define women's ability to find employment that further gets exasperated due to low demand. This has led to two kinds of situations. One, a greater incidence of unemployment in the official sense (i.e., those seeking work as a percentage of the labour force) but more importantly a higher incidence of underutilized labour (i.e., those seeking and not seeking work but out of education). It is this dimension of the inability of the state of Kerala to utilize the educated labour of women that we highlight as a spectacular failure.

Despite equipping themselves with higher levels of education and low and early completion of fertility (before 30 years of age), women find themselves trapped in households without opportunities for gainful and decent employment. If we take the working age group of 15–59 years, the progression in acquiring higher educational capabilities is truly remarkable both for men and women. In 1983, only 18 per cent of men and 15 per cent of women had an educational attainment of at least secondary level (10 years or above). By 2017–18, it increased to 57 per cent for men and 58 per cent for women. The percentage of men with at least a graduate level education was a mere 3 per cent in 1983 that increased to 19 per cent by 2017–18, while for women, it increased from 2 to 29 per cent. The lower rate of increase in graduate level and above for men could be a statistical one because of the disproportionate number of educated young men emigrating to other parts of India and abroad (mostly to Gulf countries) in search of jobs and better opportunities.

However, the outcome in the labour market is quite contrary to this progression in one of the important dimensions of human development. If we restrict ourselves to the official categorization of unemployment rate (i.e., those who are seeking work as a percentage of the labour force), we get only a partial picture. Even here, as shown in Table 8.10, the unemployment problem is one of educated unemployment with women registering twice the rate in 1980s and then three times the rate as compared to men. We think that it is necessary to recognize that a considerable proportion of women are outside

Table 8.10 *Unemployment rate – those seeking work by age, gender and education*

Category	Gender	Kerala				All-India
		1983	1987	1999–2000	2018–19	2018–19
Working age group 15–59 years						
All	Male	8.2	10.6	6.7	5.8	6.5
	Female	9.3	18.9	16.6	19.2	5.6
Secondary &	Male	16.7	19.2	11.4	10.0	10.1
above	Female	30.3	42.0	37.1	29.3	17.1
Below	Male	6.7	8.3	4.6	1.0	3.9
secondary	Female	5.7	12.1	6.2	1.7	8.8
Younger generation WAP 20–39 years (men only)						
All	Male	8.0	11.2	7.9	11.1	8.8
	Female	10.3	23.3	23.2	37.1	9.3
Secondary &	Male	18.2	22.5	15.1	15.3	13.6
above	Female	32.5	45.5	44.2	44.0	21.8
Below	Male	5.8	7.7	3.8	2.3	4.2
secondary	Female	5.2	14.5	7.8	5.0	1.2

Source: Computed from unit level data from NSS 38th, 43rd, 55th Rounds and PLFS 2018–19.

the category of seeking work while they are out of work and in education. We therefore took an accounting framework of activities of those belonging to the working age group of 15–59 in terms of workers, those engaged in education and those other than workers and in education. In addition, we separately examined the problem among the younger generation by focusing on the age group 20–39 years. Following our earlier finding (Kannan and Raveendran 2019) that the labour market in India is sharply divided, among others, by education, we take the two broad categories of (1) less educated (below secondary level); and (2) higher educated (secondary and above level). The results are presented in Table 8.11.

By measuring both unemployment (in the sense of 'seeking work') and underutilization of labour (seeking plus not seeking work but out of work and education) we get a fairly good picture of the intensity of the problem. Men have considerably low levels of both the official measure of unemployment as well as the underutilization of labour. Moreover, men in the less educated category have less 'unemployment' as well as LU as compared to the educated category. This is an interesting development for a number of reasons. First, the secular rise in educational attainment reduced the supply of labour for casual work that is wholly associated with informal work status. In fact, the shortage of men for manual casual work has led to a situation of in-migration of workers from other states in India especially from the central and eastern regions. Second, men in informal work in the informal sector is well organized in Kerala and has secured a higher wage rate than their counterparts in other states in India as well as women in Kerala. Third, they are also covered by collective care arrangements under occupation-specific 'welfare funds' (see Kannan 2002). Fourth, an overwhelming proportion of emigrants – especially to Gulf countries – are men earlier in the lower education category but now in the higher one. None of these favourable factors are available for women and hence less-educated women experience higher unemployment as well as LU for reasons of lack of adequate employment in the local economy as well as a lower mobility across space than men. It is this situation that we characterize as 'unfreedom' for women in Kerala despite their best efforts in enhancing educational and other dimensions of human capability to participate in the workforce. What is also important here is the rising aspirations among women for regular employment as opposed to casual employment.

Spectacular Failure 2: Declining Tax Collection Efficiency and the Resultant Loss of Public Resources

The assumption of a responsive state to public action focused on human development in a long-term historical perspective is not difficult to recognize but no such public action was visible in the sphere of management of public finance. This could be due to the fact that people do not experience, generally speaking, public finance as a factor in their day-to-day lives unlike education, health care and social security.

The continuing bane of unemployment, increasingly manifesting as educated unemployment, has to be characterized as a spectacular failure of Kerala's development experience that is at the root of its trapping as a low-income middle economy by global standards. While public action in the form of protests by the unemployed has been a frequent phenomenon, the state government has not yet been able to devise an action plan that focuses on the creation of decent employment. Its ability to attract private investment has been a very limited one especially in the manufacturing sector. Much of the private investment that has taken place in Kerala has been an outcome of the uninterrupted flow of outside money in the form of international remittances and its multiplier effects in consumption and in selected areas of investment as in the case of construction, food-processing, tourism, higher education and tertiary-level treatment hospitals. It has also attracted investments in quick-money ventures notably in the entertainment sector such as film production, TV channels, and retail trading shops in gold jewellery and white goods.

While these new investments have created new jobs, we have seen that more jobs were destroyed in the agricultural sector as well as in some others. The regional state's ability to create decent jobs for the educated unemployed got stymied mainly due to the lack of financial resources to strengthen infra-

Table 8.11 *Rate of labour underutilization (LU) as per cent of working age population by age, gender and education*

| Category | Gender | Kerala | | | | All-India |
		1983	1987	1999–2000	2018–19	2018–19
Working age group 15–59 years						
All	Male	10.5	12.2	9.2	8.3	8.2
	Female	45.5	53.4	56.3	57.2	62.4
Secondary &	Male	13.5	15.9	10.2	9.7	9.2
above	Female	34.3	45.8	51.6	52.8	55.8
Below	Male	9.8	11.1	8.7	6.4	7.3
secondary	Female	47.6	55.4	58.5	63.8	66.1
Younger generation WAP 20–39 years (men only)						
All	Male	9.7	12.9	9.4	12.0	9.8
	Female	50.2	59.6	62.3	66.0	69.6
Secondary &	Male	17.0	20.7	14.2	14.3	12.5
above	Female	45.2	57.0	62.8	64.2	66.7
Below	Male	7.9	10.1	6.4	6.3	6.8
secondary	Female	51.2	60.3	62.9	71.6	71.7

Note: Figures in brackets show the LU for women. WAP = Working Age Population 15 to 59 years; Sec+ means those with secondary or higher levels of education; <Sec means those with less than secondary level of education.
Source: Computed from unit level data from the NSS 38th, 43rd and 55th Rounds, and from PLFS 2018–19.

structure, start new ventures in the public sector and/or strengthen the existing ones as well as embark on public employment programmes that could be linked to the creation of new capital, especially in strengthening and improving the natural capital via land and water management, investment in renewable energy, waste management and so on. All these call for an efficient management of public finances to husband as much public financial resources as feasible. In this crucial sphere of governance, the regional state of Kerala has been a failure which we call 'spectacular' given the potential created by early investment in human development and its consequent unintended benefit in the form of a steady flow of outside money for four decades that varied between 10 per cent and 24 per cent of the state income.

What is the nature of this 'spectacular failure'? In the Indian federal context, there are two major sources of revenue for a regional state. One is called 'own revenue' sources given the state's constitutional authority to tax defined goods and services, and the other 'central transfers' that come from the national state through allocations determined by a Finance Commission and what is called transfers to implement 'centrally-sponsored schemes'. The second source is beyond the control of the regional state and partly determined by a constitutional procedure and partly by the discretion of the national government. Therefore, the focus has to be in raising own revenue and efficient management of its expenses.

Given the availability of data on basic indicators of public finance, we have calculated the own revenue of the state as a percentage of the state income. Since the official statistics on state income excludes the outside money in the form of international remittances, we have, as pointed out earlier, a revised state income called modified state income. What we find is a declining trend in the share of own revenue as a percentage of state income since 1987–88 that corresponds to the beginning of the second phase of aggregate growth that in fact witnessed an acceleration. The question then is how does one measure the tax collection efficiency or lack of it? One way is to find out the tax potential and compare it with the actual collection to find out the gap. But this requires estimates of tax potential which could have been best carried out by the government but not undertaken so far. In the absence of such a direct estimate, we opt for a second-best solution. We look at the long-term performance in tax collection and identify the period when it had reported the maximum collection as a share of state income (see Figure 8.2). In our four-period classification scheme, we find period 2 as the best period when the tax collection efficiency was the maximum with an annual average of 12.4 per cent of the state income (or 11.3 per cent of the MSI). We then find out the gap between this historically given efficient average with that of the annual average of actual collection for the other three periods. This gap is the loss of own revenue (calculated as OR Loss1 and OR Loss 2).

The loss of own revenue as a percentage of state income for the four periods are given in Table 8.12. The revenue lost is 2.6 to 2.8 times of the average annual capital expenditure for the 60-year period as a whole. To put it differently, if the own revenue had been collected to the extent of the average for period 2, the capital expenditure of the Government of Kerala could have been raised by 2.6 to 2.8 times the actual expenditure.

Spectacular Failure 3: Public Sector as a Drain on Public Resources

While the spectacular failure in collecting fully or even substantially the state government revenue is a sign of the failure of the sub-national state in sharp contrast to its shining performance in advancing human development, there is another failure, which also we would like to call as spectacular. This is due to the inability of the public sector enterprises (PSEs), taken as a group, owned by the state government. Most of the enterprises were created after the formation of the state of Kerala numbering between 90 and 100 by the beginning of period 3. Since annual data on the performance of all the enterprises as a group as well as individually are available only since the early 1980s,

Figure 8.2 *Own revenue as percentage of NSDP and MSI of Kerala*

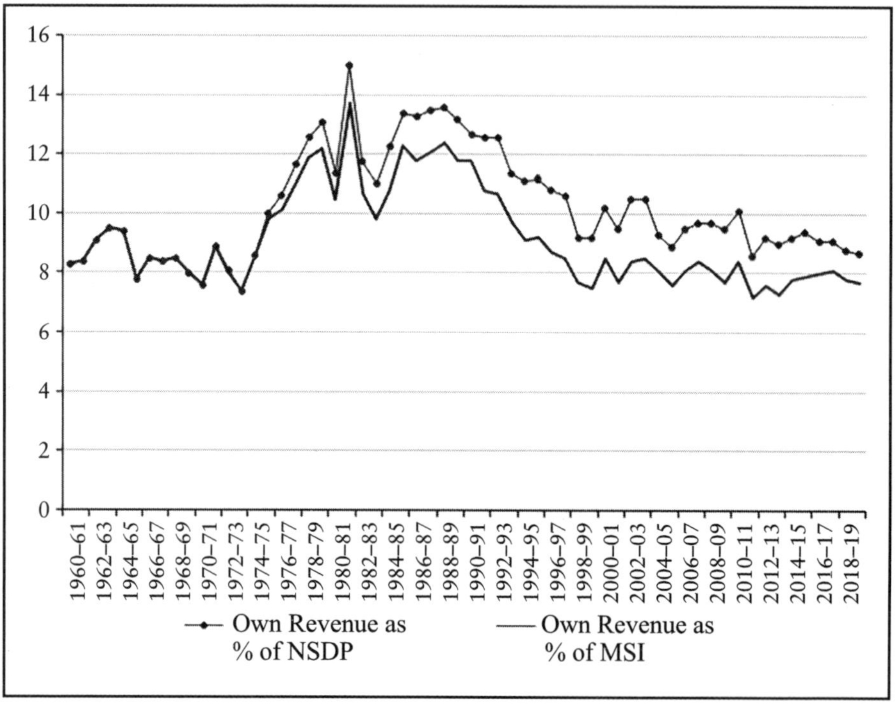

Source: Government of Kerala, *Budget in Brief*, Trivandrum, various issues.

Table 8.12 *Measurement of loss of revenue measure as per cent of state income (NSDP and MSI) and its equivalence in terms of debt and capital expenditure*

	Period 1	Period 2	First Phase	Period 3	Period 4	Second Phase	Whole Period
Own revenue as % of NSDP	8.3	12.4	11.5	11.1	9.2	9.3	9.3
Own revenue as % of MSI	8.3	11.3	10.7	9.3	7.8	7.9	7.9
Own rev lost as % of NSDP	4.1	0.0	0.9	1.3	3.2	3.1	3.1
Own rev lost as % of MSI	3.0	0.0	0.6	2.0	3.5	3.4	3.4
Capital expenditure as % of MSI	1.95	2.77	2.60	1.31	1.07	1.09	1.10
Capital expenditure as % of NSDP	1.96	3.03	2.79	1.57	1.26	1.28	1.29

Note: MSI = NSDP plus remittance from abroad.
Source: Computed from *Budget in Brief*, various issues.

our analysis refers to the thirty-one years covering the second phase of the KMD. The results of our analysis of the available data on the performance of state-owned public enterprises in Kerala should shock anyone given the stellar performance of the state in advancing human development that later led to a process of accelerated economic growth lasting for a period of thirty-one years!

Kerala has been in the lead during the 1970s and 80s in creating a number of public sector enterprises arising out of a political realization that without industrialization it can neither create what we now call decent employment to the increasing educated youth nor increase the per capita income of the people. However, management inefficiency compounded by short-term demands of politically powerful trade unions resulted in net loss year after year. Table 8.13 shows that the number of loss-making enterprises often outnumbered the number of profit-making companies. The result has been a net loss for the public sector enterprises as a whole for the two periods that come under our second phase of the KMD that was characterized by an impressive aggregate growth performance. This we call Loss-1. This comes to 2.9 per cent of the state's own revenue for the second phase as a whole; starting with a positive contribution of 6.4 per cent in equivalence to the state's own revenue but ending in 2018–19 with a negative contribution of 3.3 per cent in equivalence.

Given the scarcity of capital resources, it is perfectly reasonable to expect a profit that is at the least equal to its opportunity cost that may be taken as the average cost of capital when the public sector enterprises seek loans from the market. We have therefore taken expected profit at 10 per cent of the capital invested and added the actual losses. Viewed from this angle of adding the opportunity cost of capital, the losses incurred by the PSEs as a group works out to 14.3 per cent of the state's own revenue during the second phase and 16 per cent in equivalence to the state's own revenue starting with a negative contribution equal to 9.3 per cent in 1987–88 and reaching a high of 27.1 per cent in 1999–2000 and then declining to 11.8 per cent in 2018–19.

An argument often put forward in defence of the loss-making character of the PSEs is in terms of their employment. However, employment in the public sector enterprises, as shown above, never exceeded 2 per cent of the total employment in the Kerala economy; moreover, there has been a net decline in absolute employment arising out of the closure or liquidation of many public sector enterprises.[8]

Often loss-making PSEs are defended either because they contribute to the government towards taxes and/or fulfilling stated social objectives. The first argument of taxes does not hold much water because this would have accrued to the government even if the enterprise was not in the public domain. As for the second reasoning, it is often used as an alibi for hiding the deep internal inefficiencies and political interferences that seem to have acquired an institutional character. All these flies in the face of the larger

Table 8.13 *Summary results of the performance of public sector enterprises in Kerala*

	Period 3		Period 4	
Indicator	1987–88	1998–99	1999–00	2018–19
Total number of PSEs	93	106	107	98
Number of Loss-making PSEs	54	51	56	43
Total employment/annum (in 000s)	14.0	12.6	12.6	12.3
Loss 1 as % of state's own revenue*	6.4	(-)1.6	(-)2.4	(-)3.3
Loss 2 as % of state's own revenue*	(-)9.3	(-)24.9	(-)27.1	(-)11.8
Profit/Loss per employee in companies (Rs)	4,688	1,553	5662	(-)52,712
Loss per employee in statutory boards (Rs)	3,021	(-)15,546	(-)29,085	(-)317,007
Loss in companies (Rs in million)	340.6	102.4	369.4	(-)494.5
Loss in statutory boards (Rs in million)	456.5	(-)934.9	(-)1761.6	(-)15781.9
Total loss in all PSEs (Rs in million)	797.1	(-)832.5	(-)1392.2	(-)16276.4

Note: * actual monetary loss; ** actual monetary loss plus an assumed return of 10 per cent over invested capital.
Source: Government of Kerala, *A Review of Public Sector Enterprises in Kerala* (annual publication prepared by the Centre for Management Development), Bureau of Public Enterprises, various issues.

developmental objective of state-led industrialization in a poor developing economy. That is, efficient running of the PSEs is meant not only to generate current employment but also enable the generation of future employment through cycles of reinvestment of surplus generated over a period of time. It is this larger developmental dimension that is conspicuous by its absence when the PSEs as a group become a drain on public resources. In fact, the loss on a per capita employment basis represent the cost borne by the public at large (through budgetary support) to maintain current employment in the PSEs. With a revenue deficit year after year, the state government can ill afford such drain on its scarce public resources.

There have been several attempts made by successive regimes in Kerala to improve the functioning of the loss-making PSEs so as to stop, at the least, the drain on public resources. On the basis of a number of committees and task groups, several reforms were also carried out. While isolated cases of success have been there, the overall performance seems to have worsened in terms of the actual losses incurred (see Figure 8.3). The dramatic increase in losses is associated with the years 2012 to 2016 followed by a small recovery in the subsequent two years. Politically speaking, a UDF government was in power during the years of the dramatic increase in losses and the subsequent revival could only bring back the losses to the previous 2016 level. This spectacular nature of the failure of the public sector in the context of the 'virtuous cycle of growth' of the KMD is something that calls for detailed investigation. We think the reasons for this failure have to be sought, as in the case of the earlier examples of failures, on the failure of the state-system (successive governments) in ensuring efficient running of the PSEs. Such a failure is in sharp contrast to the success in human development realms where public action has been the principal reason. Such a notion of public action is absent in the case of the functioning of economic institutions because the people at large do not face the adverse consequences on a day-to-day basis unlike in the case of human development and social security. This state failure in delivering directly productive economic services as opposed to the success in delivery of social services arising from public action has now become a characteristic feature of the KMD.

At a disaggregated level, we find that the losses are largely contributed by major public sector enterprises that are/were statutory boards. Of the nine statutory boards, three of them contributed to around 80 per cent of the total accumulated losses of Rs 26,274 crores (as of March 2019) with the Kerala State Road Transport Corporation occupying the first place (Rs 10,955 crores). The change of the status of the two statutory boards (transport corporation and electricity board) does not seem to have changed their loss-making character in a significant way. In fact, the situation seems to have worsened in the case of the biggest loss-contributing entity, the road transport corporation.

Spectacular Failure 4: Loss of Public Resources through Exorbitant Time and Cost Overruns in Economic Infrastructure

While the first failure in effectively checking the unemployment problem, especially among the expanding segment of educated persons, is rooted in both internal and external factors, the remaining three that we highlight here are mainly due to factors internal to the governance by the successive state governments. In this section, what we therefore highlight is the loss of precious time as well as scarce resources in the implementation of public projects. We take two examples to highlight the issue. One relates to the time and cost overruns in the completion of electricity generation projects and the other relates to that of irrigation projects. Needless to say, both are critical factors in the journey of economic development of poor agrarian economies.

A detailed study on the issue of time and cost overruns of twenty power projects in Kerala was undertaken by this author jointly with another colleague as part of a larger study on the power sector (Kannan and Pillai

Figure 8.3 *Net profit/loss of all public sector enterprises in Kerala,* Rs crore

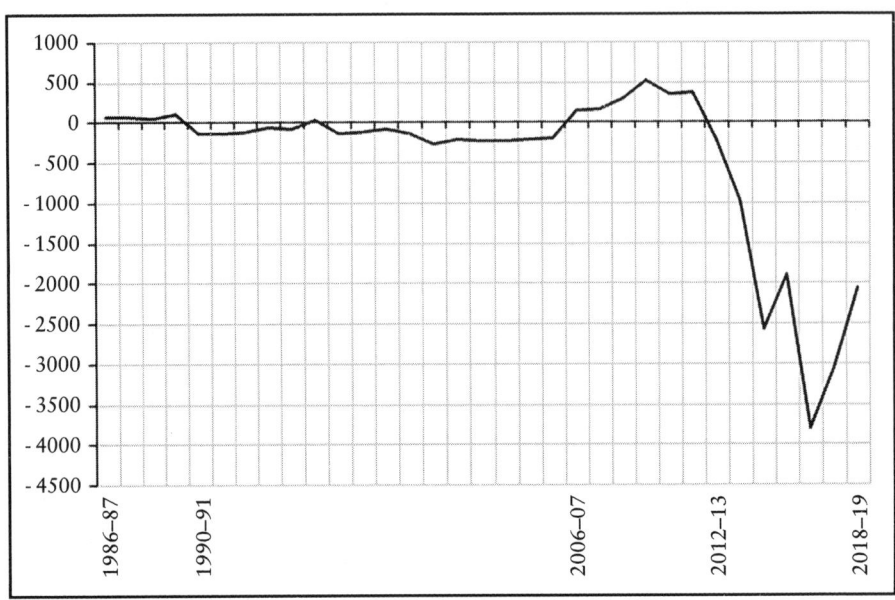

Source: Centre for Management Development, *A Review of Public Enterprises in Kerala,* annual series, Trivandrum, various issues.

2002).[9] The findings of this study are shocking given the repeated experiences of time and cost overruns. The causes for delays in time as well as several upward revisions in capital costs are several, such as changes in the technical design and feasibility reports, inadequate or incomplete data and unrealistic assumptions in original cost estimates, inefficient management, inadequate scientific and technical investigations (such as in geological characteristics) before preparing the feasibility reports, vague and ambiguous specifications and conditions of contract, sluggish decision-making at various stages of construction, unavailability of materials or lack of transport, infighting and ego clashes among different groups of the bureaucracy and technocracy of Kerala State Electricity Board, unwanted transfer of planning and supervisory staff between projects during their construction, lack of vision about the power needs of the state, labour disputes, court interventions for aggrieved contractors and so on. These causes have been analysed in some detail along with an enquiry into the political economy issues.[10]

The study covered all the power projects completed up to the year 2000. There were wide variations in both time and cost over-runs. Time over-runs ranged from 63 per cent (i.e., 0.63 times) to 500 per cent (i.e., 5 times) whereas cost over-runs ranged from 64 per cent (i.e., 0.64 times) to 777 per cent (i.e., 7.8 times). The project-wise details are given in Table 8.14.

How much is the total loss due to cost overruns? This is a question an informed citizen is likely to ask. There are technical issues in aggregating the cost overruns since the projects are undertaken in different time-points with a positive rate of inflation that makes aggregation at historical prices less meaningful.[11] The projects also vary in their size as well. By sticking to the historical cost data, the average To (i.e., number of years originally estimated) for the twenty projects works out to 5.15, whereas the Ta (i.e., number of years actually taken for completion) works out to 13.5 thus giving a ratio of 2.62. Similarly, the ratio between Co (i.e., capital cost originally estimated) and Ca (i.e., capital cost actually incurred) works out to 3.78. That is to say the cost overrun was 278 per cent higher than the original estimate whereas the time overrun was 162 per cent higher than what was originally planned. We have calculated the capital cost per unit of energy potential and computed a capital waste factor in terms of how many say, Kakkad-type projects could have been built with this excess capital cost incurred. Alternatively, one may also see this as resources lost for capital formation in general.

In order to capture the combined effect of time as well as capital cost overruns, we had also calculated what may be called a Resource (Time-cum-Cost) Waste Factor (RWF) (see Morris 1990) that is obtained as the difference between the actual capital × time (Ca×Ta) and the originally planned capital × time (Co×To) measure as a percentage of the latter (where Ca×Ta are the actual and originally planned estimates of capital cost and Ta and To are the corresponding period of commissioning. In estimating this resource waste factor, the implicit assumption is that the expenditure over the course of the project takes place uniformly. Thus, in the case of the Kakkad project, the originally planned resources were Rs 18.6 crore × 10 years = Rs 186 crore years, but the actual resources spent were Rs 153.52 crore × 23 years = Rs 33,530.96 crore years, resulting in an RWF of Rs 3,344.96 crore years or 1,798 per cent (i.e., 17.98 times or close to 18 times) of the originally planned resources. Thus, it shows that as a result of time and cost overruns, this project has eaten up about 18 times more capital and time combined than what was originally planned. In other words, if the Kakkad project had been completed as planned, the Kerala State Electricity Board could have built another eighteen Kakkad-type projects!

Apart from the loss of time as well as financial resources in capital construction, there is an additional loss in the form of loss of revenue from the electricity during the time overrun period. This has been calculated for the period 1983–84 to 1999–2000 that works out to Rs 886.3 crore as on 2000 or Rs 52 crore per year in terms of historical prices. This of course is derived by adding up the losses over the years. Viewed from present value terms, this does not take into account the inflation and consequent depreciation in the value of the rupee.

Irrigation Projects

Another mind-blowing example of exorbitant loss of public resources is the case of constructing and commissioning irrigation projects. Unlike the power projects, the accessibility and availability of relevant statistics have been quite challenging. For example, while data on the start of the projects have been reported, very little is known about the original estimate of the year of completion so as to find out the time overruns. The final costs of completed projects are often not available. What is available is the latest revision of capital costs that could be lower than the actual final cost. The data are supplied by the Department of Irrigation to the State Planning Board who is charged with preparing the annual Economic Review of the Kerala economy for tabling in the State Legislative Assembly before the presentation of the annual budget.

Table 8.15 gives a picture of the time and cost overruns of the completed projects for which we have managed to get the required data. The worst performer is the Kallada Project (in Kollam district) with the highest time overrun as well as the cost overrun. It took forty-three years to complete instead of the originally estimated six years that meant a time overrun of 617 per cent or 6.17 times. The cost overrun has been truly mind blowing that involved 5359 per cent or 53.6 times more expenditure than what was originally estimated. Next in line in terms of cost overrun is the Muvattupuzha irrigation project with almost 45 times more expenditure than the original estimate and a time overrun 557 per cent or 5.57 times more than the original estimate. What is interesting to note is that projects started before the formation of the State of Kerala reported a shorter time as well as cost overrun than those started after. What is expected is that the experience in implementing projects in earlier times becomes lessons for drawing up projects such that the newer project reports are in a position to anticipate various hurdles especially of a technical and organisational nature that are internal to the implementing agency.

There is then the question of inflation due to price rise in materials as well as wages and salaries. These are supposed to be factored in the original estimates but then limited to the estimated time for completion of the project. When time delays occur, then the subsequent revision of the capital costs will have to factor the inflation rate. Further time delays then call for further revisions both due to inflation as well as other factors. Therefore, the inefficiency in completing the projects on time leads to further cost escalation. Correcting technical and organizational flaws further contributes to this cycle of revisions in the capital costs of the projects.

Then there is the serious issue of projects that are reported as 'ongoing' or suspended or abandoned due to a variety of reasons. The capital expenditure on these projects is now in the category of 'sunk costs or costs that cannot be recovered' in any way and hence a waste of resources. The reasons for such enormous delays in completing such critical infrastructure projects might have been subjected to internal scrutiny although not many published materials are

Table 8.14 *Cost escalation of power projects, as in 1999–2000*

Name of the project	Time overrun		Cost overrun	
	To/Ta (Years)	(%)	Co/Ca (Rs Million)	(%)
Idukki II Stage	8/16	100	31.68/68.00	114.65
8/16	100	316.8/680.0	114.65	268.54
Idukki III Stage	6/16	167	41.0/151.1	268.54
Sabarigiri Augmentation	8/18	125	12.8/112.2	776.56
Idamalayar	8/17	113	234.0/900.3	284.74
Kakkad	10/23	130	186.0/1535.2	725.38
Kallada	8/19	63	118.0/180.2	52.71
Lower Periyar	8/14	75	884.3/3530.4	299.23
Malampuzha	2/12	500	29.5/67.9	130.17
Madupetty	2/11	450	29.2/47.8	63.7
Malankara	3/12	300	78.0/411.3	427.31
Chimony	3/12	300	31.4/42.5	35.35*
Peppara	3/9	200	39.2/68.1	73.72
Pooyankutty	6/21	250	2500.0/8200.0	228
Azhutha Diversion	5/11	120	29.0/144.6	398.62
Poringalkuth LB Extn	4/10	150	90.2/427.3	373.73
Kuttiar Diversion	3/12	300	21.4/94.9	343.46
Vadakkepuzha Diversn	3/12	300	13.1/51.4	292.37
Vazhikkadavu Diversion	4/12	200	18.6/159.9	759.68
Kuttiady Tail Race	4/11	175	39.7/129.2	225.44
Kuttiady Extension	4/8	100	307.3/1980.0	544.32

Note: To = Number of years originally estimated; Ta = number of years actually taken for completion; Co = Original capital cost; Ca = actual capital cost incurred.
Source: Kannan and Pillai (2002, p. 186).

available. However, in recent times there has been an attempt to examine the cases of four large irrigation projects that have been in the 'ongoing' category for far too long. A committee was formed in 2017 and a report was submitted in 2018. It would appear that as a result of the recommendations one of the projects was completed by 2020 but the fate of the other three are not known. The noteworthy findings of this committee include the brazen technical flaws in the design and construction of such seemingly not-so-complex systems such as canals (see Government of Kerala 2018).[12] It also points to the poor technical capability of the concerned government department.

Table 8.15 *Time and cost overruns of irrigation projects*

Sl. No.	Name of irrigation projects	Year of start/finish	T(o)/T(a)	Time overrun (%)	C(o) (Rs million)	C(a) (Rs million)	Cost overrun (%)	Resource waste factor (%)
1	2	3	4	5	6	7	8	9
1	Kallada	1961/2004	6/43	617	132.8	7250.0	5359	391
2	Muvattupuzha	1974/2020	7/46	557	208.6	9580.0	4493	302
3	Kanjirapuzha	1961/1995	7/34	386	36.5	1400.0	3736	186
4	Pazhassi	1961/1992	6/31	417	44.2	1500.0	3294	175
5	Chitturpuzha	1963/1992	4/29	625	10.6	257.0	2325	175
6	Periyar Valley	1956/1994	6/38	533	34.8	835.1	2300	152
7	Pampa	1961/1992	6/31	417	38.3	58.98	1440	80
8	Chamravattom	1985/2012	7/27	286	8.70	1200.0	1279	53
9	Kurtiady	1962/1993	6/31	417	49.6	507.3	923	53
10	Chimoni-Mupli	1976/1996	6/20	233	63.3@	595.8	841	31
11	Mangalam (PC1956)	1953/1966	4/13	225	4.5	10.6	136	8
12	Neyyar (PC1959)	1951/1973	4/14	250	24.8	46.1	86	7
13	Malampuzha (PC1955)	1949/1966	6/17	183	38.8	58.0	49	4
14	Walayar (PC1956)	1953/1964	4/11	175	9.2	13.2	43	4
15	Thrithala	1998/2007	4/9	125	190.0	266.0	40	3

Note: PC stands for 'partially commissioned'; C(o) and T(o) indicate original cost and time estimate, respectively, while C(a) and T(a) indicate actual cost and time taken to complete the project, respectively. Some of the final cost figures are the latest available revised cost estimates and hence the possibility of the actual cost could be higher. Resource Waste Factor = [C(o)xT(o)/C(a)xT(a)] x 100.

Source: Computed from data from *Economic Review*, Kerala State Planning Board, Government of Kerala, various issues.

In sum, the record of project implementation in major and medium irrigation and power projects in Kerala is one of huge loss of public resources as well as loss of time. Such excess expenditure became an additional burden on the state budget adding to both revenue and fiscal deficits from 1983–84 to the present without any break. This has also led to reduced capacity for new capital expenditure including in these two critical sectors.

In Lieu of a Conclusion

Our assessment of the performance of the Kerala economy since its formation covering a period of six decades show a mixed performance in the background of the famed 'model' called the Kerala Model of Development. What we have been able to bring out is the positive link between investment and attainment in human development that ultimately resulted in high economic growth despite the poor performance of the material-producing sectors of agriculture and industry. We have quantified the contribution of human development that worked through a demographic transition and found that it is a significant one. Further, it is the same human development that worked through emigration of large numbers of people, predominantly men, that ignited and sustained a high economic growth in the second phase through remittances. This has resulted in further lopsidedness of the Kerala economy dominated by the service sector.

While such a growth process also resulted in a structural transformation of Kerala's economy, much earlier than the national economy, it has resulted in heightening the intersectoral inequality. However, despite the impressive increase in per capita income along with a high human development record, Kerala continues to face the problem of unemployment with a significant underutilization of labour of both educated and less educated working age population. The main burden of educated unemployment has fallen on women adding to the problem of gender unfreedom. The state's ability to tackle this basic problem of unemployment and enhance capital expenditure has been thwarted by a declining tax collection efficiency leading to borrowing to meet both revenue and capital account deficits. Besides, the state has also failed to generate any surplus from its public sector enterprises and thus having to carry the burden of its losses. In addition, the state's record in project implementation has been a deeply disappointing one leading to waste of scarce public resources as well as time.

The overall picture emerging from this assessment is therefore one of spectacular successes in human development along with a spectacular failure on the part of the state government in managing the public finance and delivering economic services.

The time has therefore come for Kerala to re-examine its governance system and rise to the challenges posed by a society with high human development that has consequentially generated high aspirations especially among the younger generation. Two external shocks have also made it imperative for a re-examination. One is the great flood of 2018 and its devastating impact on its ecology calling for a conscious adoption of environmental sustainability as a framework for future development (see Kannan 2019). The other is the Covid-19 induced pandemic that has affected the country as a whole – along with many other countries – forcing a rethink on the neoliberal economic policies of unfettered liberalization and globalization. In that sense, the 60-year period that we have examined here with two major phases has come to an end with a structural break in the growth process. For the first time since 1987, Kerala registered a negative economic growth (of more than 7 per cent) in 2020–21. It has also thrown up new challenges in terms of coping with the emerging market for work and employment. It will also strengthen the need for a reformed or new perspective on the future course of development.

The examination and analysis of the six decades of the KMD here is anchored to an economic development perspective. Given the highly contested nature of political parties and their broad grouping into two coalitions so far, a political economy understanding of Kerala's development is likely to be of value in its future possibilities of correcting the lopsidedness in its current developmental scenario. This is a task that I intend to pay attention to in my future research work.

This essay was originally published under the same title in *The Indian Economic Journal*, vol. 71, no. 1, 2023, pp. 120–51.

Appendix

Table A1 *Sub-sectoral growth rate in Kerala, based on NSDP 1999–2000 prices*

Sector	Kerala/India	P1 1960–61 to 1974–75	P2 1975–76 to 1986–87	Phase1 1960–61 to 1986–87	P3 1987–88 to 1998–99	P4 1999–2000 to 2019–20	Phase2 1987–88 to 2019–20	WP 1960–61 to 2019–20
Real estate, OD & BS	Kerala	-0.81	5.00	9.64	3.35	8.62	15.92	8.16
	India	2.63	7.57	4.10	7.15	8.47	7.55	6.81
Transport, S & C	Kerala	6.05	-1.01	4.00	4.63	10.54	10.79	7.44
	India	5.72	5.87	5.99	6.24	9.81	9.68	7.66
Banking and insurance	Kerala	7.75	9.05	9.01	5.73	9.97	9.08	8.58
	India	5.54	7.86	6.82	9.56	10.26	9.79	8.85
Construction	Kerala	4.81	16.08	8.55	5.25	7.35	8.17	8.14
	India	7.25	5.58	6.57	8.29	6.52	6.57	5.06
Mining and quarrying	Kerala	-5.60	2.54	1.45	4.57	4.25	7.86	6.44
	India	2.91	5.37	3.88	4.78	3.29	3.75	4.46
Trade, H & R	Kerala	5.41	3.56	4.00	11.38	5.95	7.80	6.20
	India	3.83	4.85	4.36	7.2	8.15	7.95	6.31
Electricity, G & WS	Kerala	9.16	-10.87	3.81	11.19	2.14	5.93	4.60
	India	3.95	2.85	3.38	4.88	4.48	5.34	6.43
Public administration	Kerala	4.99	5.32	4.75	2.29	6.19	5.89	5.55
	India	6.35	5.79	5.63	4.75	6.18	6.11	5.88

Table A1 (continued)

Sector	Kerala/India	P1 1960–61 to 1974–75	P2 1975–76 to 1986–87	Phase1 1960–61 to 1986–87	P3 1987–88 to 1998–99	P4 1999–2000 to 2019–20	Phase2 1987–88 to 2019–20	WP 1960–61 to 2019–20
Forestry and logging	Kerala	4.07	1.71	5.63	19.64	0.94	4.78	4.61
	India	2.67	- 0.20	0.44	0.77	2.25	1.85	0.77
Manufacturing	Kerala	4.45	1.13	3.43	2.71	6.30	3.84	3.47
	India	3.89	4.45	4.09	5.90	7.72	6.65	5.40
Fishing	Kerala	13.51	-4.02	6.11	7.75	0.27	1.73	4.04
	India	3.85	3.37	3.88	6.02	4.75	4.06	4.09
Agriculture	Kerala	2.58	-0.92	0.50	3.09	- 0.14	- 0.04	0.45
	India	1.79	2.59	2.33	3.47	3.03	2.92	2.8
Other services	Kerala	5.13	- 1.51	2.74	4.47	7.45	7.54	4.78
	India	3.41	3.83	3.25	6.1	6.65	6.57	5.24

Note: P1 to P4 indicate periods; WP stands for whole period; OD & BS means Ownership of Dwellings and Business Services; G & WS means Gas and Water Supply; S & C means Storage and Communication; H & R means Hotels and Restaurants.
Source: Government of India, National Accounts Statistics, Central Statistical Organisation, New Delhi, various issues.

Notes

[1] K.N. Raj, the principal author of the CDS 1975 study and his co-authors did not certainly use the term 'model' in this first study. Amartya Sen explicitly stated that he does not think there is a Kerala Model; he preferred to call it the 'Kerala Way to Development'. 'I have, of course, said there is a lot to learn from Kerala, but not about the "Kerala model",' Sen said, while speaking at the launch of the International Centre for Human Development, a collaboration of the United Nations Development Programme (UNDP) and Shimla-based Indian Institute of Advanced Studies in Delhi (*Business Standard*, 29 January 2013).

[2] An early critique of the KMD was from the perspective of the labouring poor in agriculture (see Mencher 1980) followed by another about the same group but from a gender point of view (den Uyl 1995). My own work on the women workers in the cashew industry found that their work conditions and wages were no better than that of women agricultural labourers (Kannan 1980). The work of Anna Lindberg (2001) on cashew workers from a class, caste and gender points of view is also a powerful critique. Despite progress in many dimensions of human development, women in general and those belonging to the depressed social groups such as Scheduled Castes and Tribes in particular, have trailed behind other social groups although their position is better than their counterparts in most, if not all, other parts of India. The need to look beyond the gender-parity in basic developmental indicators was highlighted by Kodoth and Epen (2005). From the perspective of the KMD, the condition of fish workers was characterized as an 'outlier' by Kurien (2000). On the whole there were strong proponents (see, for example, the articles in Parayil, ed. [2000]) and severe critiques of the KMD (see, for example, Tharamangalam [1998] and the discussion that followed). From the point of sustainability of the KMD from a public finance point of view, George (1993) talked about the 'limits to Kerala Model of Development'. For a succinct discussion of Kerala's historical experience in development, CDS (2006). On the question of the political economy of labour and development in Kerala, see Kannan (1998).

[3] In 2018, people from households in Kerala classified as non-resident Keralites were found to be 21.22 lakhs of which 89 per cent were located in the Gulf countries. It worked out to 10.3 per cent of Kerala's working age population (15–59 years).

[4] In 1961, Kerala's population density was 429 as against 132 for India. At the time of Kerala's turnaround in growth in 1987, population density reached 707 as against 235 for all-India. Although population has stabilized in Kerala, the estimated population density in 2020 is 892 as against 408 for all-India.

[5] Kerala attained a total fertility ratio of 2 by 1990 compared to the all-India ratio of 4. See Zachariah *et al.* (1994).

[6] This poor growth performance of the primary sector, especially agriculture, has a long record (see, for example, Kannan & Pushpangadan, 1988, 1990), although the value-based land productivity levels are high comparable to Punjab and Haryana due to the cultivation of a variety of high-value cash crops (see Kannan 2011).

[7] The share of male workers in the primary sector in 1983 was 51 per cent as against 67 per cent for female workers. The latter's share in the primary sector employed declined to 49 per cent in 1999–2000 indicating that structural transformation covered the women workers as well.

[8] As of 2018–19, twenty PSEs were either closed down, liquidated or transferred/merged with other enterprises. Fifteen of them were closed down and assets were transferred to public agencies for other activities.

[9] See Chapter 5 of Kannan and Pillai (2002). Also see Pillai and Kannan (2002).

[10] See Chapter 10 in Kannan and Pillai (2002).

[11] A cash flow of capital expenditure is hard to get from published documents except some information on revised cost estimates for some years.

[12] In a rare move to examine the status of long-pending irrigation projects with considerable time and cost overruns, the State Planning Board constituted a Technical

Committee on the Ongoing Major and Medium Irrigation Projects in Kerala on 16 May 2017. Its report was submitted on 9 August 2008. The committee focused mainly on the inordinate delay in the completion of four major projects that were still in the process of construction varying from thirty-six to forty-three years as on 2017. Only one project, the Muvattupuzha Irrigation Project which started in 1974, is reported to be completed arising out of the recommendations of this committee. Although the report has not delved into all the details of the sources and forces that are responsible for the massive delays, it is worth reading to understand some of the technical and institutional aspects of delays in project implementation. In its concluding chapter, the committee stated: 'In all the projects we examined, one general drawback noticed was the poor quality of technical investigations that preceded the preparation of project proposals. These drawbacks were visible to us in terms of, among other things, the fixation of canal alignments and the accurate conduct of hydraulic investigations. What we need is the creation of a team/teams within the Irrigation Department that is/are professional and technically accurate in preparing designs and conducting field investigations. The existing IDRB [Irrigation Design and Research Board] has not been felt to us as such a professional and technically updated entity' (Government of Kerala 2018, p. 45).

References

Centre for Development Studies (CDS) (1975), *Poverty, Unemployment and Development Policy: A Case Study of Selected Issues with Reference to Kerala*, UN Department of Economic and Social Affairs.

———— (2006), *Human Development Report–2005: Kerala*, Kerala State Planning Board, Thiruvananthapuram.

Centre for Management Development, *A Review of Public Enterprises in Kerala*, Annual Series, Trivandrum, various issues.

den Uyl, M. (1995), *Invisible Barriers: Gender, Caste, and Kinship in a Southern Indian Village*, International Books.

George, K.K. (1993), *Limits to Kerala Model of Development: An Analysis of Fiscal Crisis and its Implications*, Centre for Development Studies, Thiruvananthapuram.

Government of India (GoI) (2012), *Non-profit Institutions in India: A Profile and Satellite Accounts in the Framework of the System of National Accounts (Including State-Wise Comparison of Profiles)*, Central Statistical Office, New Delhi.

Government of Kerala (2018), *Final Report of the Technical Committee on the Ongoing Major and Medium Irrigation Projects in Kerala*, State Planning Board, Thiruvananthapuram August.

———— *Budget in Brief*, Trivandrum, various issues.

Kabir, M. and T.N. Krishnan (1996), 'Social Intermediation and Health Change: Lessons from Kerala', in M. Das Gupta, L.C. Chen and T.N. Krishnan, eds, *Health, Poverty and Development in India*, New Delhi: Oxford University Press.

Kannan, K.P. (1980), 'Evolution of Unionisation and Changes in Labour Processes under Lower Forms of Capitalist Production: A Study of the Cashew Industry of Kerala', in A.N. Das, V. Nilakant and P.S. Dubey, eds, *The Worker and the Working Class: A Labour Studies Anthology*, Public Enterprises Centre for Continuing Education, New Delhi. (Reprinted from 'Evolution of Unionisation and Changes in Labour Processes Under Lower Forms of Capitalist Production: A Study of the Cashew Industry of Kerala', 1981, CDS working paper 128, Thiruvananthapuram).

———— (1998), 'Political Economy of Labour and Development in Kerala', *Economic and Political Weekly*, vol. 33, no. 52, pp. L61–L70.

———— (2002), 'The Welfare Fund Model of Social Security for Informal Workers: The Kerala Experience', *The Indian Journal of Labour Economics*, vol. 55, no. 2.

———— (2011), Agricultural Development in an Emerging Non-agrarian Regional Economy: Kerala's Challenges, *Economic and Political Weekly*, vol. 46, no. 9, pp. 64–70.

————— (2019), *The Great Kerala floods 2018*, in *Seminar*, no. 713, January, available at https:// www.india-seminar.com/2019/713/713_k_p_kannan.htm.

Kannan, K.P. and K.S. Hari (2020), 'Revisiting Kerala's Gulf Connection: Half a Century of Emigration, Remittances and Their Macroeconomic Impact, 1972–2020', *The Indian Journal of Labour Economics*, vol. 63, pp. 941–67, doi: https:// doi.org/10.1007/ s41027-020-00280-z.

Kannan, K.P. and N.V. Pillai (2002), *Plight of the Power Sector in India*, Centre for Development Studies, Thiruvananthapuram.

————— (2004), 'Public Action as Participatory Development: The Kerala Experience Reinterpreted', in A. Sengupta, A. Negi and M. Basu, eds, *Reflections on the Right to Development*, Centre for Development and Human Rights.

Kannan, K.P. and K. Pushpangadan (1988), 'Agricultural Stagnation in Kerala: An Exploratory Analysis', *Economic and Political Weekly*, vol. 23, no. 39, pp. A120–A128.

————— (1990), 'Dissecting Agricultural Stagnation in Kerala: An Analysis Across Crops, Seasons and Regions', *Economic and Political Weekly*, vol. 25, no. 36, pp. 1991–2004.

Kannan, K.P. and G. Raveendran (2019), 'From Jobless to Jobloss Growth: Gainers and Losers During 2012–18', *Economic and Political Weekly*, vol. 54, no. 44, pp. 38–44.

Kodoth, P. and M. Epen (2005), 'Looking Beyond Gender Party: Gender Inequities of Some Dimensions of Well-being in Kerala', *Economic and Political Weekly*, vol. 40, no. 30, pp. pp. 3278–86.

Kurien, J. (2000), *The Kerala Model: Its Central Tendency and the Outlier* (G. Parayil, Ed.). Zed Books.

Liebowitz, S., and S. Margolis (2000), *Encyclopaedia of Law and Economics*, Cheltenham, UK: Edward Elgar.

Lindberg, A. (2001), *Experience and Identity: A Historical Account of Class, Caste and Gender Among the Cashew Workers of Kerala*, Lund University, Sweden.

Mencher, J. (1980), 'The Lessons and Non-lessons of Kerala: Agricultural Labourers and Poverty', *Economic and Political Weekly*, vol. 15, nos 41/43, pp. 1781–802.

Nair, G.P.R. (1981), *Primary Education, Population Growth, and Socioeconomic Change: A Comparative Study with Particular Reference to Kerala*, New Delhi: Allied Publishers.

Parayil, G., ed. (2000), *Kerala: The Development Experience. Reflections on Sustainability and Replicability*, London: Zed Books.

Pillai, N.V. and K.P. Kannan (2002), 'Time and Cost Overruns of the Power Projects in Kerala', *Journal of Social and Economic Development*, vol. 4, no. 2, pp. 148–69.

Tharamangalam, J. (1998), 'The Perils of Social Development Without Economic Growth: The Development Debacle of Kerala, India', *Bulletin of Concerned Asian Scholars*, vol. 30, no. 1, pp. 23–24.

Zachariah, K.C., I. Rajan, P.S. Sarma, K. Navaneetham, P.S. Gopinathan Nair and U.S. Misra (1994), *Demographic Transition in Kerala in the 1980s*, Monograph Series, Centre for Development Studies, Thiruvananthapuram.

9

WTO Agreement on Agriculture

Worsening India's Agrarian Crisis

Biswajit Dhar

Introduction

During the past three decades, agricultural policies in major economies have been influenced by the Agreement on Agriculture (AoA), one of the most iniquitous agreements that the World Trade Organization (WTO) has been tasked to monitor. The Agreement was crafted essentially by the United States (US) and the European Union (EU), the two members of the WTO, having signed a series of bilateral agreements in 1992 (the 'Blair House Accords') on certain specificities regarding agricultural subsidies that were eventually included in the AoA. According to the US General Accounting Office, 'while the other major parties did not agree with some of these proposed changes, they accepted them for practical reasons – no agreement on agricultural reform would be possible without the support of the United States and the EU' (GAO 1994, p. 137).

With bilateral agreements between the US and the EU becoming integral parts of the multilateral trading system in the form of the AoA, it was hardly surprising that developing countries had begun to voice their concerns even before it was implemented. In the ministerial conference convened to formally endorse the formation of the WTO in 1994, the then Indian commerce minister, Pranab Mukherjee, voiced his concerns regarding the AoA. The minister argued that the 'agreement on agriculture will need to be refined in future so that greater liberalization can be achieved and trade-distorting practices disciplined without affecting in any way the developmental programmes and social objectives of developing countries' (The Uruguay Round 1994, p. 2). He underlined that the Government of India was 'firmly committed to protecting the interests of our farmers who constitute the country's lifeline and to the objective of ensuring food security for our people'. Although India's commerce minister had argued that the AoA needed to be refined to ensure that it did not adversely affect the development objectives of developing countries, the inequities embedded especially in the subsidies regime of the agreement have become progressively worse.

This essay examines two aspects of the subsidies discipline of the AoA, which could not only undermine India's subsidies regime but could also render ineffective the implementation of the National Food Security Act (NFSA), 2013 that promises subsidized food to nearly two-thirds of the country's population. The first section of the essay deals with India's administered price mechanism in agriculture, which is being subjected to intense scrutiny in the Committee on Agriculture (CoA) that 'oversees the implementation' of the AoA and 'provides a forum for members to raise and address related questions and concerns' (WTO 2022a). The second section explains the controversies over India's public stockholding (PSH) of foodgrains for food security purposes. Besides, supporting the implementation of the NFSA is also the backbone of the public procurement system that supports the farmers and is therefore critical to sustaining rural livelihoods. The importance of public procurement for the farming community was adequately demonstrated during the 2020–21 year-long farmers' protests against the now-withdrawn farm legislation.

India's Price Support Mechanism under Scrutiny

Over the past few years, India's farm subsidies have consistently been scrutinized by WTO members. In May 2018, the US tabled a detailed paper questioning the veracity of India's minimum support price (MSP) for rice and wheat, or market price support (MPS), according to the AoA. Subsequently, Australia asked similar questions regarding the fair and remunerative price (FRP), the minimum price that sugar mills must pay to the farmers, as well as the state advised price (SAP), which sugar mills located in the states must pay to their farmers for delivering sugarcane to the mills. In 2020, Australia, Brazil and Guatemala initiated disputes against India arguing that the FRP and the SAP were both WTO-incompatible. In order to understand the veracity of these claims, it is important to critically examine the basis of the so-called disciplines on MPS mechanisms in the AoA.

Basis for Estimating Market Price Support under AoA

For assessing the extent of the so-called market-distorting subsidies, the AoA estimates the 'aggregate measure of support' (AMS) for each member, which comprises the budgetary support provided to subsidise agriculture through input subsidies and subsidies resulting from MPS extended by the governments. During the Uruguay Round negotiations, MPS should be obtained by considering the differences between the administered prices and the 'external reference price' expressed in local currency using an average market rate of exchange (General Agreement on Tariffs and Trade [GATT], 1997, p. 3). Several members suggested that the external reference prices should be so selected to avoid the price volatility of agricultural commodities. In other words, external reference prices should be selected for only those years in which prices were relatively stable.

The then members of the European Community (EC), one of the leading protagonists of this approach for estimating subsidization through MPS, argued in favour of an 'external reference price' that 'should remain unchanged for the initial five-year period'. The group suggested that a review should be conducted during the fourth year and 'a different fixed external reference price could be envisaged' (GATT 1990, p. 58). The EC pointed out that several participants 'argued that a fixed external reference price did not by itself eliminate the issue of exchange rates and world price movements' and that while 'choosing an external reference price, it was important not to lose sight of the economic realities negotiators were trying to capture in an aggregate measurement'. In an earlier phase of the negotiations, the EC had also alluded to the fact that participating countries had argued in favour of using 'a moving average reference price instead of a fixed one, in order to take into account these economic realities' (GATT 1989a, pp. 1–2).

However, after the mid-term review of the Uruguay Round conducted between December 1988 and April 1989, the pendulum began to swing in favour of the adoption of a set of 'fixed external reference prices' with 1986–88 being suggested as the preferred reference years.[1] The die was cast in favour of this methodology when the then Director General of the GATT, Arthur Dunkel, presented the 'final global package of the results of the Uruguay Round'. This so-called 'Dunkel Draft' became the basis for the outcome of the eighth Round of the GATT negotiations, although the AoA became a reality only after the US and the newly formed EU were able to find common ground through the Blair House accords, as mentioned above.

MPS provided by WTO members to different agricultural commodities are, therefore, calculated by comparing their administered prices for a given year and fixed external reference prices (FERP), namely, the international prices existing between 1986 and 1988. The assumption was that this period provided a set of unbiased and stable sets of commodity prices, which, when used as the numeraire, provided the best estimates of price support granted by the WTO members. For calculating the total value of subsidies given to each crop, the difference between the current administered prices and the FERP is multiplied by the volume of production enjoying price support (called 'eligible production'). MPS below 10 per cent of the value of production of a crop is considered the *de minimis* level for a developing country member and is excluded from the aggregate measurement of support (AMS) provided by a member. It may be mentioned that besides the non-*de minimis* MPS, AMS also includes the budgetary outlays on input subsidies, or *non-product specific support*, provided subsidies of individual inputs for a developing country are below 10 per cent of the value of production.

The subsidy discipline of the AoA imposes an upper bound on the extent of AMS that a developing country may provide, which is 10 per cent of its value of production. Although MPS for individual crops or budgetary outlays for specific inputs can exceed the 10 per cent threshold, total AMS must always remain below the *de minimis*. However, if a developing country member did not report any AMS upon accession to the WTO, this member had to always limit its MPS for each crop to below 10 per cent of its value of production.[2] India is a case in point in this regard. India had reported that its product-specific support was Rs (-)2,44,422 million as the administered prices for fifteen of the seventeen crops receiving MPS during 1986–88 were below the FERP, and therefore India did not report any AMS during these years. Therefore, India must keep its MPS for all individual crops below the *de minimis* in order to conform to Article 7.2(b) of the AoA.

AoA's complex methodology for restricting the use of MPS is faulty on several counts, which we shall briefly discuss below.

Erroneous Methodology for Estimating Market Price Support

The methodology for estimating MPS has several limitations, a few of which are mentioned below.

The first and the most obvious fallacy in the methodology for estimating MPS is the assumption that the international prices with which the administered prices are compared represent competitive prices. It is a no-brainer that international prices during 1986–88 were significantly influenced by the subsidies provided by the advanced countries, especially the US and the then EC, the major players in the markets for several important commodities. In 1988, the US and the EC members dominated the exports of several major commodities, accounting for nearly 60 per cent of wheat and 80 per cent of maize exports.[3] The US had long dominated the global markets for cotton and had continued to do so in the late-1980s.

Proponents of using FERP as the basis for estimating MPS had emphasized that the prices in the reference period should be stable. However, international commodity prices during 1986–88 were generally volatile, and the same tendencies were witnessed in the prices of major commodities, including rice, wheat and maize.

De Gorter and Ingco (2002, p. 5) alluded to the methodological flaws in the estimation of AMS. They argued that in 'many cases, the AMS is overstated or understated, or meaningless because it is double counting support already provided by import barriers or export subsidies'. They argued that there are 'difficulties in comparing the AMS across commodities and countries because it is conflated with import barriers and export subsidy measures, and if the actual market price is not equal to the support price, inaccuracies arise'. For instance, 'if there are import barriers in place that keep domestic prices high, but there is no administered price, then no "market price support" is estimated for the AMS'.

The most significant criticism of the FERP is that it compares the international prices existing nearly four decades back with the current administered prices. By so doing, this methodology imposes a severe burden on WTO members, especially developing countries, which have been experiencing 'excessive rates of inflation'[4] since 1986–88. India, for instance, has witnessed CPI (consumer price index) inflation of close to 970 per cent during this period, thus rendering its AMS calculations quite meaningless. This is, no doubt, a strong case for amending AoA's methodology for calculating AMS so that it makes good economic sense.

Unfortunately, the agreement cannot be amended since it contains a weak provision that requires WTO members to give 'due consideration to the influence of excessive rates of inflation on the ability of any Member to abide by its domestic support commitments' (Article 18.4 of the AoA). This provision indicates that the drafters of the AoA were aware of the problems that inflation could cause while implementing the agreement (Matthews 2014, p. 15), but they opted against including provisions that result in renegotiations involving areas of the AoA, not least the domestic support provisions that were carefully crafted by the US and the EU.

These limitations of AoA's subsidies disciplines notwithstanding, India has been frequently questioned for providing MPS well beyond its entitlements. We will briefly discuss two instances when India's AMS on rice, wheat and sugarcane, have been questioned in the WTO.

Unjustified Questioning of India's Market Price Support to Rice and Wheat

In 2018, the US submitted a document to the WTO questioning the legality of MPS to wheat and rice. The US contented that the MPS of these two crops were well above the limits set by the AoA during 2010/2011–2013/2014 (WTO 2018a). The US argued on the basis of its calculations that India's MPS for rice was consistently above 70 per cent of the value of agricultural production since 2010–11, while the corresponding figures for wheat were above 60 per cent during the same period. These levels of MPS, claimed the US, were well above the 10 per cent threshold beyond which India was not allowed to provide support, according to the AoA rules.

In contrast, India's domestic support notifications and its inputs regarding the value of production of rice and wheat provided to the CoA show that the MSP provided to rice and wheat was well below the 10 per cent threshold during the same period. The MSP for rice was above 7 per cent until 2013–14 and declined to nearly 5.5 per cent in 2013–14.

It is obvious that the discrepancies between the 'US-calculated' figures and 'India's notified' figures in Tables 9.1 and 9.2 respectively are because of the differences in the currencies that have been used to present the figures. The figures presented by India in its notifications show the effect of the devalua-

Table 9.1 *India's market price support to rice and wheat*, in Indian rupees

Crops	Items	MY* 2010/11	MY 2011/12	MY 2012/13	MY 2013/14
Rice	US calculated MPS by value (` million)	11,21,561	13,65,406	16,52,817	17,80,185
	US calculated MPS as % of value of production	74.0	80.1	84.2	76.9
Wheat	US calculated MPS by value (` million)	6,18,688	7,31,486	9,04,191	9,64,973
	U.S. calculated MPS as % of value of production	60.1	60.9	68.5	65.3

Note: * marketing year.
Source: WTO (2018a).

Table 9.2 *India's market price support to rice and wheat*, in US dollars

Crops	Items	MY 2010–11	MY 2011–12	MY 2012–13	MY 2013–14
Rice	India's notified MPS by value ($ millions)	2,282.17	2,647.39	2,796.70	1,983.73
	India's notified MPS as % of value of production	7.22	7.44	7.68	5.45
Wheat	India's notified MPS by value ($ millions)	- 161.98	117.76	- 604.23	- 817.81
	India's notified MPS as % of value of production	- 0.73	0.48	- 2.50	- 3.53

Source: WTO (2018a).

tion of the Indian rupee on the estimated MPS of rice and wheat. By factoring in the devaluation of the rupee in its domestic support notifications, India was able to show that the MPS for rice and wheat as a share of their value of production were well below the 10 per cent threshold. But why is the US opposed to India's practice of notifying its domestic support figures in rupees instead of the US dollars?

The major criticism of the US against India is that at the conclusion of the Uruguay Round negotiations, India had submitted its domestic support notification indicating its MPS during 1986–88 in Indian rupees.[5] However, in its notifications after the implementation of the AoA in 1995, India has been notifying its MPS in terms of US dollars. The US contented that India should have continued to notify its actual levels of domestic support in Indian rupees as it had done in the first notification. This point may have some validity, but only from the point of view of consistency in reporting. However, this criticism lacks legal validity as the AoA does not advise/direct the WTO members about the currency in which they should be submitting their notifications.

From India's point of view, the advantages of reporting its domestic support notifications in US dollars instead of Indian rupees can clearly be understood from Tables 9.1 and 9.2. If India had continued to notify its MPS in Indian rupees, it would have long breached the *de minimis* threshold for developing countries. Consequently, India would have had to freeze its MPS, and it would have been prevented from increasing the MSPs every year.

By notifying its MPS in US dollars, India was in effect, getting partial compensation for the 'excessive inflation' it had experienced. Between 1986–88 and 2010–11 to 2013–14, the period covered in the US submission, the Indian rupee had depreciated by over 300 per cent, while India's CPI inflation was well over 600 per cent. In other words, India's MPS notifications in US dollars were under-compensating for the effects of 'excessive inflation' and are therefore leaving no scope for future increases in MPS for rice. In 2020–2021, MPS for rice had already exceeded 15 per cent of its value of production and was well above the *de minimis* level (WTO 2022b). Compensation for 'excessive inflation' while notifying MPS should, therefore, be India's major demand in the WTO.

Threat to India's Price Policy for Sugarcane

Like wheat and rice, India's sugarcane policies also came under scrutiny in 2018. A formal submission by Australia the WTO-consistency of FRP, the minimum price that sugar mills must pay sugarcane farmers, as well as the SAP, which sugar mills in the States must pay to their farmers for supplying sugarcane (WTO 2018b). In 2019, Brazil initiated a dispute against the FRP and SAP (WTO 2019) and was joined by Guatemala and Brazil. They had also characterized India's sugar export promotion measures as a violation of AoA.

The complainants argued that India can no longer provide MPS for sugarcane as it had exceeded 10 per cent of the value of cane production. Australia argued on the basis of its data shown in the Table 9.3, that the sugarcane farmers enjoyed subsidies that were 94.4 per cent of the value of production of the crop (WTO 2018b). The dispute settlement panel concurred with the views of the complainants that FRP and SAP are forms of MPS (WTO 2021). India contested the view of the Panel arguing that the AoA states that 'subsidy can only exist where there is a budgetary outlay or revenue foregone by governments or their agents', meaning thereby that governments must be involved in the payment of subsidies. India clarified that the central and state governments do not purchase sugarcane or pay FRP and SAPs to the farmers; these payments are made by the sugar mills, which are private entities.

However, the dispute settlement panel disagreed with India's argument that FRP and SAPs cannot be treated as subsidies. The panel's argued that the 'market price' of an agricultural product is the price of the product in

Table 9.3 *India's apparent market price support (MPS) for sugarcane, as estimated by Australia*

Items	2011–12	2012–13	2013–14	2014–15	2015–16	2016–17
MPS as % of value of production	77.7	77.1	94.1	94.4	99.8	94.4
MPS (millions, Rupees)	4,67,124	5,26,758	6,84,508	7,40,551	7,47,017	6,56,163
MPS (millions, USD)	9,332	9,403	11,444	11,832	11,375	9,918

Source: WTO (2018b).

the market, and 'price support' refers to the 'assistance from a government or other official body in maintaining prices at a certain level regardless of supply or demand'. Therefore, a mandatory minimum price set by the government would seem to constitute 'domestic support' to agricultural producers, even if the payment was made by sugar mills.

This conclusion arrived at by the dispute settlement panel that FRP and SAPs are forms of subsidy raises at least two questions. The first is whether the panel had an adequate understanding of raison d'etre for fixing the statutory minimum prices that the farmers receive from the sugar mills. The real reason why the central and state governments direct the sugar mills to pay the farmers is to ensure that the latter receive fair prices from the former. Thus, the intention of the central and state governments is to improve the livelihoods of the farmers who are already in considerable distress. In giving its ruling, the panel seemed to be ignorant of the reality that sugar farmers are in an adverse bargaining position vis-à-vis the sugar mills, and it is therefore imperative for the governments to step in to ensure that the farmers receive remunerative prices for sugarcane.

A second question against the panel's ruling against India can be raised from the way it had concluded that FRP and SAPs are forms of price support measures, or subsidies even when the sugar mills were making payments to the farmers for supplying sugarcane. This interpretation by the panel seems to have turned the definition of a subsidy given in the WTO Agreement on Subsidies and Countervailing Measures (ASCM) on its head. The definition of subsidies given in ASCM has three basic elements: (1) a financial contribution (2) by a government or any public body within the territory of a WTO member (3) which confers a benefit.[6] All three of these elements must be satisfied for a subsidy to exist. Therefore, when non-government entities like sugar mills pay FRP and SAPs to farmers, why did the panel stretch itself to categorize these payments as subsidies?

Constraints in Managing Public Stockholding of Foodgrains

Indian agriculture faces the most formidable challenge from the implementation of AoA rules in respect of Public Stockholding for Food Security Purposes (PSH). The AoA imposes two sets of conditions on WTO members maintaining food stocks to provide subsidized food for addressing the problem of domestic food insecurity. One, governments must build public stockholding of foodgrains by purchasing the grains at current market prices and must sell from food security stocks at the current domestic market prices. Two, when stocks of foodstuffs for food security purposes are acquired and released at administered prices, the difference between the acquisition price and the FERP must be accounted for in the AMS. In other words, procurement of foodgrains for building publicly held stocks is done at the administered prices, and is subjected to a set of rules that are similar to those for providing MPS, as discussed earlier. The provisions regarding PSH became important for India after the government began implementing the National Food Security Act (NFSA) in 2013. Having committed to provide subsidized foodgrains to almost two-thirds of the country's population, India was staring at a situation where the possibility of breaching the subsidies threshold of 10 per cent become imminent. If the government had continued to implement the NFSA despite breaching the subsidy limit, any other WTO member could have initiated a dispute against India. And, if India had lost the dispute, the distribution of subsidized foodgrains would have to be discontinued immediately.

However, in the run-up to the Bali Ministerial Conference in 2013 (WTO 2013), India accepted the so-called 'peace clause', an interim mechanism that provided a temporary reprieve from facing disputes even if its total AMS had exceeded 10 per cent of the value of production. However, the 'peace clause' proposed two binding conditions on the countries using 'public stock-holding'. First, India has to notify the WTO of the details regarding the PDS, including the quantity procured and distributed, and the quantities exported from the stockholding. The second condition was that food stocks procured under such programmes must not be used to distort trade or to adversely affect the food security of other members, in other words, India must refrain from exporting such subsidized stocks of foodgrains.

With this export restriction clause in place, it is hardly surprising that India's increasing exports of foodgrains during the past few years and the government's target to increase export volumes in the near term have attracted attention in the CoA discussions. WTO members have, in particular sought clarification, on whether the publicly held stocks with the Food Corporation of India are being used to trigger India's cereal exports. Clearly, the export restriction condition in the 'peace clause' can adversely impact India's ambitions to become a major exporter of cereals.

By Way of Conclusions

The Government of India's MPS mechanism faces formidable challenges from the subsidies' disciplines of the AoA. Over the past few years, India's price support policies have consistently been challenged by several WTO members who have argued that India has breached the threshold specified by the agreement in respect of most major crops. The implications of these challenges are to prevent the government from providing price support to the farming communities, which are vitally important for protecting rural livelihoods.

This essay argued that the methodology for estimating MPS, based on which India is being challenged, is deeply flawed. The AoA was established 'to establish a fair and market-oriented agricultural trading system', but its implementation has revealed that the agreement can only widen inequities among WTO members by increasing agrarian distress in the developing world. India is rapidly losing its flexibility to provide MPS and the government's inability to provide price support to the farmers could significantly worsen the agrarian crisis.

This essay was originally published under the same title in *The Indian Economic Journal*, vol. 71, no. 1, 2023, pp. 152–61.

Notes

[1] One of the early suggestions came from the Cairns Group (GATT 1989b, p. 6).

[2] Article 7.2(b) of the AoA.

[3] Data from FAOSTAT.

[4] In the negotiations to find a way through the logjam on the issue of PSH, the G-33, a developing-country grouping, focusing on food security and livelihood concerns, had proposed that inflation rates of 4 per cent or above should be considered as 'excessive' (ICTSD and FAO 2013, p. 2).

[5] At the end of the Uruguay Round negotiations, participating countries submitted the 'AGST Supporting Tables', which are specifically noted in the 'Schedules' containing their domestic support and export subsidy reduction commitments (WTO 2022a).

[6] Article 1.1(a)(1) of the Agreement of Subsidies and Countervailing Measures.

References

De Gorter, H. and M.D. Ingco (2002), *The AMS and Domestic Support in the WTO Trade Negotiations on Agriculture: Issues and Suggestions for New Rules*, Washington, DC: World Bank Group, http://documents.worldbank.org/curated/en/890891468762885475/The-AMS-and-domestic-support-in-the-WTO-trade-negotiations-on- agriculture-issues-and-suggestions-for-new-rules

General Accounting Office (GAO) (1994), 'The General Agreement on Tariffs and Trade: Uruguay Round Final Act Should Produce Overall U.S. Economic Gains', https://www.gao.gov/assets/ggd-94-83b.pdf

General Agreement on Tariffs and Trade (1989a), 'Summary of the Main Points Raised at the Fourteenth Meeting of the Negotiating Group on Agriculture (10–12 July 1989): Note by the Secretariat', MTN.GNG/NG5/W/103, http://docs.wto.org/gattdocs/q/UR/GNGNG05/W103.PDF

——— (1989b), 'Comprehensive Proposal for the Long-term Reform of Agricultural Trade: Submission by the Cairns Group Comprising Argentina, Australia, Brazil, Canada, Chile, Colombia, Hungary, Indonesia, Malaysia, New Zealand, Philippines, Thailand

and Uruguay', MTN.GNG/NG5/W/128, https://docs.wto.org/gattdocs/q/UR/GNGNG05/W128.PDF

——— (1990), 'Clarification and Elaboration of Elements of Detailed Proposals Submitted Pursuant to the Midterm Review Decision: Note by the Secretariat', MTN.GNG/NG5/W/161. http:// docs.wto.org/gattdocs/q/UR/GNGNG05/W161.PDF

——— (1997), 'Aggregate Measurement of Support: Note by the Secretariat', MTN.GNG/NG5/W/34, https://docs.wto.org/gattdocs/q/UR/GNGNG05/W34.PDF

International Center for Trade and Sustainable Development (ICTSD) and Food and Agriculture Organization (FAO) (2013), 'G-33 Proposal: Early Agreement on Elements of the Draft Doha Accord to Address Food Security', https://www.fao.org/fileadmin/templates/est/PUBLICATIONS/g33-proposal-early-agreement-on-elements-of-the-draft-doha-accord-to-address-food-security_1_.pdf

Matthews, A. (2014), 'Food Security and WTO Domestic Support Disciplines Post-Bali; ICTSD Programme on Agricultural Trade and Sustainable Development', issue paper no. 53, International Centre for Trade and Sustainable Development, https://www.files.ethz.ch/isn/182734/Food%20Security%20and%20WTO%20Domestic%20Support%20Disciplines%20post-Bali.pdf

Uruguay Round, The (1994), 'India—Statement by Mr. Pranab Mukherjee: Minister of Commerce', MTN.TNC/MIN(94)/ST/38, https://docs.wto.org/gattdocs/q/UR/TNCMIN94/ST38.PDF

World Trade Organization (WTO) (2013), 'Public Stockholding for Food Security Purposes: Ministerial Decision of 7 December 2013', WT/MIN(13)/38, WT/L/913, 11 December, https://docs.wto.org/dol2fe/Pages/SS/directdoc.aspx?filename=q:/wt/min13/38.pdf

——— (2018a), 'Certain Measures of India Providing Market Price Support to Rice and Wheat: Communication from the United States of America Pursuant to article18.7of the Agreement on Agriculture', G/AG/W/174, 9 Mayhttps://docs.wto.org/dol2fe/Pages/SS/directdoc.aspx?filename=q:/G/AG/W174.pdf&Open=True

——— (2018b), 'India's Measures to Provide Market Price Support to Sugarcane: Communication from Australia', G/AG/W/189, 16 November, https://docs.wto.org/dol2fe/Pages/SS/directdoc. aspx?filename=q:/G/AG/W189.pdf

——— (2019), 'India—Measures Concerning Sugar and Sugarcane: Request for Consultations by Brazil', WT/DS, G/L/1298, 579/1, G/AG/GEN/151, http://docs.wto.org/dol2fe/Pages/SS/directdoc.aspx?filename=q:/WT/DS/579-1.pdf&Open=True

——— (2021), 'India—Measures Concerning Sugar and Sugarcane: Reports of the Panels', WT/DS579/R, WT/DS580/R, WT/DS581/R, 14 December, https://www.wto.org/english/tratop_e/dispu_e/579_580_581r_e.pdf

——— (2022a), 'The Agriculture Committee', https://www.wto.org/english/tratop_e/agric_e/ag_work_e.htm

——— (2022b), 'Notification', G/AG/N/IND/2027, 1 April, https://docsonline.wto.org/dol2fe/Pages/SS/directdoc.aspx?filename=t:/G/AG/NIND27.docx&Open=True

10

Generalized Semiproletarianization in Africa

Paris Yeros

Introduction

We know since Marx (1990, chapter 25) that the formation of labour reserves is the basic social contradiction of capitalist development. The concrete form of labour reserve formation in the peripheries today is a generalized condition of semiproletarianization, which is the historic result of capitalist development in its mature monopoly stage. This marks the obsolescence of capitalism as a social system – which is also to say that there is no solution to this grave and multifaceted existential crisis of our times on the terms of capitalism itself: the crisis will drag on until sovereign planning with a socialist orientation takes hold.

The present article will provide some thoughts on the trajectory of labour reserves in Africa. The focus is on the period of neoliberalism, configuring the *late-neocolonial* phase of imperialism (Yeros and Jha 2020). We take our immediate cue from a specific insight as expressed by Prabhat Patnaik (2015, p. 165: see fuller statement in Patnaik & Patnaik, 2017) on the 'blurring' of economic activities and forms of labour in the peripheral reserves under contemporary globalization:

> [T]he distinction between the active and the reserve army [of labour] is being progressively blurred today owing to the proliferation of 'informal employment', 'casual employment', 'work outsourcing' and such other measures. The employment rationing rule earlier under which some people were fully employed while others were not, which was the basis for distinguishing between the 'active' and the 'reserve' armies of labour, is increasingly being replaced by another employment rationing rule under which unemployment is more widely shared out among the entire workforce.

This observation goes to the heart of what is being considered here. In what follows, some conceptual elements will first be offered with regard to the *longue durée* of Africa's social formations and the structural convergence of its marco-regions today, before sketching the growth of the continent's labour reserves. The analysis of recent trends will be based on figures sourced from the database of the World Employment and Social Outlook of the International Labour Organization (ILO 2022).

African Social Formations in Historical Perspective

The contours of Africa's social formations may be recalled briefly for the purpose of historical perspective. After the fall of ancient Egypt, autonomous social formations gradually reemerged and proliferated on the continent with evident tendencies towards tributary development. A key overall feature, nonetheless, was that political organization remained regionalized, while accumulation relied mainly on long-distance trade instead of surplus extraction from local cultivators. Local populations remained socially organized on the basis of lineage with effective village control over land and labour. These autonomous, trading social formations eventually entered into sustained conflict with the commercial requirements of the Mediterranean and Islamic worlds for the expanding tributary dynamics in these contiguous regions produced aggressive incursions and wars of enslavement south of the Sahara. These and other factors, including the defeat of the Moors in the Iberian Peninsula, set the stage for Africa's encounter with an emergent mercantile capitalism led by the Iberian and other European powers.

In this encounter, Africa was transformed into the 'periphery of the periphery', in the words of Samir Amin (1972), to serve Europe's expansion across the Atlantic and the globe. Over the ensuing centuries, the peoples of the continent were captured in the millions, transported to the Americas and subjected to mass enslavement for the purpose of accumulation in Europe (Rodney 1972; Williams 1994). The social formations of the continent underwent depopulation and reduction of the political organization into smaller warring formations. Lineage was also mobilized to establish new social hierarchies, entailing an erosion of village control over land and labour and, increasingly, at the expense of women.

Africa's trajectory acquired two further characteristics in the wider process of European colonial expansion. First, unlike in the Americas where indigenous civilization was largely destroyed during the conquest, the social basis of African civilization was not undermined, even in the course of mass enslavement and direct colonial occupation under monopoly capital. As Mafeje (1991) has argued, the 'lineage mode of social organization' remained resilient even as it came under the sway of tributary and capitalist modes of production. It is thus notable that, while the African diaspora across the Atlantic yielded a new field of economic and cultural integration, amplified by settler-colonial polarization on both sides, the social organization of African social formations retained characteristics more proximate to the peasant-based civilizations of Asia, yet also with greater control over land and labour via lineage organization. The peasantry thus survived well into the twentieth century, perpetually adjusting under the weight of monopoly capital. It is also notable that these realities presented particular challenges to the liberation movements, as recognized by Fanon (1963), Cabral (1969, 1979) and Nkrumah (1971), among others. A key question here, as we will see, is how this has continued to change and what new challenges are being posed today.

Second, colonialism created a structurally heterogeneous continent, given that diverse economic trajectories were forged under European conquest and settlement. By the turn of the twentieth century, colonialism had produced three macro-regions with distinct structural characteristics based on different *modes of integration into monopoly capitalism* and the different *labour regimes underpinning them*, as noted by Amin (1972). With some modifications to Amin's terminology, we may identify the three regions as follows: (1) the *commercial monopolies* of West Africa and the Sahel, where peasant production under lineage organization was diverted by colonial authorities towards commodity exports under the control of European trading houses (Amin 1973); (2) the *concessionary monopolies* of Central Africa where the initial pillage and terror of European commercial capital was followed by the establishment of joint stock companies with large concessions across all sectors (Depelchin 1992); and (3) the *settler monopolies* of southern and East Africa, similar to the Maghreb, where conquest took the form of a 'scorched-earth campaign' (Magubane 1979, p. 38) to deprive Africans of independent livelihood and engineer labour reserves on a regional basis for the mines, farms and industries of the settler bourgeoisie. These three macro-regions sealed the fate of the continent under monopoly capitalism. Despite the fact that in non-settler regions the peasantry for the most part retained control of the land and that the lineage mode of social organization remained resilient for production and reproduction everywhere, class formation and related shifts in gender relations under the colonial system put into motion a new type of peripheral social formation. The question posed today concerns the emergence of newer patterns of accumulation beyond the specific colonial structures.

It is also of historical significance, of course, that colonialism carved out dozens of states with arbitrary boundaries unrelated to ethnolinguistic affinities or potential economic complementarities; and that, after the First World War, colonial authorities also resorted to manipulating sub-state 'tribal' chiefdoms in the interest of 'indirect rule', to obtain control over lineage-mediated land and labour relations (Mamdani 1996). Such divide-and-rule tactics installed a series of institutional and political mechanisms which survived into the neocolonial transition. Yet, it remains important to emphasize that these institutions were never an end in themselves (Moyo and Yeros 2007). They were always *about something else*, which was precisely the control over land and labour in tropical and sub-tropical regions for the exclusive benefit of European monopolies and their settler kin.

Thus, it is of further importance, historically and at present, that the survival of the lineage mode of social organization was not due to colonial design, whose primary objective was to manipulate lineage and whose real effect was to degrade its reproductive function without providing alternatives. It survived because of the relation of forces that defended the institution against total loss of control over land and labour under colonial conditions. The struggle for control over land and labour remained the driving force of lineage organization, given its unparalleled social legitimacy for social reproduction. We may recall a conclusion reached by Cabral (1969, p. 4) in reference to the villages in colonial Guinea that had not yet succumbed to social differentiation and loss of control of land and labour:

> . . . these groups without any defined organization put up much more resistance
> against the Portuguese than the others [in 'semi-feudal' conditions] and they
> have maintained in tact their traditions of resistance to colonial penetration. This
> is the group that we found most ready to accept the idea of national liberation.

Nor, for that matter, was the weight of so-called indirect rule the same in settler and non-settler regions. The coercive nature of 'indirect rule' was even heavier in settler regions. The extensive alienation of land by settlers, the creation of 'tribal' reserves, and the rapid degradation of the social and ecological conditions directly undermined the blueprint of the indirect rule itself. Thus, it is not surprising that the underlying causes of struggle would even intensify in the course of national liberation. We might similarly recall the conclusion drawn by Fanon (1963, p. 127): '. . . the mass of the country people have never ceased to think of the problem of their liberation except in terms of violence, in terms of taking back the land from the foreigners, in terms of national struggle and of armed insurrection. It is all very simple.'

With the transition to neocolonialism, relative autonomy from imperialist and settler monopolies was finally obtained and this applies to the whole of the state apparatus including the local government bureaucracies carrying the late-colonial imprint of indirect rule. Nonetheless, state power everywhere has continued to express the evolving relation of class forces – among peasants, workers, settlers, local bourgeoisie and imperialism – *not* the ensemble of bureaucratic institutions themselves (Moyo and Yeros 2011). The underlying economic structures and their evolution under monopoly capitalism have continued to weigh heavily on the relation of forces and, hence, state power, the national question and Pan-African unity.

The correct reading of the social structure and its political potential has always been a matter of utmost significance to the national revolution. In the course of Africa's liberation, persistent efforts were made to identify the social forces capable of leading the national revolution and sustaining Pan-African unity, in the absence of a national bourgeoisie and an industrial proletariat. There was also substantial dispute over the political character and potential of existing social classes, as well the character of the state and the ideology of liberation. However, there was substantial similarity in the actual components of the social formation, which generally conformed to a five-fold structure: (1) the foreign and settler monopolies; (2) the petty bourgeoisies consisting of the liberal professions and petty commerce, including of non-African origin; (3) a small proletariat in transportation (railroads, docks), domestic services, mines and farms, which grew with industrialization; (4) the peasantry, the bulk of the population; (5) and a small lumpenproletariat in the cities.

In terms of social reproduction, the centre of gravity of this social formation remained in the countryside and rooted in land held under lineage organization. Unpaid labour outside the market undertaken disproportionately by women was fundamental to both productive and reproductive activities in the peasant sector (Amanor-Wilks 2009; O'Laughlin 2001; Tsikata 2016), alongside unpaid labour in colonial infrastructure works mainly in the case of men. Moreover, migratory labour for wages among the male population was extensive in the settler regions, but it did emerge in the other regions as well. It is indeed the case that the colonial economy set into motion, however abruptly or incrementally, the transformation of households and kinship networks into a 'hoe and wage' mode of reproduction tied to different modes of integration into monopoly capitalism (Arrighi 1970; Cordell, Gregory and Piché 1998; First 1983; Mafeje 1978, 1981). This is what we identified elsewhere as the matrix of the 'poor peasant' path, which would gain force and complexity over time as a full-fledged *semiproletarianized* reality, split between the town, country and international borders, and between wages and farming and other non-waged activities (Moyo and Yeros, eds 2005). The colonial situation marked the incipient phase of this path, whereby households and extended kin came to straddle the proletarian, peasant and reproductive functions, in all their gendered dimensions.

In Figure 10.1, we attempt a schematic approximation of the structure of this late-colonial semiproletarianized social formation in the shape of a social pyramid. The depiction includes the foreign and settler monopolies at the top of the pyramid, followed by the petty bourgeoisies, the proletariat, the peasantry, the lumpenproletariat and unpaid family labour at the base of the social formation. The latter four are placed in a *porous* relationship to each another as denoted by the horizontal dotted lines, indicating the transformation of households and kinship networks and the straddling of all these forms of labour. Although the role of the petty bourgeoisie was heavily contested, it is represented here in its overriding approximation to imperialism. The sexual division of labour is also indicated as a tilted line cutting across all these forms of labour, again in a schematic manner which is not to scale.

Semiproletarianization is hardly a new phenomenon. It has been noted everywhere in different historical moments: in late-nineteenth-century Western Europe and Russia (Kautsky 1988 [1899]; Lenin 1964 [1899]), semi-colonial

Figure 10.1 *Late-colonial social formation in Africa, 1960*

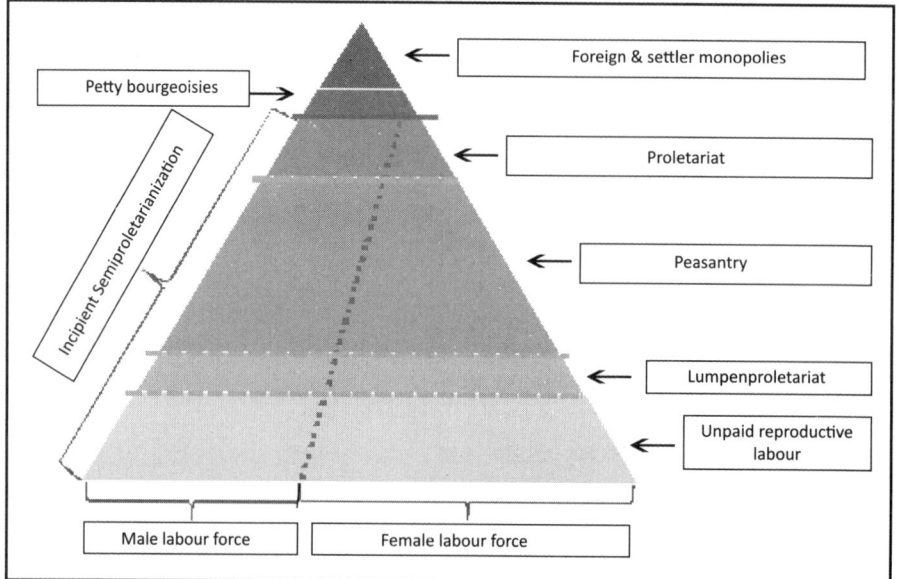

Note: Not to scale.
Source: The author.

China (Mao 2004 [1926]), post-slavery Latin America and the Caribbean (de Janvry 1981; Deere 1976; Rodney 1981), contemporary China, India, Africa and generally the South (Chambati 2022; Jacobs 2018; Jha, Chambati, Ossome, eds 2021; Li 2008; Naidu and Ossome 2016; Ossome and Naidu 2021; Prasad 2016; Zhan and Scully 2018), and in a systemic perspective by dependency and world-systems theorists (Amin 1976, 1977; Wallerstein 1983). No single conclusion has been drawn on its characteristics, function or trajectory, but in most cases, semiproletarianization has not been seen as a permanent condition in the evolution of capitalism.

For our purposes, we define the semiproletarianized condition as that in which a workforce over a significant period of time, such as a generation, does not come to rely on wages and salaried employment for its social reproduction despite having lost all or part of its means of production, but maintains or actively seeks a combination of wages, petty incomes and simple use values, alongside care work and the social policies of the state. This social condition includes ad hoc, temporary, periodic or seasonal encounters with wage labour; peasant production for own consumption; petty-commodity production for sale; direct use of natural resources from the commons; extraction of minerals and other high-value resources for commercialization; and a large range of self-employment activities in both rural and urban areas in petty trade and the service provision, situated either in the home, rented spaces, the outdoors or in transit over long distances. Ossome and Naidu (2021) have usefully resumed these labour processes in three: subsistence, petty-commodity production and wage labour. Chambati (2019) has noted in detail the synergy between wages and peasant production which includes the mobilization of wages for investment in the peasant farm. The systemic function has correctly been identified by Shivji (2017) as none other than ongoing primitive accumulation at the expense of this massive and diverse category of 'working people'.

As will be argued below, the long transition of Africa's social formation has now fallen into a systemic trap. A fuller proletarian condition in the peripheries remains unattainable under monopoly capitalism, given that social reproduction remains significantly outside the wage relation, even in highly urbanized settings, and has been deteriorating overall. In the absence of an alternative development path, via delinking, economic planning and a new mix of property relations beyond the logic of capitalism, the perverse tendencies of this social formation will remain in force: the larger the wage and income gap, the heavier the burdens of non-waged labour in productive and reproductive activities, the more intense the instrumentalization of gender, racial, ethnic, religious and other social cleavages, and the more widespread the structural – domestic, xenophobic – violence, etc. It is not entirely impossible, of course, for certain countries to overcome this systemic trap under the wing of imperialism; or to stave off its worst tendencies by palliative measures. But labour reserves being a systemic necessity, breaking out of the trap on the terms of imperialism can only be an exception, unless substantial rupture and delinking occurs. The most notable experience of delinking today – in the sense of subverting the worldwide law of value by subordinating the external environment to internal requirements – has been that of China.

The semiproletarianization trap refers us back to the 'blurring of the active and reserve armies of labour' which is denoted in Figure 10.1 by the porous boundaries between the social layers. The systemic logic of imperialism which results in this type of labour reserve is clear: to depress wages in tropical and semi-tropical regions to maintain the value of money in the imperialist centres (Patnaik 2008; Patnaik and Patnaik 2017, 2021) and perpetuate the super-exploitation of both labour and nature by means of 'dualisms' between wages or petty production and unpaid family labour (Amin 1977; Shivji 2017; Ossome and Naidu 2021). As for the exact character of these dualisms and the relationship with monopoly capital at the micro level, this may vary widely – it has even been suggested that an effective disarticulation via marginalization has occurred (Ossome and Naidu 2021) – yet the relationship with imperialism remains the structural determinant of Africa's semiproletarianized social formation.

The Convergence Hypothesis

The question that will concern us here is: what transformations have African social formations undergone since the beginning of the terminal crisis of monopoly capitalism in the 1970s? The focus will be on the neoliberal period in this current phase of the crisis which configures the *late-neocolonial* situation. This is the period of structural adjustment programmes and incessant waves of neoliberal policies. Our specific point of departure is two-fold: on the one hand, Archie Mafeje's (2003) insistence well into the 2000s that the lineage-based peasantry in non-settler Africa had still not been undermined by the encroachment of capital; and on the other, Samir Amin's (2014) notion of continuous degradation of the macro-regions, but without notable shifts in patterns of accumulation. There is room to update or revise these two positions in light of the formation of labour reserves.

This research path has been opened up by Sam Moyo, a close associate of both Mafeje's and Amin's since the 1970s – and indeed of Utsa Patnaik's and Prabhat Patnaik's from the 2000s when his views continued to evolve (see Jha, Moyo and Yeros 2017; Moyo, Yeros and Jha 2018; U. Patnaik and Moyo 2011). A substantial part of the task has been undertaken by Moyo, some of it in collaboration with other colleagues, including this author. So there is no novelty in the path chosen. But it is worth noting that Moyo advanced much further in his discussions with Mafeje, to demonstrate that the latter's argument had been overtaken by events (Moyo 2008). Moyo pointed out that structural adjustment programmes and persistent neoliberal reforms had finally produced a 'land question' in non-settler Africa as well. Moreover, he suggested that a 'tri-modal' agrarian structure, composed of poor peasants, small capitalists and large estates was spreading across the continent, from settler to non-settler Africa and even *vice versa*, as in Zimbabwe post-land reform, which expanded the peasantry against the settler monopolies. This line of argument suggested that a certain tendency towards 'structural convergence' was operating among the three macro-regions, at least in agriculture. Much also was said about the evolving food and labour questions on the continent (Moyo, Yeros and Jha 2018); the new scramble for land and other natural resources (Moyo, Yeros and Jha 2012, 2019); and trajectories of the agrarian question and labour reserves across the South (Jha, Moyo, Yeros 2017; Moyo, Jha and Yeros 2013, 2016). As the perspective evolved, a more general 'convergence hypothesis' began to be floated, but it was never fully stated or tested and the pieces of the puzzle remained scattered – for brother Sam left us too soon.

The experience of Zimbabwe is of further importance for the manner in which its revolutionary situation in the early 2000s shook up the paradigms and opened up the question of historical transition. Stubborn attempts to delink from imperialism revealed the full range of contradictions that pertain to national liberation and pan-African unity in a neoliberal world (Moyo and Chambati, eds 2013; Moyo and Yeros 2011, 2013). Not only did Zimbabwe break out of settler capitalism – a rare historical feat in itself – it also re-established conditions for accumulation from below and for a new industrialization path. Zimbabwe did so by means of radical nationalist mobilization, a land revolution, a regional mutual defence pact and active promotion of the continent's interests. This anti-imperialist posture sustained an intense struggle over the direction of the post-land reform transition, under imperialist sanctions. Above all, it demonstrated that party organization and radical mobilization remain possible, indeed fundamental, in the current conditions of generalized semiproletarianization.

This experience further suggests that, even if 'convergence' might be observed generally, its political character should not be taken at face value, for the dynamics which engulf it may come to differ greatly from one country or region to the next. So, from the start, this is an important caveat to any convergence hypothesis: objectively similar structural conditions may be underpinned by markedly different political dynamics and postures in relation to imperialism; in all cases, it is the relation of class forces in motion that must be ascertained. As Shivji (1976, p. 8) once warned us:

> In non-revolutionary situations much of the class struggle is latent and even unidentifiable as such at any particular moment. Talking about class struggle as such is really registering the fact of class struggle *ex-post facto*. The development of class and class struggle can only be talked about tendentially, in terms of historical trends. In fact, classes hardly become fully *class* conscious except in situations of intense political struggle.

This caveat applies to our analysis of the macro-regional trajectories of labour reserves presented below, where converging structural tendencies must not be taken to imply convergence in actual politics. The same structures which underpinned radical nationalist mobilization in Zimbabwe have also resulted in NGOization and ideological lumpenization under the auspices of imperialism, not mobilization for delinking.

Suffice it to reiterate in an abbreviated manner that there is a real question as to the contemporary shifts in the patterns of accumulation when put in terms of *modes of integration* into monopoly capitalism and the *labour regimes* that underpin them. As far as the mode of integration is concerned, some important tendencies may be briefly identified. A basic element of both global integration and the labour process underpinning it is the land question itself, which remains a fundamental question in a semiproletarianized social formation. This, as Moyo and others have demonstrated, has been in definite transition on the continent (Amanor and Moyo, eds 2008; Hall, Scoones and Tsikata, eds 2015; Manji 2006; Mazwi, Mudimu and Helliker, eds 2022; Moyo and Yeros 2005; Moyo, Tsikata and Diop, eds 2015; Moyo, Jha and Yeros, eds 2019; Ossome 2021; Ossome and Naidu 2021; Tsikata 2016). Since the 1980s, neoliberal pressures to reform land tenure pried open the agricultural sectors of all regions via land titling and registration, and suppression or manipulation of customary tenure. The consequence has been the deepening of land markets and the expansion of land rent and land alienation, all of which have further undermined customary guarantees to land. This trend has fuelled social differentiation to boost the position of domestic bourgeoisie and their association with external markets while impoverishing the peasantry. By the 2000s, with a more capital-friendly legal framework already in place, a new wave of land grabs struck by foreign capital itself, for the purpose of large-scale production including in regions where large-scale freehold or concessions in agriculture never existed in any significant manner.

The actual mode of agricultural integration into monopoly capitalism was promoted by neoliberal trade policy and fiscal austerity measures which shifted the accumulation pressures in agriculture by intensifying the sector's integration into global markets. This has had several notable effects. It has reinforced the logic of the production of cash crops for export while undermining food production for local consumption and nutritional requirements (Patnaik and Moyo 2011). It has pushed peasants and rural workers into contract farming within global agricultural value systems, where new dependencies are created on foreign markets, finance and technology (Amanor 2019; Chambati and Mazwi, Mudimu and Helliker, eds 2022; Martiniello and Azambuja 2019; Meagher 2019; Torvikey 2022; Tsikata 2022). It has created a myth of a 'green revolution' under the auspices of major US-based foundations, which have poured half a billion dollars in grants to a dozen countries since the mid-2000s for the purchase of commercial seeds and synthetic fertilizers from the monopolies themselves, but without delivering gains in productivity or food security (Wise 2020). It has fuelled social differentiation and gender hierarchies by favouring the more 'capable' producers, those with access to land and financial resources (Jha *et al.* 2022; Mazwi, Mudimu and Helliker, eds 2022). And it has sown social conflict over land and natural resources, often in 'ethnic', 'religious' or other such forms, while also reinforcing rural–urban and international migration.

A new agrarian 'tri-modal' pattern of accumulation has thus been emerging in agriculture. The exact mix of agricultural production units and land use changes will inevitably differ from region to region and must be analysed in its historical particularities; but the pressures towards global integration, land concentration and social differentiation are in force everywhere. The modes of integration in other industries – mining, manufacturing and services, including finance – have also been undergoing transition under the aegis of the 'generalized monopolies', in Amin's (2019) terms, as well as the rise of new commercial and investment partners among the South, especially China. We cannot delve into these in detail. We may only note that the expansion of global value systems has had uneven effects among industries and generally low impact on the continent's participation in value systems at the level of intermediate goods (AfDB, OECD and UNDP 2014).

African economies have remained fully integrated as exporters of primary materials. Beyond agriculture, a notable transition has also occurred in the energy sector, where the production of oil and gas has spread to a number of countries that previously (under colonial rule) had not been integrated as such into the world economy and are now strongly concentrated and dependent on energy exports, especially oil. This includes countries across the north and west coasts of the continent and the Sahel, and more recently, the east coast (Bush 2004; Carmody 2016; Obi 2012; Obi and Rustad, eds 2011; Yates 1996). In this sense, the concessionary mode of integration previously known to colonial Central Africa has spread to the rest of the continent, albeit under modern concessionary arrangements and with new conflicts over the appropriation of rent (Amin 2010). This further applies to minerals – gold, diamonds, uranium, platinum, coltan, copper, iron ore, bauxite, etc. – which have gained importance in old and new regions. There is an overall escalation of global integration which again is confined to the lower (primary) tiers of global industrial production and subject to volatile prices in oligopolistic sectors. Overall, in both energy and minerals, production under direct corporate control is capital-intensive, with lower absorption of labour and higher concentration of skilled labour.

Yet, it is also notable in the case of minerals that there has been a parallel accelerated expansion of artisanal mining among smaller economic agents and semiproletarianized social layers that seek their own access to minerals, but under labour-intensive, conflict-ridden and highly exploitative conditions (Bryceson and Geenen 2016; Bryceson and Jønson 2009; Geenen 2015; Hilson and Garforth 2012; Mkodzongi 2021; Mkodzongi and Spiegel 2018). In 2009, it was noted that in artisanal mining, 'about 3.7 million are directly engaged in this sub-sector and about 30 million depend on it', while predicting that the sub-sector would triple in three years (African Union 2009, p. 26). These two sides of the mining industry, therefore, differ in their technological and labour contents, even if they are both integrated into the same global value systems.

Meanwhile, manufacturing development remains stunted. Recent experiences of export-oriented growth have been subject to similar trends of integration and subordination into global value systems. The growth of industrial exports has been concentrated mainly in North and southern Africa, where four countries – Egypt, Morocco, Tunisia and South Africa – have accounted for two-thirds of manufacturing exports (AfDB *et al.* 2014, p. 168). But in terms of integration into global value systems, southern Africa remains responsible for 40 per cent of the continent's participation in the more advanced segments (ibid. p. 139). Apart from South Africa, which has retained an automotive sector, other countries which have experienced industrial growth include Ethiopia in apparel and textiles, Morocco in aerospace and Nigeria in electronics. Nonetheless, overall labour absorption in industrial production – whether with an export or local orientation – remains very low at only 12 per cent of the total workforce and this includes the mining sector (see below).

Finally, the service sectors display similar tendencies in terms of both integrations into global monopolies and export orientation, in finance, insurance and tourism, among others. However, this is the sector which has most widely split into a highly skilled component and a very large popular base which, in fact, has largely absorbed the burgeoning semiproletarianized workforce over the last half-century, across rural–urban and international boundaries.

Generalized Semiproletarianization

In a previous study dealing with global trends in reserve formation, for the period 1991–2012, it was estimated that, on a global level, the 'non-vulnerable' workforce of 'wage and salaried workers' in the ILO's terms – which in Marx's terms would correspond roughly to the 'active labour force' – was well below 50 per cent of the global labour force; this indicated a dramatic decline of the active labour force relative to the growth of labour reserves on a global scale at the turn of the century (Jha, Moyo and Yeros 2017, p. 217). The labour reserves included the 'vulnerable' workforce, counted as 'own-account workers' and 'contributing family workers', in the ILO's terms. Moreover, the 'non-vulnerable' workforce was concentrated in 'developed' countries, where the proportion of wage and salaried workers was above 80 per cent, largely in the service sectors, representing the concentration of the world's proletariat proper. The large majority of the world's workforce, therefore, in all sectors, has become trapped in labour reserves (the 'vulnerable') which are concentrated in the peripheries of the world economy (ibid.).

The ILO (2022) data for 1991–2020 with reference to Africa can shed some light. In this period, the working-age population (over fifteen years of age) in Africa, including North and sub-Saharan, doubled in size at a rate of 2.04, from 310 million to 633 million, while the rate of change for women specifically was higher than that of men, at 2.27. The whole of the population in 2020, including the under-15s, amounted to 1.3 billion, which indicates that roughly half of the population consists of youth formally outside the workforce but who will become of working age continuously in large numbers over the coming years. Moreover, the whole of the population is expected to double by 2050, such that the question of reserve formation and strategies of labour absorption cannot be brushed aside.

In fact, neoliberalism has clearly and secularly degraded the workforce over the last thirty years, as the data shows. The trends are similar in *all* sub-regions, which allows us to speak of the formation of a *continental* labour reserve, beyond the regional patterns of accumulation specific to colonialism, given that the workforce everywhere now conforms to one single semiprole-tarianized condition. The condition of generalized semiproletarianization is precisely the trap in which the continent has fallen, much like the rest of the Third World. The stage of generalized semiproletarianization differs from the incipient stage discussed earlier, by the multiplication of the forms of labour

Figure 10.2 *Late-neocolonial social formation in Africa, 2020*

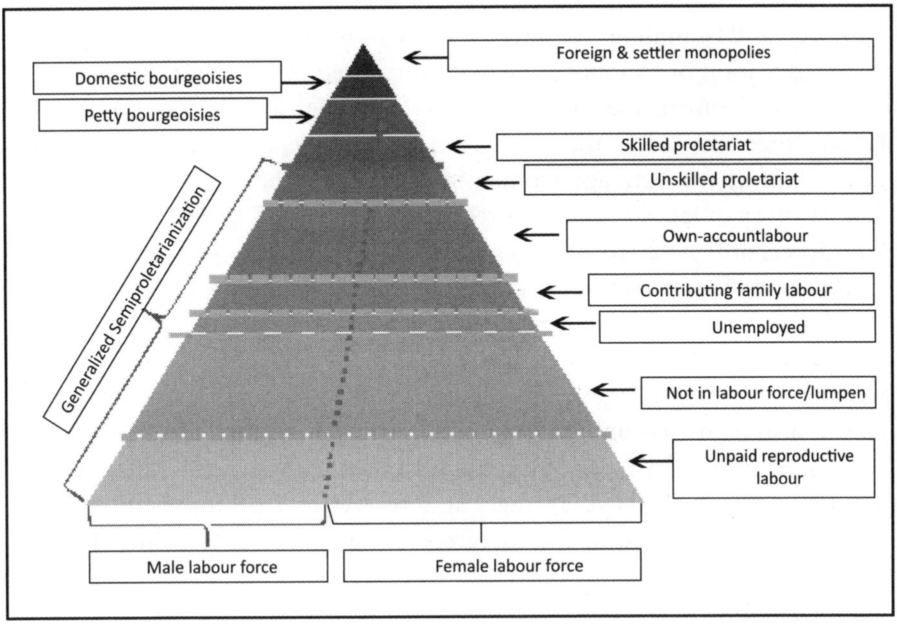

Note: not to scale.
Source: author's elaboration.

in existence today and the intensification of the 'blurring' effect among the different forms of labour.

In Figure 10.2, we attempt once again a schematic depiction of the late-neocolonial social formation. We reinsert the bourgeoisie in the schema but without considering in any detail the evolution of its fractions. We also assume that part of the wage and salaried workforce is 'skilled' and 'non-vulnerable', even though the new dataset used here itself does not provide for this distinction. We also follow the ILOs prior distinction regarding the 'non-vulnerable' 'own-account workers', who hire in wage labour – today's petty bourgeoisie, in our terms – versus the 'vulnerable' 'own-account workers', who do not hire labour, in both rural and urban settings, which again do not appear separated in our data set. We also include those counted as 'contributing family labour' specifically in production, the unemployed who are counted as still expecting to be employed, those 'not in labour force' – either temporarily or permanently withdrawn from employment, including the lumpenproletariat, in our terms – and unpaid reproductive labour, which is also not provided for in this data set.

Returning to the dataset for 1991–2020, which is suggestive of this schema (Figure 10.2) although it does not provide disaggregated data exactly as we would wish, we can observe the following. On a continental level, including North and sub-Saharan Africa, for the total working-age population of men and women together, the category that has grown fastest is that of 'not in labour force', from 35 per cent of the working-age population (80 million) to 39 per cent (214 million) (Figure 10.3a). This includes youth 'not in employment, education or training', which itself reached 59.2 million (ILO 2022).

For women, specifically, the rate of change among those outside the labour force was below the average, at 2.32 per cent, but still amounted to nearly half of working-age women in 2020, at 48 per cent (Figure 10.3b). The category of labour that most receded, from 17 to 11 per cent of the total workforce, or from 20 to 14 per cent among working-age women, was that of 'contributing family members', comprising unwaged family labour in production and services. 'Own-account labour' increased only slightly from 27 to 28 per cent of the total workforce, or from 22 to 24 per cent among women but remained the second largest category after those outside the workforce. Wage labour also increased only slightly over thirty years, from 15 to 16 per cent overall, or from 7 to 9 per cent among women, although the rate of change among women was above average, at 2.76 (versus 2.38 for the total workforce) and was, in fact, in these aggregate terms, the highest rate of change among all categories in this thirty-year period despite the still low proportion of women in the workforce. Meanwhile, formal 'unemployment' during this thirty-year period remained at a standstill at 5 per cent of the total workforce or 4 per cent among working-age women. The petty bourgeoisie which hires labour also remained at a standstill proportionally at 2 per cent overall or 1 per cent among women, which shows that the proportion of female small-scale employers remained at one-third of that of men. The rate of growth of the petty bourgeoisie has been relatively low, at 1.77 overall, or 1.6 for women.

On the basis of this dataset, we can surmise that: (1) proletarianization overall has advanced very slowly under neoliberalism, albeit at the highest pace among women; (2) the large reduction in contributing family labour (- 6 per cent) has been channelled only partly towards wage labour (+1 per cent overall or +2 per cent for women), partly to own-account labour (+1 per cent overall or +2 per cent for women) and mostly to outside the workforce, especially among men (+4 per cent overall or +2 per cent for women); (3) the petty bourgeoisie as an employer has not increased in its overall proportion and has remained concentrated among men; (4) formal unemployment has also remained low and unchanged in proportional terms for both men and women.

The sub-regional trends reveal variations to this overall picture. In 2020, the highest level of proletarianization was located in North and southern Africa at 24 per cent of the total workforce in both regions. However, in North Africa, proletarianization is very low among women (9 per cent) and thus highly concentrated among men, while it is less so in southern Africa where among women 18 per cent are proletarianized (Figures 10.4a, 10.4b). At the same time, the polarization between proletarianization and exclusion from the workforce is greatest in North Africa where 57 per cent of the total

Figure 10.3a *General employment status in Africa*, in millions

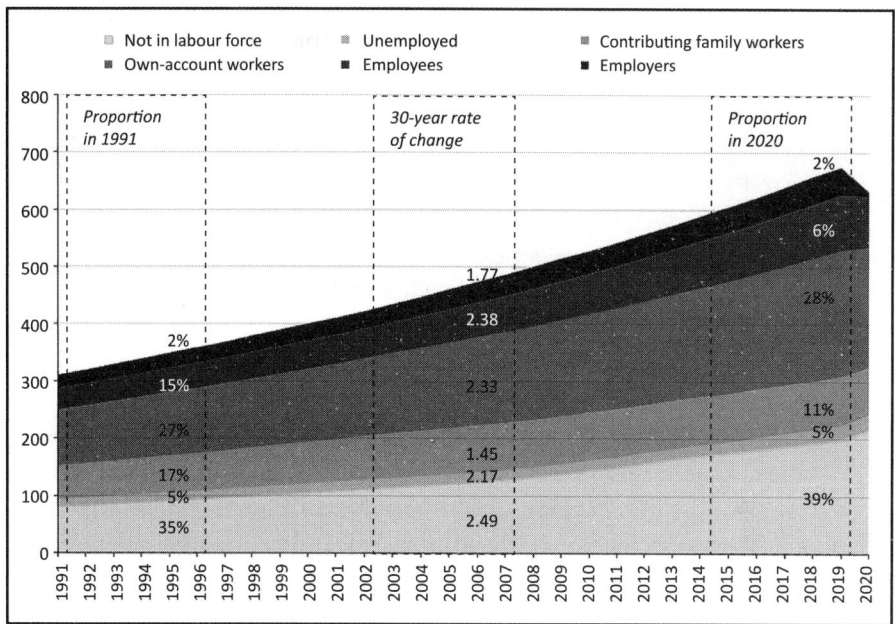

Source: ILO (2022).

Figure 10.3b *Women's employment status in Africa*, in millions

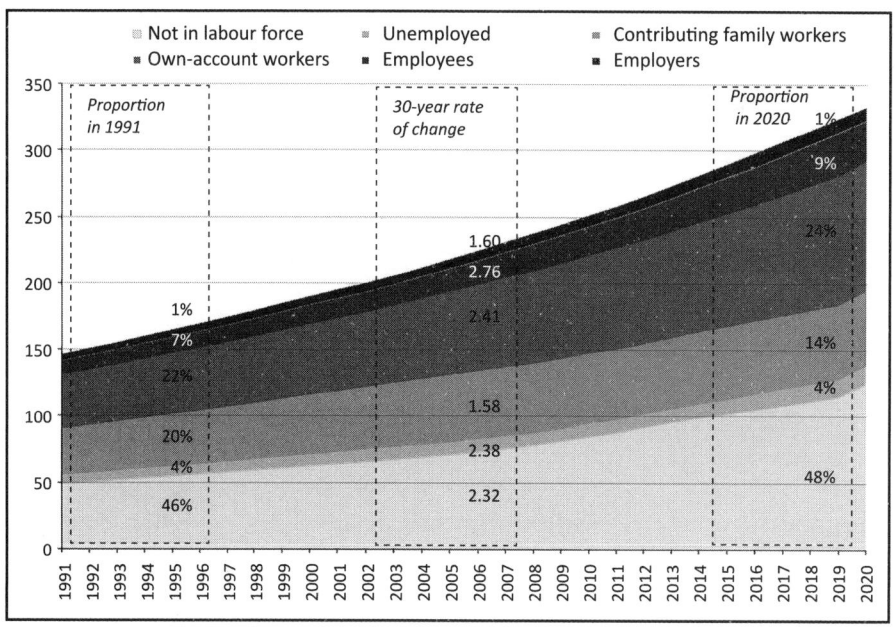

Source: ILO (2022).

working-age population is outside the workforce, a situation which is even more dramatic among women at 81 per cent. In North Africa, all the intermediate categories for both men and women – unemployed, contributing family workers and own-account workers – are much inferior in size (together they account for only 16 per cent of the total workforce or 11 per cent among women), while it is also the case that the petty bourgeoisie is very highly concentrated among men.

In southern Africa (Figures 10.5a, 10.5b), 34 per cent of the total working-age population is outside the workforce, which rises to 38 per cent among women, followed by own-account labour at 26 per cent for both men and women, which approximates the continental averages and then followed by a lower level of formally unemployed and contributing family members at 15 per cent of the total workforce or 17 per cent among women. The proportion of the petty bourgeoisie is equal to the continental average for both men and women. In other words, despite a still higher level of proletarianization in relation to most other regions, the notion of an exceptional labour question in southern Africa has eroded, insofar as it evinces comparable levels of own-account labour, labour outside the workforce and the presence of the petty bourgeoisie.

Figure 10.4a *General employment status in North Africa*, in millions

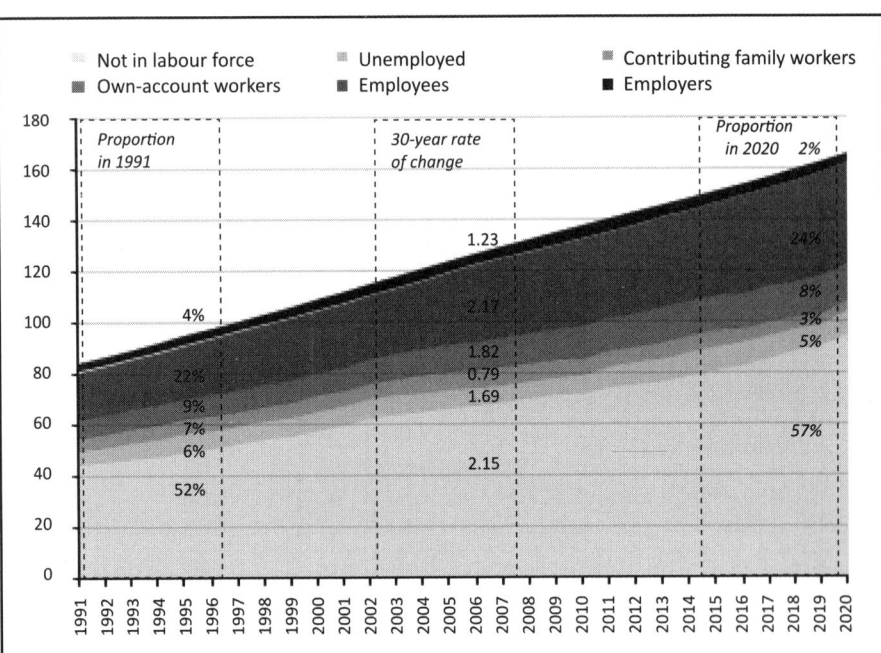

Source: ILO (2022).

Figure 10.4b *Women's employment status in North Africa*, in millions

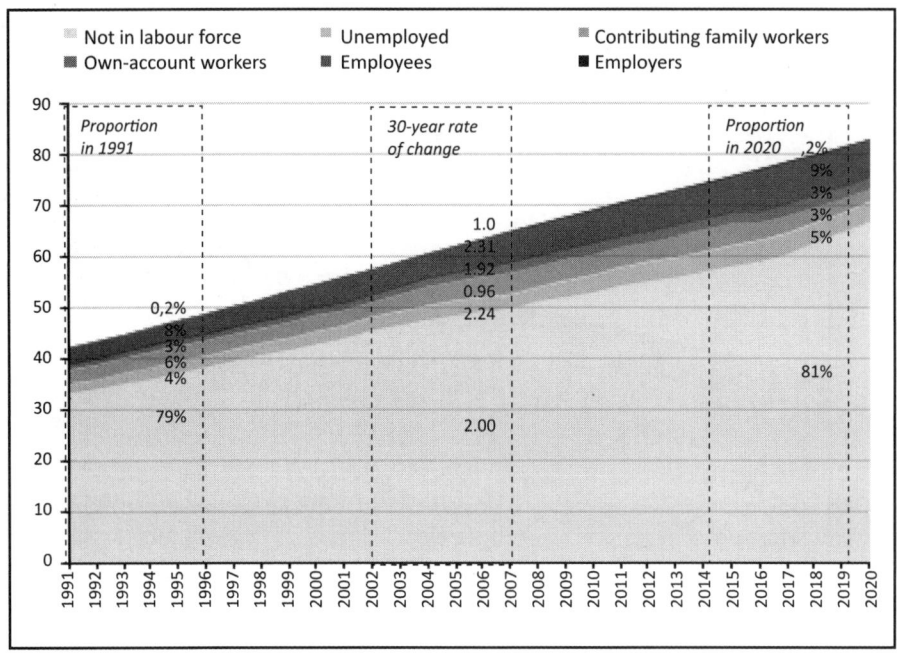

Figure 10.5a *General employment status in Southern Africa*, in millions

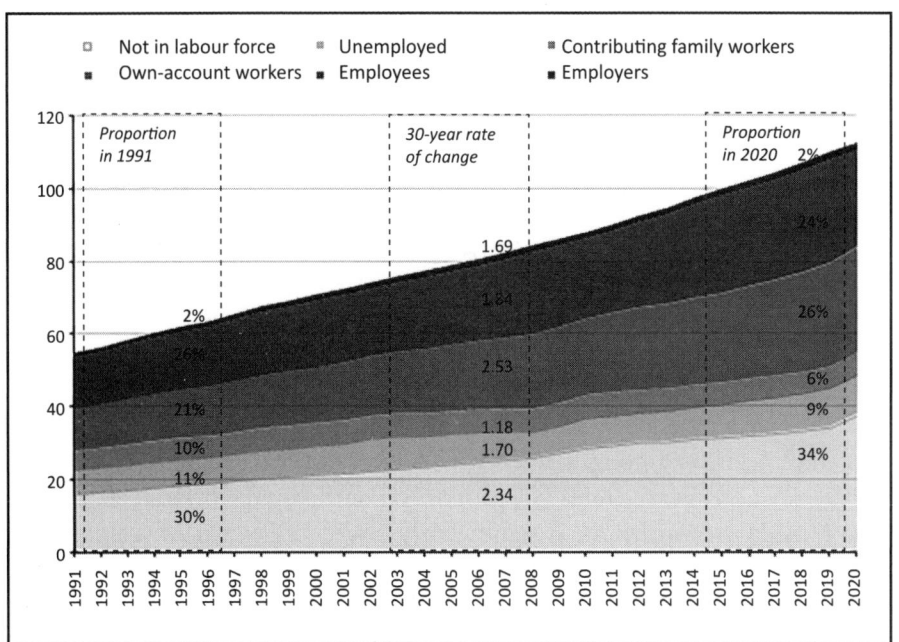

Figure 10.5b *Women's employment status in southern Africa*, in millions

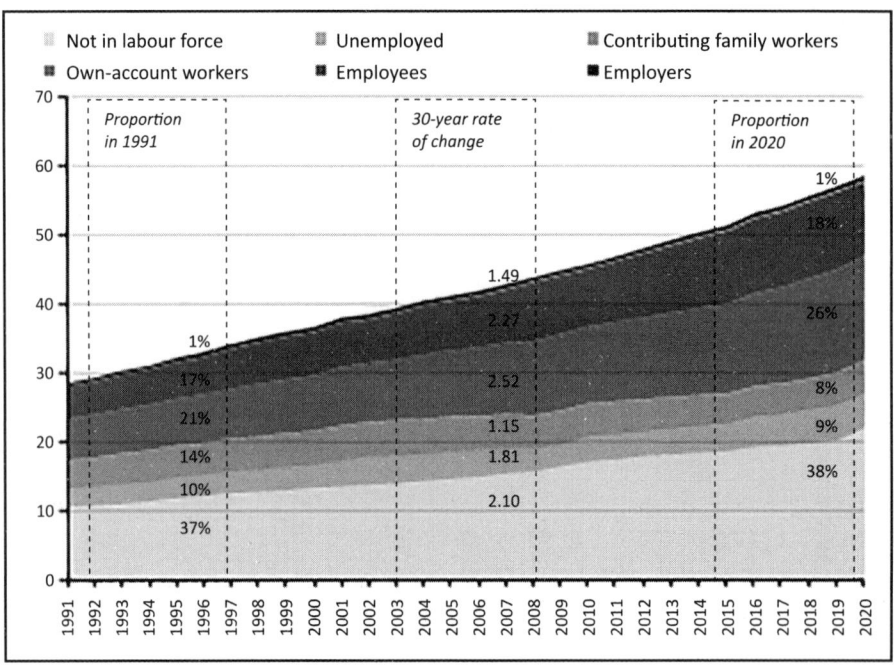

Source: ILO (2022).

West Africa (Figures 10.6a, 10.6b), by contrast, has the lowest level of proletarianization, below the continental average, at 10 per cent of the total workforce and as low as 6 per cent among women. But in this region, a larger decline of 7 per cent among the total of contributing family members, or a decline of 8 per cent among women, together with a decline of 3 per cent among own-account workers, which is concentrated among men, has been channelled partly (+2 per cent) into unemployment but mostly to those not in the labour force, which as a category gained 7 per cent for both men and women. The size of the petty bourgeoisie is also below the continental average and also concentrated among men.

Central Africa (Figures 10.7a, 10.7b) has a similar level of prole-tarianization as West Africa, at 12 per cent of the total workforce and 6 per cent among women. However, Central Africa registers the highest rate of proletarianization among women with a five-fold increase (5.42) or double the continental average rate. The proportion of the total working-age population outside the workforce is significantly lower in Central Africa at 33 per cent of the total or 38 per cent among women, but the rate of increase is also much higher at 3.22 and 3.27, respectively, compared to West Africa (2.7 and 2.62, respectively). In other words, aside from the growth in wage labour, the working-age population outside the workforce has been the category to which

Figure 10.6a *General employment status in West Africa,* in millions

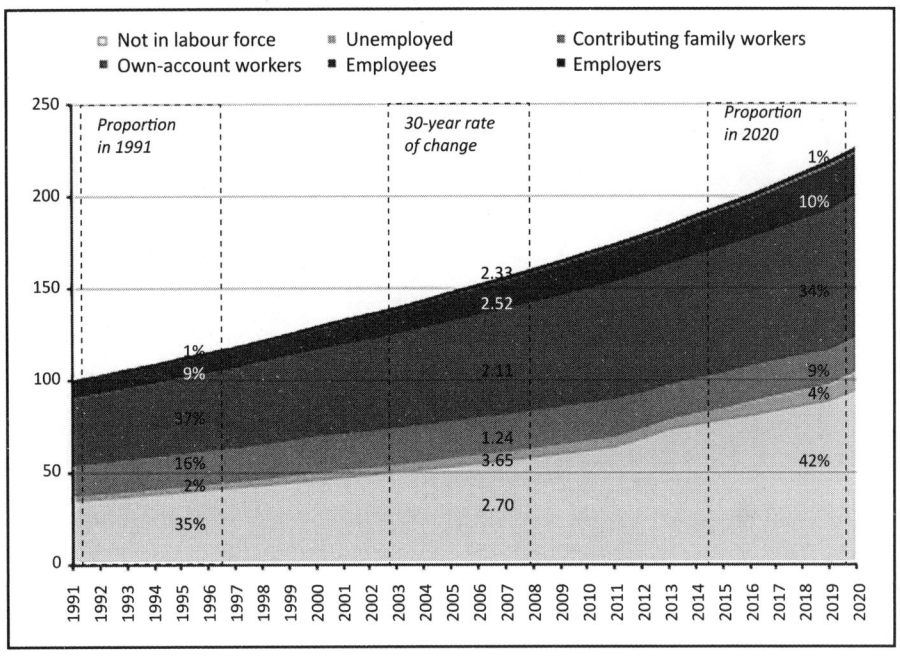

Source: ILO (2022).

Figure 10.6b *Women's employment status in West Africa,* in millions

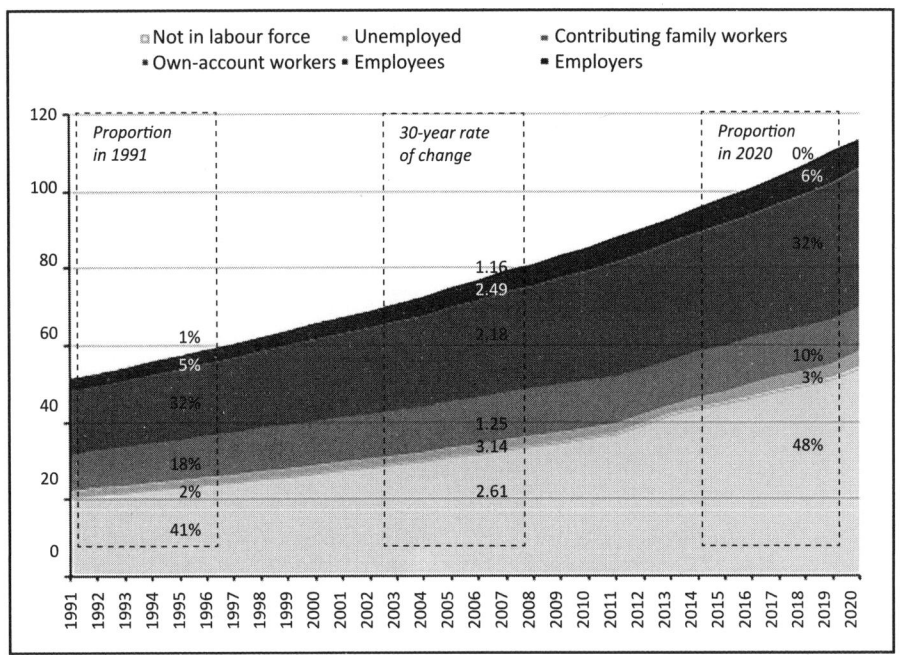

Source: ILO (2022).

Figure 10.7a *General employment status in Central Africa*, in millions

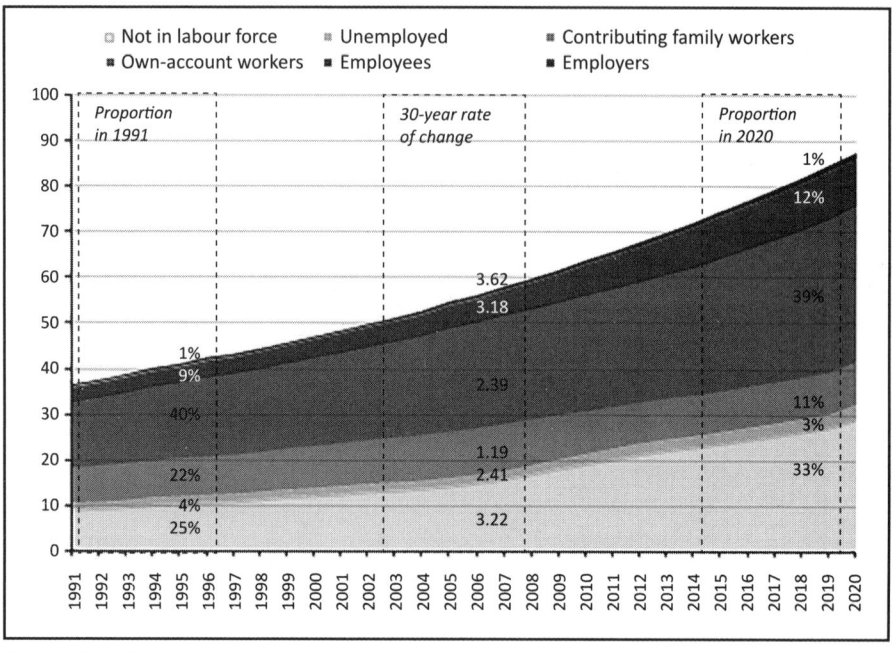

Source: ILO (2022).

Figure 10.7b *Women's employment status in Central Africa*, in millions

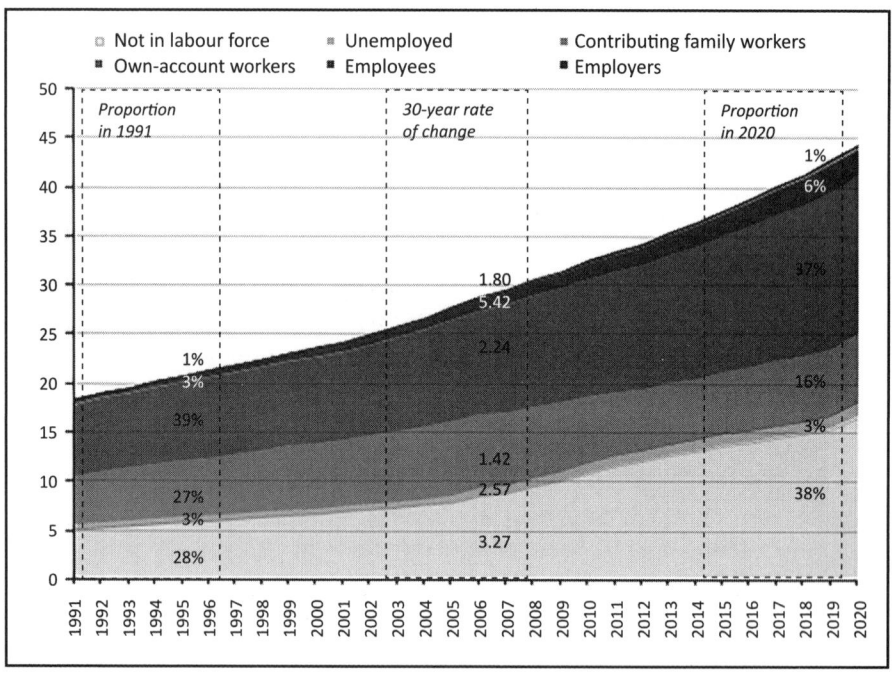

Source: ILO (2022).

the decline in other categories, especially among contributing family workers (- 11% for both men and women), has been channelled, above the category of proletarian labour. No significant change has occurred among the petty bourgeoisie, which appears to be similar among men and women.

East Africa (Figures 10.8a, 10.8b) holds a proximate position to West and Central Africa in terms of levels of proletarianization, at 14 per cent of the total and 9 per cent among women. However, the rate of proletariniazation has been higher than that of West Africa, at 3.31 for the total workforce or 3.85 for women. The category that again has declined the most is that of contributing family workers, by 6 per cent for the total workforce and 5 per cent among women. However, the decline has not been channelled significantly outside the workforce but has largely been absorbed partly by own-account labour (+1 per cent overall, or +3 per cent for women) and mostly by proletarianization (+3 per cent for both men and women). No significant change has occurred among the petty bourgeoisie, which again appears similar among men and women.

The sectoral distribution of employment is of further significance. On a continental level, the main change has been the decline in agricultural employment in this 30-year period from 60 to 49 per cent overall, which has been steeper for women, from 65 to 51 per cent (Figures 10.9a, 10.9b). This decline in employment in agriculture has been channelled almost entirely to the service sectors, which have grown overall from 28 to 38 per cent, and more so among women, from 26 to 41 per cent. Industrial employment overall has gained by only 1 per cent, which is concentrated among men, given that industrial employment among women has declined by 1 per cent. Thus, the category of own-account labour, which, as shown above, is the category to which most labour has been channelled (after those outside the labour force), is heavily concentrated in the service sectors. Therefore, it appears also that the small overall increase in proletarianization discussed earlier has not taken place in the industrial sector; in fact, for women, industrial employment has actually declined by 1 per cent.

Finally, the sectoral distribution of employment among sub-regions might give us some more clues as to the change in the patterns of accumulation (Figures 10.10a, 10.10b). In 1992, in all regions except for North Africa, agriculture was the dominant sector of employment; only in North Africa was the service sector slightly larger than agriculture in terms of employment (but both around 40 per cent). Employment in agriculture was just above 50 per cent in southern and West Africa, and above 70 per cent in Central and East Africa. Employment in services in North, southern, West, Central and East Africa stood at 40, 35, 30, 18 and 20 per cent, respectively. Industrial employment in North, southern, West, Central and East Africa stood at 21, 14, 12, 9 and 8 per cent, respectively. This distribution changed quite dramatically in the ensuing three decades, with the growth of the service sectors, but still

Figure 10.8a *General employment status in East Africa*, in millions

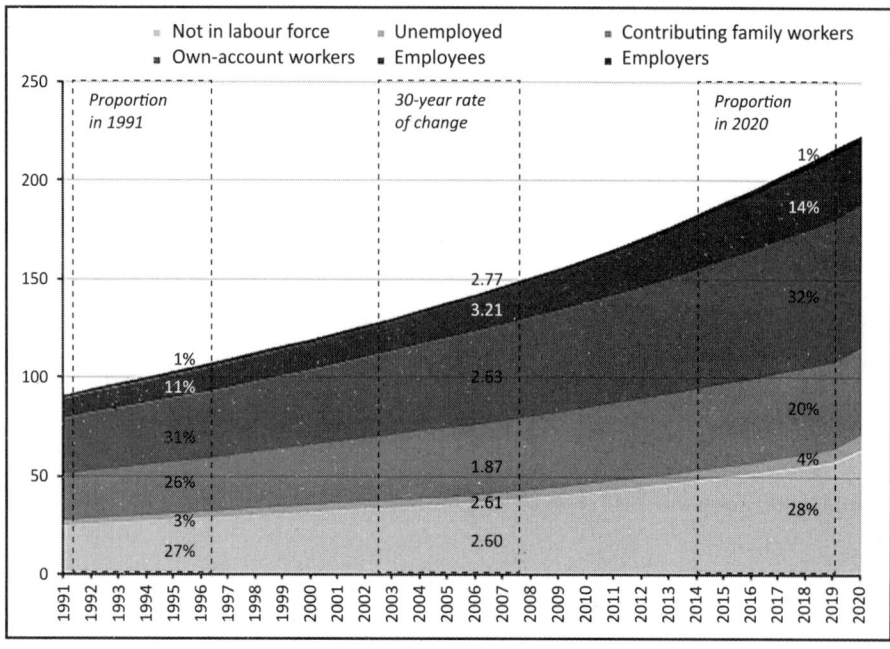

Source: ILO (2022).

Figure 10.8b *Women's employment status in East Africa*, in millions

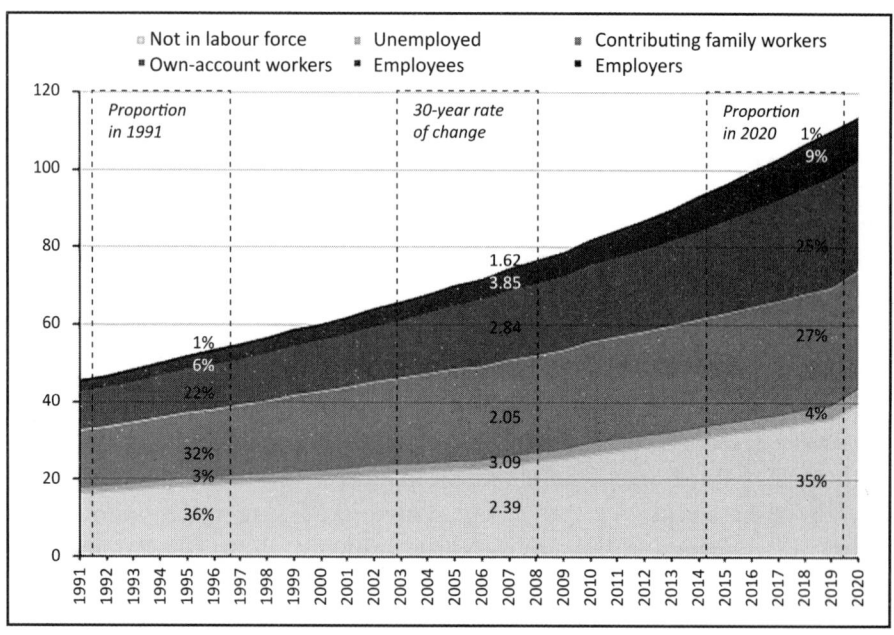

Source: ILO (2022).

Figure 10.9a *General employment by sector in Africa,* in millions

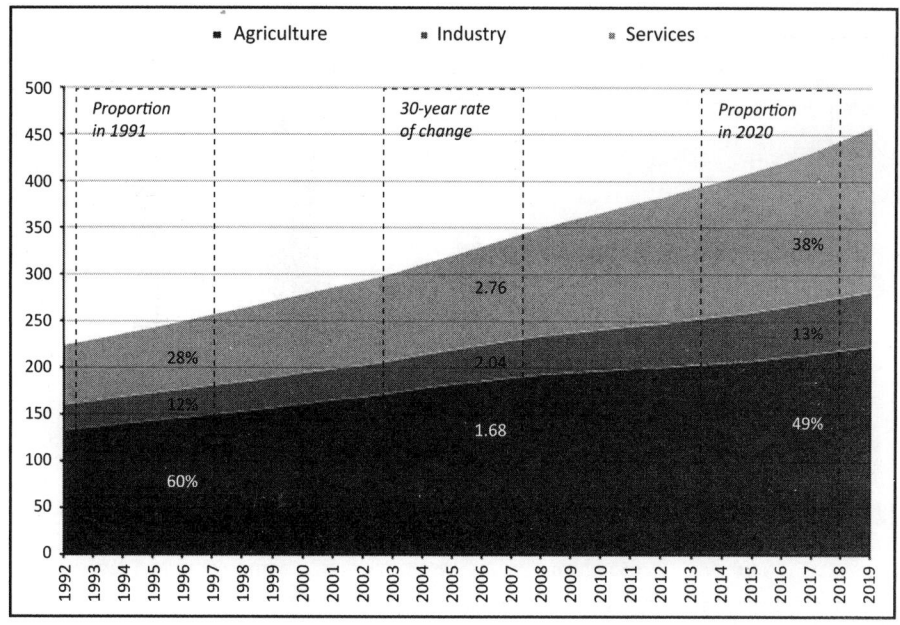

Source: ILO (2022).

Figure 10.9b *Women's employment by sector in Africa,* in millions

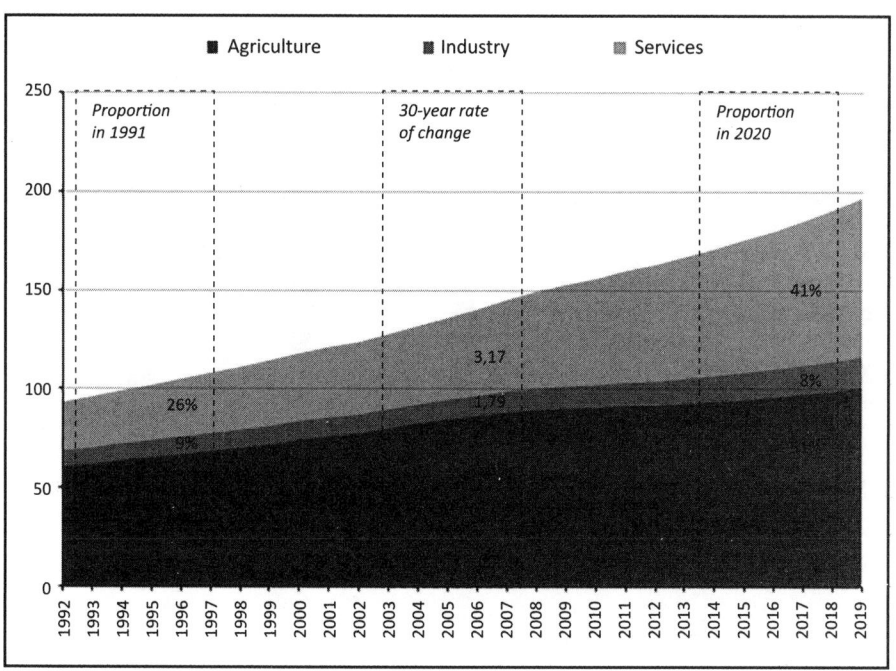

Source: ILO (2022).

Figure 10.10a *General employment by sector in the sub-regions in 1992,* employed workforce in per cent

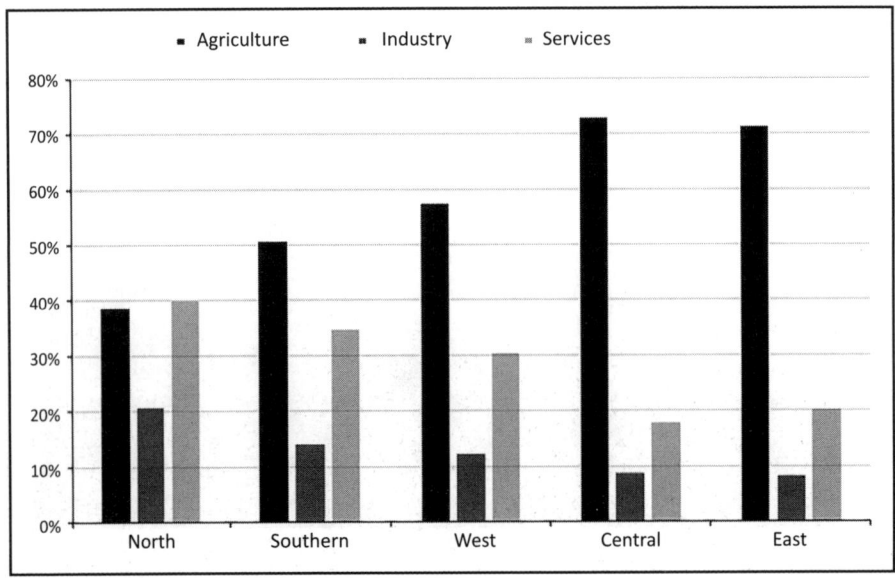

Source: ILO (2022).

Figure 10.10b *General employment by sector in the sub-regions in 2019,* employed workforce in per cent

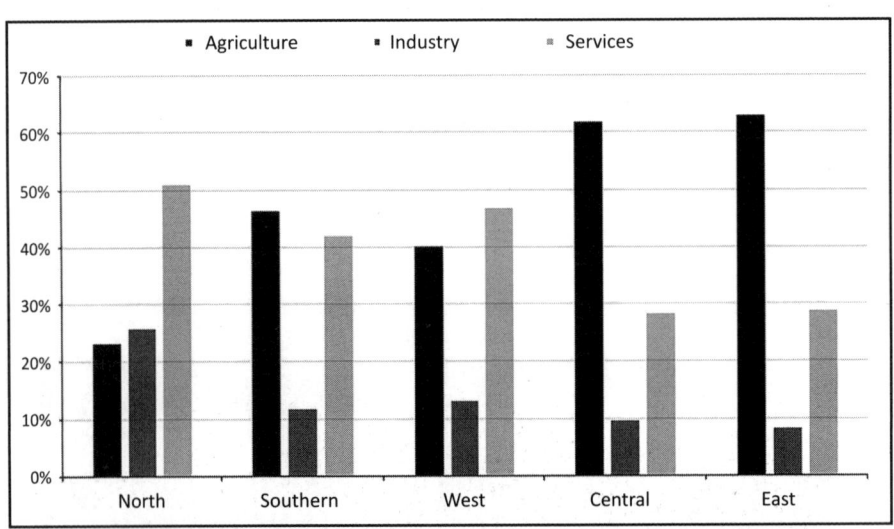

Source: ILO (2022).

unevenly. In North and West Africa, services overtook agriculture, reaching 51 versus 23 in North Africa and 47 versus 40 per cent in West Africa. Southern Africa seems to be reaching this point soon, given that employment in services, at 42 per cent, is near that of agriculture at 46 per cent. In Central and East Africa, despite the substantial growth of employment in services, up to 28 and 29 per cent, agriculture remains by far the largest sector of employment, at 62 and 63 per cent.

Industrial employment has grown mostly in North Africa, from 21 to 26 per cent; declined in Southern Africa from 14 to 12 per cent; increased marginally in West and Central Africa, from 12 to 13 per cent and 9 to 10 per cent, respectively; and stagnated in East Africa.

In terms of sectoral distribution of employment among the regions, therefore, we can surmise that North Africa stands out for the highest level of employment in industry among the regions, the lowest in agriculture and again the highest in services. West and Southern Africa have become very similar in their sectoral distribution of employment, with higher and almost equal levels of employment in agriculture and services and low and almost equal levels in industry. Central and East Africa have also become very similar in their sectoral distribution of employment, with the highest and almost equal levels of employment in agriculture, followed by lower and equal levels in services, and lowest and equal levels in industry.

Concluding Remarks on the Political Challenges

Much more remains to be said about these continental trends and also comparisons drawn with the other regions of the Third World. What has been shown here is that the trend towards structural convergence in Africa, although it involves several dimensions still to be verified, is fundamentally linked to the massive growth of labour reserves, which today are coextensive with the continent. Data from the ILO show that all macro-regions took the same path with regard to these transformations in the world of work. This finding does not eliminate the particularities of each macro-region but points to a common problem for development in the twenty-first century. It is, in fact, an existential crisis that is compounded by other crises – environmental, energy and food – generated by monopoly capitalism in this phase of late colonialism.

Clearly, the urgency is for a radical change of direction towards sovereign planning in the interest of absorbing, stabilizing and upgrading the level of social reproduction of the workforce *within a generation*. This requires not 'catching up' but delinking, in the sense given to it by Amin (1990[1985]), with a view to establishing rural–urban equilibrium in a manner that is sustainable under the changing environmental conditions. This means the opposite of promoting rural exodus; it means securing land rights for all rural and urban peoples and upgrading small-scale agricultural production alongside rural and urban industrialization.

The real question for the next generation is how to combine central planning for a petty-bourgeois economy – of micro, small and medium enterprises, which have the higher labour absorption capacity – with large public investments in infrastructure and heavy industries in support of accumulation from below. The challenge extends to guiding the social formation into collective and cooperative forms of property and organization with a view to enlarging the scale of production and the capacity for labour absorption and technical upgrading. The growth of industrial employment, in particular, must obtain a five-fold increase by 2050 in labour-absorbing industries, such as those linked to agriculture, which overall remains the highest employer in small production units, as well as to those linked to the processing of minerals and large-scale production of consumer and capital goods.

The accelerated development of the productive forces does raise anew the question of original accumulation. Insofar as a driving force is required for such accumulation, the bourgeoisie already absorbed into the foreign monopolies are incapable of vision or commitment. At best, fractions of the capitalist class might be co-opted into an introverted accumulation strategy on a national and regional basis. But this presupposes strong regional autonomy and coordination, central planning and public investment towards a strategy of development of public utilities and productive forces. And insofar as the source of accumulation is concerned, it is no longer the case of separating the producers from the means of production – for this is already far advanced – or of squeezing the peasantry, which cannot be squeezed any further. The answer lies precisely in delinking, which must include regional monetary autonomy, default on debt and nationalization of finance. However painful at first, this will free up financial resources for public investment, instead of perpetuating the drain of wealth. Delinking must also include energy and minerals and the imposition of sovereign terms on these concessions so as to enable the appropriation of rents for the purpose of public investment.

The revolutionary class that must prevail for central planning to obtain consists of none other than the semiproletarianized peasants and workers, oppressed peoples and women. As has been stressed here and elsewhere (Yeros 2021), the semiproletariat is fully capable of radical ideology and revolutionary party organization. It has nothing to lose and everything to gain. It is also capable of proletarian ideology, which remains the requirement for central planning and unity to be sustained into the next generation with a socialist orientation. It is certainly not the case that the condition of generalized semi-proletarianization requires a different ideological compass.

This essay was originally published under the same title in *The Indian Economic Journal*, vol. 71, no. 1, 2023, pp. 162–86.

This essay is the result of a study initiated during a sabbatical leave in 2021–22 at the Department of History of the University of São Paulo. The conditions for research have been maintained over a longer period by the Coordination of Personnel Development in Higher Education (CAPES) of the Brazilian Ministry of Education, including its support provided to the postgraduate programme in world political economy at the Federal University of ABC, my institutional home. The ideas presented here owe much to my research association with The Sam Moyo African Institute for Agrarian Studies in Zimbabwe and to the vigorous debates within the Agrarian South Network. This article is dedicated to Professors Utsa Patnaik and and Prabhat Patnaik, whose intellectual leadership has been an inspiration to us all. I wish to thank Praveen Jha, Lyn Ossome, Archana Prasad, Walter Chambati, Freedom Mazwi and Lincoln Secco for reading and commenting on an earlier draft.

References

African Development Bank (AfDB), Organisation for Economic Co-operation and Development (OECD) and United Nations Development Programme (UNDP) (2014), *African Economic Outlook 2014: Global Value Chains and Africa's Industrialization*, Abidjan: AfDB.

African Union (AU) (2009), *Africa Mining Vision*, African Union.

Amanor, K.S. (2019), 'Global Value Chains and Agribusiness in Africa: Upgrading or Capturing Smallholder Production?', *Agrarian South: Journal Of Political Economy*, vol. 8, nos 1–2, pp. 30–63.

Amanor, K.S. and S. Moyo, eds (2008), *Land and Sustainable Development in Africa*, London and New York: Zed Books.

Amanor-Wilks, D. (2009), 'Land, Labour and Gendered Livelihoods in a 'Peasant' and a 'Settler' Economy', *Feminist Africa*, vol. 12, no. 2, pp. 31–50.

Amin, S. (1972), 'Underdevelopment and Dependence in Black Africa: Origins and Contemporary Forms', *The Journal of Modern African Studies*, vol. 10, no. 4, pp. 503–24.

—— (1973), *Neo-colonialism in West Africa*, F. McDonagh, trans., New York: Monthly Review Press.

—— (1976), *Unequal Development: An Essay on the Social Formations of Peripheral Capitalism*, B. Pierce, trans., Sussex: The Harvester Press.

—— (1977), *Imperialism and Unequal Development*, New York: Monthly Review Press.

—— (1990[1985]), *Delinking: Towards a Polycentric World*, M. Wolfers, trans., Zed Books.

—— *The Law of Worldwide Value*, B. Pierce and S. Mage, trans., Monthly Review Press.

—— (2014), Understanding the Political Economy of Contemporary Africa, *African Development*, vol. 39, no. 1, pp. 15–36.

—— (2019), 'The New Imperialist Structure', *Monthly Review*, vol. 71, no. 3, https://monthlyreview.org/2019/07/01/the-new-imperialist-structure/

Arrighi, G. (1970), 'Labour Supplies in Historical Perspective: A Study of the Proletarianization of the African Peasantry in Rhodesia', *Journal of Development Studies*, vol. 6, no. 3, pp. 197–234.

Bryceson, D.F. and S. Geenen (2016), 'Artisanal Frontier Mining of Gold in Africa: Occupational Transformation in Tanzania and the Democratic Republic of Congo', *African Affairs*, pp. 115, no. 459, pp. 296–317.

Bryceson, D. F. and J.B. Jønson (2009), 'Gold Digging Careers in Rural East Africa: Small-scale Miners' Livelihood Choices', *World Development*, vol. 38, no. 3, pp. 379–92.

Bush, R. (2004), 'Undermining Africa', *Historical Materialism*, vol. 12, no. 4, pp. 173–201.

Cabral, A. (1969), *Brief Analysis of the Social Structure in Guinea*, www.marxists.org/subject/africa/cabral/1964/bassg.htm

—— (1979), *Unity and Struggle*, New York: Monthly Review Press.

Carmody, P. (2016), *The New Scramble for Africa*, Maldem, MA: Polity Press.

Chambati, W. (2019), *Changing Agrarian Labour Relations in Zimbabwe in the Context of the Fast Track Land Reform*, PhD thesis, University of South Africa.

—— (2022), *Trajectories of Rural Labour in Southern Africa: Revisiting the Proletarianisation, Semi-proletarianisation, De-agrarianisation and Re-peasantisation theses*, Mimeo.

Chambati, W. and F. Mazwi (2022), 'Contract Farming in Zimbabwe: Review of Issues, Debates and Practice with a Special Reference to Cotton, Tobacco and Sugar', in P. Jha, P. Yeros, W. Chambati and F. Mazwi, eds, *Farming and Working Under Contract: Peasants and Workers in Global Agricultural Value Systems*, Delhi:Tulika Books, pp. 127–57.

Cordell, D.D., J.W. Gregory and V. Piché (1998), *Hoe and wage: A Social History of a Circular Migration System in West Africa*, Boulder, CO: Westview Press.

de Janvry, A. (1981), *The Agrarian Question and Reformism in Latin America*. Johns Hopkins University Press.

Deere, C.D. (1976). Rural women's subsistence production in the capitalist periphery. *Review of Radical Political Economics*, vol. 8, no. 9, pp. 9–17.

Depelchin, J. (1992). *From the Congo Free State to Zaire, 1885–1974*, CODESRIA.

Fanon, F. (1963), *The Wretched of the Earth*, New York: Grove Press.

First, R. (1983), *Black Gold*, Susses: Harvester.

Geenen, S. (2015), *African Artisanal Mining from Inside Out: Access, Norms and Power in Congo's Gold Sector*, Abingdon: Routledge.

Hall, R., I. Scoones and D. Tsikata, eds (2015). *Africa's Land Rush: Rural Livelihoods and Agrarian Change*, Suffolk and Rochester, NY: James Currey.

Hilson, G. and C. Garforth (2012), 'Agricultural Poverty' and the Expansion of Artisanal Mining in Sub-Saharan Africa: Experiences from Southwest Mali and Southeast Ghana', *Population Research and Policy Review*, vol. 31, no. 3, pp. 435–64.

International Labour Organization (ILO) (2022), *World Economic and Social Outlook Data Finder*, https://www.ilo. org/wesodata

Jacobs, R. (2018) 'An urban Proletariat with Peasant Characteristics: Land Occupations and Livestock Raising in South Africa', *Journal of Peasant Studies*, vol. 45, nos 5–6, pp. 884–903.

Jha, P., W. Chambati and L. Ossome, eds (2021), *Labour Questions in the Global South*, Singapore: Palgrave Macmillan.

Jha, P., S. Moyo and P. Yeros (2017), 'Capitalism and 'Labour Reserves: A Note', in C.P. Chandrasekhar and J. Ghosh, eds, *Interpreting the World to Change it: Essays for Prabhat Patnaik*, Delhi: Tulika Books, pp. 205–37.

Jha, P., P. Yeros, W. Chambati and F. Mazwi (2022), *Farming and Working Under Contract: Peasants and Workers in Global Agricultural Value Systems*, Delhi: Tulika Books.

Kautsky, K. (1988 [1899]), *The Agrarian Question*, P. Burgess, trans., London and Winchester, MA: Zwan.

Lenin, V.I. (1964 [1899]), *The Development of Capitalism in Russia*, Moscow: Progress Publishers.

Li, M. (2008), *The Rise of China and the Demise of the Capitalist World Economy*, London: Pluto Press.

Mafeje, A. (1978), *Science, Ideology and Development: Three Essays on Development Theory*, Uppsala: Scandinavian Institute of African Studies.

——— (1981), 'On the Articulation of Modes of Production: Review Article', *Journal of Southern African Studies*, vol. 8, no. 1, pp. 123–38.

——— (1991), *The Theory and Ethnography of African Social Formations: The Case of the Interlacustrine Kingdoms*, Dakar: CODESRIA.

——— (2003). *The Agrarian Question, Access to Land, and Peasant Responses in Sub-Saharan Africa*, Civil Society and Social Movements Programme Paper No. 6, Geneva: United Nations Research Institute for Social Development (UNRISD).

Magubane, B.M. (1979), *The Political Economy of Race and Class in South Africa*, New York: Monthly Review Press.

Mamdani, M. (1996), *Citizen and Subject: Contemporary Africa and the Legacy of Late Colonialism*, Princeton, NJ: Princeton University Press.

Manji, A. (2006), *The Politics of Land Reform in Africa: From Communal Tenure to Free Markets*, London and New York: Zed Books.

Mao, T.-T. (2004 [1926]), 'Analysis of the Classes in Chinese Society', *Selected Works*, vol. 1, www.marxists.org/ reference/archive/mao/selected-works/volume-1/mswv1_1.htm

Martiniello, G. and R. Azambuja (2019), 'Contracting Sugarcane Farming in Global Agricultural Value Chains in Eastern Africa', *Agrarian South: Journal of Political Economy*, vol. 8, nos 1–2, pp. 208–31.

Marx, K. (1990 [1867]), *Capital*, vol. 1, London: Penguin Books.

Mazwi, F., G.T. Mudimu and K. Helliker, eds (2022), *Capital Penetration and the Peasantry in Southern and Eastern Africa: Neoliberal Restructuring*, Cham: Springer.

Meagher, K. (2019), 'Working in Chains: African Informal Workers and Global Value Chains', *Agrarian South: Journal of Political Economy*, vol. 8, nos 1–2, pp. 64–92.

Mkodzongi, G. (2021), 'Primitive Accumulation and Exploitative Labour Relations in Zimbabwe's Artisanal and Small-scale Gold Mining (ASGM) Sector: The Case of Mhondoro Ngezi', in P. Jha, W. Chambati and L. Ossome, eds, *Labour Questions in the Global South*, Singapore: Palgrave Macmillan, pp. 205–24.

Mkodzongi, G. and S. Spiegel (2018), Artisanal Gold Mining and Farming: Livelihood Linkages and Labour Dynamics after Land Reforms in Zimbabwe, *Journal of Development Studies*, vol. 55, pp. 1–17.

Moyo, S. (2008), *African Land Questions, Agrarian Transitions and the State: Contradictions of Neo-liberal Land Reforms*, Dakar: CODESRIA.

Moyo, S. and W. Chambati, eds (2013), *Land and Agrarian Reform in Zimbabwe: Beyond White-Settler Capitalism*, Dakar: CODESRIA.

Moyo, S., P. Jha and P. Yeros, eds (2019), *Reclaiming Africa: Scramble and Resistance in the 21st Century*, Singapore: Springer.

Moyo, S., D. Tsikata and Y. Diop, eds (2015), *Land in the Struggles for African Citizenship*, Dakar: CODESRIA.

Moyo, S. and P. Yeros, eds (2005), 'The Resurgence of Rural Movements under Neoliberalism', in S. Moyo and P. Yeros, eds, *Reclaiming the Land: The Resurgence of Rural Movements in Africa, Asia and Latin America*, London: Zed Books and Cape Town: David Philip, pp. 8–64.

Moyo, S. and P. Yeros (2007), 'The Zimbabwe Question and the Two Lefts', *Historical Materialism*, vol. 15, pp. 171–204.

——— (2011), 'After Zimbabwe: State, Nation and Region in Africa', in S. Moyo and P. Yeros, eds, *Reclaiming the Nation: The Return of the National Question in Africa, Asia and Latin America*, pp. 78–102, London: Pluto Press.

Moyo, S. and P. Yeros (2013), 'The Zimbabwe Model: Radicalisation, Reform and Resistance', in S. Moyo and W. Chambati, eds, *Land and Agrarian Reform in Zimbabwe: Beyond White-Settler Capitalism*, Dakar: CODESRIA, pp. 331–58.

Moyo, S., P. Jha and P. Yeros (2013), 'The Classical Agrarian Question: Myth, Reality and Relevance Today', *Agrarian South: Journal of Political Economy*, vol. 2, no. 1, pp. 93–119.

——— (2016), 'The Agrarian Question and Trajectories of Economic Transformation: A Perspective from the South', in E.S. Reinert, J. Ghosh and R. Kattel, eds, *Handbook of Alternative Theories of Economic Development*, Northampton: Edward Elgar, pp. 487–503.

Moyo, S., P. Yeros and P. Jha (2012), 'Imperialism and Primitive Accumulation: Notes on the New Scramble for Africa. *Agrarian South: Journal of Political Economy*, vo. 1, no. 2, pp. 181–203.

——— (2018), 'Peasant Farming in Sub-Saharan Africa: Contemporary Trajectories and Prospects', in A. Banerjee and C.P. Chandrasekhar, eds, *Dispossession, Deprivation and Development: Essays for Utsa Patnaik*, Delhi: Tulika Books, pp. 10–36.

Naidu, S.C. and L. Ossome (2016), 'Social Reproduction and the Agrarian Question of Women's Labour in India', *Agrarian South: Journal of Political Economy*, vol. 5, no. 1, 50–76.

Nkrumah, K. (1971), *Class Struggle in Africa*, New York: International Publishers.

Obi, C. (2012), 'Transnationalism, Africa's Resource Curse and Contested Sovereignties: The Struggle for Nigeria's Niger Delta', in S. Cornelissen, F. Cheru and T. Shaw, eds, *Africa and International Relations in the 21st Century*, New York: Palgrave Macmillan, pp. 147–61.

Obi, C., and S.A. Rustad, eds (2011), *Oil and Insurgency in the Niger Delta: Managing the Complex Politics of Petro-Violence*, London: Zed Books and Uppsala: Nordic Africa Institute.

O'Laughlin, B. (2001), *Proletarianisation, Agency and Changing Rural Livelihoods: Forced Labour and Resistance in Colonial Mozambique*, Working Paper Series, no. 354, The Hague: ISS.

Ossome, L. (2021), 'Introduction: The Social Reproductive Question of Land Contestations in Africa', *African Affairs*, https://academic.oup.com/afraf/article-abstract/121/484/e9/6 425892?redirectedFrom=fulltext

Ossome, L., and S. Naidu (2021), 'The Agrarian Question of Gendered Labour', in P. Jha, W. Chambati and L. Ossome, eds, *Labour Questions in the Global South*, Singapore: Palgrave Macmillan, pp. 63–86.

Patnaik, P. (2008), *The Value of Money*, Delhi: Tulika Books.

————— (2015), 'Capitalism and Inequality', *Agrarian South: Journal of Political Economy*, vol. 4, no. 2, pp. 153–68.

Patnaik, U. and S. Moyo (2011), *The Agrarian Question in the Neoliberal Era: Primitive Accumulation and the Peasantry*, with a preface by I.G. Shivji, Cape Town, Kakar, Nairobi, Oxford and Dar es Salaam: Pambazuka Press and the Mwalimu Nyerere Chair in Pan-African Studies, University of Dar es Salaam.

Patnaik, U. and P. Patnaik (2017), *A Theory of Imperialism*, New York: Columbia University Press.

————— (2021), *Capital and Imperialism: Theory, History and the Present*, New York: Monthly Review Press.

Prasad, A. (2016), 'Adivasi Women, Agrarian Change and Forms of Labour in Neo-liberal India, *Agrarian South: Journal of Political Economy*, vol. 5, no. 1, pp. 20–49.

Rodney, W. (1972), *How Europe Underdeveloped Africa*, Dar es Salaam: Tanzanian Publishing House.

————— (1981), 'Plantation Society in Guyana', *Review*, vol. 4, no. 4, pp. 643–66.

Shivji, I.G. (1976), *Class Struggles in Tanzania*, New York: Monthly Review Press.

————— (2017), 'The Concept of Working People', *Agrarian South: Journal of Political Economy*, vol. 6, no. 1, pp. 1–13.

Torvikey, G.D. (2022), 'The Boom and Bust of Industrial Cassava Contract Farming Scheme in South-Eastern Ghana', in P. Jha, P. Yeros, W. Chambati and F. Mazwi, eds, *Farming and Working Under Contract: Peasants and Workers in Global Agricultural Value Systems*, Delhi: Tulika Books, pp. 314–30.

Tsikata, D. (2016), Gender, Land Tenure and Agrarian Production Systems in sub-Saharan-Africa, *Agrarian South: Journal of Political Economy*, vol. 5, no. 1, pp. 1–19.

————— (2022), 'The Transmission of Global Norms and Standards to Sub-National Spaces: A View of the Coalface of Contract Farming in Ghana', in P. Jha, P. Yeros, W. Chambati and F. Mazwi, eds, *Farming and Working Under Contract: Peasants and Workers in Global Agricultural Value Systems*, Delhi: Tulika Books, pp. 255–78.

Wallerstein, I. (1983), *Historical Capitalism*, London: Verso.

Williams, E. (1994 [1944]), *Capitalism and Slavery*, Chapel Hill, NC: University of North Carolina Press.

Wise, T.A. (2020), *Failing Africa's Farmers: An Impact Assessment of the Alliance for a Green Revolution in Africa*, Working Paper no. 20–01, Boston: Global Development and Environment Institute, pp. 1–38.

Yates, D.A. (1996), *The Rentier State in Africa: Oil Rent Dependency and Neocolonialism in the Republic of Gabon*, Trenton: African World Press.

Yeros, P. (2021, August–September), 'Elements of a New Bandung: Towards an International Solidarity Front', *ASN Research Bulletin*, vol. 10, pp. 26–40.

Yeros, P. and P. Jha (2020), 'Late Neocolonialism: Monopoly Capitalism in Permanent Crisis', *Agrarian South: Journal of Political Economy*, vol. 9, no. 1, pp. 78–93.

Zhan, S. and B. Scully (2018), 'From South Africa to China: Land, Migrant Labour and the Semi-Proletarian Thesis Revisited', *Journal of Peasant Studies*, vol. 45, nos 5–6, pp. 1018–38.

11

India's GST Paradigm and the Trajectory of Fiscal Federalism

An Analysis with Special Reference to Kerala

K.J. Joseph and Anitha Kumary L.

Introduction

It is generally perceived that there is no unique goods and services tax (GST) and different models are covering a variety of activities in different countries depending on what is politically acceptable (M.G. Rao 2011). Therefore, GST adopted by over 160 countries, given its inbuilt scope for flexibility (Bird and Gendron 2007), vary from one country to another. It has also been argued that the design and implementation of GST in countries with federal constitutional structures is a rather challenging task (Tait 1988). The problems get compounded in developing country federations *inter alia* on account of intergovernmental political differences and federal constitutional structures coupled with problems of low per capita income, high-income inequalities, regional disparities in development, fiscal imbalances, poor accounting practices and weak tax administration (Bird and Gendron 2007; Gillis, Shoup and Sicat, eds 1990).

In the Indian context, GST was viewed by the states with considerable apprehension as it was perceived to be instrumental in depriving them of their autonomy which was considered a prerequisite for India to remain united as a federal democracy. Scholars of eminence, Bagchi (2006, 2007), Patnaik (2016) and R.K. Rao (2016), among others, shared the same view. Quoting the experience of the United States (US), The European Union (EU), New Zealand and others, these scholars argued that the essence of taxing power lies in the power to fix the tax rates, and thus sub-national governments must have the autonomy in matters of fixing the rates, subject only to a floor. If the state GST (SGST) rates are not allowed to vary from state to state with some provision for entry tax, the fiscal autonomy of the states might be compromised forever. The task force on GST of the Thirteenth Finance Commission noted that a conventional GST could not be implemented without the states losing their fiscal autonomy (Government of India [GoI] 2009a). Such fears have been justified in the context of growing vertical inequality wherein the states spend around 60 per cent of the combined government expenditure while collecting only around 40 per cent of the combined revenue (Thomas Isaac, Mohan and Chakraborty 2019a,b; Reddy and Reddy 2019). More importantly, as per GST design, the sales tax was to be subsumed in GST, and it has been contributing around 60–65 per cent of the state's own tax revenue over the years (Kishore 2012). Hence it is a matter of great achievement for India that it managed to come up with the new tax regime on 1 July 2017, learning from the long drawn-out deliberations for over 17 years, that changed the landscape of central and state taxes in the country.

Against this background, this essay seeks answers to three specific issues of analytical and policy significance. First, what are the unique characteristics of the GST paradigm that evolved in India *inter alia* to address the apprehensions of states regarding the loss of their autonomy? Second, how has the GST implementation impacted the trajectory of India's fiscal federalism and finally how has it impacted the tax revenue of states?

The remainder of the essay is organized as follows. The second section articulates the key attributes of the Indianized GST paradigm that are primarily in the domain of centre–state fiscal relations: revenue neutrality, tax sharing between the centre and the states and GST compensation. The second section analyses the extent to which the key attributes of India's GST paradigm have been helpful in ensuring revenue productivity of states, a *sine qua non* for building cooperative federalism in the country, the third section presents evidence on the state-level tax effort under GST followed by the last section wherein the concluding observations are presented.

Indianized GST Paradigm

The introduction of the GST in India has often been considered a landmark reform in India's tax system since its independence. GST, already functional in over 160 countries across the world, has been perceived as a win-win for India given its potential to:

(1) make India a common market and draw in more foreign investments by removing barriers to factor and product mobility;

(2) reduce complexity and hence compliance cost and litigation through a simplified GST structure with an uninterrupted chain of input tax credit transfers from one stage to another in the chain of value addition;

(3) make the Indian industry more export-competitive by removing the cascading effect of taxes and hereby reducing the overall cost of indigenous products and services; and

(4) accelerate economic growth by facilitating the more efficient[1] allocation of resources and promoting trade, business and investment (Rao, Mukherjee and Bagchi 2019).

Other expected benefits included, but were not limited to, reduced inflation, shifting the tax burden from producers and suppliers to the final consumers, and improved tax compliance and transparency (Das 2017; Kumar 2015). All these positive outcomes are expected to contribute to augmenting GDP growth by at least 1–2 per cent, tax effort (tax–GDP ratio) by 2 per cent and reducing the cost of indigenous goods by around 10 per cent.

These perceived advantages notwithstanding, M.G. Rao (2011) argued that the introduction of GST reform in India requires greater recognition of and sensitivity to the views of the states, and IMF-type 'one size fits all' could simply stall the process. Hence, it is imperative that while embarking on the GST reform agenda and achieving higher revenue productivity and minimizing distortions, there is also the need to safeguard fiscal autonomy and ensure that the reform shall not deprive states of their fiscal autonomy. The call for the need to ensure fiscal autonomy of states needs to be viewed in the context wherein the disagreement between the centre and the states in the design of GST in India centred around the issue of subsuming the sales tax in GST, the only significant revenue source for the states in India (Mukhopadhyay 2003). Thus viewed, since GST demands the states to forgo their taxing rights over their crucial source of revenue, the trajectory of fiscal federalism and the fiscal health of the states therein is bound to be conditioned by the GST paradigm adopted by the country. This takes us to an examination of the key attributes of the 'Indianized' GST paradigm, which was destined to be cognizant of the imperative of addressing various complexities involved in introducing GST in a country, which is more diverse than most continents.

Perhaps the most important attribute of India's GST paradigm, viewed from the perspective of fiscal federalism, is its explicit commitment to revenue neutrality. Since the effectiveness of any tax reform quintessentially hinges on ensuring revenue neutrality, much scholarly effort has been invested in articulating the revenue neutral rate (RNR) before the implementation of GST (Rao and Chakraborty, 2010). The RNR estimated was 13.3 per cent for the centre and 14.8 per cent for the states (Rao and Chakraborthy, 2014). The GST task force appointed by the thirteenth Finance Commission suggested a 12 per cent GST rate (7 per cent as state GST and 5 per cent as central GST). However, the report on RNR by Aravind Subramanian recommended an RNR of 15–15.5 per cent. The Committee also observed that there should not be large shifts in the tax base in moving to the GST, implying that overall compensation may not be large. The rate fitment committee appointed by GST Council recommended the rates under GST after taking into account the pre-GST period tax incidence (on account of central excise, services tax and VAT (including cascading on account of these taxes) as well as the embedded taxes and the incidence of GST, octroi, entry tax, etc. (Minutes of 14th GST Council, 18–19 May 2017; Subramanian 2015, 2018). Hence, to protect revenue neutrality, the fitment committee considered pre-GST tax incidence.

Although the experts believe that there should be only a single and uniform rate (M.G. Rao 2011), based on the neutrality principle, a system of multiple rates namely 5 per cent, 12 per cent, 18 per cent and 28 per cent has been put in place.[2] With the rate for precious metals being 3 per cent and unworked diamonds and precious stones, attracting 0.25 per cent, essential goods and services are exempted. While there is no standard rate for services, most services are taxed at 18 per cent. While GST applies to all goods and services, to offset, at least partly, the revenue loss of states, certain goods with considerable revenue potential like alcohol for human consumption and five specified petroleum products (crude oil, petrol, diesel, aviation turbine fuel [ATF] and natural gas) were excluded from GST. The centre and the states mutually agreed upon the rates on each of these components under the aegis of the GST council.

Another important characteristic of India's GST paradigm, apart from ensuring revenue neutrality, is a system of tax revenue sharing between the centre and the states. By subsuming VAT, central excise and various other indirect taxes of the centre[3] and states,[4] GST has been designed on the principle of destination-based consumption taxation, with seamless provision for the input tax credit. GST in India is a tax on the 'supply' of goods or services as against the concept of tax on the manufacture of goods or sale of goods, or on the provision of services. Cognizant of the revenue forgone by both the centre and the states, it is a dual GST with the centre and the states simultaneously levying it on a common base and shared equally between them. By design, GST revenue has three components to be shared between the centre and the states. The GST levied by the centre is called central good services tax (CGST), and that levied by the state is called state goods and services tax (SGST). Union territories without legislature levy union territory goods and services tax (UTGST). An integrated goods services tax (IGST) is levied on the interstate supply (including stock transfers) of goods or services. Import of goods is treated as interstate supplies and is subject to IGST in addition to the applicable customs duties. Import of services is also treated as interstate supplies and is subject to IGST. The revenue from interstate IGST goes to a separate account, adjusted against the input tax credit for final settlement and based on final consumption shared between the state concerned and the centre through a clearing house mechanism.

The assurance of revenue neutrality notwithstanding, considering the eventuality of GST revenue not keeping on par with the pre-GST tax revenue, the GST paradigm provided for GST compensation for the states. This is yet another unique characteristic inherent in the Indianized GST paradigm brought out by institutional innovation. Accordingly, in addition to the basic rate, most items under the 28 per cent category are subjected to a cess, the proceeds used to pay GST compensation to the states. Backed by the GST (Compensation to States) Act 2017, the states are eligible to get 100 per cent compensation for the revenue loss for five years since the implementation of GST. There have been instances of union government not living up to its commitments to provide compensation to state governments for the revenue loss they had incurred on account of the phasing out of the central sales tax, which gave rise to a trust deficit between the union and the states. This presumably has given rise to the enactment of the legislation guaranteeing the payment to the states of the deemed revenue loss on GST implementation (Bhaskar 2021). The loss of revenue to a state is computed as the difference between the actual realization to a state under the GST regime and the tax revenue it would have received under the old indirect tax regime after considering a 14 per cent increase over the base year of 2015–16.

While a range of state taxes was replaced with GST, its potentially centralizing implications for fiscal federalism are sought to be offset by mechanisms of intergovernmental coordination and dispute settlement at the instance of the Goods and Service Tax Council (GSTC). GSTC, an apex committee, chaired by the union finance minister and state finance ministers as its members, is expected to ensure that decisions about the structure, design and operation of GST are taken jointly by the centre and the states. It also holds the responsibility of modifying, reconciling or procuring any laws or regulations related to GST in India. The GST council can make any recommendation to the union and state governments on all aspects relating to GST that include, but are not limited to, inclusion and exclusion of products or services under GST and revising rates. It also has the responsibility to ensure that the laws and regulations related to GST are properly implemented. The main purpose of the GST council is to ensure that the laws and regulations related to GST are properly implemented and thus act as the guardian of cooperative federalism under GST. Nonetheless, the central government holds one-third of the total votes in the council, while the state governments, put together, account for the remaining two-thirds of the total votes. This tends to suggest that, in effect, the centre enjoys an effective veto power in the council and the relative bargaining power of states in the GST council is much less as compared to the central government (Reddy 2019).

Therefore, the Indianized GST paradigm, built on the three pillars of revenue neutrality, tax sharing between the two and GST compensation with GST council as its edifice, appears unique for helping evolve a cooperative fiscal federalism by addressing India-specific issues, especially the concerns of the states. Hence, it has been seen as a successful experiment by the centre and the states envisaging cooperative federalism (M.G. Rao 2011). At the same time, the equal sharing of GST revenue and preponderance of the centre are indicators of the fault lines in its design that augur well in fostering cooperative fiscal federalism. Nonetheless, the issue of concern is also with respect to the implementation of the paradigm and its effectiveness in ensuring revenue productivity for the states, which could be considered the primary indicator of the success of any tax reform on the one hand and cooperative fiscal federalism on the other. Exploration of these issues assumes importance not only for articulating the needed changes in the system but also in understanding the state's fiscal health, especially that of fiscally stressed ones, under the new tax regime. Before proceeding further, we hasten to add that almost all the countries that adopted GST have taken considerable time to settle down. For example, even after thirty years, GST is still evolving in Canada (Bird 2012). Hence, it may be rather heroic to undertake such an exercise for India on its fifth anniversary. Further, the introduction of GST was preceded by unexpected shocks, including demonetization and Covid-19, that succeeded and persists.

The Paradigm and Performance in Cooperative Federalism

Although fiscal federalism does not formally appear in any constitutional document, Oates (1999) and Sharma (2021) postulated that fiscal federalism is concerned with understanding which functions and instruments are best centralized and which are best placed in the sphere of decentralized levels of government. This concept applies to all forms of government: unitary, federal and confederal. Bhaskar (2014, 2021) articulated that fiscal federalism envisages the empowerment of revenue capacities and the allocation of expenditure responsibilities among the different layers of a federation and their fulfilment efficiently and effectively. Thus, in the real world, fiscal federalism goes beyond the mere allocation of fiscal powers and considers how the system functions through real-world intergovernmental relations. The performance of both the centre and the states concerning GDP growth, efficient provisioning of public services to people and tax collection on the one hand and its distribution between the centre and the states on the other are also at the core of the debate on federal fiscal relations in India.

Revenue Neutrality

The commitment to building cooperative fiscal federalism has been evident from the explicit recognition of the states' need to ensure revenue neutrality. The RNR under GST refers the tax rates that protect the prior revenue after subsuming the existing taxes. While computing the RNR for the centre is relatively simple, computing the RNR for the states individually is a difficult task at best and impossible at worst, given difficulties in estimating the projected share of service tax state-wise after allowing for input tax credit (Bhaskar and Kailash Nath 2015).

It needs to be noted that during the pre-GST period, most of the goods attracted a tax rate of 14.5 per cent by the states. With the introduction of GST, 14.5 per cent of category good has been brought under the 12 per cent or 18 per cent category, wherein the states' share is only 6 per cent or 9 per cent, respectively (M.G. Rao 2009). Only a few goods were brought under the category of 28 per cent where the share of the states is 14 per cent which is lower than the 14.5 per cent that prevailed in most states. Further, the Task Force headed by Arbind Modi appointed by the Thirteenth Finance Commission (GoI 2009b) recommended that for ensuring revenue neutrality for the states, the CGST rate shall be at 5 per cent and the SGST rate at 7 per cent. The rate recommended by the Arvind Subramanian Committee (2015) was still higher at 8 per cent and 9 per cent, respectively for the centre and the states. Thus viewed, although the revenue neutrality for the states necessitated SGST to be higher than CGST, this has not been adhered to while implementing GST in the country since GST was equally shared between the centre and the states.

Surprisingly enough, hardly three months after the introduction of GST, the central government, based on the recommendation of the GST council, in response to the demand from the business community, notified (as per notification No. 41/2017) a reduction in the tax rates of around 200 items of goods from 28 to 18 per cent. As a result, the number of commodities under the 28 per cent GST schedule declined to only 32 as compared to 229 commodities when GST was initiated (Kumary and Mathews 2019). This, in turn, reduced the tax revenue of many states and turned out to be against the revenue neutrality concept that was adhered to in the initial rate fixation. As a result, at present, 28 per cent of the GST schedule has only 32 commodities compared to 229 commodities when GST was initiated (Kumary and Mathews 2019).

Since Kerala is a consumer state with around 70 per cent of the goods being taxed at 14.5 per cent during the VAT period, a decline in the tax rate to 9 per cent (SGST) has affected the revenue collection under GST. This decline in tax rate has affected the overall GST collection of states. Table 11.3 presents our estimates on the impact of rate changes on GST collection compared to the VAT period. Before GST, the majority of commodities attracted a tax rate of 12 per cent excise duty and 14.5 per cent VAT including cascading of taxes. Under GST, for many commodities, the rates were fixed at 28 per cent by considering revenue neutrality. An analysis of rate reduction under GST compared to the VAT period found that there has been a 40 per cent reduction in tax rate and the corresponding reduction in tax revenue compared to VAT even without considering the plausible increase of sales in Kerala.

It is evident from Table 11.1 that out of nineteen commodities, thirteen of them had 14.5 per cent tax during the pre-GST period, that is, 2015–16. During the pre-GST period, the majority of the commodities were in the 14.5 per cent category of VAT. Then finance minister of Kerala argued that 70 per cent of the VAT revenue of Kerala emanated from goods that attracted the VAT rate of 14.5 per cent and made a case for 70 per cent of the goods being in 28 per cent tax slab under GST (Minutes of the 14th GST Council, 18 and 19 May 2017). It is clear that though revenue neutrality is considered during the finalization of GST rates, the concern of the states has not been addressed as only 21 per cent of the commodities came under the 28 per cent category.

Table 11.1 *Comparison of VAT and GST rates and tax collection and the changes therein for selected commodities in Kerala*, Rs crore

Sl. no.	Item	VAT Collection	Rate of tax under	SGST rate of tax as on 1 July	New SGST rate of tax from 15 November	Decline in tax collection as on 1 July	Decline in tax collection as on 15 November
		2016–17	VAT (%)	2017 (%)	2017 (%)	2017	2017
1.	Motor vehicle	2,638.33	14.5	14	14	91	91
2.	Cement	1,057.03	14.5	14	14	36	36
3.	Tobacco products	879.13	14.5	14	14	30	30
4.	Medicine	635.3	5	2.5	2.5	318	318
5.	Gold*	629.65	5	1.5	1.5	101	101
6.	White goods	456.56	14.5	14	9	16	173
7.	Iron and steel	387.6	5	2.5	2.5	194	194
8.	Electrical goods	386.29	14.5	14	9	13	147
9.	Paint	378.64	14.5	14	9	13	144
10.	Tiles	337.43	14.5	14	9	12	128
11.	Readymade garments	301.91	5	2.5/6	2.5/6	100	100
12.	Electronic goods	259.75	14.5	14	9	9	99
13.	Rubber	202.02	5	2.5	2.5	101	101
14.	Marble and granites	159.62	14.5	14	9	6	61
15.	Chicken	128.71	14.5	0	0	129	129
16.	Hill produce	124.78	5	2.5	2.5	62	62
17.	Plywood	123.66	14.5	14	9	4	
18.	Timber	123.27	14.5	14	9	4	47
19.	Glass	73.28	14.5	14	9	3	28
	Total	9,282.96				1,242	2,034

Note: *compounding; revenue loss for 40 per cent of turnover.
Source: Authors' calculation based on the data of Commercial Taxes Dept/SGST Dept, Government of Kerala.

This 21 per cent initially consisted of 229 commodities, but the number of commodities under the 28 per cent category was later reduced to only 32 in number, with significant revenue implications for the states.

The point may be illustrated by taking the case of Kerala. It is observed that the tax collection from nineteen commodities mostly coming under the 14.5 per cent slab (28 per cent under post-GST) during the pre-GST period was Rs 9,282.96 crore in Kerala. Assuming that the turnover remained the same during the GST period, the tax collection would have declined to Rs 7,010.33 crores with the GST rates. This amounted to a loss of Rs 2,034 crores (24.5 per cent) from 19 commodities (Table 11.1).

This decline has been beyond the control of the state of Kerala as the rate changes were based on the decision of the GST council. This indicates the loss of revenue neutrality due to high-pitched rate reduction. Hence any inquiry into the reasons for the less-than-expected performance of the GST revenue for the state will lead to the doorsteps of loss of revenue neutrality, a basic precondition for the acceptability of any tax reform. No wonder Kerala turned out to be one of the states wherein fiscal health is contingent on GST compensation.

Incidentally, although the tax rate was reduced to 18 or 12 per cent from 28 per cent, there has been no corresponding reduction in the price of those commodities (Kumar and Dash 2022). The intention of rate reduction was in anticipation of a corresponding reduction in the price of those commodities and thereby benefiting the consumers. But it was found that while the prices are flexible upwards with an increase in taxes, it is rigid downwards with a reduction in prices. Thus, while the states, the centre and the consumers lost, the gain has been limited to those businesses aiming at profiteering. Hence a case could be made for reinstating the rates of those commodities under 28 per cent at the initial period of GST implementation. This will improve the revenue collection of states and ensure revenue neutrality leading to a reduction in the demand for GST compensation by the states.

Tax Sharing

While there has been substantial dilution in the commitment to revenue neutrality when GST was implemented, a relevant issue for fiscal federalism is the sharing of GST revenue between the centre and the states. Table 11.2 presents data on total GST collection, its three major components – CGST, SGST and IGST – and their sharing since the introduction of GST. Out of the four years for which data is presented, data for 2017–18 is only for eight months. The terminal year refers to the period of once-in-a-century pandemic that caused unprecedented disruptions in the economy. Thus, there are only two years that could be considered a normal period. During this period, the total GST collection increased from 10.8 lakh crores in 2018–19 to 11.2 lakh crores in 2019–20, recording a growth rate of 3.7 per cent. During the subsequent year, the total collection declined to 10.5 lakh crores, with the recorded growth rate being - 6.3 per cent. However, the revenue accrued to the states through GST (SGST and IGST share) increased by 19.8 per cent during 2019 and 2020 and that of the centre recorded a much higher increase of 22.5 per cent. As is evident from Table 11.2, while the share of the states in total GST increased only by 5.31 per cent during the period under consideration (from 38.7 per cent in 2017–18 to 44 per cent in 2021–22), that of

Table **11.2** *GST collection in India during 2017–18 to 2021–22: a disaggregated picture*, in Rs crore

Category	2017–18	2018–19	2019–20	2020–21	2021–22
CGST	118,900.7	202,418	227,444.5	209,659.4	269,137.25
SGST	171,850.2	278,788	309,233.1	272,513.4	344,215.86
IGST including imports	366,450.3	598,746	586,698.8	565,514.8	762,270.35
Total	657,201.2	1,079,953	1,123,376	1,047,688	1,375,623.5
State's share of GST	254,453.2	418,898	501,742.7	452,397.5	605,713.67
Centre's share of GST	201,503.6	342,528	419,954.1	389,543.5	530,635.06
Unsettled amount in IGST account	201,244.4	318,528.6	201,679.2	205,747.0	239,274.7
Share of state's share of GST (%)	38.72	38.79	44.66	43.18	44.03
Share of centre's share of GST (%)	30.66	31.72	37.38	37.18	38.57
Percentage of balance amount in IGST account (Unsettled portion of IGST) (%)	30.62	29.49	17.95	19.64	17.40

Note: State's share of GST is the sum of SGST and state's share in IGST settlement.
Source: Authors' calculation based on GSTN data.

the centre increased by 7.91 per cent (30.7 per cent in 2017–18 to 38.6 per cent in 2021–22) indicating an unfavourable sharing of GST revenue for the states. Thus, the states had to bear the double whammy – declined tax effort coupled with adverse sharing of the lower tax revenue.

Enquiry into the less-than-expected performance of the states leads us to the sharing of IGST between the centre and the states (Mukherjee 2020a, 2020b). In the GST collection, the major share is accounted for by IGST. It constitutes around 55 per cent of the collection except in 2019–20 (Table 11.2), of which about 50 per cent comes from imports from other countries. While IGST is to be shared with the states through the clearing house mechanism facilitated by the GSTN, as it operates, there is hardly any clarity concerning its sharing, especially the IGST on imports. Table 11.2 indicates that a substantial part of the IGST remains not shared, notwithstanding a decline in the share of unshared IGST revenue from over 30 per cent in 2017–18 to 17.40 per cent in 2021–22. During the introduction of GST, it is stated that whatever amount is available in the IGST account will be distributed as SGST and CGST. However, the evidence presented above for the period under consideration shows that the actual experience belied our expectations with Rs 2.4 lakh crores remaining undistributed in 2021–22, costing dearly to the fund-starved states[5] as the clearing house remained as an unclear house!

GST Compensation

In the spirit of cooperative federalism, GST ensured revenue neutrality on the one hand and envisaged an equal sharing of GST revenue between the centre and the states. Indicative of the firm commitment to cooperative federalism and ensuring the state's fiscal health, in addition to the above provisions, an additional provision for GST compensation was also constitutionally provided for the states. The GST (Compensation to States) Act 2017 guaranteed that states would be provided full compensation for the estimated loss of their revenues based upon an assumed growth rate (14 per cent) for five years, thus helping convince the hesitant states to join GST. The basis for such a commitment to the states calls for a more precise understanding of the states' sacrifice towards the establishment of GST in India. This is mainly related to the pre-GST revenue forgone by the states and the centre.

The revenue forgone by the centre and the states has been estimated at Rs 3.28 lakh crores and Rs 3.69 lakh crores respectively (GoI 2009b). This amounted to a surrender of 51.8 per cent of the state's total tax revenue and 28.8 per cent of the centre's gross tax revenue. Thus viewed, in relative terms, the states surrendered almost twice that of the centre (Joseph and Ramalingam, 2020) in exchange for a constitutionally provided provision for compensation. Hence the various committees that dealt with the revenue-neutral rates recommended that for minimizing the revenue loss, the tax rate should be higher in the case of the states (SGST) compared to the centre (CGST). While the Thirteenth Finance Commission (GoI 2009b) recommended a CGST rate of 5 per cent and an SGST rate of 7 per cent, the rate proposed by the Report on the Revenue Neutral Rate headed by Arvind Subramanian (2015) was 8 per cent and 9 per cent, respectively. Yet, the states agreed to reduce the tax rate such that SGST is imposed at the same rate as CGST.

Tax revenue is seen to be dependent on the tax base. During the pre-GST period, the tax revenue for the centre from the industrial output (excise duty) has been limited only to the point of manufacturing, indicating a very narrow tax base. On the other hand, the states were entitled to a much wider tax base as they could levy tax on the entire supply chain up to the final consumption point (Joseph and Ramalingam 2020). Further, while the cascading of tax is generally considered inimical to economic efficiency, it used to serve as an additional source of revenue mobilization by the states during the pre-GST period. Thus, cascading, a bane to the economy, has been a boon to the states. While the centre has also been able to mobilize additional resources on account of tax cascading, the benefits used to be proportionately higher for the states given their higher tax base. In general, with the introduction of

GST, the centre expanded the tax base at the cost of the states and the states have forgone substantial revenue for building one country, one tax system.

In the above context, the provision for GST compensation may be seen as *quid pro quo* for sacrificing the various tax privileges that the states enjoyed. Further, it has been made in anticipation of a plausible shortfall in states' revenue. While these provisions are said to help strengthen cooperative federalism, the GST compensation has been limited to the initial five years of GST for unknown reasons. To the extent that the provision for compensation has been built in over and above the provision for revenue neutrality towards ensuring the fiscal health of the states, it is questionable to limit it to the initial five years. As long as there is GST, there shall be GST compensation.

The empirical evidence presented in Table 11.3 suggests that, as anticipated, the actual GST collection for most of the states fell short of the projected revenue making the case for an extended period of GST compensation in the true spirit of cooperative federalism. With an estimated shortfall of about Rs 2.35 lakh crore in GST compensation fund attributable to the Covid-induced recession, the centre reneged on its promise of compensation and held that, of the projected shortfall of about Rs 2.35 lakh crore, only Rs 97,000 crore was due to the implementation of GST. The remaining amount was attributed to the Covid-19 pandemic, which according to the finance minister and chairperson of the GST council, was an 'act of God', not related to the implementation of the GST. Hence two options where offered for the consideration of the states. The first was a special window for the states, with the approval of the Reserve Bank of India (RBI), to borrow the projected GST shortfall of 97,000 crores which would not be accounted for as a part of the states' debt and the repayment of the principal and interest on these borrowings would be made from the compensation fund by extending the period of cess collections beyond 2022. As per the second option, the states could borrow the entire Rs 2.35 lakh crore shortfall from the market but the interest cost would have to be borne by the states, and only the principal would be serviced by the compensation fund. Many of the states, including Kerala, rejected both options and made the case for the centre to borrow and provide compensation to states. Accordingly, as per the decision of the 43rd GST council meeting the centre borrowed and lent to the states on a back-to-back basis to meet the resource gap on account of the inadequate amount in the compensation fund. Accordingly, the compensation cess would continue till the borrowed amount is fully repaid implying that there would not be any provision for GST compensation beyond the initially stipulated period of five years.

In this context, an analysis (R.K. Rao 2022) of the interstate variation in the role played by GST compensation in state finances by estimating the ratio of GST compensation received to a fiscal deficit for 2020–2021 is highly revealing.[6] It was observed that the size of the compensation is considerable and end of the compensation regime in the absence of any other measures

Table 11.3 *Revenue shortfall under GST across Indian states*, in Rs crore

State	2017–18	2018–19	2019–20	2020–21	2021–22*	2021–22**
Jammu and Kashmir	- 2,494	- 2,698	- 3,485	- 4,739	- 5,659	- 5,043
Himachal Pradesh	- 2,135	- 2,541	- 2,655	- 3,695	- 4,314	- 4,203
Punjab	- 6,849	- 10,222	- 11,744	- 16,623	- 20,349	- 20,195
Uttarakhand	- 2,667	- 3,277	- 3,584	- 5,308	- 5,507	- 5,826
Haryana	- 4,519	- 5,998	- 6,869	- 11,256	- 13,361	- 11,962
Delhi	- 4,894	- 8,148	- 9,155	- 17,349	- 22,873	- 23,940
Rajasthan	- 6,332	- 4,869	- 7,361	- 13,027	- 16,475	- 13,697
Uttar Pradesh	- 6,925	- 8,282	- 9,984	- 22,994	- 29,777	- 26,040
Bihar	- 7,892	- 5,458	- 6,015	- 9,329	- 9,925	- 6,342
Sikkim	- 78	4	57	- 60	- 49	38
Arunachal Pradesh	- 13	179	360	347	642	964
Nagaland	- 90	48	170	146	312	466
Manipur	- 54	124	253	165	293	473
Mizoram	- 29	144	205	162	284	502
Tripura	- 446	- 319	- 338	- 536	- 606	- 481
Meghalaya	- 479	- 241	- 191	- 454	- 503	- 360
Assam	- 2,002	- 1,440	- 1,588	- 3,486	- 4,058	- 2,707
West Bengal	- 6,169	- 5,671	- 7,060	- 14,438	- 18,704	- 16,838
Jharkhand	- 2,638	- 2,339	- 2,674	- 4,959	- 5,951	- 4,888
Odisha	- 5,247	- 5,782	- 5,654	- 8,507	- 9,918	- 9,483
Chhattisgarh	- 2,728	- 3,877	- 4,801	- 6,803	- 8,256	- 7,580
Madhya Pradesh	- 6,792	- 5,746	- 7,123	- 12,214	- 14,759	- 12,070
Gujarat	- 7,022	- 10,722	- 14,016	- 24,897	- 32,366	- 30,791
Maharashtra	- 9,721	- 13,636	- 19,224	- 45,627	- 62,023	- 58,358
Karnataka	- 13,227	- 16,533	- 18,871	- 31,388	- 39,403	- 37,760
Goa	- 900	- 1,029	- 1,291	- 2,445	- 3,091	- 2,899
Kerala	- 3,789	- 6,536	- 9,021	- 14,719	- 19,073	- 18,189
Tamil Nadu	- 7,746	- 7,205	- 10,166	- 22,319	- 30,296	- 28,821
Puducherry	- 641	- 881	- 1,108	- 1,441	- 1,745	- 1,700
Telangana	- 3,168	- 2,453	- 3,796	- 8,716	- 11,549	- 9,622
Andhra Pradesh	- 3,338	- 1,994	- 3,651	- 8,865	- 11,542	- 8,854
Total	- 1,21,024	- 1,37,398	- 1,70,380	- 3,15,374	- 4,00,601	- 3,66,206

Notes: (1) Revenue shortfall is calculated as the difference between GST collected and projected revenue. * indicates projected revenue shortfall. For this projection, GST collection for 2021–22 is done using the annual average growth rate of the last four years. This represents the conservative scenario. ** indicates that the growth rate of 2018–19 over 2017–18 is applied to project the GST revenue collection for 2021–22. This represents the realistic scenario.
Source: GST portal.

could considerably affect the ability of the states to maintain their spending programmes without taking recourse to expenditure compression in some way. The study further noted that the problem is more pronounced for states such as Himachal Pradesh, Punjab, Karnataka and Odisha.

Tax Performance of the States

Experience across countries indicates a positive relationship between GDP growth and growth in tax collection. In sync with Wagner's law, the size of the government, viewed in terms of tax GDP ratio, rises with an increase in a country's GDP. In 1950–51, the tax GDP ratio in India remained at a low level of 6 per cent, characteristic of a backward economy with low per capita income that India inherited. It almost doubled within the next fifteen years, and despite the much castigated Hindu growth rate, the ratio increased to reach 16 per cent in 1989–90, on the eve of embarking on globalization. Although the country managed to record a turnaround in GDP growth under globalization, the tax GDP ratio stagnated (Thomas Isaac, Mohan and Chakraborty 2019b). It remained in the company of many African countries (Levin 2021), such that Raj Krishna would have christened it as a 'Hindu tax effort'. When it comes to the tax GDP ratio of the centre, the trend during the last four decades shows only a marginal improvement while that of the states increased from 3.8 per cent during the 1970s to 6.2 per cent during 2011–12 to 2016–17. Overall, the higher rate of growth in GDP did not translate into a larger revenue base (Thomas Isaac, Mohan and Chakraborty 2019a). The issue of centre–state relations came to the fore in a context wherein, along with low and stagnating tax GDP ratio, there has been a growing vertical imbalance (Thomas Isaac, Mohan and Chakraborty 2019b; Sharma 2021) between resource endowments and expenditure obligations of the centre and the states. Since the new tax reform has been put in such a context, the critical issue is to what extent the new institutional innovations that led the Indianized GST paradigm helped ensuring revenue productivity of the states a *sine qua non* for building cooperative federalism in the country.

Table 11.4 presents data on the state-level ratio of own tax revenue to GSDP of non-special category states during the pre- and post-GST period. The table also presents aggregate data for the special category states along with that of the union territories. We consider two-time points as representative years (2013–14 and 2015–16) from the pre-GST period and 2019–20 to represent the post-GST period. It is evident from Table 11.4 that out of the seventeen general category states (Telangana excluded), the tax GSDP ratio has declined in the case of thirteen states. Hence, the tax GSDP ratio for the general category states as a whole declined from 7.7 per cent in 2013–14 to 6.7 per cent in 2015–16, indicating that the tax effort has been on a declining trend even before the introduction of GST. The observed pattern was hold-

Table 11.4 *Tax effort across Indian states*

States	Own tax revenue as % of GSDP							
	2013–14	2014–15	2015–16	2016–17	2017–18	2018–19	2019–20	2020–21
1. Non- special category	7.7	7.1	6.7	6.6	6.5	6.71	6.37	6.38
Andhra Pradesh	7.9	7.5	8.1	6.5	7	6.5	6.8	5.9
Bihar	5.5	5.8	5.5	6.7	6.4	6.1	5.8	5.6
Chhattisgarh	7.9	7.7	6.7	6.5	7.8	7.7	7.2	7.7
Goa	6.9	7.3	9.6	7.3	7.2	7.1	6.7	6.5
Gujarat	8.2	7.4	6.9	6.1	5.6	5.6	5.4	5.8
Haryana	6.9	6.6	6.3	6.4	6.9	6.7	5.8	5.8
Jharkhand	5.4	5.4	4.8	5	6.6	5.2	5.0	6.4
Karnataka	10.4	10.2	7.6	7.5	7.3	6.7	6.3	6.0
Kerala	8.6	8.1	6.7	7	7.2	6.9	6.5	6.4
Madhya Pradesh	8.5	7.7	7.6	7.6	6.9	6.9	6.4	6.0
Maharashtra	7.8	7.2	6.4	6.3	6.1	7.1	7.2	6.9
Odisha	6	6.2	6.2	6.8	6.2	7.1	6.3	6.3
Punjab	7.9	7.6	6.9	6.8	7.1	6.6	6.0	5.9
Rajasthan	6.5	6.5	6.3	6.2	6.2	6.5	6.2	6.9
Tamil Nadu	9.6	8.6	7.2	6.9	6.7	6.6	6.5	6.5
Telangana			5.7	7	7.8	7.7	7.6	7.4
Uttar Pradesh	7.4	7.7	7.1	7.2	7.3	8	7.4	7.6
West Bengal	5.4	5.1	4.9	4.6	4.6	5.8	5.7	5.2
2. Special category	5.7	5.6	4.9	4.9	5.1	5.4	4.6	4.6
3. All states	6.6	6.3	6.3	6.2	6.2	6.6	6.4	6.6
NCT Delhi	6.7	6.6	5.4	5.5	5.3	5.2	4.7	4.6
Puducherry	11.4	9	8.3	9	8.8	7.5	7.1	7.7

Source: RBI State Finances for different years.

ing well in the case of special category states as a group (from 5.7 per cent in 2013–14 to 4.9 per cent in 2015–16) and the union territories.

The introduction of GST was envisaged to make a turnaround in this trend as GST was perceived to raise the tax GSDP by about 1–2 per cent. However, as we move to 2019–20, in the post-GST period, it is evident that twelve out of eighteen non-special category states showed a decline in tax GSDP ratio. For the non-special category of states as a whole, the ratio declined from 6.7 per cent in 2015–16 to 6.4 per cent in 2019–20. For the special category states, the ratio declined to 4.6 per cent in 2019–20 with the union territories also showing a decline.

Thus viewed, belying our expectations, with the introduction of GST there has been no evidence of increased tax effort among the Indian states indicating that GST has not been helpful in improving the revenue position of the states. Similar conclusion has been arrived at by M.G. Rao (2022) based on an analysis of the interstate variation in the GST revenue, that the average rate of growth prior to GST appears to be higher than that in the years subsequent to the introduction of GST.

Especially notable has been the experience of Kerala wherein, the tax GSDP was as high as 8.6 per cent in 2013–14 and declined thereafter to 7 per cent in 2016–17. With the introduction of GST, Kerala's tax GSDP ratio recorded one of the highest declines among the Indian states to reach 6.4 per cent in 2020–21. Its relatively poor performance is evident from the decline in its rank among the major states from 6 in 2013–14 to 13 in 2019–20. A comparison of VAT and GST revenue growth rates for Kerala presented in Table 11.5 reveals that the rate of growth in tax revenue has been significantly higher during the pre-GST period as compared to the post-GST period. Although the growth rate was 12.3 per cent in 2018–19 under GST, the recorded growth rate in 2019–20 and 2020–21 has been negative (- 4.9 per cent and - 0.3 per cent, respectively). Despite a higher growth rate of 10.1 per cent recorded in 2021–22, the GST revenue growth rate after its introduction turned out to be only 4.3 per cent as compared to over 13 per cent recorded during the VAT regime, from 2012–13 to 2016–17.

Table 11.5 *Growth of VAT/GST collection in Kerala*

Year	VAT/GST Collection (in crore)	Growth Rate (%)
2011–12	9,803	
2012–13	12,171	24.16
2013–14	13,513	11.03
2014–15	14,605	8.08
2015–16	16,131	10.45
2016–17	18,474	14.52
2017–18*	19,020	3.0
2018–19	21,366	12.3
2019–20	20,316	- 4.9
2020–21	20,255	- 0.3
2021–22	22,302	10.12

Note: *2017–18 data include VAT and GST collection.
Source: SGST department, Government of Kerala; compensation amount is not included in GST collection.

Concluding Observations

The design and implementation of GST within a democratic federal structure is often perceived as a difficult task. This is more so in a developing country like India wherein the states, that account for over 60 per cent of the combined expenditure with only 40 per cent of the combined revenue, were expected to surrender the sales tax, their major source of revenue leading to significant revenue loss. Hence the introduction of GST has been considered a great achievement of India's fiscal federalism. Against this background, this essay explored the unique characteristics of India's GST from a fiscal federal perspective and the tax performance of states under GST. It is argued that the Indianized GST paradigm, built on the edifice of the GST council and the pillars of revenue neutrality, equitable tax sharing between the centre and the states and the provision for GST compensation, although destined towards fostering cooperative federalism, was fraught with fault lines in its design.

With respect to its implementation, it was revealed that the revenue neutrality, a *sine qua non* for any taxable reform to be acceptable, has not been ensured on account of the equality in SGST and CGST along with high-pitched rate reduction immediately after the introduction of GST, especially for those in the 28 per cent category. There were also issues with tax sharing with substantial monies remaining unshared under IGST costing dearly to the revenue-starved states. Thus, the clearing house mechanism under IGST remained a non-clearing hose *inter alia* on account of the issues associated with the GSTN (Banerjee and Prasad 2017). With these first two pillars not being strong, most of the states had no option but to depend heavily on the third pillar – GST compensation. This pillar, along with the GST council which is an edifice of the whole paradigm, is also shown to be defective by design and also by implementation. Considering the enormous sacrifice that the states have made for the making of the GST, limiting GST compensation for the initial five years was not justified. We argued that, so long as there is GST, the states shall have the entitlement for GST compensation. Moreover, there have been instances wherein the central government reneged even with respect to the constitutionally provided GST compensation. Further, contrary to the expectations, there has been no evidence of increased tax effort among the Indian states indicating that GST has not been helpful in improving the revenue position of the states. On the whole, there is reason to believe that while the Indianized GST paradigm, by design, has been cognizant of the imperative of fostering cooperative federalism, there were fault lines in its design and implementation leading to strong tendencies towards coercive federalism.

This essay was originally published under the same title in *The Indian Economic Journal*, vol. 71, no. 1, 2023, pp. 187–203.

We are very thankful to Prof. T.M. Thomas Isaac for his guidance and encouragement. An earlier version of this essay was presented at the International Seminar on India's Experience with Goods and Services Tax organized by the Gulati Institute of Finance and Taxation, 12–13 November 2021, Thiruvananthapuram, Kerala. Authors acknowledge the participants of the seminar for their helpful comments. This essay also benefited from discussions with Dr N. Ramalingam, Dr Zakaria Siddiqui and Dr Kiran Kumar Kakarlapudi. For omissions, errors and wrong interpretations, if any, we blame each other.

Notes

[1] See Joseph (1992) for a discussion on how market segmentation affected the performance of India's industrial sector by taking the case of the television industry.

[2] On the equity implications of the GST rates, refer to Chakravartti and Siddiqui (2022).

[3] GST replaced the following taxes which were levied and collected by the centre: (a) central excise duty; (b) duties of excise (medicinal and toilet preparations); (c) additional duties of excise (goods of special importance); (d) additional duties of excise (textiles and textile products); (e) additional duties of customs (commonly known as cvd); (f) special additional duty of customs (sad); (g) service tax; and (h) cesses and surcharges insofar as they relate to supply of goods or services.

[4] State taxes which were subsumed within the GST are: (a) state VAT; (b) central sales tax; (c) purchase tax; (d) luxury tax; (e) entry tax (all forms); (f) entertainment tax (except those levied by the local bodies); (g) taxes on advertisements; (h) taxes on lotteries, betting and gambling; and (i) state cesses and surcharges insofar as they relate to supply of goods.

[5] On the implications of GST performance on debt sustainability, refer to Renjith (2022).

[6] On interstate variation in the performance of GST, refer to Dash and Kakarlapudi (2022).

References

Bagchi, A. (2006), 'Towards GST: Choices and Trade-Offs', *Economic and Political Weekly*, vol. 41, no. 14, pp. 1314–17.

———— (2007), 'International Lessons in Goods and Services Tax', *Economic & Political Weekly*, vol. 42, no. 45, pp. 28–32.

Banerjee, S. and P. Prasad (2017), 'Small Businesses in the GST Regime', *Economic and Political Weekly*, vol. 52, no. 38, pp. 18–22.

Bhaskar, V. (2014), 'Case for Including Immovable Property in the GST', *Economic and Political Weekly*, vol. 49, no. 52, pp. 27–30.

———— (2021), 'Sharing of Goods and Services Tax Revenues, A Case of Unequal Fiscal Federalism?', *Economic and Political Weekly*, vol. 46, no. 30, pp. 52–58.

Bhaskar, V. and P.S.S. Kailash Nath (2015), 'What Ails the Implementation of the Goods and Services Tax?', *Economic & Political Weekly*, vol. 50, no. 37, pp. 12–14.

Bird, R.M. (2012), *The GST/HST: Creating an Integrated Sales Tax in a Federal Country*, Working Paper, 2115620, Rotman School of Management, University of Toronto, Toronto.

Bird, R.M. and P.P. Gendron (2007), *The VAT in Developing and Transitional Countries*, Cambridge: Cambridge University Press.

Chakravartti, P. and M.Z. Siddiqui (2022), *Burden of Uniform Tax Rate by Household Consumption Expenditure Class: A study of GST in India*, GIFT Discussion Paper 2022/01, Gulati Institute of Finance and Taxation (GIFT), Thiruvananthapuram, Kerala.

Das, S. (2017), 'Some Concerns Regarding the Goods and Services Tax', *Economic and Political Weekly*, vol. 52, no. 9.

Dash, S.K. and K.K. Kakarlapudi (2022), 'What Explains Interstate Variation in GST Collection?', GIFT Discussion Paper 2022/02, Gulati Institute of Finance and Taxation, Thiruvananthapuram, Kerala.

Gillis, M., C.S. Shoup and G. Sicat, eds (1990), *Value-Added Taxation in Developing Countries*, World Bank.

Government of India (GoI) (2009a), *Report of the 13th Finance Commission*, Ministry of Finance.

——— (2009b), *Report of the Task-Force on Goods and Services Tax*, Thirteenth Finance Commission.

Joseph, K.J. (1992), 'Market Segmentation and Performance of Firms: Case Study of Indian Television Industry in 1980s', *Economic and Political Weekly*, vol. 27, no. 48, pp. M141–M148.

Joseph, K.J. and N. Ramalingam (2020), 'One Nation One Tax Wasn't an Act of God', *Mint*, available at https://www.livemint.com/ opinion/online-views/-one-nation-one-tax-wasn-t-an-act-of-god-11602256300969.html

Kishore, P. (2012), 'Administering Goods and Services Tax in India: Reforming the Institutional Architecture and Rede- signing Revenue Agencies', *Economic and Political Weekly*, vol. 57, no. 17, pp. 84–91.

Kumar, A. (2015), 'Macroeconomic Aspects of Goods and Services Tax', *Economic and Political Weekly*, vol. 50, no. 29, pp. 26–30.

Kumar, A.S. and S.K. Dash (2022), 'Impact of GST on Inflation: Evidence from Bayesian Causal Analysis', GIFT Discussion Paper 2022/03, Gulati Institute of Finance and Taxation, Thiruvananthapuram, Kerala.

Kumary, A.L. and S. Mathew (2019), 'Revenue Performance of Value Added Tax (VAT) and Goods and Services Tax (GST): An Interstate Comparison with Special Reference to Kerala', discussion paper no. 2, Gulati Institute of Finance and Taxation, Thiruvananthapuram, Kerala.

Levin, J. (2021), *Taxation for Inclusive Development: Challenges Across Africa*, Nordiska Afrikainstitutet, Uppsala, Sweden.

Mukherjee, S. (2020a), 'Performance Assessment of Indian GST: State-Level Analysis of Compliance Gap and Revenue Growth', Working Paper No. 20/301, National Institute of Public Finance and Policy, Delhi.

——— (2020b), 'Goods and Services Tax Efficiency Across Indian States: Panel Stochastic Frontier Analysis', *Indian Economic Review*, vol. 55, no. 2, pp. 225–51.

Mukhopadhyay, S. (2003), 'Classification of Goods for Taxation: Need for Artificial Definitions', *Economic and Political Weekly*, vol. 38, no. 29, pp. 3033–35.

Oates, W.E. (1999), 'An Essay on Fiscal Federalism', *Journal of Economic Literature*, vol. 37, no. 3, pp. 1120–49.

Patnaik, P. (2016), 'A Blow Against Federalism: The Implications of a Uniform Goods and Services Tax', *The Telegraph*, 28 June, available at https://www.telegraphindia.com/opinion/a-blow-against-federalism/cid/1450727

Rao, M.G. (2009), 'Goods and Services Tax: Some Progress Towards Clarity. *Economic and Political Weekly*, vol. 44, no. 51, pp. 8–11.

——— (2011), 'Goods and Services Tax: A Gorilla, Chimpanzee or a Genus like "Primates"?', *Economic and Political Weekly*, vol. 46, no. 7, pp. 43–48.

——— (2022), *Evolving Issues and Future Directions in GST Reform in India*, Working Paper No. 221/2022, Centre for Public Finance, Madras School of Economics, Chennai

Rao, R.K. (2016), 'New Assumptions, New Estimates: Scrutinising a New Report on Revenue Neutral Rate', *Economic and Political Weekly*, vol. 51, no. 4, pp. 63–66.

Rao, R.K and P. Chakraborthy (2014), *Revenue Implications of GST and Estimation of Revenue Neutral Rate: Estimates for 2011–12*, National Institute of Public Finance and Policy, New Delhi.

——— (2022), 'GST, End of Compensation Regime and Stress on State Finances', Working Paper No. 376, National Institute of Public Finance and Policy, New Delhi.

Rao, R.K. and P. Chakraborty (2010), 'Goods and Services Tax in India: An Assessment of the Base', *Economic and Political Weekly*, vol. 45, no. 1, pp. 49–54.

Rao, R.K., S. Mukherjee and A. Bagchi. (2019), *Goods and Services Tax in India*, Cambridge: Cambridge University Press.

Reddy, Y.V. (2019), 'New Approached to Fiscal Federalism in India', *Review of Development and Change*, vol. 24, no.2, pp. 163–86.

Reddy, Y.V. and G.R. Reddy (2019), *Indian Fiscal Federalism*, New Delhi: Oxford University Press.

Renjith, P.S. (2022), *GST and Debt Sustainability: The Indian Experience*, GIFT Discussion Paper 2022/04, Gulati Institute of Finance and Taxation, Thiruvananthapuram, Kerala.

Sharma, C.K. (2021), *The Political Economy of India's Transition to Goods and Services Tax*, German Institute of Global and Area Studies, Hamburg.

Subramanian, A. (2015), *Report on the Revenue Neutral Rate and Structure of Rates for the Goods and Services Tax (GST)*, available at https://gstcouncil.gov.in/sites/default/files/CEA-rpt-rnr.pdf, accessed 14 August 2025.

——— (2018), *Of counsel: The Challenges of the Modi-Jaitley Economy*, Gurgaon: Penguin Random House.

Tait, M.A.A. (1988), *Value Added Tax: International Practice and Problems*, vol. 24, International Monetary Fund.

Thomas Isaac, T.M., R. Mohan and L. Chakraborty (2019a), 'Challenges to Indian Fiscal Federalism', *Economic and Political Weekly*, vo. 54, no. 9, pp. 33–40.

——— (2019b), *Challenges to Indian Fiscal Federalism*, Delhi: LeftWord.

12

Capitalism, Imperialism and the Food Question

Arindam Banerjee

Introduction

The success and failure of capitalism have been commonly measured by the yardsticks of industrialization, technical progress and innovations in the financial markets. With the first Industrial Revolution in the eighteenth century, which catapulted Britain as the leading economy in the world, defining the markers for a successful transition to capitalism, this approach became well-entrenched among scholars of economic history and development. It is often unquestioningly assumed that the constraints of nature, and consequently the food question, hardly mattered during the emergence of capitalism in the nineteenth and early twentieth centuries. The emergence of industrial agriculture under successful capitalist transitions is supposed to have taken care of all food and raw material constraints that could have arrested the development of industrial economies and societies in the North.

This position in development scholarship has crudely evolved into the 'colonial/imperial school' which locates the causes of underdevelopment exclusively in the 'backwardness' of economic and social institutions in regions of the South. Such institutions not only embedded underdevelopment but also apparently prevented the so-called 'benefits' of imperialism from reaching and transforming these poor colonies (Morris 1983). This position commits gross violence against the historical realities of the pre-industrial world, where the European regions were perpetually struggling to keep up with the development in the East and the South (Abu-Lughod 1989). It also erases the role of 'forceful capture' of economic value, first in the sphere of trade and then in production, through an imperialist, military strategy. The more generous position in mainstream scholarship is to identify poor colonial governance in some colonies, particularly the 'non-white ones' which led to inefficient institutions that were responsible for their underdevelopment, while many of the white-settler colonies benefitted from better governance by 'just' English laws. This narrative, while it recognizes the racist dimensions of global imperialism, continues to undermine the critical role played by tropical 'non-white' colonies in the development of capitalism in both the 'old' and the 'new' world (Acemoglu, Johnson and Robinson 2001).

Scholars from the South (as well as a few from the North), who imbibed a critical enquiry of the multi-century colonial expansion and domination, have looked at development and underdevelopment as an integral process of capitalism (Amin 1977; Bagchi 1982; Frank 1967; Habib 1995; Magdoff 1978; Moyo, Jha and Yeros 2013; Patnaik and Patnaik 2016). The Western European capitalism was critically dependent on colonial exploitation in more than one way. Expropriation of surplus in the form of colonial tribute, monopolizing existing trade networks, destruction of indigenous manufacturing, transforming the use of land and natural resources in colonies to the service of industries and generating the supply of cheap, unfree labour in plantations, first as slaves and then as indentured labour, are some of the prominent economic processes during various historical imperial phases through which colonies contributed to the making of capitalist nations in the North.

The work of Utsa Patnaik stands out in this genre of development scholarship as she explored multiple aspects of the contribution of colonies to the advance of capital accumulation in the North. Using a Marxian framework to analyse internal political economy, she delves into the phenomenon of nineteenth-century 'international division of labour', the role of tropical food and raw materials exports by commercialized Southern agriculture and implication for food security in the colonies. Patnaik further located these processes within the extraction of colonial tribute and a certain ordering and redirection of the colonial economy into the path of underdevelopment and dependence.

The objective of this article is to engage with the anti-imperial scholarship of Utsa Patnaik with a specific focus on the food question in capitalism. The article also looks at more recent post-colonial debates on food policy in the South with examination of some evidence from India. In the process, we question certain myths that are dominant in mainstream agricultural and food policy discourses.

The Food Question in 'Classical' Capitalist Development

A major contribution of Utsa Patnaik in understanding the international dimensions of western European (and later northern) capitalism is her critical engagement with the international division of labour in nineteenth-century world trade and the use of the Ricardian comparative advantage theory in mainstream economics to identify that phenomenon as 'mutually beneficial' to all trading partners. The specialization of colonies of the South in exporting primary agricultural commodities and natural resources like precious metals and minerals and the specialization of a small set of Northern countries in manufacturing exports emerged as defining features of world trade in the beginning of the nineteenth century and persisted late into the twentieth century. Ricardian comparative advantage theory has been frequently used to identify (and hence justify) this specialization as an outcome of 'free trade' where each country produces and exports the goods in which she has the lower relative 'opportunity cost'.

Patnaik has questioned this normalization of the international division of labour by pointing out the incorrectness of a basic assumption of Ricardo's two-country, two-good model. According to Patnaik, the assumption of 'both countries producing both goods' was never true for the bulk of the North–South trade during the colonial period. From raw cotton exports by erstwhile American colonies to the leading industry of the English Industrial Revolution, and exports of tropical food goods like tea, coffee and cocoa for food-processing industries in the North to the export of a variety of tropical fruits and spices for direct consumption, none fitted into the 'both countries producing both goods' paradigm (Patnaik 2006).

Neither was this assumption true for Ricardo's original example of cloth and wine trade between England and Portugal. England, with her cold temperate climate, could not grow any grapes nor produce any wine. Patnaik demonstrates that the so-called 'mutual gains' of free trade to both trading partners was crucially dependent on this assumption and dropping the same led to ambiguous results regarding the gains. What Ricardo's original theory clearly camouflaged was the forcible destruction of the Portuguese cloth industry by Britain through the latter's intervention in the Iberian Peninsula and bargaining with Portugal to accept the British Navigation Acts in the mid-seventeenth century. This reduction of Portugal into a semi-colony with restricted sovereignty over her seas and trading policies, meant that the latter lost out on valuable trading profits (the foundation of Portuguese empire) and gradually also lost the edge in manufacturing to Britain, including in cloth manufacturing. Pushed towards the export of primary commodities, this 'division of labour' was clearly the beginning of the development gap between two competing imperialist nations that persists till today. What is not so well appreciated is that such 'division of labour' was more the outcome of British protectionism and not any 'free-trade induced specialization'.

While Ricardo's theory would work in case both countries produced both goods, the bulk of the North–South trade in the nineteenth and most of the twentieth centuries did not satisfy that assumption. Raw cotton from America and Asia, cocoa from Africa, tea from Asia, coffee and various fruits from Africa and South America, and a range of spices from Asia are a few examples of the long list of tropical food good exports that were entering the capitalist economies with great regularity. As indispensable raw materials, stimulants to keep the working population active for longer working days and sources of critical micronutrients not available within the local European (Northern) biodiversity, these tropical exports were essential for the continuance of capitalism as well as for raising the standards of living in the cold countries. More importantly, the cheap (often under-valued) tropical exports to the metropolitan of capitalism kept the price of the wage-good basket in control and protected the profits. In short, the core accumulation of capital in these industrializing economies was crucially dependent on tropical biodiversity.

Patnaik argues that these large sets of tropical exports were products of cultivation in the summer/ monsoon season in the land of the colonies and are impossible to produce in the cold, temperate climates. No amount of increase in agricultural productivity and farming modernization could make this possible at competitive prices.

Thus, the relative 'opportunity cost' of these tropical products cannot be computed; rather, their imports acted as a binding, necessary condition for the capitalist countries. As an example, one can say that the already existing woollen industry in England was not good enough to cause an Industrial Revolution, given the limited demand for woollen clothes. Unless England demonstrated the audacity to develop an industry (cotton textiles), the products of which had a global demand, but for which the raw material would be procured from thousands of miles away, the Industrial Revolution would clearly not have happened in the time and place that it actually did. This, of course, was never an option without the establishment of cotton plantations using African slave labour in the American South during early imperialism and the destruction of indigenous cotton goods manufacturing in India, Indonesia, China or Egypt during the later phases of imperialism. The history of industrial capitalism would have been very different without the military, imperialist machinations of the western European powers across various continents in the South.

The dependence of Northern capitalism on agriculture in the colonies is often discounted on the ground that industrialization was always preceded by significant increases in agricultural productivity in these countries and attainment of self-sufficiency in foodgrain production. This argument still misses the aspect of the restricted crop basket that exists in many of the temperate countries where industrialization was in progress. Moreover, it is also worth looking at whether the assumed self-sufficiency in grain production prior to industrialization is always true in the case of capitalist countries.

While this claim has some validity in the case of the United States, where the colonization of indigenous land after the War of Independence and the development of extensive industrial agriculture led to a burst in grain outputs, the original British capitalism (and many European experiences) do not throw up unambiguous evidence to back this claim. Patnaik investigates the claims of an 'agricultural revolution' in England prior to the Industrial Revolution by studying the available grain output data and found that there were no exceptional increases in grain production that can be deemed as a 'revolution' that later facilitated rapid industrialization (Patnaik 2011).

On the contrary, English agriculture was experiencing a most unique and difficult challenge due to the large-scale dispossession and displacement of people from rural areas – the metabolic rift. The large-scale resettlement of people in urban areas (as the potential working class) meant that soil nutrition that got embodied into agricultural food products now travelled increasingly longer distances to enter the human body and consequently found it that much more difficult to find their way back into the soil. The degradation of soil fertility reached such massive proportions that the Napoleonic wars in early nineteenth century witnessed the scavenging of battlefields for human and non-human bones that were then used as manure to replenish the fertility of English soils (Foster 2009).

It was only in the later stages of capitalism in the early twentieth century that grain and livestock product surpluses emerged in the capitalist world (in the New World comprising countries like the USA, Australia and New Zealand). The post-Second World War period witnessed the supply of cheap grain (mainly wheat and corn) from the North into the poor developing countries creating a reverse dependence and extending the erstwhile colonial arrangement of using tropical lands to cultivate crops to serve the interest of Northern capital. These new relations of interdependence in the post-colonial food question and their contradictions are discussed in greater detail in the next section.

The transfer of surplus from the colonies as tribute in a systematic manner over long periods was an integral part of colonialism. This tribute transfer outlasted the mercantile phase of imperialism and evolved well into the later industrial phase. While there were several methods for exacting tribute, including direct seizure of crops and minerals, the most sustained and organized of them was the maintenance of 'unpaid export surplus' by colonies. Patnaik (1984) brilliantly illustrated the sophisticated British method of using Council Bills to usurp precious foreign exchange that wanted to buy Indian merchandise and settle the export surplus by drawing precious resources from the Indian revenues. In Patnaik's own words, a part of internal taxation revenues is not spent within India but earmarked for expenditure abroad; the transformation of this sum in the form of rupees with the colonial government into sterling with the British government takes place . . . through the earnings of foreign exchange by India by exporting goods in excess of imports, which earnings are engrossed by Britain via the imposition of Home Charges on India. The entire amount of the exchange earnings so engrossed constitutes . . . a *minimal* estimate of the 'drain' . . . (Patnaik 1984, p. 52; emphasis in original).

This, of course, was a continuation of the peculiar fiscal-trade linkage that the East India Company (EIC) had already established by acquiring the *diwani of Bengal* in the early days of colonialism in South Asia. Thus, India paid for her own exports and maintained an export surplus for more than a century without accumulating any foreign exchange that could have been used as investments in the domestic economy. Similar processes of meeting the financial obligations imposed on colonies by imperial masters is evident from Indonesia and the Caribbean (Bagchi 1982). Patnaik estimated that in certain years during the interwar years, the Home Charges were eating into more than a quarter of the taxes collected in India.[1] Also, such exaction was continuing a century after Britain emerged as the first capitalist industrial nation using colonial tributes to finance a major part of her capital formation.[2]

In a macroeconomic sense, the 'drain of wealth' bleed colonies to fatten the capitalist economies in the North and clearly created and widened the developmental gap. What this did to the internal architecture of the colonial economies was even more profound and brings us back to the food question in the colonies. The Indian case is a good example for understanding these changing implications of colonial tribute exaction. At a time when Britain was yet to have industrialized (pre-1810 approximately), a large part of the unpaid export merchandise that the EIC drained as tribute consisted of hand-manufactured Indian cotton goods. This was, however, not compatible with British capital's interests after the Industrial Revolution led by the cotton textile industries. Indian hand-manufactures had to be forcibly snuffed out from the world trade circuits, efficiently accomplished by EIC using her monopoly charter and the discriminatory tariffs against Indian goods imposed by Britain, and also probably gave way to British machine-manufactures in the domestic market.

The destruction of India's chief export item in the early nineteenth century posed a challenge for the realization of the colonial tribute as unpaid exports (Mukherjee 2010). The new vehicles of tribute were found immediately in the forceful cultivation of commercial crops like indigo and opium in eastern India and later in the general economic coercion of a large section of Indian farmers to shift to growing commercial crops. The export of primary agricultural products remained the main carrier of the tribute for the rest of the nineteenth century and into the early twentieth century. The maintenance of an (unrequited) export surplus was chiefly achieved by an ever-increasing volume of primary commodity exports from colonial India.

The gradually increasing financial obligations imposed on the Indian colony by the British imperial apparatus witnessed major spurts due to exceptional war expenditures in the twentieth century, which led to more exports, as much as allowed by the world demand situation. This was however not the only factor which imposed an increasing demand on the agricultural lands of the subcontinent for cultivating exportable commercial crops. Often, the declining dollar prices of agricultural commodities in the world markets would reduce the 'value' of the export surplus and create more pressure to increase the 'volume' of the exports such that the size of the tribute could be maintained.

The direct implication of these processes was a shift of land resources from food cultivation for domestic consumption to commercial crop cultivation. The non-foodgrain crops grew at an annual rate of 1.31 per cent in the first half of the twentieth century, while foodgrains grew at a meagre 0.11 per cent per annum (Patnaik 1999). The declining foodgrain availability was a major developing context for rising hunger and more frequent famine conditions after 1880 till the end of the colonial rule. Patnaik further argued that this commercialization of Indian agriculture, supplying ever-increasing exportable items to the world, did not create any virtuous cycle for Indian farmers nor did it transform Indian agriculture to conditions of improved productivity. Much of the commercialization of agriculture in colonial India occurred under the coercive economic conditions of unviability and debt dependence buttressed by the oppressive land taxes in British India.

The three phenomena that we have discussed in this section come together to develop an understanding of the food question under capitalism. The import of tropical food goods by the industrializing nations and their appropriation of surplus from colonies in the form of tribute were both critical for the development of industrial capitalism. The two processes reinforced each other, as a bulk of the 'tribute' was realized in the form of unrequited exports of commercially cultivated agricultural commodities. The third phenomenon of commercialization of agriculture under economic coercion along with the 'drain of surplus' ensured a secular income deflation of the average colonial subject, depressing domestic demand and worsening of the situation of hunger and undernutrition in the colonies. The classical capitalist transition in the advanced industrial countries is a text-book example of how the core of capitalist accumulation is sustained through a critical dependence on and devouring of the non-capitalist 'outside'.

The Food Question Now: Dissecting Some Myths

In the period after the Second World War, a significant development was the emergence of a surplus foodgrain situation in the 'New World', turning the erstwhile settler colonies like the USA, Australia, New Zealand, etc. into net exporters of foodgrain and livestock products. Liberal state subsidies, particularly in the US, for channelizing the surplus foodgrain (surplus even beyond export demand) into poor countries as food-aid enabled this surplus situation to persist without any immediate constraint imposed by market demand. Concomitantly, a classical state-supported capital accumulation process ensued in the agricultural sector sowing the seeds of corporatization of agriculture.

In a couple of decades, transnational corporations (TNCs) emerged dominating value chains in agriculture through rapid and expansive vertical integration of production, processing and marketing. Subsequently, the process of globalization and trade liberalization from the 1980s onwards opened up immense opportunities for these TNCs to control global value chains in agricultural commodities. They could now carry out a renewed integration of

land and labour resources in the South within the global accumulation process, something that was prevalent during colonialism but was significantly
weakened during decolonization and its associated 'autonomous development'
projects.

This phenomenon, which critics have identified as an important
component of neo-colonialism, implied an enhanced role for big capital (now
global in nature) in the organization of global agriculture. This post-colonial
'food regime' characterized by historically unprecedented capital concentration
in global agriculture also gave rise to the understanding that the TNCs were
fundamentally changing the food question by using productivity-enhancing
cultivation techniques and bringing down the cost of food products through
their vertically integrated organization of the value chain from the 'farm' to the
'plate'. Scholars, policymakers and multilateral institutions were optimistic to
euphoric about the 'low and stable prices' in global food markets in the 1980s
and 1990s and the viability of the 'cheap food import' path for attaining food
security in the developing nations (Bernstein 1996; 2004; FAO 2003).

The 'global food crisis' of 2006–14 has now demonstrated the fragil-
ity of a food policy that depends on food imports for addressing fundamental
developmental challenges like hunger and malnutrition. However, there is
a deeper myth in the assessment of the role of TNCs in transforming global
agriculture post the 1970s oil shocks.

For the fairly long period of two decades when the food prices were
indeed 'low and stable' in the global markets, it is doubtful whether this was
because agribusiness corporations had revolutionized farming and the distribution chains. The world per-capita grain output actually declined from 341.6
kg in 1985 to 290.2 kg in 2002.[3] Despite this fall in the supply of grains, the
reason why prices remained low was the declining per capita grain consumption during this period. Between 1985 and 2000, the latter had declined from
324.3 to 303.1 kg.

Disaggregation of data clearly shows that this decline was primarily
in developing regions and there is no similar evidence from developed country
grain-consumption figures. Over the 1980s and 1990s, several developing
regions experienced a decline in grain consumption, starting with the Latin
American countries and West Asia in the 1980s and then South Asia and former
Soviet Union (FSU) countries in the 1990s. The decline in grain demand in
many developing regions was due to the neoliberal restructuring of economies
causing various crises for existing economic activities, especially informal rural
and urban occupations, and a widespread income deflation (Banerjee 2020a).

The most remarkable geopolitical development though that influenced
the global grain markets decisively was the break-up of the Soviet Union and
the subsequent dismantling of food subsidies and other welfare measures.
Between 1990 and 2000, the annual per-capita grain demand in FSU collapsed
by a massive 380.5 kg. In absolute terms, the grain demand collapse was a

gigantic 112.8 million tonnes. To put this in perspective, the total increase in the world's foodgrain consumption during 1990–2000 was 148.5 million tonnes and the FSU demand collapse compensates for 76 per cent of this. It was this disappearance of grain demand in the FSU countries that kept food prices 'low and stable' in the world markets. What was being celebrated as the 'technical revolution' of corporate agribusiness was in reality an 'unspoken silent famine' and the demographic disaster in the ex-socialist world, where the population declined by 10.2 million in a decade (Banerjee 2020a)!

There is no clear evidence since the oil shock of the 1970s till date that the global grain markets have overcome supply constraints decisively. Rather, the declining demand for grains due to economic distress/collapse in various developing/ex-socialist regions at different points of time have been repeatedly misinterpreted to attribute success to corporate farming and create an illusion that developing countries do not need to pursue the goal of self-sufficiency in food production (wherever possible, given natural constraints) and can possibly depend on food imports whenever required.

It is within this wider context that we locate a couple of myths regarding the foodgrain situation and the direction of agricultural policies that have been prevalent within policymaking and popular discourses in India. These mythical arguments have been widely quoted in the context of the three farm laws that were introduced by the central government in 2020 and has now been withdrawn in the face of intense farmers' resistance, primarily in northern India.[4] The first of these myths is that India is now a grain-surplus economy and there is hence no further requirement of guaranteeing a minimum price through the public procurement operations (GoI 2015). The second myth is that Indian farmers are subjected to a net-negative support because of state regulations, particularly export restrictions, and that this policy-driven negative producer support is the chief barrier to any improvement of farmer incomes. Let us examine these arguments in some detail.

First, the grain-surplus argument runs into some commonsensical problems. A 'foodgrain surplus' nation cannot also rank as low as India manages in the 'Global Hunger Index (GHI)'. In the GHI 2021 report, India ranked 101 among 116 nations.[5] The persistence and worsening of child stunting as shown by the recent National Family Health Survey (NHFS)-5 data further points towards pervading child undernutrition.[6] One can be fairly sure that that if the children are not eating enough, one parent (and probably both in many instances) is definitely going hungry. Earlier, the NSS Nutrition surveys had also revealed that nearly the bottom three-fourths of the population definitely suffers from inadequate energy and protein intakes.[7] Any authentic attainment of a 'food surplus' status would have implied the availability of plenty of cheap grains for domestic consumption that would have prevented all the above observations regarding hunger and nutrition in the country. Rather, the simultaneous existence of deep-seated hunger among the population and enormous grain-stocks in the government godowns point towards a policy-induced artificial creation of grain surpluses.

For the common observer, it is easy to be convinced by the 'food surplus' argument, given that the FCI stocks were at an all-time high of 97 million tonnes in June 2020. The food stocks with the government continue to remain high at around 75 million tonnes by the end of 2020, despite the additional foodgrain distribution as part of the Covid relief.[8] Similarly, more frequent and large exports of foodgrains by India over this past decade give the impression that the country produces much more excess grains than it consumes. The latter must be true if cereal exports are growing and stocks burgeoning. But is it because we are producing more grains or are we consuming less?

The per-capita domestic consumption of grains started declining in the 1990s and that trend continued for two clear decades. There has been some recovery in the last decade (2011–20) but the consumptions levels continue to remain lower than what it was in 1990 (Banerjee 2015). This decline has not been taken seriously within the academia as well as the policy establishment based on the argument that with increasing incomes, Indian middle classes were diversifying their diets. They were eating more animal products and hence the demand for grains was going down in the country. This had nothing to do with the worsening nutritional status of the population.

Interestingly amid the global food crisis, the then US President George Bush Jr. made the same argument but there, he was blaming Indian (and Chinese) middle classes for diversifying their diets, eating more animal products and thereby increasing the demand for foodgrains (as food but more so indirectly as animal feed).[9] While his argument did not stand the test of facts as the per capita domestic grain consumption in India had been declining all the while from the early 1990s to the food crisis of 2006, the theoretical logic embedded in his argument was correct. Any shift to animal products due to rising middle-class incomes do lead to increased demand for grains in an economy as the 'indirect' demand for animal feed (via livestock production and processing industries) increases much more than any stagnation/decline in the 'direct' demand for grains as food.

Thus, a decline in demand for foodgrains indicates precisely the opposite of what Indian policymakers have been arguing – that diet-diversification is not happening for the Indian middle-classes. Or more realistically, while the thin Indian elites and upper middle classes have indeed diversified their diets and consume more grains (directly and indirectly) now, that additional demand is more than compensated by the majority of the population (located in the bottom three-fourths) who are eating less grains (carbohydrates) and less animal products (proteins). In fact, the higher demand for grains by rich Indians is more than compensated as the declining per capita consumption figures represent (Banerjee 2015).

Let us examine the figures a little more closely to bust this myth. In

1990, the per year per capita domestic consumption of cereals was 186 kg. For all subsequent years in the three decades from then, it has been lower than this figure. This is a level of consumption that is usually found along with widespread hunger in society. Nations where hunger has become a phenomenon of the past, the grains demand is much more than this. Now if we assume that the average Indian did not experience any further improvement but merely maintained her grain consumption at this low 186 kg for the next thirty years, India would have required a whopping additional 430 million tonnes of foodgrains for the period 1991–2020! This only depicts to what extent structural adjustment policies driven by the neoliberal economic philosophy have systematically caused a crisis for petty production in India, leading to an 'income deflation' for the masses. This, in turn, caused a decline in food demand for the masses and consequent arrest/deterioration of their nutritional and health status.

So, if this demand disappeared (or never got generated), where did the grains go? Over the last three decades and particularly in the last ten years, India has emerged as a major cereal exporter. This is an entirely new phenomenon for India since Independence. The total grain exported in 1991–2020 is 216.5 million tonnes and this accounts for part of the disappearing demand. Some part of the grain for which there is no domestic demand accumulated in the Food Corporation of India (FCI) stocks (assuming private stocks are negligible). By December 2020, the cereal stocks were 75 million tonnes as noted above. Therefore, the exports and the current stocks account for only 291.5 million tonnes of cereals out of the 430 million tonnes of grains for which demand was absent. Where are the remaining 138.5 million tonnes of grains?

The answer is that this missing grain was actually never produced! The per capita domestic grain output was 190 kg in 1990 and had also started declining since then. By 2007, this had declined to around 169 kg after which there was a recovery. Since 1991, it is only in four years that the per capita grain output touched or crossed the 190 kg mark, which was achieved way back in 1990. Three of these four years are after 2017, depicting a situation where food producers in the country were struggling for most of the last three decades to keep their food-growing systems intact due to increasing pressure of commercialization, deregulation of inputs, ecological challenges and falling incomes from cultivation. The domestic cereal production has recovered to the 1990 levels of normative output only in the last three to four years after a long stagnation.

Clearly, there is no authentic surplus foodgrain in the country. Any surplus visible in the forms of large exports and overflowing FCI stocks can be attributed to the fact that the average Indian was not able to maintain her already low level of grain consumption over the last thirty years. All euphoria regarding 'food surpluses' are really based on the dystopia of the endless pangs of hunger, undernutrition and their consequences that the average Indian and her children have borne over the last thirty years. Needless to say, this 'average Indian' is located far away from the glittering lives of the metropolitan cities and invisibilized from the world of policymakers.

Now, let us consider the second popular argument that deregulated export–import markets are always the best policy option in Indian agriculture and any trade protectionist policies necessarily led to a negative support for farmers. Markets are complex institutions representing economic relationships embedded in the prevailing sociopolitical realities. The price formation in a particular market is dependent on the demand and supply dynamics as well as a myriad of structural factors. The balance of bargaining power between any two parties determines the price formation in a commodity market. Consequently, a buoyant demand does not necessarily guarantee a better price for the seller if the buyer is a monopolist. Similarly, the absence of a monopoly buyer does not guarantee high prices to the seller if the demand is sluggish or declining. The demand and supply itself is influenced by a number of factors that are often outside the realm of market transactions.

With globalization and a revolution in transportation, the dynamics of market demand and supply are influenced by an ever greater number of factors developing in very different and apparently unconnected faraway markets and also by factors that originate from geopolitical developments or cultural changes. For agricultural commodities, natural and weather-related events further add to the complications of the demand–supply dynamics. This has meant far greater fluctuation in agricultural commodity prices after trade liberalization. There have been periods where prices have boomed but frequently followed by massive slumps wiping out past gains for small to big farmers. In light of this, any blanket claim that deregulating markets and allowing the free play of private players will improve crop prices for farmers appears to be on shaky ground at best, and spurious at worst.

Interestingly in India, the arguments that emerged in the early 1990s favouring the opening up of agricultural commodity markets to global trade and joining a multilateral trade arrangement represented by the World Trade Organization (WTO) were based on the same premise that removing government regulations like import tariffs will necessarily lead to better prices for farmers. Gulati and Sharma (1995) argued that by protecting India's farmers from global competition through trade duties, the government was doing more harm to them. They calculated that India had a negative aggregate measure of support (AMS) for Indian farmers. This was so because while the government was extending various input subsidies (like on power, fertilizer, etc.) to farmers, by preventing them from selling at higher prices in the world agricultural commodity markets, the government was actually providing negative support to them.

They estimated that the total AMS for Indian farmers stood at (-) Rs 341.4 billion in 1992–93. This was so even as the total subsidy-based support amounted to Rs 86.5 billion. It was estimated that the Indian farmers were getting a negative support of Rs 427.9 billion because *world market prices were higher than MSPs for various crops* and government restrictions were not allowing farmers to sell in export markets (Gulati and Sharma 1995). Quite a strong argument for liberalizing trade in agricultural commodities!

Except that this kind of argument is a classic example of how not to understand markets and formulate policy based on myopic play with data. Immediately after a large number of developing countries signed the WTO agreement in 1995, agricultural prices collapsed in the global markets. This was imminent in the sense that when around 70 developing countries liberalized agricultural trade in the hope of capturing the same global market, there was a sudden excess supply of most agricultural commodities. Millions of farmers from various developing countries were made to compete with each other and supply their crops at substantially lower prices. Between 1995 and 2000, the prices of major crops declined in the range of 30–80 per cent. This precipitated an agrarian distress in rural India and triggered farmer suicides, particularly for commercial farmers, in the late 90s (Patnaik 2003).

Academic and policymaking integrity demanded that the AMS be recalculated for the year 2000 or 2001 and if found that the economic support had turned positive because the world prices have fallen substantially, India should have reconsidered her commitment to the WTO agreement. This might have prevented Indian agriculture from slipping into a long crisis. Unfortunately, often, arguments are built up erroneously to push through certain reforms and hence they are seldom re-examined. The original negative AMS argument had no understanding of the fact that what they were calculating was only true for the given time and policy environment, that is in a static sense. What can be the impact of the entire developing world opening up their trade simultaneously required far greater foresight and imagination of market dynamics than was exercised.

World agricultural commodity prices did recover after 2002 and then went into a boom period led by foodgrains. The conversion of a critical threshold of grains into ethanol in the US, high oil prices and speculative finance entering the commodity futures market all led to astronomical prices of food. While the 'net food sellers' (notably in the developed world but also thin sections of food growers in the developing countries) benefitted, a majority of the farmers (and other poor non-agricultural population) in the developing world who are 'net food buyers' were again at the receiving end of the grain price boom, enduring massive onslaughts on their diets and nutrition directly and cut-back in education and health expenditures indirectly. Liberalized food markets which promised to augment farmers' income through greater efficiency caused enormous insecurity and distress to most farmers with unmatched alacrity. Clearly, there is much more to markets than efficiency!

Post the financial crisis of 2008 and the beginning of the oil price slide in 2012 (which rendered corn ethanol as unviable), the food prices started declining. This was hardly again an undisputed relief to petty commodity producers (most farmers in the developing world) given that 2012 marked the end of the commodity boom and prices of most agricultural commodities also turned downwards, often depleting the farm incomes in real terms. In India, farmers were additionally hit by demonetization in 2016 and a general economic slowdown, keeping the crop output prices low. Globally, the prices of major crops have declined between 20 per cent and 50 per cent between 2012 and 2019 and are now made further sluggish due to the adverse economic consequences of the pandemic (Banerjee 2020b).

One aspect that emerged in the farm law debates was that the middlemen (*arhatiyas*) were bringing in inefficiency into the systems through the licensed *mandi* systems and this was yet another reason for removing government intervention entirely from the grain markets. The most important argument that is not considered when it is argued that removing the *arhatiyas* will benefit the farmers, is the structure of global value chains in agricultural commodities.

It is widely accepted now that agricultural value chains typically take the shape of an hourglass, with large number of producers and consumers having negligible bargaining power at the two ends and a few wholesalers, processors and retailers (often global TNCs or conglomerates) which control all the levers in the commodity markets and appropriate a disproportionate share of the 'value'. The *arhatiyas* and the government supervision/regulation has the provision of relatively better accountability and imparts a reasonable bargaining power to farmers, which global value-chains have systematically denied to farmers across the world. Thus, the *arhatiyas* and government fees and surcharges in the *mandis* can be identified as detrimental to surplus food growers only in a make-believe world where global corporate agribusiness does not exist and is not continuously waiting eagerly to enter newer and newer agricultural markets in developing countries.

Conclusion

To summarize the major arguments of the article, the food question in contemporary capitalism continues to be located within the realms of international political economy, interconnected across the developed, developing and underdeveloped world. Corporate capital-controlled industrial agriculture has indeed reorganized agricultural value chains through vertical integration from input-industries to retailing of processed food products. Corporate agribusiness still though faces stiff constraints when it comes to increasing their access to the best cultivable lands where alternative petty organization of farming predominates. Wherever, it is not possible to displace the farming population and directly take control of land for corporate agriculture, agribusiness lobbies usually attempt to influence governments to alter regulations to favour big business and make independent farmers (small or big) and their farm systems dependent on the corporate value chains, both in downstream and upstream agro-industries.

This ever-increasing quest for land and natural resources by TNCs is of course to colonize more and more relatively independent peasant farm systems with the purpose of capturing 'economic value' and burgeoning their profits. This 'prime mover' of this global corporate food regime is to increasingly redirect land and natural resources to the service of capitalist industry and financialization, thus trying to overcome nature's constraint, or perhaps intensifying the contradiction with nature. At the same time, the best quality food commodities are retailed for the consumption of the global rich, who will pay the highest price for the final food commodities. This has impact on poorer communities in the developing and underdeveloped world in terms of availability and access to food. The poor located in the bottom half of the world population, while attempting to attain a subsistence food basket, are put in direct competition with the rich elite. Thus, we currently have the unfortunate phenomenon of malnutrition at both ends of the population distribution, overconsumption of food and associated lifestyle ailments among the richest billion and inadequate food intakes and undernutrition for the bottom two billion (or perhaps more by yardsticks of healthier diet norms).

It is also not an unambiguous case that the incomes of farming communities are markedly enhanced when they participated in these global value chains since the distribution of value is exceptionally skewed towards the corporate entities with monopolies (or oligopolies) and monopsonies (or oligopsonies). Mostly, erstwhile independent agrarian peasants and labour lose their sovereign farm systems to serve as cheap labour for global capital. In this sense, the food question under capitalism continues to be intricately linked with the expropriative relationship that capitalism maintains with the agrarian population, in history and now.

The historical North–South dimension of the food question of the classical colonial world has been restored through the acquisitive spirit of agricultural TNCs over the last four decades. Except that now we must recognize that the North–South binary is tempered to the extent that rich elites from the South have benefitted from capitalist globalization and now count themselves among the global rich. Also, the binary gets modified to the extent that industrial centres have emerged or been relocated to the South. The food question today is therefore about protecting the rights of the petty farming communities over their land and natural resources and to preserve their farm systems. A better access to basic food necessities for the global masses requires preventing corporate takeovers of independent peasant production that is often facilitated by the withdrawal of existing state support to non-capitalist organization of agriculture. The contours of this struggle may well lie within the framework of a nation or require international solidarities depending on the emerging political economy of contemporary corporate capitalism.

This essay was originally published under the same title in *The Indian Economic Journal*, vol. 71, no. 1, 2023, pp. 204–16.

Notes

[1] The Home Charges varies between 16 and 27 per cent of the Indian revenues during the years 1875–1933 (Patnaik 1984).

[2] Patnaik estimates that as early as 1801, the total drain of wealth from India and the West Indies to Britain constituted around 84 per cent of the latter's annual capital formation (Patnaik as cited in Mukherjee 2010).

[3] All grain consumption, production and export numbers quoted in this essay are based on the data available at Foreign Agriculture Service, USDA, available at https://apps.fas.usda.gov/psdonline/. For per capita figures, the data has been normalized by population figures from FAO.

[4] This can be followed at https://www.indianexpress.com/article/india/three-farm-laws-repealed-pm-modi-7630405/lite/

[5] Refer to https://www.globalhungerindex.org/india.html for details.

[6] See https://www.orfonline.org/research/what-nfhs-5-data-shows/ for details.

[7] Refer to Patnaik (2013).

[8] Food stocks figures based on data provided by FCI.

[9] Refer to https://timesofindia.indiatimes.com/home/environment/developmental-issues/Now-Bush-blames-India-for-rising-food-prices/articleshow/3006775.cms

References

Abu-Lughod, J. (1989), *Before European Hegemony. The World System AD1250–AD1350*, New York: Oxford University Press.

Acemoglu, D., S. Johnson and J.A. Robinson (2001), 'The Colonial Origins of Comparative Development: An Empirical Investigation', *American Economic Review*, vol. 91, no. 5, pp. 1369–401. https://doi.org/10.1257/aer.91.5.1369

Amin, S. (1977), *Imperialism and Unequal Development*, New York: Monthly Review Press.

Bagchi, A.K. (1982), *The Political Economy of Underdevelopment*, New York: Cambridge University Press.

Banerjee, A. (2015), 'Contestations Over Food Subsidy Policy: An Examination of the High-Level Committee Recommendations', *Social Scientist*, vol. 43, nos 7–8, pp. 41–57.

——— (2020a), 'The "Longer Food Crisis" and Consequences for Economic Theory and Policy in the South', in P. Jha, P. Yeros and W. Chambati, eds, *Rethinking the Social Sciences with Sam Moyo*, Delhi: Tulika Books.

——— (2020b), 'Saving the Rural Economy', *Financial Express*, 29 April 2020, available at https://www.financialexpress.com/opinion/saving-the-rural-economy-the-govt-will-have-to-deepen-its-procurement-operation/1942598/, accessed 1 September 2024.

Bernstein, H. (1996), 'Agrarian Questions Then and Now', *Journal of Peasant Studies*, vol. 24, nos 1–2, pp. 22–59, doi: https://doi.org/10.1080/03066159608438630

——— (2004), 'Changing Before Our Very Eyes: Agrarian Questions and the Politics of Land in Capitalism Today', *Journal of Agrarian Change*, vol. 4, nos 1–2, pp. 190–225, doi: https://doi.org/10.1111/j.1471-0366.2004.00078.x

Food and Agriculture Organization (FAO) (2003), *The State of Food in Security in the World 2003: Monitoring Progress Towards the World Food Summit and Millennium Development Goals, Rome.*

Frank, A. (1967), *Capitalism and Underdevelopment in Latin America*, New York: Monthly Review Press.

Foster, J.B. (2009), *The Ecological Revolution: Making Peace with the Planet*, New York: Monthly Review Press.

GoI (2015), 'Report of the High-Level Committee on Reorienting the Role and Restructuring of Food Corporation of India', 19 January, New Delhi. (n.d.). November 16, 2022. https://fci.gov.in/app2/webroot/upload/News/ Report%20of%20the%20High%20Level%20Committee%20on%20Reorienting%20the%20Role%20and%20 Restructuring%20of%20FCI_English.pdf

Gulati, A. and A. Sharma (1995), 'Subsidy Syndrome in Indian Agriculture', *Economic and Political Weekly*, vol. 30, no. 39, pp. 1857–63.

Habib, I. (1995), 'Colonization of the Indian Economy', in I. Habib, *Essays in Indian History*, pp. 304–46), Delhi: Tulika Books.

Magdoff, H. (1978), *Imperialism: From the Colonial Age to the Present*, New York: Monthly Review Press.

Morris, M.D. (1983), 'The Growth of Large-Scale Industry to 1947', in D. Kumar and M. Desai, eds, *The Cambridge Economic History of India*, second edition, Cambridge: Cambridge University Press.

Moyo, S., P. Jha and P. Yeros (2013), 'The Classical Agrarian Question: Myth, Reality and Relevance Today', *Agrarian South: Journal of Political Economy*, vol. 2, no. 1, pp. 93–119.

Mukherjee, A. (2010), 'Empire: How Colonial India Made Modern Britain', *Economic and Political Weekly*, vol. 45, no. 50, pp. 73–82.

Patnaik, U. (1984), 'Transfer of Tribute and the Balance of Payments in the CEHI', *Social Scientist*, vol. 12, no. 12, pp. 43–55.

―――― (1999), 'Food Availability and Famine', in U. Patnaik, *The Long Transition Essays on Political Economy*, Delhi: Tulika Books.

―――― (2003), 'Global Capitalism, Deflation and Agrarian Crisis in Developing Countries', *Journal of Agrarian Change*, vol. 3, nos 1–2, pp. 33–66, doi: https://doi.org/10.1111/1471-0366.00050

―――― (2006), 'The Free Lunch: Transfers from the Tropical Colonies and Their Role in Capital Formation in Britain During the Industrial Revolution', in K.S. Jomo, ed., *Globalization under Hegemony: The Changing World Economy*, New Delhi and New York: Oxford University Press.

―――― (2011), 'The "Agricultural Revolution" in England: Its Cost for the English Working Class and the Colonies', in S. Moosvi, ed., *Capitalism, Colonialism and Globalization*, Delhi: Tulika Books.

―――― (2013), 'Poverty Trends in India 2004–05 to 2009–10', *Economic and Political Weekly*, vol. 48, no. 40, pp. 43–58.

Patnaik, U. and P. Patnaik (2016), *A Theory of Imperialism*, New York: Columbia University Press.

13

Imperialism of the Twenty-first Century

A Global Tripartite System

Rohit Azad and Shouvik Chakraborty

Introduction

Hardt and Negri (2001) in their highly acclaimed *Empire*, which drew rave reviews from both ends of the political spectrum, state:

> [W]e find the First World in the Third, the Third in the First, and the Second almost nowhere at all . . . *[t]he United States does not, and indeed no nation-state can today, form the centre of an imperialist project.* Imperialism is over. No nation will be world leader in the way modern European nations were. (Hardt and Negri 2001, pp. xiii-xiv; emphasis in original)

While refuting the existence of imperialism, the authors are simultaneously making a nuanced argument in favour of a theoretical construct in the form of an Empire, the logic of which is not driven by any particular nation state. Without going into the details of how they perceive today's global economy to be, our attempt here is to examine their basic premise. Is imperialism, in the sense of domination of one nation state over the global economy, indeed over?

Declaring the end of the US imperialism in the backdrop of the earlier Afghan and Iraq invasions might seem perplexing to some. But Hardt (2006) defends the argument taking precisely these as examples of the end of imperialism by drawing an interesting analogy between these unilateral US attempts and that of a defeated monster at the end of a typical horror movie. These wars were, Hardt (2006) argues, like the last ditch attempt of the dead monster (imperialism, figuratively speaking) to grab one of the protagonists, right before the credits start rolling on the screen, after which his arm is cut off to finally put him to rest. He further argues that '[t]here is no point continuing the fight against the old monster, dead and buried. Its time has passed. But we know there will be a sequel with a new monster [Empire] that requires new forms of struggle'. But is the US, the 'old monster, dead and buried' indeed?

One of the primary reasons for why in these circles imperialism is considered passe is because of the surge of China from the global South as the manufacturing workshop of the world and, perhaps India as the Silicon Valley of the South. But we would like to argue that such a diffusion of capital in the Third World or de-industrialization in the First should not be seen as a sign of weakening of the concept of imperialism. Far from it, it should be seen as a way of the US imperialism trying to resolve its inner contradictions.

While capital may have shifted to the Third World resulting in high growth and employment there, there is no denying that there is only one country's currency, somewhat weakened but, still rules the global economy – the US dollar (USD). And given that the financial system of the world economy is driven by the stability of the USD, the US continues to 'form the centre of an imperialist project'. All major currencies, including Renminbi, of the world are in effect pegged to it. International finance flies to it when the country is hit by the worst ever crisis since the Great Depression of the 1930s, the exact opposite of what would have happened to any other currency in the world. Despite multiple currencies trying to challenge its hegemony, none, whether Yen earlier or Euro and Renminbi currently, have managed to replace it as a reserve currency. Lest this point be misunderstood, it is not about the US dollar in particular. During the heydays of British imperialism, the same role was played by pound sterling. To be sure, in the aftermath of the pandemic and the Russian invasion of Ukraine, there is clamour to challenge the hegemony of dollar but it remains to be seen how far this challenge will result in removing the dollar from the pedestal. But more importantly, even if it does, such a challenge will endorse our overall argument, as argued below, instead of undermining it.

Despite multiple currencies being accepted globally, there is still one which is considered to be supreme in any epoch. Why? Is the global acceptance of one currency by all countries merely an accounting exercise? In other words, is it the case that the global reserve currency – pound then and dollar now – are merely units of account, nothing more nothing less. And since any financial system requires a unit of account, there will be one currency or another which will perform that role. This in itself does not amount to imperialism for sure. But are these reserve currencies merely units of account? They are not and herein lies the essence of imperialism. We will come back to this important question later in the essay.

In what follows, we will look at three broad Marxian accounts of contemporary imperialism to differentiate our argument from theirs. The third section, 'Imperialism Breathes Value to the US Dollar', presents some stylized facts that forms the basis for our arguments. The fourth section, 'The Modus Operandi of Modern Imperialism', builds a theoretical structure to explain the reasons for why and how imperialism sustains the global reserve currency as a universal store of value. The last section concludes the article.

Contemporary Marxian Accounts of Imperialism

There are broadly three Marxian themes, with variations within, about contemporary imperialism that we review here. The choice of themes is also driven by what comes closest to our own argument, so by no means is the account in this section exhaustive. In general, there are two somewhat divergent readings of Marx, which can be classified under one of these categories: the realization problem or the tendency of the rate of the profit to fall. Since we are dealing with contemporary imperialism, we do not get into reviewing some of the classics like Hilferding, Luxemburg, Lenin, Arendt, Baran, Magdoff, the unequal exchange or dependency school. Brewer (2002) summarizes most of these positions albeit, we believe, some more accurately than the others. For the same reason, we do not engage, except perfunctorily, with the Marxist literature which argues that imperialism is over. The purpose of this section is to show similarities and dissimilarities of our argument with the existing Marxian accounts of imperialism.

North–South Interdependence

Patnaik (1997, 2009) and Patnaik and Patnaik (2016) have argued that for a global monetary system to be stable, prices of other commodities should not be increasing without bounds. One such set of commodities the prices of which might have an ex-ante tendency to rise are agricultural commodities, mainly produced in the tropical regions of the global South. This tendency arises out of the constraints of the land mass, with 'land augmenting' measures undermined by lack of public investment, required to produce them, thereby, limiting their supply in comparison to rising ex-ante demand. Patnaik and Patnaik (2016) say '[i]mperialism is the device typically used by capitalism for [the] purpose . . . [of] ensur[ing] that the phenomenon of *increasing supply price* does not actually manifest itself' (emphasis added).

And this ex-ante rise in supply price is suppressed through an ex post deflation in demand through an income squeeze of the vast mass of working people (global reserve army) in the South. To be sure, this does not require an absolute squeeze, but a relative squeeze of the South vis-a-vis the North would serve the purpose provided the resultant global ex post demand grows in tandem with production of these commodities.

Two implications follow. One, there will be growth divergence between the North and the South resulting in an 'unequal interdependence'. Two, maintaining price stability in the North would require a consistent fall in the terms of trade against primary commodities being produced in the South (much like the Prebisch-Singer hypothesis).

The problem is that both these propositions do not seem to hold in the current phase of capitalism, at least for certain countries in the South. On the one hand, the country with the largest reserve army of labour in the world, China, has witnessed an en masse shift of the manufacturing base from the

North. As a result, let alone a growth divergence, China's share in world GDP has been steadily rising since the 1990s. On the other hand, the terms of trade have moved in favour of primary commodities since the late 1990s. We find that while the premise (of output and price instabilities in the North) of this framework is correct, the prediction (low growth rate in and adverse terms of trade for the South) is empirically questionable, particularly since neoliberalism.

Imperialism as a Spatio-Temporal Fix Against Falling Rate of Profit

Harvey's (2003) work can be located within the Marxian tradition which argues that with the development of capitalism, there is a tendency for the rate of profit to fall. Harvey argues that imperialism provides a spatio-temporal fix – the former by exporting capital (diffusion in the South) and the latter through technologies with long gestation lags (both within the North and the South), delaying introduction of techniques, expenditure on education and so on – to postpone this imminent fall in the rate of profit. Let us add a rider here. Harvey (2018), of late, has changed his position dramatically and admitted that he does not 'find the category of imperialism that compelling' and the reason is that, 'the historical draining of wealth from East to West for more than two centuries has . . . been largely *reversed* over the last thirty years' (emphasis added). We of course discuss the earlier Harvey here.

The central problem with this framework, and by inference this Marxian tradition, is that the premise on which this concept of imperialism is built is theoretically unsound. Sweezy (1991) and the monopoly capital school have critiqued this position extensively, which runs as follows. One, replacement of living labour (workers) with dead labour (machines) does not mean a rise in the organic composition of capital to begin with as Marx seems to have conflated the use value with the exchange value of machines. Two, even if the organic composition of capital (denominator in Marx's rate of profit) rises, there is no upper limit to the numerator, that is, ratio between the surplus value and labour value (s/v) may still not fall. Data on rates of profit too seem to show that there has not been any technologically induced fall in the rate of profit. There could be a fall in the rate of profit reflective of the realization problem but then that is a separate issue.

But are we just nitpicking? Does it make a difference whether the actual or the potential rate of profit falls? It actually does. The latter necessitates a technological 'limit' to capitalism (capital replacing land in Ricardo's falling productivity of land), which is what imperialism helps remove in Harvey (2003) and other such traditions, including that of Smith (2016), who we discuss below.

What if there is no such technical 'limit'? Does that mean imperialism is not required for such a system? That would be an erroneous position to take. So, in contrast to Patnaik (1997), Harvey (2003) gets the prediction (diffusion of capital in certain segments of the South) correct, but his premise is theoretically (and empirically) questionable.

Unequal Exchange

Smith (2016) and Foster (2019) try to resurrect the unequal exchange school in today's context. Since this argument seems closest to what we are going to argue, we would like to discuss this in some detail to distinguish our position from theirs.

To prevent the fall of the rate of profit, massive underutilization of capacities, corporations in the North indulge in outsourcing part or all its production. In certain cases, they may create their own subsidiaries in the South but in most cases the so-called lower end of the value chain is not owned by those on the top of the pyramid. This process of creation-of-surplus-in-the-South-but-appropriation-in-the-North, that is, imperialism of today, can continue only if there is a substantial difference in wage costs between the two regions of the world, which will continue till there are restrictions on labour mobility between them. Smith (2016) calls this a process of 'labour arbitrage', which forms the core for his premise of imperialism to stand. Much like Smith, the 'old' school of unequal exchange tried to explain how this unequal exchange comes about.[1]

Arguing on similar grounds, Foster (2019) says that the difference between the nominal and the real exchange rate (purchasing power parity) can roughly measure the extent of transfer of surplus value from the South to the North and can also be treated as a measure of this late imperialism.

A few issues, primarily theoretical, arise vis-a-vis this framework too, even though the detailed analysis of the global value chains provides some very important insights into the current world order.

One, unless the benchmark of equal exchange is specified, how does one define unequal exchange? Patnaik (1982, p. 24), in her critique of the theory of unequal exchange, argued that attaching this normative label of 'equal exchange' (carrying implications of equity and justice) to exchange at labour values is directly antithetical to Marx's treatment of exchange. The necessary implication of Marx's treatment of 'equivalent exchange' under the laws of competitive capitalism is that commodities do not exchange at labour values. However, there is no normative content to Marx's use of the term 'exchange of equivalents'. And, moreover, to define that concept of unequal exchange, one needs to compare the real wages in conjunction with 'objective' levels of labour productivities.

Two, the argument that this labour arbitrage arises because of immobility of labour even as capital remains mobile to equalize rates of profit is problematic. In the theoretical framework of this tradition, whether the old or the new avatar, while capital is mobile, labour is not and that is what creates the wage differentials. But in the abstract world of full capital mobility, wage equalization should take place even if labour itself is not mobile. It is true that in reality, there are a host of social factors which determine the levels of wages. But even if these factors are controlled for, a more macro reason for wage differential today is that both capital and labour are only partially mobile, though of course to different degrees.

Three, any attempt to 'measure' imperialism in the form of labour arbitrage (and the corresponding transfer of surplus) has a basic lacuna. If, over time, the North–South wage gap falls, as is indeed happening, as a result of capital mobility, this would imply that the 'degree' of imperialism has fallen *pari passu* but would that indeed be a correct reading?

Four, if in the distant future, the wage differential of some countries in the South and the North tends to disappear, would one conclude that these Southern countries have become part of the imperialist yolk by inference?

Imperialism Breathes Value to the US Dollar

We need to first establish whether imperialism exists today or this category needs to be discarded, as Hardt and Negri (2001) propose, given the existence of the First in the Third and Third in the First.

In the light of the unilateral military or trade aggressions that the US has made in the recent past and continues to make even today vis-a-vis West Asia, one should immediately be wary of outrightly discarding the category of imperialism. There is no doubt that the military might of the US is behind its hegemony but is that all there is to US imperialism? Moreover, there is a problem with this position. It gives the impression that if tomorrow the US were to withdraw troops or become less aggressive, imperialism would have got weakened accordingly. Moreover, Hardt and Negri (2001) would argue that this is the last leg of the US' imperialism and it is trying to desperately assert its long-lost dominance and it is just a matter of time before these aggressions become politically irrelevant and disappear.

Our argument is that if there is a proof of imperialism, it lies in the way the global reserve currency is maintained in the world economy. This holds true of the past as much as it holds today. The mechanisms may have changed but that there is global financial/trade architecture which maintains the hegemony of the US dollar today or the British pound earlier is beyond doubt. It is this architecture that defines and sustains imperialism. Almost two-thirds of the forex reserves are kept as dollars irrespective of the region we look at in the world.

To be sure, currency hegemony is merely a reflection of a complex institutional infrastructure – trade agreements, debt and capital flows, intellectual property rights – created by the North to the detriment of the South. Moreover, it does not necessarily require one currency, there could be multiple currencies from the North stacked on a global ladder but at a distinctly higher level than the currencies of the South. In fact, one could argue that the changing relative strength of these high-order currencies may reflect the extent of inter-imperialist rivalry at a point in time. The current hegemony (almost absolute) of the dollar, for example, shows the unipolarity of US imperialism.

But what gives dollar (or these currencies in certain epochs) the special place it commands? Keynes (1936) in his famous chapter 17 had argued that the net return of all commodities (what he called marginal efficiency of capital net of borrowers' and lenders' risks) falls as their production rises and the commodity whose net return falls the slowest sets the limit to production of all the other commodities. That special commodity is money because of two reasons, neither of which holds for any other commodity. On the one hand, its elasticity of production is zero since only central banks can create it. On the other hand, its elasticity of substitution is nearly zero since 'money is a bottomless sink for purchasing power' (Keynes 1936, p. 31), the demand for which cannot simply be diverted to other commodities. What is true for domestic money is true for global money as well and in that sense dollar is money par excellence.

For the elasticity of substitution of dollar to be zero, global holders of wealth have to be assured of its value against other commodities and rival currencies. For the dollar to be a preferred asset, its premium net of prices (for example, of essential commodities like oil) should not fall precipitously. No wonder the 1970s oil crisis created a scare for the USD. It took a paradigmatic change in the geopolitical landscape and economic framework altogether to bring the USD back on track. Therefore, the importance of price stability cannot be stressed more. The mechanism through which stability of dollar is maintained globally forms one of the core elements of the theory of imperialism here (as also in Patnaik 1997).

As for rival Northern currencies, *ceteris paribus*, the one whose value is most stable against each other will act as the key reserve currency. We discuss how such a *ceteris paribus* does not normally hold. One could perhaps argue that price stability is nothing unique to the dollar since the other leading currencies too more or less share this property. It needs to be noted, however, that the uniqueness of the dollar comes from the fact that it maintains its hegemony despite running huge trade and fiscal deficits with autonomous monetary policy (which are all conditions for capital flight in today's world), whereas none of the other countries with leading currencies have this liberty.

A proof of this more-equal-than-others status of dollar was best exemplified recently when global capital paradoxically flew towards the US even as its financial system was experiencing the biggest collapse since the Great Depression. Euro during the Euro crisis or Yen during its lost decades did not have the same fate. Nor would Renminbi either if China were to experience such a crisis. Such is the power of the dollar! A million-dollar question (pun intended) is: why?

Technology and Patents' Regime Backs the USD
Despite having outsourced the production of commodities to the Third World countries and running huge trade deficits with some of them, the USD

has not only maintained its supremacy, but it has also not let those countries gain the status of global reserve currency despite having huge current account surplus with the US. Any other country, which would have lost the markets in the way the US has, would have long ceased to hold the reserve currency.

The politics of patents and copyrights and its limitations are well known but within the given framework, there is no doubt that the US has the highest number of patents in the world. The first world in general has higher patents than the emerging and growth-leading economies (EAGLEs) followed by the relatively underdeveloped African subcontinent. There is a clear hierarchy between these three sets of countries as far as control over technology is concerned. And within the EAGLEs, it is essentially the Chinese and South Koreans who have pushed the ranking up while the rest of the EAGLEs are way behind on the technology ladder.

This supremacy in technical knowhow provides two distinct advantages to the US and its currency. One, whoever holds the patents holds the monopoly rents arising out of those. It provides the basis for surplus value expropriation even though the production is taking place overseas, a point which has quite succinctly been made by Smith (2016) and Foster (2019).

Two, it will always have the first-mover advantage since technological development requires heavy investments in R&D and more long-term investment in educational and research institutions. It is a self-fulfilling process. The universities which provide the best research facilities attract the best minds in the world, which feeds into newer ideas, which, by generating monopoly rents, give the holders of the patents a heads up. A part of this profit is reinvested in these research departments in the US universities and the entire process repeats. The US also creates the politico-legal framework in its favour to maintain this technological advantage. Any other country to break into this position would require a huge spike in its technological pace, which is a Herculean task though some countries can still make significant advances in this regard, as China seems to be making of late.

US Military: The Power behind the Dollar

Even though not discussed or stressed so far in our argument, a very important factor behind the dollar's hegemony has to do with the military might of the US. We have downplayed it so far both because it has been written about extensively, as also we wanted to highlight the other factors which have not been given their due in the existing literature on imperialism.

The data on defence expenditure speaks for itself. If we look at the share of the US in the global defence expenditure, it is light years ahead of other countries, First or Third World countries alike. This aggressive armament race also requires the US to be at the cutting edge of warfare technology – an offshoot of which are also technologies, for example, internet or drones, which are later used for civilian purposes. So, one could argue that heavy military expenditure feeds into the patents' race and vice versa which help the US maintain its hegemony.

This gives their military an edge over any competing country, and by corollary, currency. International finance knows that when push comes to shove, the dollar can maintain its hegemony through brute force and that expectation is based on past as well as present experiences.

The Modus Operandi of Modern Imperialism

In different frameworks of imperialism, the world has been theorized as constitutive of two parts: capitalist core (global North) and pre/semi-capitalist periphery (global South). This neat classification has been smudged by the emergence of China from the global South as a major economic player in the global economy. We argue its emergence, far from weakening imperialism, is a key factor in explaining today's imperialism. Imperialism of the twenty-first century constitutes three, not two, tiers – capitalist core, periphery's core and periphery's periphery.

Tier 1: Capitalist Core – Weakening Labour and Resurgent Capital

How has the dollar, as the lead currency, maintained its value over time? In understanding this process in the contemporary world lies the essence of imperialism of the twenty-first century. What determines the price appreciation of commodities? The mainstream tradition of economics, courtesy Milton Friedman, would have us believe that inflation is essentially a monetary phenomenon, that is, higher the supply of money, higher would be the inflation. A lot has been written about this theoretically incorrect position on account of getting the basic causality wrong, so we would not delve into it here. In sharp contrast, in the Marxian and other heterodox traditions, price determination is essentially in the terrain of class politics. Since the price vector (inclusive of wages) essentially represents the class weapon that each claimant has over the total produce, how the level of output prices and inflation are going to behave depends on the relative bargaining strengths of these different claimants.

Let us take a simple case of three claimants to begin with: workers, capitalists within the First World, primary commodity producers of the Third World selling these in the First. If the sum of their ex-ante claims is greater than one, there will be a case of increasing inflation in the First World, through the wage-price spiral in the second term, unless one (or more) of the three claimants accepts the residual. Since the claim of their working class is normally taken as a function of the level of the reserve army (measured by the rate of unemployment), there appears to be a negative relationship between unemployment and inflation (the famed Phillips curve).

Patnaik (1997) has argued that it is the primary commodity producers' share in the First World output that takes the hit, which shows itself in the fall in the terms of trade of primary commodities, thereby, absorbing most of the inflationary shocks that the core would have experienced in its absence. We have already discussed that this does not seem to be holding true since the 1990s. Irrespective of the fall or rise in the terms of trade, there is, however, a far more powerful force that globalization throws up which keeps inflation in the core under check – creation of a global reserve army of labour. Indeed, rising oil prices or even food prices in recent times has not created a destabilizing inflation in the core (the most recent pandemic- and war-induced inflation notwithstanding) and the reason is the working class in the core has become price takers.[2] The claim of the first, the capitalists in the US, (and under certain conditions, the third) can rise at the cost of the claim of the second, the working class in the US. The famous slogan of the top 1 per cent vs the rest during the Wall Street movement essentially captures this reality in the First World today.

Rohit (2013) has argued that the bargaining position of the working class in the core, which is a key source of destabilizing prices in the core, itself turns redundant as their wages get tethered to their brethren in the periphery. This is quite the opposite of the central argument of the unequal exchange school, whose theory of imperialism is premised on diverging wage levels between the two regions. The role that the domestic reserve army of labour played earlier in influencing the ex-ante wage share in the core is now being played by a global reserve army. The nature of imperialism, defined in terms of the role that the periphery plays in maintaining stability in the capitalist core, and by extension the global order, changes.

The periphery, by providing a global reserve army, plays a critical role in ensuring that inflation in the core is kept under check, thereby providing stability to the reserve currency. The link between domestic unemployment rates and inflation in the core essentially breaks down. The Phillips curve essentially breaks down under globalization. This assumes greater importance than the terms of trade route of Patnaik (1997) because over a period, as he himself acknowledges, the latter could lose its shock-absorbing capacity as its magnitude itself would keep falling. Unlike the case where the burden of adjustment fell on the share of the periphery alone, here the working class within the geographical boundaries of the capitalist system too becomes the shock absorber. It is another matter that this has the potential of aggravating political instability in the core both because the bargaining power of the working class gets severely limited as also the tendency towards stagnation reappears as we see later.

There is an added effect of globalization on the core workers' bargaining strength. Capitalists through coercion attack the rate of unionization in the core. This is reflected in the drastic decline in the rate of unionization in the private sector in the US from close to 25 per cent in the mid-1970s to 7 per cent in late-2000s. There are thus two different, yet interdependent, ways in which the ex-ante money wage share in the core is kept under control – increasing globalization and (resulting) deunionization within the core.

The bargaining chip of the workers in the core is seriously hampered since they can no more negotiate a higher wage share even if their unemployment rate is extremely low because there is always a potential threat of job flight to the labour-surplus peripheral countries. In such a situation, any increase in the monopoly power of the corporations in the core can be accommodated within the core, by suppressing the wage share, without creating any price instability. Dramatic rise in inequality, which is but one way of saying falling wage share in a politically more acceptable form across the First World is common sense today (Epstein 2017).

Though apparent in this formulation, it is not as if the workers of the periphery are responsible for the loss of the workers of the core. Rather, it is the power of the capitalists in the periphery (and indirectly of the core) which keeps the money wages down for the working people in the periphery. Moreover, as part of the neoliberal package, all possible efforts are made in the name of labour market flexibility to suppress the working-class movements in these regions. This arrangement sorts the problem of price instability in the core economies. However, the concern over price instability could arise if the workers in the periphery become more organized and negotiate for a higher money wage share even as global labour solidarity builds up. There could not be a better time to realize Marx's famous slogan, 'workers of the world unite'.

Tier 2: Periphery's Core – China Enters the Scene

Let us now look at another important aspect of contemporary imperialism. Contrary to the arguments of the World Systems school or Patnaik (1997), capital has diffused in a major way in the Third World, China being the prime example of that. And China is no small country in the periphery; it is the country with a massive reserve army of labour. It fits the bill of what defines the periphery in this literature. And yet it does not behave like a typical peripheral country. We prefer to, therefore, call it periphery's core.

That the Chinese have infiltrated the US markets and the manufacturing base has shifted to China is a subject in itself that needs to be theoretically explained and located within the broader model of contemporary imperialism. The Chinese have entered the US markets due to the competitive advantage they hold in terms of relative prices of their products. Owing to low wage costs, the terms of trade of manufacturing commodities of the periphery has declined giving them this advantage.

Manufacturing has shifted out of the US to a large extent, so it has now become an economy dominated by the services sector. Also, we can safely assume that the primary commodities, particularly those which enter as inputs for manufactured products, do not enter as a claimant in the US pie. Instead, it is the capitalists or public sector enterprises of China, who replace them as, in the form of manufactured exports, a new claimant of this pie.

What does this change bring about? While the effective exchange rate for China is falling, its overall share in the US pie is rising. Since the share of China in the US' output (rising trade surplus of China vis-a-vis the US) has been rising, they will have to eat into somebody else's share in the US pie, otherwise it will create pressures of potential price instability in the US through the wage-price spiral, which could threaten the stability of the dollar. That this tendency remains dormant is again because the share of the working class in the US is downwardly flexible, thereby, acting as the shock absorber, in this process. They may have to additionally take the burden of adjusting down as a result of the rising degree of monopoly of the US corporations. The working class in the US gets squeezed by both its own capitalists as well as those in the periphery's core. What is symptomatic of the US is equally true for the capitalist core (global North) as whole. It is not, therefore, surprising to find that the share of the working class across the First World has been declining under globalization.

Does the rising share of China in the US pie, as a result of lower international output prices for Chinese goods, mean that this gets shared with their working class? Most definitely not. This rising share is pocketed by the upper strata of the Chinese with their working class' share (not necessarily real wages which in fact have risen particularly in the last decade) declining over a period of time. In fact, that lies at the core of any export-oriented strategy since the only way you can maintain your markets is if you keep your prices low and the only way you can keep them low is if one of the claimants in the Chinese pie acts as a price-taker. That can only happen if either the Chinese workers or the miners and primary commodity producers of the peripheral South take the burden or both. The first is the source of rising inequality in China while the second constitutes relative income deflation of the vast masses in the peripheral South. If, however, the terms of trade moves in favour of primary commodities as it has in the last decade or so, then the Chinese workers' wage share would get doubly squeezed.

Tier 3: Periphery's Periphery at the Bottom of the Pyramid
And thus enters the third player in the picture: the primary commodity producers of the peripheral South. Mining can reasonably be taken as a representative commodity exported to China. In this sense, peripheral South plays the same role that periphery as a whole played in the pre-globalization period where they were the primary commodity producers and exporters of the same to the First World.

Primary commodity producers not only provide the raw materials to China so crucial for it to remain the manufacturing workshop of the world but it helps provide price advantage to the Chinese goods to remain competitive in the international market. Moreover, it also acts as the market for cheap Chinese exports much like the global economy. In the process, it keeps the Chinese prices under check and, by extension, the US dollar's value intact. In line with the working classes in both China and the US who get a raw deal in the process, the primary commodity producers in the periphery become the base of the imperialist pyramid. And we do not mean the mining oligarchs but those who work in those mines, the actual miners. So, even as the terms of trade may move in favour of primary commodities in the short run, that rise is pocketed by these oligarchs instead of getting passed on to the workers.

Today's imperialism, therefore, is characterized by a three-tier structure with the country holding the reserve currency at the top while the periphery is divided into two – manufacturing commodity producers, as a middle tier (periphery's core), who buy primary commodities from the third tier peripheral countries (periphery's periphery). Symbolically, we could say the US is at the top, China in the middle and peripheral South at the bottom.

Conclusion

A declining wage share almost across the globe provides the system price stability, particularly in the country which owns the reserve currency. Despite the increasing clout of the Chinese since the 1980s, their currency still has not replaced the USD. It may or may not. In fact, even Euro could not. While globalization provides the US with price stability, it comes at the cost of political instability since a declining wage share and outsourcing create unemployment or declining income for the workers in the US. Election of Trump, perhaps, is a reflection of that. Closing down the frontiers to bring back the jobs to the US (tariffs, Mexican wall, etc.), however, might turn out to be counter-productive since that simply exports the political instability at home abroad. At the bottom of the pyramid of price takers are the mining workers in the peripheral underdeveloped economies. Once the workers, especially in the lower two tiers become organized, it would have a ripple effect on the working class globally, which could again threaten the price stability of the system. On a positive note, all this also opens up the possibilities of international solidarity among the working classes across boundaries and, with global value chains, their striking capacity is globally effective.

This essay was originally published under the same title in *The Indian Economic Journal*, vol. 71, no. 1, 2023, pp. 217–28.

Notes
[1] See Bharadwaj (1984) for a detailed theoretical critique of the unequal exchange framework.
[2] See Azad and Das (2015) for an empirical estimation.

References
Azad, R. and A. Das (2015), 'Has Globalization Flattened the Phillips Curve?' *Economic and Political Weekly*, vol. 2, pp. 42–48.

Bharadwaj, K. (1984), 'A Note on Emmanuel's "Unusual Exchange"', *Economic and Political Weekly*, vol. 19, no. 30, pp. PE81–PE87.

Brewer, A. (2002), *Marxist Theories of Imperialism: A Critical Survey*, London: Routledge.

Epstein, G. (2017), 'Imperialism?', in S. Sen and M.C. Marcuzzo, eds, *The Changing Face of Imperialism: Colonialism to Contemporary Capitalism*, India: Routledge, Taylor & Francis, pp. 171–98.

Foster, J.B. (2019), 'Late Imperialism, Fifty Years After Harry Magdoff the Age of Imperialism', *Monthly Review*, vol. 71, no. 3, pp. 1–19.

Hardt, M. (2006), 'From Imperialism to Empire', *The Nation*, available at https://www.thenation.com/article/archive/imperialism-empire/, accessed 10 November 2022.

Hardt, M. and A. Negri (2001), *Empire*, Cambridge: Harvard University Press.

Harvey, D. (2003), *The New Imperialism*, New York: Oxford University Press.

——— (2018), 'Realities on the Ground: David Harvey Replies to John Smith', *A Review of African Political Economy*, available at http://roape.net/2018/02/05/realities-ground-david-harvey-replies-john-smith/, accessed 10 November 2022.

Keynes, J.M. (1991 [1936]), *The General Theory of Employment Interest and Money*, A Harvest Book/ Harcourt, Inc.

Patnaik, P. (1997), *Accumulation and Stability Under Capitalism*, Oxford: Clarendon Press.

——— (2009), *The Value of Money*, New York: Columbia University Press.

Patnaik, U. (1982), '"Neo-Marxian" Theories of Capitalism and Underdevelopment: Towards A Critique', *Social Scientist*, vol. 10, no. 11, pp. 3–32, November, doi: https://doi.org/10.2307/3516858

Patnaik, U. and P. Patnaik (2016), *A Theory of Imperialism*, New York: Columbia University Press.

Rohit (2013), *It's not Over: Structural Drivers of the Global Economic Crisis*, Oxford University Press.

Smith, J. (2016), *Imperialism in the Twenty-First Century: Globalization, Super-Exploitation, and Capitalism's Final Crisis*, New York: Monthly Review Press.

Sweezy, P.M. (1991), *The Theory of Capitalist Development*, Kolkata: KP Bagchi Press and Company.

14

A Tangible Concept of Imperialism

Utsa Patnaik's Estimates of Colonial Transfers from India

Vibha Iyer

Introduction

It is an honour to write for this volume celebrating the work of Professor Utsa Patnaik and Professor Prabhat Patnaik as their work and teaching has had a formative influence on my understanding of political economy. I owe an invaluable debt to Professor Utsa Patnaik whose writings on colonial transfers and the Drain theory in particular have shaped in great measure my own research in the area.

Colonial transfers in the era of British imperialism remain largely an under-researched area in the history writing of the period. The omission of transfers from mainstream Cambridge School historians' literature on colonial histories is in line with their understanding of Britain's industrial revolution and the evolution of global capitalism as an endogenous self-driven process – a perception that continues to dominate modern-day textbook theoretical representations of the capitalist system. On the other hand, the lack of attention devoted to colonial transfers in heterodox literature on colonialism is an indicator of the complexities involved in understanding the distinct nature of the colonial economy as opposed to a sovereign economy and the mechanisms involved in extracting transfers.

In the Indian context, by the late nineteenth century, Naoroji (1901) and Dutt (1902, 1904) had in the Drain theory articulated in detail about the annual flow of tax-financed transfers to Britain. Ironically, while the Drain theory served as the foundational economic critique of British colonialism upon which the Indian nationalist movement was built, there has been relatively little engagement with the theory itself among economic historians in independent India. The uncritical denial of transfers has also resulted in mainstream history writing on colonialism till date being riddled with factually incorrect and logically inconsistent statements.

Professor Utsa Patnaik's work over the last five decades on imperialism and colonial transfers in particular offers a comprehensive and coherent analysis of not only the colonial foundations of capitalism, but also insight into the continued relevance of imperialism for contemporary capitalism. Her work on tax-financed transfers from India while re-establishing the relevance of the original argument of the Drain theorists also systematically dismantles several long-standing conclusions in authoritative mainstream texts on the origins of the industrial revolution and the evolution of capitalism.

This essay focuses on two of Utsa Patnaik's methodological contributions. The first is the use of modified modern macroeconomic concepts in a sovereign economy to explicate the link between India's internal budget and external accounts that helps understand the mechanism of effecting the transfers and second is the use of Council Bills as a proxy for India's merchandise surplus that helps overcome conceptual lacunae in the existing trade data and literature about the colonial period and enables a more accurate estimation of the transfers. These methodological contributions have in turn rendered a tangibility to the concept of imperialism by providing us with a concrete measure of the extent to which colonial transfers financed the evolution of global capitalism.

Re-establishing the Relevance of the Drain Theory

The idea that Britain's industrial revolution was a self-driven one is formidably challenged by Patnaik (2011, 2012) where she presents evidence of a decline in the per capita output of cereal for the entire period of the eighteenth century, thereby countering the consensus among mainstream economic historians that Britain's industrial revolution was preceded by an agricultural revolution. The decline coupled with restricted imports due to the Corn Laws in 1815 inhibiting any augmentation in per capita food availability and the hardships of its wars with France, left Britain witnessing bread riots by the end of the eighteenth century. With industrial England's primary exports of cotton textiles itself dependent on the raw material cotton which was entirely imported, Britain's dependence on imports for its industrial revolution in terms of pre-requisites of wage goods and raw materials was near-complete. While such an industrialization process would result in substantial trade deficits and is unthinkable in the current era, Britain became the world's industrial and financial leader.

The key to understanding Britain's meteoric rise amidst glaring resource constraints lies in the transfers from its colonies in the form of slave rent, land rent and taxation. The Drain theory articulated by the early Indian nationalists Dadabhai Naoroji (1901) and R.C. Dutt (1902, 1904) was the original attempt to identify the tax-financed nature of transfers from India and present a detailed critique of the same. The essence of the Drain theory's argument was that the British colonial regime diverted a large portion of India's annual tax revenue to finance its home expenditure and therefore constituted a drain of the colony's resources. This was possible only because of India's colonial status and was unheard of in any sovereign economy.

Upon acquisition of Dewani rights of Bengal in 1765, the East India Company had secured the rights to tax a population that was four times the size of Britain. The mechanism of effecting the transfers was straightforward wherein a third of the tax revenue was set aside for purchase of imports from India. Thus, Indian producers were paid out of their own taxes and Britain was able to get its imports for free. Britain had hit upon a bounty, for it could now silence the dominant mercantilist critics who frowned upon the East India Company's trade with India that caused an outflow of £30,000 in specie and additionally re-export the unrequited imports of tropical goods from India to other parts of the sovereign world in exchange for essential temperate land goods that were inadequately produced in Britain. The significance of re-exports for Britain is seen when after correcting the prevalent authoritative trade estimates for Britain for methodological errors, Patnaik (1999) shows that Britain's total trade had reached 58 per cent of its GDP (gross domestic product) taking a three-year average centred on 1800, compared to only 36 per cent of GDP in Deane and Cole (1969) for the same years. Further, by the early years of the nineteenth century, the re-exports value had increased nearly two and half times from its 1765 level and amounted to nearly two-thirds of domestic exports (Patnaik 2006).

This method of effecting the transfers underwent a change with the Charter Acts of 1813 and 1833 ending the East India Company's trade monopoly with India and opened it to private merchants. India's role changed from primarily being an exporter to an importer of British exports of cotton manufactures flowing from its mills in Lancashire and Manchester. But this changed role created a contradiction for the 'realization of tribute' (Habib 2006) from India in the form of unrequited imports. A lasting solution was found in India's transformed export basket which after having undergone de-industrialization (Bagchi 1976) and commercialization of its agriculture, now mainly comprised agricultural goods instead of the erstwhile manufactured goods and continued to find markets all over the world. Britain's focus now turned to India's increasing foreign exchange earnings and devise a route to appropriate these as its own.

A bill of exchange termed as the Council Bill was introduced in 1861 for payment of imports from India. Foreign importers had to purchase these Council Bills from the Secretary of State in London against the requisite payment in sterling, gold or other currencies which would then be sent to the Indian exporters as payment and were encashable only in rupees. While ostensibly, the Council Bill appeared to be just an exchange instrument, the catch lay in the fact that the payment in rupees made to the Indian export-ers was from the domestic budget under an account titled Expenditure in

England or Expenditure Abroad. In other words, Indian exporters continued to be paid out of their taxes and the Council bill became the mechanism that linked India's internal budget with its trade accounts. By directly diverting all the gold and foreign exchange due on India's external account directly to London, the Council Bill served as the mediating instrument to facilitate the conversion of the domestic tax raised in rupees to meet Britain's requirement in sterling terms. Patnaik (1999) shows in diagrammatic form the link between the taxes Indian producers contributed to the budget and their export surplus earnings which stayed in London, while they were paid out of their own tax contribution using the Council Bill.

From the second half of the nineteenth century, India's exports of agricultural goods which served as industrial raw material and wage goods found markets across the world and its surpluses on the merchandise account surged. This was entirely credited to Britain's account and India's current account was always in deficit. In the accounting procedure, the transfer of the forex earnings from merchandise export surpluses was via the imposition of compulsory invisible political charges imposed upon the colony (of which the Home Charges was the main component) designated in sterling on the external account, as invisibles that India owed to Britain and included in rupees under the 'expenditure abroad' part of the budget. The 'normal' invisibles such as payments for British shipping and financial services, which India would have had to pay as all sovereign nations, comprised only a small portion of the total invisibles charged, whereas the major share comprised politically determined charges imposed to the extent of the merchandise export surplus or often exceeding it, thereby leaving India's current account perpetually in deficit.

The original Drain theorists were acutely aware of the linking of India's internal budget with its trade earnings and this is reflected in their writings. However, there is no explicit statement about the same and this was mainly due to absence of the current-day macroeconomic framework and conceptual categories at the time of their writing. For instance, Naoroji (1901) writes about the interconnectedness of the internal and external aspects to the drain of wealth from the country. The internal aspect referred to the use of tax revenue extracted from the Indian population by the British not for purposes of internal development but for financing the interests of the British empire such as war and annexation and paying home charges and interest payments accruing on debt –

> [. . .] British India's chief difficulty, is this: In England, all that is paid by the people for revenue returns back to them, is enjoyed by them, and fructifies in their own pockets; while *in India, what the people pay as revenue does not all return to them, or is enjoyed by others, and carried away clean out of the country.* (Naroji 1901, p. 248; emphasis added)

Externally, he argued that India's merchandise export surpluses earned vis-à-vis trade with countries other than Britain, were drained via unilateral transfers to Britain under various heads chargeable to India only by virtue of its colonial status.

Similarly, Dutt (1902, 1904) in his two-volume history of British India from 1757 to the beginning of the twentieth century argues, by comparing the colonial government's expenditure pattern vis-à-vis the revenue collected, that the origin of India's public debt lay in the 'tribute . . . exacted as Home Charges' (Dutt 1902, p. 220) and was in no way a repayment of any capital investment by the home country in the colony. For instance, a surplus of £32 million over forty-six years from 1792 to 1838, after financing war and civil administration, instead of being saved or invested within India, was used for dividend payments to the Company's shareholders in England. When the flow of revenue proved to be insufficient, India was made to borrow in order to keep up the dividend payments, and consequent interest payments on the debt further increased the taxation burden upon the Indian masses. A debt of £60 million in 1856 rose to £70 million by 1858 due to mutiny expenses and doubled to £140 million in 1876. This included public borrowing by the state for expansion of railways, even though the total government expenditure on railways and irrigation so far amounted to a mere £24 million. Inevitably, this rising burden of public debt was met through increasing taxation which rose by 50 per cent within twelve years of the Crown's administration. India's debt in England or sterling debt alone rose by £105 million, from £23 million in 1861 to £128 million in 1900 (Iyer 2020, p. 62). Of this, the military cost of suppressing the Mutiny and compensation to the East India Company along with guaranteed dividends resulted in an over seven-fold rise in sterling debt from about £4 million in 1857 to an annual average of £31 million during 1861–63. By 1879–81, India's average sterling debt had more than doubled to £70 million on account of financing Britain's military expeditions and borrowing for expansion of railways over the two-decade period. From the mid-1880s until 1900, borrowing on account of financing Britain's military interventions in South Africa and China and monetary gold imports to build up reserves to back India's move to the gold exchange standard added another £48 million to sterling debt. By 1900, at £128 million, India's sterling debt amounted to almost one-fifth of British India's net national income (Iyer 2020, pp. 62–65).

The linking of India's internal budget with its trade accounts becomes clear in Patnaik (2006) where she uses macroeconomic identities for a sovereign economy in a modified manner to describe the colonial economy in the following way.

The identity as in the case of an open sovereign economy is:

$$(S - I) = (G - T) + NX$$

Where S is savings, I is Investment, G is total government expenditure, T is tax and other revenue and NX is net exports, i.e., export of goods and services minus imports of goods and services.

In the colonial statistical accounts, the internal budget was divided into two parts, domestic expenditure and expenditure abroad. Correspondingly, in the identity above, G, which is the total government expenditure is modified to include these two components such that $G = GD + GA$, where GD denotes domestic expenditure and GA denotes expenditure abroad (the latter term occurs only in the case of the colony). Further, $(G - T) = 0$ since in the colony the budget is kept balanced taking both types of expenditures relative to revenues.

Similarly, on the external sector front, the colony's commodity export surplus with the whole world including Britain, denoted NX, is modified to show its division into two parts corresponding to the division of the budget.

$$NX = NX_1 + NX_2$$

where $NX_2 \geq NX_1$ and $NX_2 \geq GA$.

Here NX_1 is the commodity export surplus earnings from the world and this includes normal service payments for freight and insurance by taking imports c.i.f. (cost, insurance and freight). The second part, denoted NX_2 comprises all the administered liabilities of an invisible nature placed by the metropolis on the country, arising only from its colonial status, so adjusted by the metropolis that it at least equals the commodity export surplus earnings NX_1.

The link between the budget and trade can be expressed as $NX_2 \geq GA$, with values expressed in pound sterling, which meant that NX_2 includes all the administered 'drain' items included in the GA part of the budget, and more. Therefore, even though foreign importers made the full payment reflected in NX_1 as a large surplus, Britain ensured that NX_2 or the administered charges was a large negative figure that would surpass NX_1. Ensuring that $NX_2 \geq NX_1$ meant that the commodity export surplus inclusive of normal invisibles or NX_1 never resulted in a current account surplus. No matter how large, NX_1 was always written off by an equally large or even larger NX_2. These administered invisible liabilities in turn were kept in excess of GA, thereby forcing India to borrow.

Patnaik's framework explaining the macroeconomics of the drain mechanism succinctly summarizes the argument of the Drain theory and is key to understanding the fundamental distinction of the colonial economy from that of a sovereign one. It tells us that, since every increase in the colony's commodity trade surplus or NX_1 simply translated into an equivalent (and almost always higher) increase in the administered liabilities NX_2 which in turn was reflected in the expenditure abroad or GA component of the internal budget, the drain could be measured equivalently in terms of NX_1 or GA. It

Table 14.1 *Gross revenue, expenditure in England and gross expenditure, India 1837 to 1901*, three-year annual averages in Rs million

Year	Gross revenue	Expenditure in England	Gross expenditure	Gross revenue minus gross expenditure	Exchange rate (Rs/£)
	(1)	(2)	(3)	(4)	(5)
1837–39	207.14	25.00	211.31	- 4.17	10.00
1840–42	217.68	26.40	233.23	- 15.55	10.00
1843–45	238.41	28.24	252.94	- 14.53	10.00
1846–48	254.63	30.32	271.43	- 16.80	10.00
1849–51	276.60	26.58	270.20	6.40	10.00
1852–54	286.73	29.91	296.57	- 9.84	10.00
1855–57	314.05	43.19	348.29	- 34.24	10.00
1858–60	418.90	74.84	503.58	- 84.68	10.00
1861–63	445.29	72.57	446.35	- 1.06	10.00
1864–66	455.70	69.18	461.41	- 5.71	10.00
1867–69	495.66	97.57	523.11	- 27.45	10.00
1870–72	521.33	104.78	516.58	4.75	10.31
1873–75	550.00	111.67	593.01	- 43.00	10.89
1876–78	642.41	162.55	658.02	- 15.61	11.81
1879–81	728.03	173.99	732.24	- 4.21	12.03
1882–84	709.37	177.76	701.24	8.13	12.35
1885–87	768.54	200.37	784.04	- 15.51	13.76
1888–90	841.75	213.74	820.62	21.12	14.20
1891–93	899.60	250.62	905.98	- 6.38	15.68
1894–96	958.96	274.89	957.22	1.74	17.54
1897–99	1,002.75	247.99	993.53	9.21	15.23
1900–01	1,137.13	259.27	1087.47	49.65	15.00
Total	35,974.83	7,845.00	36,617.66	- 642.83	
Average	553.46	120.69	563.35	- 9.89	

Note: The last period is a two-year average.
Source: Annual series in Dutt (1904). The data from 1877–78 to 1901–02 were in rupees. The remaining data has been converted into rupees using the annual exchange rates provided.

should be noted, however, that both these terms underestimate the drain to the extent of borrowing that the colony was forced to undertake in order to pay for the administered liabilities in excess of its commodity trade surplus.

While India's rising commodity trade surpluses spelt cheer for Britain, the period from the late nineteenth century onwards was one of distress for the former. The last three decades of the nineteenth century which saw a continuous depreciation of the rupee in terms of sterling meant that either a larger share of the domestic tax revenue be diverted to meet the increased sterling burden of the expenditure in the England component of the budget or taxation itself be raised. The resulting impact in either case, whether through a smaller amount being available for domestic expenditure or through a squeeze in the purchasing power of the masses, entailed a deflation of the Indian economy.

In Table 14.1, we observe a continuous increase in the average gross revenue from 1837 until 1901 except for a slight fall in the triennium 1882–84. A 20 per cent fall in the average exchange value of the rupee between the last triennium of the 1860s and the first triennium of the 1870s was accompanied by only a 7 per cent increase in average expenditure in England, but its share in gross expenditure had by now reached an average of over 20 per cent. By 1882–84, expenditure in England's share averaged over a quarter of gross expenditure, continuing to rise over the 1880s and averaged at about 29 per cent of the gross expenditure by the triennium 1894–96.

The rupee's depreciation which began in the 1870s and gained pace over the 1880s and 1890s was accompanied by a rise in the rupee equivalent of the sterling burden and revenue collected. Figure 14.1 shows the widening gap between gross revenue and expenditure in England from the second half of the 1850s itself, widening further with the steepening of the gross revenue graph from the 1870s.

By the triennium ending in 1896, the average exchange rate of the rupee had reached its lowest level in the period and had registered a fall of more than 75 per cent since 1870–72 and as the sterling burden in rupee terms nearly tripled over these intervals, and now accounted for nearly 30 per cent of the gross expenditure, there was a near doubling of tax revenue to about Rs 960 million. Though the rupee recovered to an average of Rs 15.23 per pound in the last triennium of the 1890s and appreciated further to an average of Rs 15 in 1900–01, tax revenue collected rose to Rs 1,003 million and to Rs 1,137 million respectively.

Patnaik (2019) shows that in the three-decade period between 1871 and 1901, with sterling demand comprising expenditure in England maintained at the initial level, the falling rupee alone would have created an additional taxation burden of Rs 88 crores on the Indian population. However, in this three-decade period, a 60 per cent increase in sterling demand upon Indian revenue along with rupee depreciation created a total additional burden of Rs 141 crores (Patnaik 2019, pp. 14–16, Table 2). Total revenues over the

Figure 14.1 *Gross revenue and expenditure in England, India 1837 to 1901*, three-year annual averages in Rs million

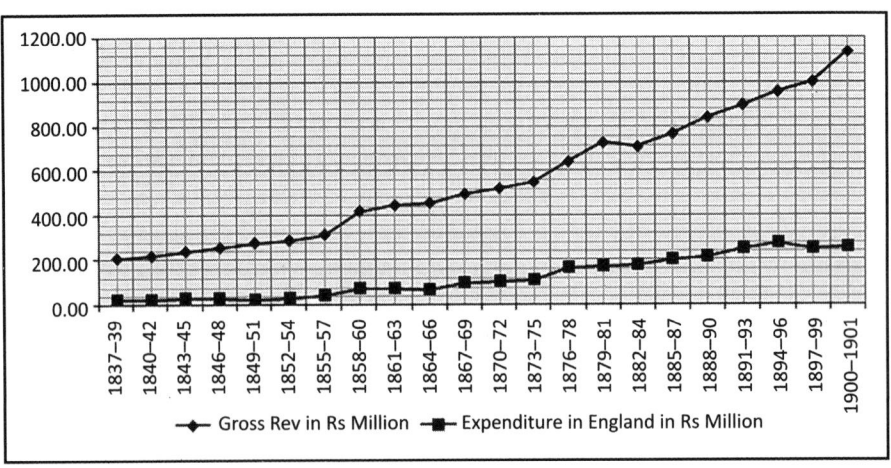

Source: Table 14.1

Table 14.2 *Expenditure in England and commodity trade surplus measured by Council Bills, India 1862 to 1900*, three-year annual averages in £ million

Period	Expenditure in England	Council Bills/ commodity trade surplus	Period	Expenditure in England	Council Bills/ commodity trade surplus
	(1)	(2)		(1)	(2)
1862–64	7.05	7.47	1886–1888	14.86	13.92
1865–67	7.42	5.58	1889–1891	15.41	15.85
1868–70	10.29	6.38	1892–1894	15.91	14.32
1871–73	10.22	12.51	1895–1897	15.81	14.01
1874–76	11.32	11.98	1898–1900	16.64	17.02
1877–79	14.13	13.11	Total	503.19	486.87
1880–82	14.31	16.26	average	12.90	12.48
1883–85	14.36	13.88			

Note: The data for column (1) from 1882–83 to 1897–98 was in rupees and was converted to pound sterling using exchange rates given in Dutt (1904).
Source: *Statistical Abstracts of British India*.

period rose by a massive Rs 159 crore with the burden being borne by the poorer Indian masses by way of increased land revenue and indirect taxes on necessities like salt.

Understanding the Role of Colonial Transfers in the Evolution of Global Capitalism

From the latter half of the nineteenth century until the outbreak of the First World War, there was an expansion of world trade, resulting in a multilateral trading network spanning several countries and continents founded upon the rising demand from the newer industrial nations of Europe and North America and large payments of interest on foreign debt. The concurrent spate of colonization that accompanied the network and colonial transfers which served as the bedrock of this network find no mention in mainstream literature.

It was through colonial transfers in the forms of rents or taxes that the colonizing countries were able to procure imports beyond their legitimate means and bring in newer countries into the trading network. The newer countries, despite not being major traders, financiers or borrowers, in turn through their own trading activities, increased the directions and the total volume of trade and facilitated the settlement of financial dues between major debtor and creditor countries. The stability of this complex system of commercial and financial transactions was hinged upon the stability of demand and multilateral settlement of dues. Britain, by performing the twin roles of providing a stable market for imports from newly industrializing countries and being the leading creditor, emerged as the epicentre of this network. Studies by Hilgerdt (1942) and Saul (1960) are extremely useful to understand the role of tax-financed transfers in the diffusion of global capitalism and the emergence of Britain as the industrial and financial leader of the capitalist world from the second half of the nineteenth century until the First World War. They show that, while Britain suffered huge current account deficits with the European continent, the United States and regions of recent European settlement, it earned huge and rising current account surpluses with its tropical colonies, India being the most significant. Without alluding to colonial transfers, the studies suggest that Britain's surpluses with the colonies helped it not only cover its rising current account deficits with the above-mentioned regions but also enabled it to export capital to these very regions, thereby incurring a huge balance of payment deficits with them.

For instance, Hilgerdt's detailed study of the origins and significance of the multilateral commodity and financial transactions network in developing a unified world market notes Britain's rising trade deficits with every other region of the world, far exceeding the trade surplus it registered solely with the tropics as well as the simultaneous increase in Britain's trade deficit and investments vis-à-vis the United States in the last three decades of the nineteenth century, but does not observe anything anomalous in this (Hilgerdt 1942, p. 42).

In Saul's study on Britain's trade with different regions, he notes the importance of India in offsetting Britain's deficits when he writes,

> The key to Britain's whole payments patterns lay in India financing as she probably did more than two-fifths of Britain's total deficits, India's trade and bullion returns for the years ending March 31, 1911, gave her an excess of exports to the rest of the Empire of £15.8m, and one of £48.6m with foreign countries. From Europe alone she earned over £30m, from China and Hong Kong over £10m, from Japan and the United States just under £7m each. But this was by no means all, for *it was mainly through India that the British balance of payments found the flexibility essential to a great capital exporting country.* (Saul 1960, p. 62; emphasis added)

The mainstream explanation for Britain's pivotal role in the network, in its grudging acknowledgement of India's role in balancing Britain's deficits, assumes that the latter was able to meet its trade deficits through its legitimate export surpluses with its colonies and its invisibles earnings (Gallagher and Seal 1981; Tomlinson 1979). By limiting India's colonial role to that of a market and a source of raw material, and maintaining a deliberate silence on the question of tax-financed transfers, the mainstream accounts of Britain's industrial and financial prowess border more on fiction than fact.

The fact is that Britain's current account surpluses with its tropical colonies were managed surpluses and possible only because the latter were captive colonies forced to keep their markets open for British exports. In addition to these manipulated surpluses, Britain also had complete control over India's foreign exchange surpluses earned from the rest of the world, which it transferred to its account by imposing invisible charges, 'adjusted in an asymmetric manner' (Patnaik 2017), to exceed its legitimate invisibles earnings from the latter.

Britain's industrial strength had been on the decline since the end of the nineteenth century and its inability to take on the newly industrialized countries such as the United States, Japan and Germany, was seen in the fall in its share of world exports in manufactures from 38 per cent in 1876–60 to 27 per cent by 1911–13, when world trade was expanding (Lewis,1969). From the 1880s, British exports had also started facing rising tariff barriers from the newly developing countries.

India helped Britain overcome its loss of markets in two ways. Firstly, re-exports of tropical goods which played a crucial role during Britain's industrialization period and had thereafter declined saw a resurgence from the closing years of the nineteenth century up to the First world War. India proved to be an important source of re-exports for Britain, as the triennium 1910–1913 saw a near doubling of the latter's re-export trade with the world from its 1870s level (Saul 1960, p. 59). Secondly, and more importantly, Britain used its control of India to overcome the loss of markets for its own goods due to the rising tariff barriers from the 1880s by newly developing countries. As India's exports faced no such tariff pressure or minimal tariffs from the rest of the world, Britain could continue to keep its own markets open for imports from the rest of the world and use India's rising trade surpluses to settle its own payments and keep up its capital exports, thereby financing the 'diffusion of capitalism to Europe, Northern America and other regions of recent European settlement' (Patnaik 2017, p. 277) and keeping the multilateral pattern of settlements steady. The 'Indian safety-valve' through its continuous transfers ensured that Britain remained steadfastly committed to free trade and the loss of its export markets outside its empire did not destabilize it.

Kindleberger (1973) argues that the stability of the capitalist system in general and particularly in recessionary conditions depends on the ability of the world capitalist leader to either keep its markets open to capitalist developing country goods and maintain production and demand in these countries, or to lend capital for their accommodation and development. The transfers from India helped Britain do both – keep its own markets open for imports from the sovereign countries in keeping with free trade and also export capital to these very countries. The transfers aided Britain's leadership in responding flexibly to the varying requirements of booms and slumps in the world economy which made 'sterling and gold virtually interchangeable' (Aldcroft 1981, p. 165), lent stability to the gold standard while allowing Britain to maintain low gold reserves (Fearon 1979)[1] and assume the position of being not only 'regulator of the British monetary system but, in great part, that of regulator of the gold standard and the international payments system' (Aldcroft 1981, p. 165). With tax-financed transfers as the bulwark of the multilateral trading and payments network and the gold standard, the drain was clearly the raison d'etre of India's colonial status.

Methodological Challenges in Estimating the Drain

Estimation of the size of the drain is not free of its methodological complexities, mainly due to the nature of trade data that is available for the colonial period. During the period of the East India Company's trade monopoly with India, the drain estimate was simply the size of Britain's unrequited import surplus vis-à-vis India. However, for the period following the end of the Company's monopoly, estimating the drain is not as straightforward.

Given the unrequited nature of its exports, the pioneering drain theorists used India's export surplus as the estimate of the drain. However, they defined 'export surplus' as 'merchandise trade balance plus treasure balance' and excluded services unlike the contemporary national income accounting measure of $(X - M)$ which always refers to the export of goods and services minus the import of the same. While the exclusion of services is justifiable on account of the high share of arbitrary administrative liabilities as discussed above, their measure suffers the shortcoming of including all treasure flows making no distinction between commodity and financial gold. This was because the Statistical Abstracts of British India, the primary source of data, only records a distinction between government and private trade in treasure and not between its commodity and financial uses due to the absence of this latter distinction even at the conceptual level.

The conflation of the gold flows, combined with the fact that India was a net importer of gold until the interwar years, led colonial administrators then and historians till date to wrongly conclude that Indians imported gold solely for hoarding in unproductive forms such as jewellery. Naoroji (1901, p. 87) had in his time confronted these allegations by arguing that apart from the fact that the absence of a modern banking system or financial instruments as in Europe led Indians to hold their savings in the form of jewellery, the bullion imports had in substantial part also been used for monetary purposes of coinage and payment. Accounting for the monetary usage of gold, left the per capita holding of gold in India over a period of 69 years from 1801 to 1869 at 33s. 6d. (33 shillings and 6 pence) – hardly different from the 30s in Britain over a much shorter period of twelve years from 1858 to 1869.

In contemporary times, transactions in gold have been classified to distinguish between commodity gold, when held as a valuable or for industrial use, monetary financial gold when held as a reserve asset by the Central Bank and non-monetary financial gold when held by financial institutions and/or bullion traders for trading purposes (Patnaik, 2017, quoting a 2006 study by the International Monetary Fund). Naoroji was absolutely correct as the colonial government did import gold for financial purposes of coinage and building reserves, but he could only limitedly prove this due to the inadequacy of data.

Patnaik (2017) ingeniously makes use of the Council Bill value which resolves the existing statistical lacuna to a substantial extent and helps achieve the twin objectives of classifying the gold flows and estimating the drain more accurately. Her argument for the use of Council Bills as an estimate of the commodity trade balance is as follows. In order to correctly measure the drain, the merchandise trade surplus would have to be adjusted for the net commodity gold flows. Since Council Bills were the de facto mechanism to pay out rupees for the trade surplus every year, their value must have represented the balance of all commodity trade, namely trade not only in merchandise but also in commodity gold, and therefore the value of Council Bills may be assumed to represent the commodity trade balance. With Council Bills value being lesser than the merchandise surplus, the difference between the two would be the negative commodity gold balance, i.e., net imports of commodity gold. Financial gold can be estimated by deducting commodity gold from the total treasure balance. While commodity gold flows would be included in the current account, financial gold flows would be a part of the capital account in the balance of payments.

The close correspondence observed between the series of Council

Figure 14.2 *Expenditure in England and commodity trade surplus (Council Bills),* *India 1862 to 1900,* three-year annual averages in £ million

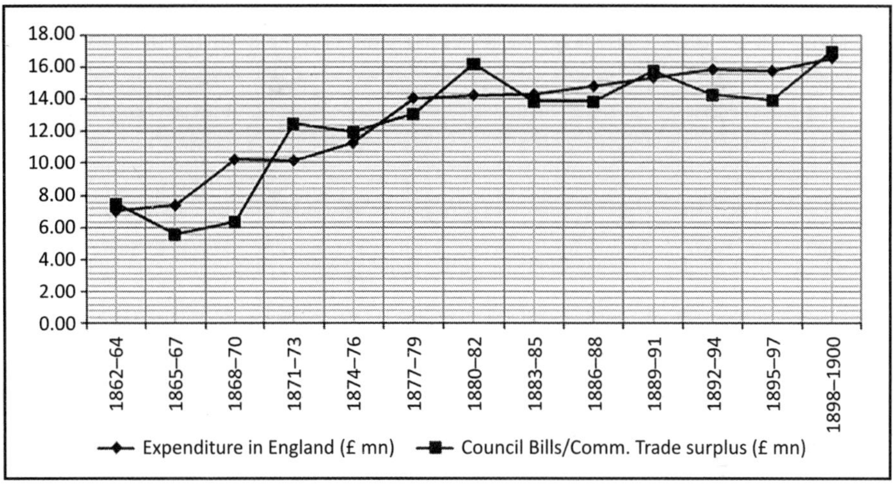

Source: Table 14.2.

Bills and the expenditure in England in Table 14.2 and Figure 14.2 vindicates the use of Council Bill values as proxy for commodity trade balance. In fact, the total value of £428.6 million for Council Bills issued against India's commodity surplus for the period of thirty years between 1871 to 1900 is seen to be identically equivalent to the total value of expenditure in England of £428.9 million for the same period (shown earlier in Patnaik 2019). The use of Council Bills took about a decade to stabilize after its introduction in 1861 and this is seen in a shortfall of £16.3 million in its total value for the period 1862 to 1870 compared to the total of expenditure in England for this period (calculated earlier in Iyer 2020).

Patnaik applies this formulation to the balance of payments aggregates estimated by Pandit (1937) and Banerjee (1963) for the time series pertaining to the pre-war period, 1898–1913, and inter-war period, 1921–38, respectively. Since imports of merchandise and gold have been calculated on c.i.f. basis the resulting commodity trade balance approximated India's normal current account balance. Consequently, the remaining invisibles listed in sterling in the external account and in rupees under the expenditure abroad account in the budget were the administered charges imposed in order to appropriate India's commodity trade surplus entirely, leaving its positive current account balance in deficit every year. For Pandit's period 1898–1913, Patnaik's adjusted calculations in sterling show that India's annual average commodity gold imports at £11.7 million comprised one-third of its annual average merchandise trade surplus (with imports at c.i.f basis) at £34.7 million (Pandit 2017, Table 4, p. 304).

Figure 14.3 *Merchandise balance, commodity trade balance/Council Bills and commodity gold balance, India 1861 to 1919*, three-year annual averages in £ million

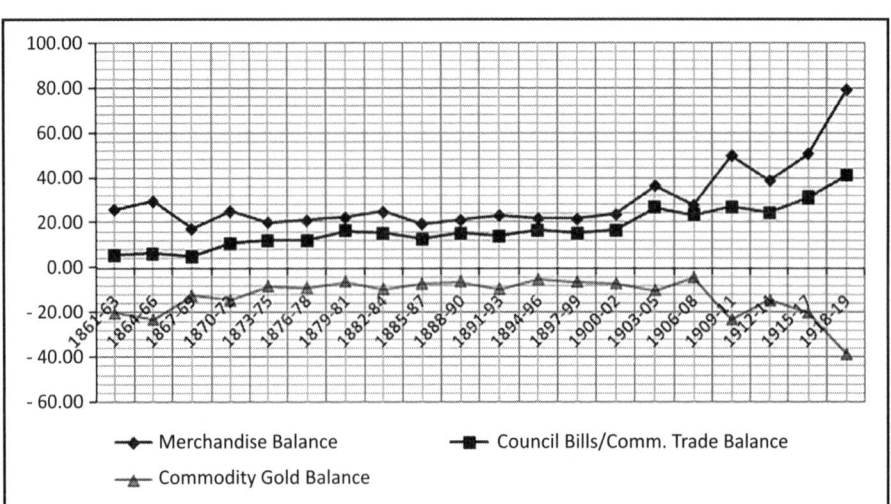

Source: Table 14.3.

When we use this method for the extended time series from 1861 to 1919, the results are telling as seen in Table 14.3 which gives the three yearly annual average commodity and financial gold flows. For the entire period of nearly six decades, we see that the annual average of commodity gold imports at £12.2 million comprised a little over two-fifths of the annual average merchandise surplus at £29.2 million. More importantly, although commodity gold imports did take place for most part of the nineteenth century, this trend was reversed from the 1877 onwards to reflect increasing gold imports for the financial purpose of building reserves for the gold exchange standard. To recollect, the increased pace of rupee depreciation from the 1880s boosted the commodity trade surplus to a total of £225 million over the fifteen-year period, 1886–1900. However, the imposition of 'abnormal' invisibles which surpassed this surplus at £235 million meant that India had to undertake these monetary gold imports through additional borrowing, resulting in an addition of about £48 million in sterling debt over this period (Iyer 2020).

As the surge in India's commodity trade surpluses continued into the first decade of the twentieth century, financial gold imports for building reserves of the Gold Standard Reserve shot up to over £16 million, forming 80 per cent of the net bullion imports in the triennium 1906–08. With India's debt burden already increasing in the war years, thanks to a 'gift' and 'popular contribution' to the tune of £145 million and additional military spending of £33 million in 1918–19 over £21 million in 1913–14 (Shah 1921, pp. 362–63, 381), the continuing financial imports which averaged at around £15 million in the biennium 1918–19 further swelled its debt levels.

Table 14.3 *Estimated commodity gold and financial gold flows, India 1861 to 1919,* three-year annual averages in £ million

Period	Merchandise balance	Treasure balance	Council Bills = commodity trade balance (approx.)	Commodity gold balance	Financial gold balance
	(1)	(2)	(3)	(4)=(3)-(1)	(5)=(2)-(4)
1861–63	25.90	-18.45	5.60	-20.30	1.84
1864–66	29.53	-18.37	6.47	-23.06	4.69
1867–69	17.26	-12.29	4.94	-12.32	0.03
1870–72	25.11	-5.52	10.90	-14.21	8.69
1873–75	20.16	-4.48	12.17	-7.99	3.51
1876–78	21.05	-7.68	12.26	-8.79	1.12
1879–81	22.27	-7.59	16.30	-5.96	-1.63
1882–84	24.80	-9.77	15.49	-9.31	-0.46
1885–87	19.54	-8.74	12.60	-6.95	-1.79
1888–90	21.17	-11.25	15.24	-5.93	-5.32
1891–93	23.27	-7.63	14.05	-9.22	1.59
1894–96	21.83	-3.60	16.70	-5.13	1.54
1897–99	21.65	-8.07	15.53	-6.12	-1.95
1900–02	23.67	-7.82	16.78	-6.89	-0.93
1903–05	36.43	-13.94	26.62	-9.82	-4.12
1906–08	27.80	-20.47	23.57	-4.23	-16.25
1909–11	50.04	-23.74	26.98	-23.06	-0.69
1912–14	38.80	-23.14	24.47	-14.33	-8.81
1915–17	50.93	-17.78	31.04	-19.89	2.11
1918–19	79.42	-53.07	41.02	-38.40	-14.67
Total	1,722.49	-797.15	1,005.20	-717.30	-79.84
Average	29.19	-13.51	17.04	-12.16	-1.35

Note: The last period is a two-year average.
The following sterling sale values have been added to column (3) prior to the calculation of three-yearly averages:
1907–08 £0.07 million
1908–09 £7.99 million
1909–10 £0.16 million
1914–15 £8.71 million
1915–16 £4.89 million
1918–19 £5.32 million
1919–20 £24.54 million.
Source: Statistical Abstracts of British India. Data from 1877–78 to 1902–03 and from 1911–12 to 1919–20 is in rupees and has been converted to sterling using the exchange rates in Dutt (1904) for the first period and in the Statistical Abstract of British India for the second period.

Figure 14.4 *Commodity trade balance and financial gold balance, India 1861 to 1919*, three-year annual averages in £ million

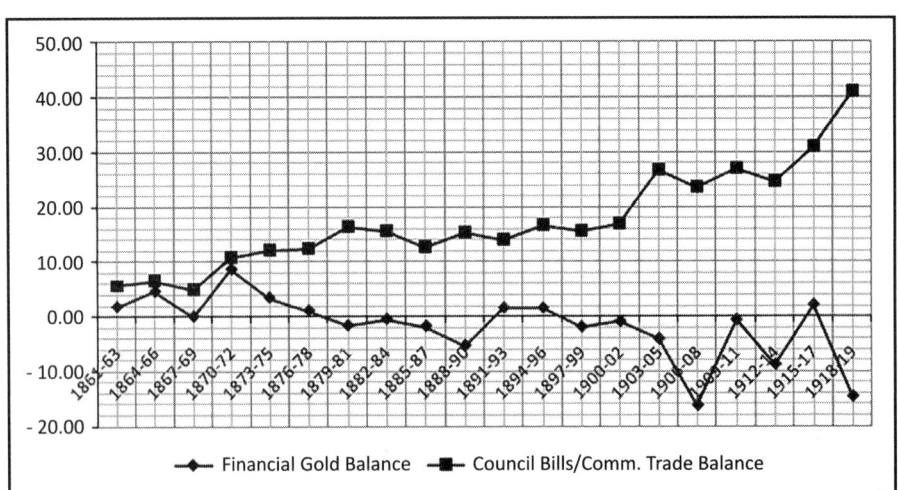

Source: Table 14.3.

Notably, while these financial gold imports over which India had no say only led to an increase in India's debt, and interest obligations became a regular source of the drain. Meanwhile, the gold reserves maintained as part of the Gold Standard Reserve in London were used for investment in British securities and extending cheap credit to leading banking houses at call and short notice at rates as low as 2 per cent, who in turn profited by reinvesting the funds in the London market at 3 per cent (de Cecco 1984, pp. 71–72).

While Council Bills do serve as a credible estimate of India's commodity trade surplus for the period from 1861 to 1919 as discussed above, their use became erratic in the interwar years. After being suspended initially for the years 1920 and 1921 when India suffered trade deficits, they were briefly resumed along with sterling purchases from 1922 to 1925. Thereafter, sterling purchases, initially by the government and from 1935 onwards by the Reserve Bank, completely replaced the use of Council Bills. The underlying reason for this can be traced ironically to the dilemma posed by India's rising export surpluses which had begun from the latter half of the nineteenth century and continued until the Depression years.

In the pre-war period itself, while India's rising commodity trade surpluses may have boosted the inflow of foreign exchange into Britain's treasury, the reimbursement of the accompanying Council Bills in rupees now absorbed a larger share of India's budgetary revenue. While the Secretary of State had started resorting to the intermittent sale of sterling from the merchandise surplus to make the rupee payments from as early as 1907, by 1916, the government was also forced to limit the sale of Council Bills, introduce controls over treasure imports and instruct Exchange Banks to finance only goods required for the war (Shah 1921). The problem got worse when the wartime demand for its exports led to a surge in India's merchandise export surpluses and Council Bill payments threatened to absorb nearly three-fourths of the central government budget, leading to a total sale of £30 million sterling for the years 1918–19 and 1919–20. The sale of sterling out of the merchandise export surplus which reduced the latter to the extent has been indicated in Table 14.3 as addition to Council Bills/commodity trade surplus for those particular years. Conversely, the fall in India's merchandise export surpluses which began during the end of the 1920s and intensified in the 1930s was accompanied by a rise in the purchase of sterling.

Therefore, for the two-decade period of the interwar years, estimation of the commodity trade surplus or the drain firstly involves estimating the commodity and financial gold flows directly from the treasure flows. This is done by treating all net imports of gold in the first decade as commodity gold imports since, there were no official imports of gold for reserves. On the other hand, in 1930s, India, for the first time in its recorded history, witnessed gold exports to the massive extent of over Rs 3.5 billion which are treated entirely as exports of financial gold.

India's rising commodity trade surpluses which could not be dented in the 1920s by the worldwide downward slide in agricultural prices from 1925 finally succumbed to the Depression of the 1930s and started to fall. This widened India's existing drain-induced current account deficit and the mounting pressure to meet Britain's relentless demands of sterling payments even in the face of falling export surpluses was resolved through the sale of the former's gold assets. These gold exports were extracted from the impoverished Indian peasantry who in an attempt to meet their rent and debt obligations and maintain their purchasing power alongside falling incomes were forced to sell their sole form of savings held as gold. Since these gold exports were used for settlement of payment, they should have been included in the capital account.

In the eighteen-year interwar time-series from 1921 to 1938, we see the exports of financial gold corresponding with the sharp fall in the merchandise surplus from 1931 onwards in Table 14.4. The average merchandise surplus for the first nine-year period, 1921 to 1929 is more than double the average for the later period 1930 to 1938. The commodity trade surplus (merchandise surplus net of commodity gold imports) for the entire period is Rs 8,944.5 million while financial gold exports over this period are also estimated at Rs 3,526 million.

Mainstream economic history writing on the interwar years which continues with its amnesic approach to transfers summarily treats this period as one of India's decolonization by arguing that its 'colonial' significance as a market for Britain declined (Tomlinson 1979). A closer examination of the data on India's transfers however tells us that far from being decolonized, its

Table 14.4 *Estimates of commodity gold and financial gold, India 1921–1938*, in Rs million

Year	Merchandise balance (adjusted for gaps)	Council bills plus net sterling purchased	Unadjusted gold balance	Commodity gold	Financial gold (in capital account)
	(1)	(2)	(3)	(4)	(5)=(3)-(4)
1921–1922	- 164.8	NA	- 136.8	NA	0
1922–1923	876.5	37.5	- 619.2	- 619.2	0
1923–1924	1,409.9	314.5	- 502.8	- 502.8	0
1924–1925	1,573.7	553.9	- 959.0	- 959	0
1925–1926	1,654.8	612.4	- 508.8	- 508.8	0
1926–1927	898.5	47.3*	- 393.1	- 393.1	0
1927–1928	942.5	377.7	- 321.9	- 321.9	0
1928–1929	1,036.0	410.2	- 343.6	- 343.6	0
1929–1930	950.8	203.9	- 262.0	- 262.0	0
1930–1931	717.7	150.0*	- 244.3	- 244.3	0
1931–1932	442.3	720.2*	556.5	- 72.6	629.1
1932–1933	106.3	472.3	649.3	- 29.9	679.2
1933–1934	429.5	599.7	572.3	- 19.6	591.9
1934–1935	282.7	498.2	525.4	- 51.9	577.3
1935–1936	351.9	455.8	363.8	- 54.5	418.3
1936–1937	868.9	708.7	144.9	- 155.1	300.0
1937–1938	491.3	332.9	143.1	- 40.1	183.2
1938–1939	511.9	340.6	124.7	- 22.3	147
Total	13,545.2#	6,835.8	- 1,074.7#	- 4,600.7	3,526
Average	796.8	402.1	- 63.2	- 270.6	207.4

Notes: From 1931 to 1938 there was every year substantial gold outflow from India to UK as a means of payment, owing to a sharp decline in India's merchandise exports combined with maintaining large administered invisible liabilities, together producing unusually large current account deficit. This financial gold outflow that belonged in the capital account was incorrectly recorded as commodity gold export. From Banerjee's figures in his Table 4 (taken by him from the *Statistical Abstracts*) for 1931–32 to 1938–39 in the above table, column (4) we have taken out the gold exports for that period and retained gold imports only, as indicating net commodity gold inflow.

Column (2) shows a combination of council bills plus sterling purchases, as there was a restriction on the sale of Council Bills in the post-war period. From 1922 to 1925, the Statistical Abstracts records a combination of Council Bills and sterling purchases by the government, from 1925 onwards, the purchase of sterling by the government and from 1935 onwards, the purchase of sterling by the RBI.

\# Totals exclude first row values.

* The following sterling sale values have been added: 1926–1927: Rs 19.2 million, 1930–31: Rs 77.5 million and 1931–32: Rs 189.8 million.

Source: Banerjee (1963), Table 4; Column (2) compiled from *Statistical Abstracts*.

'colonial' significance in terms of the drain played a particularly crucial role in helping Britain recover faster from the Depression than its counterparts in the capitalist world. If Indian tax-financed transfers had stabilized the gold standard and made the pound sterling 'as good as gold' in the pre-war years, during the inter-war years, the unabated drain and the gold outflow from India in the 1930s helped Britain now maintain a devalued pound externally to boost its exports and finance a 'cheap money' policy domestically and bailed the latter out of crisis in world capitalism (Iyer 2021). Again, contrary to the misleading assertion that the gold exports helped India post a current account surplus in the 1930s (Balachandran 1996), the correct treatment of these exports as financial gold shows that the outflow only partially neutralized its widened current account deficit, leaving it yet again as net borrower to the tune of over £89 million over the interwar period, 1921–38. Enforcing the transfers during a decade of falling export surpluses also meant subjecting an already deflated Indian economy to an additional round of income deflation comprising expenditure cuts and regressive taxation, and leaving 3 per cent of India's national income drained annually during the interwar years (Iyer 2021).

The Importance of Estimating the Drain

The present value of the drain over the period 1765–1938 cumulated up to 2017 was estimated at $45 trillion – ten times the United Kingdom's GDP in 2015 (Patnaik 2017), and the value of the drain for the period 1765–1900 alone cumulated up to 2020 is estimated at about $65 trillion – over four times the United Kingdom's estimated GDP for that year (Patnaik and Patnaik 2021). These are underestimates, since, apart from using an interest rate below market rate for compounding and excluding enforced borrowing in the estimate of transfers, it is also not possible to calculate realistically the cumulative deflationary impact on the Indian economy of the annual withdrawal of over one-third of India's domestic revenue for expenditure outside the country through the reverse operation of the Keynesian multiplier.

While it may not be realistic to expect the United Kingdom to pay India this sum as, say, reparations for colonial exploitation over two centuries, the estimate serves as crucial evidence and indicator of the extent of colonial exploitation that laid the foundations of capitalism and aided its diffusion – a fact that is obfuscated in mainstream economic history writing which deliberately dilutes the role of the colony.

Utsa Patnaik's methodological framework, by demystifying the process of effecting the drain in the Indian context, reaffirms primacy to colonial transfers in understanding the colonial phase of imperialism and provides an indispensable insight into the origins and evolution of capitalism. Her estimation of colonial transfers renders tangibility to the concept of imperialism and helps us comprehend imperialism as integral to capitalism and not merely as recourse out of crisis. This is a prerequisite to understanding contemporary capitalism as well where, in the absence of the colony as a buffer, the mechanism of income deflation continues to hold relevance as a prescription for developing countries.

This essay was originally published under the same title in *The Indian Economic Journal*, vol. 71, no. 1, 2023, pp. 229–46.

Note
¹ Britain had, during this period, liabilities in excess of its gold reserves.

References
Aldcroft, D.H. (1981), *From Versailles to Wall Street 1919–1929*, Berkeley: University of California Press.

Bagchi, A.K. (1976), 'De-industrialisation in India in the Nineteenth Century: Some Theoretical Implications', *Journal of Development Studies*, vol. 12, no. 2, pp. 135–64, doi: https://doi.org/10.1080/00220387608421565

Balachandran, G. (1996), *John Bullion's Empire: Britain's Gold Problem and India Between the Wars*, Surrey: Curzon Press.

Banerjee, A.K. (1963), *India's Balance of Payments: Estimates of Current and Capital Accounts from 1921–22 to 1938–39*, Bombay: Asia Publishing.

de Cecco, M. (1984), *The International Gold Standard: Money and Empire*, London: Francis Pinter.

Deane, P. and W.A. Cole (1969), *British Economic Growth, 1688–1959: Trends and Structure*, second edition, United Kingdom: Cambridge University Press.

Dutt, R.C. (1902), *The Economic History of India Under Early British Rule: From the Rise of the British Power in 1757 to the Accession of Queen Victoria in 1837*, volume 1, United Kingdom: Kegan Paul.

―――― (1904), *The Economic History of India in the Victorian Age: From the Accession of Queen Victoria in 1837 to the Commencement of the Twentieth Century*, volume 2, United Kingdom: Kegan Paul.

Eyre, G.E. and W. Spottiswoode (1860–1920), *British India for Various Years (Statistical Abstracts)*, H.M. Stationery office.

Fearon, P. (1979), *The Origins and Nature of the Great Slump 1929–1932*, London and Basingtoke: The MacMillan Press Ltd.

Gallagher, J. and A. Seal (1981), Britain and India Between the Wars, *Modern Asian Studies*, vol. 15, no. 3, pp. 387–414, doi: https://doi.org/10.1017/S0026749X00008647

Habib, I. (2006), *Indian Economy: 1858–1914*, A People's History of India, vol. 28, Delhi: Tulika Books.

Hilgerdt, F. (1942), *The Network of World Trade: A Companion Volume to "Europe's Trade"*, League of Nations.

Iyer, V. (2020), 'Commodity Export Surplus, Council Bills and Sterling Debt: India, 1861 to 1900', *Social Scientist*, vol. 48, nos 3–6, pp. 55–66.

―――― (2021), 'India and Britain in the World Economy during the Interwar Years', Unpublished PhD Thesis, Jawaharlal Nehru University, New Delhi.

Kindleberger, C.P. (1973), *The World in Depression 1929–1939*, USA: Allen & Unwin.

Lewis, W.A. (1969), *Economic Survey, 1919–1939*, New York: Harper & Row.

Naoroji, D. (1901), *Poverty and Un-British Rule in India*, Swan Sonnenschein and Co., Ltd.

Pandit, Y.S. (1937), *India's Balance of Indebtedness, 1898–1913*, London: George Allen & Unwin Ltd.

Patnaik, U. (1999), 'Tribute Transfer and the Balance of Payments in the Cambridge Economic History of India', in U. Patnaik, ed., *The Long Transition: Essays on Political Economy*, Delhi: Tulika Books, (reprinted from 'Transfer of Tribute and the Balance of Payments in the CEHI', 1984, *Social Scientist*, vol. 12, no. 12, pp. 43–55, doi: https://doi.org/10.2307/3517014)

—— (2006), 'The Free Lunch: Transfers from the Tropical Colonies and Their Role in Capital Formation in Britain During Industrial Revolution', in K.S. Jomo, ed., *Globalisation Under Hegemony*, New Delhi: Oxford University Press, pp. 30–70.

—— (2011), 'The "Agricultural Revolution in England": Its Cost for the English Working Class and the Colonies', in S. Moosvi, ed., *Capitalism, Colonialism and Globalisation: Studies in Economic Change*, Delhi: LeftWord Books.

—— (2012), 'Capitalist Trajectories of Global Interdependence and Welfare Outcomes: The Lessons of History for the Present', available at http://www.networkideas.org/ideasact/dec11/pdf/Utsa%20_Patnaik.pdf, accessed 30 July 2025.

—— (2017), 'Revisiting the 'Drain,' or Transfers from India to Britain in the Context of Global Diffusion of Capitalism', in S. Chakrabarti and U. Patnaik, eds, *Agrarian and Other Histories: Essays for Binay Bhushan Chaudhuri*, Delhi: Tulika Books.

—— (2019), 'The Revenue Impact on the Indian Masses of Exchange Rate Changes in the Context of the Drain of Wealth: 1871 to 1901', *Social Scientist*, vol. 47, nos 11–12, pp. 3–22.

Patnaik, U. and P. Patnaik (2021), 'The Drain of Wealth: Colonialism Before the First World War', *Monthly Review*, vol. 72, no. 9, pp. 1–19, doi: https://doi.org/10.14452/MR-072-09-2021-02_1

Saul, S.B. (1960), *Studies in British Overseas Trade 1870–1914*, Liverpool: Liverpool University Press.

Shah, K.T. (1921), *Sixty Years of Indian Finance*, Bombay: Chronicle Press [Digitised by www.archive. org (2007)].

Tomlinson, B.R. (1979), *Political Economy of the Raj 1914–1947: The Economics of Decolonization in India*, London and Basingtoke: The Macmillan Press Ltd.

15

Patriarchy and Property

Goa's Uniform Civil Code

Ritu Dewan

Introduction

Among the most contested and contentious of the myriad issues impacting gender equality worldwide is that of control over resources. This struggle over the means of production essentially centres on the access to, ownership of and control over the chief means of livelihood – that of land. Consequently, attainment of gender parity in especially developing economies focuses, in the main, on issues of land and property rights. In recognition of this central issue, the Convention on the Elimination of All Forms of Discrimination against Women (CEDAW) adopted in 1979 by the UN General Assembly has given women the right to own and administer property without discrimination (CEDAW, Article 15) as well as an equal treatment in land and agrarian reform (CEDAW, Article 14(2) (g)). Also, Article 16 ensures that both spouses have equal rights in the 'ownership, acquisition, management, administration, enjoyment and disposition of property'. Additionally, Resolution 15 (paras 1 and 3) (1998) of the Sub-Commission on the Promotion and Protection of Human Rights on 'Women and the Right to Land, Property and Adequate Housing' states that discrimination against women with respect to acquiring and securing land constitutes a violation of human rights law, and urges governments to amend and/or repeal discriminatory laws and policies and to simultaneously encourage the transformation of discriminatory customs and traditions that impede attainment of gender-equal rights.

India is a signatory to these and other conventions that make a commitment to gender equality, including the ensuring of land rights. While not going into details, suffice it to say that the Eighth Five Year Plan saw heartening policy support to gender equality, especially the guideline issued to the states in 1995 by the Department of Land Resources, Ministry of Rural Development, to issue *patta* land in the joint names of husband and wife, as well as a specific proportion to single women both unmarried and widowed. The Ninth Plan introduced, for the first time ever, individual as well as group distribution of land titles to women. The Tenth Plan recommended the distribution to women of land declared surplus under the Land Ceiling Act initiated during the 1950s and the 1960s. This process of strengthening women's land rights continued under consecutive plans, including the granting of homesteads. The Twelfth Plan emphasized the enhancement of women's land access from all three sources – direct government transfers, purchase or lease from the market and also inheritance. This was facilitated by introducing a range of initiatives including joint land titles in all government land transfers, credit support to poor women to purchase or lease land from the market, increase in legal awareness and legal support for women's inheritance rights, supportive government schemes, recording of women's inheritance shares and so on.

Consequent to these policy initiatives demanded by and combined with the impact of the burgeoning women's movements, the share of women landholders in the country rose from 10.9 per cent as per the Agricultural Census of 2000–01 to 11.7 per cent in 2005–06 to 12.78 per cent in 2010–11. Although relatively marginal, this almost 2 per cent increase is not insignificant within a short span of a decade, reflecting the success of both policy and struggle. However, it must be pointed out at the outset that there is no data available for land ownership in India, the various data sources restricting it to 'operational' holdings, defined in the Agricultural Census as: 'All land which is used wholly or partly for agricultural production and is operated as one technical unit by one person alone or with others without regard to the title, legal form, size or location.' Regrettably, since the dismantling of the Planning Commission, no policy initiatives whatsoever have been undertaken in order to ensure gender-equal control over land rights thereby constituting violation of human rights.

Women, Land Rights and the Portuguese Civil Code

The fulcrum of gender equality in all its myriad manifestations is the ownership and control over resources, and specifically in a developing economy, primarily and essentially land. However, these manifestations and also the intensity of interlinkages between gender equality and resources are to a deeply significant level determined by historical and regional specificities relating to economic as well as extra-economic factors and forces. Nowhere in India are these direct and indirect interconnects between gender equality and resources so intricate, nuanced and simultaneously complex as in the state of Goa. Goa is the only state in India that applies Article 44 of the Indian Constitution which states that '[t]he State shall endeavour to secure for the citizens a uniform civil code throughout the territory of India': the Common Civil Code which was instituted in Goa in 1867 still exists and applies to virtually all facets of life in the state, including de jure equality in land and property rights. Any analysis of gendered land rights must therefore interrelate land laws and legislations with the Portuguese Civil Code. Consequently, this requires an examination of the tightly interwoven structures of the Common Civil Code and the Family Laws: an inquiry into and the demystification of gendered land patterns must therefore be built on the prevailing intermixes of land, property and matrimonial rights, both marital and natal.

Land Rights for rural and also urban women in Goa are regulated and mediated through a vast and multiple array of laws, regulations and provisions. Those relevant to this essay are

(1) Goa Family Laws: group of laws which embody the concept of matrimonial property rights and are based on and determined by the Portuguese Civil Code, which also incorporates the Code of Usages and Customs of Gentile Hindus;

(2) Code of Comunidades: village community law that ensures common management of the land and the resources;

(3) Goa Mundkar (Protection from Eviction) Act of 1975: this law governs the rights of *mundkars* (those who lawfully reside with a fixed habitation in a dwelling house with or without obligation to render any services to the family), with the consent of the *bhatkar* (landlord).

However, before embarking on a detailed analysis, it is necessary to understand the context as well as the term 'Uniform Civil Code'. This appellation was not used during the Portuguese rule: the interchangeable terms were Portuguese Civil Code, Portuguese Civil Procedure Code, Portuguese Code of Civil Registration, Portuguese Commercial Code, Portuguese Criminal Code, Codigo Civil Portugues. Although the Portuguese Civil Code of 1867 has since been amended several times, the version of the Code as of 1936 along with the amendments consequent to the Concordat (a treaty between Portugal and the Holy See) in 1940 are the legal foundation of what are called the Family Laws of Goa. In 2016, the law called the Goa Succession, Special Notaries and Inventory Proceeding Act, 2012, was enacted, which came under in severe criticism, especially that of being delinked from the Portuguese Civil Code apart from being bad in law. This new Act of 2016 will be examined from a gendered perspective in a separate section.

Perceived within the fundamental focus of this article is the issue whether Goa's Uniform Civil Code is essentially and truly uniform and to what extent, and if at all, does it ensure gender equality specifically in the context of women's rights to own and manage property, primarily land. Importantly and additionally, does this Code incorporate substantive equality as contained in the Constitution of India. If the above are not fully integrated and not realized, then are the constraints de jure or de facto or an intermix of both.

These family laws encompass portions of the Portuguese Civil Code relating to marriage, dissolution of marriage, separation of persons and properties, annulment of marriage, succession, inheritance, inventory proceedings (initiated in court to determine the devolution of properties of a Goan deceased with properties in Goa), guardianship and adoption of children.

Code of Usages and Customs of Gentile Hindus

Included in the Family Laws of Goa is the Code of Usages and Customs of Gentile Hindus. The term 'Gentile' is somewhat derogatory, the literal meaning being a pagan or heathen, that is, a person who does not acknowledge a particular god or belief. This Code was incorporated after several Hindu groups petitioned the colonial Portuguese administration to recognize and retain their religious customs and usages. While applicable primarily to Hindus, there are provisions for other non-Catholic inhabitants of Goa to avail the limited polygamy provisions.

Article 3 states:

> However, the marriage contracted by a male Gentile Hindu by simultaneous polygamy shall not produce civil effects; except in the following cases only (1) Absolute absence of issues by the wife of the previous marriage until she attains the age of 25 years. (2) Absolute absence of male issue, the previous wife having completed 30 years of age, and being of lower age, ten years having elapsed from the last pregnancy; (3) Separation on any legal grounds when proceeding from the wife and there being no male issue, (4) Dissolution of the previous marriage as provided for in Article 5.

Article 4 states:

> The indispensable condition for the simultaneous marriage are as follows: (1) Proof of any of the circumstances mentioned in the preceding article through the court; (2) Consent of the previous wife, expressed in a public deed, in the cases falling under clauses 1 and 2 of the said Article 3.

Article 29 has provisions for other non-Catholic inhabitants of Goa to avail of the limited polygamy provisions. It states:

> The Non-Catholic inhabitants of Goa who are not Hindu Gentiles may observe the provisions of the present law, which shall be applicable to them in so far as it is not contrary to their religious rites; and in the same manner their private usages are safeguarded in so far as they are not contrary to morality and public order.

It is rather shocking that there are legal provisions for the practices of bigamy and polygamy in the Code and Customs of Gentile Hindus as contained within the Uniform Civil Code. A Hindu male is permitted to marry a second time even without divorcing the first wife in case no child is born by the time she attains the age of twenty-five, if no male child is born to the first wife when she attains the age of thirty years, and if there is a ten-year gap between pregnancies. It is claimed that this does not happen in reality and that courts can interpret. While this may be true to a large extent, there are several who do use the sexist provisions of this law. Further, under this code, adoption is permitted uniformly for a 'Hindu of any caste' when there is no male progeny. A petition challenging this provision that permits only males to be adopted by Gentile Hindus in the absence of legitimate male issues is now pending before the High Court of Bombay at Goa at the time of writing this essay.

Classification of Marriages and Matrimonial Property Rights

There are two categories of marriages that are classified under the Portuguese Uniform Code: canonical and civil (non-canonical). There are thus two kinds of marriage registrations: that for Catholics who opt for canonical marriages, and that for non-Catholics and for those who do not opt for canonical marriages. Marriage registration requires the couple to declare their intent to get married by filling a form duly signed by them and also two witnesses, combined with affirmation before the civil registrar of the *taluka* in which either one of them resides. Post this declaration, after fifteen days and before one year, the intent of marriage has to be confirmed along with the witnesses before the civil registrar or the celebrant of the nuptials in the Catholic church. The location of confirmation depends on whether the person is Catholic or non-Catholic and whether the registration as a canonical marriage is opted for by the Catholic, so that the marriage is written into the marriage registration books. Canonical marriages have the additional option of being brought to an end through annulment before the Patriarchal Tribunal of the Catholic church. Earlier it was the only option available for Catholics until a Catholic woman approached the then Judicial Commissioner's Court to get the benefit of Article 14 of the Constitution, upon which the courts agreed to apply civil law remedies. There is therefore still the option of a party seeking annulment under the Canon law from the Patriarchal Tribunal after which the order of the Tribunal is sent for confirmation to the High Court of Bombay at Goa to confirm the annulment, which then has civil effects as far as the marital status of the persons is concerned. The ecclesiastical authorities maintain that their order, on confirmation by the high court, only has civil effects when it comes to the union of the spouses, and that it is for the courts to decide on the separation of properties. However, when the courts deliberate on separation of properties in terms of either the law on separation of properties or in terms of the inventory proceedings, it is invariably the high court-approved order of the Patriarchal Tribunal that is considered.

It is said that the rights relating to succession and separation of properties are to be equally applicable to all, irrespective of religion and of whether their marriages are canonical or non-canonical. Daughters and sons formally have equal rights to parental properties. In the absence of a will, the default system of holding property upon marriage is the regime of communion of assets which means that upon marriage, unless an option is made to the contrary, all assets, including land, whether inherited, acquired before or after marriage, are held in common by the couple. There is also a limitation on parents to be being able to alienate only half of their property by a will, which in a sense in some ways takes care of the son preference and ensures that its attendant consequences do not prejudice the rights of women.

However, rights are different for parties whose marriage has been annulled as against parties whose marriage has been dissolved by divorce or death or who are separated by a decree of separation of persons and properties. In the event of a divorce, the properties are divided into equal shares. In the event of separation, if the separation was sought both of persons and properties, then the properties will be divided equally. However, there is no clarity even on this account. For instance, annulment means that the marriage never was and therefore it would follow that there is no concept of matrimonial property rights. However, technically, the law provides that the party who is at fault shall not secure any of the benefits of a marriage which is annulled while a party who is not at fault can do so. Therefore, when the civil law is circumvented by utilizing the Patriarchal Tribunal which grants annulment on grounds such as non-consummation of marriage which is not a ground for annulment under the Family Laws of Goa, it is the Tribunal's grounds of determining fault that will be upheld for division of properties.

A crucial issue is that of ownership and control over land holdings during marriage: that is, is the property marital, of neither the husband nor the wife but of the marital union? The Code of 1867 – located as it was in a feudal–patriarchal point of time – states that notwithstanding gender-equal inheritance and ownership of matrimonial property, the management and administration rights are bestowed on the male spouse except in the case of impediment. This impediment includes disability such as being 'deaf and dumb' as well as the migration of the male spouse to international destinations. An additional provision is that the male can alienate property provided he obtains the consent of his spouse, even if post facto; on the other hand, the female spouse can alienate only if she has the authorization of her husband.

Yet another provision relates to relinquishment of rights by any child who wishes to waive off inheritance. This proviso is more often than not resorted to by brothers to compel sisters to give up their rights to parental property in exchange of dowry: the argument put forward is that the sister receives her share of parental property in the form of dowry, and that by not relinquishing her rights she receives more than her legally permitted 'fair share'. The majority of Goan women agree to formally surrender their due share: data relating to relinquishment of rights are available at the sub-registrar's office and can be easily collated to quantify the information. It is therefore obvious that special safeguards are required to be put into place in order to ensure that rights of ownership and control are not wrested out of women, that there is a future for real land rights for women. Adding to this complexity is the major aspect of the harmonization of laws.

Other laws too do not take into account women's land and property rights guaranteed under the Portuguese Uniform Code. The 1969 Goa Land Revenue Code is totally delinked from family laws. The Survey and Record of Rights conducted in the late 1970s and early 1980s as well as the Land Mutation System either omitted or wrongly registered names of owners as well as of land rights. Three categories have been the most affected: tribals who did not always have births registered and also often use pet names instead of formal names; Nav Hindus who had converted to Hinduism but bore the Catholic names in their birth certificates and Hindu names in applicable land rights records; Catholic women whose names do not stand automatically changed upon marriage in the marriage certificate and therefore if their names were entered in the land records in situations where their spouses or son-less parents are dead, then their names were entered as their first name with the husband's surname. The Survey and Record of Rights excluded the dwelling houses of the *mundkars* constructed in the landlord's property, thus further compounding the case for equality in property especially for women from the marginalized sections.

The Goa Mundkar (Protection from Eviction Act) of 1975 defines heritable members of a family of a *mundkar* as his spouse, son, unmarried daughter, and includes father, mother, grandson, widowed daughter, widowed granddaughter, solely dependent on the *mundkar* for maintenance. Combined with automatic assumption of patrilocality after marriage, this provision excludes members who qualify as heirs under the family laws. The centuries-old Code of Comunidades which exists along with family laws does not confer rights to women except if they are widowed without male children, or are the unmarried daughters of son-less parents – that is, those out of the patriarchal definition of a family.

The Goa Succession, Special Notaries and Inventory Proceeding Act, 2012

In 2016, the Government of Goa enacted The Goa Succession, Special Notaries and Inventory Proceeding Act, 2012 (Goa Act 23 of 2016) which has brought several amendments to the Portuguese Civil Code. The select committee on Bill No. 13 for the formulation of The Goa Succession, Special Notaries and Inventory Proceeding Bill, 2012, was chaired first by the then chief minister Manohar Parrikar, and upon his induction as the Union Minister of Defence, by Advocate Francis D'Souza who was the deputy chief minister as well as the law minister. The committee report was adopted on 17 March 2016.

There has been much criticism of this Act on several grounds including that of constitutionality, legal correctness, separation of succession from the prevailing Portuguese Civil Code which is all-encompassing, lack of debate and discussion and so on. For one, a part of the Code has been removed and revoked and then enacted as an Act, thereby ignoring the fundamental fact that a Code and an Act are two entirely different legal entities. Also, no public consultation was conducted nor any suggestions taken even in the initial stages on whether to do away with Civil Code itself. A very short notice of barely two weeks was given for suggestions and objections as late as in 2015: many prominent lawyers and women activists speedily came together to study and analyse the Bill, but all objections were dismissed, with none of the suggestions and recommendations being taken up. This Committee on Suggestions concludes: 'The idea is retrograde and takes the law backwards. It totally overlooks jurisprudence, legal theory, Indian and western legal history, and legal culture. We are going backwards from car to bullock cart' (Government of Goa 2016).

Among the most crucial objections related directly to the central focus of this essay is that many sections go beyond succession and enter into provisions related to Law of Marriage, Divorce and Separation which are intrinsic to the Portuguese Civil Code. Seven such major illustrations of deviation are listed below, all of which need to be read in consonance:

(1) The definition of the Head of the Family is contained in Part I (2) (h): 'head of the family' means the person who is entrusted with the duty to give the list of the assets and liabilities of an inheritance and with the management of the inheritance till the finalization of the partition.

(2) Section 249: Management of the inheritance head of the family. Eldest of the spouses to be the head of the family – Where an inventory is instituted consequent upon divorce, separation or annulment of marriage, the head of the family shall, where the marriage is governed by the regime of community of assets, belong to the eldest spouse and where the marriage is governed by the regime of separation of assets, to the spouse who owns the assets; if there are any community assets, the eldest shall be the head of the family in respect thereof.

(3) Section 250: Special head of the family – The co-heirs who on the date of the opening of the inheritance, were in possession of certain properties of the inheritance and so also the heirs who have to restitute gifted properties to the estate shall be deemed heads of the family in respect of such properties.

(4) (t) 'renunciation or repudiation of heirship' means the relinquishment of the inheritance made by a person entitled to inherit by succession and to succeed.

(5) Section 26: Acceptance or renunciation by one of the spouses only – A married person is not entitled to accept or renounce an inheritance without written consent of the other spouse. The consent may be made good by an order of the Court.

(6) Section 134: Restraint on marriage – (1) The condition which pro-

hibits the heir or the legatee from getting married, or from remaining unmarried, except when the same is imposed on a widow or widower having children, by the deceased spouse or by his or her descendants or ascendants and so also the condition which compels him to take priesthood vows or to take or not to take a certain and specified profession, shall be deemed inexistent.

(7) Section 52: Order of legal succession –

   (1) The legal succession shall devolve in the following order –

     (i) on the descendants;

     (ii) on the ascendants, subject to the provisions of sub-section (2) of section 72;

     (iii) on the brothers and their descendants;

     (iv) on the surviving spouse;

     (v) on the collaterals not comprised in clause (iii) up to the 6th degree;

     (vi) on the state, provided that, in the absence of testamentary or intestate heir of a beneficial owner or of an emphyteusis, the property shall revert to the direct owner.

   (2) In respect of persons referred to in clauses (i), (ii) and (iii) of sub-section (1), the agricultural produce or fruits, gathered or growing, meant and necessary for the maintenance of the couple shall be deemed to be the personal property of the surviving spouse, provided that on the date of the opening of the inheritance, there is no suit for divorce or separation of persons and properties, pending or decreed.

Several additional factors need to be noted here. For one, the entire document refers to the head being a male, referred to as 'he' in every single one of the provisions, even though the head of the family is defined as being the 'eldest in the family'. Two, the issue of the 'eldest spouse' has to be viewed in the context of the fact that in a patriarchal society, the male spouse is invariably older than the female spouse. Several discriminatory rules and provisions have not even been attempted to be looked at: in fact, the Redrafting committee set up by the Government of Goa in the early 2000s to examine Goa's family laws that govern marriage, divorce, children, succession, wills and inventories, and to deal with suggestions and objections related to these provisions had been disbanded, and had no role whatsoever to perform in the formulation of this new Act.

Article 1057 of Goa's Code provides for the registration of marriages which lacks uniformity between Catholic and non-Catholic marriages. Intent of marriage has to be recorded by the would-be spouses before the civil registration authorities and a marriage deed signed within a minimum gap of fifteen days. Many women are neither informed of this provision and are often not even aware of the requirement of this second confirmation through signatures. The consequence, in not a few instances, is that when a dispute arises, their marriages are found and thereby declared invalid, making these women susceptible to fraud and bigamy and sometimes even extortion. Similarly, while church marriages can be annulled by the church tribunal in cases of non-consummation, for non-Christians non-consummation is not a ground of annulment or divorce. Further, under Article 1204 which deals with separation of persons and assets, the husband is permitted to get a divorce if adultery is committed by the wife: the wife however is permitted separation only if the husband commits adultery combined with public scandal, and a divorce if he abandons her and also if he keeps a mistress in the conjugal domicile.

There are four forms of pre-nuptial contracts permitted, none of which can be modified during the course of the marriage. The first system is one of total separation of properties or no communion at all: this is an extremely rare agreement signed before marriage as it does not consider the sentiments surrounding marriage. Here, the partners hold onto all their properties independently. The second form is one where there is total separation of the properties and assets owned prior to the marriage and communion of the assets and properties acquired subsequently: this form has apparently gained some prominence in recent times. The Dotal regime constitutes the third category, under which the share of the bride in her father's property and assets is given to the husband, and is often mistaken to be dowry. The husband is bound to restore all the property and assets to his partner should the marriage be dissolved.

The fourth category relates to the communion of all assets of husband and wife that are equally divided on divorce or death. While this appears to be certainly women-equitable and strengthens women's legal property rights, the provision related to the management of these properties is vested solely with the husband: the wife is not entitled to deprive the husband by way of ante-nuptial contracts from the administration of assets. Ownership and control thus are separated and delinked. The law stipulates that the management and administration of the properties and common assets of the couple, and even the exclusive properties of the wife, belongs solely to the husband. For instance, as a 'manager' the husband can rent out the premises and even transfer the shares in a cooperative society without the wife's consent. The wife is legally permitted only the right to receive part of the income from her assets for pocket expenses on the condition that this amount is not in excess of one-third of the net income.

And, finally, for those who choose to opt out of joint ownership of properties, this Act clearly reduces the ownership and succession status of the surviving spouse at number four in the order of preference of legal succession. The first right belongs to the descendants, followed by ascendants. The third right is bestowed upon the brothers and sisters and their children – gender inequality is contained even within this category, with the brother of the intestate and his descendants having primacy over sisters.

In Conclusion

The specificity of the central issue of ownership and control over land by the women of Goa is unique in that it is the only region in the entire nation that ensures – de jure – equal property rights in both marital and parental property. However, the attainment of these rights is curtailed, restricted and often denied in various ways, the intermix of different laws and provisions rendering nugatory gender equality of rights in both parental and matrimonial properties. For instance, after the liberation of Goa and its joining India in 1961, there were laws enacted for the Goa union territory and subsequently set out to be state laws, once Goa attained statehood. In the first round immediately after 1961, laws were simply imported without taking into account the family laws prevalent in Goa or even the concept of substantive equality. These include the Land Revenue Code and the Agricultural Tenancy Act. The various related laws and regulations that have a bearing on land rights need to be synchronized with the Family Laws in the matter of property rights and the same principles must reflect in the operationality of land rights without discrimination, except of course for positive discrimination where and when necessary.

The terms 'uniform' and 'uniformity' need to be demystified. What is the definition of uniformity when it applies differently to different groups, in this instance, Gentile Hindus? How does uniformity take into account those who are unequal in the system of production, especially in relation to those who are propertyless and assetless as most women and also men are? Can uniformity be imposed on those who are already marginalized and unequal? How is equality and uniformity to be legally applied to a woman who is deserted or married under fraud and deceit? Are those who are out of the patriarchal definition of a family, whether by choice or involuntarily, equal to those who by law fit into the current definition of a family? Will the levels and extent of inequality lessen or deepen? The 2016 Act has resulted in much confusion and disruption especially in the context of the fact that this Act removes and revokes part of the Code without taking into account its intrinsic character particularly in relation to the rights of women over ownership and management of property and assets, however limited these rights may be. What is required are urgent legislative, administrative and judicial reforms in order to ensure land rights and bring about gender parity, equality and empowerment.

This essay was originally published under the same title in *The Indian Economic Journal*, vol. 71, no. 1, 2023, pp. 247–55.

The inputs by Dr Albertina Almeida, Advocate-Goa are sincerely acknowledged.

References

Almeida, A. (2016), 'Goa's Civil Code Shows that Uniformity Does not Always Mean Equality', *The Wire*, 8 August.

Almeida, A. and M. Correa (2008), 'Women's Rights to Land and Housing in Goa', mimeograph, *Sandarsh*.

CEDAW (1994), *General Recommendation No. 21: Equality in Marriage and Family Relations* (13th Session), Committee on the Elimination of Discrimination Against Women, https://www.un.org/womenwatch/daw/cedaw/recommendations/recomm.htm

Goa Law Commission (2015), *Reports and Publications*, http://goalawcommission.gov.in/goa, accessed June 2022.

Government of Goa (2016), *The Goa Succession, Special Notaries and Inventory Proceeding Act, 2012*, Notification No. 7/18/2016-LA, *Official Gazette*, Series I, No. 25 (Extraordinary), Department of Law and Judiciary, Legal Affairs Division, Government of Goa, 22 September, p. 950.

Government of India (2001), *Agricultural Census 2000–01*, Ministry of Agriculture and Farmers Welfare.

Government of India (2012), *Agricultural Census 2010–11*, Ministry of Agriculture and Farmers Welfare.

Khalap, R. (2012), *Reports on Law Commission, Goa April 2009 to March 2012*, Chairman, Law Commission, Goa, mimeograph.

Press Information Bureau (2015), *Government of India, Ministry of Statistics and Programme Implementation*, Government of India, 22 July.

United Nations (1979), *Convention on the Elimination of All Forms of Discrimination Against Women* (CEDAW), United Nations Entity for Gender Equality and the Empowerment of Women, available at https://www.un.org/womenwatch/daw/cedaw/text/econvention.htm

Usgaocar, M.S. (2013), *Family Laws of Goa, Daman and Diu*, vol. 1, Vela Associates.

16

Why Inter-Caste Inequality in Educational Attainment Still Persists

Wealth and Caste Discrimination Matters

Sukhadeo Thorat and Khalid Khan

'Past may again be made to live in the present.'

– Ambedkar

Introduction

The roots of inter-caste inequality in education attainment go back very long in time when restrictions on access to education were put on low-caste people from the ancient period through the medieval age and further down during the British rule till the middle of the nineteenth century (Ambedkar 1982; Jha 2018; Moosvi 2011; Sharma 1958). It is in 1813 that the British government made a public declaration of the responsibility of promoting education among the native population. The British Parliament laid down to set apart revenue to the revival and improvement of literature and encouragement of the learned native *in India* (Ambedkar 1982, p. 409).

For the ancient period, a Manu law framed around BCE 200 states: 'One may not teach him [shudra] the law or enjoin upon him religious observances. For he who tells him [shudra] the law and he who enjoins upon him [religious] observances, he indeed together with that [shudra] sinks into the darkness of the hell' (Buhler 1886).

Thus, not only did Manu debar the Shudras from the education system but he also enacted penalties against those who might help them acquire knowledge (Ambedkar 1987). The Islamic regimes in the middle ages did not interfere much in the Hindu laws and customs including those related to education (Moosvi 2011). The British carried on with the customs and laws further quite judiciously. The first Anglo-Indian law of East India Company enacted in 1772 states: 'In suits regarding succession, inheritance, marriage, and "caste", and all religious usages and institutions, the Hindu laws – are to be considered the general rules by which the judges are to form their decision' (Jha 2018).

It is only in 1813 that the British made a public declaration regarding education of the native people. But 'unfortunately, the British also confined education to higher classes and castes that included land owners, *jagirdar*s, solider class, wealthy, highly ranked employees of government and the brahmins' (Ambedkar 1982, p. 407). The policy of confining education to higher classes and higher castes continued till 1855, when for the first time, they opened up education to the depressed castes. But even after 1855, due to stiff opposition by high castes, the depressed classes could not gain access to public schools although the laws permitted. In a memorandum to the British on 29 May 1928, Ambedkar cited the example of a Mahar[1] boy from Dharwad who was refused admission in public school by the higher castes in June 1856. In response to the Mahar boy's appeal, the then governor-general of the Bombay Presidency had stated that:

> It would not be right for the sake of single individual, the only Mahar who ever came forward to beg for admission into a school attended by the pupils of high castes and to force him into association with them, at the probable risk of making the institution practically useless for the great mass of natives. (Ambedkar 1982, p. 419)

Indeed, the opposition by the high castes was so great that the then director of public instruction reported a case where, when the admission of low-caste pupils had led to the closure of five or six large schools for two years, the huts and crops of the low-caste people were burnt in one village, and heavy punitive measures were imposed on that village for two years (Ambedkar 1982).

In the face of intense opposition by the high caste to the entry of depressed castes in public schools, the British government tried an alternative arrangement of having a separate school for children of low castes and offering grants to Christian missionary schools for admitting children from depressed castes. These measures, however, did not result in much improvement, as the enrolment of depressed classes remained close to nil in 1923 in the Bombay Presidency (Ambedkar 1982).

Although thereafter the situation improved to some extent, it remained deplorable till the adoption of the all-India education policy in independent India after 1950 which opened the gates of education for the depressed castes. Every successive higher education policy, namely, 1952, 1968, 1986 and the Programme of Action of 1992 developed measures for reducing inter-caste disparities by bringing about improvement in the education level of the Scheduled Castes (SCs), Scheduled Tribes (STs), Other Backward Castes (OBCs) and minorities. The Programme of Action of 1992 had a comprehensive package of special policies on the education of depressed castes, and that has remained the last word on policy statement till today. All later measures for improvement in the education attainment of the depressed castes have been guided by this programme (Thorat and Khan 2018).

The government followed a dual policy for mass higher education that includes setting up of public education institutions and philanthropic private aided institutions and supportive measures in the form of financial assistance, scholarship/freeship, hostel and so on for the low-class and low-caste sections of the populace. These measures brought about some improvement in the educational attainment of the depressed castes in higher education. However, later in the 1970s and 1980s, the government gradually shifted from the policy and started promoting higher education more through self-financing private commercial players along with simultaneous reduction in the role of government and philanthropic private (aided) education institutions (ibid., pp. 92–127). As a result, although the enrolment rate of lower classes and low castes has improved in higher education institutions (HEIs), the traditional gap between them and others (higher castes/classes) still persisted and the former continued to fall behind the latter in attainment of higher education.

Based on recent data, we argue that the present inter-caste disparities in higher education attainment and low enrolment rates of SCs, STs and OBCs is mainly due to an early shift in the government policy of setting up of public higher educational institutions from government/philanthropic-(aided) to commercial private sector, which made higher education unaffordable to the socially and economically disadvantaged groups and induced caste disparities at the higher education level. Using recent data for 2017–18, we present empirical evidence on unequal access of lower income classes and lower castes to HEIs and resultant inter-caste disparities in higher education. We also provide evidence on linkages of growing commercialization of higher education and the role of income and caste discrimination in low access of lower castes and lower classes to HEIs.

Growing Shift towards Commercialization of Higher Education

The increasing privatization of higher education has assumed various forms. These include the private central and state universities and colleges, which are mostly financed through very high fee-structure that students have to pay. In this category are included state private universities, deemed private universities, private colleges and institutions, and stand-alone private institutions. Privatization has also come about through self-financed courses in public educational institutions – this is back-door privatization of public institutions. Thus, today, private self-finance universities, colleges, stand-alone institutions and self-financing courses in public HEIs constitute the private sector in higher education in India (Thorat and Khan 2018; Tilak 2004; Varghese, Malik and Thorat 2017).

The relevant data for the 2017/2018 gives the total number of institutions and the share of public, private aided and private self-financing private institutions. The extent of privatization of higher education is measured in terms of percentage share of private (unaided) education institutions and of students in total education institutions and total students. In the early 1950s, all states and central universities and colleges/institutions were either government and/or private aided. By 2017/2018, the share of the private universities in the total of 993 universities/institutions was up to almost 38 per cent, of which 30.6 per cent were state private universities and 8 per cent private deemed universities. For the year 2019/2020, the provisional figure of private universities is about 40 per cent. Correspondingly, the share of government universities/institutions has reduced to 48 per cent. In the college sector, about 38,179 colleges or equivalent to 64 per cent of the total were private unaided colleges while government colleges accounted for only 22 per cent. About 66 per cent of stand-alone institutions were private HEIs.

In terms of students, the private HEIs account for about 30 per cent of the total students in higher education institutions, followed by 45 per cent in government and 24 per cent in private aided institutions. The share would go up if we include the share of self-financing courses in public institutions. Thus, both in terms of universities and colleges, and students, the private sector has begun to occupy the prime position with simultaneous decline in public sector and philanthropic private HEIs.

This is evident from the declining share of government and private aided institutions and the share of students in them (Tilak 2005). Over the passage of time, the shift towards private unaided institutions is evident from the All-India Survey on Higher Education (AISHE) by the Ministry of Education, which indicates an increase in the share of private universities from 28.6 per cent in 2011–12 to 39 per cent in 2018–19. The share of private self-financing colleges has increased from 57 per cent in 2011 to 65 per cent in 2019–20. Similarly, the share of stand-alone institutions decreased from a mere 68.3 per cent in 2011–12 to 66 per cent in 2019–20 (Table A1).

In case of students, a similar trend is clearly visible. We have taken the data on the number of students from the National Sample Survey on Social Consumption: Education. In 2017–18, the share of students in private institutions increased from 7.1 per cent in 1995 to 22.6 per cent in 2007, 33 per cent in 2014 and 30.1 per cent in 2017–18. Correspondingly, the share of students in government institutions declined from 57 per cent in 1995 to 47 per cent in 2007 and further down to 45 per cent in 2017–18. The share of private aided institutions also declined from 36 per cent in 1995 to 29 per cent in 2007, 25 per cent in 2014 and further down to 24 per cent in 2017–18 (Table A1b).

The separate figure for private universities indicates that the students' share in private self-financing institutions increased from 13.3 per cent in 2011–12 to 23.4 per cent in 2019–20 (Table A1a). Thus, the bulk of the increase in the share of students in private HEIs has come at the cost of decline of students in government institutions, universities and colleges. Similarly, for standalone institutions, the share remained high around 60 per cent in 2019–20 (Table A1a). Thus, there has been a clear shift of higher education towards private commercial education institutions along with a simultaneous decline in government and philanthropic private aided institutions. This trend has an implication for the access of students from lower-caste and low-income groups, which we examine in the next section.

Persisting Graded Caste Inequality in Educational Attainment

Educational attainment in India has showed a considerable improvement in higher education. The enrolment rate which was about 1 per cent in early 1960 increased to 25 per cent in 2017–18. The enrolment rate has improved for all economic and caste/ethnic/religious groups. However, the onward march of educational attainment has not been shared by all groups equally. In order to bridge the gap in the enrolment rate between the lower castes/STs on the one hand and high castes on the other, the rate of improvement in HEI enrolment of the former should have been faster than the latter. However, improvement in the enrolment rate of the lower castes/OBCs and the STs has not been high enough to bridge the traditional gap between them and the higher castes and classes – as the recent data show.

In 2017–18, the gross attendance rate (GAR) for students in the age group of 18 to 23 years was about 26 per cent at the all-India level. However, the GAR of the lowest income group (quintile 0–20 per cent) was about 13 per cent, which progressively increased to 19 per cent for the second quintile (20–40 per cent), 26 per cent for the third quintile, 35 per cent for the fourth and finally 53 per cent for the fifth quintile (80–100 per cent). The GAR of the bottom income group is thus four times less compared to the topmost income group, indicating a clear negative relationship between the income level and educational attainment in higher education (Table A2). The disparities by income groups are further confirmed by variations in GAR across occupations. The GAR is 14 per cent for casual wage labour which is two and a half times less compared to that of regular salaried workers.

Inter-caste graded inequality also continues to persist in the HEI attendance. As against the all-India average of 26 per cent, the GAR is 16 per cent for ST, 21 per cent for SC, 28 per cent for OBC and 41 per cent for HC. Thus, GAR of ST is two and a half times less as compared to higher castes while GAR of SC is half that of higher castes. The GAR of OBC is higher than SC/ST but it is one and a half times less than that of high caste. Graded inequality is thus quite evident; the GAR reduces as we move down in caste hierarchy, from high caste to OBC to SC and finally to ST (Table A2). Even among the casual wage labour, the GAR of ST/ SC is about 15 per cent as compared to 17 per cent of OBC casual wage labour while that of HC casual wage labour is 20 per cent (Table A2).

Thus, in higher education attainment, the inequality between the low-income and high-income group, and graded inequality between the STs, SCs, OBCs and high castes continues to persist in contemporary times. The prediction of Ambedkar that 'past may again be made to live in the present' echoes the present scenario of past suffering affecting the present education inequality (Ambedkar 1987).

Privatization Led to Low Access of Poor and Low Castes in HEIs

Privatization of HEIs has played a significant role towards the trend of unequal education attainment among castes and classes. In 2017–18, of the total students in HEIs, about one-third were in private self-financing education institutions; the percentage being a little higher in urban areas at 34 per cent compared to 27 per cent for rural areas. However, the low-income and lower-castes pupils did not receive equal access to private education institutions. Of the total students in the low-income group (quintile 0–20), about 20 per cent were in private educational institutions (unaided); this share progressively increased to 25 per cent for the second quintile (20–40 per cent), 29 per cent for the third quintile, 32 per cent for the fourth quintile and finally 38 per cent for the fifth quintile (80–100). The share of the bottom income group is thus less by about 17 per cent points compared to the top income group (Table A3). Inter-income group inequality is also reflected in the share of the bottom income group of the total number of students in private unaided institutions in the country. Of the total students in the private unaided education institutions, the bottom quintile (0–20) accounts for only 9 per cent, much lower than the 38 per cent in the top income quintile (80–100) – almost four and a half times lower than that of the bottom income group. In the middle-income group, the share varies between 12 per cent and 23 per cent. Similarly, the lower castes had lesser access to private institutions than their high caste counterparts. Of the total students in private education institutions, the share of ST was 4.8 per cent, followed by 16 per cent of SC, 48 per cent of other backward castes and 31 per cent of high castes. The share of ST is about eight times less while that of SC's is two times lower than that of high castes (Table A3).

Causes of Inter-Caste Inequality in Educational Attainment

There are obvious reasons for low educational attainment among the low-income groups and STs, SCs and OBCs. It is clear that low income and the disadvantage associated with caste identity remain a factor in lower access to higher education for low-income classes and lower castes. We have tried to estimate the likelihood of HEIs attendance across economic (income) and caste groups.

In the first logit model where income level along with other factors is considered, it is seen that the chances of attending HEIs is lower for students belonging to households whose head is less educated and family size is relatively large. The chance is low for females than males. Similarly, the chances of SC, ST, Muslim and OBC are lower than that of high castes. Further, the chance is lower for the bottom income group compared to the top income group (refer Table 16.1a).

In a second logit model where we have replaced income by occupation (due to high correlation between income level and occupation) keeping the other factors same, the result confirmed the findings of the earlier model. For instance, the chances of attending HEIs are low for households whose head has low education, and household size is relatively large. The chances are lower for female than male. Further, the chance of attending HEIs is lower among SC, ST, OBC and Muslim as compared to higher castes (Table 16.1b). The occupational group which suffers most from low access to higher education is casual wage labour; their chances of attending HEIs are the lowest compared to the regular salaried and self- employed, which confirm the impact of income (Table 16.1b).

These are very insightful results which empirically confirm that despite improvement, the enrolment rates of youth from rural areas, women, SC, ST, OBC and Muslims continue to be low in HEIs as compared to high castes. The low access to higher education is both due to economic and caste/identity. Among the economic factors, low income is the main reason for low enrolment rate. Among social factors, caste, tribal and gender identities also matter. The enrolment rate of SC, ST, OBC, Muslims and women remain low because of constraints associated with their caste/ethnic/gender identity. These results imply that although there are policies for economically disadvantaged and social groups (SC/ST/OBC/women/Muslims), they have not been adequate enough to leverage their entry into HEIs on par with the economically advantaged and high-caste groups.

Relative Role of Wealth and Caste Discrimination

We have seen that low income and caste identity influence the educational attainment of students in HEIs. Besides, the low enrolment rate of the low-income persons from SC, ST, OBC and HC (high caste) groups is also different. The enrolment rate of low-income persons within each social group declines as we move from HC to OBC to SC and ST. Thus, the enrolment rate of low-income persons from the SCs, STs and OBCs tends to be lower than the low-income person of HC. This means that SC/ST/OBC with income similar to that of the HC face additional constraints related to their caste identity, in the form of discrimination in accessing higher education. In order to know impacts of income and of caste identity separately on access to education by low castes, SC and OBC and high caste, we disaggregated the impact into endowment factors (income, education and family size) and the factors related to caste identity by using a relevant econometric technique (Madheswaran and Attewall 2010).

The decomposition exercise estimates the share of endowment factors (such as income) and of caste identity in enrolment gap between SCs and high

Table 16.1a *Logit regression with income and other factors: India, 2017–18*

Details	Coefficient
Social groups (Reference: HC)	
ST	- 0.50
SC	- 0.23
OBC	- 0.05
Muslim	- 0.48
Rest	- 0.04
Head of the household education (secondary and above or not vs below secondary)	0.56
Female (ref: male)	- 0.35
Household size	- 0.03
Income group quintile (ref: Q 5: 80%–100%)	
Q1: 0–20	- 1.16
Q2: 20–40	- 0.87
Q3: 40–60	- 0.59
Q4: 60–80	- 0.37
_cons	- 1.49

Source: Based on 75th round NSS data, 2017–18; all coefficients are statistically significant at 1 per cent.

Table 16.1b *Logit regression with occupation and other factors: India, 2017–18*

Details	Coefficient
Social groups (reference: HC)	
ST	- 0.68
SC	- 0.28
OBC	- 0.13
Muslim	- 0.54
Rest	0.12
Head of the household education (secondary and above or not vs below secondary)	0.62
Female (ref: male)	- 0.38
Household size	- 0.07
Occupational (ref: regular salaried)	
Self-employed	0.02
Casual labour	- 0.49
Others	1.20
_cons	- 1.86

Source: Based on 75th round NSS data, 2017–18; all coefficients are statistically significant at 1 per cent.

Table 16.2a *Decomposition result, India, SC vs HC*

Variable	Coefficient	% Exp
Education of head of the household (secondary and above or not)	0.013142	39.6
Gender (female or male)	0.000056	0.17
Log of Monthly Per Capital Consumption Expenditure (MPCE)	0.018175	54.8
Household size	0.001716	5.2
Total explained	0.033147	100
% explained	64.1	
% discrimination	35.9	
Gap	0.051712	

Source: Based on 75th round NSS data, 2017–18.

Table 16.2b *Decomposition result, India, OBC vs HC*

Variable	Coefficient	% Exp
Education of head of household (secondary & above or not)	0.006932	29.4
Gender (female or male)	0.000534	2.3
Log of MPCE	0.014618	62.1
Household size	0.001518	6.5
Total explained	0.023538	100.0
% explained	77.1	
% discrimination	22.9	
Gap	0.030542	

Source: Based on 75th round NSS data, 2017–18.

castes for the year 2017–18 (Table 16.2a). The endowment factors explain nearly 64 per cent of the total gap between SC and HC. Further, disaggregation of the endowment factors shows that income background explains 55 per cent and education of the household head about 40 per cent of the explained gap. The household size and gender explained 0.05 per cent and 0.7 per cent of the total explained gap, respectively. The remaining 36 per cent gap in enrolment rate remained unexplained. The unexplained part is attributed to the constraints associated with caste identity of the scheduled castes in the form of discrimination in accessing higher education (Table 16.2a).

Table 16.2b shows the decomposition result for the gap in attendance rate between OBC and HC. The endowment factors explain nearly 77 per cent of the total gap between OBC and HC while the remaining 23 per cent gap is

Table 16.3a *Result of logit regression for dropout, 2017–18, India*

	Coefficient
Social groups (reference: HC)	
ST	0.48
SC	0.11
OBC	- 0.07
Muslim	0.33
Rest	- 0.56
Education of head of the household (secondary and above or not vs below secondary)	- 0.98
Female (ref: male)	0.17
Household size	- 0.08
Income group quintile (ref: Q5: 80–100)	
Q1: 0–20	0.71
Q2: 20–40	0.72
Q3: 40–60	0.61
Q4: 60–80	0.39
_cons	- 1.27

Source: Based on 75th round NSS data, 2017–18.

Table 16.3b *Result of logit regression for dropout, 2017–18, India*

	Coefficient
Social groups (reference: HC)	
ST	0.53
SC	0.09
OBC	- 0.04
Muslim	0.34
Rest	- 0.71
Education of head of the household (secondary and above or not vs below secondary)	- 1.01
Female (ref: male)	0.18
Household size	- 0.06
Occupational (ref: regular salaried)	
Self-employed	0.02
Casual labour	0.39
Others	- 0.72
Cons	- 0.93

Source: Based on 75th round NSS data, 2017–18.

Table 16.4 *Result of logit regression for attendance in private unaided HEI, 2017–18, India*

Unaided	Coefficient
Log course fee	0.781
Scholarship received	- 0.259
Constant	- 7.513

Source: Based on 75th round NSS data, 2017–2018; all coefficients are statistically significant at 1 per cent.

attributed to the caste background. Further disaggregation of the explained gap shows that income background explains 62 per cent of the total explained gap while education of the head explains 29 per cent, followed by household size (0.06 per cent) and gender (2.3 per cent).

These results capture the contemporary reality related to the disadvantage of the low castes, namely, the SCs and OBCs in accessing the higher education. Both low income and caste discrimination matter in low access to education of the SCs and OBCs. It emerged that 62 per cent of the total gap in educational attainment between SC and the HC and 77 per cent between OBC and HC is due to endowment factors, such as low income, education of head of the household and family size. However, the endowment factors matter more in case of OBC than the SC. Conversely, caste discrimination accounts for about 36 per cent of the gap between SC and HC and 23 per cent between OBC and HC. This means that caste discrimination matters more in case of the SCs than the OBCs. This also means that the SCs face additional constraints associated with their low castes identifying much greater intensity in accessing education. While the high castes face only the constraints of low income, they continue to avail the advantage of being high castes in accessing higher education.

High Dropout as Cause of Low Education Attainment

The dropout rate also reduces the onward movement of a student in higher education and results in low enrolment rate. In 2017–18, the dropout rate in education was about 17.7 per cent, which means that, about 17 students out of 100 discontinue their onward progress towards higher education.

The dropout rate is much higher among the lower-income groups – it being 22.5 per cent for the lowest income quintile (0–20 per cent) and 6 per cent for high income groups (80–100 per cent quintile) – the dropout rate for low-income group being thrice that of the high-income group. For the middle income quintiles, the dropout rate for higher education varies between 14 and 22 per cent. The disparity in dropout rate is also clearly visible for occupational groups. It is 27.5 per cent among students from casual wage labour families as

Table 16.5 *Pattern of indicators of quality of higher education, 2017–18*

	Quintile					Social groups					
	0–20	20–40	40–60	60–80	80–100	ST	SC	OBC	HC	Muslim	Total
Share in Pvt.- unaided institution (%)	20	24.5	28.8	32	37.5	23.92	29.44	32.98	27.84	27.44	30.11
Share in professional courses (%)	13.5	15.9	21.9	28.8	49.8	18.9	26.1	28.4	34	26.7	29.3
Medium of instruction English (%)	19.1	25.1	35.1	48.6	76.9	43.5	36.5	42.7	51.4	53.9	46.3
Per student expenditure in unaided institution (Rs)	11,189	13,762	16,396	25,385	50,314	19,894	19,474	25,185	44,035	28,855	29,834

Source: Based on National Sample Survey data on Household Social Consumption: Education, 2017–18.

against 12 per cent to 16 per cent for students from self-employed and regular salaried households. Thus, the dropout rate among the casual wage labour families is twice that of the regular salaried (Table A4).

Similar disparities in dropout rate are observed between the caste and tribal groups. Figures for 2017–18 show that the dropout rate is higher among the STs and the SCs at 29 per cent and 20 per cent, respectively, as compared to 15 per cent for the OBCs and 12 per cent for the HCs, and also to the national average of 17.7 per cent. Thus, the dropout rates are high for low income and casual wage labour groups, and for the SCs and the STs among the social groups (Table A4).

There are obvious reasons for high dropout among the low-income and low-caste groups, most of which pertain to financial constraints. The National Sample Survey of 2017–18 had asked a direct question to the respondents about the reasons for dropping out. Close to one fourth (22 to 23 per cent) of the SC and ST cited financial constraints, which is higher than 21 per cent cited by OBC and 17 per cent cited by HC for discontinuing higher education. The all-India average on this count is 22 per cent. Similarly, one-fourth respondents of SC attributed their dropping out to 'lack of interest' which is again higher than OBC and HC citing the same reasons (Table A5).

We use a logit regression model to estimate the impact of economic constraints and social constrains on the dropout rate. The logit model takes dropout rate as a dependent variable and gender, education of head of the household, household size, income level, occupation and caste/ethnic/religious background as independent variable. In the model where we take these factors, but exclude occupation variable (due to high correlation between income and occupation), it emerged that the chance of dropout is high for the students if they happen to be female, or from low-income group, or belong to households whose head has low education. Similarly, the chances of dropout are high for the STs, the SCs and the Muslims than for the HC and OBC (Table 16.3a).

In a variant of this model, wherein we retain all factors and replace income by occupation, it is seen that the chance of dropout is higher for students from casual wage labour households, followed by those from self-employed households as compared with those from regular salaried households. The results also confirmed the role of education of the head of the household, gender, SC, ST, Muslim identity and household size in the dropout rate. Thus, the econometric exercise confirms that the role of low income and factors related to caste identity are significant in high dropout rates among the low-income and SC and ST groups (Table 16.3b).

High Fees as Reason for Low Access to Private (Unaided) Institutions

High fee is an important reason for low educational attainment, particularly in private unaided institutions. The fee (which includes tuition fees, examination fees, development fees and other compulsory payments) is an important component of expenditure on higher education. The average per-student fee in such institutions is Rs 17,829 per year although the fee structure varies across institutions. The fee was obviously highest for the private unaided institutions (Rs 29,834) followed by private aided (Rs 23,250), and government institutions (Rs 6,912). The fee charged by private unaided institutions is about four times higher than charged by government institutions. It is also higher than private aided institutions (Table A6).

In order to estimate the impact of high fee and scholarship on access to private unaided institutions we run a logit model. The attendance in private unaided institution is a dependent variable, which takes the value 1 if the respondent is attending a private unaided institution for higher education and zero if they are attending government and private aided institutions. The likelihood of attending an unaided institution is a dependent variable with respect to independent variables, that is (log of) course fees and scholarship. The result shows that the chances of attending unaided institution are higher for students paying higher course fees. Among students, the chances of attending private unaided institution are less for low-income groups, casual wage labour, SC, ST and female, particularly those from rural areas. Conversely, the chances are higher for students from self-employed and regular salaried backgrounds, higher income groups, HC, OBC and Muslim, and those from urban areas. The co-efficient of scholarship is negative indicating less support to students through scholarships by private unaided institutions (Table 16.4).

If the economically disadvantaged students who have low access to higher education are provided financial assistance through scholarship and freeship, it will facilitate their entry into private unaided institutions. However, the situation in the case of such institutions is somewhat different. A very low proportion of students is covered by scholarship by private unaided institutions as compared to government, and private aided institutions. In private unaided institutions, about 9 per cent of students receive scholarship, compared to 17 per cent in private aided institutions and 21 per cent in government institutions. Similarly, a low proportion of low-income students receives scholarship in private unaided education institutions. Also, a low percentage of SC students is covered under scholarship by private unaided institutes as compared to ST, OBC and higher castes. Given the high fees in private unaided institutions, one would have expected more financial assistance from these institutions.

Unequal Access to Quality Education

The low-income group and SC/ST not only suffer from low enrolment rates in HEIs, but they also lag behind the high-income group and high castes in accessing quality education. Due to limitation of data, we measured the quality of education in terms of some indirect variables which include percentage of students in private unaided universities/colleges/institutions vis-a-vis government universities/colleges, size of institutions (number of students per institution), the student–teacher ratio, the share in professional courses vis-a-vis general courses, the medium of instruction (English vis-a-vis Hindi and regional language), and expenditure on education to see whether the low-income groups and SCs/STs perform similar to students from high-income groups and high-caste households with respect to these quality indicators. The following features emerged quite clearly.

(1) The private institutions in some aspects are quality-wise better than the public universities and colleges. In terms of average size and student–teacher ratio, the private institutions are better placed than government institutions. The low access of low-income group in private institutions means that their access to quality education is also low. In 2017–18, of the total students in the bottom income group, about 20 per cent were in private unaided institutions, which is lower than the 37 per cent for top income group. It varies between 24 and 32 per cent in the middle-income groups (Table A3). Unequal access is also reflected in low share of the low-income group among total students in private unaided educational institutions. In 2017–18 of the total students in private unaided institutions those from bottom income groups were 13.5 per cent, while the top income group grabbed about 50 per cent of the seats. The share of bottom income group was nearly four times less than top income groups.

(2) The average size in terms of number of students per institution and student–teacher ratio is better in private institutions as compared with government institutions. The low share of students from the low-income group background means they are lagging in access to quality education (Tables A9a and A9b).

(3) Similarly, the share of the low-income group and SC/ST in professional courses was low, compared to HC, OBC and the Muslims. The percentage share in professional courses of the two last quintiles (0–20 and 20–40) was 13.5 per cent and 15.9 per cent, respectively, compared to 50 per cent of the top income quintile (80–100). Similarly, the share of SC/ST in professional courses was 25 per cent and 19 per cent, respectively, which is much lower than the HC share of 34 per cent in professional courses (Table 16.5 and Table A7).

Instruction in the English language gives advantage to students in general courses especially professional courses. The percentage of those with English medium was 19 per cent for bottom income group, much lower than the 77 per cent among the top income group (80–100 per cent quintile). Similarly, the proportion of ST and SC students with English as medium of instruction was 43.5 and 36.5 per cent, respectively as compared to 42.7 for OBC and 51.4 per cent for high-caste students (Table 16.5 and Table A8).

(4) The average expenditure on education (which includes fees) by bottom quintile (0–20) was four times less than the top quintile group (80–100) in case of private unaided institutions. Similarly, the SC and ST students spend less than HC and OBC. The OBC and Muslim spend more than SC and ST, but less than HC (Table 16.5 and Table A6)

Thus, judged by the indicators of the quality of education in terms of share in private unaided institutions, average size, student–teacher ratio in private unaided institutions, the students' share in professional education, the medium of instruction and expenditure on education, the low-income classes and the SC and ST significantly lag behind the high-income groups, and the OBCs and HCs. They receive low quality education compared with others.

Towards a Pragmatic Policy

In his memorandum to the British government in 1928, Ambedkar had predicted that the '[p]ast may again be made to live in the present', unless the system is reformed and policies are developed to increase the access of depressed caste/class to education and the gap between them and high castes/ class is reduced (Ambedkar 1982). The way in which government policies for the depressed classes have evolved since Independence, it is clear that the (graded) inequality in higher education persists even today despite progress in educational attainment at the overall level and for all social groups including the lower-income groups. But the progress has been unequal such that it continues to maintain the graded inequality between the low and high castes despite improved attainment rate. The policy adopted since Independence has achieved limited success in breaking the stranglehold of graded inequality by bringing the lower castes/classes on par with higher castes/classes in higher education. The results for recent years, 2017–18, clearly indicate that HEI enrolment continues to be the highest for the high castes. The OBC enrolment rate is lower than that of the high castes but higher than SC, the SC's enrolment is lower than OBC but higher than ST. Thus, the enrolment rate reduces in graded manner as we move down in caste hierarchy from high castes to lower castes/tribes, retaining the dubious unique character of the caste system.

The low-income groups from various castes are also not immune to graded inequality. Although the enrolment rate is lowest for the low-income groups, their enrolment rate from high castes is high compared with their counterparts from other castes/tribes. The enrolment rate of the low-income group in each caste reduces as we move down in the caste hierarchy from higher castes to the lowest castes and tribes. Thus, the educational attainment of low-income groups from caste/tribes also differs in a graded manner for the same income group; the enrolment rate reduces in a graded manner as we move down in caste hierarchy from high castes to lowest castes/tribes. This means that lower castes face additional constraints associated with their caste/tribal identity in the form of discrimination. It implies that the caste system with graded inequality has been the most stubborn institution, which has survived for the longest period in history witnessed anywhere in the world.

The sources of graded inequality between (inter) and within (intra) caste originated both from economic and social processes. The decomposition exercise related to gaps in enrolment rate between SC and HC and between the OBC and HC shows that among the economic factors, low income (and occupation) is the main reason for poor access of SC and OBC to higher education. The result also reveals the impact of caste identity through discrimination in access to higher education, insofar as the enrolment rate of the low-income group of SC and OBC are lower than their HC counterparts. The endowment factors, namely income, explain the 64 per cent and 77 per cent gap between SC and HC, and OBC and high castes, respectively. Conversely, about 36 per cent and 23 per cent gap between SC and HC, and OBC and high caste, respectively, is explained by the constraints related to caste identity in the form of discrimination in accessing higher education. The important difference is that the extent of caste discrimination is higher for SC than OBC, which is quite obvious: the SC suffered from discrimination on account of untouchability in worse form than any other relatively lower group in the caste hierarchy. The discrimination and atrocities experienced by the SCs in accessing higher education has now been revealed by a number of studies (Deshpande 2013; Thorat 2010; Thorat, Shah and Sujata 2020; Thorat, Shyamaprasad and Srivastava 2008). Although the government has developed policies for the SCs and the OBCs to deal with their economic and caste disadvantages, the safeguards have not been adequate enough to give them equal access on par with others. They continue to suffer from extremely low ownership of income-earning capital assets that is wealth in the form agricultural land and non-farm enterprises. The Economic Census of 2013 shows that the SC's share in total wealth in the country (that include land, building, and physical and financial asset) is 7 per cent, almost three times less than their population share in the country. The average value of wealth per household was Rs 2.9 million for higher caste, Rs 1.3 million for OBC and Rs 0.6 million for SC. The average value of wealth for SC is almost six times less compared to HC and two times less compared to OBC. The land reforms have not helped the SC in acquiring land. In 2017–18, in rural areas, only 15 per cent of SC are farmers and about 41 per cent of them depend on casual labour. Considering the limitation of land reforms, that is ceiling on land holding, Ambedkar had suggested nationalization of agricultural land in 1947 as part of the proposed idea of constitutional state socialism. But that did not happen.

The SC thus continued to suffer from low income. The empirical results clearly reveal the low income and engagement in low-earning casual wage labour as a severe handicap of the SC (as well as for others) for low access to higher education. Given the structural inequalities in ownership of wealth, the government should have developed suitable educational policies to give equal access to the low-income groups from SC and ST and other groups and not let their poor economic situation come in the way of accessing higher education on par with high income and high castes. The government did not address the problem of inequality in wealth ownership – but it could have in the minimum developed policies – to ensure equal access to education and avoided the possibility of unequal impact of unequal ownership of wealth in accessing education. In the beginning, the government developed a policy of public education along with measures of financial support such as scholarship/ freeship and hostels and other measures to facilitate access of low-income and low-caste groups to higher education. But these progressive steps were not adequate for the poor to get easy access to higher education, as revealed by their low enrolment in HEIs from the 1950s to the 1970s. To make matters worse, later in the 1970s, the government instead of providing a more pro-poor thrust to the education policy, steered it in the opposite direction by roping in the costly private commercial sector in the field of higher education. As we have seen above, this has worsened the access of low-income and low-caste group to higher education and placed them in a very precarious position.

The government also neglected another structural issue, namely, of caste discrimination: it avoided developing policies to provide safeguards against caste discrimination of the SCs, STs and OBCs in accessing education. As seen above, besides income, caste discrimination has emerged as a significant factor for low enrolment of the SCs and the OBCs in HEIs, more so for the former than the latter. Recent studies reveal discrimination of the SCs and STs both at the entry level and after entry in educational institutions, which assume various forms and result in high dropout rates among them, and in extreme cases in suicides. The government completely ignored the policy of legal and other safeguards against discrimination in educational institutions.

The issue now is: how do we overcome this mess? We feel that there is much less hope for a reversal of policies in favour of the poor and marginalized groups. The idealist solution is to bring the ownership of the entire higher education sector in public and private philanthropic institutional mode with which we began in the early 1950s following the example of several European countries. However, the political economy of higher education in which the private commercial sector is owned by those in power or their allies will make the reversal very difficult, if not impossible. Even the states where socialist governments have been in power for several decades could not avoid the political compulsion of privatization of higher education. Therefore, political constraints are too strong to reverse the present policy. The private sector in higher education now occupies about 40 per cent of universities and 64 per cent of colleges and stand-alone educational institutions. While we continue to press for public and private philanthropic sectors in education, we need to work for a pragmatic and feasible policy to give space to the poor and needy in the present system. The possible strategy which we need to push hard is to make the higher education, both public and private, affordable to those who cannot afford it. This could be done through regulation of fees and adequate financial support in the form of scholarships/freeships, subsidized hostels, interest-free easy loans and other pro-poor measures. Besides, policy to overcome discrimination in educational institutions is also required through legal and other safeguards. But this also will require deep commitment on behalf of the political party in power.

Appendix

Table A1a *Private and government sector in institutions and enrolment*

	Institution		Enrolment	
Year	2011–2012	2019–2020	2011–2012	2019–2020
Universities				
All private	28.6	38	13.3	23.4
Government	71.4	61	86.7	76.6
Colleges				
Private aided	15.5	13.3	23.8	21.3
Private unaided	57.1	64.8	38	44.9
Government	27.4	21.9	38.2	33.8
Stand-alone Institutions				
Private aided	10.4	9.2	10.1	8.6
Private unaided	68.3	66.3	59.9	58.6
Government	21.3	24.5	30	32.8

Source: All India Survey on Higher Education, 2011–12 and 2019–20.

Table A1b *Share of enrolment in higher education by types of institutions*

	Private	Government	Total
1995	7.1	92.9	100
2007	22.6	77.4	100
2017	30.6	69.4	100

Source: Based on different rounds – 52nd, 64th and 75th round for the years 1995, 2007 and 2017–18 respectively – of National Sample Survey on Education.

Table A2 *GAR by income, occupational and social groups, 2017–18*, in per cent

Social Group	ST	SC	OBC	HC	Muslim	Buddhist	Total
Quintile: 0–20 (%)	7.0	12.3	16.9	24.6	7.3	25.9	13.4
Quintile 2: 20–40 (%)	12.8	17.3	20.7	30.0	11.0	20.4	18.8
Quintile 3: 40–60 (%)	16.9	22.7	29.4	34.3	15.9	37.4	25.7
Quintile 4: 60–80 (%)	24.6	32.4	38.0	40.0	27.6	19.4	35.3
Quintile 5: 80–100 (%)	63.4	50.2	50.0	59.1	38.7	84.0	53.1
Self-employed (SE)	13.1	21.9	27.6	36.8	16.2	33.9	25.6
Regular salaried	28.2	28.7	36.3	47	26.5	41.6	36.4
Casual wage labour (CL)	7.3	15.3	17.1	20	8.1	21.3	14.3
Total	15.8	21.2	28.2	40.7	16.6	30.9	26.3

Source: Based on 75th round National Sample Survey data on Household Social Consumption: Education, 2017–18.

Table A3 *Share of institutions by income and social group, 2017–18*

Income Group Quintile	Govt.	Aided	Unaided	Total
Row %				
Q1: 0–20	53.5	26.4	20	100
Q2:20–40	52.3	23	24.5	100
Q3:40–60	49.1	21.6	28.8	100
Q4:60–80	44.1	23.9	32	100
Q5:80–100	35.5	26.6	37.5	100
Total	45.2	24.4	30.1	100
Col %				
Q1:0–20	16.1	14.7	9.0	13.6
Q2:20–40	18.5	15.0	13.0	16.0
Q3:40–60	21.5	17.5	18.9	19.8
Q4:60–80	21.4	21.4	23.3	21.9
Q5:80–100	22.6	31.4	35.9	28.8
Total	100	100	100	100
ST	46.9	27.9	23.9	100
SC	46.1	24.3	29.4	100
HOBC*	43.8	23.0	33.0	100
HHC**	45.0	26.8	27.8	100
Muslim	54.1	18.2	27.4	100
Total	45.2	24.4	30.1	100

Notes: * Higher Other Backward Castes; ** Higher Castes and Classes.
Source: Based on 75th round National Sample Survey data on Household Social Consumption: Education, 2017–18.

Table **A4** *Dropout by income and social groups, 2017–18*

Income quintiles	Drop out
Q1: 0–20	22.3
Q2: 20–40	21.8
Q3: 40–60	18.7
Q4: 60–80	14.5
Q5: 80–100	6.3
ST	29
SC	20.4
OBC	14.8
HC	12.3
Muslim	22.7
Buddhists	27.5
Total	17.7

Source: Based on 75th round National Sample Survey data on Household Social Consumption: Education, 2017–18.

Table **A5** *Reasons for dropout by social group, 2017–18*

Reasons for never enrolling	ST	SC	OBC	HC	Muslim	Buddhist	Total
Not interested in education	21.9	23.2	18.9	15.2	19	15.9	19.6
Financial constraints	23	24.1	20.9	17.3	25.4	23	22
Engaged in domestic activities	15.7	15.1	16.7	14.8	14.8	11.3	15.6
Engaged in economic activities	15	16.2	19.7	19.4	16.4	14.1	17.9
Others	24.5	21.5	23.8	33.3	24.5	35.7	24.9
Total	100	100	100	100	100	100	100

Source: Based on 75th round National Sample Survey data on Household Social Consumption: Education, 2017–18.

Table A6 *Fee in higher education by type of institution and average per student expenditure by social group, 2017–18*, in rupees

Social group	Government	Aided	Unaided	Not known	Total
ST	4,730	11,334	19,894	5,436	10,208
SC	4,748	14,710	19,474	16,550	11,520
OBC	6,312	20,479	25,185	18,461	15,823
HC	9,277	34,931	44,035	22,659	25,879
Muslim	6,076	18,079	28,855	10,543	14,521
Buddhist	5,596	7,762	17,582	24,753	8,682
Total	6,912	23,250	29,834	16,286	17,829

Source: Based on 75th round National Sample Survey data on Household Social Consumption: Education, 2017–18.

Table A7 *Share of students by social groups in general and professional courses in HEIs*

Income group (quintile)	General	Professional	Total
0–20	86.5	13.5	100
20–40	84.1	15.9	100
40–60	78.1	21.9	100
60–80	71.2	28.8	100
80–100	50.2	49.8	100
ST	81.1	18.9	100
SC	73.9	26.1	100
OBC	71.6	28.4	100
HC	66	34	100
Muslim	73.4	26.7	100
Buddhist	57.8	42.2	100
Total	70.7	29.3	100

Source: Based on 75th round National Sample Survey data on Household Social Consumption: Education, 2017–18.

Table A8 *Medium of instruction of students in HEIs*, in per cent

Income group quintile	Hindi	English	Others	Total
Q1: 0–20	62.4	19.1	18.5	100
Q2: 20–40	52.8	25.1	22.1	100
Q3: 40–60	41.1	35.1	23.8	100
Q4: 60–80	31.2	48.6	20.3	100
Q5: 80–100	15.1	76.9	8	100
ST	36.4	43.5	20.2	100
SC	39.9	36.5	23.7	100
OBC	41.8	42.7	15.4	100
HC	32.7	51.4	16	100
Muslim	27	53.9	19.1	100
Buddhist	1.1	30.5	68.5	100
Total	36.2	46.3	17.5	100

Source: Based on 75th round National Sample Survey data on Household Social Consumption: Education, 2017–18.

Table A9a *Pupil–teacher ratio in universities by types, 2019–20*

University	Pupil–teacher ratio
Central	21.24
State public university	22.01
State private university	10.33
Deemed university government	4.84
Deemed university government aided	8.06
Deemed university private	8.90
Institute of national importance	8.23
Institute under state legislature	2.45
Central open universities	1504.3
State open universities	826.87
State private open university	78.28
Total	20.38

Source: All India Survey on Higher Education, 2019–20.

Table A9b *Pupil–teacher ratio in colleges by types, 2019–20*

	Pupil–teacher ratio
Central government	7.54
State government	18.77
Local body	18.75
University	23.01
Private aided	17.85
Private unaided	9.97
Total	13.42

Source: All India Survey on Higher Education, 2019–20.

This essay was originally published under the same title in *The Indian Economic Journal*, vol. 71, no. 1, 2023, pp. 256–75.

Note
[1] A Dalit caste, which was then regarded as depressed castes.

References

Ambedkar, B.R. (1982), 'Statement Concerning the State of Education of the Depressed Classes in Bombay Presidency', in *B.R. Ambedkar: Writings Speeches*, vol. 5, Education Department, Government of Maharashtra.

——— (1987), 'The Hindu Social Order: Its Essential Features', in *B.R. Ambedkar: Writings and Speeches*, vol. 3. Higher Education Department, Government of Maharashtra.

Buhler, G. (1886), *The Laws of Manu*, Delhi: Motilal Banarsidass.

Deshpande, S. (2013), 'Towards a Biography of the General Category: Caste and Castelessness', *Economic and Political Weekly*, vol. 48, no. 15, pp. 32–39.

Jha, V. (2018), *Candala: Untouchability and Caste in Early India*, Delhi: Primus Books.

Madheswaran, S. and P. Attewall (2010), 'Wage and Job Discrimination in the Indian Urban Labour Market', in S. Thorat and K.S. Newman, eds, *Blocked by Caste: Economic Discrimination in Modern India*, New Delhi: Oxford University Press.

Moosvi, S. (2011), 'The Medieval State and Caste', *Social Scientist*, nol. 39, nos 7–8, pp. 3–22.

Sharma, R.S. (1958), *Shudra in Ancient India: A Survey of the Position of the Lower Order Down to Circa AD 500*, Delhi: Motilal Banarsidass.

Thorat, S., K.M. Shyamaprasad and R.K. Srivastava (2008), 'Report of the Committee to Enquire into the Allegation of Differential Treatment of SC/ST Students', in All India Institute of Medical Sciences, Delhi.

Thorat, S. (2010), 'Emerging Issues in Higher Education in India', in *Higher Education in India: Issue Related to Expansion, Inclusiveness, Quality, Relevance and Financing* (Report), University Grant Commission, New Delhi.

Thorat, S. and K.S. Newman, eds (2010), *Blocked by Caste: Economic Discrimination in Modern India*, New Delhi: Oxford University Press.

Thorat, S. and K. Khan (2018), 'Private Sector and Equity in Higher Education: Challenges of Growing Unequal Access', in N.V. Varghese, N.S. Sabharwal and C.M. Malish, eds, *India Higher Education Report 2016: Equity*, Delhi: Sage Publications.

Thorat, S., G. Shah and K. Sujatha (2020), *The Educational Status of Scheduled Castes*, Delhi: Rawat Publications.

Tilak, J.B.G. (2004), 'Public Subsidies in Education in India', special article, *Economic and Political Weekly*, vol. 39, no. 4, pp. 343–59.

——— (2005), 'Higher Education in "Trishanku": Hanging Between State and Market', *Economic and Political Weekly*, vol. 40, no. 37, pp. 4029–32.

Varghese, N.V., G. Malik and S. Thorat (2017), 'Higher Education Policy in India: Emerging Issues and Approaches', in N.V. Varghese and G. Malik, eds, *India Higher Education Report 2015*, Delhi: Routledge.

17

Human Resource Development in Contemporary Indian Universities and Colleges

Sudhanshu Bhushan

Introduction

Human resource development (HRD) in contemporary Indian universities and colleges has gained momentum through the technology route. The role of technology in human resource development can be conceptualized in two important ways. In managerial terms, technology is aimed at improving efficiency by providing information and utilizing information to minimize loss of time in governance and the teaching–learning process. Training is an essential component of technological integration which helps human resources to understand the use of technology to gather and disseminate information. This may be called a technological perspective. The role of the market is acknowledged to provide various platforms through which information and communication can be quickly channelized by connecting both the producers and consumers of information. There are supposed to be no barriers as technology is assumed to be equally accessed by the providers and users of information. Technology integration is considered neutral to the influences of socioeconomic and political factors.

Critical to the technological perspective, the role of technology in human resource development is not considered to be free from the influences of socioeconomic and political factors (Pal 2003). There are barriers to the use of technology and the market process emerges as one such barrier. It has asymmetric effects both on the producers and the consumers of the information as access to the market is limited to the privileged few. Technology, amongst other features, also has exclusionary influence on human resource development. The efficiency-centric argument fails to justify technology irrespective of considerations concerning inclusion. The second perspective may be critical to an efficiency-centric understanding of technology in the development process. Amidst these contestations, there is a rationale to examine the role of technology guided by an informed understanding of real situations.

Within an efficiency–centric administrator's perspective, human resource refers to employees such as teachers and administrators and the role of technology in increasing the efficiency of teachers and administrators may be assessed. However, from the perspective of the Ministry of Education, human resources also include students. The role of technology in the development of teachers, students and administrators is too large an issue as purposes vary and may even be conflicting. For example, an administrator's purpose may be to guide and supervise teaching, research and other functions efficiently rendered by a teacher. Hence, technology has a strategic role for administrators. The purpose of technology for teachers and students are also important in the process of knowledge generation and dissemination. Autonomy has intrinsic value for teachers. Hence two value goals – efficiency control and autonomy of teachers – may conflict. The substantive question of inquiry is, whether technology promotes efficiency and facilitates freedom neutrally or whether technology is an instrument of restricting freedom and the effect of technology can be assessed in a given socio-political configuration.

Against the background of the two perspectives noted above, I would like to raise a much broader question relating to HRD and technology. A broader question pertains to technology and its practice in teaching and research – including teachers and students. Attempting an answer to this question is important as it tells us how the practice of technology impacts teachers and students. It will also give us an answer to the question: what is the motive of technology? How is it conducive to creating cultural conditions in the universities such that the practice of technology for development can take place? It will also give us the clue to understand the reason for obstructing the progress of the use of technology for development

The scope of the paper is restricted to the role of technology in human resource development in the higher education sector, and specific examples are cited from higher education scenarios. The efficiency perspective is the cornerstone of the bureaucratic approach. It may be noted that the former perspective is in favour of the National Education Policy 2020 (NEP 2020), which many elite and private institutions also support. The discourse on technological determinism is also supported by those who believe in the privatization and marketization of higher education. As against this, the critical perspective looks at the reality judged from the practices of higher education. Technology in a limited sense supports efficiency. However, along with market, technology is an instrument of control and subordination in the broader context. The efficiency-centric conception of technology supports the new managerialism that infringes freedom in the name of efficiency, outcomes and accountability. (Winner 1977, 1980)

Science and its practice, in terms of technology, were the bases of rationalization. Over the last century, philosophers of science, notwithstanding its usefulness in understanding modern ways of life, have questioned the value neutrality of scientific theories. For example, Kuhn and Schlegel (1963) questioned the certainty and linearity of the progress of science. On the other hand, philosophers of technology (Jacques Elull, Heidegger and others) as well as sociologists of technology (Winner, Latour, etc.) have challenged the value neutrality of technology, pointing out the ways within which social values are encoded within technology.[1]

I have, in the essay, made use of the idea of Weber on the rationalization of science and the concept of disenchantment. Weber means to say that the discovery process is full of excitement. However, the scientific investigation demystifies the world which results in disenchantment. I have found the idea useful to explore technological rationality and how it becomes regulating, depriving the freedom of an individual. In the approach to human resource development in universities and colleges, technological rationality may become controlling and may disrupt the progress of knowledge killing the passion of teaching and research. Hence there are two points to be noted before the arguments in the essay are understood. One, science and technology are not conflated. However, both have elements of rationalization. Second, the idea of Weber's conception of science and demystification of the world leading to disenchantment is important. The author utilizes the idea to argue that technology, in a similar manner, may develop a tendency to become dominating and kill the passion of an individual. Hence, the use of technology in human resource development should, at best, be selective.

The organization of the essay is as follows. We present Weber's conception of disenchantment with increasing rationalization of science and argue that in educational administration or in knowledge generation and dissemination, technological rationalization has its limits in actual practice. Weber's value neutrality scientific project is, however, contested by Marcuse, a leading member of the Frankfurt school. Marcuse argued that an efficiency-centric technology project in the modern world is guided by domination and control. Habermas, another influential member of the Frankfurt School, argues that technological domination can be countered with communication among scientists, politicians and bureaucrats, the different stakeholders in society. However, how to build effective communication is indeed problematic. For example, the market, an ally of technology, perpetuates domination. The above perspective developed in the essay is used to examine the role of technology in educational development. NEP 2020 has high claims of benefits from technology in terms of rational, informational perspective; however, it does not explore deeply the limits of technology in the knowledge generation process which is a project embedded in economic, social and cultural context. Lastly, the author looks at the present official discourse on technology guided by a rational perspective which is information-centered and promotes commodification and standardization. On the other hand, technology is seen as a discourse that views it as a state apparatus of control. This perspective sees technology as promoting surveillance. The rhetoric is built to propagate a certain point of view that justifies it.

Further, it also restricts freedom of academia and thrusts more accountabilities.

Science and Disenchantment in Weber and its Confirmation in Technological Application

Max Weber in the lecture on 'Science as Vocation' delivered at Munich University in 1918 raises important points. First, he talks about the increasing role of science and its application towards modernization. He says scientific knowledge is boundless: 'Scientific work is chained to the course of progress. . . . Every scientific "fulfillment" raises new "questions"; it asks to be "surpassed" and outdated' (Weber 1919, p. 7). Progress of scientific knowledge has a purely practical purpose 'to orient our practical activities to the expectation that scientific experience places at our disposal' (ibid., p. 8). Second, Weber immediately negates the intellectualization and rationalization due to science. He notes that it means, there is nothing mysterious, nothing incalculable, 'one can, in principle, master all things. . . . This means the world is disenchanted' (ibid.). Even if such calculable knowledge exists that may have utilitarian value, he asks, does it provide an answer to the conditions under which we live?[2] It does not. Life conditions are varied, illusory and mysterious. The answer to the meaning of life cannot thus be provided by mere intellectualization and rationalities due to science. Third, he asks, what then is the message for the teachers of science when 'intellectual constructions of science constitute an unreal realm of artificial abstractions'? (ibid., p. 9) He says the vocation of science has to be looked at within the total life of humanity. He answers that classroom delivery is the stating and analysing of facts in a value-neutral manner. This presents students with the capacity to judge the facts and use them to search for an answer to the true meaning of life in a world that is illusory and mysterious, a large part of which is incalculable. However, the value neutrality that a teacher should maintain goes alongside the *beruf* (strange intoxication, a passion), *erlebnis* (experience) and *eingebung* (inspiration) in so far as the professional calling of a teacher is concerned. Hence, the message is that there are non-rational elements that keep a teacher enchanted through the magical influence of knowledge (Weisz 2020; Schroeder 1995).

How technology (rationality as value) is disenchanting and magic (non-rationality leading to conflict of values) is enchanting, applying Weber's perspective needs some elaboration. Technology, particularly ICT, is helpful to educational administrators in providing all sorts of information. There may be different institutions that collect information on a periodic interval and place them before educational administrators. Information is partly or wholly reviewed to further inform the consumers of education to decide concerning the choice of institution, course and programme. Based on the consumer's choice, a signal is conveyed to the providers of education to adjust to the needs of consumers. Technology helps to provide information in the fastest possible ways to reach the producers and consumers. The rational and impersonal ways of communication support bureaucrats whose decision-making power is enhanced as technology rationally does everything. Technology, for example, enables fast grading and ranking – which institutions stand where in the hierarchy. Through signalling mechanisms, institutions, teachers and students respond. Educational bureaucrats' job is done through signalling where the onus to respond falls back upon educational institutions and teachers working in those institutions. Educational administrative space leads to disenchantment as everything in decision-making is rational, calculable, fast and efficient which is communicated to all stakeholders of education. Administration is always driven by the demands of efficiency. If decision-making in educational administration is fully calculable and efficiently driven, then, from the Weberian perspective, technology and bureaucracy or, we may say, technocratic administration leads to disenchantment meaning that administration is efficiency-centric and does not solve the problems of administration that arise on account of non-rational behaviour of people. There are many cases of educational administration relating to recruitment and promotion of teachers, standards of teaching and research, and affiliation of colleges where decision-making is difficult within the complex system of rules that is to be applied uniformly in value conflict situations. Disputes take place concerning the applicability of rules. Many decisions may need contextual consideration and application of the mind grounded in practical rationality. Administrative decisions may be subject to value conflicts, say, between efficiency and equity where technology or rule, i.e. rationality, may not be of great help in dictating decisions.

We can distinguish two aspects of the pursuit of technology by academics. The first relates to the collection of heaps of information. Information must reach the desk of scholars as fast as it can. The collection of information may be free and it may involve cost as well. Technology may help in the process of collection of information efficiently and rational utilization of means enhances the efficiency by reducing time. The second relates to the process of converting the information into knowledge – scientific knowledge. Can the second aspect be subjected to rationalization? The pursuit of science certainly follows a scientific method. However, the construction of knowledge depends on various aspects which cannot be limited to rational calculation. The *beruf, erlebnis* and *eingebung*, Weber noted, are important considerations in knowledge generation. Technology cannot be a substitute for this process and cannot help in generating knowledge from information. Beyond technological rationality, there is a realm of normative or cultural sphere of the academic profession where knowledge flourishes. The normative realm is one of freedom, cooperation, reflection, questioning, refuting, breaking tradition and so on. Hence, rationality driven by technology is of help in the efficient use of means in the collection of information. It is of use also in the deployment of scientific methods in empirical sciences to prove or disprove the hypothesis. However, developing theoretical knowledge requires much more than this.

The normative and cultural considerations are important for knowledge where technology is of little use. This is the realm of magic, enchantment, norm and culture that helps in knowledge building. Weber notes 'an inner devotion', 'intuitions', 'imagination', 'hard work', 'enthusiasm', 'fate' – the realm of the non-rational, that constitutes ingredients of knowledge (Weber 1919).

Dissemination of knowledge is another important activity of educational institutions and dissemination, quite often, goes along with knowledge generation. Teaching and learning are subjected to the process of rationalization through the application of technology. Teaching methods as well as the application of technology in an online mode are encouraged. Various online learning management systems and platforms are being incorporated into the educational process. It helps in the administration and efficient management of the information concerning delivery and other functions such as documentation and tracking the progress of teaching and learning. Massive Open Online Courses (MOOCs) and virtual class platforms are encouraged. Assessment of the learning of students through various apps has been developed. The advancement of technology in teaching-learning is made possible through artificial intelligence and machine learning. It is said to further speed up the processing of information based on human behaviour and technically reach anywhere in the world. However, research shows that human behaviour guided by emotions and experience cannot be captured by artificial intelligence (Sanzogni, Guzman and Busch 2017). The need for practical understanding remains at the core of teaching and learning which cannot be taught through artificial intelligence. Hence, it may be said that there are two elements of the teaching–learning process. First is the rational element which can be managed with the help of technology to yield efficiency. Dominantly, this element of teaching–learning is increasingly put into practice and this is marginalizing the second element of teaching–learning. The second element is the emotional component of learning; emotional components such as communication, confidence, practicality, experience, responsibility, peer development, leadership, teamwork, manner, physical fitness, creativity, applied knowledge, etiquette, cooperation and talent were regarded as important (Bhushan 2019). These components can be fostered in a social context in interaction with teachers, students and peer (social) groups. The former leads to teaching–learning as a disenchanted activity guided by pure calculation and the latter an enchanted activity as reflectivity assumes importance. The meaning of education is actualized in the latter and not in the former. Teaching and learning is a social practice amidst diverse learners. The substantive role of academics in the production and dissemination of knowledge, given the efficiency-centric cage of technology, exists in the enchanting sphere. In this sense, there does exist the relative freedom of academics as well as administrators, which technology should not take away from them.

Education is a subsystem of economic modernization and cannot be immune from the larger process of development guided by bureaucracy working as the agency of direct state apparatus. The growing use of technology in education supports bureaucracy in modernization. In this, the role of technology and disenchantment leading to the loss of meaning can be summarized from the perspective of Weber as follows:

(1) In educational administration, technological rationality supports bureaucracy in enhancing the efficiency of the decision-making process. It frees bureaucracy from making decisions as technology provides information-centric signals to the users and providers of education to respond. This is considered useful as it is said to be value-free administration. It has an economic rationale in terms of saving the cost of administration. However, administration engineered by technology also leads to disenchantment as the administration is reduced to a simple calculation. Educational administration is, however, a complex process that is the interplay of power, politics, ideology and interests which are non-calculable and not value-neutral. Non-rational elements are problems of educational administration. Administrators need to use practical insights and information-based technology cannot be a substitute for it, although is important in helping decisions.

(2) The production of scientific knowledge by teachers and researchers needs information that is further subject to processing to generate knowledge. Technology helps to gather information and further supports research methods in experimentation and analysis of large data. This part of knowledge generation is rule-driven and calculable. This is the source of disenchantment as this is very mechanical. The production of knowledge cannot be guaranteed by simply following the right procedure. It is an insightful exercise. Intuition, reflection, hard work, imagination, experience and luck are important ingredients and again technology cannot be a substitute for this.

(3) Dissemination of knowledge, contained in teaching and learning, has been subjected to heavy doses of technology through online learning where learning management platforms and apps for assessment are used to record and process information. Teaching as much as learning is developing emotional components and culturally shaped. Technology cannot be a substitute for this.

Technology has been creating more and more disenchantment[3] in education and squeezing space for a meaningful social process for societal purposes. The result: 'estrangement and reification of man under industrial capitalism' (Maley 2004, p. 78).

Technology and Domination

Weber, following an idealist framework, noted that science is neutral and value-free. Science much as technology has its rational instrumental purpose in the selection of means to achieve ends and, therefore, serves an efficiency-centric role. However, Weber noted that it is the application of science in capitalist reproduction that leads to disenchantment. Marcuse, an early member of the Frankfurt School, noted that science is not value-neutral and that modern natural as well as human sciences view nature as well as humans as objects to be manipulated and controlled. This means domination is a possibility in both natural as well as human spheres. The modern period, in particular, is characterized by the domination of science over man and the domination of man over man, although there is a possibility of alternative science that may be manipulated to end domination (Lancaster University, undated). Marcuse writes: 'Domination now generates a higher rationality – that of a society which sustains its hierarchic structure while exploiting ever more efficiently the natural and mental resources, and distributing the benefits of this exploitation on an ever-larger scale' (Marcuse 2013, pp. 147–48). Marcuse notes the perpetuation of domination in political and cultural spheres.

> The scientific method which led to the ever-more-effective domination of nature thus came to provide the pure concepts as well as the instrumentalities for the ever-more-effective domination of man by man through the domination of nature. Theoretical reason, remaining pure and neutral, entered into the service of practical reason. The merger proved beneficial to both. Today, domination perpetuates and extends itself not only through technology but *as* technology, and the latter provides the great legitimation of the expanding political power, which absorbs all spheres of culture. (Ibid., p. 162)

The logic of domination is presented through the high efficiency that technology makes possible. Domination itself is rational as it enhances the capacity of the system to produce more. Marcuse can point out the limit of the Enlightenment project by pointing out the logic of domination that technological rationality brings forth. Domination is not only legitimized but is extended in all spheres. Technology is not only a means to an end, as Weber understood. It becomes an end and humans become the means in a hierarchized world. This, in other words, leads to the rationalization of 'unfreedom' and the technical impossibility of autonomous man. Technology creates the possibility of a 'one-dimensional man' in western society as technology mitigates the possibility of protest; it creates uncritical mass consciousness.[4]

Marcuse's somewhat deterministic model of technology as domination and repression, amidst its vast potential for growth, is contested by Habermas. Habermas opposes Marcuse's point that modern science and technology are historically specific to the modern period dating back to the eighteenth and the nineteenth centuries. Habermas presents a reformulation of Weber's rationalization in 'Technology and Science as Ideology' (Habermas 1971c) Habermas makes a distinction between 'work' and 'interaction'. Rationality applied to work is instrumental whereas rationality applied to interaction is communicative. The former belongs to the realm of nature and the latter to persons. Habermas notes that '[t]he rationality of language games, associated with communicative action, is confronted at the threshold of the modern period with the rationality of means–end relations, associated with instrumental and strategic action' (ibid., p. 96). The confrontation leads to the demise of traditional society and the rise of a new legitimation of domination over communicative rationality. In 'Technical Progress and Social Life World', Habermas notes that in modern times, science 'has estranged itself from humanistic culture' (Habermas 1971c, p. 55) and 'theories can become technical power while remaining unpractical, that is, without being expressly oriented to the interaction of a community of human beings' (ibid., p. 532). Further, Habermas notes a disconnect of technology and democracy as well. The result is that consensus through reflections on science in interactions is lacking. How can then the technical power be controlled in a democratic process? Habermas insists on the need for mediation between technical progress and the conduct of life. All pervasive domination of science and technology becomes the ideology of the mass, corporate world, bureaucrats, politicians, and the common man. It gives the appearance that it is the only source of knowledge. This leads to the colonization of life world by instrumental reason. Habermas, in opposition to Marcuse, notes that science and technology is not necessarily dominating, rather, it is the way we use technology to interact with society. The way forward for Habermas is a 'politically effective discussion that rationally brings the social potential constituted by technical knowledge and ability into a defined and controlled relation to our practical knowledge and will' (ibid., p. 61).

In the article 'Scientization of Politics/Public Opinion', Habermas briefly spells out the process of communication between the bureaucratic agency and scientists: 'The practical questions need to be translated into scientific questions and the translation of scientific information back into the answers of practical questions' (Habermas and Shapiro 1971b, p. 70) be made. The answer to practical questions 'in turn be translated back into the totality of historical situations in which it has a practical consequence' (ibid., p. 72). Habermas notes that the 'transposition of science into political process' (ibid.) is a dialectical one. Habermas also warns that if the rationality of technical progress intrudes unprepared into 'existing forms of life conduct' (ibid., p. 73) the confrontation between technical progress and traditional value system is bound to take place. Hence, through the communicative process, technology's fit in the society needs to be built by taking into account the need and normative order of the society. The logic of scientific technical progress should not dictate the development of the social system but rather be determined through communicative rationality.

Thus, an answer to Marcuse's domination hypothesis is a politics of deliberation with the people which is free from domination. However, the big question confronting this is, under what real conditions the ideal of communicative rationality which is free from domination be created. If it is not possible to do so in the real world then Habermas's solution is also a utopia.[5]

Technology and Market

A necessary precondition of harmony between technology and society is communicative rationality which is free from domination, Habermas argues. Despite providing the solution for creating a balance by deepening deliberative democracy and strengthening the communication between scientists, politicians, bureaucrats and the people, the influence of the market cannot be ruled out as it is a market that mediates strongly in the relationship between man and nature. If technology is non-neutral, it is also because the market impacts society differently. Hence, we cannot take our attention away from the market in judging the effect of technology.

In recent studies, the technology–society relation is viewed, not in terms of whether technology shapes society or society shapes technology. A technology discourse approach is adopted: 'Technology discourse has come to play a central role in the legitimation of a techno-political order, i.e., a political order that is legitimated by technology and techniques' (Fisher 2010, p. 231). Fisher notes that, as claimed by Harvey (2005) the post-Fordist society is appropriately dominated by a political culture of neoliberalism. 'Information technology is the most powerful symbolic weapon in the arsenal of market populism' (Frank 2000, p. 57). There is a vast literature that supports the point that digital discourse favours the free market (Aune 2001; Robins and Webster 1999). Digital discourse shows the dynamics of late capitalism where the power of capital is strengthened at the cost of labour. Fisher shows how network technology gives legitimation to a new ideology of the market as an agent of economic change.

Rational Perspective of Technology in Policy

The proponents of the new discourse on educational technology claim that technology improves efficiency by reducing the time and cost of information which is the basis of making rational decisions in educational planning and administration. In this discourse, the quality of education is sometimes synonymous with efficiency. The argument is that a blended approach to learning, flexible learning, outcome-based learning, MOOCS and assessments based on apps help to achieve effective learning output. Technology also has claimed that it supports inclusion as it can scale up the delivery of lectures to the students. It can reach anywhere in the world and the best quality lectures can be accessed by the students at affordable rates. Technology claims, on the one hand, to enhance access, equity and quality of education, and increase efficiency, effectiveness, transparency and accountability, on the other. Thus, we note that social and political legitimation of technology in the name of efficiency, access, equity, quality and excellence takes place. On the other hand, technology discourse promotes the market in education which contradicts the former claim of equity and quality.

Scanning through the NEP 2020, we observe the ambivalence found in the claim for technology and educational development. NEP 2020 envisages an apex national-level institution, the National Educational Technology Forum (NETF), to support the process of human resource development. The forum shall provide evidence-based advice to the government, build intellectual and institutional capacities, and articulate new directions for research and innovation in educational technology. It is further noted that 'NETF will maintain a regular inflow of authentic data from multiple sources including educational technology innovators and practitioners and will engage with a diverse set of researchers to analyse the data.' (GoI 2020, p. 57) Technology-based education platforms, such as DIKSHA/SWAYAM will host e-contents to be used in teaching–learning processes. For the various areas of human resource development, educational software of a rich variety shall be developed in all major Indian languages. This is said to provide access to a wide range of users, students as well as teachers, in the remotest areas where technological connectivity shall be ensured under the 'Digital India Campaign', a programme of the Government of India. Further, it is noted that 'tech-savvy teachers and entrepreneurs including student entrepreneurs' (ibid. p. 56) shall be the key to technology use and integration. There is a special mention of future technologies such as artificial intelligence and 3D/7D Virtual Reality. Future technology is called disruptive as it may disrupt the processes of human resource development by changing the contours of teaching and learning, planning and governance of education. Therefore, this may require new ways of repositioning teachers and administrators in managing future higher education scenarios. While there are dangers of this disruption, there are said to be advantages in terms of reduced cost, higher efficiency and high scale of delivery. Hence NEP 2020 notes the ways of dealing with initiating the use of artificial intelligence using research to be promoted by the National Research Foundation, an apex research foundation envisaged to promote research in India. All higher education institutions are said to raise awareness, create instructional materials, teach, research and develop skills in future technologies. Content creation, digital repositories, digital infrastructure, online teaching platforms and tools, virtual labs, training, online assessment, blended modes of learning and laying down standards are some of the key recommendations of NEP 2020 for human resource development in higher education. The specific areas of human resource development through technology are teacher preparation, professional development, teaching-learning, evaluation, educational planning and educational management including processes related to admissions and attendance (GoI 2020, p. 57).

Discourse on Technology

It is important to note that the state negotiates with the people by creating a discourse that technology is people-friendly. NEP creates a discourse to create political legitimacy in favour of technology. Discourse is information-efficiency centric. It is efficiency in information that creates possibilities for scaling up and thereby, increasing access and equity. It is efficiency that is equated with quality and excellence in teaching, learning and research as it allows flexibility in learning, greater choice for students and resources to teachers. This is said to optimize the outcome for learners. Technology is mediated through the market and it is claimed that the market promotes efficiency. Hence, technology discourse centered on efficiency also promotes the market. Efficiency is celebrated in the official discourse on technology through the National Education Policy. It is important to note that discourse is initiated by the agencies and institutions that are publicly funded as well as private stakeholders of education. In return, the former wins the support of the state, and the latter reaps profit in providing direct and indirect education services. Direct education services help to reduce costs by invoking efficiency in the production and dissemination of knowledge. Indirect education service refers to the sale of apps, learning management platforms, etc. An important point to note is that discourse on technology is information-centric. It has a claim to enhance access, equity and quality, and it supports the market process. This discourse has, therefore, three important features: information-centeredness, commodification and standardization.

Information Centredness

The collection and dissemination of information is an essential feature of the discourse on technology in education. UDISE+ (The Unified District Information System for Education Plus) captures information on schools, teachers and students in school education. The All India Survey on Higher Education collects information on higher education institutions. The entire system is now online and has been collecting data in real time. DIKSHA (Digital Infrastructure of Knowledge Sharing) platform offers teachers, students and parents engaging learning material relevant to the prescribed school curriculum. The Information and Library Network (INFLIBNET) Centre is involved in modernizing university libraries in India using state-of-the-art technologies for the optimum utilization of information. The National Testing Agency (NTA) administers efficient, transparent, fair and international-level assessments. The Annual Refresher Programme in Teaching offers online courses for the professional development of teachers. The National Academic Depository is yet another technological innovation. It is an online storehouse of all academic awards. UGC Regulations for Online Programmes, 2018 permits certificate, diploma, and degree programmes for eligible institutions. Online learning shall follow a quadrant approach which shall consist of (i) e-tutorial: video and audio contents, animation, simulations, virtual labs; (ii) e-content that shall contain PDFs or e-books or illustration, video demonstrations, documents and interactive simulations; (iii) web resources, that shall contain related links, open content on Internet, case studies, historical development of a subject, articles; (iv) self-assessment, that shall contain MCQ, problems, quizzes, assignments and solutions, discussion forum topics and setting up the FAQ, clarifications on general misconceptions. A snapshot of education technology initiatives of the Ministry of Education is given in an appendix. Human resource development is contingent upon managing the information through training the teachers and access to technology for teachers and students.

Commodification

Technology discourse is leading to the commodification of higher education. Higher education space consists of students as consumers and institutions as providers of services. Students are human capital for the labour market. Hence, education is a service meant to maximize the private return of an individual. Competition is increased between institutions using ranking and accreditation. NAAC is responsible for the grading, and the National Institutional Ranking Framework ranks institutions of higher education under different categories of institutions. Commodification supports market mechanisms in education which, in turn, shall increase the cost of education rather than reduce it. The role of a teacher is reduced to managing information and developing the skill component. Technology has enabled private players in the education market. There is a large market for apps, software, and learning management platforms. Bengaluru-headquartered Byju's, valued at $12 billion, reportedly signed the world's largest EdTech deal to acquire Aakash Educational Services.

Standardization

Technology also supports the process of standardization. Centralized admission in institutions of higher education is increasingly being adopted in state and central universities through an online admission system. Similarly, the examination is based on objective-based questions. Outcome-based education is also an attempt to quantify the outcome and assess whether such outcomes are achieved. The centralized curricula are issued by UGC (University Grants Commission). The credit system also quantifies the curricula based on the number of hours of teaching. All these reduce the space for diversity among institutions and promote standardization of higher education. Standardization makes possible the scaling up of education. It also claims to achieve quality by converging towards a certain standard. In a way, the higher education system is subject to rationalities by invoking science and technology.

Technology as State Apparatus

The popular and official discourse on technology, as noted above, is created to give political and social legitimacy. It supports the state to belief in the ideology of technology. An ideology creates a hope that technology can solve all the problems of education that relate to enhancing access, equity and quality. Ideology helps to resolve the conflict between people and state where the former submits rather willingly to the authority of the state. The state creates a dominant structure of control through bureaucracy and market. The state, like the market, strengthens the power of capital over labour. In the arena of education, technology helps the state to create domination over academia as much through surveillance as imposing accountability through various mechanisms. The accountabilities are imposed through various rationalities in the name of efficiency and quality. Reduced space of the autonomy of teachers creates a sense of 'loss of meaning' for education. Teachers miss the vibrating climate of and the passion of learning as administration as well as teaching–learning is driven not by necessity but rather by determination. Teachers feel disenchanted. Hence the line of argument of Weber, Marcuse and Habermas, as noted earlier, supports the argument that technology is a state apparatus of control, as opposed to the popular efficiency-centric discourse. Technology not only controls but creates disenchantment. This reduces teachers to a mere object. Objectification of teachers and teaching learning takes away the creative functioning and the role of teachers in education as they feel alienated from the education process.

Surveillance

Surveillance is watching. Technology helps in the process of surveilling people. Byung-Chul Han in *Psychopolitics* notes that '[t]oday, unbounded freedom and communication are switching over into total control and surveillance' (Han 2017, p. 13). He talks of digital means of information-sharing as a source of self-surveillance where the role of the state is minimized from direct observation to indirect surveillance. In the former case there is an exercise of control of freedom, but in the latter, freedom is willingly surrendered. 'The digitalized, networked subject is a panopticon of itself' (ibid., p. 51). It conducts 'perpetual auto-surveillance' (ibid.). Traditional control over teachers used to be through a self-assessment report submitted to the head of the institution. Now, with digital expansion, a teacher in a higher education institute submits information in a teacher management information system managed by the Ministry of Education. Besides, a teacher has to report on several occasions. For example, if the institution is being accredited, information is sought from a teacher. In several schemes of the government, National Institution Ranking Framework graded autonomy of colleges/universities, research funding, institutes of eminence, autonomous colleges scheme and, above all, the self-disclosure of the institution. Monthly and quarterly progress reports are submitted using digital data.

Direct surveillance also takes place. Biometric attendance is being practised in many institutions. There is a CCTV surveillance. The head of the institution can supervise the classroom teaching and examination. Many institutions are also asked by the education departments of state governments to upload photographs of the functioning of institutions daily on the websites of colleges. There are online reporting portals of the government where basic information about institutions, academic calendar and attendance of teachers is monitored at the central level. Such a degree of surveillance is the result of technological integration. It shows that in the name of transparency, legitimacy is created to have the surveillance in order, without obstruction.

Propaganda, Rumour and Rhetoric

There is an increasing claim that technology supports the process of democratization, freedom and social justice. However, social media platforms indicate how fast communication through these platforms supports propaganda and rumour and changes the discourse for political benefits or reaping profit, in turn, diverting the social issue of importance into a critical discourse. Akbar *et al.* (2021) analyse, citing the case from the film industry, the misinformation, rumour and fake claims as the basis of communication through all media platforms. Further, this leads to rhetoric and people are confused.

The Ministry of Education has social media updates. There is a minister's Twitter account that gives information, supports ideas and reports on the minister's engagement. There is also a Facebook account of the minister which conveys information and receives information mostly in conformity with the decisions. As on 8 February 2021, most of the posts on the Facebook page relate to supporting government programmes other than education, disaster and Covid-19 and to political campaigns. It turns out that the media platform is not a serious platform of constructive critique but a collection of opinions.

Autonomy

Autonomy acquires a new meaning under the latest technology regime. It is geared to facilitating the market process. 'Institutions of Excellence' and graded autonomy are new schemes of central government. Under the former, public and private institutions have been given certain privileges to run the institutions without government permission. Similarly, under graded autonomy, high-grade institutions are given academic, administrative and financial autonomy to run the institutions. Technology discourse cannot be isolated from such attempts at ensuring partly self-financing programmes in institutions of eminence or highly accredited institutions.

Conclusion

Legitimacy of the role of technology is built on the efficiency-centric argument which makes tall claims of increasing access, equity and quality of education. This sort of technological determinism is dangerous. There is, no doubt that efficiency centric role of technology is important. However, if technology becomes an ideology of the powerful and becomes an instrument to guide the process of development, it has consequences that may have harmful effects. For example, technology may become an ally of the market and perpetuate the commodification of higher education. On the other hand, it may be the instrument of the state apparatus that may infringe on the autonomy of teachers by regulating them in all the spheres of higher education. Technology may allow through surveillance and rumor the voices of the powerful to dominate over the weak.

In the higher education sector, the role of technology should not lead to technological determinism and it should not become an ideological concern to infringe upon the space of academia. Technology should help academia to preserve the academic culture and it should not be dominated by technology culture. A rational discourse on technology should be built with the help of academia, bureaucrats, politicians, students and stakeholders. Such communication should help to provide practical solutions based on evidence and research.

Appendix Table *A summary of innovative educational technology of Ministry of Education*

Programme	Description
Audio–video e-content	
SWAYAM	Massive Open Online Courses (MOOCs)
SWAYAMPRABHA	View digital courses on TV
Digital content: e-books and journals	
National Digital Library	Repository of e resource
e-PG Pathshala	Gateway for e-books upto PG
Shodhganga	A reservoir of Indian Theses
e-ShodhSindhu	e-journals
Accelerated hands-on learning	
e-Yantra	Get hands-on experience on embedded systems
FOSSEE	Free/Libre and Open-Source Software for Education
Spoken tutorial	Tutorial in IT application
Virtual labs	Web-enabled experiments for remote operation
E-governance	
University Enterprise Resource Planning (SAMARTH)	E-governance for institutions/universities
Research Network	
VIDWAN	Expert database and national research network
IRINS	Indian Research Information Network System
ShodhShudhhi	Plagiarism Detection Software (PDS)

Source: Author's compilation from various sources.

Notes

[1] Professor Dhruv Raina cautioned me not to conflate science and technology while arguing that both were the sources of rationalization. I believe, his argument is that science is a way of life which is open and depends on the contexts in which people live. On the other hand, technology closes that option and may become regulated and regulating the way of life. Technology should, therefore, be distinguished from science although both have rationalizing elements.

[2] For example, medicine may cure a disease. However, it does not provide an answer to the freeing of real conditions of life under which particular disease takes place.

[3] There is a vast literature on a new kind of re-enchantment, one in which technology seems to liberate by providing leisure and comfort. See Ellul (1964) and Germain (1995).

[4] The following lines corroborate the one-dimensional view of life: 'Technical progress, extended to a whole system of domination and coordination, creates forms of life (and of power) which appear to reconcile the forces opposing the system and to defeat or refute all protest in the name of the historical prospects of freedom from toil and domination. Contemporary society seems to be capable of containing social change-qualitative change which would establish essentially different institutions, a new direction of the productive process, new modes of human existence' (Marcuse 2013, p. xlii).

[5] 'Habermas and the whole ideology critique tradition remain bound by the Kantian assumptions' (Pippin 1927, p. 206).

References

Zainab, A.S., A. Sharma, H. Negi, A. Panda and J. Pal (2021), 'Anatomy of a Rumour: Social media and the suicide of Sushant Singh Rajput', available at https://drive.google.com/file/d/1z9RBGHKc_xaUbORETX7W4s_yzGJPhot2/view, accessed 8 February 2021.

Aune, J.A. (2001), *Selling the Free Market: The Rhetoric of Economic Correctness*, New York: The Guilford Press.

Bhushan, S. (2019), 'A Dithering Higher Education Policy', *Economic and Political Weekly*, vol. 54, no. 24, pp. 12–14.

Ellul, J. (1964), *The Technological Society*, J. Wilkinson, tran., New York: Vintage Books.

Fisher, E. (2010), 'Contemporary Technology Discourse and the Legitimation of Capitalism', *European Journal of Social Theory*, vol. 13, no. 2, pp. 229–52, doi: https://doi.org/10.1177/1368431010362289

Frank, T. (2000), *One Market Under God: Extreme Capitalism, Market Populism, and the End of Economic Democracy*, New York: Anchor Books.

Government of India (GoI) (2020), *National Education Policy 2020*, Government of India, New Delhi.

Germain, G. (1995), 'Revenge of the Sacred: Technology and Reenchantment', in A. Horowitz and T. Maley, eds, *The Barbarism of Reason: Max Weber and the Twilight of Enlightenment*, Toronto, Canada: University of Toronto Press, pp. 248–67.

Habermas, J. ([1970] 2003), 'Technical Progress and the Social Life-World', in R.C. Scharff and V. Dusek, eds, *Philosophy of Technology: The Technological Condition*, Malden, MA: Blackwell, pp. 530–35.

——— (1971a), 'Technical Progress and Social Life World', in J. Habermas, *Toward a Rational Society: Student Protest, Science, and Politics*, first edition, J.J. Shapiro, tran., Boston, USA: Beacon Press.

——— (1971b), 'Technology and Science as Ideology', in J. Habermas, *Toward a Rational Society: Student Protest, Science, and Politics*, first edition, J.J. Shapiro, tran., Boston, USA: Beacon Press.

——— (1971c), 'Scientization of Politics/Public Opinion', in J. Habermas, *Toward a Rational Society: Student Protest, Science, and Politics*, first edition, J.J. Shapiro, tran., Boston, USA: Beacon Press.

Han, B. (2017), *Psychopolitics: Neoliberalism and New Technologies of Power*, Erik Butler, tran., London: Verso.

Harvey, D. (2005), *A Brief History of Neoliberalism*, Oxford: Oxford University Press.

Heidegger, M. ([1954] 1977), *The Question Concerning Technology*, in D.F. Krell, ed., *Martin Heidgger: Basic Writings*, New York: Harper & Row, pp. 287–317.

Kuhn, T.S. and R. Schlegel (1963), 'The Structure of Scientific Revolutions', *Physics Today*, vol. 16, no. 4, p. 69, doi: https://doi.org/10.1063/1.3050879

Lancaster University (undated), Marcuse, Habermas, and Science as Ideology, Block 3 (available at: https://www.lancaster.ac.uk/users/philosophy/awaymave/404/block3.htm) (accessed on 27th January, 2021)

Maley, T. (2004), 'Max Weber and the Iron Cage of Technology', *Bulletin of Science, Technology & Society*, vol. 24, no. 1, pp. 69–86, doi: https://doi.org/10.1177/0270467604263181

Marcuse, H. (2013), *One-dimensional Man: Studies in the Ideology of Advanced Industrial Society*, London: Routledge.

Pal, J. (2003), 'The Developmental Promise of Information and Communications Technology in India', *Contemporary South Asia*, vol. 12, no. 1, pp. 103–19.

Pippin, R. (1997), *Idealism as Modernism: Hegelian Variations*, Cambridge: Cambridge University Press.

Robins, K. and F. Webster (1999), *Times of Technoculture: From the Information Society to the Virtual Life*, London and New York: Routledge.

Schroeder, R. (1995), 'Disenchantment and its Discontents: Weberian Perspectives on Science and Technology', *The Sociological Review*, vol. 43, no. 2, pp. 227–50, doi: https://doi.org/10.1111/j.1467-954x.1995.tb00602.x

Sanzogni, L., G. Guzman and P. Busch (2017), 'Artificial Intelligence and Knowledge Management: Questioning the Tacit Dimension', *Prometheus* vol. 35, no. 1, pp. 37–56, doi:10.1080/08109028.2017.1364547

Weber, M. (1919), *Science as a Vocation*, Munich: Duncker and Humblodt, Munich. originally delivered as a speech at Munich University, available at http://www.wisdom.weizmann.ac.il/~oded/X/WeberScienceVocation.pdf, accessed on 27 January 2021.

Weisz, E. (2020), 'Science, Rationalization, and the Persistence of Enchantment', *Max Weber Studies*, vol. 20, no. 1, pp. 8–24, doi:10.15543/maxweberstudies.20.1.8

Winner, L. (1977), *Autonomous Technology: Technics-out-of-Control as a Theme in Political Thought*, Cambridge, MA and London: MIT Press.

———— (1980), 'Do Artifacts Have Politics?', *Daedalus* vol. 109, no. 1, pp. 121–36.

18

Growth without Engines?

The Indian Transition to Lower Middle-Income Status

Surajit Mazumdar

India's aggregate growth has experienced several accelerations since the country achieved its independence from colonial rule. The most discussed one, and also much debated about on its relationship with the onset of liberalization in India, has been the one that is supposed to have occurred around 1980.[1] That the more important one occurred in the 1950s has also been stressed by some (Hatekar and Dongre 2005; Nayyar 2006; Balakrishnan, Das and Parameswaran 2021). The focus of this essay, however, is the growth acceleration that was experienced by India in the early years of the twenty-first century, and its story beyond the 2008 global crisis that at the least marked the end of the first phase of this high growth trajectory. It was during this course, in 2007, that India moved up from being a low-income to a lower middle-income country in the World Bank categorization.

The acceleration of growth from around 2003 to unprecedented levels was in line with a larger pattern which characterized the brief phase of globalization that preceded the 2008 crisis (Figure 18.1). During this phase that lasted barely five years, world growth picked up. Developing countries as a group not only grew faster than earlier, they also widened the gap between their growth rates and that of the advanced countries. This was especially marked in the case of the Asian developing economies. India was one among them and its growth was only overshadowed by a few countries like China. This phase of world growth, however, came to an end in 2008 with the financial crisis originating in the country which had served as its locomotive, namely the United States (US). It had also been the US which had led the advanced countries into the process of becoming net capital importers in relation to developing countries – what was termed as the 'capital flows paradox' (UNCTAD 2008). The disruption that the crisis caused to the rapid growth of the 'emerging' economies, especially in Asia, initially appeared to be temporary. However, from the early 2010s, it was clear that these economies, despite the significantly enlarged weight in the world economy they had acquired in the course of the decade, would not

Figure 18.1 *Annual percentage change in gross domestic product, constant prices, India and selected country groups, 1991 to 2023*

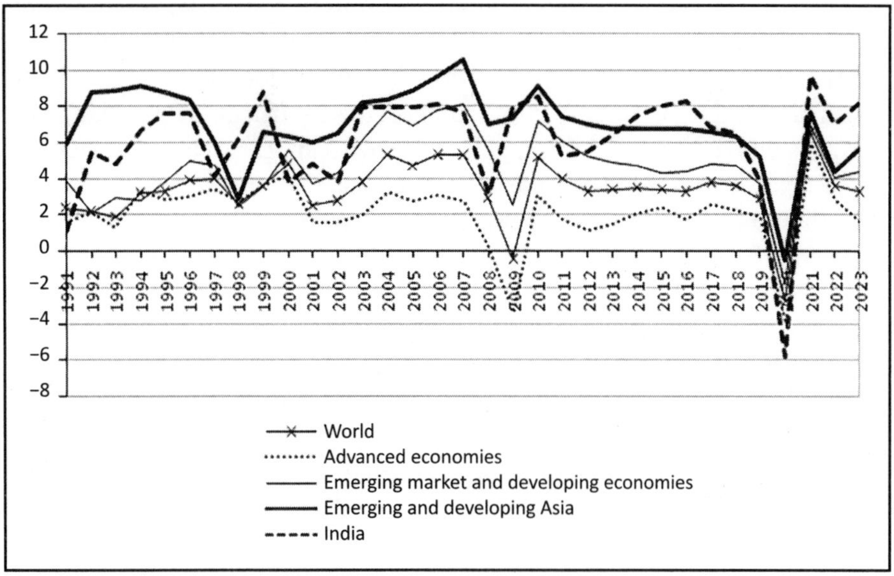

Source: Based on data from International Monetary Fund, *World Economic Outlook* database, October 2024.

be able to pull it out of the post-crisis slowdown. Instead, their own growths slowed down, though still higher than of the advanced economies.

As can also be seen in Figure 18.1, in the course of the second decade of the century that Indian growth appeared to 'recover' and diverge from even the average for emerging and developing economies as a whole and those in Asia. This divergence lasted a for a few years before India's growth got dragged down to the developing average before the Covid pandemic struck. India's 're-emergence' as one of the fastest growing economies of the world since then came on the back of an exceptionally large contraction in 2020–21 and its base effect.

The association of India's 'recovery' in the 2010s with the introduction of a new GDP (gross domestic product) series with significant changes in the methods of estimation fuelled controversy about the accuracy of India's GDP estimates (Nagaraj 2015; Mazumdar 2015; Dennis Rajakumar 2016; Subramanian 2019). The debate on the methodological changes ushered in by the new GDP series with 2011–12 as base year was never resolved, and many remain sceptical about Indian growth since 2011–12 being any faster than in the two decades after 1980. Some also firmly believe that demonetization and the introduction of the goods and services tax (GST) regime disproportionately affected India's large unorganized sector, which is not captured in GDP data (Kumar 2023). More recently, new concerns have arisen in the context of the

GDP growth in 2023–24 being based on an implicit GDP inflation rate that is far below the consumer price index-based rate (Mazumdar 2024b).

What is clear, however, is that even if India's official data are accepted at face value, Indian growth since 2011–12 has had a very different character to the rapid growth of the previous decade, a transition whose possibility had been hinted at in P. Patnaik (2007). Indeed, it is a particularly peculiar growth process where almost all the engines of growth appear to be conspicuous by their absence. Indeed, three interrelated aspects that one expects to be motoring the rapid growth of a developing capitalist economy – industrialization and industrial development, investment and capital formation, and trade expansion – have all taken adverse turns from the beginning of this period. In recent years, some additional odd features appear to have crept into the Indian growth process that relate to the emergence of apparently new employment trends. Moreover, the decade began with the shift in Indian macro policy as in the other parts of the world to retreat from the post-crisis stimulus, austerity or fiscal consolidation, with curbing of inflationary pressures being prioritized. This remained the thrust of the Indian fiscal and monetary policy throughout the decade, and the return to this path after the first year of the Covid pandemic was also very rapid. In other words, Indian growth has not even been propped up by expansionary macroeconomic policy. Instead, the demonetization of 2016, the introduction of the GST in 2017 and the lockdown measures in response to the pandemic were major policy-related shocks inflicted on the Indian economy.

Premature De-industrialization and India's Second Stagnation Decade

While Indian industrial growth had experienced a revival in the 1980s from the phase of stagnation that had set in since the mid-1960s, the upward trend in the relative importance of manufacturing in the Indian economy's production as well as employment structures was never seen again. Indeed, services as well as construction activities played a far more significant role in the post-1980s growth.[2] However, even within this broad story of Indian growth sans industrialization, the period since 2011–12 stands out as truly a decade of severe industrial crisis. If we simply look at the rates of growth of manufacturing production as measured by the index of industrial production (IIP), the rapid growth during the first decade of the century appears to have given way to what can be accurately described as India's second decade of industrial stagnation (Table 18.1). Growth rates during this period have been similar to the mid-1960s to mid-1970s period. Additionally, the post-Covid trends suggest that the stagnation has now extended well beyond a decade – the manufacturing IIP in 2023–24 was barely 11.6 per cent greater than in 2019–20, which would correspond to less than 2.8 per cent per annum growth rate on a point-to-point basis. Particularly severely affected by stagnation have been the capital goods and consumer durables sectors, whose index values in

Table 18.1 *Annual average rate of growth of the index of industrial production (IIP) of manufacturing for different periods*, percentage per annum

Period	Annual average growth rate	Period	Annual average growth rate
1956–65	7.7	1981–82 to 1990–91	7.3
1966–75	3.7	1991–92 to 2000–01	7.4
1976–80	4.6	2001–02 to 2010–11	9.8
1966–80	4.2	2011–12 to 2019–20	3.6

Source: Computed from data in Nayyar (1978); RBI, *Report on Currency and Finance*, various issues; and RBI, *Handbook of Statistics on the Indian Economy*, 2023–24.

2023–24 (with 2011–12 =100) stood at just 106.5 and 118.6, respectively.

In terms of its shares in value added and in employment, the declining trends of the manufacturing sector in this period (Figure 18.2) emphatically confirm Dani Rodrik's results that India was in the company of sub-Saharan Africa in experiencing the most 'premature' of de-industrializations (Rodrik 2015). This is despite India's participation in the rise of developing Asia's share in world manufacturing which has made it the fifth largest manufacturing economy in the world (UNIDO 2024). India's 3.2 per cent share in world manufacturing value added (MVA) is considerably lower than her share in world population which is close to 18 per cent. It also pales in comparison to China's 31.8 per cent share in world MVA.

Figure 18.2 *Share of manufacturing in Indian gross value added (GVA) and employment, 2000–01 to 2023–24*

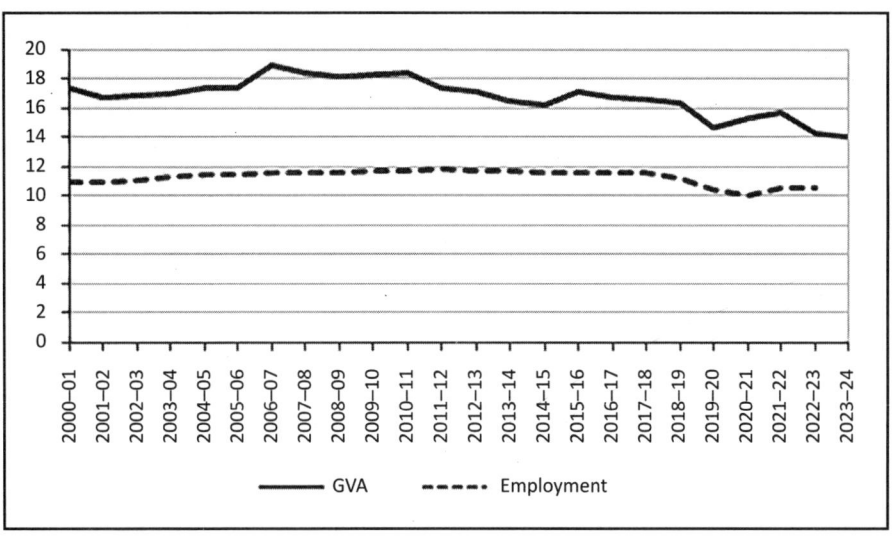

Source: Based on data from National Statistical Office, National Accounts Statistics (NAS), 2024 and 2011–12 *Base Year Back Series*, and RBI-KLEMS database, July 2024 release.

Table 18.2 *Manufacturing value added (MVA) per capita and relative importance of manufacturing in GDP and employment: India in a comparative perspective*

Country/country group	MVA per capita 2023 (2015 US$)	MVA share in GDP 2023 (%)	Manufacturing share in employment 2022 (%)
World	*1,912*	*16.7*	*13.6*
High income industrial economies	6,365	13.9	13.4
Middle-income industrial economies	2,216	23.5	18.0
Middle-income industrializing economies	314	13.0	11.4
India	*346*	*15.7*	*11.7**
Low income	65	9.2	5.5

Note: * Relates to 2021
Source: UNIDO, *International Yearbook of Industrial Statistics*, 2023 and 2024.

India's de-industrialization in fact raises questions about whether it can truly be placed in the category of middle-income *industrializing* economies. Its manufacturing value added per capita levels and the shares of manufacturing in her aggregate output an employment are certainly representative of that category (Table 18.2). All of these are significantly lower in the case of India than in middle-income *industrial* economies, while her per capita MVA levels are only a fraction of the de-industrialized or de-industrializing high-income industrial economies. India, however, does not seem to be on the path to such high-income industrial status via achieving middle-income industrial status.

Indian manufacturing of course has a distinctive feature in that it has a significant unorganized component, which is where the bulk of manufacturing employment had always been concentrated. However, unorganized manufacturing had started shrinking in importance relative to its organized counterpart even before 2011–12. A revival of growth of organized manufacturing employment was in fact a feature of the first decade of the century (Goldar 2011; Nagaraj 2011). However, even this growth decelerated in the 2010s – Annual Survey of Industries (ASI) data indicates that between 2011–12 and 2022–23, the number of workers in the factory sector increased by 40 per cent while the total persons engaged grew by 37.7 per cent. In the period between 2000–01 and 2011–12, the same increases had been 70.1 per cent and 68.1 per cent respectively – and even in absolute numbers these increases were greater than after 2011–12.

Investment Stagnation

A remarkable feature of India's economic trajectory during the boom years before the 2008 crisis was the dramatic rise in her investment ratio,

Figure 18.3 *Gross fixed capital formation (GFCF) as a percentage of GDP, 2000–01 to 2023–24*

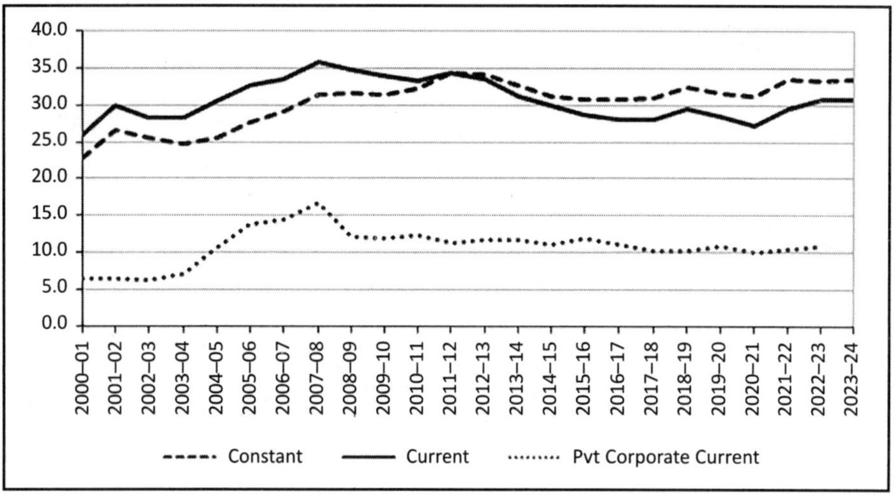

Source: Based on NAS, 2024 and 2011–12 *Base Year Back Series* data.

with private corporate investment playing the leading role in it (Figure 18.3). Investment of course has a dual character – serving to expand the fixed capital stock of the economy as well as creating demand – and fosters growth in both ways. Rangarajan and Srivastava (2017) had concluded that high savings and investment rates had not only been the main factor behind the high growth, but remained the most important basis for sustaining it. The investment-led growth of the early years of the century, however, certainly did not last into its second decade. The investment ratio itself declined quite sharply after 2008 when measured in current prices, and even when measured at constant prices, it has since 2011–12 tended to remain below that year's level. Such a sustained downward trend in the investment ratio in fact has been unprecedented in India's post-Independence development history. The ratio had been steadily moving up over the long term, and any periods of decline that emerged from time to time were of relatively short duration.

Even when seen in real or constant price terms, clearly the growth of investment significantly slowed down in the second decade of the current century in comparison to the first. This sharp deceleration is clearly visible in the comparison presented in Figure 18.4 of how the annual fixed capital formation levels moved over the two twelve-year periods starting from the base years of 2000–01 and 2011–12. What can also be observed in the figure is how closely the trends in manufacturing and aggregate investment tracked each other through both the boom as well as the subsequent slowdown. This serves as an indication of the relationship between the industrial crisis and the onset of investment stagnation – manufacturing being one of the important

Figure 18.4 *Indices of GFCF, aggregate and manufacturing, at constant prices, 2000–01 to 2011–12 and 2011–12 to 2022–23* (respective year 1 = 100)

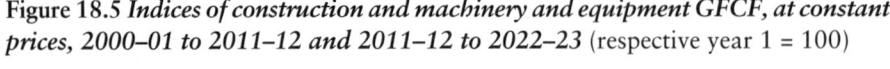

Source: Based on NAS, 2024 and 2011–12 *Base Year Back Series* data.

Figure 18.5 *Indices of construction and machinery and equipment GFCF, at constant prices, 2000–01 to 2011–12 and 2011–12 to 2022–23* (respective year 1 = 100)

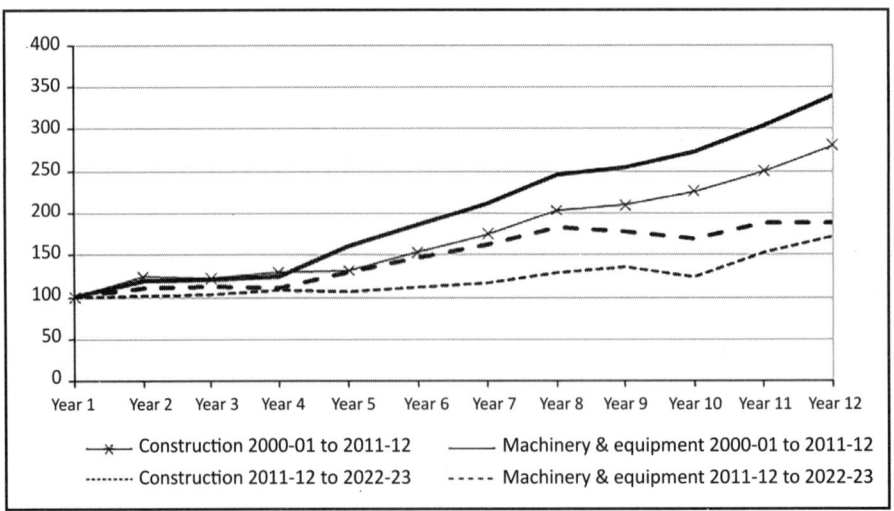

Source: Based on NAS, 2024 and 2011–12 *Base Year Back Series* data.

sectors where capital–output ratios tend to be high. On the other side, the extremely bleak picture with regard to capital goods production can be related to the demand effects of the lack of investment.

Figure 18.5 compares in a similar fashion as Figure 18.4 the trends in the two broad components of fixed capital formation.[3] The slowdown after 2011–12 and the prolonged phases of stagnation are again clear in both cases,

Table 18.3 *Distribution of the net fixed capital stock and GFCF of private corporations*

Percentage share in net fixed capital stock of private corporations		
Sector	31 March 2012	31 March 2023
Agriculture, forestry and fishing	0.2	0.3
Industry	68.5	53.7
Manufacturing	*54.1*	*41.0*
Services	31.3	46.0
Communication and services related to broadcasting	*2.7*	*7.2*
Real estate, ownership of dwelling and professional services	*4.9*	*13.5*
Percentage share in GFCF of private corporations		
Asset Type	2011–12 to 2013–14	2020–21 to 2022–23
Dwellings, Other buildings & Structures	25.8	28.9
Machinery and equipment	53.7	43.6
Cultivated biological resources	0.1	0.0
Intellectual property products	20.4	27.5

Source: Based on NAS, 2024 and 2011–12 *Base Year Back Series* data.

indicating that in addition to manufacturing investment, the boom in construction activities (real estate as well as infrastructure) had also come to an end.

The causal links between de-industrialization and the investment story also find reflection in the changing composition of private corporate investment (Table 18.3). The sharp shift away from industry towards services – mainly from manufacturing to communication services, and real estate and business services – in the private corporate sector's fixed capital stock points towards the erosion of investment opportunities in manufacturing. The same is indicated by the declining significance of machinery and equipment relative to construction and intellectual property products (primarily software) in the expenditure on capital formation.

There is an additional significance of the trends of stagnation in expenditures on machinery and equipment, which relates to its likely employment effect. Since the time of the global crisis, a pre-existing trend that has become more pronounced is that of the *cheapening* of capital goods relative to labour services even if real wages remain stagnant (Figure 18.6). The effects of productivity increases in manufacturing coupled with sustained rise in food prices have been responsible for this trend whose implication should be the

Figure 18.6 *Relative prices: ratio of index of machinery and equipment prices and the consumer price index of industrial workers (2011–12 = 1), 1990–91 to 2022–23*

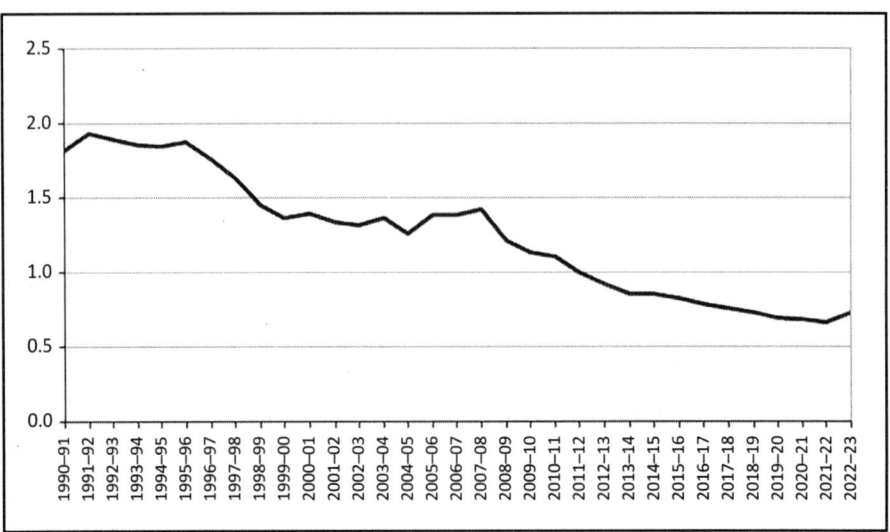

Source: Based on data in NAS, 2024 and 2011–12 *Base Year Back Series,* and RBI, *Handbook of Statistics on the Indian Economy,* 2023–24.

inducement of labour-substituting capital formation in activities where wage labour is used. Such outcomes have been found in the manufacturing sector (Sen and Das 2015). Investment stagnation in such circumstances means an even greater negative impact on the demand for labour services.

Trade and Foreign Investment

India's insertion into the process of globalization was never characterized by any trend of India emerging as a significant location of production of manufactures for the world market. Instead, it was a more manufacturing import-intensive participation in global production networks and value chains, and heavy import dependence characterized even high-export sectors like pharmaceuticals. Indeed, India's manufacturing trade was an important contributor to the sharp rise in India's merchandise trade deficit in the boom preceding the 2008 crisis (Mazumdar 2014; Chaudhuri 2013). This made India somewhat exceptional among developing countries – let alone not being a net capital exporter, India's current account actually experienced an adverse movement during the boom. This happened despite the rapid parallel growth of India's invisible earnings, which were mainly from the exports of information technology (IT) services and from remittances. These were the areas where India's 'globalization' succeeded most. However, in addition to being a low capital–output ratio activity, the IT services sector has remained largely dependent on export markets and the production of these services used very limited domestically produced inputs or capital goods. In other words, the backward and forward linkage effects, or that on the inducement of investment, of the growth of the sector were limited in nature. The stimulating effect of both this growth as well as that of the flow of remittances from Indian working abroad was mainly through the channel of personal expenditures from incomes accruing to individuals.

Clearly, therefore, India's foreign trade patterns were not of a kind that would make for any sustained process of export-led industrialization and investment-based growth. Nevertheless, in the first decade of this century, the expansionary trends in world trade as well as capital flows did spill over into the Indian economy and all indicators of India's external transactions showed a sharp rise (Table 18.4). It would be reasonable to argue that these played an important role in ensuring India's participation in the worldwide process of developing countries experiencing an acceleration in growth and beyond the effects produced by rise in invisibles receipts. India's exports of manufactured products grew and their composition as well as geographical orientation also changed (Veeramani 2012). The accompanying shift in exports away from India's traditional labour-intensive products towards more capital-using industries likely played a part in spurring manufacturing investment and growth. Portfolio capital inflows contributed to asset price increases and a credit-financed growth in construction and other capital-formation activities in the real estate and infrastructure sectors (Ghosh and Chandrasekhar 2009). The growth of imports – of capital goods and intermediates – was a result of the pace and pattern of expansion.

The trends of rapid expansion in the scales of India's external transactions did not last into the second decade of the century, and exhibited extreme stagnation till the Covid-19 pandemic, as can also be seen in Table 18.4. The exports of goods and services as a ratio of GDP too showed a downward trend (Figure 18.7). All of these were entirely in line with the global trends in trade during the same period, as was the short and sharp rise experienced in the post-Covid period partly on account of rise in prices (WTO 2024). In other words, India was no exception among developing countries and it too experienced the disappearance, after 2008, of the expansionary momentum that had previously been transmitted to developing countries by globalization. The decelerations in investment and manufacturing that in part were the result of this in turn explain the slowdown in import growth.

There is of course some indication that while the total quantum of foreign investment has tended to stagnate, there has been a change in its composition after the global crisis, with direct investment increasing in significance relative to portfolio flows (Table 18.5). However, when placed alongside the trends in both overall investment as well as trade, this FDI trend does not appear to be reflecting any significant turnaround in the nature and extent of India's importance as a location for world market production. In fact, it is very

Table 18.4 *Indices of selected key components of India's balance of payments in US dollars, 2000–01 to 2011–12 and 2011–12 to 2023–24*

Base year	Item	2001–02	2002–03	2003–04	2004–05	2005–06	2006–07
2000–01=100	Exports, f.o.b.*	98.4	118.3	145.8	187.5	231.3	283.6
	Imports, c.i.f.**	97.2	111.3	138.1	205.3	271.2	329.2
	Invisibles, net	152.9	173.9	283.9	318.9	428.9	533.2
	Foreign Investment	120.0	88.6	230.9	225.3	315.0	438.0
		2007–08	2008–09	2009–10	2010–11	2011–12	
2000–01=100	Exports, f.o.b.	365.6	415.8	401.4	563.6	681.5	
	Imports, c.i.f.	444.9	532.7	519.1	662.2	862.6	
	Invisibles, net	773.2	935.3	817.1	809.4	1139.5	
	Foreign Investment	913.0	410.6	964.3	890.9	741.6	
		2012–13	2013–14	2014–15	2015–16	2016–17	2017–18
2011–12=100	Exports, f.o.b.	99.0	102.9	102.2	86.0	90.4	99.7
	Imports, c.i.f.	100.5	93.3	92.4	79.4	78.6	93.9
	Invisibles, net	96.3	103.3	105.8	96.7	87.8	99.7
	Foreign Investment	108.7	71.1	153.8	81.9	99.2	122.3
		2018–19	2019–20	2020–21	2021–22	2022–23	2023–24
2011-12=100	Exports, f.o.b.	108.9	103.4	95.7	138.5	147.2	142.5
	Imports, c.i.f.	103.6	95.7	79.8	123.8	144.4	136.8
	Invisibles, net	110.2	119.0	113.0	135.0	177.6	196.0
	Foreign investment	85.2	112.3	186.0	83.7	73.8	141.2

Notes: * free on board; ** cost, insurance and freight.
Source: Based on data from RBI, *Handbook of Statistics on the Indian Economy*, 2023–24.

likely that much of the FDI is also of financial nature – private equity, venture capital, etc. – but categorized as direct investment because of the criteria used in generating statistics on FDI.

Indeed, little change can be seen in the broad characteristics of FDI in India over the period of more than a decade since 2011–12. As highlighted in Table 18.6, while close to half of the FDI in entities in India have remained in manufacturing, the share of the sector in sales and purchases of all foreign subsidiaries, including exports and imports, has tended to decline and that of services had increased. Moreover, foreign manufacturing subsidiaries continue

Figure 18.7 *Exports of goods and services at current prices as percentage of GDP, 2000–01 to 2023–24*

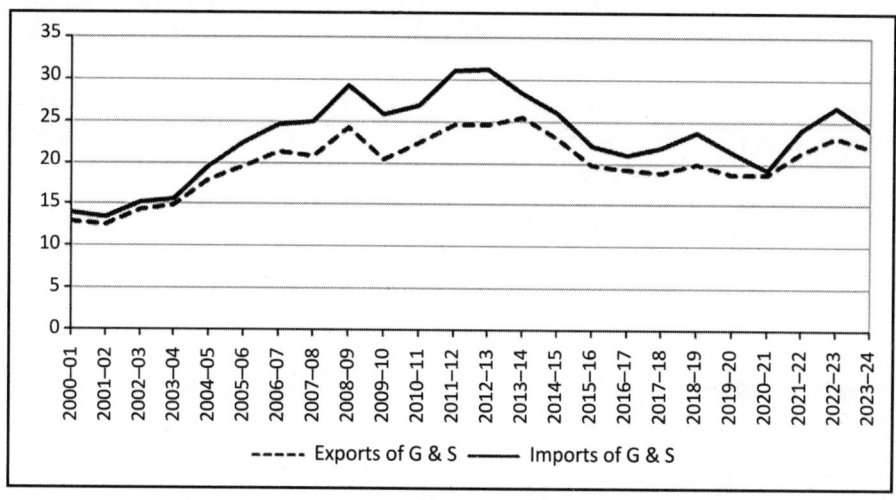

Source: Based on NAS, 2024 and 2011–12 *Base Year Back Series* data.

Table 18.5 *Foreign investment inflows, 2003–04 to 2023–24*

Period	Amount (US $ million)			Percentage shares	
	Net foreign direct investment	Net portfolio investment	Total	Net foreign direct investment	Net portfolio investment
2003–04 to 2007–08	32,721	67,630	100,351	32.6	67.4
2008–09 to 2011–12	74,233	65,829	140,062	53.0	47.0
2012–13 to 2015–16	108,655	69,788	178,443	60.9	39.1
2016–17 to 2019–20	139,623	30,512	170,136	82.1	17.9
2020–21 to 2023–24	120,318	58,289	178,607	67.4	32.6

Source: Based on data from RBI, *Handbook of Statistics on the Indian Economy*, 2023–24.

to have a high proportion of their sales in the Indian market, while imports play a much more significant role in their purchases and also exceed their exports by a wide margin (Table 18.7). This can be contrasted with the pattern of the IT sector whose share in FDI has been of significantly lower than that of manufacturing. As can be seen from Tables 18.6 and 18.7, it is this sector which has accounted for a large and an increasing share of the exports of FDI subsidiaries in India, and an even greater proportion of their net foreign currency earnings.

Table 18.6 *Sectoral distribution of FDI and transactions of FDI subsidiaries*

Item	Year(s)	Manu-facturing	Services	*Of which: Information and comm-unication*	Other activities
Total FDI of all	2012–13	50.0	39.1	*15.5*	10.9
FDI Entities	2019–20	52.6	42.1	*17.2*	5.3
	2023–24	51.4	42.4	*15.3*	6.2
Sales of foreign	2011–13	63.7	31.7	*16.7*	4.5
subsidiaries	2018–20	52.5	45.2	*21.0*	2.3
	2022–24	47.6	50.5	*25.2*	1.9
Exports of foreign	2011–13	43.9	55.2	*42.8*	0.8
subsidiaries	2018–20	32.0	67.7	*49.5*	0.3
	2022–24	29.6	69.9	*51.2*	0.5
Purchases of foreign	2011–13	72.9	22.7	*7.0*	4.4
subsidiaries	2018–20	56.3	41.3	*14.9*	2.4
	2022–24	50.0	47.8	*20.5*	2.1
Imports of foreign	2011–13	79.2	19.2	*5.2*	1.6
subsidiaries	2018–20	71.4	27.2	*7.4*	1.4
	2022–24	65.4	33.4	*11.8*	1.0

Source: RBI, *Census on Foreign Liabilities and Assets of Indian Direct Investment Entities*, various issues.

Table 18.7 *Selected export and import ratios of foreign subsidiaries*

Activity	Years	Manu-facturing	Services	*Of which: Information and communication*	All activities
Exports/sales	2011–13	21.1	53.1	*78.2*	30.6
	2018–20	19.3	47.4	*74.7*	31.7
	2022–24	22.1	49.2	*72.2*	35.5
Imports/purchases	2011–13	47.3	36.9	*32.6*	43.5
	2018–20	44.7	23.2	*17.5*	35.2
	2022–24	41.8	22.4	*18.5*	32.0
Exports/imports	2011–13	59.5	307.7	*876.4*	107.2
	2018–20	58.6	324.8	*875.8*	130.7
	2022–24	68.5	317.0	*656.9*	151.6

Source: RBI, *Census on Foreign Liabilities and Assets of Indian Direct Investment Entities*, various issues.

The Fiscal Leash

The early years of the twenty-first century saw the only episode that India experienced after liberalization of a rise in the tax revenue to GDP ratio. This had been led by direct taxes – a result of growth of corporate profits and incomes of high-income groups at a pace faster than that of incomes in the economy as a whole (Mazumdar 2014). As can be seen in Table 18.8, the rise in this ratio by 4.6 percentage points between 2001–02 and 2007–08 was the main reason why the general government fiscal deficit (centre and states combined) came down by 5.7 percentage points. During this period, the savings of public enterprises as ratios of GDP were also higher than they were to be thereafter. If we consider only the final expenditure of the public sector as a whole, including public enterprises, it is also noticeable that the ratio of such expenditure to GDP was maintained at around 18 per cent till 2007–08, with a upward drift in the capital expenditure component. In the next few years after the crisis erupted, the revenues dropped while expenditures were maintained at a slightly higher level. The rise in the government's fiscal deficit during this phase of the post-crisis stimulus led to a sustained effort to bring it down thereafter – and this retreat came to define the decade after 2011. The limits to the achievement of this objective before the Covid pandemic, its partial nature as well as the time taken, were not on account of expenditure growth. The reason lay more in the lack of recovery of revenues. In fact, the control exercised over expenditure growth is reflected in both the disbursements as well the final expenditure to the GDP levels till 2019–20 – for the most part they were even lower than during the boom period before 2008 when the fiscal deficit came down.

Even the Covid pandemic did not produce a significant upward push in public sector final expenditures. On the other hand, revenues did recover after the initial year of the lockdown, and at least as a percentage of GDP became even higher than in 2019–20. The sharp rise in the ratios to GDP of government disbursements and the fiscal deficit were, therefore, primarily attributable to transfers and interest payments and the contraction in GDP. The public sector capital formation to GDP ratio – which has remained at or under 7 per cent since 2019–20 – also shows clearly that there has been also no stimulating effect emanating from what is an apparent reorientation of central government expenditures in favour of capital, as opposed to revenue, expenditures. It confirms the argument that this reorientation was primarily an accounting rather than real story and was accompanied by a parallel reduction in investments out of their own resources by public enterprises (Mazumdar 2024a).

Table 18.8 *Receipts and disbursements of central and state governments, savings of non-departmental public enterprises and combined final expenditures of the public sector, as percentage of GDP, 2000–01 to 2022–23*

Year	Combined for central and state governments				Savings of non-depart-mental enter-prises	Final expenditures by public sector		
	Total revenue receipts	Tax revenue	Disburse-ments	Fiscal deficit		Public sector gcf	Government final consumption expenditure	Total public final expenditure
2000–01	17.7	14.1	27.8	9.3	3.7	7.0	11.9	18.9
2001–02	17.3	13.3	28.2	9.8	4.3	7.2	11.8	19.0
2002–03	18.2	14.1	28.3	9.4	4.6	6.8	11.3	18.1
2003–04	18.6	14.6	28.5	8.4	4.8	7.0	10.9	17.9
2004–05	19.3	15.2	27.3	7.4	4.6	7.4	10.4	17.8
2005–06	19.5	15.9	26.4	6.6	4.7	7.8	10.4	18.2
2006–07	20.6	17.0	26.1	5.2	4.6	8.4	9.8	18.2
2007–08	21.7	17.9	26.8	4.1	3.8	8.7	9.9	18.6
2008–09	20.3	16.8	29.0	8.5	3.3	9.0	10.5	19.5
2009–10	19.0	15.5	29.1	9.5	3.4	8.9	11.5	20.4
2010–11	20.7	16.4	28.1	7.0	3.5	8.4	11.0	19.4
2011–12	19.4	16.5	27.7	7.8	3.0	7.5	11.1	18.6
2012–13	19.8	17.0	27.1	6.9	2.6	7.2	10.7	17.9
2013–14	19.7	16.4	26.7	6.7	2.2	7.1	10.3	17.4
2014–15	19.2	16.2	26.3	6.7	2.0	7.1	10.4	17.5
2015–16	20.0	16.7	27.3	6.9	2.0	7.6	10.4	18.0
2016–17	20.3	17.0	27.7	6.9	2.2	7.2	10.3	17.5
2017–18	19.8	17.4	26.4	5.8	2.4	6.8	10.8	17.6
2018–19	20.1	17.3	26.7	5.8	1.9	7.3	10.8	18.1
2019–20	19.2	16.1	26.9	7.2	2.7	6.9	11.0	17.9
2020–21	18.6	16.1	32.0	13.1	2.3	6.7	11.6	18.3
2021–22	20.4	17.6	30.1	9.5	2.6	6.5	10.5	17.0
2022–23	21.2	17.9	31.1	9.6	2.6	7.0	10.7	17.7

Source: Based on data in NAS and RBI, *Handbook of Statistics on the Indian Economy*, 2023–24.

A Reverse Lewisian Process?

With premature de-industrialization, investment and trade stagnation, and the relative cheapening of capital goods constituting its background, and with the additional shocks being inflicted on the economy, the reversal since 2017–18 of the trend of decline in the worker–population ratio of the Indian economy would appear to be somewhat strange. The Periodic Labour Force Survey (PLFS) data which started becoming available from that year, however, has given rise to precisely this controversial result (Figure 18.8).

Indeed, if one sets the employment figures against those of capital accumulation and production (Table 18.9), then three clear stories emerge that surely would not be normally considered reflections of an economy enjoying a robust growth momentum.

The first is that Indian growth appears to be highly labour-intensive in character – relative to the increase in capital stock which has been somewhat limited, the growth of employment is quite high. This emerges particularly sharply when one looks at investment in machinery and equipment, where there has been a picture of extreme stagnation across the different institutional sectors (Table 18.10). The second is that labour productivity is not growing in the Indian economy, with production growth being limited in comparison with employment growth. This appears to be also true across different sectors of the economy – as can be seen in Table 18.9 for the manufacturing, services and agriculture sectors. The third relates to the sector that has long been

Figure 18.8 *Employment to mid-year population status and usual status (ps+ss) worker population ratios, 2011–12 to 2023–24*

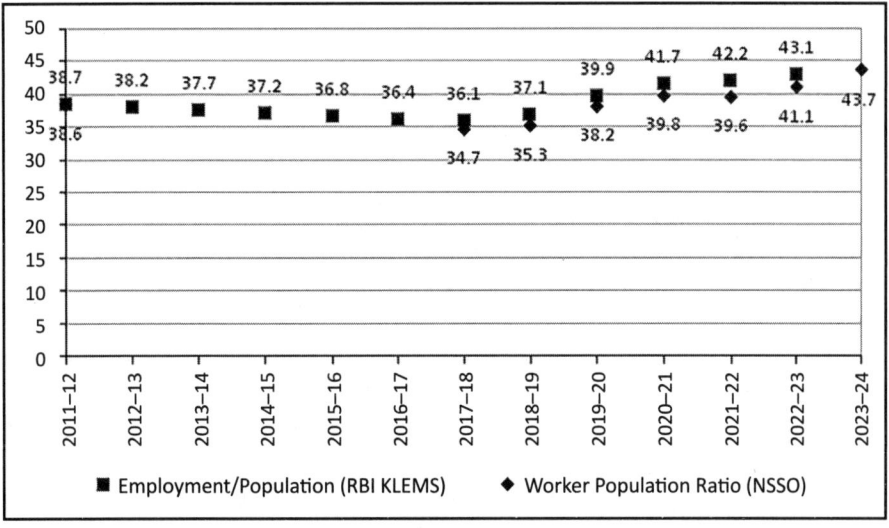

Source: Based on data from NAS, 2024 and RBI-KLEMS Database, July 2024 release; NSSO, Employment and Unemployment Situation, Report No. 554, 2014; Periodic Labour Force Survey (PLFS), various releases.

Table 18.9 *Indices of value added, employment, capital stock and labour productivity (values at constant prices and 2017–18=100), economy and main sectors, 2017–18 to 2023–24*

Variable	2017–18	2018–19	2019–20	2020–21	2021–22	2022–23	2023–24
Economy							
Value added	100	105.8	110.0	105.4	115.3	123.0	131.9
Employment	100	103.7	112.5	119.1	121.6	125.6	135.5
Capital stock	100	107.2	114.1	119.8	127.2	135.0	143.7
Labour productivity	100	102.0	98.0	88.5	94.9	98.0	97.6
Manufacturing							
Value added	100	105.4	102.3	105.4	115.9	113.4	
Employment	100	101.0	102.5	104.3	111.8	115.5	
Capital stock	100	104.9	110.5	114.3	120.0	126.0	
Labour productivity	100	104.5	99.8	101.2	103.7	98.3	
Services							
Value added	100	107.2	114.1	104.5	114.1	125.6	
Employment	100	106.8	113.1	117.2	120.0	125.0	
Capital stock	100	108.0	115.6	121.5	129.3	138.1	
Labour productivity	100	100.5	101.0	89.2	95.2	100.5	
Agriculture and Allied							
Value added	100	102.1	108.4	112.7	117.9	123.5	
Employment	100	101.3	114.8	124.0	124.0	126.4	
Capital stock	100	103.8	107.6	112.4	117.8	124.6	
Labour productivity	100	101.1	94.6	91.3	94.6	97.8	

Source: Computed from data in RBI-INDIA KLEMS Database, July 2024.

afflicted by a crisis, namely agriculture (U. Patnaik 2007). In the period since 2017–18, this sector has been apparently doing relatively well on all counts in comparison to the non-agricultural sectors, and in the case of employment even in relation to services. It is manufacturing instead that is the truly laggard sector. In other words, neither has average productivity has increased in individual sectors, nor has shift of workers from relatively low productivity activities like agriculture to higher productivity ones like manufacturing have been taking place. Clearly, therefore, the turnaround in employment trends in the Indian economy are not related to any changes in the fundamental tendencies that have been described in the previous sections as afflicting the economy since 2011–12.

To put it differently, unless the accuracy of the data is to be seriously

Table 18.10 *Indices of machinery and equipment GFCF, at constant prices (2017–18+100), 2017–18 to 2022–23*

Institutional Sector	2017–18	2018–19	2019–20	2020–21	2021–22	2022–23
All Sectors	100	113.7	109.0	101.0	113.6	112.4
Public non-financial corporations	100	132.5	126.0	101.6	99.1	104.9
Private non-financial corporations	100	106.9	98.1	95.7	114.5	115.6
Household sector	100	117.0	116.7	100.2	115.1	105.1

Source: Computed from data in NAS, 2024.

disputed, one would have to say that the Indian economy in recent years has taken a course which reflects the onset of a dynamic that is the opposite of what Arthur Lewis (1954) had suggested would be the route through which a labour-surplus economy could experience growth, capital accumulation and structural transformation. If one looks at the employment trends by the category of employment, the entire growth of such employment has been in 'self-employment' rather than wage-employment, with casual employment experiencing the steepest decline (Table 18.11). This is not surprising given the relative cheapening of machinery. Table 18.11 also shows that the increase in the worker–population ratio has been led by an apparent reversal of the much discussed trend of low and declining women's work-participation that were characteristics of the Indian economy. However, unlike in the case of men, their employment has become even more concentrated in agriculture over this period. Moreover, earnings from all of these employment have not kept pace with the rise in prices, the greatest squeeze in real earnings having been experienced by the self-employed (Figure 18.9). All of these serve to only reinforce the conclusion that the recent employment trends in the Indian economy reflect what could be described as the expansion of the 'subsistence sector' in the Lewisian framework. This is *because* of slackening of capital accumulation and limited labour-absorption in the 'capitalist sector'. The slowing down of capital accumulation in turn is *not* a result of the erosion of the capitalist sector's surplus attributable to the elimination of the unlimited supply of labour situation.

Conclusion

The phase of rapid growth that preceded India's entry into the lower middle-income category was characterized by several typical features which were consistent with that growth – a surge in trade and capital flows, a sharp rise in the investment ratio and high levels of industrial growth. Neither of these survived India's transition into middle-income status and the post-2008 context of globalization. In that sense, Indian growth, particularly since the

Table 18.11 *Indicators of the changing composition of employment, 2017–18 to 2023–24*

Category	2017–18	2018–19	2019–20	2020–21	2021–22	2022–23	2023–24
Distribution by Category of Employment (% Shares)							
Self-Employed	52.2	52.1	53.5	55.6	55.8	57.3	58.4
Helper	13.6	13.3	15.9	17.3	17.5	18.3	19.4
Regular	22.8	23.8	22.9	21.1	21.5	20.9	21.7
Casual	24.9	24.1	23.6	23.3	22.7	21.8	19.8
Worker-Population Ratios (%)							
Male	52.1	52.3	53.9	54.9	54.8	54.4	56.4
Female	16.5	17.6	21.8	24.2	24	27	30.7
Persons	34.7	35.3	38.2	39.8	39.6	41.1	43.7
Share of Agriculture in Usual Status Employment (%)							
Male	40.2	38.3	40.9	39.8	38.1	37.1	36.3
Female	50.7	55.3	59.9	62.2	62.9	64.3	64.4
Persons	44.1	42.5	45.6	46.5	45.5	45.8	46.1

Source: PLFS, various issues.

Figure 18.9 *Indices of earnings from different kinds of employment and the consumer price index (2017–18=100), April–June 2018 to April–June 2024*

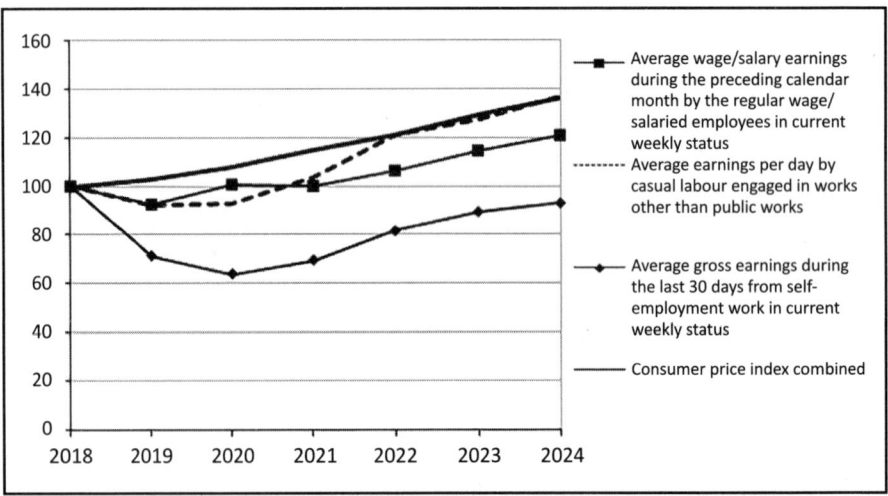

Source: Computed from data in PLFS, various issues, and RBI, *Handbook of Statistics on the Indian Economy*, 2023–24.

end of the first decade of the twenty-first century, has happened without this growth being impelled by any of the engines that usually drive rapid growth. Instead, Indian capitalist development has moved into a phase where it is unable to utilize its capital accumulation potential despite the presence, and even expansion, of a labour reserve and the consequent unbounded availability of cheap labour. Moreover, this has no causal relationship with any 'scarcity' for private capital caused by 'excessive' cornering of the surplus by the state. Instead, this has happened despite the extreme adherence to fiscal conservatism and several other attempts by the state to unleash the 'animal spirits' of private investment, including measures to attract foreign capital. It is, therefore, not in any deviation from the neoliberal path but precisely in the contradictions inherent in that path, given the specific historical context of India's economy, that one would have to locate the origins of this 'premature' exhaustion of the engines of growth.

Notes

[1] See for instance Rodrik and Subramanian (2005) and Srinivasan (2005).

[2] While the exceptional significance of services in India's post-liberalization growth is widely recognized – Soni and Bala Subrahmanya (2020) and Raj and Reddy Kalluru (2022) being two recent studies – Krishna *et al.* (2022) provide a rare contrary view. They suggest that manufacturing growth has been more impressive than measured by the standard methods and the sector has contributed significantly to overall growth. They do, however, acknowledge a fall in manufacturing's employment and investment rates in the period after the global crisis.

[3] For the purposes of facilitating comparison, the four-fold division of GFCF in the 2011–12 base year series has been converted to the two components into which GFCF was divided previously. Construction from 2011–12 onwards includes dwellings, other buildings and structures as well as cultivation of biological resources, while machinery and equipment is the sum of machinery and equipment, and intellectual property products.

References

Balakrishnan, P., M. Das and M. Parameswaran (2021), 'Growth Transitions in India: Myth and Reality', *Economic and Political Weekly*, vol. 56, no. 11, pp. 43–49

Chaudhuri, S. (2013), 'Manufacturing Trade Deficit and Industrial Policy in India', *Economic and Political Weekly*, no. 48, no. 8, pp. 41–50.

Dennis Rajakumar, J. (2016), 'Estimates of High GDP Growth for 2015–16: Not Entirely Convincing', *Economic and Political Weekly*, vol. 51, nos 26 and 27, pp. 117–20.

Ghosh, J. and C.P. Chandrasekhar (2009), 'The Costs of "Coupling": The Global Crisis and the Indian Economy', *Cambridge Journal of Economics*, vol. 33, no. 4, pp. 725–39.

Goldar, B. (2011), 'Growth in Organized Manufacturing Employment in Recent Years', *Economic and Political Weekly*, vol. 46, no. 7, pp. 20–23.

Hatekar, N. and A. Dongre (2005), 'Structural Breaks in India's Growth: Revisiting the Debate with a Longer Perspective', *Economic and Political Weekly*, vol. 40, no. 14, pp. 1432–35.

Krishna, K.L., B. Goldar, A.A. Erumban, P.C. Das and S.C. Aggarwal (2022), 'Sources of India's Post-reform Economic Growth: An Analysis Based on India KLEMS Database', *Economic and Political Weekly*, vol. 57, no. 31, pp. 36–43.

Kumar, A. (2023), 'GDP Growth: Less Than Officially Given', *Impact and Policy Research Institute*, 3 June, available at https://www.impriindia.com/insights/gdp-growth-economy/

Lewis, W.A. (1954), 'Economic Development with Unlimited Supplies of Labour', *The Manchester School of Economic & Social Studies*, vol. 22, no. 2, pp. 139–91.

Mazumdar, S. (2014), 'Globalisation and Growth: The Indian Case in Perspective, in R. Khasnabis and I. Chakraborty, eds, *Market, Regulations and Finance: Global Meltdown and the Indian Economy*, pp. 213–30, Springer.

——— (2015). Manufacturing Growth in the New GDP Series, *Economic and Political Weekly*, 50 (24): 120-21.

——— (2024a). The Great Post-Covid Reset of the Indian Economy: Union Budget 2024-25 in Perspective, *SSER*, available at https://www.indianstatistics.org/2024/02/06/budget202425.html

——— (2024b), 'The State of the Indian Economy: Myth and Reality', in S. Roy, ed, *India's Economy 2024: Disparities in Fractured Democracy*, pp. 11–19, Delhi: Aakaar Books.

Nagaraj, R. (2011), 'Growth in Organized Manufacturing Employment: A Comment', *Economic and Political Weekly*, vol. 46, no. 12, pp. 83–84.

——— (2015), 'Seeds of Doubts on New Numbers: Private Corporate Sector Overestimated?', *Economic and Political Weekly*, vol. 50, no. 13, pp. 14–17.

Nayyar, D. (1978), 'Industrial Development in India: Some Reflections on Growth and Stagnation', *Economic and Political Weekly*, vol. 13, nos 31 and 33, Special Number, pp. 1265–78.

——— (2006), 'Economic Growth in Independent India: Lumbering Elephant or Running Tiger?', *Economic and Political Weekly*, vol. 41, no. 15, pp. 1451–58.

Patnaik, P. (2007), 'A Model of Growth of the Contemporary Indian Economy', *Economic and Political Weekly*, vol. 42, no. 22, pp. 2077–81.

Patnaik, U. (2007), 'New Data on the Arrested Development of Capitalism in Indian Agriculture', *Social Scientist*, vol. 35, nos 7 and 8, pp. 4–23.

Raj, P. and S. Reddy Kalluru (2022), 'Dynamics of Economic Growth in India: An Application of Stojanovic's Matrix of Growth', *Economic and Political Weekly*, vol. 57, no. 15, pp. 62–68.

Rangarajan, C. and D.K. Srivastava (2017), 'Underlying Drivers of India's Potential Growth', *Economic and Political Weekly*, vol. 52, nos 25 and 26, pp. 69–77.

Rodrik, D. (2015), 'Premature Deindustrialization', *NBER Working Paper Series*, Working Paper 20935, available at http://www.nber.org/papers/w20935.

Rodrik, D. and A. Subramanian (2005), 'From "Hindu Growth" to Productivity Surge: The Mystery of the Indian Growth Transition', *IMF Staff Papers*, vol. 52, no. 2, pp. 193–228.

Sen, K. and D.K. Das (2015), 'Where Have All the Workers Gone? Puzzle of Declining Labour Intensity in Organised Indian Manufacturing', *Economic and Political Weekly*, vol. 50, no. 23, pp.108–15.

Soni, S. and M.H.B. Subrahmanya (2020), 'Growth and Structural Change in the Indian Economy: An Analysis of Pattern, Determinants, and Outcomes', *Economic and Political Weekly*, vol. 55, nos 26 and 27, pp. 65–70.

Srinivasan, T.N. (2005), 'Comments on "From 'Hindu Growth' to Productivity Surge: The Mystery of the Indian Growth Transition"', *IMF Staff Papers*, vol. 52, no. 2, pp. 229–33.

Subramanian, A. (2019), 'Validating India's GDP Growth Estimates', *CID Faculty Working Paper 357*, Center for International Development at Harvard University, Harvard University.

UNCTAD (2008), *Trade and Development Report: Commodity Prices, Capital Flows and the Financing of Investment*, United Nations.

UNIDO (2024), *International Yearbook of Industrial Statistics*, United Nations Industrial Development Organization.

Veeramani, C. (2012), 'Anatomy of India's Merchandise Export Growth, 1993–94 to 2010–11', *Economic and Political Weekly*, vol. 47, no. 1, pp. 94–104.

WTO Secretariat (2024), 'Thirty Years of Trade Growth and Poverty Reduction', *WTO Data Blog*, 24 April, available at https://www.wto.org/english/blogs_e/data_blog_e/blog_dta_24apr24_e.htm

Contributors

Rohit Azad teaches at Jawaharlal Nehru University (JNU), New Delhi and specializes in development economics and public policy. Known for his incisive critiques of economic reforms, he actively engages in academic and policy debates. His work emphasizes equity and structural transformation in India's economic development.

Arindam Banerjee is Professor and Dean, School of Liberal Studies, BML Munjal University, Haryana. His research interests traverse colonialism, agrarian relations and food systems. A Jawaharlal Nehru University-trained political economist, he has taught at Ambedkar University Delhi and Centre for Development Studies (CDS), Thiruvananthapuram. He has published on colonial historiography, agrarian crisis, biofuels and food security, and neoliberal economic reforms.

Sudhanshu Bhushan is former Professor and Head of the Department of Higher and Professional Education at the National Institute of Educational Planning and Administration (NIEPA), New Delhi. He specializes in internationalization, policy issues and planning in higher education. His notable works include *The Future of Higher Education in India* (2019), *Governance of Higher Education in Bihar* (2021) and *The Evolving Landscape of Higher Education in India: Post-Pandemic Policies and Transformations* (2024). He received the Amartya Sen Award in 2012 for distinguished social science research. He is the editor of *Indian Economic Journal*.

Akeel Bilgrami, a philosopher and Professor at Columbia University, is known for his significant contributions on identity, secularism and moral psychology. Bridging philosophy of mind, language and political thought, his writings engage with contemporary debates on beliefs, ethics and society, marked by intellectual clarity and humanistic concern.

Shouvik Chakraborty is a researcher at the Political Economy Research Institute (PERI), University of Massachusetts Amherst, with a PhD from Jawaharlal Nehru University, New Delhi. His work addresses progressive economic policy, focusing on energy policy, international trade, environmental justice and green job creation. Widely published, he is an advocate for equitable and sustainable development models.

C.P. Chandrasekhar taught for close to four decades at the Centre for Economic Studies and Planning, Jawaharlal Nehru University, New Delhi. He is currently Senior Research Fellow at the Political Economy Research Institute (PERI), University of Massachusetts Amherst, and Global Director of Research, International Development Economics Associates (IDEAs). He has published widely and his most recent book is *Karl Marx's Capital and the Present: Four Essays.*

Ritu Dewan is an eminent economist and gender expert, with over 350 publications on development, labour and displacement. She was the first woman to head the University of Mumbai's Economics Department. A respected policy advisor, she was the 64th President of Indian Society of Labour Economics (ISLE), President of the Indian Association of Women's Studies (IAWS) and Vice President of the Indian Society of Agriculture Economics (ISAE). She is currently Visiting Professor at the Institute of Human Development (IHD), New Delhi.

Biswajit Dhar, a leading authority on international trade and intellectual property rights, is former Professor, Centre for Economic Studies and Planning, Jawaharlal Nehru University, New Delhi and ex-Director General, Research and Information Systems for Developing Countries (RIS), New Delhi. His research emphasizes development-oriented trade policy and sustainable growth, contributing to India's strategic economic engagements in global platforms.

Gopalkrishna Gandhi is a former administrator and diplomat. He was Secretary to the President of India and High Commissioner for India to South Africa and Sri Lanka. He served as Governor of West Bengal from 2004 to 2009. A columnist with *The Hindustan Times* and *The Telegraph* (Kolkata), he currently gives a course on India's civilizations at Ashoka University, Sonepat, Haryana.

Jayati Ghosh is Professor of Economics at the University of Massachusetts Amherst, USA. Previously, she taught at Jawaharlal Nehru University, New Delhi for nearly thirty-five years. Her research focuses on development economics, gender, labour and macroeconomic policy. She has authored and edited over twenty books, including *The Making of a Catastrophe: Covid-19 and the Indian Economy* (2022) and *Women Workers in the Informal Economy* (2021). Ghosh has received numerous awards, such as the 2023 Galbraith Award and the ILO's Decent Work Research Prize (2011).

Barbara Harriss-White, Emeritus Professor at the University of Oxford, has spent nearly six decades researching rural South Asia. Her work explores agrarian transformations, informal capitalism, social institutions like caste and gender in the economy, and outcomes like malnutrition and waste. A pioneer in political economy, she brings grounded, field-based insights into the realities of poverty and social injustice.

Vibha Iyer, Associate Professor, Zakir Husain Delhi College, University of Delhi, specializes in colonial economic history and development economics. With a focus on critical thinking and analytical rigour, she is deeply engaged in fostering academic inquiry and contributes meaningfully to teaching and research in economics.

Praveen Jha is Sukhamoy Chakravarty Chair Professor of Economics at the Centre for Economic Studies and Planning (CESP), and Adjunct Professor at the Centre for Informal Sector and Labour Studies (CISLS), School of Social Sciences, Jawaharlal Nehru University (JNU), New Delhi. He has been a visiting fellow at a number of universities and institutions in Germany, China, Switzerland, South Africa and Zimbabwe, and has collaborated in research programmes with UN agencies, including the ILO, UNICEF, UNDP and FAO. He has published widely on labour and agrarian relations, the economics of education and public finance. He is an editor of *Agrarian South: Journal of Political Economy.*

K.J. Joseph, Director of the Gulati Institute of Finance and Taxation (GIFT), Thiruvananthapuram, Kerala, is a leading scholar on innovation, trade and regional development. Formerly with the Centre for Development Studies (CDS), Yale University, Jawaharlal Nehru University (JNU), Research and Information Systems for Developing Countries (RIS), and a policy consultant for the United Nations Economic and Social Commission for Asia and the Pacific (UNESCAP), his work explores IT policy, industrial transformation, issues in public finance and Kerala's development experience.

K.P. Kannan, former Director of the Centre for Development Studies (CDS), Thiruvananthapuram, Kerala, is acclaimed for his work on Kerala's development model, labour and public policy. A vocal advocate for inclusive and sustainable development, his research continues to influence fiscal and social policy discussions across India and beyond.

Khalid Khan, an economist with a PhD from Jawaharlal Nehru University, New Delhi, has over ten years of post-doctoral research and teaching experience. His work focuses on the economics of education, inequality, ageing and labour markets. Having worked with institutions like Oxfam, the Institute of Economic Growth (IEG) and the Indian Institute of Dalit Studies, he regularly speaks at national forums on socio-economic discrimination and public policy.

Martin Khor Kok Peng (1951–2020) was a prominent Malaysian economist and journalist, known for championing the rights of developing nations. As Director of the South Centre and Third World Network, he advocated on global issues such as trade, climate change and intellectual property. His legacy endures in efforts toward global equity and justice.

Anitha Kumary L., Associate Professor, Gulati Institute of Finance and Taxation (GIFT), Thiruvananthapuram, Kerala, specializes in finance, corporate governance and development economics. With a strong academic and research background, she critically engages with financial markets and institutions, offering insights into their role in shaping equitable economic growth.

Surajit Mazumdar is Professor, Centre for Economic Studies and Planning, Jawaharlal Nehru University (JNU), New Delhi. His areas of research and teaching include political economy, Indian industrialization and corporate sector dynamics. A former faculty at Ambedkar University Delhi and Institute for Studies in Industrial Development (ISID), New Delhi, his research offers critical insights into India's regulatory and economic transformations.

Issa G. Shivji, Emeritus Professor of Public Law at the University of Dar es Salaam, is a pre-eminent African scholar on constitutionalism, land rights and development. The first Julius Nyerere Chair in Pan-African Studies, he has been instrumental in shaping legal and political discourse rooted in the continent's realities.

Jomo Kwame Sundaram is a distinguished Malaysian economist and former UN Assistant Secretary-General. His extensive research spans global inequality, development strategy and critiques of neoliberalism. A public intellectual and policy advisor, his work continues to inform international debates on inclusive and sustainable economic policies.

Sukhadeo Thorat, Emeritus Professor at Jawaharlal Nehru University (JNU), New Delhi, is a distinguished economist renowned for his work on the economics of caste discrimination, and on inter-group inequality in education, employment, poverty and Dalit atrocities. A former Chairman of the University Grants Commission (UGC) and the Indian Council of Social Science Research (ICSSR), he has shaped education and social policy in India. Honoured with the Padma Shri, his scholarship continues to guide and influence inclusive development initiatives.

Paris Yeros teaches at the Federal University of ABC (UFABC), São Paulo, Brazil. He is an editor of *Agrarian South: Journal of Political Economy* and has been the coordinator of the Postgraduate Programme in World Political Economy at UFABC. His research interests include agrarian, labour and development questions in the world economy.